GRAND LODGE OF MA
OF ENGLAND ANL
DISTRICTS AND LC

YEAR BOOK

2012-2013

ONE HUNDRED AND TWENTY-EIGHTH YEAR OF ISSUE

© Grand Lodge of Mark Master Masons

MARK MASONS' HALL,
86 ST. JAMES'S STREET,
LONDON, SW1A 1PL

Telephone: 020 7839 5274
Fax: 020 7930 9750
Email: grandsecretary@mmh.org.uk
www.markbenevolence.org.uk
www.glmmm.com

Contacts
Grand Secretary: 020 7747 1163
Deputy Grand Secretary: 020 7747 1161
Assistant Grand Secretaries: 020 7747 1183
Events: 020 7747 1165/1194
Masonic Support Group: 020 7747 1183/1198
Charities: 020 7747 1187
Yearbook: 020 7747 1164
Registration Department: 020 7747 1173
Finance Department: 020 7747 1172
Grand Tyler: 020 7747 1179
Tylers Office: 020 7747 1801
Facilities Manager: 020 7747 1174
Maintenance: 020 7747 1190
Mark Masons Hall Limited: 020 7747 1177
Catering Department: 020 7747 1185

glmmm.com website
Quick Reference Tag for
Smartphone users

First published 2012

ISBN 978 0 85318 431 7

All rights reserved. No part of this book may be reproduced or transmitted in any form or by any means, electronic or mechanical, including photocopying, recording, scanning or by any information storage and retrieval system, on the internet or elsewhere, without permission from the Publisher in writing.

Published by Lewis Masonic

An imprint of Ian Allan Publishing Ltd, Hersham, Surrey KT12 4RG.

Printed in England by Ian Allan Printing Ltd, Hersham, Surrey KT12 4RG.

SECRETARIAT OF GRAND LODGE

Grand Secretary:
Bro. John Brackley, P.G.J.W., G.M.R.A.C.

Secretary:
Mrs. F. Reading

Deputy Grand Secretary:
Bro. Lt.Cdr. Angus P.D. Hannagan, *R.D.*, R.A.M.G.R.

Secretary:
Ms. K. Kopsis

Assistant Grand Secretaries:
Bro. Jonathan C. Roberts, P.G.S.D., R.A.M.G.R.
Bro. Martin B. Budds, R.A.M.G.R.

Events Manager:
Mrs. J. Millings

Commercial Manager:
Bro. M.J. Sale, P.G.S.D., R.A.M.G.R.

Shop:
Mrs. L. Corcoran

Masonic Support Group
Bro. D. Coleman
Mrs. J. Deo (Year Book Editor)

Charities:
Bro. D. Coleman

Registration Department:
Miss J. Pindoriya, (Manager)
Mrs. N. Bhudia

Finance Officer:
Mrs. J. Ridley

Accounting Staff:
Miss J. Johnson
Mrs. J. Patel
Mrs. L. Read
Mrs. I. Varatharajan

Grand Tyler:
Bro. T. Thomson, *C.P.M., M.A.*, P.G.S.D., R.A.M.G.R.

Grand Tyler's Staff:
Bro. A.P.T. Harverson
Bro. T.P. Hatton, P.A.G.D.C.
Bro. L.J. Millings, P.A.G.D.C., R.A.M.G.R.

Facilities Manager:
Mr. J. Wheeler

Maintenance:
Bro. R. Smythe

CONTENTS

Mark

	PAGE
Secretariat of Grand Lodge	3
Grand Officers, 2012-2013	6
General Board, at Mark Masons' Hall 2012-2013	12
Mark Executive Committee	12
Appeals Court and Trustees	13
Provincial and District Grand Masters—Precedence of	16
The Grand Master's Award	18
Provincial Grand Lodges	19
District Grand Lodges	50
Lodges Abroad under a Grand Inspector	63
Unattached British Lodges and Lodges Overseas	64
Roll of Mark Lodges	65
Alphabetical List of Lodges	141
Alphabetical List of Grand Officers	198
Active Grand Lodge Officers	361
Succession of Grand Masters, Pro Grand Masters, Deputy Grand Masters, Provincial Grand Masters District Grand Masters and Grand Inspectors	371
Masonic Orders – Mark Masons' Hall	390
Representatives	393
Grand Mark Lodges, Grand R.A. Chapters and Craft Lodges in Amity: Secretaries and Addresses	395
"Daughter" Grand Lodges of M.M.M.	401
Grand Master's Lodges's of Instruction Calendar	402
Mark Benevolent Fund Festival	403
Notices and Publications	404
Constitutions and Regulations	409

Royal Ark Mariner

Grand Master's Royal Ark Council, 2011-2012	12
Grand Officers 2011	14
Roll of Royal Ark Mariner Lodges	155
Alphabetical List of Grand Officers	198
Constitutions and Regulations	453

PAGE

Great Priory and Great Priory of Malta
Principal Officers, 2012-2013 390

Red Cross of Constantine
Principal Officers, 2012-2013 390

Royal and Select Masters
Principal Officers, 2012-2013 391

Order of the Allied Masonic Degrees
Principal Officers, 2012-2013 391

Order of the Secret Monitor
Principal Officers, 2012-2013 391

Order of the Scarlet Cord
Principal Officers, 2012-2013 399

Great Priory of the Knights Beneficent of the Holy City
Principal Officers, 2012-2013 399

Royal Order of Scotland
Principal Officers Prov.G.Lodge, London and
    Metropolitan Counties, 2011-2012 399

NOTE

Grand Lodge meets on the Tuesday before the second Wednesday in the months of March, June and September at Freemasons' Hall, Great Queen Street, London, WC2B 5AZ.

An Annual Assembly of Royal Ark Mariner's is held on the second Tuesday in the month of December, at Freemasons' Hall, Great Queen Street, London, WC2B 5AZ.

GRAND LODGE OF MARK MASTER MASONS
of England and Wales and its Districts and Lodges Overseas

Grand Master:
Most Worshipful Brother
HIS ROYAL HIGHNESS PRINCE MICHAEL OF KENT, *GCVO*

PRO GRAND MASTER
Most Worshipful Brother
BENJAMIN ADDY

DEPUTY GRAND MASTER
Right Worshipful Brother
MICHAEL EDWARD HERBERT

ASSISTANT GRAND MASTER
Right Worshipful Brother
HERBERT KEITH EMMERSON

Grand Officers 2012

President of the General Board at M.M.H.	Peter Hamilton Rollin, P.Prov.G.M.
Grand Senior Warden	Michael George Wenman Masters
Grand Junior Warden	Thomas Firth Jackson
Grand Master Overseer	Bryan Desmond Little
Grand Senior Overseer	Colin David Hellyer
Grand Junior Overseer	Norman Dunkeld Milburn
Grand Chaplain	Revd. Gwynfor Williams
Grand Treasurer	Stuart Ian Edwards, P.G.J.W.
Grand Registrar	His Hon. Judge Keith Charles Cutler, *C.B.E.*
President of the Mark Benevolent Fund	Raymond John Smith, P.Prov.G.M.
President of the Mark Executive Committee	John Norman George Howitt, P.G.J.W.
Deputy President of the Mark Executive Committee	Peter Hawken, *M.B.E.*, Prov.G.M.
Grand Secretary	John Brackley, P.G.J.W.
Grand Director of Ceremonies	Kessick John Jones, P.G.J.O.
Grand Inspector of Works	Neil Howard Matthews, *B.Sc., B.Arch., R.I.B.A.*, P.G.J.W.
Grand Sword Bearer	David John William Willcock
Deputy President of the General Board at M.M.H.	Dr. John Lawson William Wright, *R.D., F.R.C.S.*
Deputy Grand Chaplain	Revd. Bruce David Harry
Deputy Grand Registrar	Lloyd Lloyd
Deputy Grand Secretary	Lt.Cdr. Angus Patrick Douglas Hannagan, *R.D.*
Deputy Grand Directors of Ceremonies	Eric John Rymer
	Christopher David Davis
	Ryan Andrew Williams
Deputy Grand Inspector of Works	Vincent John Driver
Deputy Grand Sword Bearer	Derek Edward Wilton
Grand Senior Deacons	Christopher James Bowles, *J.P.*
	Antony David George Harvey
	David Keith Ramsay
	Brian Ridler
	Malcolm Robson
	David Alexander Wright

Grand Junior Deacons	Warner Barton
	Anthony Shane Trenavin Body
	Roger De Courcey-Cooke
	Christopher John Farrow
	Edward Rennie Garty
	Geoffrey Herbert Lee
Assistant Grand Chaplain	Dr. Vivian Thomas, *J.P.*
Assistant Grand Secretary	Jonathan Charles Roberts, P.G.S.D.
	Martin Bradford Budds
Assistant Grand Registrar	Christopher Granville Angus Aylwin
Assistant Grand Directors of Ceremonies	Ralph Mannings Apperley
	Robert John Hargate
	John Dudley Pinnock
	Jonathan Roberts
	Kenneth James Robinson
	Philip Wills
Assistant Grand Inspector of Works	Harry Wells, P.G.J.O.
Assistant Grand Sword Bearer	Stephen Charles Hallberg
Grand Organist	David Edward Henry Adams, *B.Mus.(Edin.), A.R.C.M., F.C.I.E.A.*
Grand Standard Bearers	David Neil Morgan
	William Alec Brown Sherlock
Deputy Grand Organist	Naunton Charles William Liles
Assistant Grand Standard Bearers	Joseph Louis Azzopardi
	Revd. Adrian Francis Pearce
Grand Inner Guard	Lance Milburn
Assistant Grand Inner Guards	Brian Harold Owen
	Neil Webster
Grand Tyler	Thomas Thomson, *C.P.M., M.A.*, P.G.S.D.

Grand Stewards:

Peter Beedle	Durham
John Charles Bicknell	West Lancashire
Maj. Dennis Bradley, *B.E.M.*	London
Kenneth Thomas D'Souza	Middlesex
Ian Alfred Eaton	Essex
Keith Thomas Fairweather	London
Richard Forster	Hertfordshire
Leslie Frederick Francis	Northumberland
Garth Ratcliffe Green	East Lancashire
Philip Harry Gunning	West Lancashire
Shaun Higson	East Lancashire
Paul Stephen Hollebone	Sussex
John David Jennings	North & East Yorkshire
Ian Brook Johnson	Berkshire
Clive Kingsley-Smith	London
David John Maddy	Bristol
Robert Alexander McMillan	Cheshire
Graham John Minett	Northamptonshire & Huntingdonshire
Phillip Nicholas Moles, *J.P.*	Monmouthshire
Graham Raven	Kent
Gerald Smith	Devonshire
Sir Paul Michael Williams, *O.B.E., C.St.J., D.L.*	South Wales
John Henry William Ellis	London

PROMOTIONS

Past Grand Junior Warden
  Keith Wallace Clayton
  Ernest Peter Donnison

Past Grand Master Overseer
  Michael Frederick Barnes, *M.Sc., B.Sc.*
  Richard William Davis
  Simon Andrew Mighall

Past Grand Senior Overseer
  Richard Anthony Barton
  Michael Lawrence Homer
  Roger Hugh Jago
  Anthony Francis Moore, *M.B.E.*

Past Grand Junior Overseer
  Cyril Acton
  William John Balderston
  Kenneth James Blackburn
  John Charles Board
  Laurence Eric Bourne, *J.P.*
  John Henry Brayford
  John Duncan Clarke
  John Collakis
  His Hon. Judge Peter Edward Copley
  Robert Corfield
  Anthony Craven
  Leonard Davies
  Robert Gorton Hall
  Harold Wilford Hampton
  Clifford Arthur Hannabuss
  Peter Hargreaves
  Stanley James Harris
  Stuart Andrew Raymond Ingram

Past Grand Senior Deacon
  Chandran Arul
  John Atta-Quayson
  Maxwell William Bayes
  Douglas Dennis Black
  MC Black
  Max Nicholas Brown
  Martin Bryan Caunter
  Raymond Charles Clarke
  Mark Samuel Livermore Corcoran
  David Philip Coupe
  David Terence Davies
  John Vincent Davis
  Robert James Douglas
  The Hon. Alexander Frank Downie, *M.L.C.*
  Brian Ennever
  Maurice Myers Evans
  Gaspar Llewellyn Gill
  David Victor Hagger
  Eddie Hayford
  Geoffrey Charles Howells
  Neville Griffith Jarrett
  Boo Khean Khoo, *K.M.N., A.M.N.*

Past Grand Junior Deacon
  Ralph Derek Allard
  Thomas Frederick Auber, *M.A.*
  Christopher Robin Baker
  Ignace Desire Laval Bany, *M.A.*
  Arthur Donald Cecil Beaver
  John Alan Bibby
  Donald Blackburn

Robert Goedbloed
Frederick Arthur Smith

Dr. Nigel Francis John Scott-Moncrieff
Alan John Vaughan
Mervyn Frank Wilson

Travers Stanton Penrose
Brian William Price
Lt. Bartel Smit

John Charles Jacobson
David Kenneth Jesson
Alan Jones
Brian Robert Kemp, *M.A.*
Percy George Larner
Richard Samuel Moss
Nigel William Penn
Brian Quartermain
Roger Francis Richardson
Jean-Pierre Robert
Derek Norman Roberts
Alan Smith, *C.B.E.*
Alan Edge Smith
Derek Thomas
Peter Reginald Vaughan
Steven John Warwick
Anthony John Waspe
Anthony Yarinakis

John MacKinnon
Joseph Kenneth Maison
David Melvin
John Brian Mitchinson
John Graham Morgan, *R.R.C., T.D., J.P.*
Michael John Murphy
Achyutkumar Chandubai Patel
Ghanshyam Maganvhai Patel
Derek Lenfesty Pilling
David George Punt, *O.B.E.*
David Barrie Richardson
John George Ridge
David Rucker
Peter Saxton
Barry Sherman
Rodney Staines
Peter Frood Turner
Richard Malcolm Walker
Barry James Williamson
Stephen John Henry Willoughby
George Robert Wood

Christopher David Boak
James Boughton
Richard Bowyer
Peter George Brassett
Frederick Brown
Michael Frank Bull
John Burden

Past Grand Junior Deacon *(cont.)*
   Andrew Burke
   Wallace Ransford Campbell
   William Agnew Caughie
   James William Doyle
   Gregory Dunham
   Andrew John Eastman
   Michael Joseph Flint
   Frederick Fox
   Brian Derek Francois
   Brian Walter Frost
   Gordon Nicholson Graves
   David Charles Greenland
   Robert William Hancock
   John Norman David Hancock
   John Willan Hudson
   Paul Graham Hurst
   Peter Frederick Johns
   Gareth Jones, *O.B.E.*
   Michael Graham Langley
   William Peter Lewis
   Mervyn David Arthur Lewis
   David George Lynn
   Geoffrey Frank Lyons-Mound
   Frederick Arthur Milgate
   Christopher Lintern Moore
   Leslie Sydney Morgan
   Alan Oldfield
   Stephen Geoffrey Overy
   Calwyn Kirwan Onslo Bonner Parkins
   Arthur John Pearson
   Ronald Richard Rawlings
   Arthur Robinson
   Ronald Brian Sankey
   John Leonard Sharp
   Ronald Andrew Smerdon
   Bernard Edward Smith
   Milton Solves
   Harald John Sommerin
   Trevor Sykes
   Barrie Whiticker Thompson
   Herman Van Wijk
   Barrie Vernon
   Raymond Edward Roy Walters
   Robert Michael Williams

Past Assistant Grand Director of Ceremonies
   Colin Birch
   Kenneth Barrington Chalkley, *M.B.E.*
   Gordon Alan MacMillan
   Frank Arthur Langlands Norman
   Roger Wallace Sargent
   Nigel Thomson
   Barry Arthur Williams

FIRST APPOINTMENTS

Past Grand Senior Deacon
   Richard John Anderson
   Colin Peter Thomas Brown
   Kenneth Michael Rondel

Past Grand Junior Deacon
   Ernesto Alberto Marcer
   Moses Oghenerume Taiga
   Geoffrey Brian Tindall
   Robin Keith Wilson

   Pieter van den Berg

Past Assistant Grand Chaplain
   Revd. Kenneth Cox
   David Thoms Youngson

Past Assistant Grand Director of Ceremonies
   Philip Charles Ablott
   Geoffrey Alexander
   His Hon. Joseph Bernard Alfred
   Robert Andrew
   John Wilberforce Ashcroft
   Rodney Frank Atkinson
   Eddy Bamford
   Robert Alan Blake
   David Bowden
   Alan William Brookes
   Peter Arthur Brown
   Thomas Maria Buchsbaum
   Reginald Arthur Laurie Bugler
   Stanley John Butcher
   Stuart Cairns
   Trevor Clarke
   William David Clarke
   Michael John Collinson
   Paul Stuart Cope
   Clive Copley
   John Isaac Crittenden
   David Stanley Cuthbert
   Christopher Dears
   John Barry Edwards
   Gerald John Charles Edwards
   Brian Elcoat
   Kenneth Joseph Elmes
   David Emmerson
   David Nicholas Fisher
   Roger Kenneth Foster
   Peter Franklin
   Ian Robert Farquharson Gager
   Philip John Gillespie
   David Greenhalgh
   Michael Ian Guile
   Col. Charles Morgan Gwynn, *T.D.*
   Rodney Stanley Hancock
   Richard Henry Hardaker
   William Henry Harding
   David Ian Hargreaves
   Keith Harding Harries
   Robert Keith Hartley
   Anthony Hattam
   Richard James Hawes
   William Hugh Haynes
   Kevin Andrew Horne
   John Edward James Housham
   Philip John Huntington
   Robert Michael Hurworth
   Leslie Hutchinson

Past Assistant Grand Director of Ceremonies *(cont.)*

Alan William Ivison
Charles Trevor James
Graham Scott Johnstone
Neil Hamilton Johnstone
John William Joughin
Paul Stewart Knight
Brian Edward Langley
Michael Jules Leroy
Thomas Broster Lewis
Albert Kingsley O'Reilly Lewis
John Kwok Heem Li, *A.E.*
Colin Ian Lias
Datuk Andrew Vun Bin Lo
Evol Washington Lyn-Cook
David Arthur McNally
Ronald Milburn
Kurtikumar Chotalal Morzaria
Frank Trevor Alfred Moss
Damodaran Asan Gopalakrishnan Nayar
Alan Keith Naylor
James Henry Newman
Robert Gibb Newton
Kirkland Hencliffe Nixon
Sing Kwee Ong
Kevin Myles Patrick O'Shaughnessy
David William Philips
John Francis Phillips
Kenneth Probert
Thomas Quinn
James Reid
Brian Alec Ruderman
Dr. Joonissait Mohamed Ismail Sait
David Keith Salton
Frederick Scott
Sydney John Smith
John Benjamin Smith
David Raynor Starritt
John Frederick Statham
Thom Erik Syrdahl
Frank Michael Noel Thompson
Ian James Thorpe
David Leonard Warren
Michael Arthur Watkin
Harold William Charles Webb
Patrick David Murray Westwood
Bruce White
Stuart Michael Wilkinson
Eric Stanley Williams
Phillip Verdun Williams
Iwan Williams
Garry David Witts
Christopher George Hider Wotton
William Young

Past Assistant Grand Sword Bearer

Richard Armstrong
David Arthur Awcock
Simon Bernard Aybes
Paul Burniston
Joseph Gorrell Cheek
Shane Aubrey Duff Clapham
Leslie George Clemens
Alan Reginald Douglas
Kenneth James Drew
Joseph Flaherty
Peter Furness
Mervyn Terence Haggett
Barry Raymond Heal
Leslie William Holland
David Alan Holloway
Clifford Frederick Holmes
Brian James Isaac
Charles James Kemp
Michael William Charles Oats
Graham Potter
Richard Randle
James Francis Rogers
Lawrence Stewart Scott
Paul Wayne Shingler
Douglas Ronald Taylor
Edward Theodore Thompson
Edwin Richard John Tunbridge
Patrick Joseph Walsh
Alan Ronald Watkins
Richard Alan Weedon
Michael Anthony Whitlock
John Ernest Terence Williams
Leslie Woodhouse

Past Grand Standard Bearer

Ardeshir Sam Aga
William John Ashton
Roger Barry Bathurst
Stanley Bibby
David Geoffrey Broadhead
Alan Carden
Peter John Stanfield Castle
Roger Edward Sydney Cawston
Anthony Kenneth Clayton
Philip Charles Coles
Thomas Stuart Crane
Geoffrey Howard Crosland
Peter Cuthbert
Christopher Thomas Brooklyn Davis
Gerard Jan Willem De Joode
Philip John Draper
Clive Evans
Michael John Foster
Ian Foster
Geoffrey Albert Gaunt
James Melrose Vance Gilmer
John Charles William Hickman
Kenneth Hickson
Gordon Westmoreland Hinder
Colin Hollingsworth
Robert Hope
Thomas Richard Lewis
John Richard Lonsdale
James Edward Matcham
Christopher Charles Matthews
Brian William Mayoh
Rodney Meerza
Roger Benjamin Nettleton-Hammond
Leslie Nevin
James Etienne Payen
Ian Dalton Potter

Past Grand Standard Bearer *(cont.)*
  Terence Edward Roebuck
  Dr. Sominder Prakash Sharma
  Michael John Shaw
  Alan Keith Smith
  Ian Geoffrey Peter Strickland

Past Assistant Grand Standard Bearer
  Peter Cambria Bailey
  Clive William Anthony Blake
  Mervyn Brian Collings
  Christopher Court
  Douglas Frank Drakard
  David Edward Ellis
  Leslie Hainsworth
  Paul Christopher Haycock
  James Paul Holder

John Michael Vooght
Jan Frederik Welle Donker
Stephen Nigel White
David William Workman

Kenneth Jackson
James Munday
Alan Christopher Murphy
Antony John Playford
Roger Paul Quinn
Vijay Motichand Shah
Montague Peter Smith
David Grant White
John Winder

GENERAL BOARD AT MARK MASONS' HALL 2012-2013

MEMBERS:

The President of the General Board at Mark Masons' Hall
The Grand Treasurer
The Grand Registrar
President of the Mark Benevolent Fund
President of the Mark Executive Committee
The Grand Secretary
The Grand Inspector of Works
The Deputy President of the General Board at Mark Masons' Hall
The Chairman of the Foreign Relations Committee

The Grand Master – Great Priory of the Temple
The Grand Sovereign – Red Cross of Constantine
The Grand Master – Royal and Select Masters
The Grand Master – Allied Masonic Degrees
The Grand Supreme Ruler – Order of the Secret Monitor
The Grand Summus – Order of the Scarlet Cord

MARK EXECUTIVE COMMITTEE 2012-2013

PRESIDENT
R.W.Bro. John Norman George Howitt, P.G.J.W.

DEPUTY-PRESIDENT
R.W.Bro. Peter Hawken, *M.B.E.*, Prov.G.M., Devonshire

EX-OFFICIO MEMBERS:

The Grand Master
The Deputy Grand Master
The Assistant Grand Master
The President of the General Board at Mark Masons' Hall
The Grand Treasurer
The Grand Registrar
The Grand Secretary
The Grand Director of Ceremonies
The Grand Inspector of Works

Appointed by the Grand Master:
R.W.Bro. R. Poxon, Prov.G.M., Derbyshire
R.W.Bro. K.P. Schofield, Prov.G.M., East Lancashire

Elected by Grand Lodge:
R.W.Bro. B.R. Ogden, Prov.G.M., Cheshire
R.W.Bro. A. Morris, Prov.G.M., Leicestershire and Rutland

The Executive Committee meets four times per year on such days as determined by its President.

GRAND MASTER'S ROYAL ARK COUNCIL 2012-2012

Members of the Mark Executive Committee who are holders of Royal Ark Mariner Grand Rank.
Non-voting members:
Members of the General Board at Mark Masons' Hall who are members of the Ancient and Honourable Fraternity of Royal Ark Mariners.

Grand Master's Royal Ark Council meets on such days as shall be determined by the Chairman.

THE APPEAL COURT
Members:
Appointed by the Grand Master:
Bro. His Hon. Judge G.H. Rooke, *T.D., Q.C., D.L.*, P.G.S.D. (President)
Bro. His Hon. Judge P.E. Copley, P.G.J.O.
Bro. Judge S.M. Samuels, P.G.J.O.
Bro. J. Bonomy, *O.B.E., J.P.*, P.G.J.W.
Bro. J.A. Ball, *C.B.E.*, P.G.J.O.
Bro. M.H. Lawson, P.G.J.W.

Elected by Grand Lodge:
Bro. R.V. Wallis, *J.P.*, P.G.J.W.
Bro. N.A.B. Grout, P.G.M.O.
Bro. H. Gould, *O.B.E.*, P.G.S.O.
Bro. D.F. Pascho, P.G.J.O.
Bro. Revd. W.D. Payne-Jeremiah, P.G.J.O.
Bro. Revd. M.C.G. Lane, *J.P.*, P.Dep.G.Chap.

TRUSTEES
Mark Benevolent Fund
Bro. J.P. Croft, Prov.G.M., Durham
Bro. J.H. Prizeman, Prov.G.M., Hampshire & Isle of Wight
Bro. G.M., Redman-Brown, P.Prov.G.M.
Bro. R.J. Smith, P.Prov.G.M.
Bro. Revd. T.J. Walker, P.Prov.G.M.
Bro. Dr. J.L.W. Wright, *R.D., F.R.C.S.*, G.S.W.
Bro. M.H. Lawson, P.G.J.W.
Bro. Dr. J.A. Elmore, P.G.J.O.
Bro. S.R.N. Fenton, P.G.Stwd.

Pension Fund
Bro. R.J. Smith, P.Prov.G.M.
Bro. M.J. Sale, P.G.S.D.
Bro. D.W. Philips, Prov.A.G.D.C.

ROYAL ARK MARINER GRAND RANK APPOINTMENTS 2011

Dennis Robert Adams
Phillip William Adamson
Christopher Colin Adkin
George Robert Atkinson
Anthony Robert Austin
Anthony William Avery
David Arthur Awcock
Simon Bernard Aybes
Bruce Baker
Luiz Alberto Ballarin
Roderick John Barker
Robert Collins Barnes
Roger Barry Bathurst
Alan William Baxendale
Frederick Colborn Bean
Beverley Edwin Bennett
Ronald John Bishop
Clive William Anthony Blake
Christopher David Boak
Derek Sidney Bontoft
Christopher Arthur Boorman
Roderick Charles Bott
Stuart Leonard Brackstone
Peter George Brassett
Eric David William Braun
Clifford Howard Bull
Trevor Charles Burton
Geoffrey Butler
Maj. Phillip Leslie Bye
Paul Richard Calderwood
Wallace Ransford Campbell
William Edward Caren
Anthony Carney
David Alan Patrick Carpenter
John Richard Caswell
Geoffrey Catterall
Karunakaran Chandramohan
Robert Charles Chappell
Ralph Ian Charlton
James Peter Childs
Philip Charles Clare
Trevor Clarke
Antony Kenneth Clayton
David Bilsland Cobb, *C.B.E.*
David Keith Combes
Philip Julian Conn
David Charles Corry
David Philip Coupe
Peter James Crawshaw
Philip John Cuff
William Arthur Daly
Ian Dalgleish Daniel

Clifford Davies
John Vincent Davis
Lawrence Meredith Davis
Hugues Jacques Julien Charles De Jaillon
Jagdish Singh Dhadialla
Keith Dinning
Walter Disley
Suresh Ramakrisna Dixit
Roy Dobson
Howard Francis Doe
Kenneth James Drew
Nigel Harry Dyke
Benjamin William Dykes
Stephen John Earl
John Michael Eldridge
Robert John Ellershaw, *J.P.*
John Henry William Ellis
Anthony Jack Espag
Brian Evangelista
Keith Thomas Fairweather
Rex Marchington Ford
Roy William Ford
Brian Gordon Fordyce
Richard Forster
Morris Freeman
Peter Frost
Jose Luiz Gambarini
John Bamborough Gibson
Keith Gilbert
Richard Glover
Gerald Leslie Goldsack
Robert Paterson Gordon
Martin Albert Granger
Peter William Thomas Hadlett
Brian William Hall
Stuart James Howard Hambleton
Anthony John Hardiman
Keith Michael Harrison
Antony David George Harvey
Christopher John Hawkey
Gordon John Hawking
Peter John Hayes
William Hugh Haynes
Trevor John Tyson Heap
Raymond Heath
Robert Muir Henderson
Marcellinus Johannes Hubertus Herpers
Gareth Raymond Hicks
Jack Higgins
Christopher William Hill
Keith Leonard Hoggard
James Paul Holder

Frederick Robert Maynard Holland
Mark Robert Holt
Alan Victor Holton
Keith Horne
Philip John Hoy
John Willan Hudson
James White Hunter
Ulysses Adolphus Michael Husbands
John Michael Jackson
Michael John Simon Jacobs
Dr. George Jayaprakash
George Alfred Johnson
Alwyn Clwyd Jones
Gerard Carl Ferdinand Kaschula
Maurice Key
Lawrence Knight
Mun-wan Lai
Jack Lakritz
Terence Allen Lansdowne
Gordon Law
Thomas Richard Lewis
Anthony Terence Littleford
Brian Harold Long, *B.Sc.(Eng.), J.P.*
Gavin James Long
Reinder Lotterman
Brian William Lown
John Eric Luttrell
Anthony Glyn Machin
John MacKinnon
Terence Sarsfield Magee
James George Maitland
John Daniel Martin
Stanley Harry Martin
Graham Jeffrey Masefield
John Massey
Dr. James Stephen Boyd Mather, *Ph.D.*
Robert Young McGown
Jose Luis Menoyo-Garcia
Kenneth Graham Morris
Gary Christopher Munday
Peter John Anthony Murray
Ronald Joseph Murtagh
Roy Norman Neville
Royston James Newman
Frank Arthur Langlands Norman
Brian Partington
John Roger Paternoster
David John Peck
John Newland Peters
Peter Lyndon Penfold
Roger John Perks
Paul Phillips

Paul Edward Platt
David Barry Platten
David Richard Powell
Frank Lucas Powell
Edward John Staite Price
William Marcel Hugh Pulman
Ralph Dementri Ransom
Norman James Reiach
Robert Ward Riches
David Richardson Robinson
Keith Henry Rogers
Clifford Ernest Rowley
Eric John Rymer
Douglas Graham Sanderson
Francis Maxwell Sanderson
Robert Sanderson
Kenneth James Saxon
John Searson
Bhupendra Motichand Shah
Adrian Shaw
Dr. Santokh Singh
David Cecil Skilleter, *J.P.*
Trevor Thomas Sleigh
John Benjamin Smith
Gerald Gill Soulsby
Peter George Stephens
Robert William Stoddard
Carl Edgar Joseph Stratford
Clifford Mark Sturt
Peter Talbot
John Taylor
Cecil Thiagarajah
Robert Todd
Archibald Iain Torrance
Reginald John Tossell
Stanley Turner
Roger Frederick Wacey
Raymond Wade
Richard Malcolm Walker
Selwyn Eric Ward
John Warwick Warren
Arthur Walter Weed
Paul Frederick Weston
Leslie William Whitton
Ivor Vivian Wilkins
Anthony Frederick Williams
Ben Trevor Williams
Keith Warren Williams
Robert Michael Williams
Gerald Winfield
Terence William Wright
Alan Raymond Zimon

TABLE OF PRECEDENCE
PROVINCIAL AND DISTRICT GRAND MASTERS

Date	Name	Province/District
9th May, 1995	James Peter Croft	Durham
22nd Oct., 2001	Peter George Halls-Dickerson	Middlesex
3rd Sept., 2002	Bryan Russell Ogden	Cheshire
26th April, 2003	Robert Poxon	Derbyshire
26th Nov., 2003	Keith Partington Schofield	East Lancashire
18th Feb., 2004	Geoffrey Francis Warwick Isaac	Cornwall
16th April, 2004	Eric Roy Gore-Browne	North & East Yorkshire
1st May, 2004	David Brian Nelson	Somerset
5th May, 2004	Raymond Stanley Henry Hussey	Surrey
19th Jan., 2005	John Charles Woodrow	Brazil
4th June, 2005	Francis Charles Spencer	Worcestershire
29th June, 2005	Anthony Morris	Leicestershire & Rutland
25th Feb., 2006	Iain Malcolm McGibbon	New Zealand
6th June, 2006	David Ieuan James	Monmouthshire
24th June, 2006	George Edward Bonham	Northamptonshire & Huntingdonshire
23rd Sept., 2006	Peter Hawken, M.B.E.	Devonshire
13th Jan., 2007	Robert Leslie Munday	Spain
17th Jan., 2007	Angus John Delano Stevenson-Hamilton	Hong Kong
18th Jan., 2007	Peter Connolly	West Lancashire
31st Jan., 2007	Christopher Martin Smith	Bedfordshire
28th Mar., 2007	Revd. Trevor John Walker	Lincolnshire
31st May, 2007	Michael George Spencer	Essex
14th June, 2007	Peter James Sands	Berkshire
1st Sept., 2007	Sybe Tunnis Booij	The Netherlands
6th Sept., 2007	John Herbert Prizeman	Hampshire & Isle of Wight
31st Oct., 2007	David Michael Edwards	Staffordshire & Shropshire
6th Dec., 2007	Alfred Henry Ryan	Gibraltar
9th Jan., 2008	Roger Henry Harley Croucher	Kent
26th Feb., 2008	Viswanathan Nagarajan	Northern India
11th April, 2008	Phillip Sherwin	East Africa
4th June, 2008	Paul Raymond Clement	South Wales
15th July, 2008	Christopher David Radmore	Hertfordshire
25th Sept., 2008	Frank Jeremy Shaw	Dorset
2nd May, 2009	Shrikrishna Gopalrao Arole	Bombay
16th June, 2009	John Douglas Arthur Platts	Bristol
25th June, 2009	Peter Nigel Isom Harborne	Buckinghamshire
22nd July, 2009	Gordon Craigs	Northumberland
19th Sept., 2009	David Zavad	Natal
20th Oct., 2009	Linton Anthony Andrews	Jamaica & Cayman Islands
11th Nov., 2009	William Philip Thompson	River Plate
28th Nov., 2009	Michael Andrew Cooper	Germany

20th Mar., 2010	Nana Dr. Fredua Mensah	Ghana
3rd June, 2010	James Albert Green	Gloucestershire & Herefordshire
17th June, 2010	Alfred Martin Jefferson Brown	Wiltshire
19th June, 2010	Fabio Venzi	Italy
9th Oct., 2010	James Edward Martin	Channel Islands
28th Oct., 2010	Paul Anthony Norman	East Anglia
6th Nov., 2010	David Robert Johnston	Transvaal
27th Nov., 2010	Theodosious Socratous Theodossiou	Cyprus
14th July, 2011	David Frederick Ashbolt	London
24th Sept., 2011	Madhavan Chellappa	Madras
21st Oct., 2011	Adediji Adedoyin	Nigeria
29th Oct., 2011	Bruce Irving Watson	Zimbabwe
27th Mar., 2012	Peter Maxwell Ball	Nottinghamshire
24th April, 2012	Charles Martin Wilson	Sussex
10th May, 2012	James Robert Guy Hilditch	Oxfordshire
31st May, 2012	Stephen Brian Cobham	South & East Caribbean
16th June, 2012	Peter Talbot	North Wales
21st June, 2012	Keith Hodgson	Cumberland & Westmorland
30th June, 2012	Ronald Jones	Dyfed
7th July, 2012	Max Nicholas Brown	South Africa (Western)
23rd July, 2012	Talija Parakrama Dambawinne, *J.P.*	Sri Lanka
28th July, 2012	Francois Hewitt Vosloo	South Africa (Eastern)
4th Aug., 2012	Justice (Ret.) Mahideen Pierre Haja Rubin	Singapore
17th Nov., 2012	James Steggles	West Yorkshire
24th Nov., 2012	Roger Stuart Mac	Warwickshire
24th Nov., 2012	David Alcoreza Marchetti	Bolivia
1st Dec., 2012	Jean Verbist	Belgium

GRAND INSPECTORS

10th Feb., 2005	David Patrick Downie, *M.B.E.*	Isle of Man
17th Oct., 2009	James Randolph Bain	Bahamas & Turks

The GRAND MASTER'S AWARD for DISTINGUISHED SERVICE TO THE DEGREE OF MARK MASTER MASONRY

		DATE OF DEATH
11th June, 1991	R.W.Bro. HAROLD DEVEREUX STILL, P.G.S.W.	10th Dec, 1996
13th June, 2000	R.W.Bro. ERNEST JOHN MORTIMER, P.G.S.W.	20th Mar., 2003
11th June, 2002	R.W.Bro. COL. ROBERT KEITH HIND, P.Prov.G.M.	
10th June, 2008	R.W.Bro. KEITH STANLEY CARMICHAEL, P.G.S.W.	

PROVINCIAL GRAND LODGES

■ Has received 150th Anniversary Keystone Lodge Collarette
K Has received Keystone Lodge Collarette
* Has a Royal Ark Mariner Lodge attached

BEDFORDSHIRE (63)
Constituted 1985.

(Formerly part of Northampton, Huntingdon and Bedford, Constituted 1894)
(9 Mark and 5 R.A.M. Lodges), (Keystone Province)
Provincial Grand Lodge meets annually as directed by the Provincial Grand Master

Provincial Grand Master:
R.W.Bro. CHRISTOPHER MARTIN SMITH
Appointed 31st January, 2007

Deputy Provincial Grand Master:
W.Bro. RUSSELL HOWARD, P.G.J.D. (2012)

Provincial Grand Secretary:
W.Bro. GEOFFREY VINCENT STONE, P.G.S.D. (2011)
44 High Street, Carlton, Bedford MK43 7LA
Tel: 01234 720786
Email: jgstone@tiscali.co.uk

405 K*	*Lea*	Luton	1538 K*	*Chiltern*	Dunstable
434 K*	*Stuart*	Bedford	1625	*Icknield*	Luton
1396 K*	*Ampthill*	Ampthill	1633	*Camestone-Inglefield*	
1406 K	*Biscot*	Luton			Kempston
1507 K*	*Sir John Cotton*	Biggleswade	1755 K	*Kipling and Burns*	Dunstable

---

BERKSHIRE (02)
Constituted 1879   Re-Constituted 1994.

(Formerly Berkshire and Oxfordshire), (19 Mark and 9 R.A.M. Lodges)
(Keystone Province)
Provincial Grand Lodge meets on second Thursday in September

Provincial Grand Master:
R.W.Bro. PETER JAMES SANDS
Appointed 14th June, 2007

Deputy Provincial Grand Master:
W.Bro. RICHARD JOHN OLLIVER, P.A.G.D.C. (2012)

Provincial Grand Secretary:
W.Bro. MICHAEL FREDERICK SANDERS (2012)
2 Howbery Farm, Crowmarsh Gifford, Wallingford, Oxfordshire OX10 8NR
Tel: 01491 201757 Mobile: 07970 146002
Email: berksmark@hotmail.co.uk

27 K*	*Porchester*	Newbury	1342 K	*Hungerford*	Newbury
235 K*	*Leopold*	Sindlesham	1398 K*	*Old Rectory*	Caversham
257 *	*Jersey*	Wokingham	1430 K	*Conrad Costin*	Sindlesham
519 K*	*Windsor Castle*	Windsor	1555 *	*Friendship and Care*	
623 K	*Valentia*	Wokingham			Sindlesham
1094 K	*Pangbourne*	Pangbourne	1568 *	*Linden Acre*	Wokingham
1162 K*	*Wallingford*	Wallingford	1616	*Cranley*	Windsor
1207	*Wantage*	Wantage	1627	*Erlegh*	Sindlesham
1330 *	*Berkshire and Oxfordshire*		1631	*Caduceus*	Wallington
	Installed Mark Masters		1657	*Charles Wilkinson*	Sindlesham
		Wallingford	1868	*Wilder*	Sindlesham

BRISTOL (03)

Constituted 1876 (7 Mark and 3 R.A.M. Lodges), (Keystone Province)
Provincial Grand Lodge meets on second Saturday in March

Provincial Grand Master:
R.W.Bro. JOHN DOUGLAS ARTHUR PLATTS
Appointed 16th June, 2009

Deputy Provincial Grand Master:
V.W.Bro. KEITH FREDERICK DOWNES, P.G.J.O. (2009)

Provincial Grand Secretary:
W.Bro. DAVID ANTHONY POWELL, P.G.S.D. (2003)
10 Banwell Close, Keynsham, Bristol BS31 1JX
Tel: 0117 986 8355
Email: davepowell.key@fsmail.net

T.I. K*	Canynges	Bristol	1423 K	Ernest Dunscombe	Bristol
183 K*	Baldwyn	Bristol	1563	Goodwin	Bristol
630 K*	Dunckerley	Bristol	1717	Bristol Installed Mark Masters	Bristol
1060 K	Brunswick	Bristol			

BUCKINGHAMSHIRE (04)

Constituted 1882 (17 Mark and 9 R.A.M. Lodges), (Keystone Province)
Provincial Grand Lodge meets at such time and place as appointed by the Provincial Grand Master

Provincial Grand Master:
R.W.Bro. Wg.Cdr. PETER NIGEL ISOM HARBORNE
Appointed 25th June, 2009

Deputy Provincial Grand Master:
V.W.Bro. JEFFERY ROBERT GREEN, P.G.J.O. (2009)

Provincial Grand Secretary:
W.Bro. DAVID EDMUND TREMAINE, P.A.G.Swd.B. (2009)
1 Sunnyview, Tingewick Road, Buckingham MK18 1ST
Tel: 01280 816805   Email: david@tremaine3928.plus.com

97 K*	St. Barnabas	Aylesbury	1629 K	Haddenham	Thame
163 K*	St. Peter and St. Paul	Newport Pagnell	1634 K*	Buckinghamshire Installed Mark Masters	Aylesbury
292 K	Watling Street	Wolverton	1648 K	Slough	Slough
376 K*	Herschel	Slough	1675	The Great Ouse Valley	Olney
480 K* ■	Wycombe	Marlow	1712	Beaconsfield	Slough
975 K*	Bernard Harvey	Slough	1768	Nightingale	Winslow
1087 K* ■	Misbourne	Beaconsfield	1779	The Chalfonts	Beaconsfield
1350 K*	Beaudesert	Linslade			
1499 K	Bletchley	Bletchley			
1510 K*	Merlaue Weir	Marlow			

CHANNEL ISLANDS (65)
Constituted 1989, (6 Mark and 4 R.A.M. Lodges)
Provincial Grand Lodge meets on second Saturday in October

Provincial Grand Master:
R.W.Bro. JAMES EDWARD MARTIN
Appointed 9th October, 2010

Deputy Provincial Grand Master:
W.Bro. DEREK ARTHUR UPTON, P.G.S.D. (2010)

Provincial Grand Secretary:
W.Bro. JOHN MICHAEL JACKSON, P.A.G.D.C. (2011)
La Tourelle, La Villette Road, St. Martin, Guernsey GY4 6QQ
Tel: 01481 236421
Email: mjax@cwgsy.net

74	*	*Caesarean*	St. Helier	1614	*	*Guernsey*	St. Martin's Guernsey
425	*	*Sarnian*	St. Martin's Guernsey	1719		*The Liberation*	St. Helier
1493	*	*Jubilee*	St. Helier	1788		*Channel Island Installed Mark Masters*	Variable

CHESHIRE (05)
Constituted 1872 (43 Mark and 24 R.A.M. Lodges), (Keystone Province)
(150th Anniversary Keystone Province)

Provincial Grand Lodge meets in March or April
on a date appointed by the Provincial Grand Master

Provincial Grand Master:
R.W.Bro. BRYAN RUSSELL OGDEN
Appointed 3rd September, 2002

Deputy Provincial Grand Master:
W.Bro. DAVID ROBINSON SELLERS, P.G.S.D. (2011)

Assistant Provincial Grand Master:
W.Bro. AUSTIN WESTBURY BAMBER, P.Dep.G.Swd.B. (2011)

Provincial Grand Secretary:
W.Bro. COLIN HAMBLETON (2012)
c/o Oaklands M.H., Beech View, Mottram Road, Hyde, Cheshire SK14 3DE
Tel (O): 0161 366 7807 Tel (H): 01477 537399
Email: secretariat@cheshiremarkmasons.co.uk

T.I. K		*Ashton District*	Dukinfield	953 K*■	*Cestrian*	Chester
T.I. K	■	*Benevolent*	Stockport	964 K*■	*Macclesfield*	Macclesfield
11 K*	■	*Joppa*	Wallasey	1016 K*	*Rivacre*	Ellesmere Port
31 K	■	*Fidelity*	Birkenhead	1024 K*■	*Altrincham*	Macclesfield
148 K*	■	*Stamford*	Sale	1072 K*	*Birkenhead*	Birkenhead
165 K		*Egerton*	Birkenhead	1081 K	*St. Hilary*	Birkenhead
196 K*		*Earl of Chester*	Chester	1090 K*	*Ashlar*	Chester
327 K*		*Sincerity*	Wallasey	1107 K	*Dukinfield*	Dukinfield
396 K*		*De Tabley*	Birkenhead	1206 K	■ *The Namptwyche*	Nantwich
532 K		*Wythenshawe*	Christleton	1275 K	* *Walter De Hereford*	Northwich
597 K*		*Stayley*	Hyde	1325 K*	*Leverhulme*	Birkenhead
600 K	■	*Wallasey*	Wallasey	1445 K*■	*Neston*	Neston
622 K*■		*Warren de Tabley*	Knutsford	1468 K*■	*East Cheshire*	Knutsford
705 K*■		*Claughton*	Birkenhead	1497 K	*West Cheshire*	Birkenhead
723 K*■		*Four Cardinal Virtues*	Crewe	1522	* *Tarporley*	Tarporley
792 K		*Doric*	Stockport	1543 K	■ *Haven*	Altrincham
795 K	■	*Deeside*	Neston	1607 K	*Eaton*	Congleton
824 K*■		*Mersey*	Runcorn	1609 K*	*Sandbach*	Sandbach
839 K*■		*Cornwall Legh*	Stockport	1780 K	*Marple*	Marple
868 K*		*Hyde*	Hyde	1825 K	■ *Cheshire Provincial Grand Stewards*	Middlewich
902 K	■	*Middlewich*	Middlewich			
922 K*		*Tuscan*	Sale	1855 K	■ *Massada*	Altrincham

CORNWALL (06)

Constituted 1867   (32 Mark and 16 R.A.M. Lodges), (Keystone Province)
Provincial Grand Lodge meets at such time and place as the
Provincial Grand Master shall appoint

Provincial Grand Master:
R.W.Bro. GEOFFREY FRANCIS WARWICK ISAAC
Appointed 18th February, 2004

Deputy Provincial Grand Master:
V.W.Bro. KEVIN JOHN HICKS, P.G.J.O.   (2012)

Assistant Provincial Grand Master:
W.Bro. PETER FREDERICK JOHNS, P.G.J.D.   (2012)

Provincial Grand Secretary:
W.Bro. CRAIG BRYANT, P.A.G.D.C.   (2009)
4 Belvedere, Truro, Cornwall TR1 1UU
Tel: 01872 274699 Mobile: 07970 541599
Email: craig.bryant@live.com

73 K	*Meridian*	Redruth		1098 K	*Carew*	Torpoint
78 K*	*Fortitude*	Truro		1188 K*	*St. Nicholas*	Bodmin
87 K*	*Cornubian*	Hayle		1231 K*	*Sir Bevil Granville*	Bude
94 K	*Love and Honour*	Falmouth		1332 K*	*Cornish Installed Mark*	
101 K*	*Boscawen*	St. Day			*Masters*	Truro
175 K*	*St. Michael's*	Helston		1367 K	*St. Piran's*	Perranporth
275 K*	*St. Austell*	St. Austell		1437 K	*William James Hughan*	
351 K*	*St. Anne's*	Looe				Falmouth
379 K*	*St. Martin's*	Liskeard		1514 K	*Sir Alfred Robbins*	Launceston
404 K*	*St. John the Baptist*	Penzance		1605	*Saint Breock*	Wadebridge
417 K	*Mount Edgcumbe*	Camborne		1632 *	*The Edwin Perry Morgan*	
700 K	*St. Columba*	St. Columb				Perranporth
787 K	*Tregenna*	St. Ives		1680 *	*Edward The Black Prince*	
831 K*	*Zetland*	Saltash				Lostwithiel
879 K*	*Three Grand Principles*	Penryn		1800	*Tintagel Castle*	Tintagel
1011 K	*St. Luke's*	Camborne		1884	*Iyver Ha Pluvenn*	Perranporth
1023 K	*Trevaunance*	St. Agnes		1885	*Cornwall Mark Provincial*	
1028 K*	*Carnanton*	Newquay			*Wardens*	Bodmin, Redruth
1030 K	*Victory*	Callington				

CUMBERLAND AND WESTMORLAND (07)
Constituted 1872 (28 Mark and 15 R.A.M. Lodges)
Provincial Grand Lodge meets at such a time and place as the Provincial Grand Master shall appoint

Provincial Grand Master:
R.W.Bro. KEITH HODGSON
Appointed 21st June, 2012

Deputy Provincial Grand Master:
W.Bro. BARRY KIRKBRIDE, P.G.J.D. (2012)

Assistant Provincial Grand Master:
W.Bro. MICHAEL KEVIN CLEMENTSON, P.G.Stwd. (2012)

Provincial Grand Secretary:
W.Bro. DAVID LOMAS, P.A.G.D.C. (2003)
23 Deer Park, Wigton, Cumbria CA7 9ND
Tel: 01697 343862
Email: d.lomas46@btinternet.com

60 K*		Cumberland	Carlisle	1020 K		John Peel	Carlisle
151	*	Whitwell	Maryport	1037	*	St. John's	Wigton
195	*	Kent Dale	Kendal	1340		Belaside	Milnthorpe
213	*	Fletcher	Cleator Moor	1345 K		Tithe Barn	Carlisle
216 K*		Henry	Frizington	1397 K		Scawfell	Seascale
229		Faithfull	Cockermouth	1466 K*		Cumbria Lodge of Installed Mark Masters	Keswick
282	*	Derwent	Workington				
421 K		Sewell	Egremont	1481 K*		Duddon	Millom
452	*	Bective	Keswick	1567		Monument	Penrith
462 K*		Inglewood	Penrith	1620		The Written Rock	Brampton
726	*	Bentinck	Kirby Lonsdale	1678	*	Wellington	Whitehaven
738	*	Gardiner	Aspatria	1761	*	Knock Murton	Cleator
779		Ehen	Cleator Moor	1814		Arthur French Sewell Lodge of Provincial Grand Stewards	
805		Loughrigg	Ambleside				
888 K		Eden Valley	Appleby				
				1821		Golden Jubilee	Workington

DERBYSHIRE (08)
Constituted 1894 (23 Mark and 11 R.A.M. Lodges), (Keystone Province)
(150th Anniversary Keystone Province)
Provincial Grand Lodge meets on Last Saturday in April

Provincial Grand Master:
R.W.Bro. ROBERT POXON
Appointed 26th April, 2003

Deputy Provincial Grand Master:
V.W.Bro. COLIN CANTRELL, P.G.J.O. (2007)

Provincial Grand Secretary:
W.Bro. Antony DAVID GEORGE HARVEY, G.S.D. (2007)
Carrfields House, 105 Nottingham Road, Long Eaton, Nottingham NG10 2BY
Mobile: 07768 746229 Fax: 0115 973 6256
Email: secretary@DerbyshireMark.org.uk

246 K*■	Duke of Connaught	Buxton	963 K	■	Derwent	Wirksworth
302 K*■	Derby	Derby	983 K	■	Trivona	Long Eaton
339 K*	William Kelly	Burton-on-Trent	1022 K		Flamsteed	Derby
353 K*■	Dove Valley	Ashbourne	1177 K	■	Peveril of the Peak	New Mills
373 K*■	Ilkeston	Ilkeston	1472 K	■	Chesterfield	Chesterfield
414 K*■	St. Martin	Alfreton	1541 K	■	Derbyshire Lodge of Provincial Grand Stewards	Belper
503 K*	Woodiwiss	Derby				
529 K*	Scarsdale	Chesterfield	1566		John Spencer	Belper
595 K*■	St. Alkmund	Belper	1664 K	■	Round Table	Dore
844 K*■	Dore	Dore	1706	*	The Derbyshire Lodge of Installed Mark Masters	Belper
855 K	Erasmus Darwin	Derby				
917 K	■ Joseph Cook	Ripley				
934 K	Melandra	Glossop	1907	■	The Scout	Long Eaton

DEVONSHIRE (09)

Constituted 1857 (46 Mark and 19 R.A.M. Lodges), (Keystone Province)
Provincial Grand Lodge meets annually as directed by the Provincial Grand Master

Provincial Grand Master:
R.W.Bro. PETER HAWKEN, *M.B.E.*
Appointed 23rd September, 2006

Deputy Provincial Grand Master:
V.W.Bro. PETER JAMES BALSOM, P.G.J.O. (2009)

Assistant Provincial Grand Master:
W.Bro. WILLIAM SAMUEL HUMPHRIES, P.G.J.D. (2012)

Provincial Grand Secretary:
R.W.Bro. KENNETH KEAST, P.G.J.W. (1993)
Woodlands, Victoria Road, Brixham, Devon, TQ5 9AR.
Tel: 01803 853415
Email: combo@kenkeast.fsnet.co.uk

No.		Name	Location
9 K*		*Fortescue*	South Molton
15 K*		*St. George*	Exeter
16 K		*Friendship*	Devonport
23 K*		*Russell*	Tavistock
35 K*		*Sincerity*	Plymouth
48 K		*Brunswick*	Plymouth
50 K		*St. John*	Plymouth
64 K*		*St. Aubyn*	Devonport
66 K		*Fortitude*	Plymouth
76 K		*Charity*	Plymouth
91 K		*Fidelity Huyshe*	Plymouth
96 K		*Metham*	Plymouth
100 K*		*Hawton*	Ivybridge
169 K		*Elliott*	Plymouth
187 K		*St. Peter's*	Tiverton
215 K		*Devon*	Newton Abbott
316 K*		*Benevolent*	Teignmouth
319 K		*Jordan*	Torquay
372 K*		*De la Pole*	Seaton
383 K*		*Lodge of St. George*	Plymouth
438 K		*Duncombe*	Plymouth
540 K*		*North Devon Union*	Ilfracombe
586 K		*Torbay*	Paignton
617 K*		*Sir Francis Drake*	Plymouth
675 K		*Pleiades*	Totnes
696 K*		*Strode*	St. Budeaux
737 K		*Dartmouth*	Dartmouth
783 K*		*Unity*	Crediton
798 K		*Caput Anguli*	Plymouth
822 K		*Perseverance*	Sidmouth
849 K		*Amity*	Exmouth
958 K		*Athelstan*	Exeter
1029 K		*St. John's*	Torquay
1038 K*		*Ashburton*	Ashburton
1075 K		*Exon*	Exeter
1076 K*		*Manadon*	Plymouth
1100 K		*Plympton Erle*	Plymouth
1116 K		*Lodge of St. Simon*	Plymouth
1159 K*		*True Love and Unity*	Brixham
1180 K		*Lodge of West Gate*	Barnstaple
1264 K*		*Benevolence*	Bideford
1284 K		*Lewis*	Torquay
1370 K		*Sanctuary*	Buckfastleigh
1495 K		*Spencer*	Yelverton
1727 K		*Holsworthy*	Holsworthy
1750 K*		*Devonshire Lodge of Installed Mark Masters*	Buckfastleigh

DORSET (10)

Constituted 1879 (14 Mark and 7 R.A.M. Lodges), (Keystone Province)
(150th Anniversary Keystone Province)
Provincial Grand Lodge meets at such venue within the Province of Dorset as the Master shall direct.

Provincial Grand Master:
R.W.Bro. FRANK JEREMY SHAW
Appointed 25th September, 2008

Deputy Provincial Grand Master:
V.W.Bro. GERALD WALTER GILLAN RIDGE, P.G.J.O. (2008)

Provincial Grand Secretary:
W.Bro. GERALD FREDERICK HAMBIDGE, P.G.J.D. (2008)
Littlebrook, 51 King John Road, Gillingham, Dorset SP8 4PG
Tel: 01747 822292
Email: g.hambidge258@btinternet.com

99 K	*St. Cuthberga*	Wimborne	1163 K	*Kinson*		Bournemouth
121 K	*St. Mary*	Blandford	1477 K*	*Branksome*		Poole
126	*All Souls*	Weymouth	1572 *	*Dorset Installed*		
132 K*	*Amity*	Poole		*Mark Masters*		Wimborne
133 K*■	*Portland*	Portland	1635	*Durnovarian*		Dorchester
634 K	*Naval and Military*	Portland	1925	Dorset Mark Stewards		
690 K*	*Victory*	Bridport				Blandford Forum
763 K*	*Anglebury*	Wareham				
1095 K*	*St. Edward the Martyr*	Shaftesbury				

DURHAM (11)

Constituted 1879 (43 Mark and 21 R.A.M. Lodges) (Keystone Province)
(150th Anniversary Keystone Province)
Provincial Grand Lodge meets on fourth Wednesday in June

Provincial Grand Master:
R.W.Bro. JAMES PETER CROFT
Appointed 9th May, 1995

Deputy Provincial Grand Master:
V.W.Bro. Prof. DENOVAN KEITH WILSON, P.G.J.O. (2011)

Assistant Provincial Grand Master:
V.W.Bro. FRANK ALEXANDER RANKIN, P.G.J.O. (2006)
V.W.Bro. STUART ANDREW RAYMOND INGRAM, P.G.J.O. (2009)

Provincial Grand Secretary:
W.Bro. DANNY GUY, P.G.S.D. (2009)
161 Byerley Road, Shildon, County Durham DL4 1HN
Tel: 01388 774984
Email: scribedannyguy@aol.com

39 K*■ *Eclectic*	Hartlepool	981 K*■ *Spennymoor*	Spennymoor
122 K*■ *Percy*	Stockton-on-Tees	1015 K ■ *Ernest Dixon*	Sunderland
124 K*■ *Union*	Sunderland	1055 K*■ *Penshaw*	Shiney Row
250 K*■ *Darlington*	Darlington	1093 K ■ *St. Lawrence*	South Shields
293 K*■ *Industry*	Gateshead	1106 K ■ *Walton*	Crook
356 K*■ *Dunelm*	Durham	1112 K*■ *Elevation*	Burnopfield
362 K*■ *Wouldhave*	Tyne Dock South Shields	1145 K ■ *St. Aidan*	Blackhill
596 K ■ *Auckland*	Bishop Auckland	1151 K ■ *Cestria*	Chester-le-Street
605 K*■ *Bede*	Sunderland	1269 K ■ *Ambrose Crowley*	Dunston
701 K ■ *Jarrow*	Jarrow	1271 K ■ *Shipley*	Gateshead
718 K ■ *Ravensworth*	Sunderland	1274 K ■ *Staindrop*	Staindrop
740 K ■ *Harte*	West Hartlepool	1339 K ■ *Hebburn*	Hebburn
761 K*■ *Hackworth*	Shildon	1492 K*■ *Durham Lodge of Installed Mark Masters*	Birtley
778 K*■ *Barnard Castle*	Barnard Castle	1511 K ■ *St. Thomas*	Stockton-on-Tees
827 K ■ *Unity*	Seaham Harbour	1551 K*■ *Stanhope*	Stanhope
846 K ■ *Steadfast*	Darlington	1560 K ■ *Ferryhill*	Ferryhill
854 K*■ *St. Andrew's*	Stanley	1626 K ■ *George Washington*	Washington
860 K*■ *Bernard Gilpin*	Hetton-le-Hole	1714 K*■ *Ryton*	Ryton
896 K*■ *Clavering*	Blaydon-on-Tyne	1806 K ■ *Chief of the Builders*	Dunston
925 K*■ *Moseley*	Birtley	1820 K ■ *Provincial Grand Stewards*	Birtley
929 K ■ *William Todd*	Bishop Auckland	1936 *Indaba*	Darlington
930 K*■ *Castle Eden*	Castle Eden		

DYFED (64)

Constituted 1989 (12 Mark and 6 R.A.M. Lodges)
Provincial Grand Lodge meets on Fourth Saturday in June

Provincial Grand Master:
R.W.Bro. RONALD JONES
Appointed 30th June, 2012

Deputy Provincial Grand Master:
W.Bro. IAN LODWICK DAVIES, P.G.S.D. (2012)

Provincial Grand Secretary:
W.Bro. GARETH RAYMOND HICKS, P.A.G.D.C. (2008)
8 Lilac Close, Milford Haven, Pembrokeshire SA73 1DF
Tel: 01646 690739 Mob: 07971 729734
Email: DyfedPGLMark@aol.com

116 K*	*Mansel*	Carmarthen		1441	*Teifi*	Cardigan
256 K*	*Five Arches*	Tenby		1535	* *Dyfed Lodge of Installed*	
297	* *Picton Castle*	Haverfordwest			*Mark Masters*	Llanelli
729	*St. Bride's*	Milford Haven		1674	*Aberystwyth*	Aberystwyth
820	* *Lliedi*	Llanelli		1700	*Gorllewin Cymru Mark*	
1102	*Penfro*	Pembroke Dock			*Grand Officers*	Llanelli
1287 K*	*Loventium*	Aberaeron		1705	*Carreg Wastad*	Fishguard

---

EAST ANGLIA (12)

Constituted 1883 (33 Mark and 22 R.A.M. Lodges), (Keystone Province)
Provincial Grand Lodge meets on Fourth Saturday in July

Provincial Grand Master:
R.W.Bro. PAUL ANTHONY NORMAN
Appointed 28th October, 2010

Deputy Provincial Grand Master:
W.Bro. RAYMOND CHARLES CLARKE, P.G.S.D. (2011)

Assistant Provincial Grand Master:
W.Bro. Dr. NIGEL CHRISTOPHER WILLIAMS (2012)

Provincial Grand Secretary:
W.Bro. DAVID STANLEY CUTHBERT, P.A.G.D.C. (2011)
40 Saddlers Place, Martlesham Heath, Ipswich, Suffolk IP5 3SS
Tel.: 01473 625180
Email: davidcuthbert@talktalk.net

70 K*	*Albert Victor*	Ipswich		1166 K*	*Ernest Hines*	Wroxham
92 K*	*Walpole*	Norwich		1187 K*	*St. Winnold*	Downham Market
105 K*	*Freeman*	Bury St. Edmunds		1210 K*	*Suthburgh*	Sudbury
112 K*	*Isaac Newton University*			1410	* *Gild of Good Fellowship*	
		Cambridge				Wisbech
317 K*	*Youell*	Great Yarmouth		1418 K	*East Anglian Installed*	
334 K*	*York*	Cambridge			*Mark Masters*	Diss
538 K*	*Philanthropic*			1427 K*	*Admiral Rous*	Newmarket
	King's Lynn and Hunstanton			1465 K	*Deben Valley*	Woodbridge
603 K*	*Stradbroke*	March		1519 K	*Breckland*	Thetford
686 K*	*Lowestoft*	Lowestoft		1597	*Yare Valley*	Norfolk
687 K*	*Barnard*	Wymondham		1659	* *Brackenbury*	Felixstowe
717 K*	*Eversley*	Cromer		1715	*Ronald Chitty*	Framlingham
770 K	*Northwic*	Norwich		1724	*Thomas Beevor*	
850 K*	*Dunwich*	Bungay				Great Yarmouth
957 K*	*Hartismere*	Diss		1847	* *Abbott Simeon*	Ely
965 K*	*Connaught*	Ipswich		1866	*Columbyne*	Stowmarket
1077 K	*The George Borrow*			1906	* *The Geoffrey Dicker*	Diss
		East Dereham		1937	*East Anglia*	
1140 K	*Waveney Valley*	Harleston			*Mark Stewards*	Diss

EAST LANCASHIRE (13)

Constituted 1870   (61 Mark and 35 R.A.M. Lodges), (Keystone Province)
Provincial Grand Lodge meets at such time and place as the Provincial Grand Master shall appoint

Provincial Grand Master:
R.W.Bro. KEITH PARTINGTON SCHOFIELD
Appointed 26th November, 2003
Deputy Provincial Grand Master:
W.Bro. DAVID ANDERSON, P.G.S.D.   (2008)
Assistant Provincial Grand Masters:
V.W.Bro. STEPHEN JOHN HOLT, P.G.J.O.   (2008)
W.Bro. JEFFREY ALAN HUDDART, P.G.J.D.   (2010)
Provincial Grand Secretary:
W.Bro. TREVOR EDWARD PARVIN, P.A.G.D.C.   (2011)
13 Tower Street, Dunkinfield, Cheshire SK16 5NE
Tel: 0161 330 5348 Mobile: 07957 399800
The Mark Provincial Office is open on Tuesday and Friday
Email: trevor@parvin.eu

No.	Name	Location
T.I. K*	*St. John's*	Bolton
18 K*	*Rectitude*	Rawenstall
20 K*	*Faith*	Manchester
24 K*■	*Roberts*	Rochdale
32 K	*Union*	Manchester
34 K*	*St. Andrew's*	Salford
56 K*	*Temperance*	Todmorden
113 K*■	*Blair*	Clayton-le-Moors
136 K*	*William Romaine Callender*	Bury
141 K*	*Skelmersdale*	Ashton-under-Lyne
142 K	*Wike*	Breighmet
156 K*	*County Palatine*	Audenshaw
159 K*	*Starkie*	Accrington
171 K*■	*Union*	Oldham
189 K*	*Scarlett*	Burnley
403 K*	*Perseverance*	Blackburn
680 K	*Goulburn*	Manchester
689 K*	*Lancastrians*	Manchester
693 K	*Priory*	Whalley
695 K	*Pendle*	Padiham
745 K	*Manchester Keystone*	Manchester
762 K	*Bolton*	Bolton
817 K	*Derby*	Salford
829 K	*Loyalty*	Accrington
852 K	*Semper Paratus*	Manchester
908 K*	*Billinge*	Blackburn
911 K*■	*Keep*	Clitheroe
939 K	*Fabric*	Rochdale
949 K*	*Constitution*	Manchester
990 K*	*East Lancashire Provincial Grand Officers'*	Manchester
994 K*	*Salford*	Salford
1001 K*■	*University of Manchester*	Manchester
1010 K*■	*Rose of York*	Ashton-under-Lyne
1014 *	*Gawthorpe*	Burnley
1034 K	*Gorton*	Manchester
1042 K	*Supera Moras*	Bolton
1059 K*	*Manchester Engineers*	Manchester
1065 K	*Adoniram*	Accrington
1080 K	*White Stone*	Manchester
1132 K*	*F. W. Broadbent*	Bolton
1165 K*	*Quatuor Legati*	Bolton
1174 K	*Elizabethan*	Nelson
1222 K*	*Ardwick*	Audenshaw
1272 K	*East Lancashire Provincial Grand Stewards'*	Manchester
1300 K*	*Turton*	Turton
1303 K*	*Middleton*	Middleton
1309 K*	*Lodge of Good Report*	Manchester
1327 K	*The Darwen*	Blackburn
1369 K*	*Integrity*	Shaw, nr. Oldham
1381 K*■	*Mossley*	Ashton-under-Lyne
1383 K	*Thomas Sharples Barlow*	Manchester
1405 K	*George Farnworth Nuttall*	Clayton-Le-Moors
1454 K*	*Stanley*	Audenshaw
1459 K	*Friendship*	Middleton
1554	*De Lacy*	Clayton-Le-Moors
1577 *	*Progress*	Manchester
1582 K	*Wycoller*	Colne
1613 *	*Robert Burns*	Salford
1649 K	*Arnold Moreton*	Manchester
1716 *	*Cornerstone*	Manchester
1932	*Secretarius*	Salford

ESSEX (14)

Constituted 1899 (46 Mark and 38 R.A.M. Lodges), (Keystone Province)
(150th Anniversary Keystone Province)
Provincial Grand Lodge meets on the Third Thursday in May
Provincial Grand Master:
R.W.Bro. MICHAEL GEORGE SPENCER
Appointed 31st May, 2007
Deputy Provincial Grand Master:
W.Bro. TERRENCE DOUGLAS SHEERN, P.A.G.D.C. (2012)
Assistant Provincial Grand Masters:
W.Bro. PAUL BADEN HUMPHREY, P.G.J.D. (2008)
W.Bro. ROBERT JOHN POTTS, P.G.J.D. (2009)
Provincial Grand Secretary:
W.Bro. RICHARD BOWYER, P.G.J.D. (2010)
23 Balgores Lane, Gidea Park, Romford, Essex RM2 5JT
Tel: 01708 745371
Email: richardbowyer1@aol.com

145 K*	*Constantine*	Colchester	1142 K*	*Tuscan Pillar*		Upminster
205 K*	*Beaconsfield*	Southend-on-Sea	1195 K*	*Upminster*		Upminster
342 K*	*Chelmer*	Chelmsford	1244 *	*Royal Oak Tree*		Chingford
377 K*	*Brentwood*	Hutton	1252 K*	*Chingford*		Chingford
413 K*	*St. Nicholas*	Harwich	1319 K*	*Saxon Shore*		Tollesbury
461 K*	*George Graveley*	Grays	1333 K*	*Wyven*		Wivenhoe
467 K*	*West Ham*	Harlow	1366 K*	*Craftsmen of Walden*		Saffron Walden
527 K*	*Dunmow*	Braintree	1380 K*	*Naze Tower*		Frinton-on-Sea
570 K*	*Grays Thurrock*	Grays	1399 K*	*Potters Clay*		Harlow
814 K*	*Aurelius*	Clacton-on-Sea	1413 K*	*Mark of Industry*		Upminster
825 K	*Beriffe*	Brightlingsea	1415 *	*Battlesbridge*		Southend-On-Sea
834 K*	*Ambresbury*	Loughton	1444 *	*Forest of Waltham*		Harlow
859 K	*Rainham*	Orsett	1463 *	*Thameside*		Wickford
864 K*	*The White Stone*	Chingford	1470 *	*Ilford St. Mary*		Hutton
944 K*	*Fillebrook*	Chingford	1480 K*	*Mark of True Friendship*		Wickford
945 K*	*Crowstone*	Southend-on-Sea	1536 *	*Mayflower*		Wickford
998 K*	*Boleyn Castle*	Brentwood	1564 *	*Viking*		Southend
1026 K*	*St. Katharine's*	Wickford	1628 *	*Langdon Hills*		Orsett
1044 *	*Essex Installed Mark Masters*	(a selected town)	1718	*Mark of Love and Rememberance*		Rochford
1056 K*	*Pymmes Park*	Witham	1735	*Stilus et Denarius*		Upminster
1092 K*	*Tudor*	Upminster	1781	*The Easterford*		Kelvedon
1096 K*	*Wayfarers*	Colchester	1804	*Centurion*		Newbury Park
1123 K*	*Essex Jubilee*	Southend-on-Sea				
1126 K	*Oakleaf*	Grays				

GLOUCESTERSHIRE AND HEREFORDSHIRE (15)

Constituted 1879 (20 Mark and 10 R.A.M. Lodges), (Keystone Province)
Provincial Grand Lodge meets on first Saturday in June

Provincial Grand Master:
R.W.Bro. JAMES ALBERT GREEN
Appointed 3rd June, 2010

Deputy Provincial Grand Master:
W.Bro. ROGER WILLIAM BLAKE, P.G.S.D. (2011)

Provincial Grand Secretary:
W.Bro. DAVID IAN HARGREAVES, P.A.G.D.C. (2011)
11 Croft Thorne Close, Up Hatherley, Cheltenham, Gloucestershire GL15 3YR
Tel: 01242 575972 Mobile: 07702 132418
Email: dave.hargreaves266@btinternet.com

No.		Lodge	Place
10	K*	Cheltenham and Keystone	Cheltenham
218	K*	Lyegrove	Downend
243	K*	St. Ethelbert	Hereford
340	K*	Royal Forest of Dean	Newnham-on-Severn
439	K*	Gloucester	Gloucester
646	K*	Avon	Avonmouth
1039	K*	Stroud	Stroud
1134	K	The Foster	Dursley
1238	K*	Tewkesbury Abbey	Tewkesbury
1338	K	Purdown	Bristol
1349	K	The Kyrle	Ross-on-Wye
1374	K*	Stow-on-the-Wold	Stow-on-the-Wold
1387	K	Old Patesian	Cheltenham
1420	K	William Bathurst	Cirencester
1429	K*	Installed Masters Lodge of Reflection	Wotton-under-Edge
1449	K	Davy	Chipping Sodbury
1650	K	Leofric	Bromyard
1677	K	Silurean	Kington
1793	K	Portus Abonae	Avonmouth
1803		Mount Sinai	Chipping Sodbury

HAMPSHIRE AND ISLE OF WIGHT (16)

Constituted 1873 (48 Mark and 27 R.A.M. Lodges), (Keystone Province)
(150th Anniversary Keystone Province)
Provincial Grand Lodge meets on fourth Saturday in April
Provincial Grand Master:
R.W.Bro. JOHN HERBERT PRIZEMAN
Appointed 6th September, 2007
Deputy Provincial Grand Master:
V.W.Bro. GEORGE JOHN DEACON, P.G.J.O. (2007)
Assistant Provincial Grand Master:
W.Bro. Lt.Col. ROGER JOHN ELLIS JENKINS, T.D., P.G.S.D. (2010)
Provincial Grand Secretary:
W.Bro. WILLIAM PETER LEWIS, P.G.J.D. (2010)
2 Arun Way, West Wellow, Romsey, Hampshire SO51 6GT
Tel: 01794 322921
Email: wpeterlewis@btinternet.com

T.I. K*■	Albany	Newport, I.O.W.		969 K*■	Winchester	Winchester
2 K*■	Phœnix	Portsmouth		973 K	William of Orange	Petersfield
17 K*	Portsmouth	Havant		988 K	Shalden	Alton
37 K*■	Wyndham	Andover		1048 K	Thistle and Shamrock	Havant
54 K*	Aldershot Military	Aldershot				
62 K*	Carnarvon	Havant		1049 K*	Hindhead	Borden
63 K*	St. Andrew's	Eastleigh		1246 K	Needles	Freshwater, I.O.W.
125 K*	Bournemouth	Boscombe		1258 K*	Chandlers Ford	
140 K*	Medina	West Cowes, I.O.W.				Chandlers Ford
305 K*	Gosport	Gosport		1279 K	The Norman	Eastleigh
320 K*	William Hickman			1296 K	Thomas Dunckerley	Gosport
		Sandown, I.O.W.		1382 K	Botley	Botley
349 K	■Aldershot Army and Navy			1385 K*	Clanfield	Horndean
		Farnborough		1395 K	Hector Young	Totton
381 K	Unity	Bournemouth		1403 K	Woolmer Forest	Bordon
611 K	New Forest	Lymington		1453 K*	Christchurch	Christchurch
613 K*	Clausentum	Woolston		1491 K*	The Mark of Education	
674 K*	Loveland	Eastleigh				Cosham
694 K	Connaught	Southampton		1687 K*	Hampshire and Isle of Wight	
739 K*	Portsdown	Cosham			Installed Mark Masters	
775 K*■	Thomas à Becket	Portsmouth				Chandler's Ford
777 K*■	Mercury	Farnborough		1733	Brocas Hyrst	New Milton
809 K	John Pounds	Portsmouth		1773 K	Forty Steps	Southampton
867 K	■ Vale of Avon	Ringwood		1785	Aldershot Meridian	Aldershot
874 K	■Stradbroke	Portsmouth		1796 *	Hampshire & Isle of Wight	
875 K*■	Harmony	Fareham			Provincial Grand Stewards	
886 K*■	Oakley	Basingstoke				Botley
910 K	■Romsey	Romsey		1798	*■Meridies	Botley
951 K	Sir Arthur Holbrook	Ryde				

HERTFORDSHIRE (17)

Constituted 1885 (39 Mark and 30 R.A.M. Lodges), (Keystone Province)
Provincial Grand Lodge meets annually as directed by the Provincial Grand Master

Provincial Grand Master:
R.W.Bro. CHRISTOPHER DAVID RADMORE
Appointed 15th July, 2008

Deputy Provincial Grand Master:
W.Bro. RICHARD MALCOLM WALKER, P.G.S.D. (2011)

Assistant Provincial Grand Master:
W.Bro. NEIL PHILLIPS, P.A.G.D.C. (2012)

Provincial Grand Secretary:
W.Bro. TREVOR CLARKE, P.A.G.D.C. (2011)
35 Appleton Fields, Thorley, Bishop's Stortford, Hertfordshire CM23 4DP
Tel: 01279 651001 Mobile: 07765 241621
Email: trevor.clarke@live.co.uk

241	K*	*Watford*	Watford	1254 K*	*Harpenden*	Harpenden and St. Albans
354	K*	*Rose and Lily*	F.M.H., London	1291 K*	*Hemel Hempstead*	Hemel Hempstead
366	K*	*Hertford*	Hertford			
367	K*	*Gladsmuir*	M.M.H., London	1315 K*	*Elstree and Radlett*	Radlett
428	K*	*Broxbourne*	Watford	1358 K*	*The Joseph Moffett*	Radlett
556	K*	*James Terry*	Cheshunt	1404 K*	*Stevenage*	Letchworth
636	K*	*Debenham*	St. Albans	1489 K*	*Halsey*	Royston
683	K*	*East Hertfordshire*	Radlett	1505 K*	*Chevalier*	Rickmansworth
872	K*■	*Digswell*	Welwyn	1508	*Fratres Scriptabacorum*	St. Albans
909	K*	*Lea Valley*	Cheshunt			
920	K*	*Ravenscroft*	Cheshunt	1529 K*	*Ayot*	St. Albans
926	K*	*William Hamilton Underhill*	Letchworth	1585	*Rosewalk*	Radlett
962	K*	*Latimer*	Radlett	1686	*Adastral*	Cheshunt
974	K*	*James Parsons*	Watford	1701	*St. Cecilia*	Watford
991	K*	*Eleanor Cross*	Cheshunt	1710 *	*Scholars in Amity*	Letchworth & St. Albans
1047	K*	*Cheshunt*	Cheshunt			
1108	K	*St. Albans*	St. Albans	1809 *	*Stanstead Abbots*	Sawbridgeworth
1109	*	*King Harold*	Cheshunt			
1114	K*	*Sprig of Acacia*	Radlett	1824	*John Burr*	St. Albans
1121	*	*Hertfordshire Installed Mark Masters*	St. Albans	1832	*White Stone*	St. Albans
				1880	*Provincial Grand Stewards*	Royston
1172	K*	*Berkhampsted*	Berkhampsted			
1236	*	*Bishop's Stortford*	Bishop's Stortford			

KENT (18)

Constituted 1872 (59 Mark and 47 R.A.M. Lodges), (Keystone Province)
(150th Anniversary Keystone Province)
Provincial Grand Lodge meets on last Saturday in September
Provincial Grand Master:
R.W.Bro. ROGER HENRY HARLEY CROUCHER
Appointed 9th January, 2008
Deputy Provincial Grand Master:
V.W.Bro. PETER DAVID WILLIAMS, P.G.J.O. (2008)
Assistant Provincial Grand Masters:
V.W.Bro. DAVID JOHN GREEN, P.G.J.O. (2008)
W.Bro. ARCHIBALD IAIN TORRANCE, G.Stwd. (2010)
Provincial Grand Secretary:
V.W.Bro. WILLIAM JOHN BALDERSTON, P.G.J.O. (2008)
66 Berengrave Lane, Rainham, Kent ME8 7NA
Tel: 01634 230889
E-mail: billbalderston@hotmail.com

6 K*	*Adams*	Sheerness	938 K*	*Whitstable*	Whitstable
44 K*	*Florence Nightingale*	London WC1H	984 K*	*Lodge of Harmony*	Faversham
			999	*	*Kent Installed Mark Masters*	Maidstone
69 K*	*United Service*	Gillingham			
129 K	*Holmesdale*	Ramsgate	1053		*St. Peter in Thanet*	Broadstairs
152 K*	*Dover and Cinque Ports*	Dover	1061		*St. George's*	Gillingham
226 K*	*Excelsoir*	Welling	1073	*	*Margate*	Margate
237 K*	*St. Andrew's*	Rochester	1083 K*	*Orpington*	Bromley
255 K*	*Robinson*	Maidstone	1089 K*	*St. Michael's*	Sittingbourne
262 K*	*St. Martin's*	Canterbury	1157 K*	*Crane*	Cranbrook
266 K*	*Amherst*	Sandgate	1168	■	*Cantwara-byrig*	Canterbury
267 K*	*King Charles the Martyr*	Tunbridge Wells	1233	*	*Pilgrims*	Wrotham
			1292		*Paddock Wood*	Paddock Wood
294 K*	*Royal Naval College*	M.M.H.	1326 K*	*Hundred of Hoo*	Hoo
309 K*	*Saye and Sele*	Sidcup	1354	*	*Westwood*	Welling
322 K*	*Temple*	Bromley	1379 K*	*The Lodge of Sympathy*	Gravesend
332 K*	*Greenwich*	M.M.H.			
364 K*	*Gordon*	Gravesend	1417 K*	*The Romney Marsh*	Dymchurch
378 K	*Invicta*	Ashford			
380 K*	*Folkestone*	Folkestone	1425 K*	*Malling Abbey*	West Malling
390 K*	*Granville*	Deal	1448	*	*Manor of Bexley*	Sidcup
416 K*	*Royal Oak*	Sidcup	1461	*	*Richard Watts*	Chatham
584 K*	*Manor of Chatham*	Gillingham	1494 K*	*The Lord Harris*	Sidcup
682 K	*Pentangle*	Rochester	1557	*	*Biggin Hill*	Sevenoaks
767 K	*Shorncliffe and Hythe*	Hythe	1584 K*	*Oakley*	Bromley
771 K	*Herne Bay*	Herne Bay	1682	*	*The North Kent*	Wilmington
797 K	*Sandwich Haven*	Sandwich	1691		*Kent Mark Stewards*	Maidstone
811 K	*Medway*	Paddock Wood	1777	*	*Eos*	Gravesend
841 K*	*Catford*	Bromley	1802	*	*Millennium*	Sittingbourne
842 K*	*St. Peter's*	Wigmore	1840	*	*St. James's*	London SW1Y
857 K *Kentish*		Welling	1886	*	*Mandalay*	Bromley
876 K*	*Knole*	Sevenoaks	1894	*	*Erdemont*	Dartford

LEICESTERSHIRE AND RUTLAND (19)

Constituted 1858 (16 Mark and 9 R.A.M. Lodges), (Keystone Province)
Provincial Grand Lodge meets on second Tuesday in May
Provincial Grand Master:
R.W.Bro. ANTHONY MORRIS
Appointed 29th June, 2005
Deputy Provincial Grand Master:
W.Bro. DR. GHANSHYAM MAGANBHAI PATEL, P.G.S.D. (2012)
Provincial Grand Secretary:
W.Bro. STEPHEN DAVISON, P.A.G.D.C. (2010)
68 Main Street, Cossington, Leicestershire LE7 4UU
Tel (O): 0116 249 0333   Mobile: 07932 165614
Email: steve.d.mes@btconnect.com

19 K*	*Fowke*	Leicester	1133 K	*St. George's*	Leicester
21 K*	*Howe*	Loughborough	1149 K	*Wyggeston*	Leicester
30 K*	*Knight of Malta*	Hinckley	1775 K	*Multum in Parvo*	Uppingham
194 K*	*Simon de Montfort*	Leicester	1783 K*	*Ashby-de-la-Zouch*	
491 K	*Fidelity*	Coalville			Ashby-de-la Zouch
751 K*	*Stony Gate*	Leicester	1786 K*	*The Progress Lodge of*	
970 K	*East Goscote*	Syston		*Installed Mark Masters*	
1051 K*	*Rutland*	Melton Mowbray			Leicester
1068 K*	*Wiclif*	Lutterworth	1881	*Joey Dunlop*	Lutterworth
1078 K	*St. Peter's*	Market Harborough			

LINCOLNSHIRE (20)

Constituted 1874 (22 Mark and 17 R.A.M. Lodges)
(Keystone Province)
Provincial Grand Lodge meets on second Saturday in April
Provincial Grand Master:
R.W.Bro. Revd. TREVOR JOHN WALKER
Appointed 28th March, 2007
Deputy Provincial Grand Master:
W.Bro. JOHN CHARLES BOARD, P.G.J.O. (2010)
Provincial Grand Secretary:
W.Bro. STEPHEN CHARLES HALLBERG, A.G.Swd.B. (2012)
15 Butt Lane, Laceby, Grimsby DN37 7BB
Tel: 01472 871005
Email: stephen.hallberg@btconnect.com

117 K*	*Remigius*	Lincoln	1203 K		*White Stone*	Lincoln
172 K*	*John o'Gaunt*	Gainsborough	1230		*Alexandra*	Long Sutton
188 K*	*Sutcliffe*	Grimsby	1239		*St. Matthew*	Barton-on-Humber
209 K*	*St. Wilfrid's*	Alford	1240	*	*Mercia*	Spalding
326 K*	*Urania*	Louth	1365 K*		*Bayons*	Market Rasen
387 K*	*St. Oswald*	Scunthorpe	1412	*	*The Leonard Anderson Lodge*	
427 K*	*Nene*	Sleaford			*of Installed Mark Masters*	
445 K*	*St. Swithun's*	Crowle				Boston
916 K*	*St. Wulfram's*	Grantham	1732 K*		*The Haven*	Cleethorpes
946 K*	*St. Botolph's*	Boston	1899	*	*Mayflower*	Spilsby
1032 K*	*Earl of Scarbrough*	Skegness	1910		*The Lincolnshire Provincial*	
1122 K*	*St. Guthlac*	Market Deeping			*Officers*	Grimsby/Grantham
1199 K	*Spurn and Humber*	Cleethorpes				

LONDON (01)

Constituted 1990 (95 Mark and 82 R.A.M. Lodges)
(150th Anniversary Keystone Province)
Provincial Grand Lodge meets on second Thursday in July
Provincial Grand Master:
R.W.Bro. DAVID FREDERICK ASHBOLT
Appointed 14th July, 2011
Deputy Provincial Grand Master:
W.Bro. WILLIAM ARTHUR DIVALL, P.G.J.D. (2011)
Assistant Provincial Grand Masters:
W.Bro. VINCENT JOHN DRIVER, Dep.G.Insp.Wks. (2009)
W.Bro. IGNACE DESIRE LAVAL BANY, P.G.J.D. (2011)
W.Bro. KEITH LESLIE FLORENCE, P.G.S.D. (2011)
W.Bro. PAUL HOWARD MUSTON, P.G.J.D. (2012)
Provincial Grand Secretary:
W.Bro. HARVEY ANDREW ROLAND, P.A.G.D.C. (2012)
25 Herbert Gardens, Kensal Rise, London NW10 3BX
Tel: 020 8969 4446   Mobile: 07710 279765
Email: secmmmlondon@talktalk.net

T.I.	2**KF**	*	*Bon Accord*	Mark Masons'Hall	633	2**K**	*	*Horus*	Mark Masons'Hall
T.I.	2**KF**	*	*Old Kent*	Mark Masons'Hall	643	3**K**	*	*Imperial*	10, Duke St., S.W.1.Y
1	1**K**	*■	*St. Mark's*	Mark Masons'Hall	647	**K**	*	*Guild of Freeman*	
4	**K**	*	*Prince of Wales*	Mark Masons'Hall					London M.C. Clerkenwell
5	**K**	*■	*Mallet and Chisel*	Mark Masons'Hall	652	**K**	*	*Alliance and Memorial*	
7	**K**	*	*Carnarvon*	Mark Masons'Hall					Mark Masons'Hall
8	3**K**	*	*Thistle*	Mark Masons'Hall	728	**K**	*	*Royal Colonial Institute*	
22	**K**	*	*Southwark*	Mark Masons'Hall					Mark Masons'Hall
104	3**K**	*	*Macdonald*	Mark Masons'Hall	742	**K**	*■	*Kelvin*	Mark Masons'Hall
107	2**K**	*	*Keystone*	Mark Masons'Hall	748	3**K**	*	*Connaught Army & Navy*	
139	**K**	*	*Panmure*	Mark Masons'Hall					Mark Masons'Hall
176	**K**	*	*New Era*	Mark Masons'Hall	786	**K**	*	*Sanitarian*	Mark Masons'Hall
197	**K**	*■	*Studholme*	Mark Masons'Hall	791	**K**	*	*Public Schools*	Mark Masons'Hall
223	**K**	*	*West Smithfield*	Mark Masons'Hall	801	**K**	*	*Vaudeville*	West London M.C.
224	**K**	*	*Athlumney Menatschim*		802	**K**	*	*Composite*	Mark Masons'Hall
				10, Duke St., S.W.11	815	4**K**		*Fitz Roy*	Armoury House, Finsbury
234	**K**	*	*Brixton*	London M.C. Clerkenwell	828	**K**	*■	*King Solomon's Quarries*	
238	**K**	*	*Prince Leopold*	Mark Masons'Hall					Mark Masons'Hall
239	**K**	*	*Royal Naval*	Mark Masons'Hall	830	3**K**	*	*Eton & Harrow*	Mark Masons'Hall
315	**K**	*	*Henniker*	West London M.C.	833	**K**		*Maguncor*	Mark Masons'Hall
361	3**K**	*■	*Onslow*	Café Royal, W.1	835	2**K**	*	*Sydenham*	S.E. London M.H. Penge
363	**K**	*	*Ruspini*	Mark Masons'Hall	856	**K**	*	*Golden Square*	Mark Masons'Hall
385	**K**	*	*King Solomon*		897	**K**	*■	*Barnet Mark Well*	Mark Masons'Hall
				London M.C. Clerkenwell	899	**K**		*Irenic*	Mark Masons'Hall
399	2**K**	*	*Euston*	Mark Masons'Hall	921	**K**	*	*Foundation*	Mark Masons'Hall
400	2**K**	*	*Egerton of Tatton*	Mark Masons'Hall	932	**K**	*	*Prudence & Verity*	Mark Masons'Hall
406	3**K**	*■	*Scots*	Mark Masons'Hall	936	3**K**	*	*Meridian*	Mark Masons'Hall
410	**K**	*	*Eclectic & Empress Britannic*		976	**K**	*■	*Johann Gutenberg*	Mark Masons'Hall
				Mark Masons'Hall	996	2**K**	*	*Isma*	Mark Masons'Hall
411	**K**	*■	*Ubique*	Mark Masons'Hall	997	2**K**	*	*Pickwick*	Royal National Hotel, WC1H
415	2**K**		*Grafton*	Mark Masons'Hall	1071	2**K**	*	*Polytechnic*	Blakemore Hotel
418	**K**	*	*Camden*	Mark Masons'Hall	1074	**K**	*	*Thea Sinensis*	Mark Masons'Hall
431	2**K**	*	*Hibernia*	Mark Masons'Hall	1091	**K**	*■	*Commemoration*	Corvino's, E.1
433	2**K**	*	*Britannic*	Mark Masons'Hall	1105	**K**	*■	*Mapesbury*	Imperial Hotel, WC1B
454	5**K**	*■	*Tuscan*	Mark Masons'Hall	1118	**K**	*	*Halcyon*	Mark Masons'Hall
458	**K**	*	*Ethical*	Mark Masons'Hall	1124	2**K**	*■	*St. John's Wood*	Mark Masons'Hall
459	2**K**	*■	*La France*	Mark Masons'Hall	1152	**K**	*	*Minchenden Oak*	Southgate M.C., N.14
469	3**K**	■	*Savage Club*	Mark Masons'Hall	1160	2**K**	*■	*Pro Minimis*	Mark Masons'Hall
487	**K**	*■	*Dramatic*	Mark Masons'Hall	1200	**K**		*Centenary*	Imperial Hotel, WC1B
489	**K**	*■	*United Servic*	Mark Masons'Hall	1227			*London Installed Mark Masters*	
569	**K**	*	*Abernethy*	Mark Masons'Hall					Mark Masons'Hall
577	**K**	*	*Wicket*	Mark Masons'Hall	1228	**K**	*	*Drury Lane*	Mark Masons'Hall
616	2**K**	*	*Carnarvon*	Mark Masons'Hall	1265		*	*Woodard*	Mark Masons'Hall

1313	K	*■	Friendship from Service Covino's E.1
1336		*	Gibraltar Mark Masons'Hall
1363	K	*	Piscator Royal National Hotel, WC1H
1389	K	*■	University of London
			Mark Masons'Hall
1457		*	London West Africa
			Mark Masons'Hall
1467			Italia Mark Masons'Hall
1473	K	*■	Semper Fidelis Mark Masons'Hall
1534			Orchestral Mark Masons'Hall
1604	K	*	London East Africa
			Mark Masons'Hall
1638	*■	City Livery Mark Masons' Hall & City of London Club
1748	*■	Euclid Mark Masons'Hall
1767		Roentgen Portal Middlesex St., E.1
1771		Epworth 10 Duke St., S.W.1
1856	*	The Mahajan Highgate, NW5
1870		London Mark Provincial Grand Stewards Mark Masons'Hall
1889	*	Equator West London Masonic Centre, Ealing
1895	*	St. James Mark Masons'Hall
1909	*	Highgate Imperial Hotel, WC1B

MIDDLESEX (21)
Constituted 1870 (50 Mark and 40 R.A.M. Lodges), (Keystone Province)
Provincial Grand Lodge meets once a year at such time and place as the Provincial Grand Master shall appoint

Provincial Grand Master:
R.W.Bro. PETER GEORGE HALLS-DICKERSON
Appointed 22nd October, 2001
Deputy Provincial Grand Master:
V.W.Bro. DAVID SPARKS, P.G.J.O. (2006)
Assistant Provincial Grand Masters:
V.W.Bro. KEITH DUNCAN ROGER WATERS, P.G.J.O. (2009)
W.Bro. BRIAN LESLIE BERRY, P.G.J.D. (2010)
Provincial Grand Secretary:
W.Bro. JOHN MILLS EDWARDS, P.A.G.D.C. (2010)
127 Upton Court Road, Slough, Berkshire SL3 7NG
Tel: 01753 711543 Mobile: 07850 633737
Email: johnmillsedwards@btinternet.com

3 K*	Keystone	London
144 K*	Grosvenor	Twickenham
173 K*	Temple	10, Duke St., S.W.1
181 K*	Sir Francis Burdett	M.M.H., London
199 K*	Duke of Connaught	Harrow
211 K*	Hammersmith	Twickenham
236 K*	Ashlar	Gun Tavern, E.1
284 K*	High Cross	Corvino's, E.1
350 K*	Emblematic	M.M.H., London
355 K*	Royal Savoy	Cheshunt
357 K*	Chiswick	M.M.H., London
448 K*	Hampton Court	Twickenham
494 K*	St. Pancras	M.M.H., London
499 K*	Star	Twickenham
504 K*	Oxford and Cambridge University	10, Duke St., S.W.1
772 K*	Enfield	Gun Tavern, E.1
858 K*	Staines	Staines
861 K*	Christopher Wren	Twickenham
869 K*	City of London	Civil Service Club SW1A
873 K	North & East Middlesex Lodge of Installed Mark Masters	M.M.H., London
883 K*	Mill Hill	London E.1 or other selected venue
892 K*	Tower Hamlets	M.M.H., London
895 K	Quadratic	Twickenham
901 K*	Kenton	Harrow
924 K	Tottenham	Staines
928 K	Star in the West	Harrow
931 K*	Headstone	Harrow
986 K*	All Hallows	Twickenham
987 K	Diligence	Harrow
1013 K*	Ealing	Twickenham
1017 K	St. Giles	Uxbridge
1054 K	Cranford Park	Gun Tavern, E.1
1063 K*	Middlesex St. David's	Harrow
1104 K	Fortis Green	Southgate
1138 *	Exedra	M.M.H., London
1190 *	North Wold	Harrow
1196 *	Hillingdon Heath	Uxbridge
1205 *	Air Unity	Twickenham
1218 *	Middlesex Installed Mark Masters	Twickenham
1251 *	All Saints	Southgate
1316 K*	The George Parker	Uxbridge
1373 K*	Alexander Burnett Brown	Harrow
1378 K*	Twickenham	Twickenham
1391 K	Haste Hill	Harrow
1393 K*	Temple of Uxbridge	Uxbridge
1469 *	Gauntlet	Harrow
1521 K*	Sub-Urban	Twickenham
1720	Prince Michael of Kent	Twickenham
1846 *	Lodge of Enlightenment	Twickenham
1911	Universal	Harrow
1921	New Morning	London, SW1Y

MONMOUTHSHIRE (22)

Constituted 1876 (16 Mark and 9 R.A.M. Lodges)

Provincial Grand Lodge meets on first Tuesday in June

Provincial Grand Master:
R.W.Bro. DAVID IEUAN JAMES
Appointed 6th June, 2006

Deputy Provincial Grand Master:
V.W.Bro. DEREK THOMAS, P.G.J.O. (2010)

Provincial Grand Secretary:
W.Bro. DAVID RICHARD POWELL, P.A.G.D.C. (2009)
Belle Vue Cottage, Belle Vue Lane, Upper Cwmbran, Cwmbran, Gwent NP44 5AL
Tel: 01633 482446
Email: dave.powell12@btinternet.com

109	*	*Keystone*	Newport	1436 K*	*Portwall*	Chepstow
185		*Ashlar*	Tredegar	1447 K*	*Monmouthshire Installed*	
214	*	*St. John's*	Abergavenny		*Mark Masters*	Pontypool
604	*	*Tylery*	Ebbw Vale	1474	*Beaufort*	Ebbw Vale
731		*Cube Stone*	Newport	1478	*St. Margaret's*	Blackwood
796	*	*Torfaen*	Pontypool	1586	*Wentloog*	Castleton, Cardiff
1031	*	*Maius*	Risca	1709 K*	*The Lady of the Lamp*	
1317	*	*Albert Edward*	Newport			Chepstow
				1836	*Utrique Fidelis Lodge*	
1422		*Llantarnam*	Pontypool		*of Grand Officers*	Chepstow

NORTHAMPTONSHIRE AND HUNTINGDONSHIRE (23)

Constituted 1985

(Formerly part of Northampton, Huntingdon and Bedford Constituted 1894)
(16 Mark and 13 R.A.M. Lodges), (Keystone Province)

Provincial Grand Lodge shall meet regularly at least once a year
at such time and place as the Provincial Grand Master shall appoint

Provincial Grand Master:
R.W.Bro. GEORGE EDWARD BONHAM
Appointed 24th June, 2006

Deputy Provincial Grand Master:
W.Bro. BRIAN ENNEVER, P.G.S.D. (2011)

Provincial Grand Secretary:
W.Bro. BRIAN JOHN ELLIOTT (2012)
7 Hathaway Close, Eaton Socon, St. Neots, Cambridgeshire PE19 8HQ
Tel: 01480 212454
Email: brianelliott@talktalk.net

245 K*	*Simon de St. Liz*	Northampton	1341 K*	*Ferrers*		Rushden
471 K*	*Lilford*	Thrapston	1346 K*	*Northampton Castle*		
477 K*	*Fitzwilliam*	Peterborough				Northampton
594 K*	*Croyland*	Wellingborough	1458 K*	*Earl of Euston*		Huntingdon
607 K*	*St. Ivo*	St. Ives	1486 K	*Beneventa*		Daventry
685 K*	*Powys*	Kettering	1643 K	*Norman Rolfe*		Peterborough
752 K*	*Steanforde*	Stamford	1645	*	*Rockingham*	Corby
794 K*	*Socrates*	Huntingdon	1871		*Ailwyn*	Ramsay
1243 K*	*The Graftonian*	Towcester				

NORTH AND EAST YORKSHIRE (24)

Constituted 1881 (31 Mark and 13 R.A.M. Lodges), (Keystone Province)
(150th Anniversary Keystone Province)
Provincial Grand Lodge meets annually as directed by the Provincial Grand Master

Provincial Grand Master:
R.W.Bro. ERIC ROY GORE-BROWNE
Appointed 16th April, 2004

Deputy Provincial Grand Master:
W.Bro. DAVID ROBERT CLANCEY, P.G.J.D. (2011)

Assistant Provincial Grand Master:
W.Bro. NEIL THOMAS WOODWARD, P.G.J.D. (2011)

Provincial Grand Secretary:
W.Bro. CLIVE COPLEY, P.A.G.D.C. (2012)
Woodlands, Highfield Lane, Nawton, York YO62 7TU
Tel: 01439 771793 Mobile: 07733 125455
Email: clivecopley1@btinternet.com

T.I. K*		*York*	York	1170 K		*Brough*	Hull
12	*	*Minerva*	Hull	1428	*	*John Ashton Wade Lodge of*
95	*	*Star in the East*	Scarborough			*Installed Mark Masters*
182	*	*Humber*	Hull				Beverley
276	*	*Middlesborough*		1452	*	*Memorial Lodge of Installed*
			Middlesbrough			*Mark Masters*	Malton
277 K*		*Fitzwilliam*	Malton	1532		*Saltburn*	Saltburn-by-Sea
281 K		*Beverlac*	Beverley	1583	*	*The Beacon Centenary*
291		*Londesborough*	Bridlington				Pocklington
329		*De la Pole*	Hull	1588		*The Victory*	Pickering
337		*Streonshalh*	Whitby	1640		*Abbot Hugh of Selby*	Selby
743	*	*St. Cuthbert's*	Howden	1671		*Sir William Crosthwaite Mark*
782 K		*Thesaurus*	Sutton			*Grand Officers*	Pocklington
785 K		*Lord Bolton Daylight*	Hull	1681		*Hoveden Lodge of Installed*
803	*	*Alexandra*	Hornsea			*Mark Masters*	Hoveden
804		*Redcar*	Redcar	1711		*Stokesley Lodge of Installed*
845 K*		*Alverton*	Northallerton			*Mark Masters*	Stokesley
1008 K*		*St. Peter's*	York	1784		*The Farmers'*	Pickering
1040 K		*Cleveland*	Stokesley	1830		*Sykes*	Driffield
1130		*The Lodge of St. Andrew*					
			Kingston upon Hull				

NORTHUMBERLAND (25)

Constituted 1870 (32 Mark and 17 R.A.M. Lodges)
Provincial Grand Lodge meets on last Saturday in September

Provincial Grand Master:
R.W.Bro. GORDON CRAIGS
Appointed 22nd July, 2009

Deputy Provincial Grand Master:
W.Bro. FREDERICK CRAIGIE MAIN, P.G.S.D. (2009)

Assistant Provincial Grand Master:
W.Bro. IAN DALGLEISH DANIEL, P.G.J.D. (2009)

Provincial Grand Secretary:
W.Bro. DAVID MOSES, P.A.G.D.C. (2011)
Provincial Mark Office, Masonic Hall, 1 Hartford Road West, Bedlington,
Northumberland NE22 6HU
Tel: 01670 815989
Email: magpie1946@hotmail.com

T.I. K*		*Northumberland and Berwick-upon-Tweed*	Newcastle upon Tyne	968 K*	*Carville*	Newcastle upon Tyne
				1033	*Risingham*	Bellingham
135	*	*Hotspur with Coquetdale*	Alnwick	1141 *	*Newgate*	Newcastle upon Tyne
				1147 K	*Grainger*	Newcastle upon Tyne
192	*	*St. Cuthbert's*	Berwick-upon-Tweed	1155	*Nepos*	Newcastle upon Tyne
				1161 *	*Hexham*	Hexham
346 K*		*Tristram*	Newcastle upon Tyne	1189 K*	*Backworth*	Shiremoor
463		*Gosforth*	Wallsend	1235	*Cramlington*	Cramlington
546	*	*Hartford*	Bedlington	1270	*De Umfraville*	Mickley
547	*	*Blagdon*	Blyth	1278	*Haltwhistle*	Haltwhistle
691 K*		*Morpeth*	Morpeth	1290 K*	*De la Val*	Whitley Bay
702 ■		*Thomas Purvis*	Newcastle upon Tyne	1439 K	*Ridley*	Blyth
				1483 *	*Adoniram Lodge of I.M.*	Blyth
708		*Unity*	Newcastle upon Tyne	1527 K	*The George Stephenson*	Wylam
750	*	*Haven*	North Shields	1540 *	*Farne*	Alnwick
780		*Amble*	Amble	1550	*Ponteland*	Ponteland
788 K*		*Whitley*	Whitley Bay	1756	*Newbiggin by the Sea*	Newbiggin by the Sea
890	*	*Ashington*	Ashington	1890	*Oriental*	Jesmond

NORTH WALES (26)

Constituted 1880 (22 Mark and 12 R.A.M. Lodges), (Keystone Province)
Provincial Grand Lodge meets on Third Saturday in June

Provincial Grand Master:
R.W.Bro. PETER TALBOT
Appointed 16th June, 2012

Deputy Provincial Grand Master:
W.Bro. PETER GORDON WATKIN, P.A.G.D.C. (2012)

Provincial Grand Secretary:
W.Bro. GRAHAM ROLAND BRADSHAW, P.A.G.D.C. (2008)
Hillberry, 25 Maelgwyn Drive, Deganwy, Conwy LL31 9UY
Tel & Fax: 01492 581651
Email: gray.brad25@googlemail.com

38 K*	*St. Davids*	Llandudno	1394 K*	*Holywell*		Rhewl
259 K*	*Snowdonia*	Bangor	1451 K*	*Maen Clo*		Llandudno
321 K	*Elffin*	Cærnarfon	1509 K	*Flint*		Flint
324 K*	*Hunter*	Rhyl	1591 K*	*North Wales Lodge of*		
360 K*	*St. Eilian*	Amlwch		*Installed Mark Masters*		
688 K	*St. Seiriol*	Holyhead				Connah's Quay
760 K*	*St. Giles*	Wrexham	1647	*	*Dyffryn Clwyd*	Denbigh
821 K*	*Idris*	Barmouth & Bala	1703 K	*Buckley*		Buckley
838 K*	*Hawarden*	Connah's Quay	1708	*Gwynedd Lodge of Installed*		
919 K	*St. Mabon*	Ruabon		*Mark Masters*		Bangor
927 K	*Eifl*	Pwllheli	1772 K	*St. Grwst*		Llanrwst
1084 K*	*Welchpool*	Welshpool	1929	*North Wales Provincial*		
1169 K	*Colwyn*	Colwyn Bay		*Grand Stewards*		Rhyl

NOTTINGHAMSHIRE (27)

Constituted 1883 (22 Mark and 11 R.A.M. Lodges), (Keystone Province)
(150th Anniversary Keystone Province)

Provincial Grand Lodge will meet at such time and place as the
Provincial Grand Master shall appoint

Provincial Grand Master:
R.W.Bro. PETER MAXWELL BALL
Appointed 27th March, 2012

Deputy Provincial Grand Master:
W.Bro. GEOFFREY BRIAN TINDALL, P.G.S.D. (2012)

Provincial Grand Secretary:
W.Bro. CHRISTOPHER COLIN ADKIN, P.A.G.D.C. (2010)
Arndale, Atkin Lane, Mansfield, Nottinghamshire NG18 5AN
Tel (O): 01623 645243 Tel (H): 01623 660799 Mobile: 07702 161622
Email: christopher.adkin@btinternet.com

T.I. K*	*Newstead*	Nottingham	1311 K	*Carnarvon*		Nottingham
265 K*	*Fleming*	Newark-on-Trent	1347 K*	*Chilwell*		Chilwell
344 K*	*St. Alban's*	Nottingham	1359 K	*Magdala*		Nottingham
500 K	*Royal York*	Nottingham	1464 K*	*Nottingham Excelsoir*		
632 K*	*Fitz Hugh*	Nottingham				Nottingham
654 K	*Mansfield Manor*	Mansfield	1482 K	*Fidelis*		Nottingham
810 K*	*Bassetlaw*	Worksop	1506 K	*Nottingham Jubilee*		
818 K	*Shelford Priory*	Nottingham				Nottingham
940 K*	*Galway*	Nottingham	1513 K	*Saint Peter's*		Mansfield
1144 K	*Woodthorpe*	Chilwell	1526 K	*Trent*		Newark-on-Trent
1146 K*	*Ashfield*	Mansfield	1808	*	*Arthur Morley Custance Lodge*	
1299 K	*Ribblesdale*	Nottingham		*of Installed Mark Masters*		
1307 K*	*West Bridgford*	West Bridgford				Nottingham

OXFORDSHIRE (69)

Constituted 1994 (13 Mark and 10 R.A.M. Lodges)
(Formerly Berkshire and Oxfordshire)
Provincial Grand Lodge meets on the Second Thursday in May

Provincial Grand Master:
R.W.Bro. JAMES ROBERT GUY HILDITCH
Appointed 10th May, 2012

Deputy Provincial Grand Master:
W.Bro. STEPHEN JOHN HENRY WILLOUGHBY, P.G.S.D. (2012)

Provincial Grand Secretary:
W.Bro. BARRY ALISTAIR PRIOR (2011)
35 Kiln Road, Emmer Green, Reading, Berkshire RG4 8UE
Tel: 0118 946 1150
Email: barry@backhouses.co.uk

55	*	*University*	Oxford	1305		*Weyland*	Bicester
225	K*	*Abbey*	Abingdon	1386	*	*Windrush*	Witney
247	K*	*Alfred*	Oxford	1443		*Wychwood*	Burford
847	K*	*Cherwell*	Banbury	1546		*Godstow*	Oxford
980	K*	*Marlborough*	Woodstock	1655	*	*Bowyer*	Chipping Norton
1183	K*	*Thames*	Henley-on-Thames	1838	*	*Menatschim*	Oxford
1242	*	*St. Marys*	Thame				

SOMERSET (28)

Constituted 1858 (24 Mark and 12 R.A.M. Lodges), (Keystone Province)
Provincial Grand Lodge meets on the first Saturday in May

Provincial Grand Master:
R.W.Bro. DAVID BRIAN NELSON
Appointed 1st May, 2004

Deputy Provincial Grand Master:
W.Bro. JOHN GRAHAM MORGAN, *R.R.C., T.D., J.P.*, P.G.S.D. (2012)

Provincial Grand Secretary:
W.Bro. SYDNEY JOHN SMITH, P.A.G.D.C. (2012)
Pinewood, Edgarley, Glastonbury, Somerset BA6 8LF
Tel: 01458 832213
email: s.john.smith@btinternet.com

T.I.	K*■	*Royal Cumberland*	Bath	781 K	*Mendip*	Glastonbury
102	K	*Else*	Weston-super-Mare	807 K	*Eldon*	Portishead
119	K*	*Carnarvon*	Keynsham	967 K*	*George Norman*	Yatton
128	K*	*Science*	Wincanton	1295 K	*Monument*	Wellington
155	K*	*Portal*	Frome	1548 *	*Nailsea*	Nailsea
162	K	*William de Irwin*	Yeovil	1608	*Somerdale*	Keynsham
177	K	*Royal Sussex*	Bath	1615	*Langdale*	Taunton
191	K*	*William Long*	Burnham-on-Sea	1652 *	*Somerset Installed Mark Masters*	Taunton
348	K*	*Fidelity and Unanimity*	Taunton	1656	*Portcullis*	Langport
571	K*	*Cerdic*	Chard	1912	*Isle of Wedmore*	Wedmore
697	K*	*Exmoor*	Minehead	1924	*St. Andrew's*	Somerset
730	K*	*Hallam*	Clevedon			
749	K	*Quantock*	Bridgwater			

SOUTH WALES (29)

Constituted 1870 (30 Mark and 21 R.A.M. Lodges)
Provincial Grand Lodge meets on First Wednesday in June
Provincial Grand Master:
R.W.Bro. PAUL RAYMOND CLEMENT
Appointed 4th June, 2008
Deputy Provincial Grand Master:
V.W.Bro. ANTHONY FRANCIS MOORE, *M.B.E.*, P.G.S.O. (2008)
Assistant Provincial Grand Master:
W.Bro. THOMAS RICHARD EIRIAN JONES, P.A.G.D.C. (2008)
Provincial Grand Secretary:
V.W.Bro. STANLEY WILLIAM JEFFREY CLARKE, P.G.M.O. (1993)
The Coach House, Rear of 128 Newport Road, Roath, Cardiff CF24 1DH
Tel: 02920 490555 Fax: 02920 491666
Email: swmark@btconnect.com

28	*	*Langley*	Cardiff	1377	*	*Porthcawl*	Porthcawl
179	*	*Talbot*	Swansea	1455 K*		*Sir Frederick Alban*	Swansea
585 K*		*Arthur Lewis*	Pontypridd	1487 K		*Ysgolion*	Pontyclun
639	*	*St. Tydfil*	Merthyr Tydfil	1528 K*		*Cambrensis*	Cardiff
758 K		*Stability*	Penarth	1573		*Cowbridge*	Cowbridge
784	*	*St. Illtyd*	Pontyclun	1590	*	*Cynon-Dare*	Aberdare
823	*	*Cambria*	Cardiff	1592	*	*Llynfi Valley*	Maesteg
950	*	*Dunraven*	Bridgend	1606	*	*De Cymru*	Cardiff
1043	*	*Barry*	Barry	1670		*Mark Lodge of Progress*	
1057	*	*Principality*	Cardiff				Caerphilly
1088 K*		*Afan*	Port Talbot	1685	*	*Sketty Hall*	Swansea
1125	*	*Neath*	Neath	1725	*	*Brychan*	Brecon
1201	*	*South Wales Installed Mark Masters*		1812		*Cwm Rhonda*	Treorchy
			Cardiff or a Selected Town	1829		*South Wales Mark Provincial Stewards*	Bridgend
1318		*Rhaeadr Gwy*	Llandrindod Wells	1845		*Trinity*	Bargoed
1348	*	*Caeffili*	Caerphilly	1914		*Dewi Sant*	Bridgend

STAFFORDSHIRE AND SHROPSHIRE (30)
Constituted 1882 (36 Mark and 20 R.A.M. Lodges), (Keystone Province)
Provincial Grand Lodge meets on the first Thursday in November
Provincial Grand Master:
R.W.Bro. DAVID MICHAEL EDWARDS
Appointed 31st October, 2007
Deputy Provincial Grand Master:
W.Bro. MICHAEL RICHARD HEENAN, P.G.S.D. (2011)
Assistant Provincial Grand Master:
W.Bro. IAN CHRISTOPHER MARSHALL SMITH, P.G.S.D. (2011)
Provincial Grand Secretary:
W.Bro. LAWRENCE KNIGHT, P.A.G.D.C. (2009)
Handsworth Masonic Hall, 21 Wretham Road, Birmingham, West Midlands B19 1ED
Tel: 0121 551 4878
Email: Lawrence_knight@sky.com

45 K*	*Gough*	Shelton		1401 K	*Noah's Ark*	Tipton
186 K*	*Wulfruna*	Wolverhampton		1416 K*	*Wulfric Spot*	Burton-upon-Trent
290 K	*Tudor Lodge of Rifle Volunteers*	Wolverhampton		1426 K*	*St. Editha's*	Tamworth
				1450 K	*Stretton Hills*	Church Stretton
318 K*	*Saint James's*	Handsworth		1484 K	*Loxley*	Uttoxeter
444 K*	*Shropshire*	Shrewsbury		1485 K	*The Jubilee*	Stafford
541 K*	*Staffordshire Knot*	Stafford		1503 K*	*Kidsgrove*	Kidsgrove
650 K*	*St. Bartholomew*	Wednesbury		1524 K	*The Croft*	Aldridge
840 K*	*North Shropshire*	Ellesmere		1581 K	*Centenary*	Market Drayton
862 K*	*Regis*	Warley		1617 K*	*Severn*	Bridgnorth
933 K*	*Noel Boardman Walsall*	Aldridge		1622	*Castle*	Newcastle
960 K	*North Staffordshire*	Shelton		1630	*Round Table and Rotary*	Newport
982 K	*St. Oswald*	Oswestry				
993 K*	*Dartmouth*	West Bromwich		1697	*Staffordshire & Shropshire, Mark Grand Officers Lodge*	Rugeley
1021 K	*Talbot*	Whitchurch				
1085 K*	*Hantune*	Wolverhampton				
1127 K*	*Beaudesart*	Rugeley		1827	*Eccleshall*	Eccleshall
1129 K*	*Wrekin*	Wellington		1922	*The Roses and Castles Boaters'*	
1150 K*	*South Shropshire*	Ludlow				
1182 K	*St. Edward's*	Leek				
1304 K*	*Robert Mummery*	Cannock				
1392 K*	*Joseph Whittall Lodge of Installed Mark Masters*	Wolverhampton/ Shrewsbury/Rugeley				

SURREY (31)

Constituted 1857 (44 Mark and 39 R.A.M. Lodges), (Keystone Province)
(150th Anniversary Keystone Province)
Provincial Grand Lodge will meet annually at such place and day as the
Provincial Grand Master shall direct

Provincial Grand Master:
R.W.Bro. RAYMOND STANLEY HENRY HUSSEY
Appointed 5th May, 2004

Deputy Provincial Grand Master:
W.Bro. DAVID JOHN BLACKBURN, P.G.J.D. (2012)

Assistant Provincial Grand Masters:
W.Bro. DAVID MALCOLM WILLMOTT, P.G.S.D. (2010)
V.W.Bro. PETER ERNEST RUBIE-TODD, P.G.J.O. (2012)

Provincial Grand Secretary:
W.Bro. IAN NELSON CLARK, P.A.G.D.C. (2010)
Tanglewood, Hillbury Close, Warlingham, Surrey CR6 9TN
Tel: 01883 626996
Email: nelsclark@yahoo.co.uk

13 K*	*Hiram*	Guildford	1268	*	*Coulsdon*	Croydon
114 K*	*Percy*	Guildford	1285 K*		*Redhill*	Croydon
198 K*	*Croydon*	Croydon	1314 K*		*Weald of Surrey*	Sutton
333 K*	*Kintore*	Croydon	1320	*	*Addiscombe*	Croydon
442 K*	*Weyside*	Guildford	1321	*	*Warlingham*	Redhill
450 K*	*Crystal Palace*	Sutton	1352 K*		*Comites Sigillorum*	Croydon
451 K*	*Bolingbroke*	Croydon	1356 K*		*The Dorking*	Croydon
505 K*	*Noel*	Surbiton	1407	*	*Frederick Wheeler*	Croydon
534 K*	*Rose*	Surbiton	1411 K*		*The Curfew*	Chertsey
806 K*	*St. Andrew's*	Farnham	1419 K*		*Lingfield*	Surrey
808 K*	*Richmond*	Surbiton	1569	*■	*Woodstock*	Surbiton
914 K*	*Loyalty*	Croydon	1576	*	*Bond of Friendship*	Croydon
955 K*	*Pleydell-Bouverie*	Godalming	1669	*	*The Collingwood*	Guildford
989 K*■	*Northern Heights*	Sutton	1704		*Fratres Calami Aerariique*	
995 K*	*Stoneleigh*	Sutton				Sutton
1050 K*■	*Esher*	Chertsey	1726		■*Mark Provincial Grand*	
1097 K	*East Croydon*	Croydon			*Stewards Lodge of Surrey*	
1111 K*	*Woodgrange*	Croydon				Croydon
1131 K*	*Camberley*	Camberley	1738	*	*Pride of Surrey*	Sutton
1167 K*■	*Manor of Bensham*	Croydon	1742	*■	*Sanderstead*	Croydon
1197 K*	*H.A. Mann*	Sutton	1839	*	*Oaktree*	Bisley
1219	*■ *Surrey Installed Mark*		1841		*Table Fellowship*	Surbiton
	Masters	Surbiton	1857	*	*Ditton*	Surbiton
1237	*■ *Welcome*	Sutton	1917		*Cranleigh Centenary*	Cranleigh

SUSSEX (32)

Constituted 1874 (39 Mark and 25 R.A.M. Lodges)
Provincial Grand Lodge meets once a year at such time and place as determined by the Provincial Grand Master

Provincial Grand Master:
R.W.Bro. CHARLES MARTIN WILSON
Appointed 24th April, 2012

Deputy Provincial Grand Master:
V.W.Bro. ROGER FRANCIS RICHARDSON, P.G.J.O. (2012)

Assistant Provincial Grand Master:
W.Bro. ANDRIES JOHANNES VAN DER BURGH, P.A.G.D.C. (2012)

Provincial Grand Secretary:
W.Bro. STUART ALEXANDER LEWIS (2012)
6 Ambleside Road, Sompting, Lancing, West Sussex BN15 9SE
Tel: 01903 779660 Mobile: 07810 205898
Email: stuartlewis@live.co.uk

75 K*	*Royal Sussex*	Brighton	1086 K*	*Abbey*		Battle
164 *	*Southdown*	Haywards Heath	1117 K*	*Hampton Parva*		Littlehampton
166 *	*East Sussex*	St. Leonards-on-Sea	1158 *	*Sussex Installed Mark Masters*		Brighton
168	*Hova*	Brighton	1234 *	*Hailsham*		Herstmonceux
386 K	*Adur*	Brighton	1241 *	*Earl of Courtown*		East Grinstead
391 K*	*Lewis*	Lewes	1245 K*	*Pulborough*		Pulborough
409 K*	*Royal Connaught*	Brighton	1375 K	*Charles H. Mosse*		Peacehaven
426 K	*Brighton*	Brighton	1490 K*	*Harold W. Richardson*		Brighton
449 *	*Mid-Sussex*	Horsham	1520 K*	*St. Margaret of Antioch*		Ifield
453 K*	*West Sussex*	Worthing	1530 K	*Heffle*		Burwash Common
484 K*	*Eastbourne*	Eastbourne	1556	*Wellington*		Rye
568 K*	*Regnum*	Chichester	1747 K	*Sussex Mark Provincial Grand Stewards*		Brighton
631 *■	*Thornton*	Uckfield				
703 *	*Hothampton*	Bognor Regis	1763	*Charmandean*		Worthing
732 K	*Persevere*	Brighton	1795 *	*James Webster*		Brighton
918 K*	*Rottingdean*	Brighton	1831 K*	*Thomas á Becket*		Worthing
978 K	*Temperance*	Brighton	1876 *	*Clifford W. Jeapes*		Peacehaven
979 K	*Arts and Crafts*	Brighton	1898 *	*West Sussex Lodge of Installed Mark Masters*		Chichester
1009 K	*Midhurst*	Midhurst				
1025 K	*Duke of Richmond*	Brighton				
1058 K*	*Bexhill*	Bexhill	1931	*Amity*		Peacehaven

WARWICKSHIRE (33)

Constituted 1876 (32 Mark and 20 R.A.M. Lodges), (Keystone Province)
Provincial Grand Lodge meets on fourth Saturday in November
Provincial Grand Master:
R.W.Bro. ROGER STUART MAC
Appointed 24th November, 2012
Deputy Provincial Grand Master:
W.Bro. DEREK JOHN GRIFFIN, P.G.J.D. (2012)
Assistant Provincial Grand Master:
W.Bro. GARETH HUGHES, P.G.J.D. (2012)
Provincial Grand Secretary:
W.Bro. MICHAEL DAMIAN SAXON, P.A.G.D.C. (2012)
47 Victoria Road, Bromsgrove, Worcestershire B61 0DW
Tel/Fax: 01527 874661
E-mail: secwarksmark@gmail.com

T.I. K	*Howe*	Birmingham	1041 K	*Holte*	Birmingham
40 K*	*Shakespeare*	Warwick	1066 K	*Lodge of Peace*	
115 K*	*Bedford*	Birmingham		*and Unity*	Birmingham
174 K*	*Athol*	Birmingham	1128 K	*St. Christopher's*	
408 K*	*Hertford Military*	Birmingham			Sutton Coldfield
430 K*	*Charity*	Birmingham	1256 K*	*Remembrance*	Birmingham
606 K*	*Seymour*	Leamington Spa	1400 K*	*Warwickshire Installed Mark*	
629 K*	*Temperance*	Birmingham		*Masters*	Birmingham
698 K*	*Machen*	Birmingham	1501 K*	*Signa Bene*	Alcester
719 K*	*Yenton*	Yenton	1574 K*	*The Harry Wilson*	Nuneaton
735 K*	*Concord*	Birmingham	1737 K*	*Thomas Arthur Wood*	Warwick
744 K*	*Central Keystone*	Birmingham	1746 K	*Progress*	Birmingham
757 K*	*Vesey*	Sutton Coldfield	1774 K	*Royal Air Force*	Edgbaston
776 K*	*Rugby*	Rugby	1811 K	*Coventry*	Coventry
870 K	*St. Paul's*	Birmingham	1818 K	*Ronald Albutt*	Birmingham
959 K	*St. Martin's*	Birmingham	1844 K	*Cyril Batham*	
972 K*	*Silhill*	Knowle			Stratford upon Avon
1012 K*	*Matthew Clarke*	Birmingham	1883 ■	*Mancetter*	Atherstone

WEST LANCASHIRE (34)
Constituted 1870 (60 Mark and 24 R.A.M. Lodges), (Keystone Province)
Provincial Grand Lodge meets on first Wednesday in May
Provincial Grand Master:
R.W.Bro. PETER CONNOLLY
Appointed 18th January, 2007
Deputy Provincial Grand Master:
V.W.Bro. KEITH ALAN BEARDMORE, P.G.J.O. (2012)
Assistant Provincial Grand Masters:
V.W.Bro. MICHAEL JOHN CLARKE, P.G.J.O. (2010)
W.Bro. IAN DOUGLAS NAIRN, P.G.J.D. (2011)
Provincial Grand Secretary:
W.Bro. GEOFFREY HERBERT LEE, G.J.D. (2010)
25 Hough Lane, Leyland, Lancs. PR25 2SB
Tel: 01772 421878 Mobile: 07836 219663
Email: wlmarkprovsec@gmail.com

T.I. K	■*Lebanon*	Liverpool	903 K*	*Prescot*	Prescot
36 K	*Furness*	Barrow-in-Furness	935 K	*Lodge of Charity*	Bryn
65 K*	*West Lancashire*	Liverpool	942 K	*Garston*	Garston
143 K*	*Preston*	Preston	956 K	*George Harradon*	Liverpool
146 K	*Garnett*	Lancaster	992 K	*Allen Pooley*	Liverpool
158 K*	*Rose and Thistle*	Wigan	1002 K*	*Leyland*	Leyland
161 K	*Walton*	Garston	1003 K	*Newton*	Bryn
268 K	*Lathom*	Southport	1006 K	*Westhoughton*	Westhoughton
296 K*■	*Fylde*	Blackpool	1007 K	*Freshfield*	Southport
313 K*	*Lawrence*	Chorley	1019 K*	*Ormskirk Priory*	Ormskirk
359 K*	*Excelsior*	Garston	1052 K	*Corinthian*	Liverpool
375 K*	*Jubilee*	Ulverston	1062 K	*The University of*	
394 K*	*Chorlton*	Chorlton-cum-Hardy		*Liverpool*	Liverpool
447 K	*Clarence*	Widnes	1099 K	*Tuscan*	Liverpool
466 K	*Prince of Wales*	St. Helen's	1103 K	*Scorton*	Garstang
473 K*	*Southport*	Southport	1113 K	*Fermor*	Southport
478 K	*Bootle*	Bootle	1173 K*	*Flixton Shepherd Eastwood*	
479 K*■	*St. Austin's*	Warrington			Urmston
490 K	*Murray*	Wigan	1176 K	*Cleveleys*	Cleveleys
523 K	*Wilbraham*	Widnes	1178 K	*Warrington*	Warrington
552 K*	*Adoniram*	Leyland	1276 K	*Imperial*	Poulton-le-Fylde
553 K*	*St. George*	Garston	1312 K	*Aeon*	Leyland
563 K	*Coronation*	Garston	1322 K*	*Leigh*	Leigh
716 K*	*Morecambe*	Morecambe	1331 K	*Queensway*	Prescot
734 K	*Ormskirk*	Ormskirk	1438 K	*New Temple*	Chorley
754 K	*Wyre*	Fleetwood	1446 K*	*Prince Setana*	
774 K	*Temperance*	Liverpool			Poulton Le Fylde
843 K	*Eccles*	Eccles	1475 K	*Cloister*	Chorlton-cum-Hardy
866 K	*Bispham with Norbreck*		1539 K*	*Ridgmont*	Horwich
		Blackpool	1549 K	*Friendship*	Southport
880 K*	*Semper Fidelis*	1594	K	*The Red Rose*	Hindley
		St. Annes-on-Sea	1646	* *Philadelphia Lodge of Installed*	
898 K*	*Progress*	Preston		*Mark Masters*	Leyland

WEST YORKSHIRE (35)

Constituted 1871 (44 Mark and 21 R.A.M. Lodges), (Double Keystone Province)
(150th Anniversary Keystone Province)
Provincial Grand Lodge meets at such time and place as the Provincial Grand Master shall direct

Provincial Grand Master:
R.W.Bro. JAMES STEGGLES
Appointed 17th November, 2012

Deputy Provincial Grand Master:
V.W.Bro. ROBERT CORFIELD, P.G.J.O. (2012)

Assistant Provincial Grand Master:
W.Bro. JOHN FRED CLOUGH, P.G.J.D. (2009)

Provincial Grand Secretary:
W.Bro. ALAN OLDFIELD, P.G.J.D. (2010)
14 High Street, Thornhill, Dewsbury, West Yorkshire WF12 0PS
Tel: 01924 465458
E-mail: alanoldfield54@gmail.com

T.I. K* *Old York*	Cleckheaton	706 K *Halifax*	Halifax
14 K*■ *Prince Edward*	Huddersfield	715 K*■ *Lightcliffe*	Hipperholme
53 K* *Britannia*	Sheffield	727 K ■ *Worth*	Keighley
58 K*■ *Fearnley*	Mirfield	753 K ■ *Brighouse*	Brighouse
110 K*■ *Integrity*	Wakefield	768 K*■ *Knaresborough Castle*	
111 K*■ *Copley*	Leeds		Knaresborough
127 K* *Portal*	Barnsley	812 K *Gilkirke*	Barnoldswick
137 K*■ *Truth*	Huddersfield	878 K*■ *Pontefract*	Pontefract
352 K ■ *Prince Leopold*	Ripon	887 K ■ *Lascelles*	Sheffield
374 K ■ *St. Chad*	Leeds	943 K ■ *Sincerity*	Sheffield
398 K ■ *Danum*	Doncaster	1004 K*■ *Thorne*	Thorne
457 K ■ *Legiolium*	Castleford	1018 K *Gothic*	Swinton
493 K ■ *Eland*	West Vale	1027 K ■ *Wharfedale*	Otley
501 K*■ *Caldene*	Hebden Bridge	1067 K ■ *White Rose*	Baildon
525 K*■ *Haywra*	Harrogate	1079 K*■ *St. Hiev*	Bingley
535 K*■ *Bronte*	Haworth	1139 K ■ *Escafeld*	Sheffield
545 K ■ *Dartmouth*	Slaithwaite	1191 K ■*Vulcan*	Sheffield
618 K ■ *Cleeves*	Sheffield	1257 K ■ *Castle*	Leeds
641 K*■ *Dewsbury*	Dewsbury	1523 K ■ *Beaumont*	Kirkburton
651 K*■ *Rother*	Rotherham	1739 K ■ *Ainsty*	Wetherby
658 K*■ *Pudsey*	Pudsey	1769 K ■ *Aireferry*	Goole
669 K ■ *Aries*	Bradford	1905 *■ *Morley*	Batley
681 K* *Peace*	Uppermill		

WILTSHIRE (36)

Constituted 1892 (13 Mark and 8 R.A.M. Lodges), (Keystone Province)
(150th Anniversary Keystone Province)
Provincial Grand Lodge meets on third Thursday in June

Provincial Grand Master:
R.W.Bro. ALFRED MARTIN JEFFERSON BROWN
Appointed 17th June, 2010

Deputy Provincial Grand Master:
W.Bro. JOHN BELL, P.G.S.D. (2010)

Provincial Grand Secretary:
W.Bro. ROBERT ALAN BLAKE, P.A.G.D.C. (2012)
15 Rock Lane, Warminster, Wiltshire BA12 9JZ
Tel: 01985 218929
Email: robert_blake1110@hotmail.co.uk

178 K*	*Wiltshire Keystone*	Devizes	1110 K*	*Warminster*		Warminster
401 K*	*Swindon Keystone*	Swindon	1143 K	■*Border*		Ludgershall
443 K*	*Elias de Derham*	Salisbury	1460 K*	*Wiltshire Installed Mark*		
599 K	*Chaloner*	Melksham		*Masters*		Chippenham
853 K	*Radnor*	Salisbury	1531 K	*St. Aldhelm*		Malmesbury
971 K*	*Geoffrey Short*	Trowbridge	1599	■*The Kennet*		Marlborough
1035 K*■	*Lansdowne*	Chippenham	1843	*	*Wiltshire Downs*	Warminster

---

WORCESTERSHIRE (37)

Constituted 1884 (22 Mark and 16 R.A.M. Lodges), (Keystone Province)
Provincial Grand Lodge meets on second Saturday in June

Provincial Grand Master:
R.W.Bro. FRANCIS CHARLES SPENCER
Appointed 4th June, 2005

Deputy Provincial Grand Master:
V.W.Bro. LAURENCE ERIC BOURNE, *J.P.*, P.G.J.O. (2010)

Provincial Grand Secretary:
W.Bro. ADRIAN WILLIAM CHURCH (2011)
527 Chester Road South, Kidderminster, Worcestershire DA0 1XH
Tel: 01562 824182 Mobile: 07580 580523
Email: secretary@worcestershiremarkpgl.org.uk

59 K*	*Lechmere*	Worcester	1334	*	*Bromsgrove*	Bromsgrove
330 K*	*Godson*	Dudley	1351		*The Malvern Priory*	Malvern
590 K*	*Athlumney*	Oldbury	1409	*	*Worcestershire Installed*	
667 K*	*Moseley*	Moseley			*Masters*	Worcester
733 K*	*Perseverance*	Halesowen	1462 K*		*All Saints Kings Heath*	
747 K*	*Stechford*	Stechford				King's Heath
893 K*	*St. Laurence*	Redditch	1623	*	*Centenary*	Birmingham
923 K*	*Vernon*	Stourport-on-Severn	1813		*Provincial Directors of*	
977 K*	*Eaton*	Birmingham			*Ceremonies*	
1135	*	*St. Egwin*	Evesham	1822 K*	*Millennium*	Birmingham
1136 K	*Mosaic*	Dudley	1901		*Quill and Key*	Birmingham
1260 K*	*Teme Valley*	Tenbury Wells	1920		*St. George's*	Bewdley
1281	*Stability*	Stourbridge				

DISTRICT GRAND LODGES
BELGIUM (67)

Constituted 1996 (9 Mark and 6 R.A.M. Lodges)
District Grand Lodge meets at a time and place the District Grand Master shall direct

District Grand Master
R.W.Bro. JEAN VERBIST
Appointed 1st December, 2012

Deputy District Grand Master
V.W.Bro. JEAN-PIERRE ROBERT, P.G.J.O. (2012)

Assistant District Grand Master
W.Bro. DANIEL SHIELDS, P.A.G.D.C. (2012)

District Grand Secretary
W.Bro. EMMANUEL JOZEF ADRIENNE PAUL CLAESSENS (2012)
Rue de l'Eglise, 36, 1060-Bruxelles, Belgium
Mobile: 00 32 477 70 7777
Email: manu.claessens@telenet.be

1587	*	*La Marque D'Alliance*	Champion	1673 K*	*Mark of Enterprise*	Bruxelles
1603 K*		*Les Disciples de Salomon*		1753 *	*Ter Duinen*	Koksijde
			Leuven	1815 K*	*La Marque de Lorraine*	Arlon
1624 K*		*La Marque d'Union*	Bruxelles	1875	*Prins van Oranje*	Antwerp
1653		*L'Esperance*	Charleroi	1928	*John of Gaunt*	Gent

BOLIVIA (74)

Constituted 2000 (9 Mark and 6 R.A.M. Lodges)
District Grand Lodge meets on

District Grand Master:
R.W.Bro. DAVID ALCOREZA MARCHETTI
Appointed 24th November, 2012

Deputy District Grand Master:
W.Bro. MARIO JAVIER EGUIA (2012)

District Grand Secretary:
W.Bro. RENÉ GONZÁLES LEYTON (2012)
Casilla 1255, La Paz, Bolivia
Tel: +591 2272 0565
Email: mundorgl@hotmail.com

1666	*	*Bond of Friendship*	La Paz	1842	*Concordia*	Oruro
1754	*	*Lealtad*	La Paz	1865 *	*Cyril H. Rees Providencia*	La Paz
1790	*	*Fraternidad*	La Paz	1879	*Luz y Concordia*	Cochabamba
1794	*	*Santa Cruz*	Santa Cruz	1891	*Chuquisaca*	Sucre
1805	*	*Cantera Del Oriente*	Santa Cruz			

BOMBAY (39)
Constituted 1870 (5 Mark and 5 R.A.M. Lodges)
District Grand Lodge meets on first Saturday in March
District Grand Master:
R.W.Bro. SHRIKRISHNA GOPALRAO AROLE
Appointed 2nd May, 2009
Deputy District Grand Master:
W.Bro. JOSEPH JANARDAN D'SILVA, P.A.G.D.C. (2012)
District Grand Secretary:
W.Bro. SURENDRA KUMAR SHAH, P.G.J.D. (2012)
Freemasons' Hall, D. Sukhadwala Road, Fort Mumbai, India 401 001
Tel: 00 91 22 2351 6840
Email: RecdGCWI@gmail.com

514 K*	*Sandhurst*	Bombay	668 K*	*St. Marks*	Poona
648 *	*Lewis*	Bombay	836 K*	*Industry and Merit*	Bombay
653 *	*Capt. Sam B. Aga*	Nagpur			

BRAZIL (40)
Constituted 1953 (11 Mark and 7 R.A.M. Lodges)
District Grand Lodge meets on second Saturday in October
District Grand Master:
R.W.Bro. JOHN CHARLES WOODROW
Appointed 19th January, 2005
Deputy District Grand Master:
W.Bro. RAPHAEL NASSIM BEHAR, P.G.J.D. (2008)
Assistant District Grand Master:
W.Bro. JOSÉ LUIZ GAMBARINI, P.G.J.D. (2008)
District Grand Secretary:
V.W.Bro. PLÍNIO VIRGÍLIO GENZ, P.G.J.O. (2008)
Rua Brasilia 45 Apt 81, Itaim, São Paulo, SP, Brazil 04534 040
Tel: 0055 11 3071 3566
Email: pliniog3@uol.com.br

961 K*	*St. Paul's*	São Paulo	1852 *	*Barão de Mauá*	São Paulo
1137 *	*Wanderers*	Santos	1854	*Harmonia*	Niterói
1156 K*	*Guanabara*	Rio de Janeiro	1888	*The Goose and Gridiron*	
1355 *	*Campos Salles*	São Paulo			Rio de Janeiro
1817 *	*Fênix*	São Paulo	1908	*Centenary*	São Paulo
1819 *	*Moses Montefiore*	São Paulo	1926	*Santa Catarina*	Florianopolis

CYPRUS (77)

Constituted 2010 (4 Mark and 1 R.A.M. Lodges)

District Grand Master:
R.W.Bro. THEODOSIOS SOCRATOUS THEODOSSIOU
Appointed 27th November, 2010

Deputy District Grand Master:
W.Bro. DUNCAN JOHN MOORE, P.G.S.D. (2010)

District Grand Secretary:
W.Bro. GERALD LESLIE GOLDSACK, P.G.S.D. (2011)
302 C(L/e) Lordos Pelagos Hill, Georgiou Griva Degeni, Chlorakas, 8220 Paphos, Cyprus
Tel: 00357 2692 3601
Email: dgsecmmm@cyprus-freemasons.org.cy

455		*St. Paul's*	Limassol	1904		*Kition*	Larnaca
1835	*	*Kypros*	Episkopi	1923		*Phoenix*	Nicosia

EAST AFRICA (42)

Constituted 1978 (9 Mark and 9 R.A.M. Lodges)
District Grand Lodge meets on the fourth Saturday in June

District Grand Master:
R.W.Bro. PHILIP SHERWIN
Appointed 11th April, 2008

Deputy District Grand Master:
W.Bro. KISHORE NAYAR, P.A.G.D.C. (2012)

Assistant District Grand Master:
W.Bro. VIJAY MOTICHAND SHAH, P.A.G.St.B. (2012)

District Grand Secretary:
W.Bro. PHIL MINOO DASTUR, P.A.G.D.C. (2012)
P.O. Box 58008, Nairobi, Kenya 00200
Mobile: +254 733 606751
Email: dusty1938@gmail.com

816	*	*Rock of Hope*	Dar es Salaam	1602	*	*Rift Valley*	Naivasha
906	*	*Mount Mawenzi*	Selia Arusha	1636	*	*Nyanza*	Kisumu
952	K*	*Kenya*	Nairobi	1776	*	*Seychelles*	Mahe
1198	K*	*Nandi Border*	Eldoret	1787	*	*East Africa Lodge of Installed Mark Masters*	Nairobi
1476	*	*Donyo Sabuk*	Ruiru				

GERMANY (60)
Constituted 1980 (12 Mark and 11 R.A.M. Lodges)
District Grand Lodge shall meet at least once a year at such time and place
as the District Grand Master shall decide
District Grand Master:
R.W.Bro. MICHAEL ANDREW COOPER
Appointed 28th November, 2009
Deputy District Grand Master:
W.Bro. JOHN MACKINNON, P.G.S.D. (2012)
Assistant District Grand Masters:
W.Bro. Dr. WOLFGANG SCHAEFER, P.G.S.D. (2012)
W.Bro. MICHAEL EDWARD BRAHAM, P.A.G.D.C. (2012)
District Grand Secretary:
W.Bro. DAVID JOHN MCDOUGALL (2012)
Haupt Strasse 9, 25489 Haseldorf, Germany
Tel: +4129 955484 Mobile: +0171 745 3972
Email: john@mcdougall.de

1432 K*	*Heinz Ritter Friendship*	Mönchengladbach-Rheindahlen	1575	*	*Sparrenburg*	Kassel
1471	*	*Britannia* Bielefeld	1600	*	*Saxony*	Berlin
1498 K*	*Rose of Minden*	Herford	1612	*	*Tremonia*	Hanover
1515	*	*Keys of Münster* Frankfurt am Main	1642	*	*Ludwig Zum Flammenden Stern*	Steinfurt-Burgsteinfurt
1518		*West Germany Installed Mark Masters* Osnabrück	1782	*	*The Rope and Anchor*	Hamburg
			1792	*	*Zum Maurischen Schloss im See*	Langenargen
1542	*	*Doric* Osnabrück				

GHANA (73)
Constituted 2010 – (Formerly a Group)
(5 Mark and 3 Royal Ark Mariner)
District Grand Lodge meets on 3rd Saturday in June in Accra.
Half-yearly communication on 2nd Saturday in December at such place
as may be appointed by the District Grand Master
District Grand Master:
R.W.Bro. Nana Dr. FREDUAH MENSAH
Appointed 20th March, 2010
Deputy District Grand Master:
V.W.Bro. Dr. JO BLANKSON, *Ph.D.*, P.G.J.O. (2010)
Assistant District Grand Master:
W.Bro. EDDIE HAYFORD, P.G.S.D. (2010)
District Grand Secretary:
W.Bro. ROBERT GARDINER EKOW DANIELS
P.O. Box KN 5474, Kaneshie, Accra, Ghana
Tel. No. (O): 00 233 302 632074 Mobile: 00 233 243 83795
Email: gdglmmms@yahoo.com

1217 K*	*Ghana*	Accra, Ghana	1887	*	*Taquah*	Tarkwa, Ghana
1672	*	*Accra* Adjabeng, Ghana	1930		*Sir Charles Tache-Menson*	Accra
1702		*Asanteman* Kumasi, Ghana				

GIBRALTAR (43)

Constituted 1884 (3 Mark and 1 R.A.M. Lodges)
District Grand Lodge meets twice a year in March and October

District Grand Master:
R.W.Bro. ALFRED HENRY RYAN
Appointed 6th December, 2007

Deputy District Grand Master:
W.Bro. MAURICE KEY, P.A.G.D.C. (2011)

District Grand Secretary:
W.Bro. EMILIO BARKER, P.G.St.B. (2008)
45 Repulse Hse., Varyl Begg Estate, Gibraltar
Tel (H.): 00 350 200 73760   (W.): 00 350 200 40202   Mob: 00 350 540 12538
Email: emilboss@gibtelecom.net

43	*	*Gibraltar*	Gibraltar	516 K	*Hammerton*	Gibraltar
278		*Mediterranean*	Gibraltar			

HONG KONG (44)

Constituted 1925 Redesignated 1964 (4 Mark and 2 R.A.M. Lodges)
(Keystone District)
District Grand Lodge meets on first Monday in June

District Grand Master:
R.W.Bro. ANGUS JOHN DELANO STEVENSON-HAMILTON
Appointed 17th January, 2007

Deputy District Grand Master:
W.Bro. HERBERT HAK KONG TSOI, *B.B.S., J.P.*, P.G.J.D. (2012)

District Grand Secretary:
W.Bro. PATRICK PURNELL-EDWARDS, P.A.G.D.C. (2008)
Flat 7a, Emerald Garden, 86 Pokfulam Road, Pokfulam, Hong Kong
Tel (H. & W.): 00 852 2834 6275   Fax: 00 852 3018 1215   Mobile: +852 9190 7683
Email: ppe88@netvigator.com

264	*	*Eothen*	Hong Kong	721 K*	*Concordia*	Hong Kong
419 K		*United*	Hong Kong	832 K	*Shameen*	Hong Kong

ITALY (76)
Constituted 2010   (4 Mark and 2 R.A.M. Lodges)
District Grand Lodge meets on second Saturday in December

District Grand Master:
R.W.Bro. FABIO VENZI
Appointed 19th June, 2010

Deputy District Grand Master:
W.Bro. ROBERTO BURSESE   (2012)

Assistant District Grand Master:
W.Bro. RINALDO ROMANI   (2010)

District Grand Secretary:
W.Bro. ANDREA BONECHI, P.A.G.D.C.   (2010)
Via A. Righi, 48, 52100 Arezzo, Italy
Mob: +39 335 350 641
Email: italy@glmmm.it

1896	*	Pico Della Mirandola	1916	*	Giorgio Vasari
		Rome and other Italian cities			Arrezo and other Italian cities
1915		John Dee	1934		Gaetano Filangieri
		Rome and other Italian cities			Genoa and other Italian cities

---

JAMAICA & CAYMAN ISLANDS (45)
Constituted 1877   (8 Mark and 7 R.A.M. Lodges)
District Grand Lodge meets on fourth Tuesday in June

District Grand Master:
R.W.Bro. LINTON ANTHONY ANDREWS, *J.P.*
Appointed 20th October, 2009

Deputy District Grand Master:
W.Bro. JEFFREY PAUL MORGAN, P.G.S.D.   (2009)

Assistant District Grand Master:
W.Bro. EVOL WASHINGTON LYN-COOK, P.A.G.D.C.   (2011)

District Grand Secretary:
W.Bro. EVAN GARFIELD KILDARE DONALDSON   (2012)
Medical Associates Hospital, 18 Tangerine Place, Kingston 10, Jamaica, West Indies
Tel/Fax: (H) 001 876 968 9705
Email: kildare@cwjamaical.com

42	*	Sussex	Kingston	1424	*	Melrose Keystone	Mandeville
240	*	Royal Keystone	Kingston	1559	*	The Friendly	Kingston
242		Phœnix	Kingston	1618	*	Cayman Keystone	
368	*	Kingston Keystone	Kingston				Grand Cayman
1232	*	Cornwall Keystone					
			Montego Bay				

MADRAS (46)

Constituted 1871 (14 Mark and 12 R.A.M. Lodges)
District Grand Lodge meets on second Saturdays in February and August

District Grand Master:
R.W.Bro. MADHAVAN CHELLAPPA
Appointed 24th September, 2011

Deputy District Grand Master:
W.Bro. ACHYUTKUMAR CHANDUBAI PATEL, P.G.S.D. (2012)

Assistant District Grand Master:
W.Bro. APPUKUTTAN PILLAI KARUNAKARAN NAIR, P.A.G.D.C. (2011)

District Grand Secretary:
W.Bro. Dr. JOONISSAIT MOHAMED ISMAIL SAIT, P.A.G.D.C. (2011)
Freemasons' Hall, 14 Ethiraj Salai, Egmore, Chennai, India 600 008
Tel (H.): +91 44 2674 4710 Tel (O.): +91 44 2822 5516
Email: drjmi.sait@gmail.com

81	*	Keystone	Secunderabad	640	*	United Service	Bangalore
157	*	Russell	Ootacamund	642	*	Lord Carmichael	Calcutta
160	*	Macdonald Ritchie	Chennai	877	*	Sivangnanam	Thiruvananthapuram
220 K	*	Sandeman Stat Veritas	Calcutta				
496		Zuriel	Calcutta	907	*	Campbell	Erode
531		Orient	Calcutta	937	*	Cauvery	Tanjore
542	*	Davoren	Wellington	1225	*	Kerala	Calicut (Kozhikode)
610	*	Chola	Trichinopoly				

NATAL (47)

Constituted 1883 (12 Mark and 8 R.A.M. Lodges), (Keystone District)
District Grand Lodge meets at such time and place as the
District Grand Master may consider necessary

District Grand Master:
R.W.Bro. DAVID ZAVAD
Appointed 19th September, 2009

Deputy District Grand Master:
V.W.Bro. DEREK NORMAN ROBERTS, P.G.J.O. (2009)

Assistant District Grand Master:
W.Bro. WAYNE NORMAN JOHNSTON (2011)

District Grand Secretary:
W.Bro. HERMAN VAN WIJK, P.G.J.D. (2010)
Unit 2-22 Assegai Road, Hayfields, Pietermaritzburg, 3317 South Africa
Tel (H): 00 27 33 3966686 (W)/Fax: 00 27 33 3961030
Email: mark.ram@satweb.co.za

252 K*	Natalia	Pietermaritzburg	575 K*	Stanger	Stanger
288 K*	Port Natal	Durban	1046 K*	Zululand	Empangeni (Zululand)
486 K	Natal Installed Masters	Pietermaritzburg	1223 K*	The Lewis	Park Rynie
515 K*	Addington	Durban	1294	The East Griqualand	Kokstad
528 K	Ladysmith	Ladysmith	1578 *	Harmony	Camperdown
566 K*■	Biggarsberg Unity	Dundee	1816	Durban Inanda	

THE NETHERLANDS (48)

Constituted 1972 (22 Mark and 16 R.A.M. Lodges)
District Grand Lodge meets on the first Saturday in September

District Grand Master:
R.W.Bro. SYBE TUNNIS BOOIJ
Appointed 1st September, 2007

Deputy District Grand Master:
W.Bro. CORNELIS VAN PUTTEN, P.G.J.D. (2012)

Assistant District Grand Master:
W.Bro. FRANK CORNELIS JOHANNES POOR, P.G.St.B. (2012)

District Grand Secretary:
V.W.Bro. DICK LANGELAAR, P.G.J.O. (1998)
Zandzegge 8, 2318 ZL Leiden, The Netherlands
Tel: 00 31 71 5232171
Email: langeld@xs4all.nl

1220	K*	*Concord*	Rotterdam	1488	*	*Libanon*	Terneuzen
1283	K*	*Jacob van Lennep*	The Hague	1504	K*	*Moriah*	Alkmaar
1324	K*	*Zaradatha*	Leiden	1516	*	*Het Sticht*	Amersfoort
1344	K*	*Adon Hiram*	Groningen	1533	*	*Twente*	Enschede
1376	K*	*Mosam Trajectum*	Roermond	1547	*	*Thuredrecht*	Dordrecht
1384		*Gijsbrecht van Amstel*	Amsterdam	1562		*Marckdael*	Breda
				1565	*	*Hollandia*	Bilthoven
1390		*Hamerkin*	Deventer	1579	*	*de Sluitsteen*	Wageningen
1414		*Schieland*	Rotterdam	1580	*	*de Keursteen*	Leeuwarden
1421		*Succoth*	Haarlem	1601	*	*Den Aks*	Eindhoven
1434	*	*The Netherlands Installed Mark Masters Lodge*	Bilthoven	1741		*Coronet*	Roermond
				1799	*	*Delta*	Goes

NEW ZEALAND (49)

Constituted 1882 Redesignated 1967 & 2002 (10 Mark and 7 R.A.M. Lodges)
(Formerly New Zealand, North Island and New Zealand, South Island)
District Grand Lodge meets on first and/or second Saturdays in August

District Grand Master:
R.W.Bro. Capt. IAIN MALCOLM MCGIBBON, *O.B.E.*
Appointed 25th February, 2006

Deputy District Grand Master:
W.Bro. JEREMY EGGLETON, P.G.J.D. (2012)

Assistant District Grand Master:
W.Bro. IAN DINGWALL, P.A.G.D.C. (2012)

District Grand Secretary:
W.Bro. DAVID MICHAEL WILDING, P.A.G.D.C. (2009)
11 Tauranga Place, Orewa, Whangaparaoa 0931, New Zealand
Tel: +64 9 426 9931
Email: davidwilding41@xtra.co.nz

49	*	*Lewis*	Auckland	579	*	*St. George*	Helensville
154	*	*Union*	Auckland	580		*Concord*	Whangarei
272	*	*Hiram*	Taradale	1064	*	*Sir Donald McLean*	Waitara
280		*Newton*	Auckland	1101	*	*Aorangi*	Wellington
300		*South Canterbury*	Christchurch	1261	*	*United Manawatu*	Palmerston North

NIGERIA (78)
Constituted 2011 (5 Mark and 3 R.A.M. Lodges)
District Grand Lodge meets in the third quarter of the year
at a date appointed by the District Grand Master
District Grand Master:
R.W.Bro. ADEDIJI ADEDOYIN
Appointed 21st October, 2011
Deputy District Grand Master:
W.Bro. BABAJIDE AKINBODE ADESOLA, P.G.S.D. (2011)
Assistant District Grand Master:
W.Bro. BABATUNDE ADEYEMI JOHNSON, P.A.G.D.C. (2011)
District Grand Secretary:
Bro. IBUKUN AYODELE WILLIAMS (2011)
P.O. Box 2783, Marina, Lagos State, Nigeria
Mobile: +234 803 2641 745
Email: williamsibukun24@yahoo.com

624	*	*Premier*	Lagos	1851 *	*Eko*	Ebute-Metta
1433	*	*Arewa*	Kaduna	1927 *	*Port Hacourt*	Port Harcourt
1850	*	*Abeokuta*	Abeokuta			

NORTHERN INDIA (51)
Constituted 1953 (5 Mark and 3 R.A.M. Lodges)
District Grand Lodge meets on third Saturday in November
District Grand Master:
R.W.Bro. VISWANATHAN NAGARAJAN
Appointed 26th February, 2008
Deputy District Grand Master:
W.Bro. KAPIL DEV JOTI (2006)
District Grand Secretary:
R.W.Bro. RADHEY SHYAM GUPTA (2009)
4962 Hauz Qazi, O.P.P. S.B.I., Delhi, India 110 066
Tel: (H) 00 98 181 14879 (B) 00 98 232 11909
Email: dglofmmmni@gmail.com

138		*Adlard*	Jullundur	1255	*Raza*	Amritsar
679	*	*Clarke*	New Delhi	1277 *	*Devi Das*	Chandigarh
1229	*	*Yadavindra*	. Patiala			

RIVER PLATE (53)
Constituted 1908 Redesignated 1974 (5 Mark and 3 R.A.M. Lodges)
(Keystone District)
District Grand Lodge meets on first Friday in November
District Grand Master:
R.W.Bro. WILLIAM PHILIP THOMPSON
Appointed 11th November, 2009
Deputy District Grand Master:
W.Bro. EUSEBIO SANDA PALACIOS, P.A.G.I.G. (2009)
District Grand Secretary:
W.Bro. ERNESTO ALBERTO MARCER, P.G.J.D. (2007)
Juez Tedin 2767, Buenos Aires, Argentina 1425
Tel: 00 54 11 48 076111
Email: ernestoa.marcer@gmail.com

481 K*	*Buenos Aires*	Buenos Aires	628 K*	*Silver River*	
507 K	*Rosario*	Buenos Aires			Montevideo, Uruguay
627 K	*Southern Cross*	Lomas de Zamora	746 K*	*Patron Saints*	Buenos Aires

SINGAPORE (79)

Constituted 2012 (3 Mark and 1 R.A.M. Lodge)
District Grand Lodge meets on the first Saturday in August

District Grand Master:
R.W.Bro. Justice (Ret.) MOHIDEEN PIERRE HAJA RUBIN
Appointed 4th August, 2012

Deputy District Grand Master in charge:
W.Bro. SHIVA PRASAD BANERJEE, P.A.G.D.C. (2012)

District Grand Secretary:
W.Bro. RONALD PAUL NG (2012)
64 Lorong M, Telok Kurau #02-05, Singapore 425365
Tel (O): +65 6235 1504 Fax: +65 6737 9257
Email: ronaldpaul.ng@gmail.com

436 K*	*Edaljee Khory*	Singapore	1935	*Perseverance*	Singapore
1286 K	*The Malaysia*	Singapore			

SOUTH AFRICA (EASTERN DIVISION) (55)

Constituted 1876 (7 Mark and 3 R.A.M. Lodges)
District Grand Lodge meets on 5th Saturday in July or August

District Grand Master:
R.W.Bro. FRANCOIS HEWITT VOSLOO
Appointed 28th July, 2012

Deputy District Grand Master:
W.Bro. DAVID SPENCER FREEMAN, P.G.J.D. (2011)

Assistant District Grand Master:
V.W.Bro. GRAHAM LESLIE BARKER, P.G.J.O. (2011)

District Grand Secretary:
W.Bro. DAVID WILLIAM CAMERON, P.A.G.D.C. (2003)
P.O. Box 571, Port Alfred 6170, South Africa
Tel: 00 27 46 624 5600
Email: david.or.cameron@gmail.com

253 K*	*Spes Bona*	Port Elizabeth	800	*Border Lodge of Installed*	
435 *	*Panmure*	East London		*Mark Massters*	Port Alfred
576 *	*Sphinx*	Port Alfred	819	*Transkei*	Queenstown
799	*Amatole*	Fort Beaufort	1148	*Good Fellowship*	
					Umtata (Transkei)

SOUTH AFRICA (WESTERN DIVISION) (57)
Constituted 1898 (11 Mark and 6 R.A.M. Lodges)
District Grand Lodge meets in July at such time and place
as the District Grand Master may appoint.

District Grand Master:
R.W.Bro. MAX NICHOLAS BROWN
Appointed 7th July, 2012

Deputy District Grand Master:
W.Bro. PIETER VAN DEN BERG, P.G.J.D. (2012)

Assistant District Grand Master:
W.Bro. RODNEY FRANK ATKINSON, P.A.G.D.C. (2012)

District Grand Secretary:
W.Bro. JOHN ALEXANDER DARNÉ, P.A.G.D.C. (2006)
48a North Road, Table View, Cape Town, South Africa
Tel: 00 27 21 557 7502 Fax: 00 27 86 530 1322
Email: johndarne@iburst.co.za

345 K	British	Cape Town	773	*	Van Der Stel	Strand
502 K*	Phœnix	Glen Cairn	985	*	Cango	Mossel Bay
551	* St. George	Cape Town	1120		Drakenstein	Worcester
558	* Israel	Cape Town	1193		Walter Weeden	Hermanus
601 K*	Cape Centenary Lodge of Installed Mark Masters	Cape Town	1216		Union	Kynsna
			1662		Gariep	Springbok

SOUTH AND EAST CARIBBEAN (75)
Constituted 2003 (17 Mark and 13 R.A.M. Lodges)
District Grand Lodge meets in the month of May

District Grand Master
R.W.Bro. STEPHEN BRIAN COBHAM
Appointed 31st May, 2012

Deputy District Grand Master:
W.Bro. LESLIE EUSTACE BINDON NANTON, P.A.G.D.C. (2012)

Assistant District Grand Master:
W.Bro. GASPAR LLEWELLYN GILL, P.G.S.D. (2010)
W.Bro. RALPH MAXWELL CRAIG, J.P., P.G.J.D. (2011)

District Grand Secretary:
W.Bro. HAMILTON LEWIS JONES, P.A.G.D.C. (2010)
P.O. Box 600, St. Thomas, U.S. Virgin Islands 00604-0600
Tel: (340) 775 6633 Mobile: (340) 690 0193
Email: hljones@islands.vi

212 K*	Albion	St. George, Barbados	1849		Guyana Installed Mark Masters	Georgetown
231 K*	Union	Georgetown, Guyana	1864	*	Montserrat	St. Michael, Barbados
1502	* Abercrombie	St. Lucia	1873	*	Dominica	Trinidad
1596	* Stabroek	Georgetown, Guyana	1874	*	Tortola	British Virgin Islands
1637	* James Jack	Georgetown, Guyana	1882	*	Ituni	Guyana
1723 K*	Antigua	Antigua	1897		Southern	Trinidad
1828	* Royal Prince of Wales	Trinidad	1913		Prince Michael of Kent	St. George, Barbados
1834	* Charlotte Amalie	St. Thomas				
1833	St. Kitts	St. Kitts				
1848	* Barbados Installed Mark Masters	St. Michael, Barbados				

SPAIN (68)
Constituted 1996 (22 Mark and 13 R.A.M. Lodges)
District Grand Lodge meets at such time and place as the District Grand Master shall direct
District Grand Master
R.W.Bro. ROBERT LESLIE MUNDAY
Appointed 13th January, 2007
Deputy District Grand Master:
W.Bro. RAFAEL RODRIGUEZ PORRÚA (2012)
Assistant District Grand Masters:
W.Bro. BARRIE ROY MANSELL, P.G.J.D. (2009)
W.Bro. BARRIE JAMES HOWARD, P.A.G.D.C. (2012)
District Grand Secretary:
W.Bro. PETER DAVID KENT (2012)
Neptuno 1837, Calle Polopos 7, Urb Camposol Golf D28, Mazarrón, Murcia 30875, Spain
Tel: +34 968 970637
Email: secretary@districtmarkspain.com

1683	*	*Barcino*	Barcelona	1789		*Euromason*	Javea
1684		*Arquimedes*	Madrid	1807		*Eivissa*	Santa Eulalia
1688	*	*Javea*	Javea	1810	*	*San Juan*	Callosa d'en Sarriá
1689		*Hesperides*		1823	*	*Oliva La Safor*	Gandia
			Las Palmas, Canary Islands	1826	*■	*Tenerife*	San Muguel de Abona
1690	*	*Andalucia*	Fuengirola	1837	*■	*Cantero*	La Azohia
1694	*	*Friendship Iberia*	Coin	1867	*	*Quesada Summer*	Rojales
1722	K*	*Madrid*	Madrid	1869		*Temple Builders*	(various)
1744		*Serendipity*	Javea	1877	*■	*Mojacar*	Mojacar
1745	*	*Torrevieja*	Torrevieja	1902	*	*Lanzarote*	Arrecife
1752		*Forest of Lebanon*	Nerja	1918	*	*Lapis Anguli*	Bilbao
1751		*Balearic*	Palma				

SRI LANKA (59)
Constituted 1959 Redesignated 1975 (4 Mark Lodges and 1 R.A.M. Lodge)
(150th Anniversary Keystone Province)
District Grand Lodge meets at a time
and place decided by the District Grand Master
District Grand Master:
R.W.Bro. TALIJA PARAKRAMA DAMBAWINNE, J.P.
Appointed 23rd July, 2012
Deputy District Grand Master:
W.Bro. DIYAL WIJEWARDENE, P.A.G.D.C. (2012)
District Grand Secretary:
W.Bro. SRITHARAN KANAPATHY (2012)
Wellington Apartments, 40-6/1 Vivekananda Road, Colombo 6, Sri Lanka 00600
Tel: 00 94 11 492 7970 Mobile: 00 94 77 7895092
Email: srithark@sltnet.lk

464	K*	*St. George of Colombo*	Colombo	865	*Duke of Connaught*	Colombo
				1250	*Melville Jennings*	Colombo
475		*Henry Byrde*	Kandy			

THE TRANSVAAL (56)
Constituted 1902 (30 Mark and 14 R.A.M. Lodges), (Double Keystone District)
District Grand Lodge meets on fourth Saturday in October
District Grand Master:
R.W.Bro. DAVID ROBERT JOHNSTON
Appointed 6th November, 2010
Deputy District Grand Master:
W.Bro. DAVID ANTHONY GURNEY, P.G.S.D. (2010)
Assistant District Grand Masters:
W.Bro. DENNIS ROY HAMMOND, P.G.J.D. (2010)
W.Bro. PETER GEORGE STEPHENS, P.G.J.D. (2010)
District Grand Secretary:
W.Bro. FRANCIS GRAHAM BENDELL, P.G.J.D. (2003)
P.O. Box 657, Bruma, 2026, South Africa
Tel: 00 27 11 622 2120
Email: markdistrict@hixnet.co.za

217	*	Cornerstone	Kimberley	941 K	King Edward	Carletonville
424 K	*	Ashlar	Johannesburg	954 K	Wilfred Hulbert	Johannesburg
508 K		Sunbeam	Germiston	966 K*	Northern Transvaal	Polokwane
557 K		Corona	Johannesburg	1153 K	Travellers	Johannesburg
588 K		United Service	Pretoria West	1186 K*	Transvaal Keystone	Rewlatch
608 K		Royal George	Johannesburg	1298 *	Swaziland	Manzini
621 K	*	Cinderella	Boksburg	1302 *	Austral	Mafikeng
707 K		Springs	Springs	1335 K*	Orkney	Gaborone, Botswana
720 K	*	Benoni	Roodepoort	1337	Doornfontein	Johannesburg
741 K	*	Hillbrow	Johannesburg	1456	Teks	Kinross
848 K	*	Kosmos	Norwood	1545	Bryanston	Johannesburg
863 K	*	Jeppestown	Johannesburg	1570	The Transvaal Installed	
885 K	*	Rising Star	Bloemfontein		Mark Masters	Johannesburg
900 K	*	Vereeniging	Mauritius	1621	White River	White River
904 K		Waldie Peirson	Johannesburg	1696	Golden Harvest	Johannesburg
905 K		Prosperity	Johannesburg			

ZIMBABWE (61)
Constituted 1956 Redesignated 1980 (5 Mark and 4 R.A.M. Lodges)
District Grand Lodge meets on second Saturday in November
District Grand Master:
R.W.Bro. BRUCE IRVING WATSON
Appointed 29th October, 2011
Deputy District Grand Master:
W.Bro. JACOBUS GERHARDUS DURAND CROUS, P.G.St.B. (2011)
District Grand Secretary:
W.Bro. TREVOR ALFRED CHARSLEY (2012)
P.O. Box FM 745, Famona, Bulawayo, Zimbabwe
Tel: (H.) 00 263 928 7725 Tel: (O.) 00 263 988 2100 Mobile: 00 263 772 245 686
Email: watsonia@zol.co.zw

550 K*	Manica	Mutare	1267		Sebakwe	Kwe Kwe
573	*	Keystone	Harare	1440	* New Sarum	Harare
881 K*	Bulawayo	Bulawayo				

GROUPS OF LODGES UNDER A GRAND INSPECTOR

ISLE OF MAN (70)
(3 Mark and 1 Royal Ark Mariner)

Grand Inspector for the Isle of Man
V.W.Bro. DAVID PATRICK DOWNIE, *M.B.E.*
Appointed 10th February, 2005

Group Secretary:
W.Bro. RONALD WILLIAM CORLETT (2011)
Mill Road, Greeba, Isle of Man IM4 3LA
Tel: 01624 801460 Mobile: 07264 498102
Email: ron.corlett@manx.net

323	*	*Peveril*	Douglas	1558 **K**	*The Carrick*	Castletown
1517 **K**		*James Herbert Cain*	Peel			

BAHAMAS AND TURKS (71)
(3 Mark and 3 Royal Ark Mariner)

Grand Inspector for the Bahamas and Turks
V.W.Bro. JAMES RANDOLPH BAIN
Appointed 17th October, 2009

Group Secretary:
W.Bro. NORMAN JAMES REIACH, P.A.G.D.C. (2006)
P.O. Box 8424, Nassau, Bahamas
Tel: 242 325 1129
Email: nreiach@gmail.com

1368 **K**	*	*Royal Victoria*	Nassau	1553	*	*Turks Island Forth* Turks Island
1552	*	*Lucayan*	Freeport			

UNATTACHED BRITISH LODGES (62)

(6 Mark and 3 R.A.M. Lodges)

	*	*Grand Masters*	1892		*The Lord Swansea*
		Mark Masons Hall			Mark Masons' Hall
	■	*Grand Stewards*	1933	*	*Entente Cordiale*
		Mark Masons Hall			Mark Masons' Hall
1000	*	*Milestone* Mark Masons Hall			
1641		*The Mark Provincial Grand Secretaries* Mark Masons Hall and in a selected Province			

UNATTACHED LODGES OVERSEAS (99)

(15 Mark and 7 R.A.M. Lodges)

33 K*	*Bermuda* Hamilton, Bermuda	1212 K		*Kafue* Kitwe, Zambia
47 *	*Victoria* Melbourne, Australia	1402		*Chandos* Sofia, Bulgaria
131	*St. Paul's* Pierrefonds, Quebec, Canada	1442 1797		*Itawa* Ndola, Zambia *Sierra Leone*
184 *	*Perseverance* Willemstad, N.A.			Freetown, Sierra Leone
644 *	*Arum* Jamestown, St. Helena	1863	*	*Broadley* Valletta, Malta
736	*Arts and Crafts* Plovdiv, Bulgaria	1893 1903	* *	*Premier Siam* Phuket, Thailand *New Quarries* Salzburg, Austria
912	*Victoria Falls* Livingstone, Zambia	1919		*Harmonia* Belgrade, Serbia

ROLL OF LODGES
(1566)

* * Has a Royal Ark Mariner Lodge attached
* F Foundation Lodge G.L.M.M.M. in 1856.
* C Has received a Centenary Warrant.
* J Authorised to wear a Commemorative Jewel (Jubilee)
* K Has subscribed the necessary Quota and received the Keystone Collarette. The figure before the **K** indicates the number of successive Quotas subscribed
* S Has received a Sesquicentenary Warrant
* ■ Has subscribed the necessary quota and received the 150th Anniversary Keystone Collarette

ABBREVIATIONS. (I.)—Installation Meeting. Tav.—Tavern. M.C.—Masonic Centre. M.H.—Masonic Hall. M.T.—Masonic Temple. M.R.—Masonic Rooms. F.M.H.—Freemasons' Hall. St.—Street. Ho.—Hotel. Mark Masons' Hall (only) or Street without Town, signifies London. F.M.—Full Moon. B.F.M.—Before Full Moon. A.F.M.—After Full Moon.

2K J		**Grand Master's**—Mark Masons' Hall. *1st Wed. April (I.), Oct.*	Feb. 14, 1881
3KCJ	■	**Grand Stewards'**—Mark Masons' Hall. *1st Mon. July; Mon. immediately before the 2nd Tues. in Dec. (I.)*	Dec. 1, 1884
2KF S	*	**Bon Accord**—Mark Masons' Hall. *3rd Thurs. Feb., April, Oct. (I.)*	Dec. 10, 1856 Con.S.C.
2KF		**Old Kent**—Mark Masons' Hall. *4th Tues. Feb., Nov.; 3rd Tues. June (I.)*	July 22, 1857 Con.Time Imml.
6KC		**Ashton District**—M.H., Old Rd., Dukinfield. *1st Tues.Jan. (I.), April, July, Oct.*	Nov. 2, 1899 Con.Time Imml.
KFJ	*■	**Royal Cumberland**—M.H. Old Orchard St., Bath. *2nd Wed. Feb. March (I.), Oct., Nov.*	Dec. 10, 1856 Con.Time Imml.
KF	*	**Northumberland and Berwick-upon-Tweed**— Newcastle East M.T., Corbridge Road, Byker, Newcastle Upon Tyne. *4th Wed. Feb., March, April, Sept., Oct., Nov. (I.)*	Nov. 28, 1857 Con.Time Imml.
3KC S	*	**St. John's**—M.H. Institute St., Bolton, Lancs. *1st Tues. March, May, Nov. (I.)*	Oct. 2, 1872 Con.Time Imml. (Con.S.C. Mar. 4, 1857) 150 yrs. Commemorative Warrant Jan 23, 2009
3KC	*■	**Old York**—The Masonic Hall, 51 Whitcliffe Rd., Cleckheaton, Bradford. *4th Tues. Oct. (I.), Nov., Jan., Feb., March, April.*	Nov. 8, 1873 Con.Time Imml.
4KCJ	*	**Canynges**—F.M.H., Park Street, Bristol. *3rd Thurs. Feb., March (I.), Oct., Nov.*	Jan. 30, 1874 Con.Time Imml. (Con.S.C. June 7, 1857) 150 yrs. Commemorative Warrant Sept. 22, 2007
3KCJ	*	**York**—M.H. St. Saviour Gate, York. *2nd Wed. Jan. (I.) March, May, Oct.*	Nov. 11, 1876 Con.Time Imml.
3K	■	**Lebanon**—Britannia Adelphi Hotel, Liverpool. *1st Mon. Feb., April (I.), Nov.*	Dec. 18, 1876 Con.Time Imml.
3K		**Howe**—M.T., Edgbaston, Birmingham. *3rd Tues. Jan. (I.) March, May, Nov.*	Jan. 22, 1878 Con.Time Imml.

ROLL OF LODGES—*continued*

K J *		Newstead—M.H. Goldsmith St., Nottingham. *3rd Tues. Feb., May (I.), Nov.*	Mar. 6, 1881 Con.Time Imml.
K *■		Albany—M.H., Langley Street, Newport, Isle of Wight PO30 5ET. *3rd Tues. Jan., March, May, Sept., Nov. (I.)*	Aug. 5, 1893 Con.Time Imml.
3KCJ ■		Benevolent—Stockport Masonic Guildhall, Wellington Rd. South, Stockport. *Last Tues. Feb., April, Sept., Nov. (I.)*	July 2, 1864 Con.Time Imml. 1955
KC *■	1	St. Mark's—Mark Masons' Hall. *3rd Tues. Feb. (I.); 4th Wed. April, Oct.*	May 4, 1867 Con.S.C.
KFJ *■	2	Phoenix—Phoenix Lodge Rooms, 110 High St., Old Portsmouth PO1 2HJ. *First Mon. Feb., April, Oct. (I.), Dec.*	July 7, 1856 Con.Oldest Lodge in the world *(Minutes, 1769)*
3KC *	3	Keystone—Mark Masons' Hall. *1st Wed. Feb. (I.), May; 4th Mon. Oct.*	July 8, 1856
2KCJ *	4	Prince of Wales—Mark Masons' Hall. *4th Mon. Jan.; 3rd Mon. May (I.); 4th Mon. Oct.*	May 22, 1884 Confirmation
KC *■	5	Mallet and Chisel—Mark Masons' Hall. *2nd Wed.Jan; 3rd Wed. April; 2nd Tues. Oct. (I.)*	Dec. 17, 1856 Con. Dec. 1, 1884
KC *	6	Adams—M.H., St. George's Ave., Sheerness. *2nd Wed. March, Sept. (I.), Nov.*	May 3, 1857
KCJS *	7	Carnarvon—Mark Masons' Hall. *3rd Thurs. Feb. (I.), May; last Thurs. Nov.*	Aug., 1857 Con. July 22, 1870
3KCJS *	8	Thistle—Mark Masons' Hall. *4th Fri. Jan.; 3rd Mon. April; 2nd Tues. Oct. (I.)*	Feb. 25, 1858 Con.S.C. Warrant of Confirmation Nov. 8, 2004
KC	9	Fortescue—M.H., South Molton. *3rd Fri. Jan., March, May (I.), July, Sept., Nov.*	June 18, 1857
2KC S *	10	Cheltenham and Keystone—M.H., Cheltenham. *1stWed. Jan., March, May, Nov. (I.)*	Jan. 24, 1862 Con.S.C. Commemorative Warrant Nov. 1, 2008
KCJ *■	11	Joppa—M.H., Manor Road, Wallasey. *1st Tues. Feb., April (I.), Sept., Nov.*	Oct. 2, 1872 Con.Time Imml.
C	12	Minerva—F.M.H., Dagger Lane, Hull. *1st Wed. Feb., April, Oct., Nov. (I.), Dec.*	Feb. 14, 1862 Con.Time Imml. *(Minutes, 1782)*
2KC *	13	Hiram—M.C., Guildford. *2nd Mon. Feb. (I.); May; 3rd Mon. Oct.*	Feb. 17, 1875 Confirmation
3KCS *■	14	Prince Edward—M.H., 70 New Hey Rd, Lindley, Huddersfield. *3rd Wed. Jan., March, May (I.), July*	May 28, 1862 Con.Time Imml.
KCS *	15	St. George—F.M.H., Gandy St., Exeter. *2nd Mon. Feb. (I.), April, May, Oct., Dec.*	Oct. 15, 1857
KC	16	Friendship—Queen Victoria M.H., Victoria Rd.,St. Budeaux, Plymouth. *2nd Thurs. March, April, June, Oct., Dec. (I.)*	Oct. 24, 1862 Con.Time Imml.

ROLL OF LODGES—continued

KCJ	*	17	**Portsmouth**—M.H., Waterloo Rd., Havant PO9 1BH. *1st Thurs. March (I.), May, Oct., Dec.*	June 10, 1863 Con.Time Imml.
KC	*	18	**Rectitude**—Rossendale M.H., Rawtenstall. *4th Tues. Feb. (I.), May, Sept., Nov.*	Dec. 20, 1864 Con.Time Imml.
2KCJ	*	19	**Fowke**—F.M.H., London Rd., Leicester. *2nd Thurs. Feb., April, Oct. (I.), Dec.*	Apr. 26, 1858
KCJ		20	**Faith**—M.C., The Pavilion, Manchester Old Road., Middleton, Manchester. *1st Mon. March, Sept. (I.), Nov.*	Feb. 10, 1865
2KCJ	*	21	**Howe**—M.H., Ashby Sq., Loughborough. *3rd Tues. Jan., March, Sept. (I.), Nov.*	Apr. 27, 1858
KCJS	*	22	**Southwark**—Mark Masons' Hall. *4th Mon. Feb. (I.); 2nd Tues. May; 3rd Tues. Oct.*	Oct. 1, 1866 Con., formerly S.C.
2K S	*	23	**Russell**—F.M.H., Tavistock. *Last Wed. March (I.); 2nd Tues. June, Sept., Nov., Dec.*	Apr. 28, 1858
2KC	* ■	24	**Roberts**—M.T., Richard St., Rochdale. *2nd Thurs. March, May, Aug. (I.), Nov.*	Dec. 1, 1869 Con.Time Imml.
		25	*Sydney—F.M. Sydney, New South Wales.* *Warrant cancelled 1889*	*1858*
		26	*Pluadis—Totnes, Devon.* *Removed from Roll 1903*	*Dec. 10, 1867*
3KCJ	*	27	**Porchester**—M.H., Newbury. *2nd Wed. Feb., March(I.), Oct., Nov.*	Apr. 30, 1858
CJS	*	28	**Langley**—M.T., Guilford Cres., Cardiff. *1st Wed. March, April, Oct. (I.), Nov.*	Dec. 30, 1869 Con., formerly S.C.
		29	*1st Devon Milita—In abeyance.* *Removed from the Roll 1903*	
3KCJ	*	30	**Knight of Malta**—M.H., Hinckley. *3rd Thurs. Jan. (I.), March, May, Oct.*	June 30, 1870 Con.Time Imml.
3KC	■	31	**Fidelity**—M.T., Clifton Rd., Birkenhead. *2nd Wed. Jan., May (I.), Sept., Nov.*	July 28, 1858
KC		32	**Union**—M.T., Bridge St., Manchester. *3rd Mon. Feb. (I.), April, Oct., Dec.*	June 18, 1860
K	*	33	**Bermuda**—M.H., Reid St., Hamilton, Bermuda. *3rd Wed. Jan., March, May (I.), Oct.*	Sept. 22, 1858
KCJ	*	34	**St. Andrew's**—Hemsley House, Salford M.H., 41 The Crescent, Salford. *3rd Tues. Jan., March (I.), May, Oct.*	Oct. 2, 1872 Con., formerly S.C.
S		35	**Sincerity**—Queen Victoria M.H., Plymouth. *4th Tues. Jan., March (I.), June, Sept., Nov.*	Nov. 8, 1858
3KC		36	**Furness**—M.H., Fairfield Lane, Barrow-in-Furness. *1st Thurs. Feb., April (I.), Sept., Nov.*	Oct. 2, 1872 Con., formerly S.C.
KC	* ■	37	**Wyndham**—M.H., East St., Andover, Hants. SP10 1EP. *4th Wed. Jan., April (I.), July, Oct.*	Nov. 23, 1858
KC	*	38	**St. David's**—F.M.H., Llandudno. *1st Wed. Feb., April, Oct., Dec. (I.)*	Oct. 22, 1872 Con., formerly S.C.
2KC	* ■	39	**Eclectic**—M.H., Raby Rd., Hartlepool. *4th Tues. Jan., March (I.), April, Sept., Nov.*	Dec. 31, 1858

ROLL OF LODGES—continued

KC *	40	**Shakespeare**—M.R., Alderson House, High St., Warwick. *2nd Tues. Jan. (I.), March, Oct., Nov.*	Jan. 8, 1880 Con.Time Imml.
		41 Adelaide—F.M.H. Adelaide, South Australia. *Transferred to the G.L.M.M.M. of South Australia 1906*	*Nov. 26, 1894*
J *	42	**Sussex**—M.T., 45-47 Barbados Ave., Kingston 5, Jamaica. *3rd Mon. Feb., June (I.), Oct.*	Mar. 28, 1860
C S *	43	**Gibraltar**—Mas. Institute, Gibraltar. *4th Tues. Jan.,Oct. (I.)*	Jan. 28, 1859
KCJ *	44	**Florence Nightingale**—The Royal National Hotel, 38-51 Bedford Way, London WC1H 0DG. *3rd Mon. Jan; 2nd Tues. May (I.); 4th Mon. Nov.*	Feb. 16, 1880 Con., formerly S.C.
2KCJ *	45	**Gough**—M.H., Shelton. *1st Tues. Feb. (I.), April,Oct., Dec.*	Oct. 24, 1881 Con., formerly S.C.
		46 Union—M.R. New Cross, Manchester. *No returns after 1880*	*June 18, 1860*
C S *	47	**Victoria**—Williamstown M.C., Melbourne. *2nd Tues. March, July, Nov. (I.)*	May 25, 1859
KCS	48	**Brunswick**—St. Aubyn M.H., Devonport Rd., Stoke, Plymouth. *2nd Wed. Feb., April (I.), June, Aug., Oct., Dec.*	June 18, 1860
KCJ *	49	**Lewis**—455-461 Dominion Road, Mt. Eden, Auckland, New Zealand. *1st Thurs. March, June, Aug. (I.), Nov.* Warrant of confirmation July 12, 1889	
KCS	50	**St. John**—St. Aubyn M.H., Devonport Road, Stoke, Plymouth. *2nd Thurs. Feb., April, June, Oct. (I.), Dec.*	June 18, 1860
		51 Loyalty—Barnstaple, Devon. *Lodge never consecrated*	
		52 Economy—M.H. adjoining Black Swan Hotel, Winchester. *Warrant surrendered 1895*	*Sept. 14, 1860*
3KCJS *	53	**Britannia**—Tapton Hall, Shore Lane, Fulwood, Sheffield 10. *1st Thurs. March, April, May, June, Oct. (I.), Nov., Dec.*	Jan. 21, 1861
KC *	54	**Aldershot Military**—M.H., Edward St., Aldershot, Hants. GU11 3DR. *4th Tues. Feb., May, Sept., Nov. (I.)*	Apr. 2, 1867
CS *	55	**University**—F.M.H., 333 Banbury Rd., Oxford. *4th Sats. Hilary (I.) and Trinity Term*	Aug. 20, 1862
KCS *	56	**Temperance**—M.H., Market Place, Todmorden. *3rd Thurs. Feb., March, April, Oct. (I.)*	Sept. 19, 1862
		57 Nelson—Nelson in the Island of New Zealand. *Only one Master W.Bro. Joseph Shiphand 1873-74*	*Sept. 19, 1862*
2KCJS *■	58	**Fearnley**—Masonic Hall, 14 King Street, Mirfield. *2nd Wed. Feb., April (I.), Oct., Dec.*	Oct. 13, 1862
C	59	**Lechmere**—M.H., Worcester. *3rd Tues. Feb., April, Oct. (I.)*	Apr. 22, 1863
KCJ *	60	**Cumberland**—M.H., 10 Portland Sq., Carlisle CA1 1PY. *Last Fri. Jan., March, May (I.), Sept., Nov.*	Jan. 30, 1863
		61 St. Marks Lodge in the East—Madras or within 3 miles. *Transferred to the G.L.M.M.M. of India 1965*	*Apr. 11, 1863*
KCJ *	62	**Carnarvon**—M.H., Waterloo Rd., Havant, Hants PO9 1BH. *3rd Tues. March (I.), May, Sept., Nov.*	Apr. 11, 1863
KC *	63	**St. Andrew's**—M.H., 2 Cranberry Road, Eastleigh, Hants. SO50 5HA *4th Wed. Feb., April, Oct. (I.), Nov.*	June 10, 1863
KCJ *	64	**St. Aubyn**—St. Aubyn M.H., Devonport. *4th Mon. Jan., March, May, Sept., Nov. (I.)*	Sept. 22, 1863

ROLL OF LODGES—continued

3KC	*	65	**West Lancashire**—Liverpool M.H., 22 Hope Street, Liverpool L1 9BY. *1st Wed. March, Sept., Nov. (I.)*	Jan. 9, 1864
KC		66	**Fortitude**—St. Aubyn M.H., Devonport Rd., Stoke, Plymouth. *3rd Tues. Feb., April (I.), June, Oct.; 2nd Mon. Dec.*	Apr. 2, 1864
		67	*Benevolent Mark Lodge—Stockport, Chester. Warrant surrendered 1955*	July 2, 1864
C		68	**Victoria-in-Burma**—F.M.H., 65 Goodliffe Rd., Rangoon, Burma. *1st Fri. Feb., June, Aug., Sept. (I.)*	June 15, 1864
2KCJ	*	69	**United Service**—F.M.H. Balmoral Rd., Gillingham. *2nd Wed. Jan., March, April, Oct (I.)*	July 25, 1864
2KCJ	*	70	**Albert Victor**—M.H., Ipswich. *1st Wed. Feb., April, Oct. (I.), Dec.*	Aug. 24, 1864
		71	*St. Louis—Port St. Louis in the island of Mauritius. Removed from the Roll 1925*	Sept. 30, 1864
		72	*The Holmesdale Lodge in the East—F.M.H. Bombay. Transferred to the G.L.M.M.M. of India 1965*	Oct. 31, 1864
3KC		73	**Meridian**—M.H., Redruth, Cornwall. *4th Tues. Jan., March, May, Sept., Nov. (I.)*	Jan. 12, 1865
C	*	74	**Caesarean**—M.T., St. Helier, Jersey. *3rd Wed. Feb.(I.), April, Oct.; 1st Thurs. Dec.*	Mar. 10, 1865
2KCJ	*	75	**Royal Sussex**—Sussex M.C., Queens Rd, Brighton. *2nd Tues. Jan. (I.), March, Oct.*	Mar. 10, 1865
2KC		76	**Charity**—St. Aubyn M.H., Devonport Road, Stoke, Plymouth. *2nd Thurs. Jan., March (I.), May, Sept, Nov.*	May 1, 1865
		77	*Wilmin Figg—*	Apr. 29, 1865
KC	*	78	**Fortitude**—M.H., Cyril Rd., Truro. *1st Thurs. Feb., March, April, Oct. (I.), Nov., Dec.*	May 4, 1865
		79	*Philanthropy—Moulmein, Burma. Removed from the Roll 1953*	June 22, 1865
		80	*Cape Stone—Calcutta, India. Transferred to the G.L.M.M.M. of India 1965*	July 19, 1865
C	*	81	**Keystone**—St. John's Hall, Secunderabad, Andhra Pradesh. *3rd Thurs. Jan. (I.), April, July, Oct.*	Aug. 26, 1865
		82	*Hiram Lodge—Bangalore. Transferred to the G.L.M.M.M. of India 1965*	Sept. 30, 1865
		83	*Astroea—Thyetuyo, Burma. Warrant surrendered 1901*	Oct. 30, 1865
		84	*Stanley—Meerut, Bengal. Only one Master Lt.Col. Al Greelaw 1865*	Nov. 22, 1865
		85	*Wilmin Figg—Akyab. Province of British East Indies*	Nov. 24, 1865
		86	*Samson and Lion Lodge—M.H. Tavern, London. Removed from the Roll 1925*	Nov. 24, 1865
KC	*	87	**Cornubian**—F.M.H., Hayle, Cornwall. *Thurs. following 3rd Wed. Jan. (I.); 3rd Wed. March, May, July, Sept., Nov.*	Dec. 22, 1865
J	*	88	**Star of Burma**—F.M.H., 65 Goodliffe Rd., Rangoon, Burma. *1st Wed. Feb., May, July, Aug. (I.), Nov.*	Mar. 19, 1866
		89	*Lodge Umballa—Umballa, Bengal. No returns after 1878*	Mar. 28, 1866
		90	*Sirius—Bombay. No returns after 1872*	Apr. 27, 1866
KC		91	**Fidelity Huyshe**—Oreston M.H., Plymouth. *3rd Tues. Jan., March, May, July, Sept., Nov. (I.)*	May 11, 1866

ROLL OF LODGES—continued

KC	*	92	**Walpole**—M.H., 47 St. Giles St., Norwich. *3rd Mon. Feb. (I.), May; 4th Mon. Nov.*	May 14, 1866
		93	*James Edward—Cannanose, Madras.* *Removed from the Roll 1902*	*July 5, 1866*
KC		94	**Love and Honour**—M.H., Church St., Falmouth. *3rd Mon. Feb., April, June, Oct. (I.), Dec.*	June 19, 1866
CJ	*	95	**Star in the East**—M.H., St. Nicholas' Cliff, Scarborough YO11 2ES. *4th Fri. Feb., March, Oct., Nov. (I.)*	Nov. 15, 1866
KCJ		96	**Metham**—Manadon M.H., Crownhill, Plymouth. *2nd Mon. Feb., April (I.), Oct., Dec.*	Dec. 14, 1866
2KCJ	*	97	**St. Barnabas**—M.H., Aylesbury. *1st Thurs. March (I.), June, Oct., Dec.*	Jan. 3, 1867
		98	*Fidelity—Lahose.* *Transferred to the G.L.M.M.M. of India 1965*	*Dec. 3, 1867*
2KC		99	**St. Cuthberga**—M.H., Wimborne, Dorset. *2nd Mon. Feb. (I.), April, Oct., Nov.*	Dec. 3, 1867
KC	*	100	**Hawton**—M.H., Ivybridge, Devon. *3rd Wed. Jan., March, June, Sept., Nov. (I.)*	Feb. 10, 1868
KC	*	101	**Boscawen**—M.R., St. Day, Cornwall. *1st Tues. March, May, July, Sept., Nov. (I.)*	Apr. 18, 1868
2KC		102	**Else**—M.T., Weston-super-Mare. *3rd Tues. Jan., March, May, Nov. (I.)*	Nov. 30, 1868
		103	*St. Georges Lodge—Brisbane, Australia.* *Transferred to the G.L.M.M.M. of Queensland 1932*	*May 18, 1869*
3KC	*	104	**Macdonald**—M.M.Hall. *lst 5th weekday (Sat.excepted) Jan., March, Oct. (I.)*	June 10, 1869
2KCJ	*	105	**Freeman**—M.H., Bury St. Edmunds. *3rd Thurs. Fcb., April (I.), Sept., Nov.*	June 28, 1869
		106	*Aubrey Launders—Bellary, Madras.* *Transferred to the G.L.M.M.M. of India 1965*	*Sept. 24, 1869*
2KCJ	*	107	**Keystone**—Mark Masons' Hall. *2nd Thurs. Feb. (I.), May, Nov.*	Dec. 1, 1869
		108	*St. Botolphs—Peacock Hotel, Boston, Lincolnshire.* *Warrant surrendered 1871*	*Oct. 20, 1899*
C	*	109	**Keystone**—M.H., Newport. *2nd Wed. Jan., March, May, Sept., Nov. (I.)*	Mar. 29, 1870
2KC	* ■	110	**Integrity**—M.H., Zetland St., Wakefield. *Last Thurs. Jan., Feb., March, Sept. (I.), Oct., Nov.*	May 11, 1870
4KC	* ■	111	**Copley**—The Allerton, Nursury Lane, Morley, Leeds. *3rd Tues. Jan., March (I.), April, Sept., Nov., Dec.*	June 20, 1870
KCJ	*	112	**Isaac Newton University**—F.M.H., Bateman St., Cambridge. *3rd Tues. Feb.; 2nd Sat. June; 2nd Tues. Nov. (I.)*	June 9, 1870
KCJ	* ■	113	**Blair**—M.H., Mill House, Whalley Rd., Clayton-le-Moors, Accrington. *3rd Wed. Jan., March, Sept., Nov. (I.)*	July 11, 1870
KC		114	**Percy**—South West Surrey M.Ctr., Hitherbury Close, Guildford GU2 4DR. *1st Wed. May, Oct., Dec. (I.)*	July 28, 1870
3KCJ	*	115	**Bedford**—M.T. Clarendon Rd. Edgbaston, Birmingham. *1st Mon. Feb., April (I.), Oct., Dec.*	Aug. 10, 1870
KCJ	*	116	**Mansel**—M.H., Carmarthen. *1st Tues. Feb. (I.) April, Oct, Dec.*	Aug. 23, 1870
KCJ	*	117	**Remigius**—County Assembly Rooms, Bailgate, Lincoln. *3rd Mon. Feb, April, Dec.;* *also Festival of St. Michael and All Angels, Sept. 29 (I.)*	Sept. 5, 1870
		118	*Northumberland—Grotto Hotel, Twickenham, London.* *Removed from the Roll 1925*	*Sept. 19, 1870*

ROLL OF LODGES—continued

2**KCJ**	*	119	**Carnarvon**—M.H., Keynsham, Somerset. 3rd Mon. Feb., April (I.), June, Oct., Dec.	Sept. 20, 1870
		120	*Armstrong—Mooltan, Bengal.* *No returns after 1881*	*Oct. 8, 1870*
K		121	**St. Mary's**—M.H. West St., Blandford Forum. Last Thurs. Jan., March, May (I.), Sept., Nov.	Nov. 16, 1870
KC	* ■	122	**Percy**—M.H., Stockton-on-Tees. 2nd Thurs. Feb., April, Oct. (I.), Nov.	Nov. 28, 1870
4**KC**		123	*Callender—M.H., Parsons Lane, Bury, Lancs.* *Warrant surrendered Aug. 3, 2010*	*Dec. 6, 1870*
KC	* ■	124	**Union**—M.T, Burdon Rd. Sunderland. 4th Thurs. Jan., Feb., March, April (I.), Oct., Nov.	Jan. 9, 1871
2**KC**	*	125	**Bournemouth**—M.H., Knowle Rd., Bournemouth BH1 4DH. 2nd Wed. April, Oct.; 4th Wed. Feb. (I.), Nov.	Jan. 16, 1871
C		126	**All Souls'**—M.H., Weymouth. 3rd Tues. Jan., March (I.), Sept., Nov.	Jan. 19, 1871
2**KC**		127	**Portal**—M.H., Eastgate Barnsley. 3rd Thurs. Jan. April (I.), Oct., Dec.	Jan. 25, 1871
2**KCJ**	*	128	**Science**—M.H., Wincanton. 3rd Thurs. Jan., April, Sept., Nov. (I.)	Feb. 20, 1871
2**KCJ**		129	**Holmesdale**—M.T., St. Lukes Avenue, Ramsgate. 3rd Wed. Jan., March (I.), May, Oct.	Feb. 20, 1871
		130	*Boston—The Peacock Hotel, Lincoln.* *Only one Master L. Thomas 1871*	*Apr. 4, 1871*
KCJ		131	**St. Paul's**—Harmony Hall, 14100 Pierrefonds Boulevard, Pierrefonds, Quebec H9A 1A8, Canada. 4th Fri. Feb. (I.); 2nd Fri. April; 4th Fri. Oct.; 1st Thurs. Dec.	Apr. 4, 1871
KC	*	132	**Amity**—M.H., Poole. 2nd Thurs. Feb. (I.), May, Sept., Nov.	Apr. 25, 1871
KCJ	* ■	133	**Portland**—M.H., Portland. 2nd Wed. Jan., Feb. (I.), March, Oct., Nov., Dec.	May 3, 1871
		134	*Mallet & Chisel—M.H. Povia, Bombay, India.* *Transferred to the G.L.M.M.M. of India 1965*	*May 8, 1871*
KC	*	135	**Hotspur with Coquetdale**—M.H., Prudhoe St., Alnwick. 3rd Wed. Feb., April (I.), Oct., Dec.	May 8, 1871
2**KC**	*	136	**William Romaine Callender**—M.H., Parsons Lane, Bury, Lancashire. 2nd Tues. Jan. (I.), March; 1st Tues. May, Oct.	July 18, 1871
2**KC**	* ■	137	**Truth**—M.H., Greenhead Road, Huddersfield. 3rd Thurs. Oct. to March (I. Nov.)	Aug. 9, 1871
KC		138	**Adlard**—F.M.H., Jullundur, India. 4th Wed. Jan., March (I.), May, July, Sept., Nov.	Nov. 1, 1882
KC	*	139	**Panmure**—Mark Masons' Hall. 4th Wed. Feb.; 3rd Wed. May; 3rd Wed. Nov. (I.)	Aug. 15, 1871
KCJ	*	140	**Medina**—M.H., 26 Castle Road, West Cowes, I.O.W. PO31 7QZ. 3rd Thurs. Feb. (I.), April, June, Oct., Dec.	Sept. 22, 1871
KCJ	*	141	**Skelmersdale**—M.H., Albert Terr., Ashton-under-Lyne. 3rd Tues. Feb. (I.), May, Oct., Dec.	Nov. 8, 1871
2**KCJ**	*	142	**Wike**—Radcliffe Mas.H., Breightmet. 2nd Wed. Feb. (I.), May, Sept., Nov.	Jan. 1, 1872
2**KCJ**	*	143	**Preston**—M.T., Saul St., Preston, Lancs. 1st Thurs. Jan., March, Sept. (I.), Nov.	Jan. 10, 1872
2**KC**	*	144	**Grosvenor**—Twickenham District M.C., Cole Court, 150 London Rd., Twickenham, Middx. 4th Wed. Feb.; 2nd Thurs. June (I.); 5th Tues in Sept., Oct. or Nov.	Feb. 23, 1872

ROLL OF LODGES—continued

KCJ	*	145	**Constantine**—St. Giles M.C., 5 St. John's Green, Colchester CO2 7EZ. 3rd Tues. Jan., April (I.), Nov.; 4th Wed. Sept.	Mar. 4, 1872
KC		146	**Garnett**—M.H., Lancaster. Last Mon. Jan., March (I.), Sept., Nov.	Mar. 4, 1872
		147	*Bective—Keswill, Cumberland. No returns after 1874*	*Mar. 30, 1872*
2KC	*■	148	**Stamford**—M.H., Tatton Rd., Sale. 4th Mon. Jan. (I.), Feb., April, Oct.	Mar. 23, 1872
		149	*Huiam—Hazareebagh, Bengal. Removed from the Roll 1904*	*Mar. 30, 1872*
		150	*Lewis—Tuchinopoly, Madras. Removed from the Roll 1902*	*Mar. 30, 1872*
C	*	151	**Whitwell**—F.M.H., High Street, Maryport CA5 6EJ. 4th Thurs. Jan., March, May, July, Sept., Nov. (I.)	Apr. 19, 1872
KCJ	*	152	**Dover and Cinque Ports**—M.H., Snargate St., Dover. 2nd Tues. Feb., April, June, Nov. (I.)	May 14, 1872
		153	*Wellington—Wellington, New Zealand. Removed from the Roll 1904*	*May 16, 1872*
CJ	*	154	**Union**—M.H., Robert Street, Auckland, New Zealand. 2nd Tues. March, May, July (I.), Sept.	June 10, 1872
2KC	*	155	**Portal**—M.H., Frome. Last Thurs. Feb. (I.), April, Oct.	June 24, 1872
K		156	**County Palatine**—Stanley House, Manchester Rd., Audenshaw, Manchester. 2nd Mon. Feb. (I.), May, Nov.	July 6, 1872
	*	157	**Russell**—F.M.H., Ootacamund, Madras, India. Thur. Before 2nd Fri., Feb., June (I.), Oct.	July 10, 1872
2KC	*	158	**Rose and Thistle**—Pemberton M.H. 1st Wed. Feb.; 2nd Wed. April (I.), Oct., Dec.	Aug. 2, 1872
KCJ	*	159	**Starkie**—M.H., Adelaide St., Accrington. 4th Fri. April (I.), June, Oct.	Nov. 6, 1872
CJ	*	160	**Macdonald Ritchie**—F.M.H., Madras. 3rd Mon. Jan. (I.), April, July, Oct.	Nov. 13, 1872
3KC		161	**Walton**—M.H., Island Rd. South, Garston, Liverpool. 1st Wed. March, Sept., Nov. (I.)	Dec. 31, 1872
2KCJ		162	**William de Irwin**—M.H., Yeovil, Somerset. Last Thurs. Jan., March, Sept. (I.), Nov. and the penultimate Thurs. in May.	Jan. 30, 1873
2KC	*	163	**St. Peter and St. Paul**—M.H., The Square, Wolverton. 2nd Tues. Jan.; 3rd Tues. April (I.), Oct.	Mar. 26, 1873
4KCJ	*	164	**Southdown**—Birch Hotel, Lewes Road, Haywards Heath, Sussex. 2nd Wed. April, May, June; last Wed. Sept. (I.)	Apr. 5, 1873
4KC		165	**Egerton**—M.H., Oliver St., Birkenhead. 3rd Fri. Jan., March (I.), Nov.	Apr. 9, 1873
C	*	166	**East Sussex**—M.T., East Ascent, St. Leonards-on-Sea. 3rd Tues. Feb., Nov.; 3rd Wed. May (I.), Sept.	Apr. 10, 1873
		167	*Washington—F.M.H. Beechworth, Victoria. Transferred to the G.L.M.M.M. of South Australia 1906*	*Sept. 2, 1873*
C		168	**Hova**—Sussex M.C., Queen's Rd., Brighton. 1st Thurs. Feb. (I.), May, Oct.	Sept. 9, 1873
KC		169	**Elliott**—Queen Victoria M.H., St. Budeaux, Plymouth, Devon. 3rd Tues. Jan., March, May, July, Sept. (I.), Nov.	Sept. 29, 1873
		170	*No Lodge Formed— Lodge never Consecrated*	
KC	*■	171	**Union**—Rochdale Masonic Hall, Richard Street, Rochdale OL11 1DU. 4th Fri. Feb. (I.), April, Nov.	Nov. 24, 1873

ROLL OF LODGES—*continued*

KC	*	172	**John o'Gaunt**—32 North Marsh Road, Gainsborough. *3rd Mon. Jan., April (I.), Sept., Nov.*	Jan. 15, 1874
2KCJ	*	173	**Temple**—10 Duke St., St. James's, S.W.1. *3rd Thurs. Feb. (I.); 4th Mon. Sept.; 3rd Mon. Dec.*	Jan. 16, 1874
2KCJ	*	174	**Athol**—Warwickshire M.T., Clarendon Rd., Birmingham. *2nd Wed. Feb. (I.), April, Oct.*	Feb. 7, 1874
KC	*	175	**St. Michael's**—M.H., Helston, Cornwall. *2nd Tues. Jan., March, May, Sept., Oct. (I.)*	Feb. 14, 1874
KCJ	*	176	**New Era**—Mark Masons' Hall. *3rd Sat. Jan., April, Oct. (I.)*	Mar. 31, 1874
2KCJ		177	**Royal Sussex**—M.H., Bath, Somerset. *4th Mon. March (I.), Sept., Nov.*	Apr. 10, 1874
KCJ	*	178	**Wiltshire Keystone**—M.H., Devizes, Wilts SN10 1NU. *2nd Fri. Feb., April, Oct. (I.), Dec.*	May 23, 1874
J	*	179	**Talbot**—M.T., Swansea. *4th Wed. Jan., March; 2nd Fri. Oct. (I.)*	Aug. 18, 1874
		180	*Ramsay—Muvree, Bengal.* *Removed from the Roll 1896*	*Nov. 27, 1874*
2KC	*	181	**Sir Francis Burdett**—M.M.H., London SW1. *1st Thurs. March (I.); 1st Wed. Sept.*	Jan. 20, 1875
C	*	182	**Humber**—M.H., Beverley Rd., Kingston upon Hull. *3rd Thurs. Feb, April, June (I.), Oct., Dec.*	Feb. 6, 1875
2KC	*	183	**Baldwyn**—F.M.H., Park St., Bristol. *4th Fri. Jan., March (I.), April, Oct., Nov.*	Feb. 23, 1875
KC	*	184	**Perseverance**—M.H., 3 Gravenstraat, Willemstad, Curacao, Netherlands Antilles. *1st Sat. Feb., April (I.), June, Aug., Oct., Dec.*	Apr. 2, 1875
C		185	**Ashlar**—M.H., Tredegar. *4th Thurs. March, June; 3rd Thurs. Sept. (I.); 1st Thurs. Dec.*	Apr. 7, 1875
KCJ	*	186	**Wulfruna**—M.H., 211 Tettenhall Rd., Wolverhampton. *3rd Fri. Feb., May, Sept. (I.), Nov.*	June 1, 1875
2KCJ		187	**St. Peter's**—M.H., Castle St., Tiverton, Devon. *3rd Wed. Jan., March, May, Sept. (I.), Nov.*	June 6, 1875
KC	*	188	**Sutcliffe**—M.H., Cambridge Rd., Grimsby. *2nd Fri. Jan., March, Sept., Nov. (I.)*	Aug. 29, 1875
KC	*	189	**Scarlett**—M.T., Nelson Sq., Burnley. *3rd Thurs. April, Oct. (I.), Dec.*	Oct. 21, 1875
		190	*Adoniram—Mussoosie, Bengal.* *Warrant surrendered 1896*	*Nov. 5, 1875*
2KC	*	191	**William Long**—M.H., Burnham-on-Sea. *3rd Fri. Jan., March, May, Oct. (I.)*	Feb. 29, 1876
CJ		192	**St. Cuthbert's**—F.M.H., Berwick-on-Tweed. *3rd Wed. Jan., March, May (I.), Sept., Nov.*	Mar. 18, 1876
		193	*Worthy Apprentices—Umballa, Bengal.* *Warrant surrendered 1943*	*May 15, 1876*
2KCJ	*	194	**Simon de Montfort**—F.M.H., London Rd., Leicester. *1st Thurs. Jan.; 4th Thurs. Feb., April, Nov. (I.)*	Aug. 29, 1876
CJ	*	195	**Kent Dale**—M.H., Station Road, Kendal LA9 6BT. *1st Thurs. Feb., April (I.), Oct., Dec.*	Aug. 29, 1876
KCJ	*	196	**Earl of Chester**—F.M.H., Plough Lane, Christleton, Chester. *3rd Wed. Feb. (I.), April, Sept., Nov.*	Nov. 11, 1876
KC	* ■	197	**Studholme**—Mark Masons' Hall. *1st Thurs. May; 4th Thurs. Nov. (I.)*	Nov. 18, 1876
2KCJ	*	198	**Croydon**—M.H., Croydon. *3rd Wed. March, May (I.), Nov.*	Jan. 11, 1877

ROLL OF LODGES—continued

K	*	199	**Duke of Connaught**—Harrow District, M.C. *4th Thurs. Jan.; 3rd Thurs. March; 4th Thurs. June; 1st Thurs. Nov. (I.);*	Feb. 17, 1877
		200	*Lazar—M.H.Hotitika, New Zealand.* *Warrant surrendered 1904*	Mar. 12, 1877
		201	*Wahab—Sealkoti, Bengal.* *Warrant surrendered 1930*	Mar. 12, 1877
		202	*St. Marks-in-the-South—Launcestow, Tasmania.* *Removed from the Roll 1925*	Mar. 12, 1877
		203	*Voussoir—Meerut, Bengal.* *Transferred to the G.L.M.M.M. of India 1965*	May 12, 1877
		204	*Frontier—Peshawor, Bengal.* *No returns after 1887*	May 31, 1877
2KCJ	*	205	**Beaconsfield**—Southend M.C., Saxon Hall, Aviation Way, Southend-on-Sea, Essex SS2 6UN. *1st Wed. Feb. (I.); 2nd Wed. May; 3rd Tues. Oct.*	July 12, 1877
		206	*Fort—Red Lion Hotel, Newquay.* *Warrant surrendered 1904*	July 11, 1877
		207	*Lebanon—Allahabad, Bengal.* *Warrant surrendered 1947*	July 20, 1877
		208	*Rough Ashlar—Kamptee, Madras.* *Removed from the Roll 1902*	Apr. 4, 1876
KC	*	209	**St. Wilfrid's**—M.H., Alford, Lincs. *4th Mon. Feb., Oct., Nov. (I.); Tues after 3rd Mon. March, Dec.*	Aug. 6, 1877
		210	*Vale of Brislington—Brislington, Bristol.* *No returns after 1877*	Sept. 8, 1877
K	*	211	**Hammersmith**—Twickenham District M.C., Cole Court, London Rd., Twickenham. *4th Mon. Feb.; 1st Mon. April (I.), Oct.*	Oct. 31, 1877
KC	*	212	**Albion**—Masonic Centre, Salters, St. George, Barbados. *3rd Tues. Feb., May (I.), Aug. Nov.*	Oct. 31, 1877
C	*	213	**Fletcher**—Cleator Moor Civic Hall and M.C. CA25 5AR. *1st Fri. Jan., March (I.), April, Oct., Dec.*	Nov. 15, 1877
C		214	**St. John's**—M.H., St. John's St., Abergavenny. *3rd Wed., Feb., March, May, Sept., Oct. (I.). Nov.*	Nov. 17, 1877
KC		215	**Devon**—F.M.H., Newton Abbot. *1st Tues. Feb., April (I.), June, Oct., Dec.*	Jan. 22, 1878
KC	*	216	**Henry**—F.M.H., Frizington Road, Frizington, Cumberland CA26 3QU. *3rd Wed. Feb., April (I.), Oct., Nov.*	Jan. 22, 1878 Con., formerly S.C.
C	*	217	**Cornerstone**—M.T., Kimberley, South Africa. *4th Wed. Jan., April, July, Oct. (I.)*	Feb. 7, 1878
KCJ	*	218	**Lyegrove**—M.H., Shrubbery Rd., Downend, Bristol. *3rd Wed. April (I.), Sept., Nov.; 1st Wed. June.*	Feb. 8, 1878
K J	*	219	**Ardvorlich**—F.M.H., Karachi, Pakistan. *4th Thurs. Jan., Feb. (I.), Nov.*	Feb. 11, 1878
K J	*	220	**Sandeman Stat Veritas**—F.M.H., 19 Park St., Calcutta. *2nd Tues. Jan. (I.), May, July, Nov.*	Feb. 16, 1878
		221	*St. Johns—Meean, Bengal.* *Warrant surrendered 1911*	Mar. 16, 1878
		222	*Kingston—M.H. in the City of Tunis, North Africa.* *Removed from the Roll 1912*	Apr. 11, 1878
KCJ	*	223	**West Smithfield**—Mark Masons's Hall. *3rd Thurs. Jan.; 2nd Thurs. April; 4th Thurs. Nov. (I.)*	Apr. 16, 1878
KCJ	*	224	**Athlumney Menatschim**—10 Duke St., St. James, London SW1Y 6BS *2nd Wed. Feb. (I.), Oct.*	May 4, 1878

ROLL OF LODGES—*continued*

KCJ		225	**Abbey**—The Council Chambers, Abingdon.	
			3rd Thurs. Feb.; last Thurs. April, Sept. (I.), Nov.	May 9, 1878
KCJ	*	226	**Excelsior**—Westwood M.C., Welling, Kent.	
			1st Sat. Feb. (I.), May, Nov.	May 11, 1878
		227	*Hereward—Bowine, Lincolnshire.*	
			No returns after 1880	*July 16, 1878*
		228	*Garnet—Diuaport, Bengal.*	
			Warrant surrendered 1903	*June 14, 1878*
C		229	**Faithfull**—M.H., Challoner St., Cockermouth CA13 9QS.	
			2nd Wed. Jan., March, May, Oct., Nov. (I.)	July 13, 1878
		230	*Clifton Mount Keystone—Friendly Lodge Rooms, Kingston, Jamaica.*	
			Warrant surrendered 1916	*July 13, 1878*
K J	*	231	**Union**—F.M.H., Georgetown, Guyana.	
			3rd Thurs. Feb. (I.); 4th Mon. June; 4th Thurs. Sept.	Constituted Aug. 9, 1878
				Re-constituted Jan. 15, 1947
		232	*Cyprus—Benares, Bengal.*	
			Warrant surrendered 1965	*Aug. 21, 1878*
		233	*Headstone of the Corner—Lucknow, Bengal.*	
			Transferred to the G.L.M.M.M. of India 1965	*Oct. 3, 1878*
KC	*	234	**Brixton**—Central London M.C., Clerkenwell.	
			4th Tues. Feb.; 2nd Tues. April (I.); 4th Tues. Nov.	Oct. 3, 1878
KCJ	*	235	**Leopold**—The Berkshire Mas. Centre, Sindlesham, Berkshire.	
			Last Mon. Jan., March, Sept. (I.)	Oct. 30, 1878
KCJ	*	236	**Ashlar**—The Gun Public House, 54 Brushfield Street, London E1.	
			4th Tues. Feb; 2nd Tues. April; 4th Tues. Nov. (I.)	Oct. 31, 1878
KCJ	*	237	**St. Andrew's**—M.C. Franklin Road, Gillingham, Kent.	
			1st Mon. Sept., Feb. (I.), April, Nov.	Dec. 18, 1878
KCJ	*	238	**Prince Leopold**—Mark Mason's Hall.	
			3rd Mon. March; 4th Wed. June (I.); 2nd Thurs. Sept.	Dec. 18, 1878
KCJ	*	239	**Royal Naval**—Mark Masons' Hall.	
			3rd Thurs. Jan. (I.), April, June.	Jan. 1, 1879
CJ		240	**Royal Keystone**—M.T., 45-47 Barbados Avenue, Kingston 5, Jamaica, W.I.	
			3rd Mon. April (I.), Aug., Dec.	Jan. 6, 1879
				Warrant of Confirmation April 4, 1996
2KCJ	*	241	**Watford**—Halsey M.H., Watford, Herts.	
			3rd Fri. Jan. (I.), April, Oct.	Jan. 13, 1879
		242	**Phœnix**—M.T., 45-47 Barbados Avenue, Kingston 5, Jamaica.	
			3rd Mon. Jan., May (I.), Sept.	Jan. 21, 1879
KC	*	243	**St. Ethelbert**—M.H., Kyrle St., Hereford.	
			2nd Tues. Jan., March, May; 2nd Wed. Oct. (I.)	Feb. 25, 1879
	.	244	*Trinity College—Trinity College, Weymouth, Middlesex.*	
			Warrant surrendered 1920	*Mar. 8, 1879*
2KC	*	245	**Simon de St. Liz**—F.M.H., St. George's Ave., Northampton.	
			2nd Tues. Jan., Oct.; 3rd Wed. March (I.)	Apr. 23, 1879
2KC	* ■	246	**Duke of Connaught**—M.H., George St., Buxton.	
			3rd Tues. Feb., April, Oct. (I.), Dec.	Apr. 26, 1879
KCJ	*	247	**Alfred**—Oxfordshire M.C., 333 Banbury Rd., Oxford.	
			3rd Wed. Feb., Oct. (I.), Dec.	May 10, 1879
		248	*Ramsey—Vallette, Malta.*	
			Warrant surrendered 1972	*July 14, 1879*
		249	*Empress of India—Woollahia, New South Wales, Australia.*	
			No returns after 1883	*July 14, 1879*
KCJ	* ■	250	**Darlington**—F.M.H., Archer St., Darlington.	
			2nd Wed. Jan., March, May, Sept., Nov. (I.)	Nov. 20, 1879

ROLL OF LODGES—*continued*

		251	Mount Moriah—Princes Hall, Princes Road, Essex. Warrant surrendered 1907	Dec. 15, 1879
KC	*	252	**Natalia**—Masonic Temple, Camperdown. *1st Tues. Feb., May, Aug. (I.)*	Dec. 19, 1879
KCJ	*	253	**Spes Bona**—F.M.H., 17 Parliament St., Port Elizabeth, *4th Thurs. Jan., March, May, July (I.), Sept. Nov.*	Jan. 1, 1880
		254	Saint Louis—M.H. Tunis, Malta. Removed from the Roll 1912	Jan. 30, 1880
2KCJ	*	255	**Robinson**—Masonic Centre, Maidstone, Kent. *4th Tues. Feb., March, May (I.), Oct.*	Feb. 10, 1880
KCJ	*	256	**Five Arches**—M.H., Tenby. *1st Mon. Feb., Nov.; 3rd Thurs. April (I.)*	Feb. 19, 1880
2KC	*	257	**Jersey**—Wokingham. *1st Thurs. Mar.; 2nd Thurs. Apr.; 1st Fri. Oct. (I.); 3rd Thurs. Dec.*	Mar. 1, 1880
		258	Gutley—Ferozepore, East India. Warrant surrendered 1907	Mar. 8, 1880
KCJ	*	259	**Snowdonia**—M.T., Bangor. *3rd Wed. Feb., March, Oct., Nov. (I.)*	Mar. 15, 1880
		260	Comet—M.H. Rockhampton, Queensland, Australia. No returns after 1883	Mar. 24, 1880
		261	Zealandia Marine—M.H. Port Chalmers, New Zealand. Removed from the Roll 1927	Apr. 17, 1880
KCJ	*	262	**St. Martin's**—M.T., 38 St. Peter's St., Canterbury. *4th Fri. Jan. (I.), March, April, Oct.*	Apr. 20, 1880
		263	Union of Malta—M.H. Valletta, Malta. Warrant surrendered 1972	Apr. 27, 1880
KC	*	264	**Eothen**—Zetland Hall, Hong Kong. *3rd Tues. March (I.), May, Sept., Nov.*	May 18, 1880
3KC	*	265	**Fleming**—M.H., Newark-on-Trent. *4th Thurs. Feb., April, Sept. (I.), Nov.*	July 7, 1880
KCJ	*	266	**Amherst**—Mason Hall, Gough Road, Sandgate, Kent CT20 3RU. *4th Thurs. Jan., March, April (I.), Nov.*	July 14, 1880
2KCJ	*	267	**King Charles the Martyr**—M.H., Royal Tunbridge Wells. *30th Jan. or nearest weekday; 3rd Fri. May; 2nd Tues. Oct.*	July 19, 1880
3KCJ		268	**Lathom**—M.H., Southport. *4th Mon. Feb., April, Oct. (I.); 3rd Mon. Dec.*	July 31, 1880
		269	Prinsep—Bareelly, Bengal. Warrant surrendered 1942	Oct. 18, 1880
		270	Albert—Morak Gwalios, Bengal. No returns after 1885	Oct. 18, 1880
		271	Brychan—Brecon, South Wales. No returns after 1882	Oct. 25, 1880
J	*	272	**Hiram**—Omarunui M.Ctr., Elbourne Street, Taradale, N.Z. *Fri. before 3rd Sat. March (I.), May, Aug., Nov.*	Dec. 1, 1880
		273	Rutland—Wanganui, New Zealand. No returns after 1887	Dec. 1, 1880
		274	Tasmania—M.T. Hobart, Tasmania. Warrant surrendered 1982	Dec. 1, 1880
2KC	*	275	**St. Austell**—M.H., St. Austell, Cornwall. *1st Mon. Feb., March, April (I.), Oct., Nov., Dec.*	Jan. 1, 1881
C	*	276	**Middlesborough**—M.H., Roman Rd., Middlesbrough. *1st Mon. Feb., April (I.), June, Oct.*	Feb. 17, 1881
KC		277	**Fitzwilliam**—F.M.H., New Malton. *1st Tues. Feb., April (I.), June, Oct, Dec.*	Mar. 5, 1881

ROLL OF LODGES—continued

C	278	**Mediterranean**—Masonic Institute, Gibraltar. 2nd Thurs. Jan., May (I.), Nov.	Mar. 7, 1881
	279	*Pinnacle*—*Limla, Bengal. Transferred to the G.L.M.M.M. of India 1965*	*Apr. 12, 1881*
CJ	280	**Newton**—F.M.H., 455-461 Dominion Rd., Mt. Eden, Auckland. 3rd Tues. Feb., May (I.), Aug., Nov.	May 12, 1881
KCJ	281	**Beverlac**—M.H., Trinity Lane, Beverley. 3rd Mon. Feb. (I.), Mar., April, May, Oct., Dec.	May 16, 1881
CJ *	282	**Derwent**—M.H., Gordon Street, Workington CA14 2EN. 1st Wed. Feb., March, April, Oct., Nov., Dec. (I.)	June 8, 1881
	283	*William Pearl*—*Mysore, Madras. Warrant surrendered 1897*	*June 9, 1881*
2KCJ *	284	**High Cross**—M.M. Hall. 3rd Tues. Jan. (I.); 2nd Wed. March; 1st Wed. Sept.	June 24, 1881
	285	*Kirly*—*Jaidpur, Bengal. Warrant surrendered 1927*	*July 12, 1881*
	286	*Cheena*—*Muvree, Bengal. Warrant surrendered 1926*	*July 20, 1881*
	287	*Carlo Eduardo Coffey*—*Lyacuse, Sicily. Removed from Roll 1902*	*July 22, 1881*
KC *	288	**Port Natal**—M.T., Berea Rd., Durban. 4th Mon. Feb. (I.), April, June, Aug., Oct.	Aug. 4, 1881
	289	*Dalhousie*—*Oddfellows Hall, Victoria. Transferred to the G.L.M.M.M. of Victoria 1901*	*Aug. 11, 1881*
KC	290	**Tudor Lodge of Rifle Volunteers**—M.H., Wolverhampton. 2nd Wed. Jan., March, May, Nov. (I.)	Sept. 30, 1881
CJ	291	**Londesborough**—M.H., St. John's Ave., Bridlington. 2nd Wed. Feb., April (I.), June, Oct., Dec.	Sept. 30, 1881
2KC	292	**Watling Street**—M.H., 22 Market Sq., Wolverton. 3rd Thurs. March (I.), Sept., Nov.	Oct. 24, 1881
KC * ■	293	**Industry**—M.H., Alexandra Rd., Gateshead. 1st Mon. Feb. (I.), March, April, Oct., Nov., Dec.	Nov. 15, 1881
2KCJ	294	**Royal Naval College**—M.M.H. 4th Mon. Feb., Oct.; 2nd Mon. May.	Dec. 7, 1881
	295	*Loyalty*—*Zealand Island, Bermuda. Warrant surrendered 1982*	*Feb. 1, 1882*
2KCJ * ■	296	**Fylde**—M.H., Adelaide St., Blackpool. 4th Thurs. Jan., March, April, Sept., Nov. (I.)	Feb. 24, 1882
C *	297	**Picton Castle**—M.H., Haverfordwest. 4th Tues. Feb. (I.), May, Oct., Nov.	Mar. 30, 1882
	298	*Yaj Mehal*—*Agsa, Bengal. Transferred to the G.L.M.M.M. of India 1965*	*Mar. 31, 1882*
	299	*Davy*—*Swan Hotel, Woffonunder Edge. Removed from the Roll 1902*	*Apr. 8, 1882*
J	300	**South Canterbury**—M.T., Wordsworth St., Christchurch, N.Z. 2nd Wed. April, June, Oct. (I.)	Apr. 20, 1882
	301	*Victoria*—*Monkeal, Canada. Removed from the Roll 1900*	*May 8, 1882*
KCJ * ■	302	**Derby**—Derby Mas.Hall, 457 Burton Rd., Littleover, Derby. 2nd Mon. March, May, Sept., Nov. (I.)	June 28, 1882
	303	*Aroha*—*Winchester, Canterbury, New Zealand. No returns after 1883*	*Aug. 7, 1882*
	304	*Orient Mark Lodge of Japan*—*Yokohama, Japan. Removed from the Roll 1964*	*July 17, 1882*

ROLL OF LODGES—*continued*

KC	*	305	**Gosport**—M.H., Clarence Rd., Gosport, Hants. PO12 1BB. *4th Wed. Feb., May, Sept., Nov. (I.)*	July 28, 1882
		306	*St. Thomas's—St. Thomas's Mount, Madras.* *Warrant surrendered 1901*	*Aug. 23, 1882*
		307	*Zaredatha—Parzabad, Bengal.* *Warrant surrendered 1941*	*Sept. 1, 1882*
		308	*Ehuscan—M.H. Caroline, Staffordshire.* *Warrant surrendered 1906*	*Sept. 30, 1882*
KC	*	309	**Saye and Sele**—M.H., Church Road, Sidcup DA14 6BX. *3rd Mon. Jan. (I.), April; 4th Tues. May*	Oct. 20, 1882
		310	*South Melbourne—Emerald Hall, South Melbourne, Australia.* *Warrant surrendered 1900*	*Nov. 20, 1882*
		311	*Egypt—Cairo, Egypt.* *Amalgamated with Friendship Lodge No. 536 in 1963*	*Nov. 22, 1882*
		312	*Joppa—Delhi, India.* *Removed from the Roll 1896*	*Jan. 1, 1883*
KCJ	*	313	**Lawrence**—M.H., Cuncliffe St., Chorley. *3rd Thurs. Jan., March, May, Sept., Nov. (I.)*	Jan. 29, 1883
		314	*Henniker—Monkeal, Canada.* *Removed from the Roll 1900*	*Jan. 20, 1883*
KCJ	*	315	**Henniker**—West Ealing, M.C., Westfield House, Churchfield Rd., Ealing, W13 9NF. *1st Fri. Feb., Nov. (I.); 2nd Fri. May.*	Feb. 26, 1883
3KCJ	*	316	**Benevolent**—M.H., Hollands Road, Teignmouth. *3rd Fri. Feb., April, June, Sept., Nov. (I.)*	Mar. 1, 1883
2K	*	317	**Youell**—Masonic Royal Assembly Rooms, Great Yarmouth. *4th Mon. Jan. (I.), April, Nov.*	Mar. 5, 1883
KCJ	*	318	**St. James's**—M.H., Wretham Rd., Handsworth. *3rd Mon. Jan., (I.), Oct.*	Mar. 16, 1883
KC	*	319	**Jordan**—M.T., Tor Hill Rd., Torquay. *3rd Mon. Feb., April, Sept. (I.); 1st Mon. Dec.*	Mar. 31, 1883
KC	*	320	**William Hickman**—M.H., Melville St., Sandown, I.O.W. PO36 8LF. *Last Tues. Jan., Feb., March, Oct., Nov. (I.)*	June 19, 1883
2KCJ		321	**Elffin**—M.H., Castle Street, Caernarvon. *3rd Fri. Feb., March, Sept. (I.), Nov.*	Aug. 4, 1883
KC	*	322	**Temple**—M.H., Bromley, Kent. *2nd Sat. Jan., June (I.); 3rd Sat. Nov.*	Aug. 21, 1883
CJ		323	**Peveril**—F.M.H., Woodbourne Rd., Douglas, I.O.M. *4th Wed. Feb. (I.); 1st Thurs. May; 4th Wed. Sept., Nov.*	Sept. 17, 1883
KCJ	*	324	**Hunter**—M.H., Grange Rd., Rhyl. *1st Mon. Jan., March, Nov. (I.); 1st Wed. May*	Nov. 2, 1883
		325	*Lebanon—M.T. Cornwall.* *Warrant surrendered 1900*	*Nov. 5, 1883*
KC	*	326	**Urania**—M.H., Queen St., Louth, Linc. *2nd Tues. Feb., March, Oct., Nov.; 2nd Thurs. Dec. (I.)*	Nov. 9, 1883
KC	*	327	**Sincerity**—M.H., Manor Rd., Wallasey. *4th Fri. Feb. (I.), April, Oct.*	Dec. 8, 1883
		328	*St. George—Evandale, Tasmania.* *Only one Master*	*Dec. 8, 1883*
C		329	**De La Pole**—M.H., Beverley Rd., Hull. *3rd Fri. April (I.), June, Sept., Nov.*	Dec. 22, 1883
KCJ	*	330	**Godson**—M.H., Wellington Rd., Dudley. *3rd Thurs. Feb., Sept. (I.), Nov.*	Jan. 1, 1884
		331	*Davison—8th Red Lion Square, London.* *Warrant surrendered 1921*	*Feb. 21, 1884*

ROLL OF LODGES—continued

2KCJ	*	332	**Greenwich**—Mark Masons' Hall.

4th Thurs. Sept. (I.); 2nd Thurs. Dec. and April.   Feb. 23, 1884

2KCJ   *   333   **Kintore**—Croydon and District Masonic Halls Plc, 73 Oakfield Rd., Croydon.
3rd Mon. March, May, Nov. (I.)   Feb. 25, 1884

KCJ   *   334   **York**—F.M.H., Bateman St., Cambridge.
3rd Wed. Feb., May (I.); 1st Wed. Dec.   Mar. 8, 1884

335   *Behar—Bengal.*
Removed from the Roll 1905   *Mar. 10, 1884*

336   *Combermere—F.M.H. Melbourne, Victoria.*
Transferred to the G.L.M.M.M. of Victoria 1901   *Mar. 12, 1884*

C   337   **Streonshalh**—F.M.H., John St., Whitby.
2nd Mon. Jan., March, April, May (I.), Oct., Nov.   Mar. 27, 1884

338   *Umvoti—F.M.H. Greytown, Natal.*
No returns after 1893   *May 29, 1884*

KCJ   *   339   **William Kelly**—F.M.H., Ashby Rd., Burton-on-Trent.
1st Wed. Jan., March, May, Sept., Nov. (I.)   June 6, 1884

2KC   *   340   **Royal Forest of Dean**—M.H., Newham-on-Severn.
4th Thurs. March, May (I.), Sept., Nov.   June 21, 1884

341   *Egerton of Tatton—M.H. Red Lion Square, London.*
Lodge never Consecrated   *July 8, 1884*

KCJ   *   342   **Chelmer**—F.M.H., Rainsford Road, Chelmsford CM1 2PZ.
2nd Wed. Jan., April, July, Oct. (I.)   Aug. 6, 1884

343   *Metropolitan—M.H. Melbourne, Victoria.*
No returns after 1892   *Aug. 6, 1884*

2KC   *   344   **St. Albans**—M.H., 25 Goldsmith St., Nottingham NG1 5LB.
4th Thurs. Feb., Nov.; 3rd Thurs. Sept. (I.)   Sept. 13, 1884

KCJ   345   **British**—M.C., Pinelands, Cape Town, S.A.
4th Mon. Jan., April, July (I.), Oct.   Sept. 13, 1884

3KC   *   346   **Tristram**—Neville Hall, Westgate, Newcastle upon Tyne.
2nd Tues. Feb., March, Oct. (I.), Nov., Dec.   Dec. 2, 1884

347   *Albert Edward—St. Thomas, Danish West India.*
Removed from the Roll 1922   *Dec. 16, 1884*

2KCJ   *   348   **Fidelity and Unanimity**—M.H., The Crescent, Taunton.
Last Tues. Jan., March, May, Oct. (I.)   Feb. 16, 1885

2KCJ   ■   349   **Aldershot Army and Navy**—M.H., Alexandra Road, Farnborough GU14 6BS.
4th Fri. Mar.; 3rd Fri. Nov. (I.)   Feb. 16, 1885

KC   *   350   **Emblematic**—M.M.H.
2nd Thurs. Jan.; 4th Thur. April (I.), Oct.   Feb. 16, 1885

KC   *   351   **St. Anne's**—M.H., Castle Street, Looe, Cornwall PL13 1DD.
2nd Tues. Jan., March, May, Sept., Nov. (I.)   Feb. 19, 1885

3KCJ   ■   352   **Prince Leopold**—M.H., Skellgate, Ripon.
2nd Fri. Feb., April (I.), Oct., Dec.   Mar. 3, 1885

2KC   * ■   353   **Dove Valley**—M.H., Ashbourne.
3rd Mon. Feb., May (I.), Sept., Nov.   Mar. 16, 1885

KCJ   354   **Rose and Lily**—F.M.H., Gt. Queen St., London.
2nd Sat. May (I.); 2nd Sat. Sept.   Mar. 27, 1885

KCJ   *   355   **Royal Savoy**—Halsey M.H., Cheshunt, Herts.
2nd Tues. Oct. (I.), Feb., April.   Mar. 31, 1885

2KCJ   * ■   356   **Dunelm**—M.H., Old Elvet, Durham.
4th Thurs. Feb. (I.), March, May, Sept., Oct., Nov.   Apr. 15, 1885

3KCJ   357   **Chiswick**—Mark Masons' Hall, London SW1A 1PL.
2nd Wed. Jan.; 1st Tues. June; 1st Fri. Sept. (I.)   June 1, 1885

358   *Finnemore—M.H. Addington, Natal.*
Warrant surrendered 1895   *July 2, 1885*

ROLL OF LODGES—continued

KCJ *	359	Excelsior—M.H., Island Rd. South, Garston, Liverpool 19. 3rd Thurs. Feb. (I.), April, Oct.	Aug. 22, 1885
KC	360	St. Eilian—M.H., Amlwch, Anglesey. 2nd Wed. Feb., April, Sept. (I.), Nov.	Oct. 7, 1885
3KCJ * ■	361	Onslow—Farmers' and Fletchers' Hall, 3 Cloth St., Smithfield, London EC1A 7LD. 2nd Thurs. March; 1st Tues. July; 3rd Thurs Nov. (I.)	Nov. 16, 1885
KCJ * ■	362	Wouldhave Tyne Dock—M.H., Ingham St., South Shields. 3rd Wed. March (I.), May, Sept., Nov.	Nov. 27, 1885
KCJ	363	Ruspini—Mark Masons' Hall. 3rd Thurs. June; 4th Thurs. Sept. (I.)	Feb. 22, 1886
KC *	364	Gordon—M.H., Gravesend. 2nd Mon. Jan.; 4th Mon. April, (I.); 2nd Mon. Sept.	Feb. 22, 1886
	365	*Hesperus—New South Wales, Australia.* *No returns after 1887*	*Mar. 22, 1886*
2KCJ *	366	Hertford—Mayflower Place, Hertingfordbury. 2nd Mon. Feb., June (I.); 1st Mon. Oct.	Mar. 30, 1886
KC *	367	Gladsmuir—M.M.H, London, SW1A 1PL. 4th Tues. Feb.; 1st Mon. June; 4th Tues. Oct. (I.)	May 26, 1886
C *	368	Kingston Keystone—M.T., 45-47 Barbados Avenue, Kingston 5, Jamaica. 3rd Mon. March (I.), July, Nov.	Sept. 1, 1886
	369	*Rangoon—M.T. Rangoon.* *Warrant surrendered 1898*	*Sept. 1, 1886*
	370	*Jamestown—Jamestown, St. Helena.* *Warrant surrendered 1900*	*Nov. 10, 1886*
	371	*Waranga—Murchison, Victoria, Australia.* *Warrant surrendered 1898*	*Nov. 15, 1886*
KCJ *	372	De La Pole—M.H., Queen St., Seaton. 4th Wed. Feb. (I.); 1st Wed. June, Sept., Dec.	Dec. 1, 1886
KCJ * ■	373	Ilkeston—M.H., High Street, Ilkeston. 4th Wed. Jan., April (I.), Sept., Nov.	Dec. 1, 1886
3KC ■	374	St. Chad—M.H., Castle Grove, Moor Road, Leeds 6. 2nd Thurs. Feb. (I.), March, April, Sept., Oct., Nov.	Dec. 18, 1886
5KCJ *	375	Jubilee—M.H., Kings Rd., Ulveston. 1st Fri. March, Sept., Oct. (I.), Nov. Dec.	Feb. 1, 1887
KCJ *	376	Herschel—M.H., Slough. Last Thurs. Feb., April (I.); 4th Thurs. Nov.	Feb. 8, 1887
KCJ *	377	Brentwood—Hutton M.H., Mount Avenue, Brentwood, Essex CM13 2NS. 4th Mon. Feb. (I.), Nov.; 1st Mon. June.	Feb. 11, 1887
2KC	378	Invicta—M.T., North St., Ashford, Kent. 2nd Wed. Jan., March, May (I.), Nov.	Feb. 19, 1887
*	379	St. Martin's—M.H., Liskeard. 2nd Tues. Feb. (I.), April, June, Oct., Dec.	Mar. 8, 1887
2KCJ *	380	Folkestone—M.H., High Street, Sandgate. 3rd Tues. Jan., March, Oct. (I.), Nov.	May 19, 1887
2KCJ	381	Unity—M.H., Knowle Rd., Bournemouth BH1 4DH. 4th Wed. Jan., Mar., May, Sept. (I.)	May 24, 1887
2K *	382	*Gottlieb—Dewan Freemason, 136 Jalan Utama, Penang, Malaysia.* *Transferred to the G.L.M.M.M. South East Asia – August 2012*	*July 1, 1887*
2KC *	383	Lodge of St. George—Manadon M.H., Crownhill, Plymouth. 3rd Thurs. Jan., March, May (I.), July, Sept., Nov.	July 12, 1887
	384	*Mandalay—Mandalay, Burma.* *Removed from the Roll 1953*	*Sept. 1, 1887*
KC *	385	King Solomon—London Mas. Centre, Clerkenwell Green, E.C.1. 4th Tues. Jan. (I.); 1st Thurs. May, Nov.	Oct. 15, 1887

ROLL OF LODGES—continued

KC		386	**Adur**—Sussex M.C., Queens Rd., Brighton. *3rd Thurs. Jan. (I.), March, Oct.*	Dec. 15 1887
KC	*	387	**St. Oswald**—M.T., Normanby Rd., Scunthorpe. *2nd Tues. Jan., March, May, (I.), Sept., Nov.*	Feb. 18, 1888
		388	*Victoria*—*M.H. Bridgetown, Barbados.* *Warrant surrendered 1902*	*Mar. 14, 1888*
		389	*Cowra—Cowra, New South Wales.* *Lodge never Consecrated*	*Mar. 31, 1888*
2KCJ	*	390	**Granville**—M.H., Sondes Rd., Deal. *3rd Mon. Feb., May (I.), Oct., Dec.*	Apr. 20, 1888
KC	*	391	**Lewis**—F.M.H., High Street, Lewes. *4th Tues. Jan., March, May, Nov. (I.)*	June 29, 1888
		392	*Sanford—Dugshai, East India.* *No returns after 1893*	*Sept. 1, 1888*
		393	*Liverpool—The Bears Paw.* *Warrant surrendered 2002*	*Sept. 11, 1888*
2KCJ	*	394	**Chorlton**—Urmston Masonic Hall, Westbourne Road, Urmston. *1st Wed. Feb. (I.), April, Oct., Dec.*	Sept. 27, 1888
		395	*Combermere—Abbury, New South Wales.* *Lodge never Consecrated*	*Oct. 10, 1888*
K	*	396	**De Tabley**—M.H., Oliver St., Birkenhead. *4th Mon. Feb., April, Sept., Nov. (I.)*	Oct. 17, 1888
		397	*Cumberland County—Paramatta, New South Wales.* *Only one Master*	*Dec. 19, 1888*
3KC	■	398	**Danum**—M.H., Priory Place, Doncaster. *2nd Fri. Feb., March, April (I.), Oct., Nov.*	Dec. 12, 1888
KC	*	399	**Euston**—Mark Masons' Hall. *3rd Fri. Jan. (I.); 3rd Thurs. June.*	Mar. 1, 1889
2K J	*	400	**Egerton of Tatton**—Mark Masons' Hall. *2nd Mon. May (I.); 1st Thurs. Nov.*	Mar. 8, 1889
KC	*	401	**Swindon Keystone**—M.T., The Planks, Swindon, Wilts SN3 1QP. *2nd Wed. March (I.), May, Nov.*	Mar. 18, 1889
		402	*Burwood—School of Arts, Burwood, Nr. Sydney.* *Warrant surrendered 1901*	*Apr. 24, 1889*
2KC	*	403	**Perseverance**—M.H., Richmond Terr., Blackburn. *2nd Mon. Jan. (I.), March, May, Sept., Nov.*	July 10, 1889
KC	*	404	**St. John the Baptist**—M.H., Prince's St., Penzance. *2nd Wed. Feb. (I.), April, June, Oct., Dec.*	Sept. 6, 1889
KCJ	*	405	**Lea**—M.H., The Pavillion, Bowling Green Lane, Luton. *1st Thurs. March, Oct. (I.); 3rd Thurs. Nov.*	Sept. 13, 1889
3KC	■	406	**Scots**—Mark Masons' Hall. *3rd Mon. Feb. (I.), Oct.*	Oct. 1, 1889
		407	*Bisley—National School Rooms, Bisley.* *Warrant surrendered 1900*	*Dec. 2, 1889*
2KCJ		408	**Hertford Military**—M.H., Severn St., Birmingham. *2nd Thurs. Jan., March (I.), Oct., Nov.*	Mar. 1, 1890
KCJ	*	409	**Royal Connaught**—Sussex M.C., 25 Queen's Road, Brighton, East Sussex. *4th Fri. Feb., Oct.; 4th Wed. May (I.)*	Mar. 7 1890
KC		410	**Eclectic & Empress Britannic**—Mark Masons' Hall. *3rd Thurs. March (I.); 3rd Mon. May; 2nd Mon. Nov.*	Mar. 12, 1890 *Warrant of Confirmation* Nov. 8, 2004
KC	*■	411	**Ubique**—Mark Masons' Hall. *3rd Thurs. Feb. (I.); 4th Mon. June*	Mar. 31, 1890
		412	*Movia—Benalla, Victoria, Australia.* *Warrant surrendered 1899*	*Apr. 21, 1890*

ROLL OF LODGES—continued

KCJ *	413	St. Nicholas—M.H., 42 Main Road, Harwich CO12 3LP. 3rd Thurs. Jan., April (I.), Sept., Nov.	Apr. 30, 1890
KC ■	414	St. Martin—Mas. Lodge Rooms, Chesterfield Rd., Alfreton, Derbyshire. 4th Tues. Jan., March, May, Nov. (I.)	May 17, 1890
2KC	415	Grafton—Mark Masons' Hall. 2nd Thurs. March (I.); 4th Thurs. Oct.	June 12, 1890
2KC *	416	Royal Oak—M.H., Sidcup. 2nd Tues. Jan. (I.); 3rd Tues. May, Sept.	July 1, 1890
KC *	417	Mount Edgcumbe—M.H., Cross St., Camborne. 4th Wed. Jan. (I.), March, Sept., Oct., Nov.	Aug. 9, 1890
KCJ *	418	Camden—Mark Masons' Hall. 3rd Wed. March (I.); 4th Wed. May; 3rd Tues. Oct.	Sept. 1, 1890
KCJ	419	United—Zetland Hall, 1 Kennedy Rd., Hong Kong. 4th Thurs. Jan., March (I.), May, Sept., Nov.	Sept. 3, 1890
	420	Pulney Andy—Madras. Warrant surrendered 1901	Sept. 16, 1890
KC	421	Sewell—M.H., Bookwell, Egremont, Cumberland CA22 2LS. Last Thurs. Jan., Feb., March, Sept., Oct. (I.), Nov.	Sept. 24, 1890
	422	Fairtbough—Freetown, Sierra Leone. Removed from the Roll 1911	Sept. 30, 1890
C	423	Keystone-David—M.H., Riverside Rd., Gonubie, Eastern Cape. Amalgamated with Pannure Lodge No. 435 – March 2012	Oct. 7, 1890
5KCJ *	424	Ashlar—F.M.H., Park Lane, Parktown, Johannesburg. 2nd Mon. Feb., April (I.), June, Oct.	Nov. 6, 1890
C *	425	Sarnian—M.T., St. Martin's, Guernsey. 2nd Mon. Feb., April (I.), Oct., Dec.	Nov. 27, 1890
KC	426	Brighton—Sussex M.C., Queen's Road, Brighton. 2nd Tues. Feb., Sept., Nov. (I.); 3rd Tues. April.	Nov. 29, 1890
K J *	427	Nene—M.R., Sleaford. Last Thurs. Jan. (I.), March, Sept., Nov.	Dec. 18, 1890
KC *	428	Broxbourne—Halsey M.H., Watford. 1st Sat. Feb. (I.), Oct.; 3rd Sat. May.	Dec. 20, 1890
	429	Frontier—Peshawor, Bengal. No returns after 1893	Feb. 26, 1891
3KCJ *	430	Charity—Edgbaston Assembly Rooms, Stirling Rd., Edgbaston, Birmingham. 1st Wed. Feb., April, Oct. (I.), Dec.	Apr. 20, 1891
2KCJ *	431	Hibernia—Mark Masons' Hall. 3rd Mon. March (I.); 3rd Thurs. Nov.	May 6, 1891
	432	Moonta—Moonta, South Australia. Transferred to the G.L.M.M.M. of South Australia 1906	May 12, 1891
2K J *	433	Britannic—Mark Masons' Hall. 2nd Tues. April, Oct.; 2nd Fri. Dec. (I.)	May 14, 1891
K J *	434	Stuart—The Keep, Bedford Rd., Kempston. 3rd Thurs. Feb., April, Oct. (I.)	July 23, 1891
*	435	Panmure—F.M.H., Croydon Road, Cambridge, East London. 4th Tues. Feb., May, Nov.; 1st Sat. Sept. (I.)	July 23, 1891
KCJ *	436	Edaljee Khory—F.M.H., Coleman St., Singapore. 1st Fri. Feb., April, June, Aug., Oct. (I.)	Aug. 11, 1891
	437	Pyramid—Barkley East, South Africa. Removed from the Roll 1926	Aug. 26, 1891
KC	438	Duncombe—Queen Victoria M.H., St. Budeaux, Plymouth. 3rd Thurs. Feb. (I.), April, June, Oct., Dec.	Oct. 1, 1891
KC *	439	Gloucester—M.H., Cross Keys Lane, Gloucester. 1st Wed. Feb., April (I.), Oct., Dec.	Nov. 30, 1891

ROLL OF LODGES—continued

		No.	Name and details	Date
		440	Sincerity—Cairo, Egypt. Warrant surrendered 1921	Feb. 3, 1892
		441	St. Michael—Bridgetown, Barbados. No returns after 1897	Mar. 29, 1892
2KCJ	*	442	Weyside—Mas. Centre, Weybourne House, Portsmouth Rd., Guildford. 1st Fri. Feb., April (I.), Oct.	Mar. 30, 1892
2KCJ	*	443	Elias de Derham—M.H., Salisbury SP1 2QD. 1st Fri. Feb., April, Oct., Dec. (I.); 3rd Fri. May	Apr. 7, 1892
KC	*	444	Shropshire—F.M.H., Crewe St, Shrewsbury. 1st Thurs. March (I.), Oct., Dec.	Apr. 26, 1892
KC		445	St. Swithun's—M.H., Park View Estate, Crowle. 4th Wed. March, May, June, Sept. (I.), Oct.	May 7, 1892
		446	Prince of Wales—Brighton, England. Warrant surrendered 1899	May 10, 1892
5KC		447	Clarence—Masonic Hall, Widnes. 1st Mon. March, Oct. (I.), Dec.	July 13, 1892
KC	*	448	Hampton Court—Cole Court, London Rd., Twickenham. 3rd Fri. May; 1st Fri. July (I.)	Sept. 14, 1892
C		449	Mid-Sussex—Normandy Centre, Horsham. 1st Mon. March, July (I.), Nov., Dec.	Sept. 28, 1892
KCJ	*	450	Crystal Palace—M.H., Sutton, Surrey. 2nd Wed. Feb. (I.); 4th Wed. Sept.; 1st Wed. June.	Oct. 5, 1892
KCJ	*	451	Bolingbroke—M.H., Oakfield Road, West Croydon. 2nd Sat. Jan. (I.), May; 3rd Sat. Sept.	Oct. 12, 1892
C	*	452	Bective—M.T., St. John St., Keswick CA12 5AP. On the Monday following 2nd Tues. Feb., March, Oct., Nov.	Oct. 20, 1892
C	*	453	West Sussex—Charmandean Centre, Forest Rd., Worthing. 2nd Thurs. Feb.; 3rd Thurs. April (I.); 2nd Thurs. Oct.; 3rd Thurs. Dec.	Nov. 28, 1892
5KCJ	*■	454	Tuscan—Mark Mason's Hall. 3rd Mon. June (I.); 1st 5th weekday Oct.	Dec. 5, 1892
		455	St. Paul's—Masonic Rooms, 8 Jerusalem Street, Limassol, Cyprus. 4th Fri. Jan; 1st Fri. May; 4th Fri. Sept. (I.),	Jan. 4, 1893 Reponement Oct. 15, 2005
		456	Royal George—M.H. Bermuda. Warrant surrendered 1933	Jan. 4, 1893
4KC	■	457	Legiolium—M.H., Powell St., Castleford. 1st Fri. March (I.), May, Oct., Nov., Dec.	Jan. 9, 1893
KCJ	*	458	Ethical—Mark Masons' Hall. 1st Mon. March (I.); 4th Tues. June; 4th Tues. Oct.	Jan. 21, 1893
2KCJ	*■	459	La France—Mark Masons' Hall. 3rd Mon. April, June (I.), Oct.	Feb. 23, 1893
		460	Avondale—St. Johns Island, Anbiqua. Warrant surrendered 1935	Feb. 24, 1893
3KCJ	*	461	George Graveley—Thurrock M.H., Lenthall Ave., Grays RM17 5AA. 2nd Mon. March, May, July (I.)	Mar. 6, 1893
KCJ	*	462	Inglewood—M.H., Portland Place, Penrith CA11 7DN. 1st Thurs. Feb., April, Nov. (I.), Dec.	Mar. 25, 1893
C		463	Gosforth—Wallsend M.H., Station Road, Wallsend NE28 6TA. 4th Mon. Feb., April, Sept. (I.), Oct., Nov.	June 5, 1893
K J	*	464	St. George of Colombo—Victoria M.T., Colombo 03, Sri Lanka. 3rd Mon. Feb., May, Aug., Nov. (I.)	June 13, 1893
		465	Beluchistan—Zuetta. Warrant surrendered 1935	June 20, 1893
KC		466	Prince of Wales—M.H., Hall St., St. Helens, Lancs. 3rd Tues. Feb., April, Oct. (I.), Dec.	Aug. 3, 1893

ROLL OF LODGES—continued

K	*	467	West Ham—M.H., Church Road, Potter St., Harlow CM17 9HD. *1st Thurs. Dec. (I.); 4th Thurs. Oct., April.*	Aug. 3, 1893
		468	Quarries—*Jhanis, India.* *Removed from the Roll 1933*	*Nov. 20, 1893*
3KCJ		469	**Savage Club**—Mark Masons' Hall. *2nd Wed. March, Oct., Dec. (I.)*	Dec. 7, 1893
		470	*Ballarat—Ballarat, Victoria, Australia.* *Removed from the Roll 1940*	*Dec. 18, 1893*
KC	*	471	**Lilford**—Chicheley Lodge Rms., Thrapston, Northants. *2nd Wed. Feb. (I.), Oct., Dec.*	Dec. 27, 1893
		472	*New Capestone—Mozufferpore, Bengal, India.* *Transferred to the G.L.M.M.M. of India 1965*	*Dec. 28, 1893*
2KC	*	473	**Southport**—M.H., Duke St., Southport. *1st Thurs. Jan., March (I.), Nov.*	Feb. 14, 1894
K J	*	474	**Ashlar**—F.M.H., Karachi. *4th Fri. Jan., Feb. (I.), Nov.*	Apr. 23, 1894
		475	**Henry Byrde**—Kandy M.T., Siebel Place, Kandy, Sri Lanka. *3rd Sat. March, July, Nov. (I.)*	Aug. 27, 1894
		476	*Justicia—Mark Masons' Hall, London.* *Warrant surrendered 1907*	*Sept. 8, 1894*
2KC	*	477	**Fitzwilliam**—M.H., Peterborough. *4th Thurs. Jan., March, Sept., Nov. (I.)*	Oct. 10, 1894
2KC		478	**Bootle**—M.H., 50-52 Sefton Road, Litherland, Liverpool L21 7PQ. *4th Mon. Feb., April, Oct. (I.); 3rd Mon. Dec.*	Oct. 18, 1894
2KCJ	*■	479	**St. Austin's**—M.H., Warrington. *3rd Mon. Feb., April (I.), Oct., Dec.*	Jan. 7, 1895
2KCJ	*■	480	**Wycombe**—M.C.St., Peters St., Marlow, Bucks. *1st Wed. Feb. (I.), May, Oct.*	Mar. 8, 1895
KC	*	481	**Buenos Aires**—Calle Peru 1134, Buenos Aires 1068 Argentina. *3rd Mon., April, June, Aug., Oct . (I.)*	Mar. 8, 1895
		482	*Orient—Shanghai, China.* *Warrant surrendered 1954*	*Mar. 18, 1895*
		483	*York—Jubbelpors, Bombay, India.* *Warrant surrendered 1955*	*Mar. 20, 1895*
KC	*	484	**Eastbourne**—M.T., South St., Eastbourne. *3rd Fri. Feb., April, Oct. (I.); 2nd Thurs. Dec.*	Apr. 23, 1895
		485	*Highbury—The Cock Tavern, Highbury, London.* *Warrant surrendered 1901*	*Apr. 24, 1895*
K		486	**Natal Installed Mark Masters**—N.M.R. Masonic Temple, Durban. *Fifth Thurs., in months where there are 5, except Dec.,* *(I.) 2nd 5th Thurs. in year.*	June 25, 1895
KC	*■	487	**Dramatic**—Mark Masons' Hall. *2nd Mon. Feb. (I.); 2nd Thurs. May; 1st Tues. Oct.*	Oct. 8, 1895
		488	*Goulbum Valley—Shepparton, Victoria.* *Warrant surrendered 1899*	*Oct. 9, 1895*
KC	*■	489	**United Service**—Mark Masons' Hall. *2nd Tues. Feb.; 3rd Wed. May; 2nd Tues. Nov. (I.)*	Nov. 14, 1895
2KC		490	**Murray**—M.H., Pemberton, Wigan. *1st Tues. Feb., April (I.), Oct., Dec.*	Jan. 4, 1896
2KCJ		491	**Fidelity**—F.M.H., Coalville. *1st Mon. Feb.; 4th Mon. April (I.); 1st Mon. Oct., Dec.*	Jan. 16, 1896
		492	*Saint George—Limos sol, Cyprus.* *Warrant surrendered 1900*	*Jan, 27, 1896*
2KC	■	493	**Eland**—M.H., Willow Royd, West Vale, nr. Halifax. *Last Tues. Jan., Feb, March, April, Sept., Oct. (I.)*	Jan 28, 1896

ROLL OF LODGES—continued

KC	*	494	St. Pancras—Mark Masons' Hall. 2nd Fri. March (I.), May	Mar. 25, 1896
		495	Keystone—Barrackpore, Bengal. Transferred to the G.L.M.M.M. of India 1965	Mar. 30, 1896
		496	Zuriel—F.M.H., 19 Park St., Calcutta, Bengal. 2nd Mon. Feb., April, Oct., Dec. (I.)	Apr. 21, 1896
		497	Sir John Edge—Cawnpore, Bengal, India. Transferred to the G.L.M.M.M. of India 1965	Apr. 21, 1896
		498	Massy—Jullumdue, Punjab, India. Warrant surrendered 1911	May 24, 1896
KC	*	499	Star—Twickenham District M.C., Cole Court, London Rd., Twickenham. 3rd Thurs. Feb., Oct. (I.); 4th Wed., May	May 31, 1896
2KC		500	Royal York—M.H., Nottingham. 1st Thurs. Feb., April; 2nd Thurs. Oct. (I.)	June 5, 1896
3KC	*■	501	Caldene—M.H., Hangingroyd Lane, Hebden Bridge. 1st Tues. May, June, Oct. (I.), Nov.	June 15, 1896
KC	*	502	Phoenix—M.T., Glen Cairn, C.P., South Africa. 4th Wed. Jan., April, July; 1st Sat. Nov. (I.)	June 22, 1896
2KC		503	Woodiwiss—Derby M.H., 457 Burton Rd. 2nd Mon. Feb. (I.), April, Oct., Dec.	Nov. 6, 1896
2KC	*	504	Oxford and Cambridge University—M.H., 10 Duke St., St. James's, S.W.1. 4th Thurs. Jan.; 2nd Thurs. March (I.), Nov.	Apr. 5, 1897
KC	*	505	Noel—M.H., Surbiton. 3rd Mon. March, May, Sept. (I.), Nov.	June 14, 1897
		506	Mizpah—M.C., Ringwood Drive, Pinelands, S.A. Amalgamated with St. George No. 551. 4th October 2007.	July 9, 1897
KC		507	Rosario—M.T., Calle Peru 1134, Buenos Aires 1068, Argentina. 2nd Thurs. May, July, Sept. (I.), and Nov.	Oct. 13, 1897
2KCJ		508	Sunbeam—M.T., Haley Av., Germiston, S.A. 1st Mon. Feb. (I.), April, June, Aug., Oct.	Nov. 1, 1897
		509	Sellenborck—Sellenborck, Cape Colony, South Africa. Warrant surrendered 1908	Dec. 1, 1897
		510	Ragheb—Cairo, Egypt. Removed from the Roll 1925	Dec. 3, 1897
		511	Nubia—The New Masonic Hall, Cairo, North Africa. Removed from the Roll 1967	Dec. 21, 1897
		512	Happiness—Lagazig, Egypt, North Africa. Warrant surrendered 1902	Jan. 1, 1898
		513	Al Hakeeka—Cairo, Egypt. Warrant surrendered 1902	Jan. 12, 1898
K	*	514	Sandhurst—F.M.H., Fort, Bombay. 4th Thurs. April, July, Nov., Jan. (I.)	Jan. 11, 1898
KC	*	515	Addington—Umlazi M.T., Old Main Road, Bellair, Durban. 3rd Mon. March, May, July, Oct. (I.)	Apr. 12, 1898
C		516	Hammerton—Masonic Institute, Gibraltar. 4th Tues. Feb., April (I.), Nov.	May 2, 1898
		517	Kedad—Minieh, Upper Egypt. Removed from the Roll 1902	May 6, 1898
		518	Yeatman Biggs—Dayeeling, Bengal. Warrant surrendered 1968	May, 9, 1898
2KC	*	519	Windsor Castle—M.H., Windsor. 3rd Wed. Jan., March, Nov. (I.)	Sept. 1, 1898
		520	Toowong—M.H. Toowong, Queensland. Warrant surrendered 1950	Sept. 26, 1898

ROLL OF LODGES—continued

	521	*Charters Towers*—Charters Towers, Queensland. Transferred to the G.L.M.M.M. of Queensland 1932	Jan. 2, 1899
	522	*Phoenix*—Gympie, Queensland. Warrant surrendered 1926	Jan. 2, 1899
2KCJ *	523	**Wilbraham**—Widnes M.H., Kingsway, Widnes. 2nd Thurs. March, April (I.), Oct., Dec.	Jan. 30, 1899
	524	*Kyrle*—M.H. Ross, Hereford. Warrant surrendered 1909	Mar. 29, 1899
3KC * ■	525	**Haywra**—M.H., Station Av., Harrogate. 1st Tues. Feb., April, Sept., Nov. (I.)	May 8, 1899
	526	*Courtenay Luck*—North Pine, Queensland. Warrant surrendered 1950	June 5, 1899
3KC *	527	**Dunmow**—Howard Hall, 36 Bocking End, Braintree, Essex CM7 9AA. 3rd Mon. Feb., May (I.), Nov.	Aug. 2, 1899
C	528	**Ladysmith**—M.T., Ladysmith, Natal. 2nd Mon. March, June; 2nd Sat. Sept. (I.), Dec.	Aug. 25, 1899
KCJ *	529	**Scarsdale**—M.H., Chesterfield. 1st Wed. Jan., March, May, Nov. (I.)	Sept. 13, 1899
	530	*Irrawaddy*—Sagaing, Burma. Warrant surrendered 1907	Oct. 23, 1899
	531	**Orient**—F.M.H., Calcutta, Bengal. 4th Mon. Feb. (I.), June, Sept.; 3rd Mon. Dec.	Dec. 4, 1899
KC	532	**Wythenshawe**—F.M.H., Cheshire View, Plough Lane, Christelton. 1st Thurs. May, Nov. (I.)	Dec. 15, 1899
KC *	533	*Empress Britannic*—Mark Masons' Hall. Amalgamated with Eclectic Lodge No. 410, October 2008	Jan. 20, 1900
KC *	534	**Rose**—Surbiton M.H., 6 The Crescent, Surbiton, Surrey, KT6 4BN. 3rd Sat. Feb. (I.); 2nd Wed. June; 1st Sat. Oct.	Feb. 1, 1900
3KC * ■	535	**Bronte**—M.H., Haworth. 1st Mon. A.F.M. Jan., March (I.), April, Oct., Nov., Dec.	Feb. 14, 1900
	536	*Friendship*—M.H., Cairo, Egypt. Amalgamated with Egypt Lodge No. 311 in 1953	Mar. 2, 1900
	537	*Union*—Mansaunah, Egypt. Warrant surrendered 1911	Mar. 3, 1900
KC *	538	**Philanthropic**—New M.C., Hamburg Way, King's Lynn. 3rd Mon. March (I.), Sept., Nov.	Mar. 5, 1900
	539	*Bundaberg*—Bundaberg, Queensland, Australia. Transferred to the G.L.M.M.M. of Queensland 1932	Mar. 12, 1900
KC *	540	**North Devon Union**—M.T., Northfield Road, Ilfracombe. 4th Wed. Feb, April, Sept., Nov. (I.)	May 22, 1900
KC *	541	**Staffordshire Knot**—M.H., Stafford. 4th Tues. Jan., March, Oct. (I.)	July 2, 1900
C *	542	**Davoren**—M.H., Wellington, Nilgiris, Madras, India. 4th Wed. Jan., May (I.), Sept.	July 20, 1900
	543	*Bassein*—Bassein, Burma. In abeyance 1921	Oct. 15, 1900
KC	544	*Unity*—M.H., 22 Hope St., Liverpool. In abeyance – March 2012	Nov. 26, 1900
4KC ■	545	**Dartmouth**—M.H., Slaithwaite. 1st Wed. Feb., March, April, Oct. (I.), Nov., Dec.	Nov. 26, 1900
C *	546	**Hartford**—M.H., Bedlington, Northumberland. 2nd Tues. Jan., March, May (I.), Sept., Nov.	Jan. 21, 1901
C *	547	**Blagdon**—M.H., Beaconsfield St., Blyth, Northumberland. 1st Wed. Feb., March, April (I.), Oct., Dec.	Jan. 21, 1901

ROLL OF LODGES—continued

		548	Temple—Shillong, Bengal. Warrant surrendered 1965	July 1, 1901
		549	Prosonno Coomar Dutt—Cooch Bepar, Bengal. Warrant surrendered 1923	July 1, 1901
K J	*	550	**Manica**—M.H., Mutare, Zimbabwe. 1st Thurs. July, Aug., Sept.; 2nd Sat. after 1st Thurs. Oct.	Aug. 7, 1901
	*	551	**St. George**—M.C., Pinelands, Cape Town. 4th Tues. Feb., May, Nov. (I.)	Oct. 15, 1901
2KC	*	552	**Adoniram**—M.H. Wellington Park, Church Road, Leyland. 3rd Wed. March, Nov. (I.)	Oct. 15, 1901
KC	*	553	**St. George**—M.H., Island Rd., Garston L19 5NT. 2nd Mon. Feb., April, Oct. (I.), Dec.	Dec. 4, 1901
		554	Towsville—Townsville, Queensland, Australia. Transferred to the G.L.M.M.M. of Queensland 1932	Feb, 24, 1902
		555	Cairo—M.H. Cairo, Egypt. Warrant surrendered 1947	Apr. 5, 1902
KC	*	556	**James Terry**—Halsey M.H., Cheshunt, Herts. 1st Tues. March (I.), Oct.; 2nd Tues. May.	May 13, 1902
2K		557	**Corona**—F.M.H., Parktown, Johannesburg, Gauteng. 2nd Wed. Feb., May, Aug. (I.), Nov.	May 13, 1902
	*	558	**Israel**—M.C., 37 Ringwood Drive, Pinelands, Cape Town, S.A. 1st Mon. Feb., July, Oct.; last week March (I.)	June 3, 1902
		559	Carnarvon—M.C. Pinelands, Cape Town, S.A.	June 3, 1902
		560	Menzies—Menzies, Western Australia. Warrant surrendered 1906	Aug. 22, 1902
		561	Angus—M.H. Wallsend. In abeyance	Aug. 19, 1902
		562	Metropolitan—M.C., Pinelands, Cape Town, S.A.	Sept. 30, 1902
3KC		563	**Coronation**—Garston M.H., Island Rd., Garston, Liverpool. 1st Thurs. Feb. (I.), April, Oct., Dec.	Dec. 2, 1902
		564	Demison—Bowen, Queensland, Australia. Transferred to the G.L.M.M.M. of Queensland 1932	Feb. 16, 1903
		565	Virtue—Ranikhet, Bengal, India. Warrant surrendered 1956	Nov. 10, 1903
K J	*	566	**Biggarsberg Unity**— 2nd Sat. March; 2nd Weds. Sept. at Beaconsfield St., Dundee. 2nd Weds. June; 1st Weds Dec. at Newcastle Lodge, Kirkland St., Newcastle.	Feb. 10, 1904
		567	Samson—Freemantle, Western Australia. Warrant surrendered 1912	Mar. 8, 1904
2KC	*	568	**Regnum**—M.H., 7 South Pallant, Chichester. 2nd Thurs. Jan., March, June, Nov. (I.)	Apr. 8, 1904
KCJ	*	569	**Abernethy**—Mark Masons' Hall. 4th Thurs. Jan.; 1st Thurs. April (I.); 2nd Mon. Oct.	May 17, 1904
KC	*	570	**Grays Thurrock**—Thurrock M.H., Lenthall Avenue, Grays RM17 5AA. 2nd Wed. Feb., April, Nov. (I.)	May 17, 1904
2KC	*	571	**Cerdic**— M.H., Chard, Somerset. 3rd Wed. Feb., April, Oct. (I.); 2nd Wed. Dec.	June 5, 1904
		572	Trinity—Caius, Queensland, Australia. Warrant surrendered 1928	Jan. 11, 1904
CJ	*	573	**Keystone**—M.T., Glenara Ave, Harare, Zimbabwe. 3rd Wed. March (I.), June, Sept.	Nov. 4, 1904
K J	*	574	**Maymyo**—F.M.H., Maymyo, Burma. 3rd Sat. April, July, Oct., Nov. (I.)	Jan. 10, 1905

ROLL OF LODGES—*continued*

KC	*	575	**Stanger**—Victoria County Masonic Hall, Umhlali, S.A. *4th Wed. March, May (I.), July, Sept., Nov.*	Jan. 17, 1905
	*	576	**Sphinx**—Mas. Complex, Masonic Street, Port Alfred. *Last Sat. Jan. (I.); 2nd Mon., April, July, Oct.*	Apr. 20, 1905
KC	*	577	**Wicket**—Mark Masons' Hall. *1st Fri. Feb. (I.), Nov.*	Apr. 26, 1905
		578	*Vryheid—Vryheid, Natal.* *Warrant surrendered 1911*	*Nov. 21, 1905*
J	*	579	**St. George**—M.H., Helensville, N.Z. *1st Tues. March, June (I.), Sept., Dec.*	Dec. 19, 1905
C		580	**Concord**—Masonic Centre, 17 Albert Street, Whangarei. *4th Fri. Feb., April, June (I.), Oct.*	Dec. 19, 1905
		581	*Edward—Port Elizabeth, South Africa.* *Removed from the Roll 1926*	*Jan. 3, 1906*
		582	*Pirie—Port Pirie, South Australia.* *Warrant cancelled*	*Jan. 22, 1906*
		583	*The Northern Lodge of China—Liu Kun Fao Wee Hai Wei, North China.* *Warrant surrendered 1915*	*Apr. 9, 1906*
3KCJ	*	584	**Manor of Chatham**—M.T., Franklin Rooms, Gillingham, Kent. *4th Mon. April; 1st Thurs. Sept. (I.), Nov.*	Apr. 17, 1906
KC	*	585	**Arthur Lewis**—M.H., Pontypridd. *2nd Tues. Oct. (I.), Feb., April; 3rd Tues. June.*	Apr. 17, 1906
KCJ		586	**Torbay**—M.H., Courtland Rd., Paignton. *2nd Fri. March, May (I.), Oct., Nov., Dec.*	Apr. 17, 1906
		587	*Multan—Multan, India.* *No Returns after 1933*	*Sept. 27, 1906*
2K		588	**United Service**—151 Industria Road, Pretoria West, South Africa. *2nd Sat. Jan. (I.), April, July, Oct.*	Nov. 20, 1906
		589	*Stannite—Herberton, Queensland, Australia.* *Transferred to the G.L.M.M.M. of Queensland 1932*	*Jan. 23, 1907*
KCJ	*	590	**Athlumney**—Talbot Ho., Stourbridge. *1st Thurs. Jan. (I.), March, Nov.*	Mar. 7, 1907
		591	*Plattberg—Harrismith, River Colony, South Africa.* *Warrant surrendered 1932*	*Mar. 7, 1907*
		592	*Larmour—Kidderpore, Bengal, India.* *Removed from the Roll 1928*	*Apr. 27, 1907*
		593	*Victory—Mossman, Queensland, Australia.* *Warrant surrendered 1926*	*Apr. 29, 1907*
KC	*	594	**Croyland**—M.H., Mill Rd., Wellingborough. *2nd Thurs. March, Dec.; last Thurs. Sept. (I.)*	June 11, 1907
KC	* ■	595	**St. Alkmund**—Belper M.H., Campbell St., Belper. *1st Thurs. Jan., April (I.), June, Oct.*	Feb. 1, 1908
KC	■	596	**Auckland**—M.H., Victoria Ave., Bishop Auckland. *3rd Wed. Jan., March, May (I.), Sept., Nov.*	Feb. 3, 1908
2KC		597	**Stayley**—Oaklands Masonic Club, Mottram Road, Hyde, Cheshire. *1st Thurs. Feb., May (I.), Sept., Nov.*	Feb. 4, 1908
		598	*Rock—Jalmalfur, Bengal, India.* *Warrant surrendered 1942*	*Jan. 5, 1908*
KC		599	**Chaloner**—M.H., Melksham, Wilts SN12 6LS. *1st Tues. Feb., April, Oct. (I.), Dec.*	May 9, 1908
KC	■	600	**Wallasey**—M.H., Manor Rd., Wallasey, Cheshire. *4th Wed. Jan. (I.), March, Sept., Nov.*	Nov. 27, 1908
K	*	601	**Cape Centenary Lodge of Installed Mark Masters**—M.C., Pinelands, Cape Town. *4th Wed. Jan.; 2nd Wed. April (I.), July, Oct.*	Jan. 29, 1909

ROLL OF LODGES—*continued*

		602 Sudan—Khartoum, Egypt. Removed from the Roll 1971	Apr. 15, 1909
KC	*	603 **Stradbroke**—M.R., High St., March, Cambs. 2nd Tues. Feb., April, Dec.; 1st Tues. Oct. (I.)	Apr. 17, 1909
C	*	604 **Tylery**—M.H., Ebbw Vale, Blaenau Gwent NP23 6ET. 3rd Tues. March; 4th Tues. May; 3rd Tues. Sept. (I.), Nov.	Apr. 27, 1909
KC	* ■	605 **Bede**—M.H., Burdon Road, Sunderland. 2nd Fri. Feb., March, Oct. (I.), Nov., Dec.	Apr. 30, 1909
2KC	*	606 **Seymour**—M.R., Leamington Spa. Last Tues. Jan., March, Sept., Nov. (I.)	July 17, 1909
2KC	*	607 **St. Ivo**—M.H., St. Ives, Huntingdonshire. 4th Wed. Feb., April, Oct. (I.)	Aug. 31, 1909
K		608 **Royal George**—Kensington Hall, Cr. Roberts Ave. and Ivanhoe St. 4th Wed. Feb., April, June, Aug., Oct. (I.); 1st Thurs. Dec.	Sept. 21, 1909
2KC	*	609 **Batu Bertanda**—Dewan Freemason, 213 Jalan Tun Razak, Kuala Lumpur. Transferred to the G.L.M.M.M. of South East Asia – August 2012	Oct. 16, 1909
	*	610 **Chola**—M.T., Trichinopoly, Madras. 1st Sat. March (I.), June, Sept., Dec.	Oct. 18, 1909
2KC		611 **New Forest**—M.H., 10 High Street, Lymington, Hants. SO41 9AA. 2nd Mon. Jan., Feb. (I.), April, Sept., Nov.	Nov. 9, 1909
		612 Earl of Shaftesbury—Bridport, Dorset. Warrant never issued	Nov. 22, 1909
2KCJ	*	613 **Clausentum**—M.H., Manor Road, Woolston, Southampton SO19 2DS. 3rd Wed. Feb. (I.), April, June, Oct.; last Wed. Nov.	Nov. 24, 1909
		614 Taquah—Tarkwa, Gold Coast Colony, West Africa. Warrant surrendered 1915	Dec. 6, 1909
		615 Bahia Balance—Bahia Balance, Argentine. Warrant surrendered 1962	Jan. 17, 1910
2KC	*	616 **Carnarvon**—Mark Masons' Hall. 2nd Sat. Feb. (I.), June, Oct.	Jan. 19, 1910
2KC		617 **Sir Francis Drake**—Manadon M.H., Smallack Drive, Crownhill, Plymouth. 4th Thurs. Feb., April (I.), Sept., Nov.	Jan. 21, 1910
3KC	■	618 **Cleeves**—Tapton Hall, Shore Lane, Sheffield 10. 3rd Wed. Jan., May (I.), Sept., Nov.	Mar. 11, 1910
		619 St. David—Geraldton, Queensland, Australia. Transferred to the G.L.M.M.M. of Queensland 1932	Apr. 11, 1910
		620 Chillagoe—Chillagoe, Queensland, Australia. Warrant surrendered 1927	Apr. 11, 1910
2KC	*	621 **Cinderella**—Central East Rand Temple, Boksburg, 66 Jubilee Rd., Gauteng. 3rd Mon. Jan., March, May, July, Nov.; 3rd Sat. Sept. (I.)	June 21, 1910
3KC	* ■	622 **Warren de Tabley**—Leicester-Warren Hall, Bexton Lane, Knutsford, Cheshire. Last Fri. Jan., March; 4th Mon. Sept., Nov. (I.)	Aug. 18, 1910
2KC		623 **Valentia**—M.H., Wokingham. 4th Wed. Feb., April, Oct. (I.), Nov.	Oct. 7, 1910
K J	*	624 **Premier**—Ebute Metta M.H., 22 Odaliki Street, Ebute Metta, Lagos, Nigeria. 4th Wed. March, May, Sept., Nov. (I.)	Oct. 19, 1910
		625 Julian—F.M.H. Kasaull, Punjab, India. Warrant surrendered 1930	Nov. 30, 1910
2KC	*	626 **Maitland Coffin**—Mark Masons' Hall. In abeyance July 2012	Dec. 1, 1910
K		627 **Southern Cross**—Calle Colombres 146, Lomas de Zamora, Argentine. 2nd Tues. April, June, Aug., Oct. (I.)	Dec. 5, 1910
K	*	628 **Silver River**—M.T., Calle Canelones 1429, Montevideo, Uruguay. 4th Tues. April, July (I.), Oct.	Dec. 13, 1910

ROLL OF LODGES—continued

2KC	*	629	**Temperance**—Warwickshire M.T., Stirling Rd., Birmingham. *1st Fri. March (I.), May*	Feb. 8, 1911
2KCJ	*	630	**Dunckerley**—F.M.H., Park St., Bristol. *2nd Tues. Feb., March, April (I.), Oct., Nov.*	May 10, 1911
C	* ■	631	**Thornton**—M.H., Church Street, Uckfield. *1st Mon. Feb., April, Oct. (I.), Dec.*	May 17, 1911
2KC	*	632	**Fitz Hugh**—M.H., Nottingham. *2nd Fri. Jan., March, Nov. (I.)*	June 8, 1911
2KCJ	*	633	**Horus**—Mark Masons' Hall. *Last Mon. Jan.; 3rd Mon. May; 2nd Mon. Oct. (I.)*	Oct. 14, 1911
KC		634	**Naval and Military**—Shaftsbury Hall, Portland. *1st Mon. Feb., April, June, Oct., Dec. (I.)*	Nov. 6, 1911
		635	*Coronation Masters—Mark Masons' Hall, Great Queen Street, London. Warrant surrendered 1924*	Nov. 29, 1911
KC	*	636	**Debenham**—Ashwell House, 167 Verulam St., St. Albans, Herts. *1st Thurs. Feb., April, Oct. (I.)*	Jan. 22, 1912
	*	637	*Meeanee—F.M.H., Karchi, Lind, India. Transferred to the G.L.M.M.M. of India 1965*	May 23, 1912 Reconstituted July 11, 1949
		638	*Hannay—Yizagapatam, Madras, India. Transferred to the G.L.M.M.M. of India 1965*	July 29, 1912
J	*	639	**St. Tydfil**—M.T., Park Terrace, Merthyr Tydfil. *3rd Thurs. March, May, Nov.; 4th Thurs. Sept. (I.)*	Aug. 20, 1912
	*	640	**United Service**—F.M.H., Bangalore, Karnataka State. *Last Thurs. Feb. (I.), May, Aug., Nov.*	Sept. 20, 1912
2KC	* ■	641	**Dewsbury**—Masonic Temple, Halifax Road, Dewsbury. *3rd Mon. Jan., March, May, Oct. (I.), Dec.*	Oct. 28, 1912
	*	642	**Lord Carmichael**—F.M.H., 19 Park St., Calcutta. *2nd Wed. Jan. (I.), April, Aug., Nov.*	Mar. 14, 1913
3K		643	**Imperial**— 10 Duke St., SW1Y 6BS. *2nd Tues. March; 1st Wed. May (I.); 4th Wed. Oct.*	Mar. 28, 1913
J	*	644	**Arum**—F.M.H., Jamestown, St. Helena. *4th Tues. Jan., April, July (I.), Oct.*	Oct. 5, 1913
		645	*Koyaji—Ajmer, Bombay, India. In abeyance 1934*	Sept. 6, 1913
K	*	646	**Avon**—M.H., Park Road, Stapleton, Bristol. *4th Tues. Jan.; 3rd Tues. Feb., April; 4th Wed. Oct. (I.); 3rd Tues. Nov.*	Sept. 22, 1913
K J	*	647	**Guild of Freemen**—London Masonic Centre, Clerkenwell. *1st Thurs. Jan. (I.) (5th Thurs. when a Public Holiday), March, Nov.*	Oct. 17, 1913
J	*	648	**Lewis**—F.M.H., Bombay, India. *4th Wed. Jan. (I.), March, July; last working day in Nov.*	Dec. 16, 1913
		649	*Irvinebank—Irvinebank, Queensland, Australia. Warrant surrendered 1926*	Feb. 12, 1914
K	*	650	**St. Bartholomew**—M.T., Russell St., Wednesbury. *3rd Tues. March, April (I.), Oct.*	Feb. 21, 1914
4K	■	651	**Rother**—M.H., High St., Wellgate, Rotherham. *3rd Thurs. Jan., March (I.), Oct., Nov.*	Mar. 3, 1914
K J	*	652	**Alliance Memorial**—Mark Masons' Hall. *1st Tues. March; 4th Tues. May (I.); 1st Tues. Nov.*	Mar. 16, 1914
	*	653	**Capt. Sam B. Aga**—M.H., Civil Lines, Nagpur, India. *2nd Fri. Feb., May, Aug. (I.), Nov.*	June 10, 1914
2K J		654	**Mansfield Manor**—M.H., Mansfield, Notts. *Last Wed. Feb., April, Oct. (I.); 1st Thurs. Dec.*	July 3, 1914
		655	*Unity— Lodge never Consecrated*	

			656	*Chera—Palamcotta, Madras, India.* *Transferred to the G.L.M.M.M. of India 1965*	*Nov. 24, 1914*
			657	*Kudal—Madura, Madras, India.* *Transferred to the G.L.M.M.M. of India 1965*	*Nov. 25, 1914*
2K		* ■	**658**	**Pudsey**—M.H., Pudsey. *2nd Mon. Jan., Feb., March, April, Oct., Nov. (I.)*	Sept. 2, 1915
			659	*Coromandel—Bezwada, Madras, India.* *Transferred to the G.L.M.M.M. of India 1965*	*Oct. 17, 1915*
			660	*Limestone—Ipswich, Queensland, Australia.* *Warrant surrendered 1937*	*Oct. 12, 1915*
			661	*Welcome—Grand Hotel, Sheffield.* *Removed from the Roll 1937*	*June 18, 1916*
			662	*Friendship & Harmony—Inqatpuri, Bombay, India.* *Transferred to the G.L.M.M.M. of India 1965*	*Feb. 14, 1916*
2K		*	**663**	**Perak**—Dewan Freemason, Tiger Lane, Ipoh, Malaysia. *3rd Sat. Jan., April (I.), July, Oct.*	Sept. 29, 1916
			664	*Athlumney—The Imperial Restaurant, Regent Street, London.* *Amalgamated with the Menatschim Lodge No. 224 in 1983*	*Nov. 13, 1916*
			665	*Lukis—Delhi, India.* *Transferred to the G.L.M.M.M. of India 1965*	*Dec. 6, 1916*
2			*666*	*Jampatrao—Baroda, Bombay, India.* *Transferred to the G.L.M.M.M. of India 1965*	*Mar. 1, 1917*
K		*	**667**	**Moseley**—Moseley M.H., Alcester Road South, Birmingham B14 6DT. *1st Mon. March, June, Dec.; 4th Mon. Sept. (I.); 1st Mon. Dec.*	Sept. 1, 1917
			668	**St. Mark's**—F.M.H., Poona. *3rd Tues. Feb., May, Aug., Nov. (I.)*	Nov. 1, 1917 *Warrant of Confirmation* April 4, 1996
2K	J	■	**669**	**Aries**—The Midland Hotel, Forster Square, Bradford BD1 4HU. *2nd Thurs. March (I.), June, Aug., Dec.*	Dec. 4, 1917
			670	*Saint John's—St. Georges' Hall, Lagos Nigeria.* *In abeyance 1934*	*Dec. 4, 1917*
			671	*Mulgrave—Gordonvate, Queensland, Australia.* *Transferred to the G.L.M.M.M. of Queensland 1932*	*Dec. 6, 1917*
			672	*Moreton—Wynnum, Brisbane, Queensland, Australia.* *Warrant surrendered 1932*	*Dec. 8, 1917*
		*	*673*	*Ravi—F.M.H., Lahore, Pakistan.* *Transferred to the G.L.M.M.M. of India 1965*	*May 1, 1918*
K	J	*	**674**	**Loveland**—M.H., 2 Cranberry Road, Eastleigh, Hants. SO50 5HA *1st Tues. Feb., March (I.), Oct., Nov., Dec.*	May 1, 1918
	J		**675**	**Pleiades**—M.H., Totnes, Devon. *2nd Tues. Jan. (I.), March, May, Sept., Nov.*	June 28, 1918
			676	*Pennock—Dharwar, Bombay, India.* *Warrant surrendered 1929*	*June 28, 1918*
			677	*Universal Brotherhood—* *Lodge never Consecrated*	
			678	*East & West—F.M.H., Limla, India.* *Removed from the Roll 1964*	*June 28, 1918*
		*	**679**	**Clarke**—M.H., New Delhi, India. *3rd Mon. May, July (I.); 3rd Tues. Nov.*	Dec. 6, 1918
K			**680**	**Goulburn**—F.M.H., Bridge St., Manchester. *4th Wed. Jan., March, Nov. (I.)*	Sept. 5, 1918
3K		*	**681**	**Peace**—M.H., Brownhill Vale, Uppermill, Yorks. *4th Thurs. Feb., April, Oct. (I.); 3rd Thurs. Dec.*	Sept. 21, 1918
2K			**682**	**Pentangle**—M.H., Rochester, Kent. *4th Fri. Jan. (I.), April, Nov.*	Oct. 25, 1918

ROLL OF LODGES—continued

2K	*	683	East Hertfordshire—M.H., Radlett. 4th Mon. March (I.), April, Sept.	Nov. 1, 1918 Warrant of Confirmation May 15, 1996
		684	Doon—Rookee, Bengal, India. Warrant surrendered 1930	Jan. 23, 1919
K	*	685	Powys—M.H., York Rd., Kettering. Last Mon. Jan., March (I.), Oct.	Jan. 30, 1919
K	*	686	Lowestoft—M.H., 101 The Avenue, Lowestoft. 1st Mon. April (I.), Oct., Dec.	Feb. 26, 1919
K	*	687	Barnard—M.H., Wymondham. 1st Thurs. Feb., April (I.), June, Oct.	Mar. 1, 1919
K		688	St. Seiriol—M.H., Holyhead. 3rd Tues. Feb. (I.), April, Sept., Nov.	Apr. 12, 1919
2K J	*	689	Lancastrians—F.M.H., Bridge St., Manchester. 2nd Tues. April, Nov. (I.)	May 1, 1919
2K	*	690	Victory—M.H., Bridport, Dorset. 4th Mon. Jan., March, May, Sept., Nov. (I.)	June 25, 1919
K	*	691	Morpeth—F.M.H., Dacre St., Morpeth. 3rd Thurs. Feb., April, Oct., Dec. (I.)	June 30, 1919
		692	Patricia—Ahmedagar, Bombay India. Warrant surrendered 1946	July 7, 1919
4K J		693	Priory—M.R., Whalley, Lancs. 1st Wed. March (I.), Oct., Dec.; 3rd Wed. June	July 10, 1919
K		694	Connaught—M.H., Manor Road, Woolston, Southampton SO19 2DS. 1st Mon. March, May, July, Sept., Nov. (I.)	July 12, 1919
K		695	Pendle—M.H., Guy St., Padiham, Lancs. 2nd Wed. Jan. (I.), March, May, Aug., Nov.	July 14, 1919
K J	*	696	Strode—Queen Victoria M.H., 76 Victoria Road, St. Budeaux, Plymouth. 1st Thurs. Feb., June, Sept., Nov. (I.)	July 21, 1919
K J	*	697	Exmoor—M.H., Minehead, Somerset. 2nd Thurs. May (I.); 1st Thurs. Oct., Dec., March.	July 29, 1919
2K J	*	698	Machen—The Warwickshire M.T., Clarendon Rd., Birmingham 16. 4th Wed. March, Sept. (I.), Nov.	July 30, 1919
		699	Eureka—St. Georges' Hall, Lagos Nigeria. Removed from the Roll 1954	July 31, 1919
K		700	St. Columba—F.M.H., St. Columb, Cornwall. 4th Wed. Feb., April, June, Sept., Oct. (I.)	Sept. 16, 1919
K	■	701	Jarrow—F.M.H., Grange Rd., Jarrow. 3rd Mon. Jan. (I.), Feb., March, April, Oct., Nov.	Sept. 20, 1919
	■	702	Thomas Purvis—M.H., Maple Terrace, Newcastle upon Tyne. 4th Mon. Jan., March, May, Sept. (I.)	Sept. 25, 1919
		703	Hothampton—F.M.H., Canada Grove, Bognor Regis. 3rd Wed. Jan., March (I.), May, Nov.	Sept. 29, 1919
		704	Tientsin—Tientsin, Northern China. Warrant surrendered 1953	Oct. 3, 1919
2K	*■	705	Claughton—M.T., Clifton Rd., Birkenhead. 3rd Mon. Jan. (I.), March, Nov.	Oct. 10, 1919
3K		706	Halifax—Southwood, Birdcage Lane, Halifax. 2nd Wed. Jan., March, Sept. (I.), Nov.	Oct. 11, 1919
2K		707	Springs—M.H., 1st Avenue, Springs, Gauteng. 2nd Wed. March, May, July, Nov.; 2nd Sat. Sept. (I.)	Oct. 14, 1919
	J	708	Unity—F.M.H., Headlam St., Newcastle upon Tyne. 2nd Thurs. Feb., March, April (I.), Oct., Nov., Dec.	Oct. 30, 1919 Warrant of Confirmation July 8, 1998

ROLL OF LODGES—continued

		No.	Lodge	Date
		709	Cloncurry—Cloncurry, Queensland, Australia. Transferred to the G.L.M.M.M. of Queensland 1932	Nov. 4, 1919
		710	Jubilee—M.H. Brisbane, Australia. Transferred to the G.L.M.M.M. of Queensland 1932	Nov. 5, 1919
		711	Southern Cross—M.H. Toowoomba, Queensland, Australia. Warrant surrendered 1928	Nov. 6, 1919
		712	Old Sidsagar—Nazira, Libsagar, Assam, India. Warrant surrendered 1927	Nov. 17, 1919
		713	Conjuncta—10 Dukes Street, St. James's, S.W.1. Warrant surrendered 1931	Mar. 12, 1920
		714	Alma—Nairi Tal, India. Warrant surrendered 1942	Mar. 2, 1920
7K	*■	715	**Lightcliffe**—M.H., Whitehall Rd., Hipperholme. *3rd Fri. Jan., Feb., March, Oct. (I.), Nov., Dec.*	Mar. 11, 1920
K		716	**Morecambe**—M.H., Morecambe. *2nd Mon. Feb., April, Oct. (I.), Dec.*	Mar. 29, 1920
K	*	717	**Eversley**—M.R., Sheringham. *2nd Wed. Jan., March, Oct. (I.), Dec.*	June 7, 1920
K J	■	718	**Ravensworth**—F.M.H., Queen St. East, Sunderland. *4th Wed. Jan., March, Sept. (I.), Nov.*	June 9, 1920
2K J	*	719	**Yenton**—Yenton Assembly Rooms, Erdington, Birmingham. *1st Mon. March, June, Nov. (I.)*	June 12, 1920
2K	*	720	**Benoni**—Horizon M.C., Andrew St., Roodepoort, S.A. *1st Tues. March (I.), May, July, Sept., Nov.*	June 15, 1920
2K	*	721	**Concordia**—Zetland Hall, 1 Kennedy Road, Mid-levels, Hong Kong, S.A.R. *2nd Thurs. Jan. (I.), March, May, Sept., Nov.*	Aug. 5, 1920
		722	Abernethy—Mark Masons' Hall, Great Queen Street, London. Amalgamated with Dimsdale Lodge No. 569 in March 1935	Aug. 5, 1920
K	*■	723	**Four Cardinal Virtues**—M.H., Wybunbury Rd., Willaston, Nantwich. *2nd Mon. Feb., April (I.), Oct., Dec.*	Aug. 14, 1920
		724	Tigris—F.M.H. Bassah, Mesopotamia. Removed from the Roll 1965	Aug. 13, 1920
		725	Excelsoir—F.M.H., Accra, Gold Coast, West Africa. Warrant surrendered 1928	Sept. 12, 1920
	J	726	**Bentinck**—M.R., 7 Fairbank, Kirkby Lonsdale LA6 2BD. *4th Fri. Feb., April (I.), Sept., Nov.*	Oct. 19, 1920
2K J	■	727	**Worth**—M.R., Cooke St., Keighley. *3rd Mon. Jan., Feb., March, April, Oct., Nov. (I.)*	Dec. 11, 1920
K	*	728	**Royal Colonial Institute**—Mark Masons' Hall. *2nd Fri. March (I.); 3rd Fri. June; 1st Fri. Dec.*	Dec. 11, 1920
		729	**St. Bride's**—M.T., Milford Haven. *2nd Tues. March, May, Sept., Nov. (I.)*	Jan. 6, 1921
2K	*	730	**Hallam**—M.H., Albert Road, Clevedon. *4th Wed. Sept., Nov., Feb., April (I.)*	Jan. 6, 1921
		731	**Cube Stone**—M.H., Newport, Monmouthshire. *3rd Tues. Feb. (I.), April, Nov.: 2nd Thurs. Sept.*	Feb. 18, 1921
K		732	**Persevere**—Sussex M.C., Queens Road, Brighton. *2nd Fri. Feb. (I.), Oct.*	Mar. 1, 1921
2K J	*	733	**Perseverence**—M.H., Nedfields, Halesowen. *3rd Mon. Feb., April, Oct., Dec. (I.)*	Mar. 7, 1921
3K J		734	**Ormskirk**—M.H., Park Road., Ormskirk. *2nd Thurs. Jan., March, Nov. (I.)*	Apr. 5, 1921
7K	*	735	**Concord**—M.H., Severn Street, Birmingham. *1st Fri. Feb., April, Oct., Dec. (I.)*	Apr. 16, 1921

ROLL OF LODGES—continued

11K	J	*	736	**Arts and Crafts**—Severn Hills Hotel, 6 Zhiten Pazar Str., Plovdiv, 4000 Bulgaria. *3rd Wed. March, June, Nov.* — Apr. 21, 1921; Reponement Nov. 19, 2011
2K	J		737	**Dartmouth**—Hauley M.H., Dartmouth. *3rd Thurs. Feb., March, April (I.), May, Oct., Nov.* — May 18, 1921
	J	*	738	**Gardiner**—M.H., Temple Terrace, Aspatria CA7 3BH. *1st Tues. Feb., March, April, Oct., Nov., Dec. (I.)* — June 14, 1921
2K		*	739	**Portsdown**—M.H., Albert Rd., Cosham, Hants. PO6 3DD. *1st Mon. March, Sept., Nov. (I.); 2nd Fri. May.* — Aug. 4, 1921
K		■	740	**Harte**—M.T., Hart, Rd., West Hartlepool. *2nd Mon. Feb. (I.), April, Oct., Dec.* — Aug. 18, 1921
2K		*	741	**Hillbrow**—F.M.H., Park Lane, Parktown, Johannesburg. *1st Mon. Feb., June, Aug., Oct. (I.)* — Sept. 6, 1921
K		*■	742	**Kelvin**—Mark Masons' Hall. *4th Tues. Jan., March (I.); 1st Tues. Nov.* — Sept. 24, 1921
			743	**St. Cuthbert's**—M.H., Howden, East Yorkshire. *1st Tues. March (I.), Sept., Nov.; 1st Wed. May* — Sept. 30, 1921
3K	J	*	744	**Central Keystone**—Warwickshire M.T., 2 Stirling Rd., Edgbaston, Birmingham. *1st Thurs. Feb., May, Nov. (I.)* — Sept. 30, 1921
K			745	**Manchester Keystone**—F.M.H., Bridge St., Manchester. *4th Mon. Jan., Sept.; 1st Tues. June (I.)* — Oct. 1, 1921
K		*	746	**Patron Saints**—M.T., Calle Perú 1134, Buenos Aires. *4th Thurs. March; 4th Mon. May, July (I.), Sept., Nov.* — Oct. 1, 1921
K	J	*	747	**Stechford**—M.H., Bordersley Green East, Stechford, Birmingham. *4th Sat. Jan., March, Sept., Nov. (I.)* — Oct. 14, 1921
3K	J	*	748	**Connaught Army and Navy**—Mark Masons' Hall. *2nd Wed. July (I.); 1st Tues. Dec.* — Oct. 18, 1921
3K	J		749	**Quantock**—M.T., King Sq., Bridgwater. *1st Wed. Feb., March (I.), Oct. Nov.* — Nov. 5, 1921
		*	750	**Haven**—M.H., Albion Rd., North Shields. *2nd Mon. Feb., April (I.), Oct., Dec.* — Nov. 15, 1921
3K		*	751	**Stony Gate**—F.M.H., Leicester. *2nd Fri. Jan., March (I.), Nov.* — Nov. 23, 1921
K		*	752	**Steanforde**—Mas. Centre, All Saints' St., Stamford. *Last Wed. March, Sept. (I.), Nov.* — Dec. 30, 1921
4K	J	■	753	**Brighouse**—M.H., Assembly Rooms, Briggate, Brighouse. *2nd Mon. Jan., Feb. (I.), March, Oct., Nov., Dec.* — Jan. 3, 1922
K			754	**Wyre**—M.H., 32 Esplanade, Fleetwood. *3rd Wed. Feb., April (I.), Oct. Dec.* — Jan. 9, 1922
			755	*Yarraman*—Yarraman, Queensland, Australia. Transferred to the G.L.M.M.M. of Queensland 1932 — Jan. 16, 1922
			756	*Tezpur*—Tezpur, Assam, Bengal, India. Warrant surrendered 1935 — Jan. 18, 1922
3K		*	757	**Vesey**—M.H., Sutton Coldfield. *4th Tues. Jan., March (I.), Oct., Nov.* — Jan. 30, 1922
K			758	**Stability**—M.H., Penarth, Glamorgan. *2nd Mon. Oct., Dec., Feb., March; 4th Thurs. April (I.)* — Mar. 3, 1922
			759	*Tyne Dock*—M.H. Whitehead Street, South Shields. Warrant surrendered 1994 — Mar. 15, 1922
K		*	760	**St. Giles**—M.T., Wrexham. *1st Thurs. Feb., April, Sept., Nov. (I.)* — Mar. 15, 1922
K		■	761	**Hackworth**—M.H., Shildon, Durham. *1st Tues. Feb., April, June (I.), Oct., Dec.* — Apr. 12, 1922
2K			762	**Bolton**—F.M.H., Institute St., Bolton. *1st Fri. Feb., April, Nov. (I.)* — Apr. 12, 1922

ROLL OF LODGES—continued

K		763	**Anglebury**—M.H., Wareham. 2nd Wed. May (I.), Nov.; M.H., Swanage. *2nd Wed. Jan., March*	Apr. 12, 1922
		764	**Octavum**—M.H. Atherton, Queensland, Australia. Warrant surrendered 1926	*Apr. 12, 1922*
		765	**Lewis**—Colesberg, South Africa. Removed from the Roll 1946	*Apr. 12, 1922*
		766	**Barcoo**—Blackall, Queensland, Australia. Transferred to the G.L.M.M.M. of Queensland 1932	*June 6, 1922*
2K	J	767	**Shorncliffe and Hythe**—M.H., Windmill St., Hythe. *3rd Wed. Feb., April (I.), Oct.; 2nd Wed. Dec.*	June 6, 1922
2K	* ■	768	**Knaresborough Castle**—M.H., Knaresborough. *2nd Fri. Jan., March (I.), May, Sept., Nov.*	June 6, 1922
		769	**Nagpur**—Nagur, India. Transferred to the G.L.M.M.M. of India 1965	*June 6, 1922*
2K	J	770	**Northwic**—47 St. Giles St., Norwich. *2nd Fri. Jan., March, Nov. (I.)*	June 26, 1922
K		771	**Herne Bay**—M.T., Herne Bay. *1st Wed. Feb., April (I.), Oct., Dec.*	July 13, 1922
K J	*	772	**Enfield**—Corvino Ristorante Italiano, Beaufort House, 7 Middlesex St., London E1 7AA. *4th Mon. May, July; 1st Wed. Sept. (I.)*	July 13, 1922
				Warrant of Confirmation May, 2004
	*	773	**Van der Stel**—Masonic Centre, Strand, C.P., South Africa. *1st Wed. Feb. (I.), May, Dec.*	July 20, 1922
K		774	**Temperance**—M.H., Brook St., Liverpool. *1st Tues. Feb. (I.), April, Sept. Nov.*	July 20, 1922
K J	*	775	**Thomas á Becket**—R.N. & R.A.Y.C., 17 Pembroke Road, Portsmouth PO1 2NT. *1st Thurs. Feb. (I.), April, June, Sept., Nov.*	Oct. 31, 1922
4K	*	776	**Rugby**—M.H., Rugby. *3rd Mon. Jan., March, May (I.), Nov.*	Oct. 31, 1922
K	* ■	777	**Mercury**—Brook House M.C., Botley, Hampshire SO30 2ER. *2nd Fri. March (I.), May, Nov.*	Oct. 31, 1922
K J	* ■	778	**Barnard Castle**—M.H., Barnard Castle. *3rd Fri. Feb., April, June, Oct. (I.)*	Oct. 31, 1922
	J	779	**Ehen**—Cleator Moor Civic Centre and M.H., Cumbria CA25 5AR. *1st Fri. Feb., May, Sept., Nov. (I.)*	Dec. 5, 1922
		780	**Amble**—M.H., Gloucester Terr., Amble, Northumberland. *4th Wed. Jan., March (I.), May, Sept., Nov.*	Dec. 5, 1922
2K		781	**Mendip**—M.H., Glastonbury, Somerset. *3rd Tues. Jan.; 4th Tues. March (I.), May, Oct.*	Dec. 30, 1922
K J		782	**Thesaurus**—M.H., College Street, Sutton-on-Hull, Hull HU7 4UP. *4th Thurs. Feb., April, Sept., Nov. (I.)*	Dec . 30, 1922
2K J		783	**Unity**—M.H., Crediton. *1st Thurs. Feb., April (I.), June, Oct., Dec.*	Jan. 29, 1923
	J *	784	**St. Illtyd**—M.H., Brynadler, Pontyclun. *2nd Thurs. Feb., March, April, Oct. (I.), Nov.*	Jan. 29, 1923
`K J		785	**Lord Bolton Daylight**—M.H., Beverley Rd., Hull. *3rd Fri. Feb. (I.), May, Oct.*	Feb. 22, 1923
K J	*	786	**Sanitarian**—Mark Masons' Hall. *4th Wed. Feb.; 4th Mon. June (I.); 3rd Mon. Sept.*	Feb. 22, 1923
2K		787	**Tregenna**—M.H., St. Ives, Cornwall. *Last Wed. Feb., April (I.), June, Aug., Oct.; 3rd Fri. Dec.*	Mar. 14, 1923
K	*	788	**Whitley**—M.H., Norham Rd., Whitley Bay. *4th Wed. March, April, Sept., Nov. (I.)*	Mar. 27, 1923

ROLL OF LODGES—continued

		789	*Universal Brotherhood*—F.M.H. Bombay. Transferred to the G.L.M.M.M. of India 1965	Apr. 7, 1923
K	*	790	**Umlazi**—M.T., Bellair, Natal. In abeyance – Nov. 2011	Apr. 7, 1923
K J	*	791	**Public Schools**—Mark Masons' Hall. 2nd Wed. Feb.; 1st Wed. June (I.)	May 3, 1923
K J		792	**Doric**—Oaklands M.H., Beech View, Mottram Road, Hyde, Cheshire SK14 3BH. 3rd Mon. Jan. (I.), March, Nov.	May 3, 1923
		793	*Vedra*—The Palatine Hotel, Sunderland, Durdem. Warrant surrendered 1997	May 16, 1923
K J	*	794	**Socrates**—The Priory, Huntingdon. 2nd Tues. Jan. (I.); 1st Tues. Oct.; 2nd Tues. Nov.	June 10, 1923
K		795	**Deeside**—M.H., Bushell Road, Neston. 2nd Wed. Feb., April, Oct. (I.)	July 4, 1923
J	*■	796	**Torfaen**—M.H., Pontypool. 1st Wed. Oct.; 2nd Wed. Dec. (I.); 4th Wed. March, May	Aug. 20, 1923
2K		797	**Sandwich Haven**—M.T., Sandwich. 4th Tues. Feb., March, Oct., Nov. (I.)	Aug. 20, 1923
K		798	**Caput Anguli**—St. Aubyns M.H., Stoke, Plymouth. 2nd Wed. Jan., March (I.), May, Sept., Nov.	Dec. 17, 1923
		799	**Amatole**—M.H., Durban Street, Fort Beaufort, Eastern Cape. 4th Thurs. July, Sept., Nov.; 1st Sat. March (I.)	Dec. 17, 1923
		800	**Border Mark Lodge of Installed Masters**—Masonic Complex, Masonic Street, Port Alfred, S. Africa. Usually 2nd Sat. July (same as District meeting); 4th Sat. Oct.	Dec. 17, 1923
K J	*	801	**Vaudeville**—Imperial Hotel, Russel Square, London. 2nd Mon. Jan. (I.); 4th Tues. June; 1st Mon. Oct.	Mar. 3, 1924 Warrant of Confirmation Jan. 4, 2007
K J		802	**Composite**—Mark Masons' Hall. 4th Thurs. April Sept. (I.); 2nd Thurs. Dec.	Mar. 6, 1924
J	*	803	**Alexandra**—F.M.H., Alexandra Rd., Hornsea. 2nd Wed. Feb., March, Oct. (I.), Dec.	Apr. 17, 1924
J		804	**Redcar**—F.M.H., Redcar. 3rd Mon. Jan., March, May, Sept., Nov. (I.)	Apr. 17, 1924
		805	**Loughrigg**—Jubilee Rooms, Ellerthwaite Rd., Windermere LA23 2AH. 1st Thurs. Jan., March, Oct. (I.), Nov.	May 1, 1924
K J	*	806	**St. Andrew's**—M.H., Farnham. 4th Thurs. Jan., March, Oct. (I.), Nov.	June 3, 1924
2K		807	**Eldon**—Masonic Hall, Albert Road, Clevedon. 1st Thurs. Feb., April, June, Oct. (I.)	July 3, 1924
K J	*	808	**Richmond**—M.H., 6 The Crescent, Surbiton, Surrey. Last weekday Jan.; 3rd Mon. June; 2nd Mon. Oct. (I.)	July 25, 1924
K		809	**John Pounds**—M.H., Albert Rd., Cosham, Hants. PO6 3DD. 2nd Tues. Feb., April, June, Oct., Dec.	Sept. 3, 1924
K	*	810	**Bassetlaw**—M.H., Worksop. 4th Tues. Jan., March, Sept. (I.), Nov.	Sept. 3, 1924
K		811	**Medway**—M.H., Paddock Wood, Kent. 4th Tues. Jan., March, May, Nov. (I.)	Sept. 5, 1924
2K J		812	**Gilkirke**—Masonic Hall, Barnoldswick. 3rd Tues. March, April, May, Oct. (I.), Nov.	Nov. 18, 1924
		813	*Kashmir*— Lodge never Consecrated	
K J	*	814	**Aurelius**—Colvin Memorial Temple, 7 Holland Road, Clacton-on-Sea CO15 6EG. 2nd Fri. Feb., April (I.), Oct., Dec.	Feb. 26, 1925

ROLL OF LODGES—continued

4K		815	**FitzRoy**—Armoury House, City Road, London EC1Y 2BQ.
			4th Mon. March (I.), (if Public Holiday, 3rd Mon. March), Sept.;
			1st Mon. June — Feb. 5, 1925
	*	816	**Rock of Hope**—M.H., Dar-es-Salaam, Tanzania.
			3rd Fri. March, June (I.), Sept. — Feb. 26, 1925
2K		817	**Derby**—F.M.H., Helmsley House, The Crescent, Salford M5 4PE.
			3rd Thurs. Feb., April, Sept. (I.) — Feb. 26, 1925
2K		818	**Shelford Priory**—M.H., Nottingham.
			4th Fri. Jan., April (I.), Oct. — Feb. 26, 1925
		819	**Transkei**—Star in the East Masonic Complex, 3 Alexandra Rd., Queenstown, E. Cape.
			3rd Sat. Feb., May, Aug. (I.), Nov. — Feb. 26, 1925
	*	820	**Lliedi**—M.H., Llanelli.
			Last Mon. Feb., April, Oct. (I.); 3rd Mon. Dec. — May 13, 1925
K J		821	**Idris**—M.H., Water Street, Barmouth & M.H., Mount Street, Bala.
			Barmouth: 2nd Wed. April, Dec.; Bala: 2nd Wed. Feb. (I.), Nov. — June 5, 1925
2K J		822	**Perseverance**—M.H., Sidmouth.
			4th Wed. Jan., April, June (I.), Oct. — July 15, 1925
K	*	823	**Cambria**—M.T., Cardiff.
			3rd Fri.March, May, Oct. (I.) — Oct. 1925
K	* ■	824	**Mersey**—M.T., York St., Runcorn.
			4th Wed. Jan. (I.), April, Sept., Nov. — Oct. 26, 1925
K J		825	**Beriffe**—M.H., Tower Street, Brightlingsea, Essex CO7 0AL.
			2nd Tues. Feb. (I.), May, Oct.; 1st Tues. Dec. — Oct. 29, 1925
		826	*Wynberg—Mas. Centre, Pinelands, South Africa.*
			Amalgamated with British Lodge No. 345 in 2009 — Dec. 22, 1925
K	■	827	**Unity**—M.H., Seaham Harbour.
			1st Thurs. April (I.), June, Oct. — Jan. 13, 1926
K	* ■	828	**King Solomon's Quarries**—The Royal Quarries, Jerusalem and Mark Masons' Hall, London.
			4th Thurs. Jan., April (I.), Nov. — Feb. 3, 1926
2K		829	**Loyalty**—M.H., Accrington.
			3rd Wed. Jan., March (I.), May, Nov. — Mar. 1, 1926
3K		830	**Eton and Harrow**—Mark Masons' Hall.
			3rd Mon. June (I.); 4th Tues. Nov. — Mar. 15, 1926
3K	*	831	**Zetland**—M.H., Saltash.
			3rd Wed. March, May (I.), Sept., Nov. — Mar. 16, 1926
K J		832	**Shameen**—Zetland Hall, Kennedy Rd., Hong Kong.
			2nd Fri. Jan., May, Sept., Nov.; 2nd Tues. March (I.) — May 10, 1926
K J		833	**Maguncor**—Mark Masons' Hall.
			2nd Wed. March (I.), July, Oct. — May 11, 1926
2K	*	834	**Ambresbury**—M.H., 16 High Beech Road, Loughton, Essex IG10 4BL.
			4th Fri. Jan., April, Oct. (I.) — June 16, 1926
2K	*	835	**Sydenham**—S.E. London M. Club, Avenue Road SE20 7RT.
			3rd Sat. Feb.; 1st Sat. April, Oct. (I.) — July 1, 1926
K	*	836	**Industry and Merit**—F.M.H., Bombay.
			3rd Mon. Jan. (I.), April, July, Oct. — Oct. 6, 1926
		837	*Toril—The Corinthian Hall, Kobe, Japan.*
			Warrant surrendered 1959 — Oct. 22, 1926
K	*	838	**Hawarden**—Fairfield Hall, Connahs Quay, N. Wales.
			2nd Thurs. Feb. (I.), April, Oct., Dec. — Nov.9, 1926
K	* ■	839	**Cornwall Legh**—Masonic Guildhall, Stockport.
			4th Wed. Jan., March, Sept., Nov. (I.) — Nov. 9, 1926
K J	*	840	**North Shropshire**—Ellesmere Town Hall, Ellesmere.
			2nd Thurs. Feb., April (I.); 3rd Thurs. Sept.; 2nd Thurs. Dec. — Nov. 9, 1926

ROLL OF LODGES—*continued*

2K	*	841	Catford—M.H., Oakley House, Bromley Common, Kent.	
			1st Wed. April, June, Dec. (I.)	Nov. 9, 1926
2K	*	842	St. Peter's—Howard Memorial Hall, Woodside, Wigmore, Gillingham.	
			1st Thurs. Jan., March (I.), June, Nov.	Dec. 1, 1926
9K		843	Eccles—Eccles M.H., 'Elm Bank', Half Edge Lane, Eccles.	
			2nd Fri. Jan., March (I.), Sept., Nov.	Feb. 7, 1927
K	*■	844	Dore—M.H., Dore, Derbyshire.	
			4th Mon. Jan., March (I.), May, Sept., Nov.	Mar. 28, 1927
3K J	*	845	Alverton—M.H., Bedale.	
			3rd Tues. Feb., April, Oct. (I.), Dec.	June 2, 1927
K	■	846	Steadfast—F.M.H., Darlington.	
			1st Wed. Feb., March, April, Oct., Nov., Dec. (I.)	June 19, 1927
K J		847	Cherwell—M.H., Banbury.	
			Last Tues. Jan., March, Sept. (I.), Nov.	June, 10, 1927
2K	*	848	Kosmos—F.M.H., Park Lane, Parktown, Johannesburg, Gauteng.	
			3rd Thurs. Jan., March, May, July, Sep., Nov. (I.)	June 10, 1927
2K J		849	Amity—M.H., St. Andrew's Rd., Exmouth.	
			3rd Mon. Feb. (I.), June, Sept., Nov.	July 4, 1927
K J	*	850	Dunwich—Masonic Rooms, Chaucer Street, Bungay, Suffolk.	
			4th Thurs. March, Sept. (I.); 3rd Thurs. May.	Aug. 30, 1927
		851	Stellenbosch—M.T., Bird Street, Stellenbosch, S.A.	
			In abeyance 02/05/07.	Nov. 10, 1927
3K		852	Semper Paratus—Stanley House, Manchester Rd., Audenshaw, Manchester M34 5GB.	
			2nd Tues. Feb., May (I.), Sept.	Dec. 20 1927
2K		853	Radnor—F.M.H., Crane St., Salisbury, Wilts SP1 2QD.	
			2nd Mon. Jan., March, May (I.), Nov.	Feb. 8, 1928
K	*■	854	St. Andrew's—M.H., Stanley, Co. Durham.	
			4th Thurs. Sept. to April except Dec. and Jan. (I. Sept.)	Mar. 1, 1928
K J		855	Erasmus Darwin—M.H., The Grange, 457 Burton Rd., Littleover, Derby.	
			3rd Wed. Jan., March, May, Sept., Nov. (I.)	Mar. 1, 1928
K	*	856	Golden Square—Mark Masons' Hall.	
			3rd Wed. Feb. (I.); 2nd Wed. April, Oct.	May 16, 1928
K J	*	857	Kentish—Westwood Mas.Centre, Welling, Kent.	
			1st Tues. March; 4th Tues. Sept. (I.); 1st Tues. Dec.	Mar. 19, 1928
3K J	*	858	Staines—Staines District M.C.	
			2nd Fri. March, July (I.), Nov.	Mar. 26, 1928
K J		859	Rainham—M.H., Rectory Road, Orsett, Essex RM16 3EH.	
			4th Sat. Feb. (I.); 1st Sat. May; 3rd Sat. Dec.	Mar. 26, 1928
			Warrant of Confirmation	Mar. 23, 2010
2K J	*■	860	Bernard Gilpin—M.H., Hetton-le-Hole, Durham.	
			2nd Tues. Feb., March, May, Oct. (I.), Nov., Dec.	Apr. 11, 1928
K J	*	861	Christopher Wren—Cole Court, London Rd., Twickenham.	
			1st Thurs. April (I.); 4th Thurs. Sept.	Apr. 11, 1928
K J	*	862	Regis—M.R., 395 Halesowen Road, Cradley Heath, Warley.	
			2nd Thurs. Feb., April, Oct. (I.), Dec.	Apr. 18, 1928
2K J	*	863	Jeppestown—F.M.H., 8 Park Lane, Park Town, Johannesburg, S. Africa.	
			2nd Wed. March, June (I.), Sept., Dec.	Apr. 23, 1928
3K J	*	864	The White Stone—M.H., Station Road, Chingford, London E4 7AZ.	
			3rd Mon. Oct. (I.); 4th Mon. April.	June 6, 1928
		865	Duke of Connaught—Victoria M.T., Columbo, Sri Lanka.	
			4th Thurs. Jan. (I.), April, July, Oct.	Sept. 9, 1928
4K		866	Bispham-with-Norbreck—M.H., Adelaide St., Blackpool.	
			2nd Fri. Jan., Feb. (I.), April, Oct., Nov.	Sept. 9, 1928
K J	■	867	Vale of Avon—Unity Hall, Southampton Road, Ringwood, Hants. BH24 1HY.	
			1st Thurs. Feb., March, Oct., Nov. (I.)	Oct. 4, 1928

ROLL OF LODGES—continued

3K	*	868	**Hyde**—M.H., Mottram Rd., Hyde. 3rd Fri. Feb. (I.), April, Sept., Nov.	Nov. 12, 1928
K	*	869	**City of London**—Civil Service Club, 13/15 Great Scotland Yard, London SW1A 2HJ. 4th Mon. Jan., March, Nov. (I.)	Nov. 12, 1928
3K	J	870	**St. Paul's**—M.T., Stirling Rd., Birmingham 16. 3rd Thurs. Feb., April, Oct. (I.), Nov.	Nov. 12, 1928
		871	*Flinders—M.T. Julia Creek, Queensland, Australia.* *Transferred to the G.L.M.M.M. of Queensland 1932*	*Nov. 19, 1928*
2K	* ■	872	**Digswell**—The Cloisters, Barrington Road, Letchworth SG6 3TH. 3rd Wed. March, May (I.); 4th Wed. June	Jan. 3, 1929
K	J	873	**North and East Middlesex Lodge of Installed Mark Masters**— M.M.H., London or other selected venue within the Province. *1st fifth weekday in April (I.), Sept.*	Feb. 1, 1929
K	J ■	874	**Stradbroke**—M.H., Albert Rd., Cosham, Hants. PO6 3DD. 3rd Fri. Feb., April (I.), June, Sept., Nov.	Feb. 4, 1929
K	J * ■	875	**Harmony**—M.H., Queens Rd., Fareham, Hants. PO16 0NN. 3rd Tues. Jan., April, June, Oct. (I.), Nov.	Feb. 7, 1929
2K	*	876	**Knole**—M.Ctr., 119a St. John's Hill, Sevenoaks, Kent. 2nd Fri. March, Oct. (I.), Dec.	Mar. 25, 1929
		877	**Sivangnanam**—F.M.H., Trivandrum, Madras. 1st Sat. Jan., April, Oct.; 4th Sat. July	Apr. 17, 1929
4K	* ■	878	**Pontefract**—M.H., Carleton Close, Pontefract. 4th Thurs. Jan., Feb., March (I.), April, Sept., Oct., Nov.	May 1, 1929
K	J *	879	**Three Grand Principles**—M.H., Penryn, Cornwall. 4th Mon. Jan., March, April (I.), Sept., Nov.	May 3 1929
3K	*	880	**Semper Fidelis**—The Palace, Garden St., St. Anne's-on-Sea. 3rd Mon. Feb. (I.), April, Oct., Dec.	May 10, 1929
K	*	881	**Bulawayo**—F.M.H., Sadie Kaplan Ave, Parkview, Bulawayo, Zimbabwe. 2nd Mon. March, June (I.), Sept., Dec.	May 30, 1929
		882	*Port Curtis—Gladstone, Queensland, Australia.* *Transferred to the G.L.M.M.M. of Queensland 1932*	*June 1, 1929*
K	*	883	**Mill Hill**—Cafe Naz at Corvino, 7 Middlesex Street, London E1 7AA. 4th Sat. June; 3rd Sat. Dec. (I.)	Sept. 9, 1929
		884	*Mackay—Macay, Queensland, Australia.* *Transferred to the G.L.M.M.M. of Queensland 1932*	*Sept. 16, 1929*
K	*	885	**Rising Star**—M.C., van Blerk Ave., Spitskop, Bloemfontein, S. Africa. 4th Sat. Jan. (I.), April, July; 1st Sat. Oct.	Sept. 30, 1929
K	* ■	886	**Oakley**—M.H., Victoria St., Basingstoke, Hants. RG21 3BT. 3rd Tues. Jan., March, May, Oct. (I.)	Oct. 2, 1929
7K	■	887	**Lascelles**—Tapton Hall, Shore Lane, Sheffield S10 3BU. 1st Tues. Feb. (I.), April, July, Oct.	Oct. 8, 1929
K		888	**Eden Valley**—M.H., Boroughgate, Appleby, Westmorland CA16 6XB. 4th Thurs. Jan., March, April, Oct. (I.)	Nov. 1, 1929
		889	*Yeoman—M.H. Valletta, Malta.* *Warrant surrendered 1997*	*Nov. 6, 1929*
J	*	890	**Ashington**—M.H., Ashington, Northumberland. 1st Thurs. Feb. (I.), April, June, Oct., Dec.	Dec. 2, 1929
K	*	891	*Isthmian—Chingford M.H., Station Rd., Chingford.* *In abeyance June 2009*	*Feb. 7, 1930*
3K	*	892	**Tower Hamlets**—Mark Masons' Hall. 2nd Mon. Jan.; 1st Mon. June, Sept. (I.)	June 12, 1930
K	*	893	**St. Laurence**—M.H., Redditch. 2nd Mon. Sept. (I.), Nov., March	June 14, 1930
		894	*Astrul—Helsinki, Finland.* *Transferred to the G.L.M.M.M. of Finland 1971*	*June 30, 1930*

ROLL OF LODGES—continued

4K		895	**Quadratic**—Twickenham Dist.Mas.Centre, Cole Court, London Rd., Twickenham. *3rd Mon. April; 2nd Mon. Sept., Dec. (I.)*	July 3, 1930
K	* ■	896	**Clavering**—New F.M.H., Blaydon-on-Tyne, Co. Durham. *3rd Thurs. March, April, Oct., Nov. (I.) Dec.*	Sept. 22, 1930
4K	* ■	897	**Barnet Mark Well**—Mark Masons' Hall. 4th Tues. May; *3rd Mon. Sept. (I.); 1st Tues. Dec.*	Nov. 15, 1930
5K	*	898	**Progress**—Ashlar House, Saul St., Preston. *2nd Mon. Feb., April, Oct. (I.), Dec.*	Jan. 28, 1931
K		899	**Irenic**—Mark Masons' Hall, 86 St. James's Street, London SW1A 1PL. *3rd Wed. April (I.), Oct.*	Feb. 14, 1931
2K J	*	900	**Vereeniging**—Masonic Hall, Phoenix, Mauritius. *1st Mon. March, June, Sept. (I.), Dec.*	May 22, 1931
2K	*	901	**Kenton**—Harrow Mas.Centre, Northwick Circle, Kenton. *4th Thurs. March; 2nd Thurs. June; 4th Thurs. Nov. (I.)*	June 16, 1931
2K	■	902	**Middlewich**—M.H., Kinderton Street, Middlewich. *4th Mon. Jan. (I.), April, Sept., Nov.*	Aug. 31, 1931
K	*	903	**Prescot**—M.H., High St., Prescot. *Last Mon. Feb. (I.), April, Oct.; 3rd Mon. Dec.*	Aug. 31, 1931
5K		904	**Waldie Peirson**—Kensington M.H., Cnr. Roberts Ave. and Ivanhoe St., Johannesburg. *2nd Thurs. Feb. (I.), May, Aug., Nov.*	Nov. 4, 1931
3K		905	**Prosperity**—F.M.H., Park Lane, Parktown, Johannesburg. *4th Wed. Jan., March (I.), June, Sept.*	Nov. 8, 1931
		906	**Mount Mawenzi**—M.H., Selian, Arusha, Tanzania. *3rd Tues. March, June, Nov. (I.)*	Nov. 21, 1931
				Warrant of Confirmation July 1, 1998
	*	907	**Campbell**—Yaley Residency, Brough Road, Erode-1, Tamil Nadu, India. *Last Sat. Feb., May, Aug. (I.), Nov.*	Jan. 7, 1932
				Warrant of Confirmation Feb. 1, 2007
2K		908	**Billinge**—M.H., Richmond Terr., Blackburn, E. Lancs. *3rd Thurs. Jan., March, Oct. (I.)*	Feb. 4, 1932
K J	*	909	**Lea Valley**—Halsey M.H., Cheshunt. *3rd Tues. March; 4th Tues. June; 3rd Tues. Oct. (I.)*	June 28, 1932
K J	■	910	**Romsey**—M.H., Albion Place, Southampton SO14 2DD. *4th Mon. Jan. (I.), Feb., April, Oct., Nov.*	Aug. 24, 1932
3K	* ■	911	**Keep**—M.R., Conservative Club, Castle St, Clitheroe. *4th Thurs. Jan., March, May, Sept., Nov. (I.)*	Sept. 26, 1932
K		912	**Victoria Falls**—M.T., Livingstone, Zambia. *Last Sat. Feb. (I.), June, Oct.*	Oct. 19, 1932
		913	*Britannic Lodge of Madeira—Quinta, Bichinhe, Funchal, Madeira. Warrant surrendered 1985*	*Nov. 9, 1932*
7K	*	914	**Loyalty**—M.H., Oakfield Rd., Croydon. *1st Fri. March (I.), Oct.; 2nd Fri. June.*	Dec. 9, 1932
		915	*Srinagar—Srinagar, Kashmir, Punjab, India. Warrant surrendered 1944*	*Jan. 17, 1933*
K	*	916	**St. Wulfram's**—M.H., Chambers St., Grantham. *4th Thurs. Feb., March (I.), Oct., Nov.*	Jan. 20, 1933
K	■	917	**Joseph Cook**—M.H., Ripley, Derbyshire. *4th Mon., Feb. (I.), April; 2nd Thurs. Oct., Dec.*	Feb. 1, 1933
K	*	918	**Rottingdean**—Brighton M.C., Queens Rd., Brighton. *2nd Mon. March; 1st Mon. Oct. (I.); 1st Tues. Dec.*	Feb. 27, 1933
3K		919	**St. Mabon**—Wynnstay M.T., Duke Street, Ruabon. *4th Mon. Feb., March, Oct., Nov. (I.)*	Feb. 28, 1933
K J	*	920	**Ravenscroft**—Halsey M.C., Turners Hill, Cheshunt, Herts. *3rd Mon. Feb., May (I.), Nov.*	Mar. 19, 1933

ROLL OF LODGES—continued

K	*	921	Foundation—Mark Masons' Hall, London SW1A 1PL.	
			4th Mon. March (I.), Sept.	Apr. 7, 1933
				Warrant of Confirmation Sept. 28, 2009
3K		922	Tuscan—M.H., Tatton Rd., Sale, Cheshire.	
			3rd Thurs. Feb., April (I.), Oct.	June 1, 1933
K	*	923	Vernon—M.H., Stourport-on-Severn.	
			2nd Tues. Feb., April, Oct. (I.); 2nd Mon. Dec.	June 13, 1933
2K J		924	Tottenham—Staines M.H., Thames St., Staines, Middlesex.	
			2nd Thurs. June (I.); 3rd Mon. July; 3rd Wed. Dec.	June 28, 1933
2K	*■	925	Moseley—M.H., Birtley, Co. Durham.	
			3rd Fri. Feb., April, May, Oct. (I.), Dec.	July 3, 1933
K J	*	926	William Hamilton Underhill—The Cloisters, Barrington Rd., Letchworth.	
			3rd Mon. April (I.), Sept., Nov.	Aug. 30, 1933
K J		927	Eifl—M.H., Pwllheli.	
			3rd Tues. Feb., April, Sept., Nov. (I.)	Aug. 31, 1933
K		928	Star in the West—Harrow M.C., Kenton.	
			3rd Mon. Feb., May, Nov. (I.)	Oct. 26, 1933
K	■	929	William Todd—M.H., Victoria Ave., Bishop Auckland.	
			3rd Tues. Feb., April, June, Oct. (I.), Dec.	Nov. 15, 1933
K	*■	930	Castle Eden—M.H., Castle Eden, Durham.	
			4th Wed. March, May (I.), July, Sept., Nov.	Nov. 28, 1933
2K J	*	931	Headstone—M.C., Northwick Circle, Harrow, Middx.	
			4th Mon. Feb. (I.); 2nd Wed. May; 1st Wed. Nov.	Dec. 27, 1933
K J	*	932	Prudence and Verity—Mark Masons' Hall.	
			3rd Mon. Feb. (I.); 3rd Tues. Oct.	Dec. 28, 1933
K J	*	933	Noel Boardman Walsall—M.T., High St., Aldridge.	
			2nd Mon. May (I.); 1st Mon. Oct., March; 3rd Mon. Jan.	Mar. 14, 1934
2K		934	Melandra—Spencer M.H., Hague Street, Whitfield, Glossop, Derbyshire SK13 8NS.	
			3rd Mon. April; 4th Mon. June, Sept. (I.)	June 28, 1934
5K		935	Lodge of Charity—M.H., Bryn, nr. Wigan.	
			3rd Mon. Feb. (I.), April, Sept., Nov.	June 29, 1934
3K J	*	936	Meridian—M.M.H., London SW1A 1PL.	
			4th Wed. Jan., April; 3rd Wed. Sept. (I.)	July 12, 1934
	*	937	Cauvery—F.M.H., Tanjore, Madras.	
			1st Sat. March, June, Sept. (I.), Dec.	Oct. 3, 1934
2K	*	938	Whitstable—M.T., Cromwell Road, Whitstable.	
			3rd Wed. Jan. (I.), March, Sept., Nov.	Nov. 1, 1934
2K		939	Fabric—M.T., Richard St., Rochdale.	
			3rd Tues. Feb., April, Oct. (I.), Dec.	Dec. 21, 1934
4K	*	940	Galway—M.H., Goldsmith St., Nottingham.	
			3rd Tues. March, Sept. (I.), Nov.	Dec. 22, 1934
2K		941	King Edward—M.H., Corner Garnett and Jade Streets.	
			4th Thurs. Jan., May, Sept.; 2nd Sat. March (I.)	Feb. 18, 1935
2K		942	Garston—M.H., Island Rd. South, Garston, Liverpool.	
			1st Wed. Feb.; 3rd Wed. May; 2nd Wed. Nov. (I.)	Feb. 26, 1935
6K J	■	943	Sincerity—Tapton Hall, Shore Lane, Sheffield 10.	
			2nd Thurs. Jan., March, May, Sept. (I.), Oct., Nov.	Mar. 1, 1935
K	*	944	Fillebrook—M.H., Station Road, Chingford, London E4 7AZ.	
			2nd Wed. March (I.), June; 3rd Thurs. Oct.	Apr. 27, 1935
K	*	945	Crowstone—Southend M.C., Saxon Hall, Aviation Way, Southend-on-Sea SS2 6UN.	
			3rd Thurs. Jan., April, Nov. (I.)	May 16, 1935
K J	*	946	St. Botolph's—M.H., Main Ridge, Boston, Lincs.	
			Last Tues. Feb. (I.), April, Oct., Nov.	May 22, 1935
		947	Barnet—Mark Masons' Hall, Great Queen Street, London.	
			Amalgamated with Mark Well No. 897 (Warrant surrendered)	July 3, 1935

ROLL OF LODGES—continued

			948	Mount Figmont—The Temple, New Plymouth, New Zealand. Warrant surrendered 1969	Sept. 5, 1935
10K	J		949	**Constitution**—F.M.H., Bridge St., Manchester. 2nd Tues. Jan. (I.), March, Nov.	Oct. 9, 1935
	J	*	950	**Dunraven**—M.T., Bridgend, Glamorgan. 1st Tues. Feb., March, April (I.), Oct., Dec.	Nov. 6, 1935
K	J		951	**Sir Arthur Holbrook**—M.H., John Street, Ryde, I.O.W. PO33 2PY. 4th Wed. Feb., April, Oct., Nov. (I.)	Nov. 7, 1935
K		*	952	**Kenya**—F.M.H., Nairobi, Kenya. 2nd Thurs. Jan. (I.), April, July, Oct.	Nov. 22, 1935
2K	J	■	953	**Cestrian**—F.M.H., Queen St., Chester. 2nd Fri. Jan. (I.), March, Nov.	Dec. 6, 1935
4K	J		954	**Wilfred Hulbert**—F.M.H., Park Lane, Parktown, Johannesburg, S.A. 4th Tues. Feb. (I.), April, June, Aug., Oct.	Jan. 30, 1936
K		*	955	**Pleydell-Bouverie**—M.H., Godalming. 4th Tues. Jan., April (I.), Oct.	May 12, 1936
5K			956	**George Harradon**—M.H., Hope St., Liverpool. 3rd Thurs. Feb., May, Nov. (I.)	May 12, 1936
2K		*	957	**Hartismere**—F.H., Diss. 1st Tues. Feb., May, Nov.; 3rd Tues. Sept. (I.)	June 15, 1936
3K			958	**Athelstan**—F.M.H., Topsham, Exeter EX3 0EU. 4th Fri. Jan. (I.), March, April, Oct., Nov.	June 22, 1936
3K			959	**St. Martin's**—M.H., Severn St., Birmingham. 3rd Thurs. Jan., March, Sept. (I.), Nov.	July 7, 1936
K	J		960	**North Staffordshire**—M.H., Shelton, Stoke-on-Trent. 4th Tues. Feb., April; 1st Tues. Nov. (I.)	July 8, 1936
K		*	961	**St. Paul's**—M.T., Rua Lisboa 1120, Sao Paulo, Brazil. 2nd Tues. Feb. (I.), May, Aug., Nov.	July 21, 1936
K		*	962	**Latimer**—Ashwell House, St. Albans, Herts. 4th Wed. Jan.; 4th Fri. April; 3rd Fri. Sept. (I.)	Sept. 14, 1936
3K		■	963	**Derwent**—Moot Hall, Wirksworth. 1st Fri. Feb., April, Oct. (I.), Dec.	Dec. 18, 1936
3K		*■	964	**Macclesfield**—M.T., Macclesfield. 4th Tues. Feb. (I.), March, Sept., Nov.	Jan. 4, 1937
K		*	965	**Connaught**—F.M.H., Soane St., Ipswich. 3rd Tues. Jan., March (I.), May; 1st Tues. Nov.	Jan. 5, 1937
2K		*	966	**Northern Transvaal**—M.H., Voortrekker St., Polokwane (formerly Pietersburg), South Africa. 4th Sat., March, June (I.), Sept., Nov.	Apr. 29, 1937
2K		*	967	**George Norman**—M.H., Yatton, Somerset. Last Mon. Jan., March, Sept., Nov. (I.)	July 6, 1937
4K		*	968	**Carville**—F.M.H., Headlam St., Newcastle upon Tyne 6. 1st Fri. Feb., April (I.), Oct., Dec.	Dec. 23, 1937 Warrant of Confirmation Sept., 1 1998
K	J	■	969	**Winchester**—Winchester M.C., 124 Alresford Rd., Winchester SO21 1MB. 4th Mon. Feb., April, Oct. (I.), Nov.	Jan. 24, 1938
2K	J		970	**East Goscote**—M.H., Broad St., Syston, nr. Leicester. 4th Tues. Feb., April (I.), Oct., Dec.	Feb. 7, 1938
K		*	971	**Geoffrey Short**—M.H., Yerbury St., Trowbridge, Wilts BA14 8DP. 4th Wed. Jan., March, Sept. (I.), Nov.	June 8, 1938
4K		*	972	**Silhill**—M.R., Warwick Road, Knowle. 4th Thurs. Jan., March, Sept. (I.), Nov.	July 8, 1938
K			973	**William of Orange**—M.H., Windsor Road, Petersfield, Hants. GU32 3ER. 3rd Wed. Feb., April, Sept., Nov. (I.)	Aug. 8, 1938

ROLL OF LODGES—*continued*

K	*		974	**James Parsons**—Halsey M.H., Watford. *2nd Wed. Feb., May, Nov. (I.)*	Feb. 7, 1939
K	*		975	**Bernard Harvey**—Mas. Centre, Slough. *2nd Mon. March (I.), May, Nov.*	May 31, 1939
K	* ■		976	**Johann Gutenberg**—Mark Masons' Hall. *1st Tues. March (I.); 4th Tues. Sept.*	July 6, 1939
K J	*		977	**Eaton**—Moseley M.H., Alcester Rd. South, King's Heath, Birmingham. *3rd Fri. Feb., April, Nov. (I.)*	June 14, 1940
K			978	**Temperance**—Sussex M.C., Queen's Rd., Brighton. *3rd Fri. Jan.; 1st Fri. June; 1st Thurs. Sept. (I.)*	June 14, 1940
K			979	**Arts and Crafts**—Sussex M.C., Queen's Rd., Brighton. *3rd Sat. Jan.; 2nd Sat. Oct. (I.); 3rd Sat. May*	Aug. 12, 1941
3K	*		980	**Marlborough**—M.H., Woodstock, Oxfordshire. *2nd Tues. Feb., July (I.), Oct., Nov.*	Feb. 24, 1942
K	* ■		981	**Spennymoor**—M.H., Dundas St, Spennymoor. *1st Thurs. Jan., March, May (I.), July, Sept., Nov.*	Aug. 14, 1942
K J			982	**St. Oswald**—M.H., Roft St., Oswestry. *4th Tues. Feb., April (I.), Oct.*	Mar. 23, 1943
2K	* ■		983	**Trivona**—M.H., Elm Ave., Long Eaton. *3rd Thurs. Feb., April (I.), Oct., Dec.*	Mar. 23, 1943
K	*		984	**Lodge of Harmony**—M.T., Faversham. *2nd Mon. Feb., April (I.), Oct., Nov.*	Mar. 9, 1943
	*		985	**Cango**—M.T., 45 Marsh Street, Mossel Bay, Western Cape, S. Africa. *1st Sat. March, June, Dec.; Sat. following first Fri. Sept. (I.)*	Mar. 9, 1943
3K	*		986	**All Hallows**—Twickenham District M.C., Cole Court, 150 London Rd., Twickenham, Middx. *3rd Mon. Feb. (I.); 2nd Mon. July; 4th Mon. Oct.*	Ma. 15, 1943
3K			987	**Diligence**—Harrow District M.C., Northwick Circle, Harrow, Middx. *2nd Tues. Jan.; 3rd Tues. April (I.), Oct.*	May 6, 1943
K			988	**Shalden**—M.H., Market St., Alton, Hants. GU34 1HA. *1st Wed. March, May (I.), Oct., Dec.*	May 14, 1943
K	■		989	**Northern Heights**—M.H., Grove Road, Sutton, Surrey. *2nd Thurs. March, Dec. (I.); 3rd Mon. May*	June 11, 1943
3K	*		990	**East Lancashire Provincial Grand Officers**—F.M.H., Bridge St., Manchester 3. *Last Tues. April, Oct. (I.)*	June 11, 1943
K J	*		991	**Eleanor Cross**—Halsey M.H., Cheshunt, Herts. *3rd Wed. Feb., May, Oct. (I.)*	Oct. 14, 1943
K			992	**Allen Pooley**—Britannia Adelphi Hotel, Ranelagh Place, Liverpool L3 5UL. *2nd Wed. Feb., April, Oct.*	Oct. 22, 1943
K J	*		993	**Dartmouth**—M.H., Edward St., West Bromwich. *4th Mon. April (I.), Sept., Nov.*	Nov. 9, 1943
2K	*		994	**Salford**—M.H., Crescent, Salford 5. *1st Thurs. Feb. (I.) April, Oct., Dec.*	Feb. 10 1944
K	*		995	**Stoneleigh**—Sutton M.H. *2nd Fri. Jan., March (I.), Sept.*	Nov. 24, 1943
2K	*		996	**Isma**—Mark Masons' Hall. *4th Tues. Feb.; 1st Wed. May; 3rd Wed. Oct. (I.)*	Dec. 13, 1943
2*K*	*		997	**Pickwick**—Royal National Hotel, 38-51 Bedford Way, London WC1H 0DG. *2nd Thurs. March; 3rd Wed. June; 4th Wed. Sept. (I.)*	Mar. 15, 1944
5K	*		998	**Boleyn Castle**—Hutton M.H., Mount Ave., Brentwood, Essex CM13 2NS. *4th Tues. March; 4th Thurs. June (I.); 4th Tues. Oct.*	Mar. 27, 1944
	*		999	**Kent Installed Mark Masters**—M.H., Tovil, Maidstone, Kent or at such other venue within the Province as the W.M. shall direct. *4th Sat. June; 1st Sat. Nov. (I.)*	Apr. 1, 1944

ROLL OF LODGES—continued

2K	*	1000	**Milestone**—Mark Masons' Hall. *1st Thurs. April (I.); 1st Thurs. Oct.*	Apr. 1, 1944
3K	* ■	1001	**University of Manchester**—F.M.H., Bridge St., Manchester 3. *2nd Mon. June; 4th Mon. Nov.*	Apr. 1, 1944
3K	*	1002	**Leyland**—M.H., Church Road, Leyland. *2nd Thurs. Jan. (I.), March, May, Sept., Nov.*	Apr. 1, 1944
K J		1003	**Newton**—Bryn. M.H., Ashton-in-Makerfield. *3rd Mon. Jan., March (I.), May, Oct.*	June 1, 1944
2K J	* ■	1004	**Thorne**—M.H., Stonegate, Thorne, Yorks. *1st Thurs. Feb., March (I.), May, Oct., Nov.*	June 1, 1944
2K		1005	**Composite**—Masonic Guildhall, Wellington Rd. South, Stockport. Warrant surrendered June 2011	June 1, 1944
K		1006	**Westhoughton**—M.H., Peel St., Westhoughton. *2nd Thurs. Feb., April, Oct., Dec. (I.)*	June 1, 1944
2K		1007	**Freshfield**—M.H., Duke St., Southport. *4th Fri. Feb., Oct.; 3rd Fri. April (I.), Dec.*	June 1, 1944
K		1008	**St. Peter's**—M.H., St. Saviourgate, York. *1st Mon. March, Sept., Nov. (I.); 1st Tues. May.*	Aug. 22, 1944
K		1009	**Midhurst**—M.H., Bepton Rd, Midhurst. *4th Tues. Jan., March (I.), April, Oct.*	Oct. 18, 1944
2K	* ■	1010	**Rose of York**—F.M.H., Westholme, Stockport Road, Mossley, Lancs. *2nd Fri. Feb., May (I.), Sept.*	Sept. 22, 1944
K		1011	**St. Luke's**—M.H., Camborne. *4th Mon. Jan., Feb., March, April, Sept., Nov. (I.)*	Sept. 1, 1944
3K J	*	1012	**Matthew Clarke**—M.H., Severn St., Birmingham. *2nd Sat. Feb., April, Oct. (I.), Nov.*	Oct. 1, 1944
K	*	1013	**Ealing**—Cole Court, 150 London Road, Twickenham. *1st Fri. April, July, Nov. (I.)*	Oct. 1, 1944
2K	*	1014	**Gawthorpe**—M.T., Nelson Sq., Burnley. *2nd Thurs. Jan., March, May (I.), Nov.*	Oct. 1, 1944
K	■	1015	**Ernest Dixon**—Wearside M.T., Burdon Rd., Sunderland. *3rd Tues. Jan., March, April, Sept. (I.), Nov.*	Oct. 10, 1944
K	*	1016	**Rivacre**—M.H., 141 Chester Rd., Ellesmere Port, Cheshire. *3rd Wed. Feb., May (I.), Sept., Nov.*	Dec. 7, 1944
K		1017	**St. Giles**—Uxbridge M.C., Hercies Road, Hillingdon, Uxbridge, Middx. *2nd Wed. Feb. (I.); 3rd Wed. May; 2nd Thurs. Nov.*	Dec. 7. 1944
3K J		1018	**Gothic**—M.H., Station St., Swinton. *1st Tues. March (I.), Oct., Nov., Dec.*	Jan. 9, 1945
3K	*	1019	**Ormskirk Priory**—M.H., Park Rd., Ormskirk. *4th Thurs. Jan., March, Nov. (I.)*	May 4, 1945
K J		1020	**John Peel**—M.T., 10 Portland Sq., Carlisle CA1 1PY. *2nd Mon. Feb., April, May (I.), Oct., Dec.*	Mar. 6, 1945
K J		1021	**Talbot**—The N. Shropshire M.R., Castle Hill, Whitchurch, Shropshire. *4th Wed. March, in the event of the Installation meeting falling in the same week as Spring Bank Holiday the meeting shall be held on the next following Wed., May (I.), July, Sept.*	Mar. 6, 1945
2K		1022	**Flamsteed**—M.H., 457 Burton Rd., Littleover, Derby. *2nd Thurs. Feb., April (I.), Sept., Nov.*	Apr. 1, 1945
K J		1023	**Trevaunance**—M.H., Rosemundy, St. Agnes, Cornwall. *3rd Fri. Jan., March, May, Sept., Nov. (I.)*	Apr. 26, 1945
6K	* ■	1024	**Altrincham**—Macclesfield M.H., Oakleigh House, 1 Riseley St., Macclesfield. *4th Fri. Feb. (I.), March, Oct.*	Apr. 26, 1945
2K		1025	**Duke of Richmond**—Sussex M.C., Queen's Rd., Brighton. *3rd Wed. Feb.; 3rd Mon. May (I.); 2nd Mon. Oct.*	Apr. 26, 1945

ROLL OF LODGES—*continued*

2K	*	1026	St. Katharine's—Fraternity Hall, 288 Eastwood Road North, Southend-on-Sea, Essex SS9 4LT. *4th Sat. Jan., March, Sept., Nov. (I.)* — Apr. 26, 1945
6K J	■	1027	Wharfdale—M.H., Westbourne House, Otley, W. Yorks. *1st Thurs. April, May (I.), July, Oct., Nov.* — June 6, 1945
K	*	1028	Carnanton—M.H., Newquay, Cornwall. *2nd Fri. Feb., March, Oct. (I.), Nov.* — June 6, 1945
2K J		1029	St. John's—M.H., Parkhill Road, Torquay, Devon. *Last Mon. Jan., March, Sept., Nov. (I.)* — June 7, 1945
3K J		1030	Victory—M.H., Callington, Cornwall. *3rd Tues. Jan., March, May, July, Sept., Nov. (I.)* — June 6, 1945
K	*	1031	Maius—M.H., Risca, Monmouthshire. *1st Thurs. Jan., March, May, Nov.* — June 6, 1945
K	*	1032	Earl of Scarbrough—M.H., Rutland Rd., Skegness. *2nd Wed. Jan., Feb., March, Nov., Dec. (I.)* — July 12, 1945
J		1033	Risingham—M.H., Manchester Square, Bellingham, Northumberland. *2nd Tues. March, June, Sept., Oct. (I.)* — Sept. 4, 1945
2K		1034	Gorton—Audenshaw M.H., Stanley House, Manchester. *1st Thurs. Feb., April (I.), Oct., Dec.* — Sept. 4, 1945
K	* ■	1035	Lansdowne—M.H., Emery Lane, Chippenham, Wilts SN15 3PJ. *4th Mon. Jan., April, Oct. (I.); 3rd Mon. Dec.* — Sept. 20, 1945
		1036	Purcell—M.T., Maple Terrace, Newcastle upon Tyne. Warrant surrendered May 2012 — *Sept. 4, 1945*
J	*	1037	St. John's—M.R., Water St., Wigton, Cumbria CA7 9AN. *2nd Mon. Jan., Feb., March (I.), Oct., Dec.* — Oct. 1, 1945
3K J		1038	Ashburton—M.H., Church Road, Ashburton. *2nd Thurs. Feb., April, July, Sept., Nov. (I.)* — Oct. 18, 1945
K	*	1039	Stroud—M.H., The Hill, Merrywalks, Stroud. *2nd Fri. Feb., April (I.), Oct., Dec.* — Oct. 18, 1946
K		1040	Cleveland—M.H., Stokesley, Yorks. *1st Fri. Feb., March, May, Oct. (I.), Dec.* — Oct. 18, 1945
3K J		1041	Holte—M.H., Severn St., Birmingham. *2nd Mon. Feb., April (I.), Oct.* — Dec. 1, 1945
2K		1042	Supera Moras—F.M.H., Institute St., Bolton, Lancs. *3rd Wed. Jan., March (I.), May, Oct.* — Dec. 1, 1945
J	*	1043	Barry—M.T., Broad St., Barry, Glam. *1st Mon. March, May (I.), Sept.* — Nov. 11, 1945
	*	1044	Essex Installed Mark Masters'—Such venues as the Prov.G.M. shall direct. *3rd Tues. March (I.); 2nd Thurs. Sept.* — Dec. 6, 1945
		1045	Asbestos—Freemasons Hall, Bulawayo. Warrant surrendered 2007 — *Mar. 12, 1946*
K	*	1046	Zululand—M.T., Empangeni, Zululand, Natal. *4th Thurs. Feb., April, June (I.), Aug., Oct.* — Mar. 12, 1946
K J	*	1047	Cheshunt—Halsey M.H., Cheshunt, Herts. *3rd Thurs. March; 4th Thurs. June; 1st Thurs. Nov. (I.)* — Jan. 13, 1946
2K J		1048	Thistle and Shamrock—M.H., Waterloo Road, Havant PO9 1BH. *3rd Thurs. Jan., March (I.), April, Oct., Nov.* — Feb. 1, 1946
K	*	1049	Hindhead—Bordon M.C., High St., Bordon, Hampshire GU35 0AL. *3rd Thurs. Jan., May, Sept. (I.)* — Feb. 28, 1946
K J	* ■	1050	Esher—M.H., Masonic Hall Road, Chertsey. *3rd Mon. Feb. (I.), June, Sept.* — Feb. 28, 1946
2K J		1051	Rutland—F.M.H., Burton Road, Melton Mowbray. *2nd Wed. Feb., May (I.), Oct., Dec.* — Feb. 25, 1946
2K		1052	Corinthian—M.H., Hope St., Liverpool. *4th Thurs. Feb., April, Oct. (I.)* — Mar. 18, 1946

ROLL OF LODGES—continued

K J		1053	St. Peter-in-Thanet—M.T., Broadstairs, Kent. 2nd Tues. Feb., May, Oct., Dec. (I.)	May 18, 1946
K		1054	Cranford Park—The Gun Public House, 54 Brushfield Street, London. 2nd Tues. July; Mon. following 2nd Wed. Dec. (I.)	Apr. 24, 1946
K	*■	1055	Penshaw—M.H., New Building, Shiney Row, Philadelphia, Co. Durham. 2nd Thurs. Jan., March, May, June, Sept., Nov. (I.)	Apr. 26, 1946
K J*		1056	Pymmes Park—M.H., Maldon Road, Witham, Essex CM8 1HN. 3rd Wed. Oct., April (I.); 2nd Wed. June.	
J	*	1057	Principality—M.T., Guildford St., Cardiff. 3rd Wed. Feb., March, Sept. Oct. (I.)	May 30, 1946
K	*	1058	Bexhill—M.T., Wilton Rd., Bexhill. 4th Thurs. Feb., April, Oct., (I.), Nov.	June 5, 1946
2K	*	1059	Manchester Engineers—F.M.H., Bridge St., Manchester. 3rd Thurs. Feb. (I.), April, Oct., Dec.	June 11, 1946
5K J		1060	Brunswick—F.M.H., Park St., Bristol, BS1 5NH. 2nd Tues. Dec.; 4th Tues. Feb., May; 2nd Mon. Nov. (I.)	June 24, 1946
K J		1061	St. George's—M.H., Franklin Rd., Gillingham. 3rd Mon. March, June, Sept., Nov. (I.)	July 31, 1946
K J		1062	The University of Liverpool—Liverpool Medical Institution, 114 Mount Pleasant, Liverpool. 3rd Mon. Feb. (I.), Sept.; 4th Mon. April	Aug. 7, 1946
K J	*	1063	Middlesex St. David's—Harrow Dist.Mas.Centre, Northwick Circle, Kenton, Middx. 3rd Wed. Feb.; 2nd Wed. June; 4th Wed. Sept. (I.)	Aug. 19, 1946
J	*	1064	Sir Donald McLean—M.H., Domett St., Waitara, N.Z. 3rd Thurs. March, May, July, Sept. (I.)	Sept. 12, 1946
2K J		1065	Adoniram—M.H., Accrington. 4th Tues. Jan., March, May, Sept., Nov. (I.)	Sept. 12, 1946
4K		1066	Lodge of Peace and Unity—M.T., Clarendon Rd., Edgbaston, Birmingham. 3rd Fri. Jan. (I.), March, May, Nov.	Sept. 23, 1946
4K J	■	1067	White Rose—M.H., Hoyle Court, Otley Rd., Baildon. 2nd Mon. Jan., Feb., March, April, Nov., Dec. (I.)	Oct. 24, 1946
K J	*	1068	Wiclif—F.M.H., Lutterworth, Leics. 4th Wed. Jan., March (I.), Sept.	Nov. 12, 1946
		1069	Gordinia changed name to Ben Simon 2/11/1972—Upington, South Africa. Warrant surrendered 1988	Nov. 6, 1946
	*	1070	Joseph Van Praagh—M.T., Vryburg, Cape Province, S.A. In abeyance May 2010	Nov. 6, 1946
2K J		1071	Polytechnic—Mark Masons' Hall. 3rd Tues. April, June (I.); 1st Wed. Oct.	Nov. 29, 1946
2K	*	1072	Birkenhead—Wallasey Masonic Hall. 2nd Tues. Jan., Sept. (I.); 1st Tues. April	Dec. 4, 1946
J	*	1073	Margate—M.T., New Cross St., Margate. 2nd Thurs. Jan., March (I.), Oct., Nov.	Jan. 24, 1947
K J	*	1074	Thea Sinensis—Mark Masons' Hall. 3rd Thurs. April (I.); 4th Thurs. Oct.; 1st Wed. Feb.	Jan. 27, 1947
3K J		1075	Exon—F.M.H., Gandy St., Exeter. 4th Wed. Jan., March, May (I.), Nov.; 3rd Wed. Sept.	Feb. 4, 1947
2K	*	1076	Manadon—M.H., Crownhill, Plymouth. 2nd Mon. Jan., March, May, July, Sept. (I.), Nov.	Mar. 3, 1947
K J		1077	The George Borrow—M.H., East Dereham, Norfolk. 2nd Wed. Feb., April (I.), Oct., Dec.	Ma. 6, 1947
K J		1078	St. Peter's—M.H., King's Rd., Market Harborough. 1st Wed. Feb., April, Oct. (I.)	Apr. 2, 1947
5K J	■	1079	St. Hiev—M.H., Charles St., Bingley. 2nd Mon. Jan., Feb., March, Oct. (I.), Nov., Dec.	Apr. 9, 1947

ROLL OF LODGES—continued

K		1080	**White Stone**—F.M.H., Bridge St., Manchester 3. *3rd Fri. Jan., Sept. (I.)*	June 1, 1947
K		1081	**St. Hilary**—M.T., Clifton Rd., Birkenhead. *2nd Sat. Feb; 3rd Sat. Sept. (I.)*	June 2, 1947
2K J	*	1082	**West Croydon**—Croydon & District M.H., 73 Oakfield Road, Croydon. Warrant surrendered 2006 (Warrant of Confirmation Oct. 8, 1992)	June 10, 1947
K J	*	1083	**Orpington**—M.H., Bromley, Kent. *1st Wed. Feb., May, July, Nov. (I.)*	June 16, 1947
K	*	1084	**Welchpool**—M.T., Berriew St., Welshpool, Mont. *1st Thurs. Feb., March, Oct. (I.), Nov.*	June 26, 1947
K J	*	1085	**Hantune**—The Red House, High Street, Albrighton. *3rd Mon. Jan., April, Sept. (I.), Nov.*	July 8, 1947
K	*	1086	**Abbey**—M.H., 3 North Trade Rd., Battle. *4th Mon. Jan. (I.); 1st Fri. June; 1st Mon. July; 1st Fri. Oct.*	July 14, 1947
2K J	*■	1087	**Misbourne**—M.H., Beaconsfield. *3rd Wed. Feb., June, Oct. (I.)*	July 15, 1947
K J	*	1088	**Afan**—M.T., Forge Rd., Port Talbot. *3rd Mon. Feb., March, Nov. (I.), Dec.*	July 21, 1947
2K J	*	1089	**St. Michael's**—M.H., Albany Rd., Sittingbourne. *3rd Thurs. Jan. (I.); 4th Thurs. March, May, Oct.*	Aug. 6, 1949
K	*	1090	**Ashlar**—F.M.H., Plough Lane, Christleton, Chester. *2nd Tues. Jan., March, Nov. (I.)*	Oct. 2, 1947
K J	■	1091	**Commemoration**—Corvinos Restaurant (Café Naz), 7 Middlesex Street, London E1 7AA. *2nd Fri. Feb. (I.); 4th Wed. May, Oct.*	Oct. 3, 1947
3K J	*	1092	**Tudor**—M.H., Deyncourt Gardens, Upminster, Essex RM14 1DF. *1st Tues. March, May; 2nd Tues. Oct. (I.)*	Nov. 6, 1947
K	■	1093	**St. Lawrence**—Hedworth M.T., South Shields. *2nd Mon. Jan. (I.), May, Sept.*	Nov. 11, 1947
2K J		1094	**Pangbourne**—M.H., Pangbourne. *2nd Fri. March (I.), May, July, Sept.*	Dec. 3, 1947
K	*	1095	**St. Edward the Martyr**—M.H., Shaftesbury. *3rd Fri. Jan., March (I.), May, Sept., Nov.*	Jan. 2, 1948
K J		1096	**Wayfarers**—St. Giles M.C., 5 St. John's Green, Colchester CO2 7EZ. *1st Thurs. Feb.; 2nd Thurs. April (I.); 1st Thurs. Oct., Dec.*	Jan. 6, 1948
K	*	1097	**East Croydon**—Croydon and District M.H., Oakfield Rd., Croydon. *3rd Wed. Jan., April (I.), Sept.*	Jan. 12, 1948
4K		1098	**Carew**—M.H., Torpoint, Cornwall. *2nd Thurs. Jan., March, May, Sept. (I.), Nov.*	Jan. 21, 1948
K		1099	**Tuscan**—M.H. Hope Street, Liverpool. *3rd Mon. March, Oct., Dec. (I.)*	Jan. 26, 1948
3K	*	1100	**Plympton Erle**—F.M.H., Ridgeway, Plympton, Devon. *3rd Wed. Feb., May (I.), Sept., Nov.*	Feb. 10, 1948
J	*	1101	**Aorangi**—M.H., Philip Street, Johnsonville, Wellington, N.Z. *1st Tues. April, June, Aug., Oct. (I.)*	Mar. 3, 1948
J		1102	**Penfro**—M.T., Bush St., Pembroke Dock. *2nd Fri. Feb., April (I.), Oct., Dec.*	Mar. 8, 1948
4K		1103	**Scorton**—M.H., Garstang, Lancs. *2nd Tues. Feb. (I.), March, Oct., Nov.*	Mar. 12, 1948
K		1104	**Fortis Green**—Southgate M.C., 88 High St, London N14 6EB. *1st Thurs. May (I.); 2nd Wed. July; 1st Thurs. Sept.*	Apr. 1, 1948
K J	*■	1105	**Mapesbury**—Imperial Hotel, Russell Square, London WC1H 0DG. *2nd Wed. May (I.); 3rd Thurs. July; 1st Thurs. Sept.*	Apr. 1. 1948

ROLL OF LODGES—continued

2K	■ 1106	**Walton**—M.H., Church St., Crook, Co. Durham.		
		1st Mon. Feb., March, May, July, Oct., Dec. (I.)		Apr. 12, 1948
4K	1107	**Dukinfield**—M.H., Dukinfield.		
		2nd Wed. Jan., April, Oct. (I.)		Apr. 12, 1948
K J	1108	**St. Albans**—Ashwell House, St. Albans.		
		1st Wed. Feb.; Last Mon. April (I.); 2nd Wed. Sept.		May 6, 1948
K *	1109	**King Harold**—Halsey M.H., Cheshunt.		
		4th Sat. March (I.); 3rd Sat. Dec.		June 2, 1948
K *	1110	**Warminster**—M.H., Warminster, Wilts BA12 9AW.		
		2nd Tues. March, May, Oct. (I.), Dec.		June, 10, 1948
K *	1111	**Woodgrange**—Croydon & District M.H., 73 Oakfield Rd., Croydon.		
		2nd Mon. Feb.; 4th Mon. June, 1st Thurs. Oct. (I.)		June 10, 1948
3K	* ■ 1112	**Elevation**—M.H., Front Street, Burnopfield, Co. Durham.		
		2nd Thurs. Feb., April, Oct. (I.), Dec.		June 29, 1949
3K	1113	**Fermor**—M.H., Duke St., Southport.		
		1st Tues. Feb., April, Oct. (I.), Dec.		July 1, 1948
K *	1114	**Sprig of Acacia**—M.H., Radlett, Herts.		
		4th Sat. Feb., June; 2nd Sat. Nov. (I.)		July 14, 1948
	1115	*Coquetdale—M.H., Alnwick, Northumberland.*		
		Amalgamated with Hotspur Lodge No. 135 on 4/10/07.		*July 16, 1948*
3K J	1116	**Lodge of St. Simon**—The St. Aubyn M.H., 33 Devonport Rd., Stoke, Plymouth, Devon.		
		3rd Mon. March (I.), May, June, Sept., Nov.		July 19, 1948
K	1117	**Hampton Parva**—M.H., Church St., Littlehampton.		
		1st Thurs. Feb., April, Oct. (I.), Dec.		July 27, 1948
2K *	1118	**Halcyon**—Mark Masons' Hall.		
		3rd Thurs. Jan.; 1st Thurs. June; 3rd Thurs. Nov. (I.)		Aug. 10, 1948
	1119	*The White Stone Unity—M.T. Durban, Natal.*		
		Warrant surrendered Feb. 26, 2002		*Oct. 26, 1948*
	1120	**Drakenstein**—M.T., Beck Ave., Langerug, Worcester, S.A.		
		Last Tues. Feb., May (I.), Aug., Nov.		Nov. 15, 1948
	1121	**Hertfordshire Installed Mark Masters**—Ashwell House, 167 Verulam Rd., St. Albans.		
		1st Tues. June Nov. (I.)		Dec. 7, 1948
K	1122	**St. Guthlac**—M.H., Market Deeping.		
		Last Mon. March, April, Oct. (I.), Nov.		Feb. 14, 1949
K J *	1123	**Essex Jubilee**—Saxon Hall, Aviation Way, Southend-on-Sea SS2 6UN.		
		1st Fri. Sept. (I.); 2nd Fri. Feb., May.		Mar. 8, 1949
2K J	* ■ 1124	**St. John's Wood**—M.M. Hall.		
		1st Mon. March (I.); 4th Wed. May; 1st Wed. Nov.		Apr. 5, 1949
	* 1125	**Neath**—M.T., Queen St., Neath, South Wales.		
		2nd Wed. Feb., April (I.), Oct., Dec.		Apr. 8, 1949
K J	1126	**Oakleaf**—Thurrock M.H., Lenthall Ave., Grays RM17 5AA.		
		4th Thurs. Jan.; 1st Thurs. April (I.); 3rd Thurs. Nov.		May 2, 1949
K J *	1127	**Beaudesart**—Rugeley & District Masonic Centre, Chase Golf Club, Penkridge.		
		2nd Tues. Feb., April (I.), Oct.		June 1. 1949
2K J	1128	**St. Christopher's**—M.H., Mill Street, Sutton Coldfield B72 1TH.		
		4th Mon. Jan., March, Sept. (I.), Nov.		June 7, 1949
K J *	1129	**Wrekin**—M.H., Constitution Hill, Wellington, Telford, Shrops.		
		2nd Thurs. Feb., April, Oct. (I.), Dec.		June 14, 1949
	1130	**The Lodge of St. Andrew**—M.H., 69 Beverley Rd., Kingston upon Hull.		
		4th Wed. Feb., April, Sept., Nov. (I.); 3rd Fri. Dec.		June 22, 1949
J *	1131	**Camberley**—M.H., Agincourt Hall, London Road, Camberley, Surrey GU15 3JA.		
		4th Mon. Feb. (I.), April, Sept.		June 22, 1949

ROLL OF LODGES—*continued*

2K		* 1132	F. W. Broadbent—F.M.H., Institute St., Bolton. *3rd Wed. Feb. (I.), April, Nov.*	June 28, 1949
3K	J	1133	St. George's—F.M.H., London Rd., Leicester. *1st Wed. Jan., March, Nov. (I.)*	June 30, 1949
2K		1134	The Foster—Masonic Hall, Venns Acre, Wotton-under-Edge, Glos. *4th Mon. Jan., March, Sept. (I.), Nov.*	July 11, 1949
		1135	St. Egwin—M.H., Swan Lane, Evesham. *1st Mon. Feb., April, June (I.), Oct.*	July 28, 1949
K		1136	Mosaic—M.H., Wellington Rd., Dudley, West Midlands. *1st Fri. March, May, Last Fri. Oct. (I.)*	Aug. 18, 1949
		* 1137	Wanderers—Masonic Temple, Rua da Constituição 293, Santos. *3rd Thurs. Feb. (I.), April, July, Oct.*	Sept. 27, 1949
	J *	1138	Exedra—M.M.M. *2nd Mon., Jan. (I.); 1st Tues. May; 1st Mon. Oct.*	Dec. 2, 1949
4K	■	1139	Escafeld—Tapton Hall, Sheffield. *3rd Wed. Feb., April (I.), June, Oct.*	Feb. 20, 1950
K		1140	Waveney Valley—Mas. Rms., Harleston, Norfolk. *1st Mon. Feb., April (I.), Nov., Dec.*	Mar. 21, 1950
		* 1141	Newgate—F.M.H., 1 Headlam St., Newcastle upon Tyne 6. *1st Mon. Feb., April (I.), Oct., Dec.*	May 18, 1950
2K	J *	1142	Tuscan Pillar—M.H., Deyncourt Gardens, Upminster RM14 1DF. *3rd Fri. Jan. (I.), March, Oct.*	June 1, 1950
2K	J	■ 1143	Border—M.H., Ludgershall, Wilts. SP11 9LX. *1st Wed. Feb., April, Sept. (I.), Nov.*	June 13, 1950
3K		1144	Woodthorpe—M.H., High St., Chilwell, Nottingham. *3rd Wed. Feb., April, Oct. (I.)*	Aug. 9, 1950
K		■ 1145	St. Aidan—F.M.H., Blackhill, Co. Durham. *2nd Mon. March (I.), May, Oct., Dec.*	Sept. 15, 1950
3K	*	1146	Ashfield—M.H., Mansfield. *2nd Mon. March (I.), May, Nov.*	Nov. 9, 1950
7K		1147	Grainger—M.H., Hugh Street, Wallsend, Newcastle upon Tyne 4. *4th Fri. Jan., Feb., March, April, Sept. (I.)*	Nov. 30, 1950
		1148	Good Fellowship—M.H., Craister St., Umtata, Eastern Cape. *4th Sat. March (I.); 4th Thurs. June, Sept. Nov.*	Dec. 5, 1950
K		1149	Wyggeston—F.M.H., London Rd., Leicester. *2nd Tues. April (I.), Oct.; 3rd Tues. Feb., Dec.*	Feb. 15, 1951
K	*	1150	South Shropshire—M.H., Brand Lane, Ludlow, Shrops. *2nd Wed. Nov., Feb., April; 1st Wed. June (I.)*	Apr. 10, 1951
K		■ 1151	Cestria—M.H., Station Rd., Chester-le-Street, Co. Durham. *1st Tues. Feb., March, April, Oct. (I.), Nov., Dec.*	Apr. 18, 1951
K		1152	Minchenden Oak—Southgate Mas. Centre, High St., Southgate, N.14. *2nd Wed. March; 3rd Wed. June; 1st Wed. Sept. (I.)*	Apr. 20, 1951
2K		1153	Travellers—Masonic Centre Kensington Hall, Roberts Ave, Kensington, Johannesburg. *2nd Thurs. March, July, Oct., Jan. (I.)*	May 1, 1951
K		*1154*	*Holmroyd—Holmroyd, Burnley Rd., Bacup.* *Warrant surrendered May 2006*	*May 10, 1951*
		1155	Nepos—M.H., Headlam St., Newcastle upon Tyne 6. *3rd Tues. March (I.), May, Sept., Nov.*	May 22, 1951
K	*	1156	Guanabara—M.T., Rua da Matriz, 76, Rio de Janeiro, R.J. Brazil. *2nd Thur. April (I.), June, Aug., Oct.*	June 18, 1951
2K	*	1157	Crane—M.H., Hartley, Cranbrook. *2nd Tues. Feb., April (I.), Oct., Dec.*	Aug. 29, 1951
		1158	Sussex Installed Mark Masters—Sussex M.C. Queen's Road, Brighton. *Last Sat. June (I.); Last Wed. Oct.*	Nov. 5, 1951

ROLL OF LODGES—continued

3K	*	1159 **True Love and Unity**—M.H., Brixham. 4th Thurs. April, June, Oct. (I.); 3rd Thurs. Dec.	Dec. 27, 1951
2K	* ■	1160 **Pro Minimis**—Mark Masons' Hall. 1st Thurs. March (I.), June, Dec.	Jan. 18, 1952
	*	1161 **Hexham**—M.H., Westfield Terr., Hexham. 2nd Wed. Feb., April, June (I.), Oct., Dec.	Feb. 13, 1952
3K J	*	1162 **Wallingford**—M.H., Wallingford. Last Wed. June (I.); 2nd Wed. April, Sept., Dec.	Mar. 28, 1952
2K		1163 **Kinson**—M.H., Ferncroft Rd., Kinson, Bournemouth. 4th Mon. Jan., March, June, Oct. (I.)	Apr. 18, 1952
		1164 Caterham Valley—Croydon M.H., 73 Oakfield Road, Croydon. *Warrant surrendered 2008.*	*July 2, 1952*
K		1165 **Quatuor Legati**—F.M.H., Institute St., Bolton. 2nd Tues. Feb. (I.), May., Oct.	Nov. 4, 1952
K		1166 **Ernest Hines**—M.R., Wroxham. Last Tues. April (I.); 2nd Mon. June; 4th Mon. Sept.	Nov. 14, 1952
K	* ■	1167 **Manor of Bensham**—Croydon and District M.H., Oakfield Rd., Croydon. 3rd Fri. March; 2nd Fri. Oct., Dec. (I.)	Nov. 26, 1952
K	■	1168 **Cantwara-byrig**—M.T., Canterbury. 3rd Thurs. March (I.), Sept., Nov.	Dec. 24, 1952
K		1169 **Colwyn**—M.H., Bay View Rd., Colwyn Bay. 1st Thurs. Jan., March (I.), May, Nov.	Dec. 29, 1952
K		1170 **Brough**—Brough M.H., College St., Sutton, Hull. 2nd Tues. Feb., April (I.), Oct., Dec.	Jan. 2, 1953
		1171 Lutece—65 Boulevard, Oineau, Paris, France. *Transferred to the G.L.M.M.M. of France 1997*	*Feb. 20,1953*
K J	*	1172 **Berkhampstead**—Ashwell House, St. Albans. 3rd Thus. Feb.; 4th Wed. May, Nov. (I.)	Apr. 28, 1953
2K	*	1173 **Flixton Shepherd Eastwood**—Urmston M.H., Westbourne Rd., Urmston, Manchester. 4th Mon. Feb., Oct. (I.); 2nd Fri. May	June 16, 1953
5K		1174 **Elizabethan**—M.T., Bradshaw St., Nelson. 2nd Tues. Feb., April (I.), Oct., Dec.	June 30, 1953
		1175 Rhodes Centenary (changed name to Gatooma Sept. 1980)—Gatooma, South Rhodesia. *Warrant surrendered 1982*	*July 6,1953*
2K		1176 **Cleveleys**—M.H., West Drive, Cleveleys, Lancashire. 2nd Tues. Jan., March (I.); 3rd Wed. Sept., Nov.	July 7, 1953
K	■	1177 **Peveril of the Peak**—M.H., New Mills, Derbyshire. 1st Wed. Feb., April, Oct. (I.), Dec.	Aug. 10, 1953
K		1178 **Warrington**—M.H., Winmarleigh St., Warrington. 2nd Wed. Jan.; 1st Wed. March, Sept., Nov. (I.)	Jan. 11. 1954
		1179 Jabulani—M.T. Eshowe, Natal. *Warrant surrendered*	*Jan. 11, 1954*
2K		1180 **Lodge of the West Gate**—M.H., 4 Trafalgar Lawn, Barnstaple. 1st Thurs. April, June (I.), Aug., Dec.	Feb. 18, 1954
		1181 Pirkka—Hameenpuisto 22, Tampere, Finland. *Transferred to the G.L.M.M.M. of Finland 1971*	*Mar. 3, 1954*
K		1182 **St. Edward's**—M.H., King St., Leek. 3rd Thurs. Feb., April (I.), Oct., Dec.	Apr. 15, 1954
2K	*	1183 **Thames**—M.H., Henley-on-Thames. Last Fri. Jan., April (I.), Sept., Nov.	June 14, 1954
		1184 Vale of Darenth—Westwood M.C., Bellegrove Rd., Welling. *Warrant surrendered August 2010*	*June 15, 1954*
		1185 Penmon—M.H. Beaumaris, Anglesey, North Wales. *Warrant surrendered 1967*	*July 5, 1954*

ROLL OF LODGES—continued

2K	*	1186	**Transvaal Keystone**—M.T., Glensands Ave., Rewlatch, Johannesburg. 1st Tues. March, June, Sept. (I.), Dec.	Aug. 24, 1954
2K	*	1187	**St. Winnold**—M.H., Downham Market. 4th Thurs. Feb. (I.), April, Oct.	Sept. 28, 1954
8K	*	1188	**St. Nicholas**—M.H., Bodmin. 3rd Thurs. Feb., April (I.), June, Aug., Oct.	Dec. 1, 1954
K	*	1189	**Backworth**—M.H., Shiremoor, Northumberland. 2nd Tues. March, April, Sept., Oct., Nov. (I.)	Feb. 1, 1955
	*	1190	**North Wold**—Harrow District M.C., Northwick Circle, Kenton, Middx. 3rd Fri. Feb.; 4th Thurs. May (I.), Oct.	Feb. 21, 1955
2K	■	1191	**Vulcan**—Tapton Hall, Shore Lane, Fulwood, Sheffield. 4th Mon. Feb., April (I.), Oct., Nov.	Feb. 25, 1955
		1192	*Paris—65 Boulevard, Oineau, Paris, France.* *Transferred to the G.L.M.M.M. of France 1997*	*May 2, 1955*
		1193	**Walter Weeden**—M.T., Royal St., Hermanus, C.P., S.A. 3rd Fri. Jan., April, July; 2nd Sat. Oct. (I.)	May 16, 1955
		1194	*Lahti—Konserttitalo, Lahti, Finland.* *Transferred to the G.L.M.M.M. of Finland 1971*	*June 3, 1955*
K	*	1195	**Upminster**—M.H., Deyncourt Gardens, Upminster RM14 1DF. 3rd Mon. April, Nov. (I.); 1st Mon. Sept.	June 20, 1955
	*	1196	**Hillingdon Heath**—New Uxbridge M.C. 3rd Wed. Jan., April; 2nd Wed. Sept. (I.)	July 11, 1955
K	*	1197	**H.A. Mann**—M.H., Sutton. 4th Fri. Feb. (I.), Oct.; 4th Thurs. April.	Jan. 18, 1956
K	*	1198	**Nandi Border**—M.T., Eldoret, Kenya, E. Africa. 2nd Fri. Feb. (I.), June, Oct.	Jan. 24, 1956
K		1199	**Spurn and Humber**—M.H., Kings Rd., Cleethorpes. 2nd Tues. Jan., March, May (I.), Nov.	Mar. 26, 1956
K		1200	**Centenary**—Imperial Hotel, Russell Square, London.. 1st Mon. April; 2nd Mon. June (I.); 3rd Mon. Oct.	Apr. 4, 1956
	*	1201	**South Wales Installed Mark Masters**—M.T., Bridgend. *31st March (I.), and at a selected town in the Province on the 4th Sat. Sept.*	Apr. 4, 1956
		1202	*Christ's Hospital—M.T. Horsham, Sussex.* *Warrant surrendered 1999*	*Aug. 20, 1956*
K		1203	**White Stone**—The County Assembly Rooms, Bailgate, Lincoln. 3rd Mon. Jan. (I.), March, Sept., Nov.	Sept. 10, 1956
		1204	*Heart of Glendale—M.H. Wooler, Northumberland.* *Warrant surrendered 1997*	*Sept. 12, 1956*
	*	1205	**Air Unity**—Cole Court, London Road, Twickenham. 2nd Mon. Feb. (I.), June; 4th Wed. Sept.	Oct. 12, 1956
K	■	1206	**The Namptwyche**—Parish Hall, Acton, Nantwich. 1st Mon. Feb., April, Oct. (I.), Dec.	Oct. 16, 1956
		1207	**Wantage**—M.C. Alfred Street, Wantage. 2nd Mon. Jan., May (I.), Sept.	Feb. 28, 1957
		1208	*Shyam and Narendra—F.M.H. Calcutta.* *Transferred to the G.L.M.M.M. of India 1965*	*Mar. 7, 1957*
		1209	*Salem—F.M.H. Suramangalm, Madras, India.* *Transferred to the G.L.M.M.M. of India 1965*	*Mar. 11, 1957*
K	*	1210	**Suthburgh**—M.H., North Street, Sudbury. 2nd Fri. Feb., April, Oct. (I.), Nov.	Mar. 25, 1957
		1211	*Stella—Itapuisto 1, Pori, Finland.* *Transferred to the G.L.M.M.M. of Finland 1971*	*May 31, 1957*
K		1212	**Kafue**—F.M.H., Kitwe, Zambia. 1st Mon. Feb., May (I.), Aug., Nov.	June 3, 1957

ROLL OF LODGES—continued

		1213	Saamwerk I.M.M. (changed name from Mimosa 1973)—M.H. Zastron, South Africa. Removed from the Roll 1991	June 17, 1957
		1214	Fennia—M.T. North Esplanade No. 35, Helsinki. Transferred to the G.L.M.M.M. of Finland 1971	July 5, 1957
		1215	Aura—Auraktu 1, Turku, Finland. Transferred to the G.L.M.M.M. of Finland 1971	July 11, 1957
		1216	Union—M.T., Unity St., Kynsna, C.P., S.A. 4th Thurs. Feb., May, Nov.; 1st Fri. Sept. (I.)	July 15, 1957
K	*	1217	Ghana—F.M.H., Adjabeng, Accra, Ghana. 2nd Fri. April June, Oct. (I.)	Aug. 1, 1957
		1218	Middlesex Installed Mark Masters— TDMC Cole Court, 150 London Road, Twickenham TW1 1HD. Last Tues. Jan. (I.); last Mon. June.	Aug. 15, 1957
	*■	1219	Surrey Installed Mark Masters—M.H., Surbiton. 3rd Wed., June; 4th Thurs. Sept. (I)	Nov. 1, 1957
K J	*	1220	Concord—F.M.H., Rotterdam, The Netherlands. 4th Sat. Jan., April (I.), Oct.	Apr. 26, 1958
		1221	No Lodge Formed— Petition not approved	
3K	*	1222	Ardwick—Stanley House, Manchester Rd., Audenshaw, Manchester. 4th Wed. Jan., March, May, Oct. (I.)	Jan. 2, 1958
K	*	1223	The Lewis—M.T., Park Rynie, Natal. 1st Tues. June (I.); 2nd Tues. Nov.	Apr. 3, 1958
		1224	Flixton—Urmston M.H., Westbourne Rd., Urmston. Warrant surrendered October 2007.	June 18, 1958
	*	1225	Kerala—F.M.H., Calicut, Kozhikode, Madras. 4th Sat. Feb., May, Aug. (I.), Nov.	July 8, 1958
		1226	Unitas—M.H., Milner St., Graaff-Reinet, Eastern Cape. Warrant surrendered Nov. 2003	July 29, 1958
		1227	London Installed Mark Masters—Mark Masons' Hall. 4th Mon. Feb.; the Mon. before 2nd Wed. Sept. (I.)	Oct. 2, 1958
K	*	1228	Drury Lane—Mark Masons' Hall. 4th Thurs. May; 3rd Thurs. Oct.; 2nd Thurs. March (I.)	Dec. 19, 1958
	*	1229	Yadavindra—F.M.H., Shimla-171001, Northern India. 1st Sat. April (I.), June, Aug., Oct.	Dec. 22, 1958
		1230	Alexandra—M.H., Long Sutton, Lincs. 4th Tues. Jan., March (I.), Sept., Nov.	Jan. 22, 1959
2K	*	1231	Sir Bevil Granville—M.H., Bude, Cornwall. 1st Fri. March, April, May (I.), Oct., Nov., Dec.	Mar. 6, 1959
	*	1232	Cornwall Keystone—M.T., Davis Ave., Red Hills, Montego Bay, Jamaica. 4th Mon. Feb., May (I.), Aug., Nov.	Mar. 9, 1959 Warrant of Confirmation June 15, 2010
2K	*	1233	Pilgrims—M.H., Wrotham, Kent. 4th Mon. Feb., April (I.), Nov.	Mar. 23, 1959
	*	1234	Hailsham—M.H., Herstmonceux, East Sussex BN27 4LJ. 1st Thurs. March, May, Nov. (I.)	Mar. 26, 1959
		1235	Cramlington—M.H., School Lane, Cramlington, Northumberland. 3rd Mon. March, April, May, Sept. (I.)	May 26, 1959
		1236	Bishop's Stortford—M.H., Hadham Rd., Bishop's Stortford. 4th Wed. April; 1st Wed. July, Sept. (I.)	July 7, 1959
2K	■	1237	Welcome—M.H., Grove Rd., Sutton. 3rd Thurs. Jan., April, Nov. (I.)	July 31, 1959
2K J	*	1238	Tewkesbury Abbey—M.H., Trinity Walk, Tewkesbury GL20 5NP. 4th Tues. Feb., April, June, Oct. (I.)	Aug. 5, 1959

ROLL OF LODGES—continued

		1239	**St. Matthew**—M.T., Brigg Rd., Barton-on-Humber. *2nd Tues. Feb., April, Oct. (I.), Dec.*	Aug. 19, 1959
	*	1240	**Mercia**—M.H., Pinchbeck Rd., Spalding. *3rd Wed. March, April, Oct., Nov. (I.)*	Aug. 27, 1959
		1241	**Earl of Courtdown**—M.H., St. James's Rd., East Grinstead, West Sussex. *1st Mon. March; 2nd Mon. May (I.), Nov.*	Oct. 26, 1959
	*	1242	**St. Mary's**—M.H., Thame. *1st Fri. March, June; 3rd Fri. Oct. (I.)*	Oct. 26, 1959
3K	*	1243	**The Graftonian**—M.H., Towcester. *2nd Thurs. March, Oct.; 4th Thurs. May (I.)*	Dec. 15, 1959
	*	1244	**Royal Oak Tree**—Chingford M.C., Station Road, London E4 7AZ. *3rd Tues. Feb. (I.); 2nd Tues. May, Oct.*	Dec. 16, 1959
K	*	1245	**Pulborough**—M.H., Station Rd., Pulborough. *4th Tues. Feb., May (I.), Sept., Nov.*	Dec. 18, 1959
K		1246	**Needles**—M.H., Solent Hill, Freshwater, I.O.W. PO40 9TG. *3rd Mon. Jan., March, Sept. (I.), Nov.*	Jan. 5, 1960
		1247	*Aurora—M.T. North Esplanade No. 35, Helsinki.* *Transferred to the G.L.M.M.M. of Finland 1971*	*Feb. 1, 1960*
		1248	*Halla—Nasilinnankatu 34, Tampers, Finland.* *Transferred to the G.L.M.M.M. of Finland 1971*	*Mar. 21, 1960*
K	*	1249	**Kirkstone**—M.H., Hope St., Liverpool. *Surrendered Warrant 2005*	*Apr. 20, 1960*
		1250	**Melville Jennings**—Victoria M.T., Colombo 03, Sri Lanka. *2nd Tues. March, June, Sept. (I.), Dec.*	June 21, 1960
	*	1251	**All Saints**—The Southgate Mas. Centre, N14. *3rd Tues. Jan., March, Oct. (I.)*	July 29, 1960
K	*	1252	**Chingford**—M.H., Station Rd., Chingford, London E4 7AZ. *3rd Fri. March (I.), June, Sept.*	Oct. 20, 1960
		1253	*David—M.T. Donkin Street, Bedford.* *Amalgamated with South Africa (Eastern Division)*	*Dec. 5, 1960*
K	*	1254	**Harpenden**—Ashwell House, Verulam Road, St. Albans. *1st Wed. March, May; 4th Mon. Oct. (I.)*	Feb. 10, 1961
3K	*	1256	**Remembrance**—Warwickshire M.T., Edgbaston, Birmingham. *2nd Tues. Feb., April (I.), Oct., Dec.*	Mar. 9, 1961
2K	■	1257	**Castle**—Castle Grove, M.H., Moor Rd., Leeds. *1st Mon. Feb., Sept., Nov.; 4th Mon. April (I.), June*	Apr. 19, 1961
K	*	1258	**Chandlers Ford**—Kings Court M.H., Chandlers Ford, Eastleigh SO53 2GG. *4th Thurs. Jan., March, Sept. (I.), Nov.*	May 9, 1961
		1259	*Star of Pakistan—Chittagong, Bengal, India.* *Warrant surrendered 1973*	*May 15, 1961*
K J		1260	**Teme Valley**—M.H., Church St., Tenbury Wells, Worc. *2nd Wed. March, Oct. (I.); 3rd Wed. May.*	July 17, 1961
J	*	1261	**United Manawatu**—Masonic Lodge Rooms, Church St., Palmerston North, New Zealand. *2nd Tues. April (I.), June, July, Sept.*	Nov. 28, 1961
		1262	*Loosi Pohja—Kokkola, Finland.* *Transferred to the G.L.M.M.M. of Finland 1971*	*Dec. 13, 1961*
		1263	*Arx Nova—Savonlinna, Finland.* *Transferred to the G.L.M.M.M. of Finland 1971*	*Mar. 14, 1962*
3K	*	1264	**Benevolence**—M.H., Bridgeland St., Bideford. *1st Thurs. March, May, July, Sept., Nov. (I.)*	May 21, 1962
	*	1265	**Woodard**—Mark Masons' Hall. *4th Tues. March; 2nd Wed. June; 3rd Wed. Oct. (I.)*	May 24, 1962
		1266	*Concoria—Vaasa, Finland.* *Transferred to the G.L.M.M.M. of Finland 1971*	*May 31, 1962*

ROLL OF LODGES—continued

		1267	**Sebakwe**—M.T., Kwe Kwe, Zimbabwe. *1st Wed. March, Sept., Dec.; 3rd Sat. May (I.)*	June 12, 1962
	*	1268	**Coulsdon**—Croydon M.H., Oakfield Road, Croydon. *2nd Thurs. March; 3rd Thurs. June; 4th Thurs. Oct. (I.)*	June 15, 1962
K	■	1269	**Ambrose Crowley**—M.H., Holmside Ave., Dunston, Co. Durham. *3rd Tues. Feb., March, April, Oct. (I.), Nov.*	June 26, 1962
		1270	**De Umfraville**—Prudhoe M.H., Mickley, Northumberland. *2nd Mon. March, May, Oct. (I.), Dec.*	Aug. 8, 1962
K	■	1271	**Shipley**—M.H., Queens Terrace, Gateshead. *4th Tues. Feb., April (I.), Oct., Nov.*	Aug. 8, 1962
K		1272	**East Lancashire Provincial Grand Stewards'**—F.M.H., Bridge St., Manchester 3. *2nd Fri. Jan.; 1st Fri. Sept. (I.)*	Oct. 5, 1962
		1273	*Durga—F.M.H. Allahabad, Bengal, India.* *Transferred to the G.L.M.M.M. of India 1965*	*Dec. 17, 1962*
K	■	1274	**Staindrop**—M.H., North Green, Staindrop, Co. Durham. *1st Mon. April, June, Sept., Nov. (I.)*	Dec. 18, 1962
K	■	1275	**Walter de Hereford**—John St. Social Club, John St., Northwich, Cheshire. *3rd Thurs. March (I.), Nov.; 3rd Wed. Oct.*	Feb. 22, 1963
2K		1276	**Imperial**—M.H., Poulton-Le-Fylde. *1st Fri. Feb., April, Oct., Dec. (I.)*	Feb. 28, 1963
	*	1277	**Devi Das**—F.M.H., Daon, Chandigarh. *3rd Sat. Jan., Feb. (I.), March, Sept.*	May 6, 1963
		1278	**Haltwhistle**—M.H., Haltwhistle, Northumberland. *3rd Thurs. March, April, May, Oct. (I.)*	May 17, 1963
K		1279	**The Norman**—Kings Court M.H., Winchester Road, Chandlers Ford, Eastleigh SO53 2GG. *1st Wed. Feb., March, Oct. (I.), Nov.*	May 28, 1963
		1280	*Jamshedpur—F.M.H. Jamshedpur, Bengal, India.* *Transferred to the G.L.M.M.M. of India 1965*	*Dec. 2, 1963*
		1281	**Stability**—Talbot Ho., Stourbridge. *2nd Tues. Feb, April (I.), Oct.*	Jan. 6, 1964
		1282	*Republic—F.M.H. Dinubhai, Bombay, India.* *Transferred to the G.L.M.M.M. of India 1965*	*Jan. 6, 1964*
K	*	1283	**Jacob van Lennep**—M.H., The Hague, Netherlands. *Last Fri. April (I.), Oct.*	Jan. 10, 1964
3K		1284	**Lewis**—M.T., St. Margaret's Rd., Torquay. *3rd Fri. March (I.), May, Dec.; 2nd Fri. Nov.*	Jan. 14, 1964
K	*	1285	**Redhill**—Croydon & District M.C., Oakfield Rd., Croydon. *2nd Wed., Jan., April, Oct. (I.)*	Feb. 7, 1964
2K		1286	**The Malaysia**—F.M.H., Coleman St., Singapore. *4th Tues. Feb., April, June, Aug., Oct. (I.)*	Feb. 24, 1964
3K		1287	**Loventium**—M.H., Aberaeron. *1st Fri. Feb., Oct.; 2nd Fri. May (I.), Dec.*	Mar. 4, 1964
		1288	*Hakkri—Rauma, Finland.* *Transferred to the G.L.M.M.M. of Finland 1971*	*Apr. 13, 1964*
		1289	*Kirkala—Lahti, Finland.* *Transferred to the G.L.M.M.M. of Finland 1971*	*Apr. 13, 1964*
K		1290	**De La Val**—M.H., Seaton Delaval, Northumberland. *2nd Thurs. Jan., March, May, Sept. (I.), Nov.*	June 4, 1964
K	*	1291	**Hemel Hempstead**—Ashwell House, Verulam Rd., St. Alban's. *2nd Thurs. April, July; 1st Thurs. Nov. (I.)*	Aug. 6, 1964
K		1292	**Paddock Wood**—M.T., Paddock Wood, Kent. *4th Wed. Feb., April (I.), Oct.*	Aug. 10, 1964
		1293	*Ravensmead—Oakley House, 358 Bromley Common, Bromley, Kent.* *Warrant surrendered 08/05/2008*	*Oct. 9, 1964*

ROLL OF LODGES—continued

		No.	Lodge	Date
		1294	**East Griqualand**—Tullibardine Farm, Kokstad, South Africa. *4th Thurs. March, June, Sept.; 4th Sat. Nov. (I.)*	Oct. 15, 1964
2K		1295	**Monument**—M.H., Wellington, Somerset. *3rd Wed. Jan., March, Sept. (I.), Nov.*	Nov. 5, 1964
K		1296	**Thomas Dunckerley**—M.H., Clarence Rd., Gosport, Hants. PO12 1BB. *3rd Wed. Feb., April (I.), June, Oct.*	Nov. 10, 1965
		1297	*United Goldfields—Mas. Centre, Odendaallsrus, O.F.S., South Africa.* *Warrant surrendered 2008*	*Dec. 16, 1964*
	*	1298	**Swaziland**—Pim Lorentz Memorial Masonic Hall, Manzini. *3rd Wed. Feb., May, Nov.; 3rd Sat. Aug. (I.)*	Apr. 13, 1965
2K		1299	**Ribblesdale**—M.H., Goldsmith St., Nottingham. *4th Mon. April, June, Sept. (I.)*	Apr. 26, 1965
8K	*	1300	**Turton**—Last Drop Village, Bromley Cross, Nr. Bolton. *3rd Tues. March (I.), Aug., Oct.*	May 13, 1965
		1301	*Kuopio—Kuopio, Finland.* *Transferred to the G.L.M.M.M. of Finland 1971*	*June 11, 1965*
	*	1302	**Austral**—M.T., 13 Tillard St., Mafikeng, South Africa. *1st Mon. Feb., Aug., Nov.; 1st Sat. May (I.)*	June 14, 1965
3K	*	1303	**Middleton**—M. Club, Manchester Old Rd., Middleton. *1st Wed. Feb., April, Oct. (I.)*	June 25, 1965
K	*	1304	**Robert Mummery**—Rugeley & District M.C., The Chase Golf Club, Pottal Pool, Penkridge. *3rd Wed. Jan., March, Sept. (I.), Nov.*	July 14, 1965
		1305	**Weyland**—Weyland Hall, Bicester, Oxon. OX26 6ND. *2nd Wed. May; 3rd Wed. Sept.; 1st Tues. Dec. (I.)*	Aug. 26, 1965
		1306	*Kyminlinna—Karhula, Finland.* *Transferred to the G.L.M.M.M. of Finland 1971*	*Aug. 26, 1965*
2K		1307	**West Bridgford**—The Freemasons Halls, West Bridgford. *4th Tues. Feb., April, Oct. (I.)*	Oct. 13, 1965
		1308	*Valli—Lauritsala, Kauppatori 7, Finland.* *Transferred to the G.L.M.M.M. of Finland 1971*	*Oct. 22, 1965*
2K	*	1309	**Lodge of Good Report**—Stanley House, Manchester Rd., Audenshaw, Manchester M34 5GB. *3rd Wed. Feb. (I.), May, Sept.*	Nov. 23, 1965
		1310	*Hiram—Pohjoinen Esplanaadikatu 35, Finland.* *Transferred to the G.L.M.M.M. of Finland 1971*	*Dec. 3, 1965*
3K		1311	**Canarvon**—M.H., Goldsmith St., Nottingham. *3rd Wed. Jan., April (I.), Sept.*	Jan. 6, 1966
4K		1312	**Aeon**—M.H., Church Rd., Leyland, Lancs. *3rd Thurs. Feb., April; 4th Thurs. Oct. (I.)*	Jan. 21, 1966
K	*■	1313	**Friendship from Service**—Mark Masons' Hall. *1st Fri. Jan.; 1st Mon. July (I.); 1st Thurs. Sept.*	Feb. 2, 1966
K	*	1314	**Weald of Surrey**—M.H., Grove Road, Sutton, Surrey. *2nd Thurs. Jan., April (I.); 4th Thurs. Oct.*	Feb. 2, 1966
K	*	1315	**Elstree and Radlett**—M.H., Rose Walk, Radlett, Herts. *2nd Fri. March, May, Oct. (I.)*	Feb. 3, 1966
K	*	1316	**The George Parker**—Uxbridge M.C., Hillingdon, Middlesex. *4th Mon. March; 4th Wed. Oct. (I.)*	Mar. 3, 1966
		1317	**Albert Edward**—M.H., Castleton, Gwent. *1st Thurs. Oct. (I.); 1st Fri. Nov., Feb., April; 2nd Fri. May.*	Mar. 4, 1966
		1318	**Rhaeadr Gwy**—Hotel Commodore, Llandrindod Wells. *2nd Sat. April, June (I.); 3rd Sat. Sept.*	Apr. 20, 1966
3K	*	1319	**Saxon Shore**—M.H., East Street, Tollesbury, Essex CM9 8QE. *1st Wed. March (I.), Oct., Dec.*	July 11, 1966

ROLL OF LODGES—continued

	*	1320	**Addiscombe**—M.H., Oakfield Rd., Croydon, Surrey. *2nd Tues. Feb.; 4th Tues. April; 3rd Tues. Oct. (I.)*	July 3, 1966
	*	1321	**Warlingham**—Nutfield M.C., Redhill. *1st Mon. March, Dec. (I.); 2nd Mon. May.*	July 3, 1966
K	*	1322	**Leigh**—M.H., 61 Ellesmere St., Leigh, Lancs. *3rd Mon. Jan. (I.), March, Sept., Nov.*	July 4, 1966
		1323	*Mikael*—M.T. Rauhankatu 15, Turku, Finland. *Transferred to the G.L.M.M.M. of Finland 1971*	Sept. 8, 1966
K	*	1324	**Zaradatha**—F.M.H., Steenschuur 6, Leiden, Netherlands. *2nd Wed. Feb. (I.), May, Nov.*	July 4, 1966
5K	*	1325	**Leverhulme**—M.T., Clifton Road, Birkenhead, *3rd Tues. Feb., April, Oct. (I.)*	Oct. 4, 1966
K	*	1326	**Hundred of Hoo**—M.H., Main Rd., Hoo, Rochester. *3rd Wed. March (I.), Nov.*	Oct. 13, 1966
2K		1327	**The Darwen**—M.H., Darwen, Lancs. *3rd Mon. Jan., March, May, Oct. (I.)*	Oct. 14, 1966
	■	1328	*Memorial*—Mark Masons' Hall. *Amalgamated with Alliance Lodge No. 652 – March 2012*	Nov. 21, 1966
		1329	*Harju*—Kauppakatu 5, Jyvaskyla, Finland. *Transferred to the G.L.M.M.M. of Finland 1971*	Dec. 7, 1966
		1330	**Berkshire and Oxfordshire Installed Mark Masters**—M.H., Wallingford. *1st Fri. May (I.); 4th Fri. Oct.*	Jan. 1, 1967
K		1331	**Queensway**—Prescott M.H., Prescott. *1st Fri. May, Sept. (I.)*	Mar. 14, 1967
K	*	1332	**Cornish Installed Mark Masters**—M.H., Truro. *3rd Fri. March, June, Oct. (I.)*	May 22, 1967
K	*	1333	**Wyven**—M.H., 26 The Avenue, Wivenhoe, Essex CO7 9AH. *4th Thurs. Feb., April, Sept. (I.), Nov.*	May 23, 1967
	*	1334	**Bromsgrove**—M.H., Churchfield, Bromsgrove, Worc. *2nd Fri. May (I.), July, Sept.*	June 20, 1967
2K	*	1335	**Orkney**—M.T., Gaborone, Republic of Botswana. *3rd Fri. Jan., April, June; 2nd Sat. Nov. (I.)*	July 6, 1967
	*	1336	**Gibraltar**—Mark Masons' Hall. *1st Sat. Feb. (I.), Nov.; 3rd Sat. June.*	Aug. 31, 1967
		1337	**Doornfontein**—F.M.H., Park Lane, Parktown, Johannesburg. *1st Thurs. March, June, Sept. (I.)*	Sept. 12, 1967
2K		1338	**Purdown**—M.H., Stapleton, Bristol. *4th Thurs. Feb., April, Sept., Nov. (I.)*	Oct. 3, 1967
K	*■	1339	**Hebburn**—M.H., Hebburn. *1st Fri. May, June, Sept., Oct., Dec. (I.)*	Feb. 5, 1968
		1340	**Belaside**—Flowerden House, Church Street, Milnthorpe, Cumbria LA7 7DX. *4th Fri. March; 3rd Fri. May; 4th Fri. Oct. (I.)*	May 9, 1968
K	*	1341	**Ferrers**—M.H., Rushden, Northants. *4th Tues. Jan. (I.), April; 3rd Tues. Sept.*	May 28, 1968
K		1342	**Hungerford**—M.H., London Road, Newbery RG14 1JN. *2nd Tues. April (I.), July, Sept.*	June 5, 1968
		1343	*Louhos*—Aleksanterinkatu 9, Oulu, Finland. *Transferred to the G.L.M.M.M. of Finland 1971*	June 11, 1968
K	*	1344	**Adon Hiram**—F.M.H., Groningen, Holland. *3rd Sat. Jan., April (I.), Sept.*	July 1, 1968
K		1345	**Tithe Barn**—M.H., 10 Portland Sq., Carlisle CA1 1PY. *1st Fri. Feb., April, June, Oct., Dec.*	July 10, 1968
2K	*	1346	**Northampton Castle**—F.M.H., St. George's Ave., Northampton. *1st Mon. March; 2nd Fri. May; 3rd Tues. Nov. (I.)*	July 22, 1968

ROLL OF LODGES—continued

2K	*	1347	**Chilwell**—M.H., High Rd., Chilwell, Notts. *3rd Mon. May (I.), Oct., Dec.*	Aug. 7, 1968
		1348	**The Caerffili**—M.T., Caerphilly, South Wales. *2nd Thurs. March, May, Sept., Nov. (I.)*	Aug. 27, 1968
K		1349	**The Kyrle**—M.T., Ross-on-Wye, Herefordshire. *2nd Mon. March, May, June, Nov. (I.)*	Sept. 16, 1968
4K		1350	**Beaudesert**—Gables Hall, Linslade, Bucks. *4th Wed. March (I.), April, Sept., Nov.*	Oct. 9, 1968
		1351	**The Malvern Priory**—M.H., Belle Vue Terr., Malvern, Worcs. *1st Wed. March; 2nd Wed. May, Sept., Nov.*	Nov. 5, 1968
K	*	1352	**Comites Sigillorum**—M.H., Oakfield Rd., Croydon. *1st Tues. Feb. (I.); 2nd Tues. May; 1st Tues. Nov.*	Dec. 30, 1968
		1353	*Sumeri—M.T. Kasarmikatu 16D, Helsinki, Finland.* *Transferred to the G.L.M.M.M. of Finland 1971*	*Dec. 30, 1968*
K	*	1354	**Westwood**—Westwood Mas. Centre, 168 Bellegrove Rd., Welling, Kent. *4th Thurs. Feb. June; 3rd Tues. Dec. (I.)*	Dec. 31, 1968
	*	1355	**Campos Salles**—Rua Lisboa No. 1120, Sao Paulo, Brazil. *1st Tues. Feb., May (I.), Aug., Nov.*	Jan. 1, 1969
K	*	1356	**The Dorking**—Croydon & District M.H., 73 Oakfield Rd., Croydon. *3rd Tues. Feb., April (I.), Oct.*	Jan. 23, 1969
		1357	*Rapola—M.T. Valkeakoski, Finland.* *Transferred to the G.L.M.M.M. of Finland 1971*	*Feb. 5, 1969*
2K		1358	**Joseph Moffett**—Radlett M.Ctr., The Rose Walk, Radlett WD7 7JS. *4th Fri. March; 3rd Fri. June, Nov. (I.)*	Feb. 5, 1969
3K		1359	**Magdala**—M.H., Goldsmith St., Nottingham. *4th Mon. Feb.; 2nd Fri. May (I.); 2nd Wed. Sept.*	Feb. 25, 1969
		1360	*Faros—M.T. Hopearanta, Finland.* *Transferred to the G.L.M.M.M. of Finland 1971*	*Mar. 4, 1969*
		1361	*Ilves—M.T. Riihimaki, Finland.* *Transferred to the G.L.M.M.M. of Finland 1971*	*Apr. 22, 1969*
		1362	*Marlborough—The Church Hall, Marlborough, Central Africa.* *Warrant surrendered*	*May 2, 1969*
K	*	1363	**Piscator**—Royal National Hotel, Bedford Way, Russell Square, London WC1H 0DG. *2nd Fri. Jan. (I.); 4th Fri. April; 4th Thurs. Oct.*	July 1, 1969
		1364	*Mtilikwe—M.H. Triangle, Rhodesia, Central Africa.* *Warrant surrendered 1981*	*July 16, 1969*
K	*	1365	**Bayons**—M.H., Jameson Bridge St., Market Rasen, Lincs. *4th Thurs. March, May, Oct. (I.)*	Sept. 23, 1969
K	*	1366	**Craftsmen of Walden**—M.H., Church St., Saffron Walden, Essex CB10 1JW. *1st Tues. May (I.); 2nd Tues. Aug.; 3rd Tues. Oct.*	Sept. 24, 1969
K		1367	**St. Piran's**—M.H., Liskey Hall, Perranporth. *3rd Tues. Feb., March, May, Nov. (I.)*	Nov. 5, 1969
K	*	1368	**Royal Victoria**—M.T., Nassau, Bahamas. *4th Wed. March (I.), May, Oct.*	Dec. 5, 1969
5K	*	1369	**Integrity**—M.H., Kershaw St., Shaw, Nr. Oldham. *2nd Tues. Feb., April, Oct., Dec.*	Feb. 27, 1970
2K		1370	**Sanctuary**—F.M.H., Buckfastleigh, Devon. *3rd Thurs. Jan., March, May, Sept. (I.), Nov.*	Apr. 22, 1970
		1371	*Lodge of Installed Mark Masters of Zimbabwe—Bulawayo, Central Africa.* *Removed from the Roll 1986*	*June 1, 1970*
		1372	*Dilmun—M.T. Manama, Bahrain.* *Warrant surrendered 1976*	*June 8, 1970*
K	*	1373	**Alexander Burnett Brown**—Harrow District M.C. *3rd Fri. Sept., Jan. (I.); 4th Fri. May.*	Jan. 5, 1971
			Warrant of Confirmation	June 17, 1995

ROLL OF LODGES—continued

2K	* 1374	**Stow-on-the-Wold**—M.H., Stow-on-the-Wold, Glos. *3rd Mon. April, May (I.); 2nd Mon. Oct.; 1st Mon. Dec.*	Jan. 11, 1971
K	1375	**Charles H. Mosse**—East Brighton M.C., Seaview Rd., Peacehaven, East Sussex. *3rd Mon. March, May, Sept. (I.)*	Jan. 21, 1971
K	* 1376	**Mosam Trajectum**—F.M.H., Kerklaan 7, Roermond, Netherlands. *Last Tues. Jan., April, Oct. (I.)*	Feb. 11, 1971
	* 1377	**Porthcawl**—M.H., New Rd., Porthcawl, Glam. *1st Tues. March; 2nd Thurs. May, Oct., Dec. (I.)*	Mar. 15, 1971
K	* 1378	**Twickenham**—M.C., Cole Court, Twickenham, Middx. *2nd Wed. Feb.; 4th Wed. April; 1st Thurs. Nov. (I.)*	Apr. 7, 1971
2K	* 1379	**The Lodge of Sympathy**—M.H., Gravesend, Kent. *2nd Wed. June, Dec., Feb.; 4th Wed. Sept.*	May 12, 1971
2K	1380	**Naze Tower**—Frinton & Walton M.H., Station Rd., Kirby Cross, Essex CO13 0LU. *4th Wed. Jan., March, May; 3rd Wed. Nov. (I.)*	May 18, 1971
2K	■ 1381	**Mossley**—M.H., Westholme, Stockport Rd., Mossley, Ashton-under-Lyne, Lancs. *2nd Mon. Jan., April, Sept., Nov.*	July 30, 1971
K	1382	**Botley**—M.H., Brook House, Botley, Hants. SO30 2ER. *2nd Thurs. Feb., April, May, Oct. (I.), Dec.*	Aug. 27, 1971
K	1383	**Thomas Sharples Barlow**—F.M.H., Bridge St., Manchester. *1st Mon. April, Nov. (I.)*	Oct. 21, 1971
	1384	**Gijsbrecht van Amstel**—F.M.H., Amsterdam, Netherlands. *3rd Fri. Jan., March, Oct. (I.)*	Nov. 22, 1971
3K	* 1385	**Clanfield**—M.H., 19a Five Heads Rd., Horndean, Hants. PO8 9NW. *2nd Thurs. Jan., March, May (I.), Sept., Nov.*	Jan. 4, 1972
	1386	**Windrush**—M.T., Church Green, Witney, Oxon. *1st Fri. April (I.); 3rd Fri. May; 2nd Fri. Nov., Dec.*	Jan. 6, 1972
K	1387	**Old Patesian**—M.H., Portland St., Cheltenham. *Sat. following 1st Wed. March, May, Nov. (I.)*	Jan. 12, 1972
	1388	*Alexandra—* Lodge never Consecrated	Feb. 1, 1972
K	■ 1389	**University of London**—Mark Masons' Hall. *2nd Thurs. Feb.; 1st Wed. May; 2nd Thurs. Dec. (I.)*	Feb. 15, 1972
	1390	**Hamerkin**—F.M.H., Rijkmansstraat 10, Deventer, Netherlands. *3rd Fri. March, May, (I.) Oct.*	Feb. 22, 1972
2K	1391	**Haste Hill**—Harrow Mas.Centre, Middx. *1st Wed. April (I.), June, Dec.*	Mar. 2, 1972
K	* 1392	**Joseph Whittall Lodge of Installed Mark Master**— (a) Rugeley & District Masonic Centre, Chase Golf Club, Penkridge, Staffs. *4th Thurs. Jan., May (I.);* (b) F.M.H., Crewe St., Shrewsbury. *1st Mon. Sept.*	Mar. 29, 1972
2K	1393	**Temple of Uxbridge**—Uxbridge M.Ctr., 4a Hercies Rd., Uxbridge, Middlesex UB10 0NA. *1st Wed. March; 3rd Fri., May (I.); 2nd Thurs. Dec.*	May 2, 1972
K	* 1394	**Holywell**—Lady Augusta M.H., Rhewl, Flintshire. *2nd Thurs. Jan., March (I.), Sept., Nov.*	May 17, 1972
K	1395	**Hector Young**—M.H., Lexby Rd., Totton, Hants. SO40 9HD. *1st Thurs. April, June, Sept. (I.), Dec.*	May 18, 1972
2K	1396	**Ampthill**—M.R., Ampthill, Beds. *Last Fri. Feb., May, Oct.*	June 1, 1972
K	1397	**Scawfell**—M.H., Seascale, Cumberland. *1st Fri. Feb., May, Sept. (I.), Nov.*	July 7, 1972
4K	* 1398	**Old Rectory**—M.H., Henley Rd., Caversham, Reading. *1st Thurs. Feb. (I.), May, Nov.*	July 21, 1972

ROLL OF LODGES—continued

K   *   **1399**   **Potters Clay**—M.H., Church Road, Potter Street, Harlow CM17 9HD.
4th Wed. Feb., April, Nov. (I.)   July 21, 1972

4K   *   **1400**   **Warwickshire Installed Mark Masters**—M.T., Stirling Rd., Edgbaston, Birmingham.
Last weekday Jan., April (I.)   Aug. 25, 1972

K   **1401**   **Noah's Ark**—Royal Oak Hotel, Dudley Port, Tipton, West Midlands.
1st Wed. March, May, Nov. (I.)   Oct. 4, 1972

    1402   **Chandos**—Sofia, Bulgaria.
    Oct. 4, 1972

K   **1403**   **Woolmer Forest**—M.H., High Sreet, Bordon, Hants. GU35 0AL.
3rd Thurs. Feb., April; 2nd Thurs. June (I.); 3rd Thurs. Oct.   Nov. 7, 1972

K   *   **1404**   **Stevenage**—The Cloisters, Barrington Rd., Letchworth.
4th Tues. Jan.; 1st Tues. May (I.); 4th Tues. Oct.   Dec. 11, 1972

5K   **1405**   **George Farnworth Nuttall**—F.M.H., Mill House, Claydon-le-Moors, Accrington.
1st Thurs. March, May, Sept. (I.), Nov.   Jan. 5, 1973

K   **1406**   **Biscot**—M.H., The Pavillion, Bowling Green Lane, Luton.
4th Mon. April; 3rd Mon. June (I.); 4th Mon. Sept.   Jan. 11, 1973

  *   **1407**   **Frederick Wheeler**—Croydon & District M.H., 73 Oakfield Rd., Croydon.
4th Thurs. April
Surbiton M.H., Glenmore House, 6 The Crescent, Surbiton.
3rd Wed. Oct. (I.)   Jan. 12, 1973

K   *1408*   *Canon Taylor—Hemsley House, 41 The Crescent, Salford, Manchester M5 4PE.*
Warrant surrendered Aug. 2009   *Mar. 30, 1973*

    1409   **Worcestershire Installed Masters**—M.H., Rainhill, Worcester.
1st Sat. March, June; 2nd Sat. Oct. (I.)   Apr. 26, 1973

    1410   **Gild of Good Fellowship**—M.R., The Crescent, Wisbech, Cambs.
2nd Mon. Jan., April, Nov. (I.)   June 14, 1973

2K   *   **1411**   **The Curfew**—M.H., Chertsey, Surrey.
4th Tues. Feb. (I.); 3rd Thurs. May; 1st Tues. Dec.   June 14, 1973

    1412   **The Leonard Anderson Lodge of Installed Mark Masters**—
M.H., Main Ridge, Boston.
3rd Thurs. June; 2nd Wed. Sept. (I.)   June 19, 1973

2K   *   **1413**   **Mark of Industry**—M.H., Deyncourt Gardens, Upminster, RM14 1DF.
2nd Sat. Feb.; 3rd Sat. June; 3rd Sat. Nov. (I.)   July 2, 1973

    1414   **Schieland**—F.M.H., Oostmaasiaan 950, Rotterdam, Netherlands.
1st Mon. Feb., June, Oct. (I.)   July 27, 1973

K   *   **1415**   **Battlesbridge**—Saxon Hall, Aviation Way, Southend-on-Sea SS2 6UN.
2nd Tues. Jan.; 3rd Mon. March (I.); 2nd Mon. Nov.   July 31, 1973

K   *   **1416**   **Wulfric Spot**—F.M.H., Ashfield House, 218 Ashby Rd., Winshill, Burton-upon-Trent.
3rd Thurs. Feb., April, Oct. (I.), Dec.   Aug. 15, 1973

2K   *   **1417**   **The Romney Marsh**—M.H., High St., Dymchurch, Kent.
2nd Fri. April, June; 4th Fri. Oct. (I.)   Oct. 24, 1973

K   **1418**   **East Anglian Installed Mark Masters**—M.T., Diss, Norfolk.
1st Sat. April (I.); 1st Mon. June; 1st Wed. Sept.   Dec. 12, 1973

2K   *   **1419**   **Lingfield**—Nutfield M.Ctr., Redhill, Surrey.
2nd Fri. Jan. (I.); 1st Fri. April; 3rd Fri. Nov.   Nov. 27, 1973
    Warrant of Confirmation Jan 9, 1996

K   **1420**   **William Bathurst**—M.H., The Avenue, Cirencester.
4th Fri. March, May, Oct. (I.)   Feb. 11, 1974

    1421   **Succoth**—F.M.H., Ripperdastraat 13, Haarlem, The Netherlands.
3rd Tues. Feb. (I.), Nov.   Mar. 21, 1974

    1422   **Llantarnam**—M.H., Pontypool.
1st Thurs. Feb.; Last Thurs. May (I.); 1st Wed. Dec.   Apr. 17, 1974

2K   **1423**   **Ernest Dunscombe**—F.M.H., Park St., Bristol.
2nd Mon. Jan., May, Oct. (I.)   Apr. 30, 1974

ROLL OF LODGES—*continued*

		1424	**Melrose Keystone**—M.T., Ward Ave., Mandeville, Jamaica. *1st Mon. March, July, Nov. (I.)*	May 5, 1974
2K	*	1425	**Malling Abbey**—M.H., West Malling, Kent. *3rd Wed. Feb.; 1st Wed. June; 4th Wed. Sept., Nov. (I.)*	May 22, 1974
K	*	1426	**St. Editha's**—M.R., 29 Lichfield St., Tamworth. *3rd Wed. May; 1st Wed. Sept. (I.), Dec.*	July 26, 1974
2K	*	1427	**Admiral Rous**—M.H., Newmarket, Suffolk. *Last Fri. Feb.; 1st Fri. May, Oct. (I.)*	July 30, 1974
		1428	**The John Ashton Wade Lodge of Installed Mark Masters**— M.H., Trinity Lane, Beverley, Yorks. *4th Mon. June (I.), July; 3rd Mon. Sept.*	Aug. 7, 1974
K	*	1429	**Installed Masters Lodge of Reflection**—M.H., Wotton-under-edge or such other M.H. within the Province as approved by the Provincial Grand Master. *2nd Fri. May; 1st Fri. Sept. (I.)*	Oct. 16, 1974
2K		1430	**Conrad Costin**—Berkshire M.C., Mole Rd., Sindlesham. *4th Tues. Feb. (I.); 3rd Thurs. May; 1st Tues. Nov.*	Nov. 7, 1974
		1431	*Damara*—F.M.H., (P.O. Box 21493), Windhoek, Namibia. *In abeyance Nov. 2008*	*Nov. 20, 1974*
K	*	1432	**Heinz Ritter Friendship**—M.R., 35a Stadtwald Str, Mönchengladbach, Rheindahlen. *4th Wed. May, Nov., March (I.); 2nd Wed. Sept.*	Nov. 21, 1974
	*	*1433*	*Arewa*—M.T., College Rd., Kaduna, Nigeria. *In abeyance*	*Jan. 16, 1975*
K	*	1434	**The Netherlands Installed Mark Masters Lodge**— F.M.H., Jan Steenlaan 27, Bilthoven, Netherlands. *5th Sat. in each month (except Jan., June, July, Aug. and Dec., the day prior to a recognised religious day, a recognised religious day and national holidays) (I.) at 1st meeting in the calendar year*	Jan. 28, 1975
		1435	*Amanzimtoti*—M.T. Amanzimtoti, Natal. *Warrant surrendered*	*Feb. 12, 1975*
5K		1436	**Portwall**—M.T., Chepstow, Gwent. *2nd Wed. Feb.; 1st Mon. April (I.); 1st Wed. Sept.; 1st Mon. Nov.*	Mar. 11, 1975
K		1437	**William James Hughan**—M.H., Church St., Falmouth, Cornwall. *1st Mon. Jan., March, Nov.; 1st Thurs. May (I.)*	Apr. 14, 1975
K		1438	**New Temple**—M.H., Cunliffe St., Chorley. *3rd Thurs. Feb., April, Oct., Dec.*	Apr. 14, 1975
K		1439	**Ridley**—M.H., Beaconsfield St., Blyth. *4th Thurs. Feb., April, Sept., Oct.*	May 6, 1975
		1440	**New Sarum**—M.T., Glenora Ave., Harare, Zimbabwe. *4th Tues. Feb., May, Aug., Nov. (I.)*	June 12, 1975
		1441	**Teifi**—M.H., Cardigan. *3rd Mon. March, May, Sept. (I.)*	June 12, 1975
		1442	**Itawa**—M.T., Ndola, Zambia. *3rd Mon. Jan., April (I.), July, Oct.*	July 11, 1975
		1443	**Wychwood**—M.H., Sheep Street, Burford, Oxon. *2nd Thurs. March; 3rd Thurs. May, June; 4th Thurs. Oct. (I.)*	July 24, 1975
K	*	1444	**Forest of Waltham**—M.H., Church Rd., Potter St., Harlow, Essex CM17 9HD. *4th Sat. Feb.; 3rd Sat. June, Nov. (I.)*	July 28, 1975
2K	* ■	1445	**Neston**—Neston M.H., Bushell Rd., Neston. *3rd Fri. Feb., April, Nov. (I.)*	Aug. 7, 1975
3K	*	1446	**Prince Setanta**—M.H., Poulton Le Fylde. *2nd Thurs. Feb. (I.), April, Oct., Dec.*	Aug. 28, 1975
	*	1447	**Monmouthshire Installed Mark Masters**—M.H., Pontypool on *4th Fri. April (I.) and at such other venue within the province as the W.M. shall direct on 2nd Fri. Oct.*	Aug. 28, 1975

ROLL OF LODGES—continued

K	*	1448 Manor of Bexley—M.H., Sidcup. *2nd Sat. March (I.), May, Dec.*	Sept. 2, 1975
K		1449 Davy—M.H., Hatters Lane, Chipping Sodbury. *1st Fri. Feb. (I.), April, Nov.; 1st Wed. Sept.*	Sept. 11, 1975
K		1450 Stretton Hills—M.H., 65 High St., Church Stretton. *3rd Fri. Jan.; 2nd Fri. May (I.), Oct.*	Sept. 29, 1975
2K	*	1451 Maen Clo—F.M.H., Llandudno. *5th Mon. when it occurs March, April, May, Sept., Oct., Nov.*	Oct. 21, 1975
		1452 Memorial Lodge of Installed Mark Masters—M.H., Malton. *4th Tues. April (I.), June, Sept.*	Dec. 5, 1975
3K	*	1453 Christchurch—M.H., Warren Ave., Mudeford, Christchurch BH23 3JY. *3rd Tues. Feb., April; 3rd Fri. Sept. (I.), Nov.*	Dec. 16, 1975
2K	*	1454 Stanley—Stanley House M.H., Manchester Road, Audenshaw. *2nd Wed. Jan.; 1st Wed. May (I.), Sept.*	Dec. 17, 1975
K	*	1455 Sir Frederick Alban—M.H., St. Helen's Rd., Swansea. *1st Mon. Feb. (I.), March, Nov.*	Dec. 22, 1975
		1456 Teks—Mendel Spitz Temple, 18 Joel Road, Kinross, S.A. *1st Sat. March (I.); 1st Wed. May, Aug., Nov.*	Dec. 28, 1975
	*	1457 London West Africa—Mark Masons' Hall. *3rd Fri. March; 2nd Fri. June, Sept. (I.)*	Jan. 14, 1976
K	*	1458 Earl of Euston—Mas. RMS., The Green, Eaton Socon, St. Neots. *4th Fri. Feb., Nov.; 2nd Fri. May (I.)*	Feb. 5, 1976
2K		1459 Friendship—Middleton Mas.Club., Manchester Old Rd., Middleton. *4th Tues. Jan., March, Sept. (I.), Nov.*	Feb. 6, 1976
3K	*	1460 Wiltshire Installed Mark Masters—M.H., Emery Lane, Chippenham SN15 3PJ or such a place as the Master directs. *Last Working Day April (I.), Sept.*	Feb. 13, 1976
K	*	1461 Richard Watts—St. George Ho., New Road Ave., Chatham, Kent ME4 6BB. *5th Thurs. of each month except in Feb., June, July, Aug., Dec.;* *4th Thurs. June (I.)*	Mar. 12, 1976
K	*	1462 All Saints Kings Heath—M.H., Alcester Rd., Kings Heath, Birmingham. *2nd Thurs. May (I.); 2nd Tues. July, Sept.*	Mar. 23, 1976
K	*	1463 Thameside—M.H., Rectory Road, Orsett, Essex RM16 3EH. *1st Thurs. Oct. (I.); 2nd Thurs. Dec.; 1st Thurs. March*	Mar. 23, 1976
K	*	1464 Nottingham Excelsior—M.H., Nottingham. *4th Tues. Jan., May, Sept. (I.)*	Apr. 2, 1976
K		1465 Deben Valley—M.H., New St., Woodbridge, Suffolk. *2nd Thurs. Jan., March, May. Last working day Oct. (I.)*	May 12, 1976
K		1466 Cumbria Lodge of Installed Mark Masters—M.T., St. John St., Keswick CA12 5AP. *Last weekday (excepting Sat.) in the months of March, Sept.* *and on the Last Sat. Nov. (I.)*	May 24, 1976
		1467 Italia—Mark Masons' Hall, London. *2nd Mon. June; 3rd Mon. Oct. (I.)*	July 5, 1976
K	* ■	1468 East Cheshire—Leicester-Warren Hall, Knutsford. *2nd Fri. March, Nov. (I.)*	Aug. 25, 1976
	*	1469 Gauntlet—Harrow District M.C., Northwick Circle, Kenton, Harrow, Middx. *4th Tues. March, May, Nov. (I.)*	Sept. 16, 1976
	*	1470 Ilford St. Mary—Hutton M.H., Mount Avenue, Brentwood, Essex CM13 2NS. *4th Wed. Jan.; 3rd Thurs. May; 1st Wed. Nov. (I.)*	Sept. 17, 1976
	*	1471 Britannia—Lessinghaus, Lessingstr 3, 33604 Bielefeld, Germany. *1st Sat. March (I.); 4th Sat. May; 2nd Sat. Nov.*	Sept. 24, 1976
2K	■	1472 Chesterfield—M.H., Chesterfield. *3rd Thurs. Jan., March, May, Sept. (I.)*	Sept. 27, 1976
K	* ■	1473 Semper Fidelis—Mark Masons' Hall. *1st Thurs. April (I.); 4th Wed. June; 3rd Wed. Dec.*	Oct. 14, 1976

ROLL OF LODGES—continued

		1474 **Beaufort**—M.H., Ebbw Vale, Blaenau Gwent NP23 6ET.	
		4th Mon. Jan., April (I.), Sept., Nov.	Oct. 19, 1976
2K		1475 **Cloister**—Heaton Moor Mas. Club, 35 Heaton Moor Road, Stockport SK4 4PB.	
		2nd Tues. Jan., March (I.), Sept., Nov.	Nov. 10, 1976
	*	1476 **Donyo Sabuk**—F.M.H., Ruiru, Kenya.	
		3rd Fri. Feb. (I.), June, Sept.	Nov. 18, 1976
2K	*	1477 **Branksome**—Branksome M.H., Poole.	
		1st Mon. Feb. (I.), June, Sept., Nov.	Dec. 9, 1976
		1478 **St. Margaret's**—M.H., Blackwood, Gwent.	
		1st Wed. Jan., March, May (I.), Sept., Nov.	Jan. 5, 1977
		1479 Prieska—Prieska, Cape Province, South Africa.	
		Warrant surrendered 1996	*Feb. 9, 1977*
3K	*	1480 **Mark of True Friendship**—	
		Southend M.C., Saxon Hall, Aviation Way, Southend-on-Sea SS2 6UN	
		2nd Wed. March (I.); 4th Wed. May; 1st Wed. Sept.	Feb. 28, 1977
2K	*	1481 **Duddon**—M.H., Cambridge St., Millom, Cumbria LA18 5BD.	
		1st Mon. Feb., April, June (I.), Oct., Dec.	Feb. 28, 1977
K		1482 **Fidelis**—M.H., Nottingham.	
		1st Tues. May (I.); 1st Fri. Oct.; 1st Mon. Dec.	Mar. 2, 1977
	*	1483 **Adoniram Lodge of Installed Masters**—M.H., Blyth.	
		2nd Fri. March, June, Nov. (I.)	Mar. 28, 1977
K		1484 **Loxley**—St. John Hall, Carter Street, Uttoxeter.	
		2nd Thurs. Jan., April, Sept. (I.), Nov.	May 27, 1977
K		1485 **The Jubilee**—M.H., Gaol Sq., Stafford.	
		3rd Thurs. Feb.; 2nd Thurs. May, Nov. (I.)	June 2, 1977
K		1486 **Beneventa**—M.H., 14 High St., Daventry.	
		3rd Wed. Nov. (I.), Jan; 4th Wed. April.	June 2, 1977
3K		1487 **Ysgolion**—M.T., Pontyclun.	
		Last Fri. Jan., March, Sept. (I.), Oct., Nov.	June 24, 1977
		1488 **Libanon**—F.M.H., Spui 23, Terneuzen, Netherlands.	
		2nd Sat. Jan., May (I.), Sept.	June 24, 1977
K	*	1489 **Halsey**—Royston M.H., Royston, Jepps Lane.	
		2nd Tues. Jan., April; 3rd Thurs. Nov. (I.)	July 4, 1977
K	*	1490 **Harold W. Richardson**—Sussex M.C., 25 Queens Rd., Brighton.	
		4th Fri. April; 4th Tues. Oct. (I.)	July 12, 1977
K		1491 **The Mark of Education**—M.H., Albert Rd., Cosham, Hants. PO6 3DD.	
		1st Fri. Dec., Feb., June, Oct. (I.)	July 14, 1977
K	■	1492 **Durham Lodge of Installed Mark Masters**—M.H., Birtley Lane, Birtley, Durham.	
		4th Mon. Feb., Oct. (I.); 3rd Mon. May.	July 22, 1977
K	*	1493 **Jubilee**—M.T., St. Helier, Jersey.	
		3rd Mon. March, May, Nov. (I.)	July 28, 1977
K	*	1494 **The Lord Harris**—M.H., Church Rd., Sidcup, Kent.	
		3rd Fri. Feb.; 2nd Fri. May (I.); 2nd Tues. Dec.	July 28, 1977
K		1495 **Spencer**—Queen Victoria M.H., 76 Victoria Rd, St Budeaux, Plymouth.	
		4th Mon. Jan., March, June (I.), Nov.	Aug. 4, 1977
		1496 Flanders—Hotel Marmin, 10 Rue Monsigny, Boulogne-Jur-Mer, France.	
		Transferred to the G.L.M.M.M. of France 1997	*Aug. 17, 1977*
K		1497 **West Cheshire**—M.T., Clifton Rd., Birkenhead.	
		2nd Mon. March (I.), Sept.	Oct. 6, 1977
K	*	1498 **Rose of Minden**—Loganhaus, Logenplatz 2-4, 32052 Herford, Germany.	
		3rd Tues. Jan.; 1st Wed. July (I.), Nov.	Oct. 17, 1977
6K		1499 **Bletchley**—Bletchley M.C.	
		2nd Thurs. Jan. (I.), March, Nov.	Oct. 18, 1977
		1500 Le Maillet Et Le Ciseau—Morges, Switzerland.	
		Transferred to the G.L.M.M.M. of Switzerland 1996	*Apr. 2, 1992*

ROLL OF LODGES—*continued*

3K	*	1501	**Signa Bene**—Town Hall, Alcester. *3rd Tues. March, June (I.); 2nd Tues. Sept., Jan.*	Oct. 25, 1977
	*	1502	**Abercrombie**—M.H., Vigie, Castries, St. Lucia, W.I. *4th Thurs. Jan. (I.), April, July, Oct.*	Nov. 15, 1977
K	*	1503	**Kidsgrove**—M.H., Kidsgrove. *4th Mon. Jan., March (I.), Oct.*	Nov. 22, 1977
K	*	1504	**Moriah**—F.M.H., Gedempte Nieuwesloot 153, Alkmaar, Netherlands. *3rd Fri. Jan. (I.); 2nd Fri. April; 1st Fri. Oct.*	Dec. 8, 1977
K	*	1505	**Chevalier**—Royal Masonic School for Girls, Rickmansworth. *1st Tues. Feb.; Last Wed. June (I.); 1st Wed. Dec.*	Jan. 16, 1978
K		1506	**Nottingham Jubilee**—M.H., Goldsmith St., Nottingham. *2nd Wed. Feb., April, Nov.*	Jan. 26, 1978
2K		1507	**Sir John Cotton**—St. Andrews Rooms, Biggleswade. *2nd Mon. June, Sept.; 1st Mon. Dec. (I.)*	Mar. 8, 1978
		1508	**Fratres Scriptabacorum**—Ashwell House, St. Albans. *3rd Tues. June; 4th Tues. Oct.*	Mar. 31, 1978
K		1509	**Flint**—M.H., Halkyn St., Flint. *3rd Thurs. Jan.; 1st Mon. March (I.); 2nd Mon. Sept.; 2nd Tues. Nov.*	June 29, 1978
K	*	1510	**Merlaue Weir**—Marlow Mas.Centre, Marlow, Bucks. *3rd Sat. Jan., March; 1st Sat. Oct. (I.)*	July 18, 1978
K	■	1511	**St. Thomas**—F.M.H., Wellington St., Stockton-on-Tees. *4th Tues. Jan., March, April, Oct. (I.)*	July 19, 1978
4K		1512	*Audenshaw—M.H., Stanley House, Manchester Rd., Audenshaw, Manchester.* *Warrant surrendered August 2010*	July 19, 1978
K		1513	**Saint Peter's**—M.H., Mansfield. *2nd Thurs. Jan., March (I.), May, Nov.*	Aug. 22, 1978
K		1514	**Sir Alfred Robbins**—M.H., Tavistock Rd., Launceston. *4th Tues. Jan., March (I.), Sept., Nov.*	Aug. 23, 1978
	*	1515	**Keys of Munster**—ACGL Centre, Kruppstr 134, 60388 Frankfurt am Main. *Last Sat. Feb. (I.), June, Oct.*	Sept. 8, 1978
		1516	**Het Sticht**—F.M.H., Amersfoort, Van Persijnstraat 9, Netherlands. *1st Mon. May, Nov. (I.)*	Sept. 12, 1978
			Warrant of Confirmation Jan. 17, 2003	
3K		1517	**James Herbert Cain**—F.M.H., Peel. *4th Thurs. Jan., March, Nov. (I.)*	Nov. 3, 1978
	*	1518	**West Germany Installed Mark Masters**— Park Hotel, Am Heger Holz, Edinghausen 1, Onsnabrück. *Last Sat. June, Nov. (I.)*	Nov. 7, 1978
K		1519	**Breckland**—M.H., Bridges Walk, Thetford, Norfolk IP24 3BX. *2nd Fri. Feb. (I.); 1st Fri. June; 2nd Fri. Oct.*	Nov. 8, 1978
2K	*	1520	**St. Margaret of Antioch**—Crawley M.H., Ifield, Crawley. *3rd Sat. Feb., April; 1st Sat. Oct. (I.)*	Nov. 23, 1978
K		1521	**Sub-Urban**—Cole Court, 150 London Rd., Twickenham, Middx. *1st Tues. March (I.), June, Oct.*	Dec. 5, 1978
	*	1522	**Tarporley**—Portal Premier, Forest Road, Tarporley. *2nd Tues. April, Sept. (I.), Dec.*	Dec. 5, 1978
2K	■	1523	**Beaumont**—M.H., Shelley Lane, Kirkburton. *1st Thurs. March, April (I.), Oct., Nov., Dec.*	Dec. 13, 1978
K		1524	**The Croft**—M.H., Aldridge, Staffs. *4th Wed. March (I.); 3rd Wed. May; 4th Wed. Oct.*	Jan. 10, 1979
		1525	*Khotso—M.T., 13 Prinsloo Street, Ladybrand 9745.* *Warrant surrendered 2008*	Feb. 2, 1979
K		1526	**Trent**—M.H., The Avenue, Newark-on-Trent. *1st Fri. March; 4th Thurs. May (I.), Sept., Dec.*	Mar. 16, 1979

ROLL OF LODGES—continued

K		1527 **The George Stephenson**—M.H., Wylam. *1st Thurs. March, May (I.), Sept., Nov.*	Mar. 19, 1979
K	*	1528 **Cambrensis**—M.T., Guildford St., Cardiff. *3rd Thurs. Jan.; 1st Thurs. April (I.); 4th Tues. Sept.*	May 9, 1979
K		1529 **Ayot**—Ashwell House, Verulam Rd., St. Albans. *2nd Mon. March, July (I.), Nov.*	May 22, 1979
K		1530 **Heffle**—M.H., Stonegate Road., Burwash Common. *4th Wed. Jan., April, June; 3rd Wed. Oct. (I.)*	Sept. 18, 1979
K		1531 **St. Aldhelm**—M.H., Silver St., Malmesbury SN16 9BU. *1st Tues. Mar., June, Sept., Nov. (I.)*	Oct. 2, 1979
		1532 **Saltburn**—M.H., Marine Pde., Saltburn-by-Sea. *1st Mon. March, Sept., Nov. (I.); 3rd Mon. June.*	Nov. 22, 1979
	*	1533 **Twente**—F.H., Enschede, Netherlands. *1st Mon. Feb., April (I.), Oct.*	Jan. 7, 1980
		1534 **Orchestral**—Mark Masons' Hall. *2nd Mon. June, Sept. (I.); 1st Mon. July.*	Jan. 10, 1980
		1535 **Dyfed Lodge of Installed Mark Masters**—M.T., Llanelli, Carmarthenshire. *3rd Mon. June(I.), 2nd Mon. Dec.*	Mar. 7, 1980
		1536 **Mayflower**—Simpson's Rest., Wickford, Essex. *1st Thurs. Feb., May (I.); 3rd Wed. Nov.*	Apr. 10, 1980
		1537 Karibu—Port Natal M.T., 381 Berea Rd., Durban, Natal. *In abeyance March 7, 2011*	*Apr. 10, 1980*
K	*	1538 **Chiltern**—Dunstable Mas. Centre, Cemetery Lane, Dunstable, Beds. *1st Tues. April, July (I.), Nov.*	Apr. 10, 1980
K	*	1539 **Ridgmont**—M.H., Ridgmont House, Horwich, *3rd Fri. Jan., May (I.), Sept.*	Apr. 10, 1980
		1540 **Farne**—M.H., Prudhoe Street, Alnwick. *4th Fri. April, June (I.), Oct.*	Apr. 14, 1980
K	■	1541 **Derbyshire Lodge of Provincial Grand Stewards**—M.H., Belper, Derbyshire. *3rd Mon. March; 2nd Thurs. May; Last Tues. Oct. (I.)*	Apr. 24 1980
	*	1542 **Doric**—Lortzinghaus, An der Katherinenkirche 3, 49088, Osnabrück, Germany. *4th Wed. Jan., April, Oct.; 1st Wed. June (I.)*	May 1, 1980
K	■	1543 **Haven**—Altrincham M.H., Clay Lane, Timperley, Altrincham, Cheshire. *3rd Thurs. Feb., May (I.), Oct.*	June 2, 1980
		1544 Usambara—M.H., Tanga, Tanzania. *Returned Warrant 2003.*	*June 25, 1980*
		1545 **Bryanston**—F.M.H. 8 Park Road, Parktown, Johannesburg, S. Africa. *1st Tues. Feb., May, Aug., Nov. (I.)*	June 26, 1980
		1546 **Godstow**—F.H., 333 Banbury Road, Oxford. *2nd Wed. Oct. (I.); 1st Wed. March, June*	June 30, 1980
	*	1547 **Thuredrecht**—F.M.H., Muntgang 9, Dordrecht, Netherlands. *3rd Wed. Oct. (I.), Jan., March.*	July 14, 1980
	*	1548 **Nailsea**—M.H., Nailsea Park, Nailsea. *2nd Mon. Jan., March, May, Nov. (I.)*	July 30, 1980
K		1549 **Friendship**—M.H., Duke St., Southport. *2nd Mon. Feb., May (I.), Oct.*	Sept. 4, 1980
		1550 **Ponteland**—War Memorial Hall, Ponteland, Northumberland. *Last Thurs. Jan., April, Oct. (I.)*	Sept. 12, 1980
K	■	1551 **Stanhope**—M.H., Green Bank, Stanhope, Bishop Auckland. *3rd Mon. March (I.); 4th Mon., June, Sept., Nov.*	Sept. 12, 1980
	*	1552 **Lucayan**—M.T., East Sunrise Highway, Freeport, Grand Bahama Island. *3rd Wed. Feb., April (I.), Sept.*	Nov. 13, 1980
	*	1553 **Turks Island Forth**—M.T., Grand Turk, Turks Island, W.I. *3rd Thurs. March, June (I.), Sept.; 2nd Thurs. Dec.*	Nov. 13, 1980

ROLL OF LODGES—continued

K		1554 **De Lacy**—M.H., Millhouse, Clayton-le-Moors, nr. Accrington, Lancs. 2nd Thurs. Feb., April (I.), Oct., Dec.	Dec. 3, 1980
	*	1555 **Friendship and Care**—Berkshire Mas. Centre, Mole Rd., Sindlesham, nr. Workingham, Berk. 3rd Tues. Jan. (I.), March Nov.	Dec. 11, 1980
		1556 **Wellington**—The Temple, Turkeycock Lane, Rye, E. Sussex. 1st Wed. March, May, July, Sept. (I.)	Jan. 12, 1981
	*	1557 **Biggin Hill**—Sevenoaks M.H., St. Johns Hill, Sevenoaks, Kent. 3rd Mon. March (I.); 4th Mon. April; 2nd Mon. Nov.	Jan. 12, 1981
K		1558 **The Carrick**—M.H., Hope St., Castletown, I.O.M. 3rd Mon. May (I.), Nov., Feb.	Jan. 13, 1981
	*	1559 **The Friendly**—M.T., 45-47 Barbados Ave., Kingston 5, Jamaica. 4th Mon. March (I.), Aug, Nov.	Jan. 29, 1981
K	■	1560 **Ferryhill**—M.H., Ferryhill, Co. Durham. 2nd Thurs. Jan., March, May, Sept. (I.), Nov.	Mar. 30, 1981
		1561 Israel—Garston Masonic Hall, Island Road, South Liverpool. Amalgamated with Garston Lodge No. 942, May 2003	*Apr. 10, 1981*
		1562 **Marckdael**—Freemasons Hall, Ginnekenweg 141, Breda, Netherlands. 3rd Tues. Feb. (I.), May, Nov.	Apr. 10, 1981
		1563 **Goodwin**—F.M.H., Park St., Bristol BS1 5NH. 2nd Thurs. Jan.; 3rd Tues. March; 1st Mon. Oct. (I.)	May 13, 1981
	*	1564 **Viking**—Southend M.C., Saxon Hall, Aviation Way, Southend-on-Sea SS2 6UN. 3rd Tues. Sept.; 1st Tues. March; 1st Tues. June (I.)	May 29, 1981
	*	1565 **Hollandia**—F.M.H., Bilthoven, Netherlands. 3rd Fri. May, Sept. (I.)	June 6, 1981
		1566 **John Spencer**—M.R., Campbell St., Belper, Derbys. 3rd Tues. March, May, Sept. (I.), Nov.	June 4, 1981
		1567 **Monument**—M.H., Portland Place, Penrith, Cumbria CA11 7QN. 4th Tues. Jan., March, May, Oct. (I.)	June 5, 1981
	*	1568 **Linden Acre**—Wokingham M.H., Reading Rd., Wokingham. 2nd Tues. April; 2nd Tues. Oct. (I.);	June 8, 1981
	*■	1569 **Woodstock**—Surbiton M.H., 6 The Crescent, Surbiton, Surrey. 1st Tues. July; 2nd Sat. Feb. (I.); 4th Mon. May.	June 8, 1981
		1570 **The Transvaal Installed Mark Masters**—F.M.H., Parktown, Johannesburg, R.S.A. 4th Mon. Feb., May, Aug. (I.), Oct.	June 22, 1981
		1571 Demeter—M.T. 7 Vur de la Verite, 95 Montmorency, France. Transferred to the G.L.M.M.M. of France 1997	*Oct. 17, 1981*
		1572 **Dorset Installed Mark Masters**—M.H., Old Corn Market, Wimborne, Dorset. 2nd Wed. July; 1st Sat. Nov. (I.)	Aug. 27, 1981
		1573 **Cowbridge**—Town Hall, Cowbridge, South Glam. 3rd Fri. Feb. (I.), April, Oct.; 4th Fri. June.	Sept. 2, 1981
K	*	1574 **The Harry Wilson**—M.T., Nuneaton, Warwickshire. 2nd Mon. Jan. (I.), March, Nov.	Oct. 12, 1981
		1575 **Sparrenburg**—FO-Logenhaus, Murhardstr 6, 34119 Kassel. 2nd Sat. Jan, Sept. (I.); 4th Sat. May	Nov. 9, 1981
		1576 **Bond of Friendship**—M.H., Croydon. 3rd Fri. Jan.; 1st Thurs. May; 4th Fri. Nov. (I.)	Nov. 23, 1981
		1577 **Progress**—M.T., Bridge St., Manchester. 2nd Mon. Jan. (I.); The Tues. immediately before 1st Wed. Sept.	Nov. 23, 1981
		1578 **Harmony**—M.T., Bishop Street, Camperdown. 1st Mon. March (I.), June, Sept., Dec.	Dec. 1, 1981
	*	1579 **De Sluitsteen**—F.M.H., Dr. Niemeijerstraat 4, Wageningen, The Netherlands. 2nd Fri. Feb., May (I.); 1st Fri. Nov.	Jan. 1, 1982
	*	1580 **De Keursteen**—F.M.H., Leeuwarden, Netherlands. 4th Sat. Jan., April (I.), Sept.	Jan. 7, 1982

ROLL OF LODGES—continued

K	1581	**Centenary**—Grove House, 6th Form College, Grove School, Market Drayton, Shrops. *3rd Tues. Jan., Sept.; 2nd Mon. May (I.)*	Jan. 8, 1982
K	1582	**Wycoller**—M.H., Colne. *3rd Wed. Feb., April., Aug. (I.), Oct.*	Apr. 27, 1982
	1583	**The Beacon Centenary**—M.H., Pocklington, York. *3rd Tues. Feb., April (I.), Oct., Dec.*	May 27, 1982
K *	1584	**Oakley**—M.C., Oakley House, Bromley Common, Bromley. *4th Thurs. Feb.; 2nd Tues. May (I.), Sept.*	June 14, 1982
	1585	**Rosewalk**—M.H., Radlett. *3rd Fri. March; 1st Fri. June; 2nd Fri. Dec. (I.)*	July 12, 1982
	1586	**Wentloog**—M.H., Castleton, nr. Cardiff. *4th Fri. Jan., March, Sept. (I.), Nov.*	July 27, 1982
*	1587	**La Marque D'Alliance**—Rue Alexandre Colin, 24, 5020 Champion, Belgium. *2nd Sat. March, Oct., Dec. (I.)*	Jan. 20, 1982
	1588	**The Victory**—M.H., Bridge St., Pickering. *4th Wed. Feb., April, June, Aug., Oct. (I.)*	Sept. 3, 1982
	1589	*Heinz Ritter—33a Stadjwaldstrasse, Rheindahlen, Germany. Removed from the Roll*	*Jan. 28, 1983*
	1590	**Cynon-Dare**—M.H., Aberdare. *3rd Tues. Nov., Jan., April, May (I.)*	Apr. 29, 1983
K *	1591	**North Wales Lodge of Installed Mark Masters**—Fairfield Hall, Connah's Quay. *1st Sat. May (I.) Feb. and Sept. meetings at other Masonic venues within the Province*	May 26, 1983
	1592	**Llynfi Valley**—M.T., Castle St., Maesteg. *2nd Wed. Sept.; 1st Wed. Nov. (I.), March, April.*	June 10, 1983
	1593	*Justice and Liberty—M.H., Rose Walk, Radlett. Warrant surrendered May 2012*	*June 21, 1983*
K	1594	**The Red Rose**—Hindley M.H., Hindley. *4th Mon. Jan.; 2nd Mon. May; 4th Mon. Nov. (I.)*	June 27, 1983
	1595	*Mount Bardon—Rue de l'Hotel De Ville, Ballon pres La Rochelle, France. Transferred to the G.L.M.M.M. of France 1997*	*June 29, 1983*
*	1596	**Stabroek**—F.M.H., Company Path, Georgetown, Guyana. *1st Tues. Feb. (I.); 2nd Mon. June; 1st Wed. Sept.; 1st Tues. Nov.*	July 29, 1983
*	1597	**Yare Valley**—The Oaklands Hotel, 89 Yarmouth Rd., Norwich, Norfolk. *2nd Tues. Jan., March, Nov. (I.)*	July 19, 1983
	1598	*Palantinate—2 Augustastrasse, D-6750 Kaiserslautern, West Germany. Removed from the Roll*	*Sept. 14, 1983*
■	1599	**The Kennet**—M.H., Oxford St., Marlborough SN8 1AP. *1st Thurs. Feb., April, Nov. (I.)*	Sept. 14, 1983
	1600	**Saxony**—Grosse National Mutterloge "Zu Den Drei Weltkugeln"- 3WK-Logenhaus, Heerstr 28, 14052 Berlin. *3rd Sat. Feb., April; Last Sat. Oct. (I.)*	Nov. 4, 1983
*	1601	**Den Aks**—Potgieterstraat 41, Eindhoven, Netherlands. *4th Tues. Jan., April, Oct. (I.)*	Dec. 19, 1983
*	1602	**Rift Valley**—M.H., Naivasha, Kenya. *3rd Sat. Feb., June, Oct. (I.)*	Jan. 20, 1984
K	1603	**Les Disciples De Salomon**—M.H., Minckelersstraat, 115, B-3000 Leuven. *2nd Fri. Feb., May (I.), Oct.*	Jan. 25, 1984
K	1604	**London East Africa**—M.M.H., 86 St. James's St., SW1A 1PL. *4th Sat. Feb.; 3rd Sat. May (I.)*	Mar. 19, 1984
	1605	**Saint Breock**—M.H., Trevanion Rd., Wadebridge. *1st Wed. Jan., March (I.), Sept., Nov.*	May 8, 1984
*	1606	**De Cymru**—M.T., Port Talbot on *4th Wed. June (I.)* M.T., Caerphilly on *1st Wed. Dec.*	May 15, 1984

ROLL OF LODGES—continued

K		1607 Eaton—M.H., Mill St., Congleton. 3rd Fri. Feb., April, Oct. (I.), Dec.	June 8, 1984
		1608 **Somerdale**—M.H., Bath Rd., Keynsham, Avon. 3rd Fri. Jan., March (I.), Nov.; 2nd Fri. Sept.	June 25, 1984
	*	1609 **Sandbach**—M.H., Sandbach. 1st Fri. Feb., May, Oct. (I.)	June 28, 1984
		1610 *Le Luc—M.T. rue de Verdun 83340, Le Cannet de Maures.* *Transferred to the G.L.M.M.M. of France 1997*	*July 27, 1984*
		1611 *Occitania—32-34 Reu Gabriel Peri F31000, Toulouse, France.* *Transferred to the G.L.M.M.M. of France 1997*	*July 30, 1984*
	*	1612 **Tremonia**—Willy-Tager-Haus, Heiligengeiststrabe 1, 30173 Hannover, Germany. 3rd Sat. Jan., June, Nov. (I.)	Aug. 22, 1984
K	*	1613 **Robert Burns**—M.H., The Crescent, Salford. 4th Mon. Jan., March, Sept., Nov. (I.)	Aug. 30, 1984
		1614 **Guernsey**—M.C., St. Martin's, Guernsey. 3rd Thurs. Nov.; Last weekday, Sat. excepted in Jan. (I.); 3rd Thurs. March	Sept. 11, 1984
		1615 **The Langdale**—M.H., The Crescent, Taunton TA1 4EB. 4th Tues. April; 4th Mon. Sept. (I.)	Oct. 10, 1984
		1616 **Cranley**—M.H., Church Lane, Windsor. 2nd Mon. April (I.); 3rd Mon. Oct.	Jan. 7, 1985
K	*	1617 **Severn**—Comrades Club, Listley Street, Bridgnorth, Shrops. 2nd Tues. Jan., April (I.), Oct.	Feb. 26, 1985
		1618 **Cayman Keystone**—M.T., Prospect Park, Grand Cayman, B.W.I. 1st Fri. April (I.), July, Nov.	Mar. 28, 1985
		1619 *Florence—Mark Masons' Hall.* *Warrant surrendered July 31, 2005*	*Mar. 28, 1985*
		1620 **The Written Rock**—Lawson M.H., Craw Hill, Brampton CA8 1TN. 3rd Tues. Feb., June (I.), Sept., Nov.	Apr. 1, 1985
		1621 **White River**—White River M.Ctr., Cnr. Japie Theron and Rob Street, White River, Mpumalanga, South Africa. 2nd Thurs. Feb., Aug., Nov.; 3rd Sat. May (I.)	Apr. 25, 1985
		1622 **Castle**—M.H., Garden Street, Newcastle, Staffs. 2nd Thurs. March, May, Sept. (I.)	Sept. 12, 1985
		1623 **Centenary**—Moseley M.H., Alcester Road South, Kings Heath, Birmingham. 1st Fri. May, July; 3rd Fri. Sept. (I.)	Oct. 15, 1985
K		1624 **La Marque d'Union**—Masonic Hall., Fondation Isi Collin, Rue de Suède, 41/B-1060-Bruxelles. 2nd Sat. Feb.; 2nd Tues. May (I.); 4th Sat. Nov.	Dec. 3, 1985
		1625 **Icknield**—M.H., The Pavillion, Bowling Green Lane, Luton. 2nd Wed. March (I.), May; 3rd Wed. Sept.	Dec. 19, 1985
K	■	1626 **George Washington**—M.H., Concord Washington. 2nd Fri. May, (I.), Oct., Dec., Feb.	Jan. 2, 1986
		1627 **Erlegh, Berkshire**—M.C., Sindlesham. 4th Sat. March (I.); 3rd Sat. May; 2nd Sat. Sept.	Jan. 10, 1986
	*	1628 **Langdon Hills**—M.H., Rectory Road, Orsett, Thurrock RM16 3EH. 3rd Wed. April (I.), June, Sept.	Jan. 15, 1986
K		1629 **Haddenham**—M.H., Thame. 2nd Tues. Feb.; 3rd Tues. May (I.), Oct.	Jan. 23, 1986
		1630 **Round Table and Rotary**—M.H. Newport. 3rd Mon. March; 1st Tues. Sept. (I.); 4th Fri. Nov.	Apr. 21, 1986
		1631 **Caduceus**—M.H., Goldsmith's Lane, Wallingford. 1st Mon. March (I.), July, Sept.	May 12, 1986

ROLL OF LODGES—continued

	1632	The Edwin Perry Morgan—M.H., Perranporth, Cornwall. Last working day of May; 4th Fri. Sept. (I.)	May 23, 1986
	1633	Camestone-Inglefield—Bedford M.C., The Keep, Bedford Rd., Kempston. 3rd Sat. Sept., Nov.; 4th Sat. April (I.)	June 13,1986
K *	1634	Buckinghamshire Installed Mark Masters—M.H., Ripon St., Aylesbury. 1st fifth weekday Oct. (I.), March.	June 25, 1986
	1635	Durnovarian—M.H., High West St., Dorchester. 1st Tues. March, May, Oct. (I.); 4th Tues. Nov.	July 15, 1986
*	1636	Nyanza—M.T., Kisumu, Kenya. 2nd Sat. Feb. (I.), June, Sept.	July 18, 1986
*	1637	James Jack—F.H., Georgetown, Guyana. 3rd Thurs. March, June, Dec. (I.)	Sept. 5, 1986
* ■	1638	City Livery—M.M.H., St. James. 1st Mon. March, (I.); 4th Wed. June; 2nd Wed. Dec.	Feb. 2, 1987
	1639	Septimania—Enclos Ranc, rue Burnier Montpellier, France. Transferred to the G.L.M.M.M. of France 1997	Feb. 25, 1987
	1640	Abbot Hugh of Selby—M.H., Church Hill, Selby. 4th Wed. Feb., April (I.), June, Oct.	Mar. 12, 1987
	1641	The Mark Provincial Grand Secretaries—M.M. Hall, London or in a Province selected by the Master. Last Sat. May before Spring Bank Holiday; 3rd Sat. Oct. (I.)	Sept. 7, 1987
*	1642	Ludwig Zum Flammenden Stern—Bagno Restaurant, Hollich 156, 48565 Steinfurt-Burgsteinfurt. 1st Fri. March, Nov.; 1st Sat. June (I.)	May 18, 1987
K	1643	Norman Rolfe—M.H., Peterborough. 2nd Mon. Feb. (I.), April, Oct., Dec.	Sept. 14, 1987
	1644	Exile—M.T. 9 rue Keller, Paris, France. Transferred to the G.L.M.M.M. of France 1997	Oct. 14, 1987
	1645	Rockingham—M.H., Rockingham Road, Corby. 3rd Thurs. Feb., Sept. (I.); 4th Thurs. May.	Nov. 17, 1987
	1646	Philadelphia Lodge of Installed Mark Masters—M.H., Leyland. 2nd Mon. Jan. (I.), Sept.	Dec. 7, 1987
	1647	Dyffryn Clwyd—Masonic Buildings, Tower Hill, Denbigh on the 3rd Thurs. Jan., March, May, Oct. (I.)	Dec. 14, 1987
K	1648	Slough—M.C., Slough. 3rd Thurs. April, June (I.) Dec.	Jan. 11, 1988
K	1649	Arnold Moreton—F.M.H., Bridge St., Manchester. 3rd Fri. May (I.), Dec.	Feb. 3, 1988
K	1650	Leofric—Leominster M.H., Bromyard, Herefordshire. 1st Fri. April, May (I.), Oct.; 2nd Fri. Nov.	Feb. 16, 1988
	1651	Roi Arthur—3 rue de la Tour, Le Legue, Perin, France. Transferred to the G.L.M.M.M. of France 1997	Feb. 18, 1988
*	1652	Somerset Installed Mark Masters—M.H., Taunton. 4th Mon. May (I.), or 1st Wed. June (I.) (if 4th Mon. is a Bank Holiday); 1st Mon. Sept.	Feb. 23, 1988
	1653	L'Esperance—M.H., Hostellerie du Boubier, Rue de Couillet, 487/B-6200, Chatelet, Charleroi, Belgium. 3rd Thurs. Feb., Sept. (I.), Nov.	Mar. 4, 1988
	1654	Nemausus—34 rue de Beaucaire, Nimes, France. Transferred to the G.L.M.M.M. of France 1997	June 13, 1988
	1655	Bowyer—M.H., Chipping Norton. 2nd Mon. March (I.), June, Sept.	July 11, 1988
K	1656	Portcullis—St. Mary's Chapel, The Hill, Langport, Somerset. 3rd Tues. Feb., April, Sept., Nov. (I.)	July 26, 1988

ROLL OF LODGES—*continued*

1657 Charles Wilkinson—Berkshire M.C., Sindlesham.
1st Thurs. Oct. (I.); 4th Thurs. April. Sept. 19, 1988

*1658 Stella Maris—14 Bis rue Gusse, Bayonne, France.
Transferred to the G.L.M.M.M. of France 1997* Sept. 15, 1988

1659 Brackenbury—M.H., 19 Orwell Rd., Felixstowe.
4th Thurs. Feb., Sept., Nov. (I.); 1st Thurs. May. Dec. 16, 1988

*1660 Duquesne—56 Rue de Bammeville, Rouen, France.
Transferred to the G.L.M.M.M. of France 1997* Dec. 20, 1988

*1661 Ruscino—3 Rue Adam, Perpignan, France.
Transferred to the G.L.M.M.M. of France 1997* Feb. 21, 1989

1662 Gariep—M.T., Springbok, Northern Cape, South Africa.
3rd Sat. Feb., May, Aug.; 2nd Sat. Nov. (I.) Apr. 4, 1989

*1663 Palladia Tolosa—32-34 Rue Gabriel Peri F31000, Toulouse, France.
Transferred to the G.L.M.M.M. of France 1997* Apr. 26, 1989

K ■ **1664 Round Table**—Dore M.H., Dore, Sheffield S17 3LA.
4th Wed. Feb., July, Sept., Nov. (I.) May 15, 1989

*1665 Aquitania—13 bis, Place de Stalingrad, Bordeaux, France.
Transferred to the G.L.M.M.M. of France 1997* May 26, 1989

* **1666 Bond of Friendship**—Avda Ballivian, No. 2810, Dep. No. 6,
Cota Cota, La Paz, Bolivia.
1st Mon. Feb., May, Nov.; 2nd Sat. Aug. (I.) June 12, 1989

*1667 Dunkerque—Chateau Lowbry, 59240 Dunkirk, France.
Transferred to the G.L.M.M.M. of France 1997* June 16, 1989

1668 Luanshya—M.T. Luanshya, Zambia.
Unattached Overseas June 30, 1989

* **1669 The Collingwood**—Weybourne House, Portsmouth Road, Guildford, Surrey.
4th Fri. Jan.; 3rd Fri. April, Sept. (I.) July 31, 1989

1670 Mark Lodge of Progress—M.T., Princes Avenue, Caerphilly.
3rd Sat. March; 1st Sat. Oct. (I.) Sept. 8, 1989

1671 Sir William Crosthwaite Mark Grand Officers—M.H., The Mile, Pocklington.
3rd Wed. April, Oct. (I.) Oct. 5, 1989

* **1672 Accra**—William Galloway Memorial Temple, Liberia Road, Accra, Ghana.
3rd Mon. Feb., May (I.), Aug., Nov. Oct. 24, 1989
Warrant of Confirmation July 23, 1999

K **1673 Mark of Enterprise**—M.H., 265 Rue Royale, B-1030 Bruxelles, Belgium.
2nd Thurs. Feb.; 1st Sat. June (I.); 2nd Thurs. Oct. Feb. 22, 1990

1674 Aberystwyth—M.H., Market St., Aberystwyth, Ceredigion.
2nd Tues. Feb. (I.); 2nd Sat. Oct.; 2nd Wed. Dec. Mar. 15, 1990

1675 The Great Ouse Valley—United Reformed Church, High Street, Olney,Bucks.
2nd Mon. Jan., April, Oct. (I.) Apr. 3, 1990

*1676 Turonia—8 Rue de la Bourde, Tours, France.
Transferred to the G.L.M.M.M. of France 1997* May 2, 1990

K **1677 Silurean**—M.H., Headbrook, Kington, Herefords.
Last Wed. Feb., April, Sept. (I.), Nov. June 18, 1990

* **1678 Wellington**—M.H., Duke St., Whitehaven CA28 7NZ.
4th Fri. Feb., June, Oct.; 1st Sat. Dec. (I.) July 6, 1990

*1679 Badge of Innocence—M.C. Nutfield, Nutfield Road, Redhill, Surrey.
Warrant surrendered* Nov. 26, 1990

* **1680 Edward the Black Prince**—St. Andrew M.H., Tywardreath.
3rd Mon. Feb., March, May (I.), Oct., Dec. Dec. 3, 1990

1681 Hoveden Lodge of Installed Mark Masters—M.H., Howden.
3rd Fri. May (I.); 2nd Wed. Sept., Nov. Jan. 4, 1991

* **1682 The North Kent**—M.H., Wilmington, Kent.
4th Sat. March (I.); 3rd Sat. Aug., Dec. Jan. 16, 1991

ROLL OF LODGES—continued

     1683 **Barcino**—M.H. Gran Via Dels Corts Catalanes 617, Barcelona, Spain.
           4th Tues. Jan., May, Sept. (I.)   Apr. 10, 1991

     1684 **Arquimedes**—M.H., Juan Ramon Jiménez 6, Madrid, Spain.
           2nd Sat. Jan. (I.), May, Oct.   Apr. 24, 1991
                                                                   Warrant of Confirmation Apr. 1, 2010

*   1685 **Sketty Hall**—M.H. St. Helens Road, Swansea.
           1st Wed. Nov., March; 2nd Fri. June (I.)   June 3, 1991

     1686 **Adastral**—Halsey M.H., Cheshunt, Herts.
           2nd Mon. May; 3rd Mon. Sept. (I.); 3rd Tues. Dec.   July 4, 1991

K   1687 **Hampshire and Isle of Wight Installed Mark Masters**—
           M.H., Kings Court, Chandler's Ford.
           1st 5th Wed. after 1st Feb.; 1st 5th Wed. after 1st Sept. (I.)   Aug. 20, 1991

*   1688 **Javea**—M.H., Puerto de Javea, Alicante, Spain.
           4th Fri. Mar. (I.), Oct., Nov.   Sept. 24, 1991
                                                                   Warrant of Confirmation Apr. 20, 2007

     1689 **Hesperides**—Masonic Hall, Calle Italia No. 49, Las Palmas de Gran Canaria,
           Canary Islands, Spain.
           4th Fri. Jan., May, Sept. (I.), Nov.   Oct. 14, 1991

*   1690 **Andalucia**—M.C. (Baja), Eos, Bougainvilla, Avda, Gaviotas,
           Los Bauches Fuengirola, Malaga, Spain.
           1st Thurs. Feb., May, Nov. (I.)   Oct. 14, 1991

     1691 **The Kent Mark Stewards**—M.H., Maidstone. Masonic Hall,
           Wrotham and other Masonic Centres as convenient.
           1st Wed. March (I.) Sept.   Dec. 3, 1991

     1692 *Axis Mundi—Nangy, Haute-Savoie, France.*
           Transferred to the G.L.M.M.M. of France 1997   *Mar. 3, 1992*

     1693 *Arvernia—M.H. Clemont Ferrand, France.*
           Transferred to the G.L.M.M.M. of France 1997   *Apr. 6, 1992*

*   1694 **Friendship Iberia**—Acacia M.Cr., Cuidad del Cine, 29100 Coin, Spain.
           3rd Tues. Feb., May, Oct. (I.)   May 14, 1992

     1695 *Lugdunum—22 Rue Montesquieu, Lyon, France.*
           Transferred to the G.L.M.M.M. of France 1997   *Oct. 31, 1992*

     1696 **Golden Harvest**—F.M.H., Park Lane, Parktown, Johannesburg.
           4th Mon. (mornings) Feb., May, Aug., Nov. (I.)   July 20, 1992

     1697 **Staffordshire and Shropshire Mark Grand Officers Lodge**—
           Rugeley & District M.C., Chase Golf Club, Penkridge.
           2nd Fri. March at above venue;
           3rd Thurs. Sept. at venue to be decided by Master.   March 13, 1993

     1698 *Pericle Maruzzi—2 Rue de la Pripiniere, Paris, France.*
           Transferred to the G.L.M.M.M. of France 1997   *July 20, 1992*

     1699 *Sainte Cecile—M.T. 25 Rue du Centeral-Leclerc 81060 Albi, France.*
           Transferred to the G.L.M.M.M. of France 1997   *Aug. 27, 1992*

     1700 **Gorllewin Cymru Mark Grand Officers**—M.H., Harris Avenue, Llanelli.
           4th Sat. June; 1st Mon. Nov. (I.)   Sept. 24, 1992

     1701 **St. Cecilia**—Halsey M.H., Watford, Herts.
           4th Tues. Sept., Feb., June (I.) and the 22nd day of Nov.
           (St. Cecelias Day)   March 30, 1993

     1702 **Asanteman**—Ashanti Temple, Old Bekwai Road, Kumasi.
           1st Fri. Jan., May (I.), Nov.   May 8, 1993

K   1703 **Buckley**—M.R., Mold Road, Buckley, Flintshire.
           1st Mon. Sept. (I.), Nov., Feb.; 2nd Mon. May.   April 24, 1993

     1704 **Fratres Calami Aerariique**—M.H., Grove Road, Sutton, Surrey.
           1st Mon. July (I.); 1st Sat. Feb.   May 17, 1993

     1705 **Carreg Wastad**—M.H., Fishguard.
           2nd Tues. Jan.; 3rd Wed. June (I.); 2nd Mon. Sept; 1st Thurs. Nov.   April 30, 1993

ROLL OF LODGES—continued

K 1706 **The Derbyshire Lodge of Installed Mark Masters**—M.R., Belper, Derbyshire.
   2nd Wed. April, Sept. (I.) Sept. 25, 1993

   1707 Steinmetz—M.H. Murbach Strassr 15, 6003 Lucerne, Switzerland.
   Transferred to the G.L.M.M.M. of Switzerland 1996 *Sept. 11, 1993*

   1708 **Gwynedd Lodge of Installed Mark Masters**—M.T., Deiniol Rd., Bangor.
   3rd Fri. May; Last Fri. Sept. (I.) Sept. 4, 1993

* 1709 **The Lady of the Lamp**—M.H., Chepstow, Gwent.
   3rd Tues. March (I.), June; 3rd Mon. Sept. May 17, 1993

* 1710 **Scholars in Amity**—The Cloisters, Barrington Road, Letchworth and Ashwell House, 167 Verulam Road, St. Albans.
   Last day (except Sunday), March, June (I.), Sept. June 30, 1993

   1711 **Stokesley Lodge of Installed Mark Masters**—M.H., West Green, Stokesley.
   3rd Fri. April, June (I.), Oct. Aug. 14, 1993

   1712 **Beaconsfield**—Slough M.C., Ragstone Road, Slough.
   2nd Tues. Feb., Nov. (I.); 3rd Tues. Sept. Oct. 14, 1993

   1713 Rouvray—65 Boulevard Bineau a 92200 Neuilly-Sur-Seine, France.
   Transferred to the G.L.M.M.M. of France 1997 *Oct. 20, 1994*

K * ■ 1714 **Ryton**—M.H., Oakfield House, Ryton.
   2nd Fri. April, June, Sept. (I.), Nov. Dec. 4, 1993

   1715 **Ronald Chitty**—M.H., New Road, Framlingham, Suffolk.
   3rd Fri. June; 1st Fri. March (I.), Nov. Nov. 6, 1993

   1716 **Cornerstone**—F.M.H., Bridge Street, Manchester.
   2nd Fri. Dec. (I.); 1st Fri. June. Dec. 10, 1993

   1717 **Bristol Installed Mark Masters**—F.M.H., Park St., Bristol.
   2nd Sat. Jan., March (I.); 1st Sat. Oct. March 19, 1994

   1718 **Mark of Love and Remembrance**—M.H., The Old Court House, 24 South Street, Rochford SS4 1BQ.
   2nd Sat. Feb.; 1st Sat. April; 3rd Sat. Nov. (I.) April 16, 1994

   1719 **The Liberation**—M.T., Stopford Rd., St. Helier, Jersey, C.I.
   2nd Fri. Dec.; 3rd Fri. June (I.); 4th Thurs. April. May 7, 1994

   1720 **Prince Michael of Kent**—Twickenham M.C.
   3rd Thurs. July; 1st Fri. Dec. (I.) May 10, 1994

   1721 Reunio Insula—Temple Emile Payet la, Possession Ile de la Reunion, France.
   Transferred to the G.L.M.M.M. of France 1997 *Mar. 11, 1995*

K 1722 **Madrid**—M.H., Juan Ramon Jiménez 6, Madrid, Spain.
   1st Sat. Feb., May, Nov. (I.) May 20, 1994

K * 1723 **Antigua**—M.H., St. Johns, Antigua, W. Indies.
   3rd Thurs. Jan., May, Aug., Nov. (I.) Feb 24, 1995

   1724 **Thomas Beevor**—Masonic Royal Assembly Rooms, Great Yarmouth.
   2nd Mon. Jan., March, June, Nov. (I.) Nov 1, 1994

   1725 **Brychan**—M.H., Brecon.
   3rd Wed. March; 1st Thur., May (I.); 1st Wed. Oct. Sept. 22, 1994

■ 1726 **Mark Provincial Grand Stewards Lodge of Surrey**—Croydon and District Masonic Hall, Oakfield Road, Croydon, Surrey.
   4th Mon. Feb.; 4th Mon. Sept. (I.) Sept. 27, 1994

K 1727 **Holsworthy**—M.H., Bodmin St., Holsworthy, Devon.
   3rd Mon. March, May (I.), Sept., Nov. Dec. 3, 1994

   1728 Arelate—Primotel, Arles, France.
   Transferred to the G.L.M.M.M. of France 1997 *Aug. 26, 1994*

   1729 Terre Du Soleil—Temple Pythagore 11, Bd Gambetta, Grenoble, France.
   Transferred to the G.L.M.M.M. of France 1997 *Aug. 27, 1994*

   1730 Augustodunum—The Temple, 10 Rue du Docteur Rebiclard, le Creuset, France.
   Transferred to the G.L.M.M.M. of France 1997 *Nov. 12, 1994*

   1731 Alestum—Ales en Cevennes, Temople des Brousses, France.
   Transferred to the G.L.M.M.M. of France 1997 *Aug. 26, 1994*

ROLL OF LODGES—continued

2K * 1732 **The Haven**—M.H., Kings Road, Cleethorpes, Sth. Humberside.
1st Fri. Oct., Nov., March, June (I.) Oct. 1, 1994

1733 **Brocas Hyrst**—M.H., Avenue Road, New Milton, Hants. BH25 5JP.
2nd Thurs. March (I.), May, Sept., Nov. Nov. 12, 1994

*1734 Builders of The Silent Cities—202 Rue Jean Jaures 59650, Ville Neuve D'ascq, France.
Transferred to the G.L.M.M.M. of France 1997* Oct. 22, 1994

1735 **Stilus et Denarius**—M.H., Upminster.
4th Fri. March, Oct. (I.) Oct. 29, 1994

*1736 Aurelianis—The Temple, Rue du Hamean 45400, Saran, France.
Transferred to the G.L.M.M.M. of France 1997* Oct. 21, 1994

K * 1737 **Thomas Arthur Wood**—St. Magdalen Chapel, Guys Cliffe, Warwick.
2nd Mon. Feb., Dec. (I.); 3rd Mon. July. Dec. 10, 1994

* 1738 **Pride of Surrey**—M.H., Grove Road, Sutton, Surrey.
2nd Mon. Sept.; 1st Tues. Jan.; 3rd Thurs. March (I.) Jan. 3, 1995

3K ■1739 **Ainsty**—M.H., Deighton Road, Wetherby.
3rd Wed. Jan., Feb., March (I.), April, Oct., Nov. March 4, 1995

*1740 Adoration Des Mages—65 Boulevard Bineau a 92200 Neuilly-Sur-Seine, France.
Transferred to the G.L.M.M.M. of France 1997* Feb. 6, 1995

1741 **Coronet**—F.M.H., Kerklaan 7, Roermond, Netherlands.
1st Tues. March, May (I.); Nov. March 11, 1995

* ■ 1742 **Sanderstead**—M.H., Oakfield Road, Croydon.
1st Wed. Oct.; 2nd Thurs. March (I.); 4th Thurs. May. April 20, 1995

*1743 Narbo Martius—Domaine de Grand Boutes, 11100 Narbonne, France.
Transferred to the G.L.M.M.M. of France 1997* Mar. 24, 1995

1744 **Serendipity**—M.H., Puerto de Javea, Alicante, Spain.
3rd Fri. Feb., Oct. (I.), Nov. June 3, 1995

1745 **Torrevieja**—M.H., Calle Toledo 14, Cuidad, Quesada, Rosales, Alicante, Spain.
1st Fri. Feb., April, Oct. (I.), Nov. June 2, 1995

K 1746 **Progress**—Yenton M.H., 73 Gravelly Hill, Birmingham.
4th Thurs. May; 3rd Thurs. July; 2nd Thurs. Sept. May 20, 1995

K 1747 **Sussex Mark Provincial Grand Stewards**—
Sussex M.C., 25 Queens Road, Brighton BN1 3XA.
3rd Mon. June (I.), Oct. June 15, 1995

■ 1748 **Euclid**—M.M.H.
3rd Tues. Jan. (I.); 1st Wed. June; 4th Tues. Oct. June 8, 1995

*1749 La Croix Du Sud—65 Boulevard Bineau a 92200 Neuilly-Sur-Seine, France.
Transferred to the G.L.M.M.M. of France 1997* Nov. 6, 1995

K * 1750 **Devonshire Lodge of Installed Mark Masters**—M.H., Buckfastleigh.
1st Fri. July (I.) Sept. 30, 1995

1751 **Balearic**—The Provincial Temple, Calle Monterrey 63, Palma, Mallorca, Spain.
Mon. preceeding 4th Wed. Feb., March (I.), Oct. June 2, 1995

1752 **Forest of Lebanon**—M.T., Hotel Avelon, Punta Lara, Nerja, Malaga, Spain.
1st Thurs. Feb., May, Nov. (I.) June 2, 1995

1753 **Ter Duinen**—Hotel "Soll Cress", Koninklijke Baan 225, B-8670 Koksijde, Belgium.
3rd Sat. Jan., May; Last Sat. Aug. (I.) Oct. 7, 1995

1754 **Lealtad**—M.T., Calle 28, Cota Cota, La Paz, Bolivia.
1st Wed. Feb., May, Nov.; 2nd Sat. Aug. (I.) Aug. 19, 1995

K 1755 **Kipling and Burns**—Dunstable M.C., Cemetery Lane, Dunstable.
2nd Wed. Sept. (I.), Dec., April. Sept. 30, 1995

1756 **Newbiggin by the Sea**—
M.H., Homelyn House, Newbiggin by the Sea, Northumberland.
1st Mon. March, (I.) Sept., Oct., Nov. Nov. 18, 1995

*1757 La Pierre Briarde—2 Rue des Ferrieres, 77600 Bussy Street, Georges, France.
Transferred to the G.L.M.M.M. of France 1997* Nov. 4, 1995

ROLL OF LODGES—continued

1758 Segodunum—Chateau de Carcenac 12120, Cassagnes-B, France.
Transferred to the G.L.M.M.M. of France 1997   Aug. 25, 1995

1759 Gergovia—10 Rue Fontgieve 63000 Clermont-Ferrand, France.
Transferred to the G.L.M.M.M. of France 1997   Aug. 26, 1995

1760 Saint Semin—32-34 Reu Gabriel Peri F31000, Toulouse, France.
Transferred to the G.L.M.M.M. of France 1997   Aug. 25, 1995

* 1761 **Knock Murton**—M.H., Trumpet Road, Wath Brow, Cleator CA23 3EH.
3rd Mon. March (I.), May, July, Sept., Nov.   Oct. 12, 1995

1762 Capricorn—M.H. Masaaserstrasse 35, 7000 Chur, Switzerland.
Transferred to the G.L.M.M.M. of Switzerland 1996   Dec. 2, 1995

1763 **Charmandean**—Charmandean Centre, Forest Rd, Worthing, West Sussex.
2nd Mon. March; 1st Tue. May; 3rd Mon. Nov.   Oct. 30, 1996
    Warrant of Confirmation Oct. 28, 1998

1764 La Clef De Voute—M.C. Marges, Switzerland.
Transferred to the G.L.M.M.M. of Switzerland 1996   Dec. 2, 1995

1765 La Marque D'Argentoratum—12 Rue Finkmatt, 67000 Strasbourg, France.
Transferred to the G.L.M.M.M. of France 1997   Nov. 4, 1995

1766 District Grand Officers Lodge of France—
65 Boulevard Bineau a 92200 Neuilly-Sur-Seine, France.
Transferred to the G.L.M.M.M. of France 1997   Nov. 17, 1995

1767 **Roentgen Portal**—Imperial Hotel, Russel Square, London WC1B 5BB.
1st Thurs. March; 2nd Thurs. June; 2nd Tues. Oct. (I.)   Nov. 8, 1995

1768 **Nightingale**—Eliot Hall, Church St, Winslow, Buckinghamshire.
3rd Thurs. Feb., June, Oct. (I.)   Jan 27, 1996

2K 1769 **Aireferry**—M.H., Belgravia, Goole.
3rd Mon. May (I.), July, Sept., Nov.   Mar. 2, 1996

1770 Concord—M.T. Greuterhof, 8546 Islikon, Switzerland.
Transferred to the G.L.M.M.M. of Switzerland 1996   Dec. 2, 1995

1771 **Epworth**—M.H., 10 Duke St., St. James', London, SW1.
3rd Mon. Feb.; 4th Fri. May (I.); 1st Fri. Nov.   May 24, 1996

K 1772 **St. Grwst**—M.H., Llanrwst, Gwynedd.
4th Wed. May, June; 4th Mon. Sept.; 4th Wed. Oct. (I.)   May 22, 1996

K 1773 **Forty Steps**—M.H., Albion Place, Southampton, Hants. SO14 2DD.
3rd Tues. Jan., March, May (I.); 2nd Tues. Nov.   June 29, 1996

1774 **Royal Air Force**—Warwickshire M.T., Edgbaston, Birmingham.
1st Fifth weekday, Mar., May, Oct. (I.)   Oct. 20, 1996

K 1775 **Multum in Parvo**—Cricket Pavilion, Seaton Road, Uppingham.
1st Mon. Sept. (I.), Nov, Jan.   Sept. 24, 1996
    Warrant of Confirmation Nov. 29, 2005

1776 **Seychelles**—M.H., Marie Larue Drive, Mt. Simpson Estate, Belombre, Mahe. Seychelles.
1st Wed. April, June (I.), Nov.   Nov. 30, 1996

* 1777 **Eos**—M.H., Wrotham Rd., Gravesend, Kent.
In the morning of 1st Mon. March (I.), June, Nov.   Feb. 26, 1997

1778 Cosmopolitan—M.H. Fiat Lux, Murbacherstrasse, 15 in 6003 Lucerne, Switzerland.
Transferred to the G.L.M.M.M. of Switzerland 1996   Aug. 31, 1996

1779 **The Chalfonts**—Beaconsfield M.C., Windsor End, Beaconsfield, Bucks.
4th Wed. Feb (I.); 3rd Wed. Sept.; 1st Wed. Dec.   Feb. 26, 1997

K 1780 **Marple**—Shepley Hall, Church Lane, Marple, Cheshire.
4th Wed. Jan., March (I.), Sept., Nov.   March 15, 1997

1781 **The Easterford**—M.T., Kelvedon, Essex CO5 9DX.
2nd Wed. May (I.), Oct.   April 19, 1997

* 1782 **The Rope and Anchor**—Logenhaus, Welckerstr 8, 20358 Hamburg, Germany.
1st Sat. Feb., April (I.); 4th Sat. Sept.   April 12, 1997

ROLL OF LODGES—*continued*

K	1783	**Ashby-de-la-Zouch**—M.H., Lower Church St, Ashby-de-la-Zouch, Leics. *1st Sat. Feb., April (I.); 4th Sat. Sept.*	April 29, 1997
	1784	**The Farmers'**—M.H., Pickering. *2nd Fri. March, Nov.; 4th Fri. June, (I.)*	Nov. 20, 1997
	1785	**Aldershot Meridian**—M.H., Edward St., Aldershot, Hants. GU11 3DR. *1st Thur. April, May, Sept. (I.)*	Oct. 11, 1997
K	1786	**The Progress Lodge of Installed Mark Masters**—F.M.H., 80 London Rd., Leicester. *3rd Sat. April; 1st Wed. Sept. (I.)*	Nov. 8, 1997
*	1787	**The East Africa Lodge of Installed Mark Masters** —F.M.H., Nairobi, Kenya. *4th Sat. June (I.); 2nd Sat. May*	Feb 26, 1998
	1788	**Channel Islands Installed Mark Masters**— M.T., Stopford Road, St. Helier, Jersey or at such other venues within the Province as the W.M. shall direct. *Last Sat. Feb. (I.), Sept.*	March 28, 1998
	1789	**Euromason**—M.H., Puerto De Javea, Alicante, Spain. *4th Tues. Jan. (I.), March, Oct.*	April 24, 1998
	1790	**Fraternidad**—Calle 28, Cota Cota, La Paz, Bolivia. *1st Tues. Feb., May, Nov.; 2nd Sat. Aug. (I.)*	Aug. 31, 1998
	1791	**Cape Centenary Lodge of Installed Mark Masters**— M.C., Pinelands, Cape Town, South Africa. *4th Wed. March, June, Sept. (I.)*	Aug. 22, 1998
*	1792	**Zum Maurischen Schloss im See**—Münzhof, Marktplatz 24, 88085 Langenargen/Lake Constance, Germany. *1st Sat. April; 2nd Sat. July (I.); 3rd Sat. Oct.*	Oct. 31, 1998
K	1793	**Portus Abonae**—M.H., Portview Road, Avonmouth, Bristol. *3rd Tues. Jan., March, Oct. (I.), Nov.*	Oct. 31, 1998
*	1794	**Santa Cruz**—Santa Cruz de la Sierra, Calle, Ayacucho 431, Bolivia. *3rd Wed. Nov., March, May, Aug. (I.)*	Aug. 15, 1998
	1795	**James Webster**—Sussex M.C., Queens Road, Brighton. *1st Mon. April, July; 2nd Mon. Sept. (I.)*	Oct. 30, 1998
K	1796	**Hampshire & Isle of Wight Provincial Grand Stewards**— M.C., Brook House, Brook Lane, Botley, Hants. SO30 2ER. *2nd Mon. March, June, Oct. (I.)*	Nov. 14, 1998
	1797	**Sierra Leone**—M.T., Tower Hill, Freetown, Sierra Leone. *3rd Sat. Feb.(I.), May, Nov.*	Feb. 2, 1999
■	1798	**Meridies**—M.C., Brook House, Brook Lane, Botley, Hants. SO30 2ER. *2nd Mon. Feb., May (I.), Oct.*	Feb. 14, 1999
*	1799	**Delta**—F.M.H., Beestenmarkt 5, Goes, The Netherlands. *1st Mon. March (I.), June, Nov.*	Feb. 27, 1999
	1800	**Tintagel Castle**—King Arthur's Hall, Tintagel. *4th Fri. Feb., April (I.), Nov.; 4th Thurs. Sept.*	Apr. 23, 1999
*	*1801*	*Malacca—Dewan Freemason, Jalan Chan Koon Cheng, Malacca.* *Transferred to G.L.M.M.M. of South East Asia – August 2012*	*Jan. 22, 2000*
*	1802	**Millennium**—M.H. Sittingbourne, Kent. *4th Sat. Jan. (I.); 3rd Sat. June, Oct.*	Jan. 8, 2000
	1803	**Mount Sinai**—M.H., Chipping Sodbury. *3rd Wed. May (I.); 2nd Wed. Oct.*	Dec. 4, 1999
	1804	**Centurion**—Thurrock M.H., Lenthall Avenue, Grays, Essex RM17 5AA. *3rd Tues. March, July, Nov. (I.)*	Mar. 18, 2000
*	1805	**Cantera Del Oriente**—Calle Ayacucho 431, Santa Cruz, Bolivia. *3rd Thurs. Feb., May, Aug. (I.), Nov.*	Mar. 15, 2000
K	■ 1806	**Chief of the Builders**— F.M.H., Holmside Avenue, Dunstan, Gateshead, Tyne & Wear NE11 9TJ *3rd Fri. March (I.), Oct.*	July 21, 2000
	1807	**Eivissa**—Can Balafi De Baix, Sta. Eulalia, Ibiza, Spain. *4th Wed. Feb., Nov.; 2nd Thurs. April (I.)*	

ROLL OF LODGES—*continued*

	*	1808	Arthur Morley Custance, Lodge of Installed Mark Masters—M.H., Goldsmith St., Nottingham. *1st Fri Jan.; 3rd Tues. June (I.)*	Oct. 14, 2000
	*	1809	Stanstead Abbots—M.H., Vantorts Road, Sawbridgeworth, Herts. CM21 9AJ. *2nd Wed. Feb., May (I.), Oct.*	May 31, 2000
		1810	San Juan—Restaurante Casa Caty, Ctra, Benidorm Callosa d'en Sarriá, Alicante, Spain. *3rd Mon. Feb. (I.), April, Oct.*	May 31, 2000
K		1811	Coventry—Coventry M.H., Coventry. *4th Tues. April; 1st Mon. June; 3rd Wed. Sept. (I.)*	Nov. 11, 2000
		1812	Cwm Rhondda—R.A.F. Association Club, Bute St., Treorchy, Rhondda. *4th Mon. Feb., Nov.; 3rd Mon. May (I.)*	Mar. 3, 2001
		1813	Provincial Directors of Ceremonies— Moseley M.H., Alcester Rd. South Kings Heath, Birmingham B14 6DT. *1st Sat. Feb. (I.), Oct.*	Feb. 2, 2001
		1814	Arthur French Sewell Lodge of Provincial Grand Stewards— M.H., Wath Brow. *Last working day (not Sat.) of Feb., May, Nov. (I.)*	May 23, 2001
K	*	1815	La Marque de Lorraine—M.T., rue Nicolas Berger 66/B-6700, Arlon, Belgium. *1st Wed. March, June (I.), Oct.*	May 12, 2001
			Warrant of Confirmation	Dec. 22, 2005
		1816	Durban Inanda—Masonic Temple, Walter Gilbert Road, Durban. *4th Mon. Jan., March, July, Nov. (I.)*	Aug. 30, 2001
	*	1817	Loja Fênix de Mestres Maçons da Marca— M.T., Rua Lisboa, 1120, São Paulo or M.T., Rua São Joaquim, 457, São Paulo, Brazil. *Last Thurs. Feb., May, Aug, Nov.; Installation 3rd regular meeting of year*	Nov. 28, 2001
K		1818	Ronald Albutt—Yenton M.T., Erdington, Birmingham. *1st Tues. March, Sept. (I.)*	Nov. 3, 2001
	*	1819	Moses Montefiore—M.T., Rua Artur de Azevedo, 1781, São Paulo, S.P. Brazil. *1st Mon. Feb., April, June, Aug., Oct., Dec. (I.)*	Nov. 29, 2001
K	■	1820	Durham Lodge of Provincial Grand Stewards—Birtley M.H., Birtley Lane, Birtley. *Last Wed. April, Oct. (I.); 1st Wed. July*	Oct. 31, 2001
		1821	Golden Jubilee—M.H., Gordon St., Workington CA14 2EN. *1st Fri. July (I.); and other venues within the Province as the W.M. shall direct on 1st Thurs. Sept. and 3rd Tues. May*	Feb. 16, 2002
		1822	Millennium—Northfield M.H., 641 Bristol Rd. South, Birmingham B31 2JS. *1st Thurs. April (I.), Sept.*	Dec. 15, 2001
	*	1823	Oliva La Safor—Restaurante Flor Azahar, Ctra, Albaida, Gandia, Spain. *Thurs. after 3rd Tues. Feb. (I.), May, Nov.*	Feb. 21, 2002
		1824	John Burr—Ashwell House, 167 Verulam Road, St. Albans, Herts. AL3 4DW. *1st Wed. March, May (I.); 1st Thurs. Sept.*	May 27, 2002
K	■	1825	Cheshire Provincial Grand Stewards— M.H., Kinderton Street, Middlewich, Cheshire CW10 0JE. *1st Tues. Feb.; 3rd Fri. May (I.); 2nd Tues. Oct.*	June 29, 2002
	*■	1826	Tenerife—Restaurante Las Chafiras, San Miguel De Abona, Tenerife, Spain. *3rd Thurs. Feb. (I.), March, Nov.*	May 11, 2002
		1827	Eccleshall—M.R., Kings Arms Ho., Eccleshall. *2nd Sat. May (I.); 2nd Mon. Sept., Dec.*	Sept. 14, 2002
	*	1828	The Royal Prince of Wales— M.T., 7 Alexandra Street, St. Clair, Port of Spain, Trinidad. *2nd Thurs. Jan., April (I.), July.*	May 12, 2003
		1829	South Wales Mark Provincial Stewards—M.T., Bridgend. *4th Fri. May; 1st Fri. Nov. (I.)*	Mar. 12, 2003
		1830	Sykes—M.H., Lockwood St., Driffield. *5th Wed. in those months of the year with 5 Weds. (excluding Dec.)*	Mar. 15, 2003
K	*	1831	Thomas á Becket—Charmandean Centre, Worthing. *3rd Wed. Jan., March, May, Oct. (I.)*	May 29, 2003

ROLL OF LODGES—continued

1832 **White Stone**—Ashwell House, 167 Verulam Rd., St. Albans.
2nd Thurs. April (I.), Nov. May 29, 2003

1833 **St. Kitts**—M.H., St. John's, Antigua, West Indies.
1st Fri. Feb., June, Sept., Nov. (I.) May 8, 2003

* 1834 **Charlotte Amalie**—
M.H., 10 Wimmelskaft Gade, Charlotte Amalie, St. Thomas, Virgin Islands (U.S.).
2nd Wed. March (I.), May, Nov. May 10, 2003

* 1835 **Kypros**—Apollo Rooms, Episkopi, Cyprus.
2nd Fri. Jan., March, Oct. (I.) Oct. 8, 2003

1836 **Utrique Fidelis Lodge of Mark Grand Officers**—
M.H., Chepstow on *3rd Mon. May;* Nov. 17, 2003
M.H., Castleton on *3rd Mon. Nov. (I.)* Warrant of Confirmation Sept. 2011

* ■ 1837 **Cantero**—Meson Aquario, La Azohia (Murcia).
3rd Tues. Jan., Feb., March, Nov. (I.) Oct. 8, 2005

* 1838 **Menatschim**—Oxfordshire M.C., 333 Banbury Rd., Oxford.
4th Mon. March; 1st Mon. Sept. (I.) Nov. 8, 2003

1839 **Oak Tree**—Sit Perpetuum Temple, Bisley, Surrey.
2nd Thurs. Jan. (I.), April, Sept. Dec. 16, 2003

* 1840 **St. James's**—10 Duke St., St. James's, London SW1.
1st Mon. Jan. (I.), July (except for public holidays,
when the meeting will be held on the 5th Mon. of the same month) Nov. 21, 2003

1841 **Table Fellowship**—Glenmore House, Surbiton, Surrey.
1st Thurs. Feb. (I.); 2nd Wed. May; 4th Wed. Sept. Jan. 29, 2004

1842 **Concordia**—M.T., 6 de Octubre St.4979, Oruro, Bolivia.
1st Fri. March, June, Aug. (I.), Nov. Mar. 13, 2004

* 1843 **Wiltshire Downs**—M.H., Warminster, Wiltshire BA12 9AW.
3rd Wed. March (I.), May, Sept. Mar. 17, 2004

1844 **Cyril Batham**—M.H., Great William St., Stratford upon Avon.
1st Fri. Jan. (I.); 3rd Fri. April; 2nd Wed. Oct. Mar. 3, 2004

1845 **Trinity**—M.T., Cardiff Road, Bargoed, South Wales.
3rd Tues. March (I.), May, Oct.; 1st Mon. Dec. Mar. 16, 2004

* 1846 **Lodge of Enlightenment**—Cole Court, London Rd., Twickenham.
2nd Thurs. Feb. (I.) and any Masonic venue in the Province of Middlesex
on 2nd Thurs. June, Oct. Apr. 22, 2004

* 1847 **Abbot Simeon**—M.R., Ely.
2nd Fri. March; 1st Mon. Sept. (I.); 4th Thurs. Nov. May 15, 2004

* 1848 **Barbados Installed Mark Masters**—M.H. Belleville, St. Michael, Barbados.
2nd Tues. March (I.), Sept. Apr. 4, 2004

1849 **Guyana Installed Mark Masters**—F.H. Company Path, Georgetown.
1st Mon. Feb., May, Nov. (I.) May 3, 2004

* 1850 **Abeokuta**—Lisabi Masonic Hall, 4 Aivetoro Road, Lafenwa, Abeokuta.
3rd Sat. Jan. (I.), May, Sept. Unattached Nigeria Aug. 14, 2004

1851 **Eko**—Ebute-Metta Masonic Hall, 22 Odaliki Street, Ebute-Metta, Nigeria.
4th Thurs. Jan., April, Aug., Oct. Feb. 11, 2006

* 1852 **Barão de Mauá**—Av. Ricardo Medina Filho, 577, São Paulo, SP 05057-100 Brazil.
3rd Thurs. March, Sept. (I.), Nov. June 30, 2004

1853 **Sabah**—Dewan Freemason, Sibuga Road, Sandakan, Sabah, Malaysia.
Transferred to the G.L.M.M.M. of South East Asia – August 2012 June 25, 2004

1854 **Harmonia**—M.T., Rua Coronel Miranda 37, Niteroi, Rio de Janeiro, Brazil.
1st Sat. March (I.), June, Sept., Dec. Aug. 14, 2004

K ■ 1855 **Massoda**—M.H., Branksome, Clay Lane, Timperley, Altrincham.
1st Wed. May, Sept. (I.), Dec. Sept. 1, 2004

* 1856 **The Mahajan**—Mansfield Bowling Club, Croftdown Road, Highgate, London.
2nd Mon. March; 1st Wed. May, Nov. (I.) Nov. 3, 2004

ROLL OF LODGES—*continued*

* 1857 **Ditton**—Masonic Hall, Surbiton.
  2nd Fri. April (I.); 1st Tues. Sept.; 4th Wed. Nov.   Jan. 24, 2005

    1858 *Loja Crivo da Razao de Mestre Macons da Marca—*
R. Vigario Albernaz, 683-Sao Paulo, Brazil.
Transferred to the G.L.M.M.M. of Brazil 2005   Dec. 11, 2004

    1859 *Loja Madras de Mestre Macons da Marca—*
Rua Rodrigo de Barros, 107-Sao Paulo, Brazil.
Transferred to the G.L.M.M.M. of Brazil 2005   Dec. 11, 2004

    1860 *Loja Paul Harris de Mestre Macons da Marca—*
Rua Augusta, 719 1st Floor, Sao Paulo, Brazil.
Transferred to the G.L.M.M.M. of Brazil 2005   Dec. 11, 2004

    1861 *Loja Cosmos de Mestre Macons da Marca—*
Rua Augusta, 719 1st Floor, Sao Paulo, Brazil.
Transferred to the G.L.M.M.M. of Brazil 2005   Dec. 11, 2004

    1862 *Hairoun—*
Not yet Consecrated

* 1863 **Broadley**—"Casa Viani", 6/7 Marsamxett Street, Valletta, Malta.
  Unattached Malta 1st Sat. May (I.), Oct.   May 9, 2005

* 1864 **Montserrat**—M.H. Belleville, St. Michael, Barbados.
  2nd Sat. March (I.), July, Nov.   May 21, 2005

* 1865 **Cyril H. Rees Providencia**—
  Temple "Cyril H. Rees", Calle 8, No. 8084, Calacoto, La Paz, Bolivia.
  3rd Tues. Feb., May, Aug. (I.), Nov.   Sept. 3, 2005

    1866 **Columbyne**—Masonic Hall, Stowmarket, Suffolk.
1st Fri. Feb., May (I.), Oct.   Sept. 22, 2005

* 1867 **Quesada Summer**—Sociedad Compas, Ciudad Quesada, Rojales, Alicante.
  3rd Mon. June, July, Sept.   Sept. 2, 2005

    1868 **Wilder**—Berkshire Masonic Centre, Mole Road, Sindlesham.
4th Tues. April, Oct. (I.)   Dec. 12, 2005

    1869 **Temple Builders**—3 times per year: the day before and at the same
venue as the Annual Meeting of Dist.G.L. of Spain; May: At a venue to be
determined by the W.M.; *Nov. (I.): At the Master Elect's home Lodge*   Nov. 18, 2005

    1870 **London Mark Province of Grand Stewards**—
Mark Masons' Hall, 86 St. James's Street, London SW1A 1PL.
1st Thurs. June; 1st fifth weekday Nov. (I.)   Nov. 29, 2005

    1871 **Ailwyn**—The Abbey Rooms, Ramsay, Cambs.
1st Thurs. April (I.), Sept.; 2nd Fri. Jan.   Mar. 25, 2006

* 1872 **Batu Utama**—15 Jalan 18/16, Taman Kanagapuram, H6000,
  Petaling, Jaya, Malaysia.
      June 23, 2006

* 1873 **Dominica**—Masonic Hall, Lower Morne Bruce, P.O. Box 2112,
  Roseau, Dominica, West Indies.
  3rd Mon. May (I.), Aug., Nov.   May 15, 2006

* 1874 **Tortola**—M.T., Johnson's Ghut, Road Town Tortola, British Virgin Islands.
  2nd Fri. Jan., April, Nov. (I.)   May 11, 2006

    1875 **Prins Van Oranje**—Masonic Hall, Genuastraat, 15, B-2000, Antwerpen, Belgium.
3rd Fri. Jan., May (I.), Oct.   Sept. 30, 2006

* 1876 **Clifford W. Jeapes**—East Sussex M.C., Seaview Road, Peacehaven.
  1st Thurs. June; 4th Wed. Nov. (I.)   Sept. 29, 2006

* ■ 1877 **Mojacar**—Kimrick Restaurant, Mojacar Playa, Almeria, Spain.
  2nd Mon. Feb., March, Sept., Dec. (I.)   Sept. 30, 2006

    1878 **Knightsbridge**—South West Surrey Masonic Centre, Guildford.
2nd Mon. April, June, Oct. (I.)   Oct. 31, 2006

    1879 **Luz Y Concordia**—GLB Temple, Av. Ayacucho No. 0-165 Cochabamba, Bolivia.
3rd Fri. Feb., May, Aug. (I.), Nov.   Sept. 15, 2006

ROLL OF LODGES—*continued*

1880 **Provincial Grand Stewards**—Masonic Hall, Jepps Lane, Royston, Herts SG8 9JH.
   5th weekday in March; 5th weekday in Oct.   Oct. 20, 2006

1881 **Joey Dunlop**—Masonic Hall, Lutterworth.
   3rd Sat. May; 2nd Sat. June; 3rd Sat. Aug. (I.)   June 9, 2007

1882 **Ituni**—Masonic Hall, Ferry Street, New Amsterdam, Guyana, South America.
   3rd Sat. Feb., July, Nov. (I.)   May 21, 2007

■ 1883 **Mancetter**—M.H. 106 Long Street, Atherstone, Warwickshire CU9 1AN.
   2nd Thurs. May; 1st Thurs. June; 3rd Wed. Dec. (I.)   May 26, 2007

1884 **Iyver Ha Pluvenn**—Masonic Hall, Perranporth, St. Day, Cornwall.
   2nd Tues. July (I.) at Perranportyh Masonic Hall.
   Oct. meeting at date and place of Worshipful Master's choice
   2nd Fri. Dec. at St. Day Masonic Hall   Sept. 29, 2007

1885 **Cornwall Mark Provincial Wardens**—
   Bodmin Masonic Hall *1st Tues. June*
   Redruth Masonic Hall. *1st Thurs. Nov. (I.)*   Sept. 29, 2007

* 1886 **Mandalay**—M.C., Oakley House, Bromley Common, Bromley, Kent.
   3rd Thurs. Jan.; 2nd Thurs. May; 2nd Thurs. Nov. (I.)   Oct. 17, 2007

* 1887 **Taquah**—Tarkwa Masonic Temple, P.O. Box 42, Tarkwa, Ghana.
     Dec. 8, 2007

1888 **The Goose and Gridiron**—M.T., Av. das Américas No. 5001, Midtown,
   Barrada Tijuca, Rio de Janeiro, Brazil.
   Last Sat. March, July, Sept., Nov. (I.)   Nov. 24, 2007

* 1889 **Equator**—West London Masonic Centre, Churchfield House,
   Churchfield Road, West Ealing, London W13 9NF.
   3rd Fri. Feb., May, Oct. (I.)   Nov. 21, 2007

1890 **Oriental**—M.H., Fern Avenue, Jesmond, Newcastle Upon Tyne.
   1st Mon. March, June, Oct. (I.)   Jan. 07, 2008

1891 **Chuquisaca**—GLB Temple, Av. Juana Azurduy de Padilla, Sucre, Bolivia.
   2nd Fri. Jan., April, July, Aug. (I.)   Jan. 11, 2008

1892 **Lord Swansea**—Mark Masons' Hall.
   1st Wed. April (I.); Last Wed. July   Mar. 27, 2008

* 1893 **Premier Siam**—Hilton Phuket Arcadia Resort and Spa, 333 Patak Road,
   Karon Beach, Muang, Phuket 83100, Thailand.
   3rd Sat July; 2nd Sat. Sept., Nov. (I.)

* 1894 **Erdemont**—M.H., West Hill, Dartford, Kent.
   2nd Thurs. Feb., April (I.), Sept.   June 12, 2008

* 1895 **St. James**—Mark Masons' Hall.
   3rd Thurs. Oct. (I.); 4th Thurs. March   July 9, 2008

* 1896 **Pico Della Mirandola**—
   Such venues in Rome or other cities in Italy as W.M. shall designate.
   3rd Sat. Feb., May (I.), Nov.   July 26, 2008

1897 **Southern**—The Temple, Mount Horeb, Ruth Avenue,
   Les Efforts West, San Fernando, Trinidad, West Indies.
   4th Mon. April (I.); 1st Sat. July; 3rd Mon. Nov.   May 12, 2008

* 1898 **West Sussex Lodge of Installed Mark Masters**—
   M.H., 7 South Pallant, Chichester, West Sussex.
   2nd Fri. July (I.); 2nd Sat. Jan.   July 19, 2008

* 1899 **Mayflower**—M.H., Halton Road, Spilsby PE23 5JZ.
   Last Tues. Jan.; 1st Tues. May (I.), Dec.   Apr. 25, 2009

1901 **Quill and Key**—
   Northfield Masonic Hall, 643 Bristol Road South, Birmingham B31 2JS.
   4th Tues. March (I.), Oct.   May 8, 2009

* 1902 **Lanzarote**—Masonic Centre, Arrecife, Lanzarote.
   Fri. before 2nd Sat. April, Sept. (I.), Dec.   Apr. 24, 2009

1903 **New Quarries**—Salzburg or any other venue in Austria.
   3rd Sat. Jan., April; Last Sat. Sept. (I.)   May 22, 2009

ROLL OF LODGES—*continued*

1904 **Kition**—San Remo Hotel, Larnaca, Cyprus.
3rd Mon. Feb. (I.), May, Sept. Oct. 7, 2009

* ■ 1905 **Morley**—Blenheim House, Batley Field Hill, Batley, West Yorkshire WF17 0BG.
1st Wed. May, Sept., Nov. (I.) Sept. 23, 2009

* 1906 **The Geoffrey Dicker**—F.M.H., Parkfields, Diss, Norfolk IP22 4LE.
Twice a year on days selected by the Provincial Grand Master Dec. 14, 2009

■ 1907 **The Scout**—Long Eaton M.H., Derbyshire (I.) and other venues of the W.M.'s direction.
3rd Sat. Feb. (I.), June, Nov. Oct. 31, 2009

1908 **Centenary**—M.T. Rua Lisbon, Nr 1120, São Paulo, S.P., Brazil.
3rd Thurs. Jan., April (I.), July, Oct. Nov. 28, 2009

* 1909 **Highgate**—Imperial Hotel, Russell Square, London WC1B 5BB.
1st Sat. April (I.); 2nd Sat. July, Nov. Jan. 22, 2010

* 1910 **The Lincolnshire Provincial Officers**—
31st day of May: M.H., Chambers Street, Grantham; *31st day of Oct. (I.)*
M.H., Cambridge Road, Grimsby – unless these days are a Sat. or Sun.
in which case it will meet on the following Mon. May 8, 2010

1911 **Universal**—Harrow District M.C., Middlesex.
3rd Tues. Jan., 1st Thurs. May (I); 2nd Wed. Nov. May 20, 2010

1912 **Isle of Wedmore**—M.H., Church Street, Wedmore, Somerset, BS28 4AB.
2nd Wed. May (I.), June, Sept. May 12, 2010

1913 **Prince Michael of Kent**—Masonic Centre, Salters, St. George, Barbados, West Indies.
2nd Wed. March; 2nd Tues. June (I.); 2nd Thurs. Sept.; 2nd Wed. Dec. May 15, 2010

1914 **Dewi Sant**—Bridgend M.H., Coychurch Road, Bridgend, CF31 2AP.
2nd Mon. March (I.); 3rd Mon. Sept.; 4th Mon. Nov. Apr. 15, 2010

1915 **John Dee**—Venues in Rome or other cities in Italy as the W.M. shall designate.
2nd Sat. April, June (I.), Dec. June 18, 2010

* 1916 **Giorgio Vasari**—Venues in Arezzo or other cities in Italy as the W.M. shall designate.
4th Thurs. Jan, March, June (I.), Oct. June 19, 2010

1917 **Cranleigh Centenary**—Cranleigh M.H., Cranleigh, Surrey.
3rd Wed. Feb., May, Sept. (I.) Nov. 24, 2010

* 1918 **Lapis Anguli**—Bilbao, Spain.
4th Sat. in months in which there are five Saturdays July 3, 2010

1919 **Harmonia**—R.G.L.S. Temple, Kursulina Street, Belgrade, Serbia.
Last Sat. May, Sept. (I.); 3rd Sat. Dec. May 29, 2010

1920 **St. George's**—Ramada Hotel, Habberley Road, Bewdley, Worcestershire DY12 1LJ.
23rd April (I.); 1st Mon. Sept., 30th Nov. Sept. 6, 2010

1921 **New Morning**—10 Duke Street, St. James's, London SW1Y 6BS.
3rd Wed. Jan., June (I.) Nov. 24, 2010

1922 **The Roses and Castles Boaters'**—At a venue as directed by the Worshipful Master.
4th Mon. May, June; 2nd Fri. Dec. (I.) Dec. 2, 2010

1923 **Phoenix**—M.R., 6 Charalambous Mikhail Street, Nicosia, Cyprus.
1st Tues. June (I.), Sept.; 2nd Tues. Dec. Nov. 26, 2010

1924 **St. Andrew's**—M.H., Redfield Road, Midsomer Norton, Somerset.
3rd Mon. Jan. (I.), May, July Jan. 17, 2011

1925 **Dorset Mark Stewards**—Blandford M.H., West Street, Blandford Forum,
Dorset DT11 7AW.
1st Wed. June (I.); Last Wed. Nov. June 1, 2011

1926 **Santa Catarina**—Rua Bernardino Vaz, 177 1°a, Florianopolis, SC, Brazil.
2nd Sat. March, May, July (I.), Sept. Nov. July 9, 2011

1927 **Port Harcourt**—Port Harcourt M.H., 26 William Jumbo Street, Port Harcourt, Nigeria.
1st Sat. Feb., April, Aug., Oct. Aug. 27, 2011

1928 **John of Gaunt**—Grondwetlaan, 83, Bel-9040, St. Amandsberg, Gent, Belgium.
5th Sat. in those months of the year with five Saturdays Oct. 29, 2011

ROLL OF LODGES—*continued*

1929 **North Wales Provincial Grand Stewards**—
2nd Sat. March: at a venue chosen by the Worshipful Master.
2nd Sat. Nov. (I.): Elwy Hall, Grange Road, Rhyl, Denbighshire
LL18 4RG. Nov. 12, 2011

1930 **Sir Charles Tache-Menson**—William Galloway Memorial Temple, Liberia Road, Accra, Ghana.
3rd Mon. Jan., July; 3rd Sat. Sept. (I.) Nov. 28, 2011

1931 **Amity**—E.B.M.C., Jerrom Hall, Seaview Road, Peacehaven, East Sussex, BN10 8PX.
3rd Tues. March (I.); 1st Tues. Nov. Jan. 31, 2012

1932 **Secretarius**—
2nd Fri. May (I.): Hemsley House, 41 The Crescent, Salford M5 4PE;
3rd Fri. Nov.: at a location to be determined by the Master May 11, 2012

* 1933 **Entente Cordial**—M.M.H., London SW1A 1PL.
4th Sat. Jan., June; 3rd Sat. Oct. (I.) Mar. 10, 2012

1934 **Gaetano Filangieri**—Genova or other cities in Italy as directed by the W.M.
2nd Sat. Jan., May (I.); 3rd Sat. Sept. June 30, 2012

1935 **Perseverance**—F.M.H., 23a Coleman Street, Singapore 179806.
3rd Fri. Jan., May; 1st Fri. Sept. (I.) Aug. 3, 2012

1936 **Indaba**—F.M.H., Archer Street, Darlington DL3 6LS.
1st and 2nd fifth Fri. every year; 4th Fri. Nov. (I.) Nov. 23, 2012

1937 **East Anglia Mark Stewards**—M.H., Denmark Street, Diss IP22 4LE.
3rd Tues. Nov. (I.); and at a date between 1st of April and the 2nd week in May at a venue within the Province as directed by the W.M. Nov. 20, 2012

ALPHABETICAL LIST OF MARK LODGES
Has a Royal Ark Mariner Lodge attached

Name	No.
*Abbey, Abingdon	225
*Abbey, Battle	1086
*Abeokuta, Abeokuta, Nigeria	1850
*Abercrombie, St. Lucia, W.I.	1502
*Abernethy, Mark Masons' Hall	569
Aberystwyth, Aberystwyth	1674
Abbot Hugh of Selby	1640
*Abbott Simeon, Ely	1847
*Accra, Accra, Ghana	1672
*Adams, Sheerness	6
Adastral, Cheshunt	1686
Addington, Durban	515
*Addiscombe, Croydon	1320
Adlard, Jullundur, India	138
Adon Hiram, Groningen, Holland	1344
*Adoniram, Blyth	1483
*Adoniram, Leyland	552
Adoniram, Accrington	1065
*Admiral Rous, Newmarket	1427
Adur, Brighton	386
Aeon, Leyland	1312
*Afan, Port Talbot	1088
Ailwyn, Ramsey, Cambs.	1871
Ainsty, Wetherby	1739
*Air Unity, Twickenham	1205
*Albany, Newport, I.O.W.	T.I.
*Albert Edward, Newport	1317
*Albert Victor, Ipswich	70
*Albion, St. George, Barbados	212
Aldershot, Army and Navy, Aldershot	349
Aldershot, Meridian, Aldershot	1785
*Aldershot Military, Aldershot	54
*Alexander Burnett Brown, Kenton	1373
Alexandra, Hamilton, N.Z.	1388
*Alexandra, Hornsea	803
Alexandra, Long Sutton	1230
*Alfred, Oxford	247
Allen Pooley, Liverpool	992
*All Hallows, Twickenham	986
*Alliance and Memorial, M.M.H.	652
*All Saints' Kings Heath, Kings Heath	1462
*All Saints, Southgate N14	1251
All Souls', Weymouth	126
*Altrincham, Macclesfield	1024
*Alverton, Bedale	845
Amanzimtoti, Amanzimtoti	1435
Amatole, Fort Beaufort, S.A.	799
Amble, Amble	780
*Ambresbury, Loughton	834
Ambrose Crowley, Dunston, Co. Durham	1269
*Amherst, Sandgate	266
*Amity, Poole	132
Amity, Exmouth	849
Amity, Peacehaven	1931
*Ampthill, Ampthill	1396
*Andalucia, Fuengirola, Spain	1690
Anglebury, Swanage and Wareham	763
*Antigua, West Indies	1723
*Aorangi, Wellington, N.Z.	1101
*Arewa, Kadune, Nigeria	1431
*Ardvorlich, Karachi, Pakistan	219
*Ardwick, Audenshaw, Manchester	1222
Aries, Bradford	669
Arnold Moreton, Manchester	1649
Arquimedes, Madrid, Spain	1684
Arthur French Sewell Lodge of Provincial Grand Stewards	1814
*Arthur Lewis, Pontypridd	585
*Arthur Morley Custance, Nottingham	1808
Arts and Crafts, Brighton	979
Arts and Crafts, Plovdiv, Bulgaria	736
*Arum, St. Helena	644
Asanteman, Kumasi, Ghana	1702
*Ashburton, Ashburton	1038
*Ashby-de-la-Zouch	1783
*Ashfield, Mansfield	1146
*Ashington, Ashington	890
Ashlar, Tredgar	185
*Ashlar, The Gun Tavern, Brushfield St., E1	236
*Ashlar, Johannesburg, S.A.	424
*Ashlar, Karachi, Pakistan	474
*Ashlar, Chester	1090
Ashton District, Dukinfield	T.I.
Athelstan, Exeter	958
*Athlumney, Stourbridge	590
*Athlumney Menatschin, 10 Duke St., St. James	224
*Athol, Birmingham	174
Auckland, Bishop Auckland	596
*Aurelius, Clacton-on-Sea	814
*Austral, Mafikeng, C.P., South Africa	1302
*Avon, Avonmouth	646
*Ayot, St. Albans	1529
Backworth, Shiremoor	1189
*Baldwyn, Bristol	183
Balearic, Palma de Majorca, Spain	1751
*Barão de Mauá, São Paulo, Brazil	1852
*Barcino, Barcelona, Spain	1683
*Barbados Installed Mark Masters, St. Michael	1848
*Barnard, Wymondham	687
Barnard Castle, Barnard Castle	778
*Barnet Mark Well, M.M.H.	897
*Barry, Barry	1043
Bassein, Bassein, Burma	543
*Bassetlaw, Worksop	810
*Bata Utama, Jaya, Malaysia	1872
*Battlesbridge, Southend-on-Sea	1415
Bayons, Market Rasen	1365
*Beaconsfield, Southend-on-Sea	205
Beaconsfield, Slough	1712
*Beaudesart, Rugeley	1127
*Beaudesert, Linslade	1350
Beaufort, Ebbw Vale	1474
*Beaumont, Huddersfield	1523
*Bective, Keswick	452
*Bede, Sunderland	605
*Bedford, Birmingham	115
Belaside, Milnthrope	1340
Beneventa, Daventry	1486
*Benevolence, Bideford	1264
Benevolent, Stockport	T.I.
*Benevolent, Teignmouth	316
*Bentinck, Kirkby Lonsdale	726
*Benoni, Roodepoort, S.A.	720
Beriffe, Brightlingsea	825

141

ALPHABETICAL LIST OF MARK LODGES—continued

Lodge	No.
*Berkhampstead, St. Albans	1172
*Berkshire and Oxfordshire Installed Mark Masons', Wallingford	1330
*Bermuda, Hamilton, Bermuda	33
*Bernard Gilpin, Hetton-le-Hole	860
*Bernard Harvey, Slough	975
Beverlac, Beverley	281
Bexhill, Bexhill	1058
*Biggarsberg Unity, Dundee, Natal	566
*Biggin Hill, Sevenoaks	1557
Billinge, Blackburn	908
*Birkenhead, Birkenhead	1072
Biscot, Luton	1406
Bishop's Stortford, Bishop's Stortford	1236
Bispham-with-Norbeck, Blackpool	866
*Blagdon, Blyth	547
*Blair, Clayton-le-Moors, Accrington	113
Bletchley, Bletchley	1499
*Boleny Castle, Brentwood	998
*Bolingbroke, Croydon	451
Bolton, Bolton	762
Bon Accord, Mark Masons' Hall	T.I.
*Bond of Friendship, La Paz, Bolivia	1666
Bond of Friendship, Croydon	1576
Bootle, Bootle	478
Border Lodge of Installed Mark Masters, Port Alfred, S.A.	800
Border, Ludgershall	1143
*Boscawen, St. Day	101
Botley, Botley, Hants.	1382
*Bournemouth, Boscombe	125
*Bowyer, Chipping Norton	1655
*Brackenbury, Felixstowe	1659
Branksome, Poole	1477
Breckland, Thetford	1519
*Brentwood, Brentwood	377
Brighouse, Brighouse	753
Brighton, Brighton	426
Bristol Installed Mark Masters, Bristol	1717
*Britannia, Bielefeld, Germany	1471
*Britannia, Sheffield	53
Britannic, Mark Masons' Hall	433
British, Cape Town, South Africa	345
*Brixton, Piccadilly Hotel, W1	234
*Broadley, Valletta, Malta	1863
Brocas Hyrst, New Milton	1733
*Bromsgrove, Bromsgrove	1334
*Bronte, Haworth	535
Brough, Hull	1170
*Broxbourne, Watford	428
Brunswick, Plymouth	48
Brunswick, Bristol	1060
Bryanston, Johannesburg	1545
Brychan	1725
*Buckinghamshire Installed Mark Masters, Aylesbury	1634
Buckley, Buckley, Clwyd	1703
*Buenos Aires, Argentina	481
*Bulawayo, Bulawayo	881
Caduceus, Wallingford	1631
*Caerffili, Caephilly	1348
*Caesarean, St. Helier, C.I.	74
*Caldene, Hebden Bridge	501
*Camberley, Camberley	1131
*Cambrensis, Cardiff	1528
*Cambria, Cardiff	823
*Camden, Mark Masons' Hall	418
Camestone-Inglefield, Kempston	1633
*Campbell, Erode, S. India	907
Campos Salles, Sao Paulo	1355
*Cango, Mossel Bay, S. Africa	985
*Cantera Del Oriente, Santa Cruz, Bolivia	1805
*Cantero, La Azohia, Murcia, Spain	1837
Cantwara Byrig, Canterbury	1168
*Canynges, Bristol	T.I.
*Cape Centenary Lodge of I.M.M., Cape Town, South Africa	601
Capt. Sam. B. Aga, Civil Lines, Nagpur, India	653
Caput Anguli, Plymouth	798
Carew, Torpoint	1098
*Carnanton, Newquay	1028
*Carnarvon, Mark Masons' Hall	7
*Carnarvon, Havant	62
*Carnarvon, Keynsham	119
*Carnarvon, Mark Masons' Hall	616
Carnarvon, Nottingham	1311
Carreg Wastad, Fishguard	1705
*Carville, Newcastle upon Tyne	968
*Castle Eden, Castle Eden, Durham	930
Castle, Headingley, Leeds	1257
Castle, Newcastle	1622
*Catford, Bromley	841
*Cauvery, Tanjore, Madras	937
Cayman Keystone, Grand Cayman	1618
Centenary, Birmingham	1623
Centenary, London	1200
Centenary, Market Drayton	1581
Centenary, São Paulo, Brazil	908
*Central Keystone, Birmingham	714
Centurion, Newbury Park	1804
*Cerdic, Chard	571
Cestria, Chester-le-Street	1151
Cestrian, Chester	953
Chaloner, Melksham	599
*Chandlers Ford, Chandlers Ford	1258
Chandos, Sofia, Bulgaria	1402
Charity, Plymouth	76
*Charity, Birmingham	430
Charles H. Mosse, Peacehaven	1375
Charles Wilkinson, Sindelsham	1657
Charlotte Amalie	1834
Charmandean, Worthing	1763
*Chelmer, Chelmsford	342
*Cheltenham and Keystone, Cheltenham	10
Chewell, Banbury	847
Cheshire Provincial Grand Stewards, Middlewich	1825
*Cheshunt, Cheshunt	1047
Chesterfield, Chesterfield	1472
*Chevalier, Rickmansworth	1505
Chief of the Builders, Dunston	1806
*Chiltern, Dunstable	1538
Chilwell, Chilwell	1347
*Chingford, Chingford, E4	1252
Chiswick, Mark Masons' Hall	357
*Chola, Trichinopoly, Madras	610
*Chorlton, Chorlton-cum-Hardy	394

142

ALPHABETICAL LIST OF MARK LODGES—continued

Lodge	No.
*Christopher Wren, Twickenham	861
Christchurch, Christchurch	1453
Chuquisaca, Sucre, Bolivia	1891
*Cinderella, Boksburg North	621
*City Livery, London	1638
*City of London, Civil Service Club SW1A	869
*Clanfield, Horndean	1385
Clarence, Widnes	447
*Clarke, New Delhi, N. India	679
*Claughton, Birkenhead	703
*Clausentum, Southampton	613
*Clavering, Blaydon-on-Tyne	896
Cleeves, Sheffield	618
Cleveland, Stokesley	1040
Cleveley's, Cleveleys, Blackpool	1176
Cloister, Stockport	1475
*Clifford W. Jeapes, Peacehaven	1876
Columbyne, Stowmarket	1866
Colwyn, Colwyn Bay	1169
*Comites Sigillorum, Croydon	1352
*Commemoration, Corvino's, 7 Middlesex St. E.1	1091
Composite, Mark Masons' Hall	802
Concord, Whangarei, N.Z.	580
*Concord, Birmingham	735
*Concord, Rotterdam	1220
*Concordia, Hong Kong	721
Concordia, Oruro, Bolivia	1842
*Connaught, Ipswich	965
Connaught, Southampton	694
*Connaught Army and Navy, Mark Masons' Hall	748
Conrad Costin, Sindlesham	1430
*Constantine, Colchester	145
Constitution, Manchester	949
*Copley, Leeds	111
Corinthian, Liverpool	1052
*Cornerstone, Kimberley	217
*Cornerstone, Manchester	1716
Cornish Installed Mark Masters, Truro	1332
*Cornubian, Hayle	87
Cornwall Keystone, Montego Bay, Jamaica	1232
*Cornwall Legh, Stockport	839
Cornwall Mark Provincial Wardens, Bodmin & Redruth	1885
Coronation, Liverpool	563
Coronet, Roermond, Netherlands	1741
Corona, Johannesburg, S.A.	557
Coulsdon, Caterham	1268
*County Palatine, Audenshaw	156
Coventry, Coventry	1181
Cowbridge, Cowbridge	1573
*Craftesmen of Walden, Saffron Walden	1366
Cramlington, Cramlington	1235
*Crane, Cranbrook	1157
Cranford Park, London	1054
Cranleigh Centenary, Cranleigh	1917
Cranley, Windsor	1616
*Croydon, Croydon	198
*Croyland, Wellingborough	594
*Croystone, Southend-on-Sea	945
*Crystal Palace, Sutton	450
Cube Stone, Newport	731
Cumberland, Carlisle	60
*Cumbria Lodge of Installed Mark Masters, Keswick	1466
Cwm Rhondda Treorchy	1812
*Cynon-Dare, Aberdare	1590
Cyril Batham, Stratford upon Avon	1844
*Cyril H. Rees, Provedencia, La Paz, Bolivia	1865
Danum, Doncaster	398
*Darlington, Darlington	250
Dartmouth, Slaithwaite	545
Dartmouth, Dartmouth	737
*Dartmouth, W. Bromwich	993
Darwen, Blackburn	1327
Darvoren, Wellington, Madras	542
Davey, Chipping Sodbury	1449
Deben Valley, Woodbridge	1465
*Debenham, St. Albans	636
De Cymru, Cardiff	1606
Deeside, Neston	795
*De Keursteen, Leeuwarden, Netherlands	1580
De la Pole, Hull	329
*De la Pole, Seaton	372
De Lacy, Clayton-le-Moors	1554
De La Val, Whitley Bay	1290
Delta	1799
Den Aks, Eindhoven, Netherlands	1601
*Derby, Littleover	302
Derby, Salford	817
Derbyshire Lodge of Provincial Grand Stewards, Belper	1541
Derwent, Wirksworth	963
*Derwent, Workington	282
*De Sluitsteen, Velp, Netherlands	1579
*De Tabley, Birkenhead	396
De Umfraville, Mickley	1270
*Devi Das, Chandigarh	1277
Devon, Newton Abbot	215
Devonshire Lodge of Installed Mark Masters, Buckfastleigh	1750
Dewi Sant, Bridgend	1914
*Dewsbury, Batley	641
*Digswell, Hatfield	872
Diligence, Kenton	987
*Ditton, Surbiton	1857
*Dominica, Dominica, W.I.	1873
*Donyo Sabuk, Ruiru, Kenya	1476
Doornfontein, Parktown	1337
*Dore, Dore	844
Doric, Osnabrück, Germany	1542
Doric, Stockport	792
*Dorking, Dorking	1356
*Dorset Installed Mark Masters, Wimborne	1572
Dorset Mark Stewards, Blandford Forum	1925
*Dover and Cinque Ports, Dover	152
*Dove Valley, Ashbourne	353
Drakenstein, Worcester, S.A.	1120
*Dramatic, Mark Masons' Hall	487
*Drury Lane, Mark Masons' Hall	1228
*Duddon, Millom	1481
*Duke of Connaught, Kenton	199
Duke of Connaught, Buxton	246
*Duke of Connaught, Colombo	865
Duke of Richmond, Brighton	1025
Dukinfield, Dukinfield, Cheshire	1107

ALPHABETICAL LIST OF MARK LODGES—*continued*

*Dunckerley, Bristol	630	Erasmus Darwin, Littleover	855
Duncombe, Plymouth	438	*Erdemont, Dartford	1894
*Dunelm, Durham	356	Erlegh, Sindlesham	1627
*Dunmow, Braintree	527	Ernest Dixon, Sunderland	1015
*Dunraven, Bridgend	950	Ernest Dunscombe, Bristol	1423
*Dunwich, Bungay	850	Ernest Hines, Wroxham	1166
Durban Inanda	1816	Escafeld, Sheffield	1139
Durham Lodge of Installed Mark		*Esher, Esher	1050
Masters, Birtley	1492	*Essex Installed Mark Masters	1044
Durnovarian, Dorchester	1635	*Essex Jubilee, Southend-on-Sea	1123
*Dyfed Installed Mark Masters, Llanelli	1535	*Ethical, M.M.H.	458
*Dyffryn Clwyd, Denbigh	1647	Eton and Harrow, Café Royal, W1	830
		*Euclid, M.M.H.	1748
*Ealing, Twickenham	1013	Euromason, Javea, Alicante, Spain	1789
*Earl of Chester, Chester	196	*Euston, M.M.H.	399
*Earl of Courtown, E. Grinstead	1241	Eversley, Cromer	717
*Earl of Euston, Huntingdon	1458	*Excelsoir, Welling	226
*Earl of Scarborough, Skegness	1032	*Excelsoir, Liverpool	359
Eastbourne, Eastbourne	484	Exedra, M.M.H.	1138
East Anglia Mark Stewards, Diss	1937	*Exmoor, Minehead	697
East Anglican Installed Mark Masters, Diss	1418	Exon, Exeter	1075
*East Cheshire, Knutsford	1468		
East Croydon, Croydon	1097	Fabric, Rochdale	939
East Goscote, Syston	970	*Faith, Manchester	20
East Griqualand, Kokstad, S.A.	1294	Faithfull, Cockermouth	229
*East Hertfordshire, Radlett	683	Farne, Alnwick	1540
*East Lancashire Provincial Grand		*Fearnley, Halifax	58
Officers, Manchester	990	*Fênix, São Paulo	1817
East Lancashire Provincial Grand		Fermor, Southport	1113
Stewards', Manchester	1272	*Ferrers, Rushden	1341
East Sussex, St. Leonards-on-Sea	166	Ferryhill, Co. Durham	1560
*Eaton, Birmingham	977	Fidelis, Nottingham	1482
Eaton, Congleton	1607	Fidelity, Birkenhead	31
Eccles, Eccles, Lancs.	843	Fidelity, Coalville	491
Eccleshall, Eccleshall	1827	Fidelity Huyshe, Plymouth	91
*Eclectic, Hartlepool	39	Fidelity and Unanimity, Taunton	348
Eclectic & Empress Britannic,		*Fillebrook, Buckhurst Hill	944
Mark Masons' Hall	410	Fitz Hugh, Nottingham	632
*Edaljee Khory, Singapore	436	FitzRoy, Armoury House, EC1	815
Eden Valley, Appleby	888	*Fitzwilliam, Malton	277
Edward The Black Prince	1680	*Fitzwilliam, Peterborough	477
Egerton, Birkenhead	165	*Five Arches, Tenby	256
*Egerton of Tatton, Mark Masons' Hall	400	Flamsteed, Littleover	1022
Ehen, Cleator Moor	779	*Fleming, Newark-on-Trent	265
Eifl, Pwllheili	927	*Fletcher, Cleator Moor	213
Eivissa, Cala Llonga, Ibiza, Spain	1807	Flint, Flint	1509
Eko, Ebute-Metta, Nigeria	1851	*Flixton Shepherd Eastwood, Flixton	1173
Eland, W. Vale, nr. Halifax	493	*Florence Nightingale, Royal National Hotel,	
Eldon, Portishead	807	London WC1H	44
*Eleanor Cross, Cheshunt	991	*Folkestone, Folkestone	380
*Elevation, Burnopfield	1112	Forest of Lebanon, Nerja, Malaga, Spain	1752
Elffin, Caernarvon	321	*Forest of Waltham, Harlow	1444
*Elias de Derham, Salisbury	443	*Fortescue, South Molton	9
Elizabethan, Nelson	1174	Fortis Green, Southgate	1104
Elliott, Plymouth	169	*Fortitude, Truro	78
Else, Weston-Super-Mare	102	Fortitude, Plymouth	66
Elstree and Radlett, Radlett	1315	Foster, Dursley	1134
*Emblematic, M.M.H.	350	Foundation, Mark Masons' Hall	921
*Enfield, Gun Tavern,	772	*Four Cardinal Virtues, Nantwich	723
*Entente Cordiale, London SW1A	1933	Forty Steps	1773
*Eos, Gravesend	1777	*Fowke, Leicester	19
*Eothen, Victoria, Hong Kong	264	Fraternidad, La Paz, Bolivia	1790
Epworth, 10 Duke St., London SW1	1771	Fratres Calami Aearlique, Sutton	1704
*Equator, London W13	1889	Fratres Scriptabacrum, St. Albans	1508

ALPHABETICAL LIST OF MARK LODGES—continued

Frederick Wheeler, Croydon	1407	*Guernsey, St. Peter Port	1614
*Freeman, Bury St. Edmunds	105	*Guild of Freeman, London M.C., Clerkenwell	647
Freshfield, Southport	1007	Guyana Installed Mark Masters, Georgetown	1849
*Friendship and Care, Sindlesham	1555	Gwynedd Lodge of Installed Mark Masters,	
Friendship, Plymouth	16	Bangor	1708
Friendship, Middleton	1459		
Friendship, Southport	1549	*H. A. Mann, Sutton	1197
*Friendship, Iberia, Coin, Spain	1694	*Hackworth, Shildon	761
*Friendship from Service	1313	Haddenham, Thame	1629
Furness, Barrow-in-Furness	36	*Hailsham, Hertsmonceux	1234
*F. W. Broadbent, Bolton	1132	*Halcyon, Mark Masters' Hall	1118
*Fylde, Blackpool	296	Halifax, Halifax	706
		*Hallam, Clevedon	730
Gaetano Filangieri, Genova & various	1934	*Halsey, Royston	1489
Galway, Nottingham	940	Haltwhistle, Haltwhistle	1278
*Gardiner, Aspatria	738	Hamerkin, Deventer, Netherlands	1390
Gariep, Springbok, South Africa	1662	Hammerton, Gibralta	516
Garnett, Lancaster	146	*Hammersmith, Twickenham	211
Garston, Liverpool	942	Hampshire and Isle of Wight Installed	
*Gauntlet, Harrow	1469	Mark Masters, Chandler's Ford	1687
*Gawthorpe, Burnley	1014	Hampshire and Isle of Wight Provincial	
*Geoffrey Short, Trowbridge	971	Grand Stewards, Botley	1796
George Borrow, E. Dereham	1077	*Hampton Court, Twickenham	448
George Farnworth Nuttall, Accrington	1405	Hampton Parva, Littlehampton	1117
*George Graveley, Grays	461	*Hantune, Wolverhampton	1085
George Harradon, Liverpool	956	Harmonia, Rio de Janiero	1854
*George Norman, Yatton	967	Harmonia, Belgrade, Serbia	1919
*George Parker, Uxbridge	1316	*Harmony, Fareham	875
George Washington, Washington	1626	*Harmony, Camperdown, S.A.	1578
*Ghana, Accra	1217	*Harold W. Richardson, Brighton	1490
*Gibraltar, Gibraltar	43	Harpenden, Harpenden and St. Albans	1254
*Gibralta, M.M.H.	1336	Harte, West Hartlepool	740
Gijsbrecht van Amstel, Amsterdam,		*Hartford, Bedlington	546
Netherlands	1384	*Hartismere, Diss	957
*Gild of Good Fellowship, Wisbech	1410	Haste Hill, Kenton	1391
Gilkirke, Barnoldswick	812	Haven, N. Shields	750
*Giorgio Vasari, Arezzo & various	1916	Haven, Altrincham	1543
*Gladsmuir, M.M.H., London	367	*Hawarden, Hawarden	838
*Gloucester, Gloucester	439	*Hawton, Ivybridge	100
*Godson, Dudley	330	*Haywra, Harrogate	525
Godstow, Oxford	1546	*Headstone, Kenton	931
Golden Harvest, Parktown, Johannesburg	1696	Hebburn, Hebburn	1339
Golden Jubilee, Workington	1821	Hector Young, Totton	1395
*Golden Square, M.M.H.	856	Heffle, Burwash Common	1530
Good Fellowship, Umtata, S. Africa	1148	*Heinz Ritter Friendship,	
Goodwin, Bristol	1563	Mönchengladbach, Germany	1432
*Gordon, Gravesend	364	*Hemel Hempstead, St. Albans	1291
Gordon, Manchester	1034	*Henniker, West Ealing M.C., London	315
Gorllewin Cymru Mark Grand		*Henry, Frizington	216
Officers, Llanelli	1700	Henry Byrde, Kandy, Sri Lanka	475
Gosforth, Wallsend	463	Herne Bay, Herne Bay	771
*Gosport, Gosport	305	*Herschell, Slough	376
Gothic, Mexborough	1018	*Hertford, Hertford	366
*Gough, Shelton	45	*Hertford Military, Birmingham	408
Goulburn, Manchester	680	*Herts Installed Mark Masters, St. Albans	1121
Grafton, Mark Masons' Hall	415	Hesperides, Santa Brigada, Canary Islands	1689
Grainger, Newcastle upon Tyne	1147	*Het Sticht, Amersfoort, Netherlands	1516
Grand Masters', M.M.H.		*Hexham, Hexham	1161
Grand Stewards', M.M.H.		*Hibernia, M.M.H.	431
*Granville, Deal	390	*High Cross, M.M.H.	284
*Grays Thurrock, Grays	507	*Highgate, London WC1B	1909
*Greenwich, M.M.H.	332	*Hillbrow, Johannesburg	741
*Grosvenor, Twickenham	144	*Hillingdon Heath, Uxbridge	1196
*Guanabara, Rio de Janeiro	1156	Hindhead, Bordon, Hants.	1049

145

ALPHABETICAL LIST OF MARK LODGES—continued

*Hiram, M.M.H.	13	*John o'Gaunt, Gainsborough	172
*Hiram, Taradale, New Zealand	272	John Peel, Carlisle	1020
*Hollandia, The Hague	1565	John Pounds, Portsmouth	809
Holmersdale, Ramsgate	129	John Spencer, Belper	1566
Holsworthy, Devon	1727	*Joppa, Wallasey	11
Holte, Birmingham	1041	*Jordan, Torquay	319
*Holywell, Holywell	1394	Joseph Cook, Ripley	917
*Horus, Mark Masons' Hall	633	*Joseph Moffett, Radlett	1358
*Hothampton, Bognor	703	*Joseph Whittall, Lodge of Installed	
*Hotspur with Coquetdale, Alnwick	135	Mark Masters, Wolverhampton	
Hova, Brighton	168	Shrewsbury, Rugeley	1392
Hoveden Lodge of Inst. M.M., Howden	1681	*Jubilee, Ulverston	375
Howe, Birmingham	T.I.	*Jubilee, St. Helier, C.I.	1493
*Howe, Loughborough	21		
*Humber, Hull	182	Kafue, Kitwe, Zimbabwe	1212
*Hundred of Hoo, Hoo (Rochester)	1326	*Keep, Clitheroe	911
Hungerford, Newbery	1342	*Kelvin, Mark Masons' Hall	742
*Hunter, Rhyl	324	*Kent Dale, Kendal	195
*Hyde, Hyde	868	*Kent Installed Mark Masters, Maidstone	999
		*Kentish, Welling	857
Icknield, Luton	1625	*Kenton, Kenton	901
*Idris, Barmouth & Bala	821	*Kenya, Kenya	952
Ilford St. Mary, Shenfield	1470	Kerala, Calicut, Madras	1225
*Ilkeston, Ilkeston	373	*Keys of Münster, Frankfurt, am Main	
Imperial, London, SW1Y	643	Germany	1515
Imperial, Blackpool	1276	*Keystone, Mark Masons' Hall	3
Indabo, Darlington	1936	*Keystone, Secunderabad, Madras	81
Industry, Gateshead	293	*Keystone, M.M.H., London	107
*Industry and Merit, Bombay	836	*Keystone, Newport	109
*Inglewood, Penrith	462	*Keystone, Harare, Zimbabwe	573
Integrity, Shaw, nr. Oldham	1369	*Kidsgrove, Kidsgrove	1503
*Integrity, Wakefield	110	*King Charles the Martyr, Tunbridge Wells	267
*Installed Masters Lodge of		King Edward, Carletonville, Transvaal	941
Reflection, Wotton-under-Edge	1429	*King Harold, Cheshunt	1109
Invicta, Ashford	378	*King Solomon, London Masonic	
Irenic, Mark Masons' Hall	899	Centre, EC1	385
*Isaac Newton University, Cambridge	112	*King Solomon's Quarries, Mark Masons' Hall	828
Isle of Wedmore, Wedmore	1912	*Kingston Keystone, Kingston, Jamaica	368
*Isma, Mark Masons' Hall	996	Kinson, Bournemouth	1163
*Israel, Cape Town, S.A.	558	*Kintore, Croydon	333
*Israel, Liverpool	1561	Kipling and Burns, Dunstable	1755
Italia, Mark Masons' Hall	1467	*Kirkstone, Liverpool	1249
Itawa, Naola, Zambia	1442	Kition, Larnaca, Cyprus	1904
*Ituni, Berbice, Guyana	1882	*Knareborough Castle, Knareborough	768
Iyver Ha Pluvenn, Perranporth	1884	*Knight of Malta, Hinckley	30
		*Knock Murton, Cleator	1761
Jabulani, Eshowe, Zululand	1179	*Knole, Sevenoaks	876
*Jacob Van Lennep, The Hague, Netherlands	1283	*Kypros, Episkopi, Cyprus	1835
James Herbert Cain, Peel, I.O.M.	1517	Kyrle, Ross-on-Wye	1349
*James Jack, Georgetown, Guyana	1637		
*James Parson, Watford	974	L'Esperance, Belgium	1653
*James Terry, Cheshunt	556	Ladysmith, Ladysmith, S.A.	528
James Webster, Brighton	1795	*La France, Mark Masons' Hall	459
Jarrow, Jarrow	701	*La Marque D'Alliance, Champion, Belgium	1587
*Javea, Javea, Alicante, Spain	1688	La Marque de Lorraine	1815
Jeppestown, Park Town, Johannesburg	863	*La Marque d'Union, Brussels	1624
*Jersey, Twyford	257	*Lancastrians, Manchester	689
Joey Dunlop, Lutterworth	1881	*Langdon Hills, Orsett	1628
*Johann Gutenberg, Mark Masons' Hall	976	*Langley, Cardiff	28
*John Aston Wade, Lodge of I.M.M.,		*Lansdowne, Chippenham	1035
Beverley	1428	*Lanzarote, Arrecife	1902
John Burr, St. Albans	1824	*Lapis Anguli, Bilbao	1918
John Dee, Rome & various	1915	Lascelles, Sheffield	887
John of Gaunt, Gent	1928	*Lathom, Southport	268

ALPHABETICAL LIST OF MARK LODGES—continued

*Latimer, St. Albans	962	*Macdonald, Mark Masons' Hall	104
Lawrence, Chorley	313	*Macdonald Ritchie, Madras	160
Lealtad, La Paz, Bolivia	1754	*Machen, Birmingham	698
*Lea, Moat Lane, Luton	405	*Macclesfield, Macclesfield	964
*Lea Valley, Cheshunt	909	*Madrid, Madrid, Spain	1722
Lebanon, Liverpool	T.I.	*Maen Clo, Llandudno	1451
*Lechmere, Worcester	59	Magdala, Nottingham	1359
Legiolium, Castleford	457	Maguncor, Mark Masons' Hall	833
*Leigh, Leigh	1322	*Maius, Risca	1031
Leofric, Bromyard	1650	Malaysia, Singapore	1286
*Leopold, Sindlesham	235	*Mallet and Chisel, Mark Masons' Hall	5
Les Disciples de Salomon, Louvain, Belgium	1603	*Malling Abbey, Malling	1425
*Leverhulme, Birkenhead	1325	Malvern Priory, Malvern	1351
*Lewis, Auckland, New Zealand	49	*Manadon, Plymouth	1076
*Lewis, Lewes	391	Mancetter, Atherstone	1883
*Lewis, Bombay, India	648	*Manchester Engineers, Manchester	1059
Lewis, Torquay	1284	Manchester Keystone, Manchester	745
*Lewis, Park Royal, Natal	1223	Manchester University, Manchester	1001
*Leyland, Leyland	1002	*Mandalay, Bromley	1886
*Libanon, Terneuzen, Netherlands	1488	*Manica, Mutare, Zimbabwe	550
*Lightcliffe, Hipperholme	715	*Manor of Bensham, Croydon	1167
*Lilford, Thrapston	471	Manor of Bexley, Sidcup	1448
*Linden Acre, Wokingham	1568	*Manor of Chatham, Gillingham	584
Lingfield, Redhill	1419	*Mansel, Carmarthen	116
Liverpool, Liverpool	393	Mansfield Manor, Mansfield	654
*Lliedi, Llanelli	820	*Mapesbury, The Gun Tavern, E1 6AG	1105
Llantarnam, Cwmbran	1422	Marckdael, Breda, Netherlands	1562
Llynfi Valley, Maesteg	1592	*Margate, Margate	1073
Lodge of Charity, Byrn, Wigan	935	*Mark of Industry, Orsett	1413
Lodge of Enlightenment, Twickenham	1846	Mark of Enterprise, Brussels, Belgium	1673
*Lodge of Good Report, Manchester	1309	Mark of Love and Remembrance, Rochford	1718
*Lodge of Harmony, Faversham	984	Mark Lodge of Progress, Caerphilly	1670
Lodge of Installed Mark Masters of Zimbabwe, Bulawayo	1371	*Mark of True Friendship, Wickford	1480
Lodge of Peace and Unity, Birmingham	1066	Mark Provincial Grand Stewards Lodge of Surrey, Croydon	1726
Lodge of St. Andrew, Kingston Upon Hull	1130	*Marlborough, Woodstock	980
*Lodge of St. George, Plymouth	383	Marple	1780
Lodge of St. Simon, Plymouth	1116	Massada, Altrincham	1855
Lodge of Sympathy, Gravesend	1379	*Matthew Clarke, Birmingham	1012
Lodge of the West Gate, Barnstaple	1180	*Mayflower, Wickford	1536
Londesborough, Bridlington	291	*Mayflower, Spilsby	1899
*London East Africa, Mark Masons' Hall	1604	*Maymyo, Maymyo, Burma	574
*London Installed Mark Masters, Mark Masons' Hall	1227	*Medina, Cowes, I.O.W.	140
		Mediterranean, Gibraltar	278
London Mark Provincial Grand Stewards Mark Masons' Hall	1870	Medway, Paddock Wood	811
		*Meeanee, Karachi, Pakistan	637
*London West Africa, Mark Masons' Hall	1457	Melandra, Glossop	934
Lord Bolton Daylight, Hull	785	*Melrose Keystone, Jamaica	1424
*Lord Carmichael, Calcutta, India	642	Melville Jennings, Colombo, Sri Lanka	1250
Loughrigg, Ambleside	805	Memorial Lodge of Installed Mark Masters, Malton	1452
Love and Honour, Falmouth	94	*Menatschim, Oxford	1838
*Loveland, Eastleigh	674	Mendip, Glastonbury	781
*Loventium, Aberayron	1287	*Mercia, Spalding	1240
*Lowestoft, Lowestoft	686	*Mercury, Farnborough	777
Loxley, Uttoxeter	1484	Meridian, Redruth	73
Loyalty, Accrington	829	*Meridian, Mark Masons' Hall	936
*Loyalty, Croydon	914	Meridies, Botley	1798
Luanshya, Zambia	1668	*Merlaue Weir, Marlow	1510
*Lucayan, Freeport, Bahamas	1552	*Mersey, Runcorn	824
*Ludwig Zum Flammenden Stern, Steinfurt Burg, Germany	1642	Metham, Plymouth	96
		*Middlesborough, Middlesbrough	276
Luz Y Concordia, Cochabamba, Bolivia	1879	*Middlesex Installed Mark Masters, Twickenham	1218
*Lyegrove, Downend, Bristol	218		

147

ALPHABETICAL LIST OF MARK LODGES—continued

*Middlesex St. David's, Kenton	1063
*Middleton, E. Lancs.	1303
Middlewich, Middlewich	902
Midhurst, Midhurst	1009
*Mid-Sussex, Horsham	449
*Milestone, Mark Masons' Hall	1000
Millennium, Sittingbourne	1802
*Mill Hill, London E.1	883
*Minchenden Oak, Southgate, N.14	1152
*Minerva, Hull	12
*Misbourne, Beaconsfield	1087
*Mojacar, Mojácar, Almeria, Spain	1877
*Monmouthshire Installed Mark Master, Pontypool	1447
*Montserrat, St. Michael, Barbados	1864
Monument, Penrith	1567
Monument, Wellington	1295
*Morecambe, Morecambe	716
Moriah, Alkmaar, Netherlands	1504
*Morley, Batley	1905
*Morpeth, Morpeth	691
Mosaic, Dudley	1136
*Mosam Trajectum, Maastricht, Netherlands	1376
*Moseley, Moseley	667
*Moseley, Birtley	925
*Moses Montefiore, São Paulo	1819
*Mossley, Ashton-under-Lyne	1381
Mount Edgumbe, Cambourne	417
*Mount Mawenzi, Selian, Arusha, Tanzania	906
Mount Sinai	1803
Multum in Parvo	1775
Murray, Wigan	490
*Nailsea, Nailsea	1548
Namptwyche, Nantwich	1206
*Nandi Border, Eldoret, Kenya	1198
Natal Installed Mark Masters, Pietermaritzburg	486
*Natalia, Pietermaritzburg, Natal	252
Naval and Military, Portland	634
*Naze Tower, Frinton-on-Sea	1380
*Neath, Neath	1125
Needles, Freshwater, I.O.W.	1246
*Nene, Sleaford	427
Nepos, Newcastle upon Tyne	1155
*Neston, Neston	1445
*New Era, Mark Masons' Hall	176
New Forest, Lymington	611
New Morning, London SW1Y	1921
*New Quarries, Salzburg, Austria	1903
*New Sarum, Harare, Zimbabwe	1440
New Temple, Chorley	1438
Newbiggin by the Sea, Newbiggin by the Sea	1756
*Newgate, Newcastle upon Tyne	1141
*Newstead, Nottingham	T.I.
Newton, Auckland, N.Z.	280
Newton, Ashton-in-Makerfield	1003
Nightingale, Winslow	1768
Noah's Ark, Tipton	1401
*Noel, Surbiton	505
Noel Boardman, Walsall, Aldridge	933
Norman, Eastleigh	1279
Norman Rolfe, Peterborough	1643
North and East Middlesex Lodge of Installed Mark Masters, M.M.H. or various	873
*North Devon Union, Ilfracombe	540
*North Shropshire, Ellesmere	840
North Staffordshire, Stoke-on-Trent	960
North Wales Lodge of Installed Mark Masters, Connah's Quay	1591
North Wales Provincial Grand Stewards, Rhyl	1929
*North Wold, Kenton	1190
*Northampton Castle, Northampton	1346
Northern Heights, Sutton	989
*Northern Transvaal, Polokwane	966
*Northumberland and Berwick-upon-Tweed, Newcastle upon Tyne	T.I.
Northwic, Norwich	770
Nottingham Excelsior, Nottingham	1464
Nottingham Jubilee, Nottingham	1506
*Nyanza, Kisumu, Kenya	1636
*Oak Tree, Bisley, Surrey	1839
Oakleaf, Grays	1126
*Oakley, Basingstoke	886
Oakley, Bromley	1584
Old Kent, Mark Masons' Hall	T.I.
Old Patesian, Cheltenham	1387
*Old Rectory, Caversham	1398
*Old York, Bradford	T.I.
*Oliva La Safor, Gandia, Valencia, Spain	1823
*Onslow, Café Royal, W.1	361
Orchestral, Mark Masons' Hall	1534
Orient, Calcutta, Bengal	531
Oriental, Jesmond	1890
*Orkney, Gaborone, Botswana	1335
Ormskirk, Ormskirk	734
*Ormskirk Priory, Ormskirk	1019
Orpington, Bromley	1083
*Oxford and Cambridge University, 10 Duke St., St. James's, W.1	504
Paddock Wood, Paddock Wood	1292
Pangbourne, Pangbourne	1094
*Panmure, Mark Masons' Hall	139
*Panmure, East London, S.A.	435
*Patron Saints, Buenos Aires, Argentina	746
*Peace, Uppermill	681
Penfro, Pembroke Dock	1102
Pendle, Padiham	695
*Penshaw, Philadelphia	1055
Pentangle, Rochester	682
*Perak, Ipoh, Malaysia	663
*Percy, Guildford	114
*Percy, Stockton-on-Tees	122
Persevere, Brighton	732
*Perseverance, Curacao, N.A.	184
*Perseverance, Blackburn	403
*Perseverance, Halesowen	733
Perseverance, Sidmouth	822
Perseverance, Singapore	1935
*Peveril, Douglas, I.O.M.	323
Peveril of the Peak, New Mills	1177
Philadelphia of Inst. M.M., Leyland	1646
*Philanthropic, Kings Lynn and Hunstanton	538
*Phoenix, Portsmouth	2
Phoenix, Kingston, Jamaica	242

148

ALPHABETICAL LIST OF MARK LODGES—continued

Name	No.
*Phoenix, Glen Cairn, C.P., S. Africa	502
Phoenix, Nicosia, Cyprus	1923
*Pico Della Mirandola, Roma and other Italian cities	1896
*Pickwick, London WC1H	997
*Picton Castle, Haverfordwest	297
Pilgrims, Wrotham	1233
*Piscator, London WC1H	1363
Pleiades, Totnes	675
*Pleydell-Bouverie, Godalming	955
Plympton Erle, Plympton	1100
*Polytechnic, Blakemore Hotel	1071
*Pontefract, Pontefract	878
Ponteland, Ponteland	1550
*Porchester, Newbury	27
Portal, Barnsley	127
*Portal, Frome	155
Portcullis, Langport	1656
*Porthcawl, Porthcawl	1377
*Portland, Portland	133
Port Harcourt, Port Harcourt, Nigeria	1927
*Port Natal, Durban, Natal	288
*Portsdown, Cosham	739
*Portsmouth, Havant	17
Portus Abonae, Avonmouth	1793
*Portwall, Chepstow	1436
Potters Clay, Harlow	1399
*Powys, Kettering	685
*Premier, Lagos, S. Nigeria	624
*Premier Siam, Phuket, Thailand	1893
*Prescot, Prescot	903
*Preston, Preston	143
Pride of Surrey, Sutton	1738
*Prince Edward, Sowerby Bridge	14
*Prince Leopold, Mark Masons' Hall	238
Prince Leopold, Ripon	352
Prince Michael of Kent, Twickenham	1720
Prince Michael of Kent, St. George, Barbados	1913
Prince Setanta, Poulton Le Fylde	1446
*Prince of Wales, Mark Masons' Hall	4
*Prince of Wales, St. Helens	466
*Principality, Cardiff	1057
Prins van Oranje, Antwerp	1875
Priory, Whalley	693
*Progress, Audenshaw	1577
*Progress, Preston	898
Progress, Birmingham	1746
*Pro Minimis, Mark Masons' Hall	1160
Prosperity, Johannesburg	905
Provincial Directors of Ceremonies	1813
Provincial Grand Stewards, Royston	1880
*Prudence and Verity, Mark Masons' Hall	932
*Public Schools, Mark Masons' Hall	791
Pudsey, Pudsey	658
*Pulborough, Pulborough	1245
Purdown, Bristol	1338
*Pymmes Park, Buckhurst Hill	1056
Quadratic, Twickenham	895
Quantock, Bridgwater	749
*Quatuor Legati, Bolton	1165
Queensway, Liverpool 3	1331
Quesada Summer, Alicante	1867
Quill and Key, Birmingham	1901
Radnor, Salisbury	853
Rainham, Orsett	859
*Ravi, Lahore, Pakistan	673
Ravenscroft, Barnet	920
Ravensworth, Sunderland	718
Raza, Amritsar, N. India	1255
*Rectitude, Rawtenstall	18
Redcar, Redcar	804
*Redhill, Redhill	1285
*Regis, Old Hill	862
*Regnum, Chichester	568
*Remembrance, Birmingham	1256
*Remigius, Lincoln	117
Rhaeadr Gwy, Llandrindod Wells	1318
Ribblesdale, Nottingham	1299
*Richmond, Richmond	808
*Richard Watts, Chatham	1461
*Ridgmont, Bolton	1539
Ridley, Blyth	1439
*Rift Valley, Naivasha, Kenya	1602
*Rising Star, Bloemfontein, S.A.	885
Risingham, Bellingham	1033
*Rivacre, Ellesmere Port	1016
*Robert Burns, Manchester	1613
*Robert Mummery, Cannock	1304
*Roberts, Rochdale	24
*Robinson, West Malling	255
Rock, Jamalpur, Bengal	598
*Rock of Hope, Dar-es-Salaam	816
*Rockingham, Corby	1645
Roentgen Portal, London	1767
Romsey, Southampton	910
Ronald Chitty, Framlingham	1715
Rosario, Buenos Aires, Argentina	507
*Rose, Croydon	534
*Rose and Lily, F.M.H., London	354
Rose and Thistle, Wigan	158
*Rose of Minden, Herford, Germany	1498
*Rose of York, Ashton-under-Lyne	1010
Rosewalk, Radlett	1585
*Rother, Rotherham	651
*Rottingdean, Brighton	918
Round Table, Dore	1664
*Round Table and Rotary, Newport	1630
Royal Air Force	1774
Royal Colonial Institute, Mark Masons' Hall	728
Royal Connaught, Brighton	409
*Royal Cumberland, Bath	T.I.
*Royal Forest of Dean, Newham-on-Severn	340
Royal George, Kensington	608
*Royal Keystone, Kingston, Jamaica	240
*Royal Naval, Mark Masons' Hall	239
*Royal Naval College, Mark Masons' Hall	294
*Royal Oak, Sidcup	416
*Royal Oak Tree, Buckhurst Hill	1244
*Royal Prince of Wales, Trinidad	1828
*Royal Savoy, Cheshunt	355
*Royal Sussex, Brighton	75
Royal Sussex, Bath	177
*Royal Victoria	1368
Royal York, Nottingham	500
*Rugby, Rugby	776
Ruspini, Mark Masons' Hall	363

ALPHABETICAL LIST OF MARK LODGES—continued

Lodge	No.
*Russell, Tavistock	23
*Russell, Ootacamund, Madras	157
*Rutland, Melton Mowbray	1051
*Ryton, Ryton	1714
Saint Breock, Wadebridge	1605
St. Aidan, Blackhill	1145
St. Alban's, Nottingham	344
St. Alban's, St. Alban's	1108
St. Aldhelm, Malmesbury	1531
*St. Alkmund, Duffield	595
*St. Andrew's, Salford	34
*St. Andrew's, Eastleigh	63
*St. Andrew's, Gillingham	237
*St. Andrew's, Farnham	806
St. Andrew's, Stanley	854
St. Andrew's, Midsomer Norton	1924
*St. Anne's, Looe	351
*St. Aubyn, Devonport	64
*St. Austell, St. Austell	275
*St. Austin's, Warrington	479
*St. Barnabas, Aylesbury	97
*St. Bartholomew, Wednesbury	650
*St. Botolph, Boston	946
St. Bride's, Milford Haven	729
St. Cecilia, Watford	1701
St. Chad, Mirfield	374
St. Christopher's, Sutton Coldfield	1128
St. Columba, St. Columb	700
St. Cuthberga, Wimbourne	99
*St. Cuthbert's, Berwick-upon-Tweed	192
*St. Cuthbert's, Howden	743
*St. David's, Llandudno	38
*St. Editha's, Tamworth	1426
*St. Edward the Martyr, Shaftesbury	1095
St. Edward's, Leek	1182
*St. Egwin, Eversham	1135
*St. Eilian, Amlwch	360
*St. Ethelbert, Hereford	243
*St. George, Exeter	15
*St. George, Cape Town, S.A.	551
St. George, Liverpool	553
*St. George, Helensville, N.Z.	579
St. George of Colombo, Colombo, Sri Lanka	464
*St. George's, Gillingham	1061
St. George's, Leicester	1133
St. George's, Bewdley	1920
*St. Giles', Wrexham	760
St. Giles', Uxbridge	1017
St. Grwst, Llanrwst	1772
St. Guthlac, Market Deeping	1122
*St. Hiev, Bingley	1079
St. Hilary, Birkenhead	1081
St. Illtyd, Brynadler	784
*St. Ivo, St. Ives	607
*St. James, Handsworth	318
*St. James, M.M.M.	1895
*St. James's, 10 Duke St.	1840
St. John, Plymouth	50
*St. John's, Bolton	T.I.
*St. John's, Abergavenny	214
St. John's, Torquay	1029
*St. John's, Wigton	1037
*St. John's Wood, M.M.H.	1124
*St. John the Baptist, Penzance	404
*St. Katherine's, Wickford	1026
St. Kitts, St. Kitts	1833
*St. Laurence, Redditch	893
St. Lawrence, South Shields	1093
St. Luke's, Camborne	1011
St. Mabon, Ruabon	919
*St. Margaret of Antioch, Ifield	1520
St. Margaret's, Blackwood	1478
*St. Mark's, Mark Masons' Hall	1
St. Mark's, Poona	668
*St. Martin's, Canterbury	262
*St. Martin, Alfreton	414
*St. Martin's, Liskeard	379
St. Martin's, Birmingham	959
St. Mary's, Blandford	121
*St. Mary's, Thame	1242
St. Matthew, Barton-on-Humber	1239
*St. Michael's, Helston	175
*St. Michael's, Sittingbourne	1089
*St. Nicholas, Harwich	413
*St. Nicholas, Bodmin	1188
*St. Oswald, Scunthorpe	387
St. Oswald, Oswestry	982
*St. Pancras, M.M.H.	494
St. Paul's, Pierrefonds, Quebec	131
St. Paul's, Limassol, Cyprus	455
St. Paul's, Birmingham	870
*St. Paul's, Sao Paulo, Brazil	961
*St. Peter's, Castlegate, York	1008
St. Peter's, Market Harborough	1078
St. Peter's, Tiverton	187
*St. Peter's, Wigmore, Gillingham	842
Saint Peter's, Mansfield	1513
St. Peter and St. Paul, Newport Pagnell	163
St. Peter-in-Thanet, Broadstairs	1053
St. Piran's, Perranporth	1367
St. Seiriol, Holyhead	688
*St. Swithun's, Crowle	445
St. Thomas, Stockton-on-Tees	1511
*St. Tydfil, Merthyr Tydfil	639
*St. Wilfrid's, Alford	209
*St. Winnold, Downham Market	1187
*St. Wulfram's, Grantham	916
*Salford, Salford	994
Saltburn, Saltburn-on-Sea	1532
Sanctuary, Buckfastleigh	1370
*Sandbach, Sandbach	1609
*Sanderman Stat Veritas, Calcutta, Bengal	220
*Sanderstead, Croydon	1742
*Sandhurst, Bombay, India	514
Sandwich Haven, Sandwich	797
*Sanitarian, Mark Masons' Hall	786
*San Juan, Callosa d'en Sarriá Alicante, Spain	1810
Santa Catarina, Florianopolis	1926
*Santa Cruz	1794
*Sarnian, Guernsey	425
Savage Club, Mark Masons' Hall	469
*Saxon Shore, Tollesbury	1319
*Saxony, Berlin, Germany	1600
*Saye and Sele, Sidcup	309
Scarlett, Burnley	189
*Scarsdale, Chesterfield	529
Scawfell, Seascale	1397

ALPHABETICAL LIST OF MARK LODGES—*continued*

Schieland, Rotterdam, Netherlands	1414	*Spennymoor, Spennymoor	981	
*Scholars in Amity, Letchworth & St. Albans	1710	*Spes Bona, Port Elizabeth, S.A.	253	
*Science, Wincanton	128	*Sphinx, Port Alfred, S.A.	576	
Scorton, Garstang	1103	*Sprig of Acacia, Barnet	1114	
Scots, Mark Masons' Hall	406	Springs, Springs, Transvaal	707	
Sebakwe, Kwe Kwe, Zimbabwe	1267	Spurn and Humber, Cleethorpes	1199	
Secretarius, Salford	1932	Stability, Penarth	758	
*Semper Fidelis, St. Anne's-on-Sea	880	Stability, Stourbridge	1281	
*Semper Fidelis, M.M.H., London	1473	Stabroek, Georgetown, Guyana	1596	
Semper Paratus, Manchester	852	*Staffordshire Knot, Stafford	541	
Serendipity, Javea, Alicante, Spain	1744	Staindrop, Staindrop	1274	
*Severn, Bridgnorth	1617	*Staines, Staines	858	
Sewell, Egremont	421	Stamford, Sale	148	
Seychelles	1776	Stanger, Stanger, Natal	575	
*Seymour, Leamington Spa	606	*Stanley, Andenshaw	1454	
*Shakespeare, Warwick	40	*Stanstead Abbots, Sawbridgeworth	1809	
Shalden, Alton	988	*Star, Twickenham	499	
Shameen, Hong Kong	832	*Star in the East, Scarborough	95	
Shelford Priory, Nottingham	818	Star in the West, Kenton	928	
Shipley, Gateshead	1271	*Star of Burma, Rangoon, Burma	88	
Shorncliffe and Hythe, Hythe	767	*Starkie, Accrington	159	
*Shropshire, Shrewsbury	444	*Stayley, Hyde	597	
Sierra Leone	1797	Steadfast, Darlington	846	
*Signa Bene, Alcester	1501	*Steanforde, Stamford	752	
*Silhill, Knowle	972	*Stechford, Stechford, Birmingham	747	
*Silver River, Montevideo, Uruguay	628	*Stevenage, Letchworth	1404	
Silurean, Kington	1677	Stilus et Denarius, Upminster	1735	
*Simon de Montfort, Leicester	194	Stokesley Lodge of Inst. M.M.	1711	
*Simon de St. Liz, Northampton	245	*Stoneleigh, Sutton	995	
*Sincerity, Plymouth	35	Stony Gate, Leicester	751	
Sincerity, Sheffield	943	Stow-on-the-Wold, Stow-on-the-Wold	1374	
*Sincerity, Wallasey	327	*Stradbroke, March	603	
Sir Alfred Robbins, Launceston	1514	Stradbroke, Cosham	874	
Sir Arthur Holbrook, Ryde, I.O.W.	951	Stanhope, Stanhope	1551	
*Sir Bevil Granville, Bude	1231	Stanstead Abbots	1809	
Sir Charles Tache-Menson, Accra, Ghana	1930	Stratton Hills, Church Stratton	1450	
*Sir Donald McLean, Waitara, N.Z.	1064	Streonshalh, Whitby	337	
*Sir Francis Burdett, M.M.H.	181	*Strode, Plymouth	696	
*Sir Francis Drake, Plymouth	617	*Stroud, Stroud	1039	
*Sir Frederick Alban, Swansea	1455	*Studholme, Mark Masons' Hall	197	
*Sir John Cotton, Biggleswade	1507	*Stuart, Kempston	434	
Sir William Crosthwaite Mark Grand Officers, Pocklington	1671	*Sub-Urban, Twickenham	1521	
		Succoth, Haarlem, Netherlands	1421	
*Sivangnanam, Trivandrum, Madras	877	Sunbeam, Germiston, Transvaal	508	
*Skelmersdale, Ashton-under-Lyne	141	Supera Moras, Bolton	1042	
*Sketty Hall	1685	*Surrey Installed Mark Masters, Croydon	1219	
Slough, Slough	1648	*Sussex, Kingston, Jamaica	42	
*Snowdonia, Bangor	259	*Sussex Installed Mark Masters, Brighton	1158	
*Socrates, Huntingdon	794	Sussex Mark Provincial Grand Stewards, Brighton	1747	
Somerdale, Keynsham	1608			
*Somerset Installed M.M., Taunton	1652	*Sutcliffe, Grimsby	188	
South Canterbury, Christchurch, N.Z.	300	*Suthburgh, Sudbury	1210	
*South Shropshire, Ludlow	1150	*Swaziland, Manzini, Swaziland	1298	
*South Wales Installed Mark Masters, Cardiff	1201	*Swindon Keystone, Swindon	401	
South Wales Mark Provincial Stewards, Bridgend	1829	*Sydenham, Penge, S.E.20	835	
*Southdown, Haywards Heath	64	Sykes, Driffield	1830	
Southern, San Fernando, Trinidad, W. Indies	1897	Table Fellowship, Surbiton	1841	
Southern Cross, Lomas de Zamora Argentina	627	*Talbot, Swansea	179	
		Talbot, Whitchurch	1021	
*Southport, Southport	473	*Taquah, Tarkwa, Ghana	1887	
*Southwark, M.M. Hall	22	*Tarporley, Tarporley	1522	
*Sparrenburg, Kassel, Germany	1575	Teks, Kinross, South Africa	1456	
Spencer, Yelverton, Devon	1495	Teifi, Cardigan	1441	

ALPHABETICAL LIST OF MARK LODGES—continued

Lodge	No.
*Teme Valley, Tenbury Wells	1260
*Temperance, Todmorden	56
*Temperance, Birmingham	629
Temperance, Liverpool	774
Temperance, Brighton	978
*Temple, 10 Duke St., St. James's, S.W.1	173
*Temple, Bromley	322
Temple Builders, various, Spain	1869
*Temple of Uxbridge, Uxbridge	1393
*Tenerife, Tenerife, Spain	1826
*Ter Duinen, Belgium	1753
*Tewkesbury Abbey, Tewkesbury	1238
*Thames, Henley-on-Thames	1183
*Thameside, Grays	1463
The Aireferry, Goole	1769
*The Beacon Centenary, York	1583
The Carrick, Isle of Man	1558
The Chalfonts, Beaconsfield	1779
The Croft, Aldridge	1524
*The Collingwood, Guildford	1669
*The Curfew, Chertsey	1411
*The Derbyshire Lodge of Installed Mark Masters, Belper	1706
*The East Africa Lodge of Installed Mark Masters, Nairobi	1787
The Easterford, Kelvedon	1781
*The Edwin Perry Morgan, Perrinporth, Cornwall	1632
The Farmers', Reading	1784
*The Friendly, Kingston, Jamaica	1559
*The Geoffrey Dicker, Diss	1906
The George Stephenson, Wylam	1527
The Goose and Gridiron, Rio de Janeiro	1888
*The Graftonian, Towcester	1243
The Great Ouse Valley, Olney	1675
*The Harry Wilson, Nuneaton	1574
*The Haven	1732
The Jubilee, Stafford	1485
The Kennet, Marlborough	1599
The Kent Mark Stewards, Maidstone	1691
*The Lady of the Lamp, Chepstow	1709
The Langdale, Somerset	1615
*The Leonard Anderson Lodge of Installed Mark Masters, Boston, Lincs.	1412
The Liberation, St. Helier	1719
*The Lincolnshire Provincial Officers, Grimsby/Grantham	1910
*The Lord Harris, Sidcup	1494
The Lord Swansea, M.M.H.	1892
The Ludwig Zum Flammenden Stern, Burg Steinfurt, West Germany	1642
*The Mahajan, Highgate, London	1856
*The Mark of Education, Cosham	1491
The Mark Provincial Grand Secretaries	1641
*The Netherlands Installed Mark Masters Lodge, Leiden, Netherlands	1434
*The North Kent, Wilmington	1682
The Progress Lodge of Installed Mark Masters, Leicester	1786
The Red Rose, Hindley	1594
*The Romney Marsh, Dymchurch	1417
*The Rope and Anchor, Hamburg, Germany	1782
The Roses and Castles Boaters'	1922
The Scout, Long Eaton	1907
The University of Liverpool, Liverpool	1062
The Victory, Pickering	1588
*The Written Rock, Brampton	1620
Thea Sinensis, Mark Masons' Hall	1074
Thesaurus, Sutton, Hull	782
*Thistle, Mark Masons' Hall	8
Thistle and Shamrock, Havant	1048
*Thomas à Becket, Worthing	1831
*Thomas à Beckett, Portsmouth	775
*Thomas Arthur Wood, Warwick	1737
Thomas Beevor, Gt. Yarmouth	1724
Thomas Dunckerley, Gosport	1296
Thomas Purvis, Newcastle upon Tyne	702
Thomas Sharples Barlow, Manchester	1383
*Thorne, Thorne	1004
Thornton, Uckfield	631
*Three Grand Principles, Penryn	879
*Thuredrecht, Dordrecht,	1547
Tintagel Castle, Tintagel	1800
Tithe Barn, Carlisle	1345
Torbay, Paignton	586
Torfaen, Pontypool	796
*Torrevieja, Torrevieja, Spain	1745
*Tortola, British Virgin Islands	1874
Tottenham, Staines	924
*Tower Hamlets, Mark Masons' Hall	892
Transkei, Queenstown, S.A.	819
Transvaal Installed Mark Masters, Parktown	1570
Transvaal Keystone Mark, Rewlatch	1186
Travellers, Kensington, Johannesburg	1153
Tregenna, St. Ives	787
*Tremonia, Hanover, Germany	1612
Trent, Newark-on-Trent	1526
Trevaunance, St. Agnes	1023
Trinity, Bargoed, South Wales	1845
*Tristram, Newcastle upon Tyne	346
Trivona, Long Eaton	983
*True Love and Unity, Brixham	1159
Truth, Huddersfield	137
Tudor Lodge of Rifle Volunteers, Wolverhampton	290
*Tudor, Upminster	1092
*Turks Island Forth, Turk Island, W. Indies	1553
*Turton, Bromley Cross, nr. Bolton	1300
*Tuscan, Mark Masons' Hall	454
Tuscan, Sale	922
Tuscan, Liverpool	1099
*Tuscan Pillar, Romford	1142
*Twente, Enschede, Netherlands	1533
*Twickenham, Twickenham	1378
Tylery, Ebbw Vale	604
*Ubique, Mark Masons' Hall	411
Unanimity and Fidelity, Taunton	348
Union, Manchester	32
*Union, Sunderland	124
*Union, Auckland, N.Z.	154
*Union, Oldham	171
*Union, Georgetown, Guyana	231
Union, Kynsna, C.P., S.A.	1216
United, Hong Kong	419
*United Manawatu, Palmerston North, N.Z.	1261
*United Service, Gillingham	69
*United Service, Mark Masons' Hall	489

ALPHABETICAL LIST OF MARK LODGES—continued

Lodge	No.
United Service, Pretoria, S.A.	588
United Service, Bangalore, Madras	640
Unity, Ringwood	381
Unity, Heaton, Newcastle	708
*Unity, Crediton	783
Unity, Seaham Harbour	827
Universal, Harrow	1911
*University, Oxford	55
*University of London, Mark Masons' Hall	1389
University of Manchester, Manchester	1001
*Upminster, Upminster	1195
*Urania, Louth	326
Utrique Fidelis Lodge of Grand Officers, Chepstow	1836
Valentia, Wokingham	623
Vale of Avon, Ringwood	867
*Van der Stel, Strand, C.P., S. Africa	773
*Vaudeville, West London M.C., Ealing	801
*Vereeniging, Phoenix, Mauritius	900
*Vernon, Stourport-on-Severn	923
*Vesey, Sutton Coldfield	757
*Victoria, Melbourne	47
Victoria in Burma, Rangoon, Burma	68
Victoria Falls, Livingstone, Zambia	912
*Victory, Bridport	690
Victory, Callington	1030
*Viking, Rochford	1564
Vulcan, Sheffield	1191
Waldie Peirson, Johannesburg	904
Wallasey, Wallasey	600
*Wallingford, Wallingford	1162
*Walpole, Norwich	92
Water de Hereford, Northwich	1275
Walter Weedon, Hermanus, S.A.	1193
*Walton, Liverpool	161
Walton, Crook	1106
Wanderers, Santos, Brazil	1137
Wantage, Wantage	1207
*Warlingham, Warlingham	1321
*Warminster, Warminster	1110
*Warren de Tabley, Knutsford	622
Warrington, Warrington	1178
Warwickshire Installed Masters, Edgbaston, Birmingham	1400
Watling Street, Stony Stratford	292
*Watford, Watford	241
Waveney Valley, Harleston	1140
Wayfarers, Colchester	1096
*Weald of Surrey, Sutton	1314
*Welchpool, Welshpool	1084
*Welcome, Sutton	1237
Wellington, Rye	1556
*Wellington, Whitehouse	1678
Wentloog, Castleton, Cardiff	1586
West Bridgford, West Bridgford	1307
West Cheshire, Birkenhead	1497
West Croydon, Croydon	1082
West Germany Installed Mark Masters, Osnabrück, Germany	1518
*West Ham, Buckhurst Hill	467
Westhoughton, Westhoughton	1006
*West Lancashire, Liverpool	65
*West Smithfield, Mark Masons' Hall	223
*West Sussex, Worthing	453
*West Sussex Lodge of Installed Mark Masters, Chichester	1898
*Westwood, Welling	1354
Weyland, Bicester	1305
*Weyside, Guildford	442
Wharfedale, Otley	1027
White River, E. Transvaal	1621
White Rose, Baildon	1067
White Stone, Manchester	1080
*White Stone, Chingford	864
White Stone, Lincoln	1203
White Stone, St. Albans	1832
*Whitley, Whitley Bay	788
*Whitstable, Whitstable	938
*Whitwell, Maryport	151
*Wicket, Mark Masons' Hall	577
*Wiclif, Lutterworth	1068
Wike, Breightmet	142
*Wilbraham, Widnes	523
Wilder, Sindlesham	1868
Wilfred Hulbert, Johannesburg	954
William Bathurst, Cirencester	1420
William de Irwin, Yeovil	162
*William Hamilton Underhill, Letchworth	962
*William Hickman, Sandown, I.O.W.	320
William James Hughan, Falmouth	1437
William of Orange, Petersfield	973
*William Kelly, Burton-on-Trent	339
*William Long, Burnham-on-Sea	191
*William Romaine Callender, Bury	136
William Todd, Bishop Auckland	929
*Wiltshire Installed Mark Masters, Chippenham	1460
*Wiltshire Keystone, Devizes	178
*Wiltshire Downs, Warminster	1843
Winchester, Winchester	969
*Windrush, Witney	1386
*Windsor, Castle, Windsor	519
*Woodard, Mark Masons' Lodge	1265
*Woodgrange, Croydon	1111
*Woodiwiss, Derby	503
*Woodstock, Surbiton	1569
Woodthorpe, Chilwell	1144
Woolmer Forest, Bordon	1403
*Worcestershire Installed Mark Masters, Worcester	1409
Worth, Keighley	727
*Wouldhave Tyne Dock, South Shields	362
*Wrekin, Wellington	1129
*Wulfric Spot, Burton-on-Trent	1416
*Wulfruna, Wolverhampton	186
Wycoller, Colne	1582
*Wycombe, Gerrards Cross	480
Wychwood, Burford	1443
Wyggeston, Leicester	1149
*Wyndham, Andover	37
Wyre, Fleetwood	754
*Wythenshawe, Christleton	532
*Wyven, Wivenhoe	1333
*Yadavindra, Patiala, N. India	1229
Yare Valley, Norfolk	1597

ALPHABETICAL LIST OF MARK LODGES—continued

*Yenton, Yenton	719
*York, York	T.I.
*York, Cambridge	334
*Youell, Great Yarmouth	317
Ysgolion, Pontyclun	1487
*Zetland, Saltash	831
*Zululand, Empangeni, Natal	1046
Zuriel, Calcutta Bengal	496
*Zaradatha, Leiden, Holland	1324
*Zum Maurischen Schloss im See, Langenargen, Germany	1792

ROLL OF ROYAL ARK MARINER LODGES
(978)

J Authorised to wear a Commemorative Jewel (Jubilee)
K Has received a Keystone Collarette
(I.) Denotes Installation
C Has received a Centenary Warrant.
■ Has received a 150th Anniversary Keystone Collarette

ABBREVIATIONS. Tav.—Tavern. M.C.—Masonic Centre. M.H.—Masonic Hall. M.T.—Masonic Temple. M.R.—Masonic Rooms. F.M.H.—Freemasons' Hall. St.—Street. Ho.—Hotel. Mark Masons' Hall (only) or Street with Town, signifies London. F.M.—Full Moon. B.F.M.—Before Full Moon. A.F.M.—After Full Moon.

K		**Grand Masters**—Mark Masons' Hall. *1st Wed. April, Oct. (I.)*	Mar. 2, 1989
		Bon Accord—Mark Masons' Hall. *3rd Thurs. Feb. (I.), April, Oct.*	May 6, 1976
K		**Old Kent**—Mark Masons' Hall. *4th Tues. Feb.; 4th Tues. April (I.); 4th Tues. Nov.*	Apr. 2, 1987
K		**Bath**—M.H., Old Orchard St., Bath. *1st Wed. March, April, Nov. (I.)*	July 5, 1945
C		**Northumberland and Berwick-upon-Tweed**—M.T., Cramlington. *4th Wed. Jan., May, June (I.); 3rd Wed. Nov.*	Mar. 25, 1887
C		**Mount Horeb**—F.M.H., Institute St., Bolton. *3rd Sat. March (I.), Oct., Dec.*	Apr. 8, 1910
2KC ■		**Old York**—M.H., Waitcliffe Rd., Cleckheaton. *5th Thurs. whenever occuring except in July, Aug., Dec. (I.) first meeting in year.*	July 22, 1896
2K		**Harris**—F.M.H., Park St., Bristol. *3rd Tues. April (I.); last Wed. Feb., June, Oct.*	May 2, 1912
K		**York**—M.H., St. Saviourgate, York. *3rd Wed. Feb. (I.); 4th Wed. May; 2nd Wed. Nov.*	Feb. 18, 1872
K		**Byron**—M.H., Nottingham. *1st Wed. Jan.; March (I.); 4th Wed. Oct.*	Sept. 2, 1965
		Peace—M.H., Newport, I.O.W. *4th Thurs. Jan., March, May, Nov. (I.)*	Sept. 1, 1919
C	1	**Mother**—Mark Masons' Hall. *3rd Tues. Feb.; 3rd Mon. June (I.)*	Jan. 29, 1872
K	2	**Phœnix**—Phoenix Lodge Rooms, 110 High Street, Old Portsmouth. *1st Mon. Jan., March (I.), Nov.*	July 8, 1856
K	3	**Keystone**—M.M.H., St. James's, S.W.1. *1st Wed. May (I.); 4th Mon. Oct.*	Mar. 7, 1974
KC	4	**Prince of Wales**—Mark Masons' Hall. *4th Mon. Jan. (I.), Oct.; 3rd Mon. May.*	Feb. 22, 1886
J ■	5	**Mallet and Chisel**—Mark Masons' Hall. *2nd Wed. Jan. (I.); 3rd Wed. April; 2nd Tues. Oct.*	May 7, 1931
	6	**Adams**—M.H., St. George's Ave., Sheerness. *2nd Wed. Jan., May, Oct. (I.)*	July 14, 1914
K	7	**Carnarvon**—Mark Masons' Hall. *3rd Thurs. Feb., May; last Thurs. Nov. (I.)*	May 13 1879
J	8	**Thistle**—Mark Masons' Hall. *4th Fri. Jan.; 3rd Mon. April; 2nd Tues. Oct. (I.)*	June 4, 1953

ROLL OF ROYAL ARK MARINER LODGES—*continued*

K	9	**Fortescue**—F.M.H., New Rd., Sth. Molton, Devon. *2nd Mon. Oct., Feb., April; 1st Mon. June (I.)*	March 27, 1993
K	10	**Cheltenham and Keystone**—M.H., Portland St., Cheltenham. *1st Fri. Jan., March, June (I.)*	May 5, 1966
CJ	11	**Joppa**—M.T., Clifton Rd., Birkenhead. *2nd Sat. May; 1st Sat. Nov. (I.)*	Dec. 20, 1895
	12	**Minerva**—M.H., Prince St., Dagger Lane, Hull HU1 2LU. *4th Tues: Jan., March, Sept., Nov. (I.)*	Ma. 1, 1990
	13	**Hiram**—M.C., Guildford. *2nd Mon. Feb., May (I.); 3rd Mon. Oct.*	Apr. 25, 1929
K J ■	14	**Prince Edward**—M.H., Willow Road, West Vale, Greetland, Halifax HX4 8AH. *4th Thurs. March, Sept. (I.); 3rd Fri. May.*	June 5, 1947
K J	15	**St. George**—F.M.H., Gandy St., Exeter. *4th Fri. March; 3rd Fri. May; 4th Fri. Sept. (I.)*	Aug. 5, 1920
KC	17	**Portsmouth**—M.H., Waterloo Road, Havant, Hampshire. *1st Thurs. April, June, Sept. (I.), Nov.*	Feb. 1, 1894
K	18	**Rectitude**—Rosendale M.H., Ashay Lea, Rawtenstall. *4th Wed. May (I.), Nov.*	Oct. 6, 1988
CJ	19	**William Kelly**—M.H., Broad St., Syston. *2nd Mon. April, Oct., Dec. (I.)*	Feb. 3, 1882
■	20	**Faith**—Middleton Masonic Club, Manchester Old Road, Middleton. *1st Mon. March, Sept., Nov. (I.)*	Nov. 14, 1997
K	21	**Howe**—M.H., Ashby Sq., Loughborough. *2nd Mon. Jan., March (I.), Nov.*	Mar. 4, 1965
KC	22	**Southwark**—M.M. Hall, St. James. *4th Mon. Feb.; 2nd Tues. May (I.); 3rd Tues. Oct.*	Jan. 24, 1881
K	23	**The Russell**—F.M.H., Pym St., Tavistock, Devon. *4th Tues. March, May, July, Oct. (I.)*	Feb. 3, 1966
K	24	**Prince**—M.T., Richard St., Rochdale. *1st Thurs. March; 1st Tues. May (I.); 2nd Thurs. Jan.*	June 6, 1946
	27	**Porchester**—M.H., Newbury. *1st Wed. Feb. (I.), Nov.; 2nd Wed. Nov.*	Feb. 7, 1963
	28	**St. John's**—M.T., Guildford St., Cardiff. *3rd Wed. April (I.), Nov.*	Apr. 29, 1874
	30	**Knight of Malta**—M.H., St. Mary's Road, Hinckley. *3rd Thurs. March, May, Nov. (I.)*	Feb. 4, 1988
KCJ	33	**Bermuda Loyalty**—F.M.H., Reid St., Hamilton, Bermuda. *3rd Thurs. March, May, Oct. (I.)*	Feb. 13, 1895
K	34	**United Manchester**—M.H., Audenshaw. *3rd Sat. Jan., March (I.); 2nd Sat. Oct.*	Mar. 13, 1879
KC	35	**Sincerity**—Queen Victoria M.H., 76 Victoria Road, St. Budeaux, Plymouth PL5 1RD. *4th Tues. Feb. (I.), April, July, Oct.*	Sept. 25, 1873
K	37	**Wyndham**—F.M.H., East St., Andover. *4th Wed. Feb., May (I.), Sept., Nov.*	June 6, 1965
K	38	**Yr Ysgallen**—F.M.H., Llandudno. *2nd Fri. Feb., April, Oct. (I.), Dec.*	Mar. 7, 1946
K	39	**Ecletic**—M.H., West Hartlepool. *1st Mon. April, June, Oct. (I.), Dec.*	Aug. 30, 1920

ROLL OF ROYAL ARK MARINER LODGES—*continued*

K	40	**Shakespeare**—M.R., Alderson House, High St., Warwick. *2nd Tues. Nov.; last Thurs. May (I.)*	Mar. 2, 1961
	42	**Sussex**—M.T., Kingston, Jamaica. *4th Wed. March, June, Sept. (I.)*	Nov. 7, 1991
	43	**Cockburn**—Gibraltar Mas. Institute, 47a Prince Edward's Road, Gibraltar. *4th Tues. March, May, Sept. (I.)*	Mar. 26, 1881
	44	**Florence Nightingale Lodge**—Royal National Hotel, 38-51 Bedford Way, Russel Square, London WC1H 0DG. *3rd Mon. Jan.; 2nd Tues. May; 4th Mon. Nov. (I.)*	Mar. 23, 1998
K	45	**Gough**—M.H., Snow Hill, Shelton, Stoke-on-Trent. *1st Thurs. May (I.); 1st Tues. Oct.; 4th Thurs. Jan.*	Jan. 2, 1930
C	47	**Victoria**—Williamstown M.C., Melbourne. *2nd Tues. May, Sept., Nov. (I.)*	Jan. 7, 1884
	49	**Lebanon**—M.H. 455 Dominion Road, Mt. Eden, Auckland, N.Z. *1st Thurs. April (I.), July, Sept.*	Reopened Aug. 2008
2K	53	**Wentworth**—Tapton Hall, Sheffield. *2nd Wed. March, June, Nov. (I.)*	June 8, 1875
K	54	**The Naval and Military**—M.H., Alexandra Road, Farnborough. *1st 5th Fri. in the periods March-May; Sept.-Nov. (I.) If during either of these periods there is no 5th Fri. then the Lodge will meet on the 1st 5th working day of the said period.*	Aug. 26, 1916
	55	**Oxford University**—F.M.H., 333 Banbury Rd., Oxford. *4th Sat. Trinity Term, Michaelmas Term (I.)*	Mar. 17, 1873
	56	**Temperance Lodge**—The Masonic Hall, White Heart Fold, Todmorden. *4th Mon. Jan. (I.), March*	Mar. 20, 2006
KC ■	58	**Fearnley**—Southwood M.R.—Birdcage Lane, Halifax. *3rd Wed. June, Aug. Nov. (I.)*	Jan. 25, 1887
C	59	**Ark**—M.H., Worcester. *3rd Tues. Feb., April, Dec. (I.)*	Nov. 19, 1881
J	60	**Cumberland**—M.T., 10 Portland Sq., Carlisle CA1 1PY. *Last Fri. Feb., April, Oct. (I.), Dec.*	May 1, 1947
KC	62	**Carnarvon**—M.H., Waterloo Road, Havant. *3rd Tues. Feb., April (I.), Oct., Dec.*	Feb. 20, 1871
K	63	**Solent**—M.H., Southampton. *3rd Wed. Fri., April, Oct., Dec. (I.)*	Sept. 9, 1873
K	64	**St. Aubyn**—St. Aubyn M.H., 33 Devonport Rd., Stoke, Devonport. *3rd Fri. Jan., March, June, Oct. (I.)*	June 4, 1918
	65	**West Lancashire**—M.H., 22 Hope St., Liverpool L1 9BY. *3rd Sat. Feb; 2nd Sat. April, Nov. (I.)*	July 22, 1919
J	69	**United Service**—M.H., Balmoral Rd., Gillingham. *2nd Wed. Feb., April; 1st Mon. Nov. (I.)*	Sept. 25, 1900
CJ	70	**Henniker**—F.M.H., Ipswich. *1st Wed. Feb., April (I.), Oct., Dec.*	Jan. 23, 1889
	74	**Caesarean**—M.T., St. Helier, Jersey. *3rd Wed. Feb., (I.), April, Oct.; 1st Thurs. Dec.*	Feb. 7, 1985
C	75	**Sussex**—Sussex M.C., Queens Road, Brighton. *3rd Mon. Feb. (I.), April, Nov.*	Mar. 1, 1887
K	78	**Fortitude**—M.H., Perranporth. *4th Fri. Jan., Feb., March, April, Oct. (I.)*	Sept. 6, 1945

ROLL OF ROYAL ARK MARINER LODGES—continued

C	81	**Triangle**—St. John's Hall, Secunderabad, Andhra Pradesh. *3rd Thurs. Jan. (I.), April, July, Oct.*	Feb. 18, 1904
K	87	**Cornubian**—M.H., Hayle, Cornwall. *3rd Wed. Feb. (I.), April, June, Oct.*	Oct. 6, 1966
	88	**Stella**—F.M.H., 65 Goodliffe Rd., Rangoon. *4th Mon. Feb., May, Aug., Sept. (I.)*	Mar. 5, 1885
	92	**Bridgman**—M.H., 47 St. Giles St., Norwich. *1st Fri. Jan.; 1st Fri. June (I.); 3rd Thurs. Sept.*	Feb. 22, 1899
J	95	**Scarborough**—M.H., St. Nicholas Cliff, Scarborough. *3rd Fri. Jan., March, May (I.), Nov.*	June 5, 1947
	97	**St. Barnabas**—M.H., Aylesbury. *1st Thurs. Feb., Nov.; 2nd Thurs. May (I.)*	July 9, 1924
K	100	**Hawton**—M.H., Ivybridge. *Last Wed. Jan., April, July, Oct. (I.)*	June 5, 1975
KCJ	101	**Boscawen**—M.H., Redruth. *1st Mon. Jan., March, June, Sept., Oct. (I.), Nov.*	Feb. 26, 1895
	104	**Macdonald**—Mark Masons' Hall. *2nd Mon. March, Nov. (I.)*	Nov. 16, 1882
C	105	**Edmondsbury**—M.H., St. Edmunds. *1st Mon. Nov. (I.); 2nd Mon. May.*	Mar. 14, 1903
C	107	**Hospitallers**—M.M.H., 86 St. James's St., SW1A 1PL. *2nd Thurs. Feb., May (I.), Nov.*	Sept. 7, 1880
	109	**Keystone**—M.H., Dock St., Newport. *3rd Tues. Jan., March, May, Oct. (I.)*	Nov. 6, 1920
2K	110	**The Carl Whitehead**—Tapton Hall, Shore Lane, Sheffield. *2nd Sat. May (I.); 1st Sat. Oct.*	June 29, 1996
K ■	111	**Elmete**—M.H., The Allerton, Nursury Lane, Leeds. *3rd Tues. Feb., June (I.), Oct.*	Dec. 1, 1899
	112	**Isaac Newton University**—F.M.H., Bateman, Street, Cambridge. *3rd Tues. Feb. (I.); 2nd Sat. June; 2nd Tues. Nov.*	Apr. 29, 1874
	113	**Hargreaves**—M.H., Ashday Lea, Rossendale BB4 9QX. *4th Wed. March (I.), Sept.*	June 3, 1873
K	114	**Percy**—South West Surrey M.Ctr., Hitherbury Close, Guildford GU2 4DR. *1st Wed. May (I.), Oct., Dec.*	Oct. 3, 1946
KCJ	115	**Bedford-Charity**—M.T., 2 Stirling Rd., Edgbaston, Birmingham 16 9SB. *2nd Tues. March, May, Nov. (I.)*	Feb. 23, 1893
	116	**Coracle**—M.H., Carmarthen. *2nd Wed. March, May (I.), Oct., Nov.*	Nov. 6, 1930
KC	117	**Remigius**—County Assembly Rooms, Bailgate, Lincoln. *1st Thurs. Feb., April, Nov. (I.)*	Feb. 20, 1890
C	119	**Irwin**—M.H., Keynsham. *3rd Mon. Sept., March (I.), Nov.*	Apr. 13, 1873
K	122	**Stockton-on-Tees**—M.H., Stockton-on-Tees. *3rd Tues. Jan. (I.), March, Sept., Nov.*	July 28, 1919
K C	124	**Union**—M.H., Queen St. East, Sunderland. *2nd Wed. Feb., April, Sept. (I.), Dec.*	Dec. 3, 1897
	125	**Bournemouth**—M.H., Knole Rd., Boscombe. *1st Wed. March, May, Sept.; 2nd Wed. Dec. (I.)*	Nov. 7, 1946

ROLL OF ROYAL ARK MARINER LODGES—*continued*

2K	127	**Portal**—M.H., Eastgate, Barnsley, S. Yorks. *4th Wed. Feb., April, June, Oct.*	Mar. 2, 1989
2K	128	**Herbert Fuller**—M.H., Wincanton, Somerset. *4th Mon. Feb. (I.), Sept.; 1st Mon. May.*	July 4, 1968
K	132	**Amity**—M.H., Poole. *4th Tues. Jan., March (I.), June, Nov.*	Apr. 22, 1919
K J ■	133	**Portland**—M.H., Portland. *1st Wed. March, May, Oct. (I.), Dec.*	May 2, 1946
	135	**Hotspur**—Prudhoe St., Alnwick, Northumberland. *4th Thurs. May, Sept., Nov. (I.)*	Sept. 5, 1974
4KC	136	**Lathom**—M.H., Parsons Lane, Bury. *1st Tues. Feb. (I.), April, Sept., Nov.*	May 31, 1884
2K ■	137	**Truth**—The Masonic Hall, New Hey Road, Lindley, Huddersfield HD3 4AJ. *3rd Thurs. May (I.), June, Sept.*	Mar. 3, 1974
KC	139	**Panmure**—Mark Masons' Hall. *4th Wed. Feb. (I.); 3rd Wed. May; 3rd Wed. Nov.*	Sept. 15, 1879
KC	140	**Medina**—M.H., Castle Road, Cowes, I.O.W. *1st Tues. Feb., April, Oct. (I.), Dec.*	Nov. 12, 1907
	141	**Skelmersdale**—Albert House, Jowetts Walk, Ashton-under-Lyne. *3rd Tues. May, Oct.*	May 1, 1969
	143	**Preston**—M.H., Garstang, Lancs. *4th Tues. March, Nov. (I.)*	Dec. 5, 1929
K J	144	**Grosvenor**—Twickenham District M.C., Cole Court, 150 London Rd., Twickenham, Middlesex. *4th Wed. Feb.; 2nd Thurs. June (I.); 1st Wed. Nov.*	Mar. 25, 1879
K J	145	**Constantine**—St. Giles M.C., 5 St. John's Green, Colchester CO2 7EZ. *4th Thurs. Jan.; 4th Wed. April; 2nd Thurs. Oct. (I.)*	Sept. 6, 1928
2K	148	**Stamford**—M.H., Tatton Rd., Sale. *2nd Mon. Jan., April, Oct. (I.)*	Jan. 6, 1948
CJ	151	**Collin**—F.M.H., High St., Maryport CA5 6EJ. *2nd Thurs. Jan. (I.); 1st Thurs. May, Oct.*	Sept. 24, 1890
J	152	**Dover and Cinque Ports**—M.H., Snargate St., Dover. *2nd Tues. Feb., April, June, Oct. (I.)*	Feb. 6, 1947
CJ	154	**Ararat**—M.H., 455 Dominion Rd., Auckland, N.Z. *2nd Tues. April, June, Aug. (I.)*	Jan. 23, 1878
	155	**Portal**—M.H., North Parade, Frome. *3rd Wed. Feb., Sept. (I.); 2nd Wed. June*	Sept. 20, 2006
K	156	**County Palatine**—F.M.H., Bridge Street, Manchester. *4th Thurs. Jan. (I.), April, Oct.*	Sept. 3, 1970
	157	**Mathews Philip**—M.H., Ootacamund, The Nilgiris, Madras. *Last day March, July, Nov. (I.).*	Sept. 3, 1970
2KC	158	**Mount Ararat**—M.H., Bryn Rd, Ashton-in-Makerfield. *3rd Fri. March, Oct. (I.)*	Apr. 17, 1873
	159	**Starkie**—M.H., Accrington. *4th Fri. Jan., April, June (I.), Oct.*	Apr. 5, 1945
C	160	**Vepery**—F.M.H., Madras. *1st Fri. Feb., May, Aug., Nov. (I.)*	Sept. 7, 1889
	163	**Bradwell Abbey**—M.H., Wolverton. *1st Fri. March, May, Nov. (I.)*	June 6, 1985

ROLL OF ROYAL ARK MARINER LODGES—continued

K	164	**Southdown**—The Birch Hotel, Lewes Road, Haywards Heath, West Sussex. *2nd Wed. April, June; 3rd Thurs. Oct. (I.)*	Oct. 3, 1963
KC	166	**East Sussex**—M.H., East Ascent, St. Leonards-on-Sea TN38 0DR. *2nd Thurs. May; 4th Wed. Aug.; 4th Mon. Nov. (I.)*	June 20, 1899
■	171	**Union**—F.M.H., Union St., Oldham. *4th Fri. Feb., April (I.), Nov.*	Dec. 1, 1988
	172	**Trent**—M.T., 32 North Marsh Rd., Gainsborough. *3rd Wed. Jan., April, Oct. (I.)*	Sept. 6, 1956
2K	173	**Temple**—10 Duke St., St. James's, SW1. *4th Tues. May (I.); 3rd Mon. Dec.*	Apr. 2, 1883
K	174	**Athol**—Warwickshire M.T., Clarendon Rd., Birmingham. *2nd Wed. May (I.), Dec.*	Oct. 30, 1920
2K	175	**St. Michael's**—Helston, Cornwall. *3rd Tues. Feb. (I.), May, Sept., Nov.*	Oct. 7, 1965
	176	**New Era**—Mark Masons' Hall. *3rd Sat. Jan. (I.), April, Oct.*	June 1, 1933
KC	178	**Wiltshire Anchor**—M.H., Devizes SN10 1NU. *1st Fri. Feb., May (I.), Sept., Nov.*	Apr. 14, 1887
J	179	**Abertawe**—M.T., Swansea. *4th Wed. Jan., March; 4th Mon. Sept. (I.)*	Dec. 6, 1945
	181	**Sir Francis Burdett**—M.M.H. *1st Thurs. March; 1st Wed. Sept. (I.)*	Dec. 14, 1926
	182	**Hull**—M.H., Beverley. *5th Tues. in months in which there are 5 Tuesdays, 2nd Mon. March (I.) next regular meeting after March*	Mar. 27, 1878
	183	**Powell**—F.M.H., Park Street, Bristol. *4th Tues. Jan.; 4th Fri. May (I.); 2nd Fri. Oct.*	Nov. 11, 2010
	184	**Perseverance**—Willemstad, Curacao. *2nd Wed. Feb. (I.), June, Nov.*	Sept. 4, 1986
KC	186	**Wolverhampton**—M.H., Tettenhall Road, Wolverhampton. *3rd Fri. Jan., April (I.), Oct.*	Feb. 20, 1912
K	188	**Heneage**—M.H., Cleethorpes. *2nd Fri. Feb., Oct., Dec. (I.)*	Aug. 28, 1916
	191	**William Long**—M.H., Burnham-on-Sea, Somerset. *4th Fri. Jan., March, Oct. (I.)*	July 7, 1977
	192	**St. Cuthbert's**—M.H., The Parade, Berwick-upon-Tweed. *1st Wed. May, Oct. (I.)*	Sept. 6, 1956
K	194	**Simon de Montfort**—F.M.H., London Road, Leicester. *4th Mon. May (I.); Last weekday in June; 2nd Thurs. Sept.*	May 24, 2004
	195	**Kent Dale**—M.H., Station Road, Kendal LA6 6BT. *2nd Mon. Feb., April, Sept., Dec. (I.)*	July 4, 1963
C	196	**Cestrian**—F.M.H., Plough Lane, Christleton, Chester. *3rd Wed. Feb., April, Sept., Nov. (I.)*	Oct. 26, 1904
C	197	**Studholme**—Mark Masons' Hall. *1st Thurs. May (I.); 4th Thurs. Nov.*	Apr. 10, 1894
J	198	**Croydon**—M.H., Croydon. *3rd Wed. March, May, Nov. (I.)*	Mar. 25, 1891
	199	**Duke of Connaught**—Harrow District M.C. *4th Thurs. Jan.; 3rd Thurs. March (I.); 4th Thurs. June; 1st Thurs. Nov.*	Jan. 4, 1990

ROLL OF ROYAL ARK MARINER LODGES—continued

J 205 **Beaconsfield**—Southend M.C., Saxon Hall, Aviation Way, Southend-on-Sea, Essex SS2 6UN.
1st Wed. Feb.; 2nd Wed. May (I.); 3rd Tues. Oct. June 5, 1918

C 209 **St. Wilfrid's**—M.H., Alford.
4th Mon. Jan., April, Sept.; Tues after the 3rd Mon. May (I.) Mar. 6, 1879

J 211 **Hammersmith Jubilee**—Twickenham District M.C., Cole Court, London Road, Twickenham.
4th Mon. Feb.; 1st Mon. Dec. (I.) Nov. 1, 1928

212 **Albion**—Masonic Centre, Salters, St. George, Barbados.
3rd Tues. Feb., May (I.), Aug., Nov. Jan. 7, 1987

CJ 213 **F. R. Sewell**—Cleator Moor Civic and M.C. CA25 5AR.
Last Mon. Feb., April, Sept., Nov. Dec. 10, 1887

214 **St. John's**—Masonic Hall, Abergavenny.
3rd Wed. Jan., April, Sept; 1st Mon. Dec. (I.)

216 **Dent**—M.H., Frizington Road, Frizington CA26 3QU.
3rd Wed. March (I.), June, Sept., Dec. Dec. 11, 1920

217 **Cornerstone**—M.T., Kimberley.
4th Wed. Jan., April, July, Oct. (I.) Nov. 1, 1951

K 218 **Lyegrove**—M.H., Downend, Bristol.
4th Mon. April (I.); 1st Mon. Sept.; 3rd Mon. Dec. July 2, 1964

220 **Olive**—F.M.H., 19 Park St., Calcutta 16.
2nd Tues. Jan., May, July (I.), Nov. Feb. 22, 1905

K J 223 **West Smithfield**—Mark Masons' Hall.
3rd Thurs. Jan.; 2nd Thurs. April; 4th Thurs. Nov. (I.) Oct. 8, 1907

224 **Athlumney Menatschim**—10 Duke Street, St. James.
1st Thurs. March (I.); 2nd Wed. Oct. Dec. 12, 1899

225 **Abbey**—Council Chambers, Abingdon.
1st Fri. Feb. (I.), Nov. July 5, 1945

226 **Excelsior**—Westwood M.C., Welling.
1st Sat. Feb., May (I.), Nov. Sept. 5, 1946

K 231 **Union**—F.M.H., Company Path, Georgetown, Guyana.
3rd Thurs. Feb.; 4th Mon. June; 4th Thurs. Sept. (I.) Nov. 5, 1959

K 234 **Brixton**—C.L.M.C., Sessions House, Clerkenwell Green, London EC1R 0NA.
4th Tues. Feb.; 2nd Tues. April; 4th Tues. Nov. (I.) Mar. 5, 1931

235 **Leopold**—M.H., Reading Road, Wokingham, Berks.
Last Mon. Feb. (I.); 2nd Mon. Oct. May 22, 1900

236 **Ashlar**—
Corvino Ristorante Italiano, Beaufort House, 7 Middlesex St., London E1 7AA.
3rd Wed. Oct.; 3rd Thurs. Feb.; 4th Thurs. April (I.) Apr. 9, 1931

C 237 **Dewar**—M.H., Rochester.
4th Wed. May (I.); 2nd Wed. Sept. Mar. 23, 1882

K 238 **Prince Leopold**—Mark Mason's Hall.
3rd Mon. March; 4th Wed. June; 2nd Thurs. Sept. (I.) Apr. 9, 1886

KCJ 239 **Royal Naval**—Mark Masons' Hall.
3rd Thurs. Jan., April, June (I.) Apr. 18, 1906

240 **Royal**—Masonic Buildings, 45-47 Barbados Ave., Kingston 5, Jamaica.
1st Thurs. Feb., May, Aug., Oct. July 3, 1992

K 241 **Watford**—Halsey M.H., Watford.
3rd Fri. April, Oct.; 2nd Fri. Dec. (I.) May 3, 1934

ROLL OF ROYAL ARK MARINER LODGES—continued

	243	**St. Ethelbert**—M.H., Kryle Street, Hereford. *2nd Wed. Feb., April (I.), Sept., Nov.*	Feb. 7, 1991
KC	245	**Vikings**—F.M.H., St. George's Ave., Northampton. *3rd Tues. Feb.; 4th Tues. April (I.); 3rd Wed. Sept.*	Apr. 7, 1884
K	246	**Duke of Connaught**—M.H., George St., Buxton. *1st Wed. March, May, Sept. (I.), Nov.*	May 7, 1964
	247	**Alfred**—F.M.H., 333 Banbury Rd., Oxford. *2nd Wed. April; 3rd Wed. Dec., Feb. (I.)*	Mar. 5, 1931
K	250	**Darlington**—M.H., Archer St., Darlington. *2nd Wed. Feb., April (I.), June, Oct. Dec.*	Mar. 1, 1920
C	252	**Natalia**—M.T., Pietermaritzburg, Natal. *1st Tues. Feb., May, Aug. (I.)*	Apr. 5, 1880
	253	**Spes Bona**—Freemasons Hall, Parliament St., Port Elizabeth. Eastern Cape. *4th Thurs. Jan., March, May, July, Sept., Nov. (I.)*	July 9, 1935
	255	**Robinson**—M.C., Tovil, Maidstone. *3rd Tues. Jan., Feb., April (I.), Nov.*	Mar. 27, 1923
	256	**De Valence**—M.T., Tenby. *1st Mon. Feb., Oct., Dec.; 1st Fri. May (I.)*	Apr. 11, 1933
	257	**Jersey**—Windsor M.H., Church Lane, Windsor. *1st Wed. June (I.); 2nd Wed. Nov.*	Jan. 6, 1972
	259	**Y Geninen**—M.T., Deiniol Road, Bangor, Gwynedd. *3rd Wed. Jan. (I.); 2nd Thurs. March, May, Sept.*	Dec. 11, 1920
K	262	**St. Vincent**—M.T., Canterbury. *4th Sat. Jan. (I.); 4th Fri. April; 3rd Fri. Sept.*	Mar. 7, 1935
CJ	264	**Ararat**—Zetland Hall, 1 Kennedy Rd., Mid-levels, Hong Kong S.A.R., P.R. of China. *1st Wed. Feb., March, Oct., Dec. (I.)*	Mar. 28, 1889
K	265	**Newark on Trent**—M.H., The Avenue, London Rd., Newark. *2nd Tues. March, May (I.), Sept.*	Apr. 3, 1975
	266	**Amherst**—M.H., Sandgate High St., Folkestone. *1st Thurs. March, May (I.), Nov.*	Sept. 6, 1962
	267	**King Charles the Martyr**—M.H., St. John's Rd., Tunbridge Wells. *1st Thurs. March, May (I.), Nov.*	Oct. 1, 1970
	272	**Wickliffe**—Omarunui M.Ctr., Elbourne Street, Taradale, New Zealand. *Fri. before 3rd Sat. March (I.), May, Aug., Nov.*	
K	275	**St. Austell**—M.H., St. Austell. *4th Mon. Jan., March, April, Oct. (I.), Nov.*	June 7, 1962
	276	**Middlesbrough**—M.H., Middlesbrough. *4th Mon. Feb., April, Sept. (I.), Nov.*	Sept. 16, 1913
	277	**Ryedale**—M.H., Malton. *4th Thurs. March, June, Sept., Nov. (I.)*	Nov. 30, 1993
J	282	**Derwent Valley**—M.H., Gordon St., Workington CA14 2EN. *3rd Fri. Jan., March, June, Oct. (I.)*	May 2, 1946
	284	**High Cross**—M.M.H., London. *2nd Wed. March (I.); 1st Wed. Sept.; 3rd Tues. Jan.*	Nov. 3, 1983
C	288	**Port Natal**—M.H., Durban, Natal. *4th Mon. April, June, Aug.; 3rd Mon. Nov. (I.)*	Aug. 5, 1881
K	293	**Industry**—M.H., Holmeside Ave., Dunston. *3rd Tues. Jan., May, Sept. (I.)*	Nov. 1, 1934

ROLL OF ROYAL ARK MARINER LODGES—*continued*

    294 **Royal Naval College**—M.M.H., London.
           2nd Mon. May; 4th Mon. Oct.

K   296 **Edmund Taylor**—M.H., Adelaide St., Blackpool.
           3rd Tues. Feb., April, Oct. (I.), Dec.   May 6, 1913

    297 **Dyfed**—F.M.H., Haverfordwest.
           2nd Mon. March, April, Oct. (I.)   Feb. 2, 1956

K   302 **Beadon Woodford**—Derby M.H., 457 Burton Rd., Littleover, Derby.
           1st Tues. Feb., Dec., April (I.), Oct.   July 26, 1919

C   305 **Gosport**—Masonic Hall, Gosport.
           4th Wed. Jan. (I.), March, June, Oct.   Nov. 16,1882

    309 **Saye and Sele**—M.H., Church Road, Sidcup, Kent DA14 6BX.
           3rd Mon. April; 4th Tues. May; 3rd Mon. Nov. (I.)   May 1, 1919

    313 **Lawrence**—M.H., Cunliffe Street, Chorley.
           3rd Wed. May, Nov. (I.)   Feb. 7, 1980

    315 **Henniker**—West Ealing M.C., Westfield House, Churchfield Rd., Ealing W13 9NF.
           1st Fri. Feb. (I.), Nov.; 2nd Fri. May.   July 5, 1945
           Warrant of Confirmation Feb. 2003

K   316 **Benevolent**—M.H., Hollands Rd., Teignmouth, Devon.
           3rd Tues. Jan., March, May (I.), Nov.   June 14, 1973

    317 **Martyn**—Royal Mas. Assembly Rms., Albert Square, Gt. Yarmouth.
           4th Mon. Feb. (I.), Sept.   Mar. 15, 1891

K   318 **St. James**—Handsworth M.H., Wretham Rd., Handsworth, Birmingham.
           3rd Mon. March, Nov. (I.)   Aug. 11, 1914

KC   319 **Jordan**—M.T., Tor Hill Rd., Torquay.
           1st Mon. Jan., March, June, Nov. (I.)   Oct. 1, 1888

KC   320 **Sandown Bay**—M.H., Sandown, I.O.W.
           2nd Tues. Feb., April (I.), Oct., Nov.   Aug. 20, 1887

    322 **Temple**—M.H., Bromley, Kent.
           2nd Sat. Jan., June; 3rd Sat. Nov. (I.)   June 18, 1926

2K   323 **Peveril**—Masonic Buildings, Stanley Road, Peel, I.O.M.
           4th Mon. Jan., April, Sept.   Oct. 2, 1980

    324 **Hunter**—M.T., Grange Rd., Rhyl.
           3rd Wed. Feb., April (I.), Oct., Dec.   Nov. 5, 1964

2K   326 **St. Mary**—M.H., Queen St., Louth, Lincs.
           2nd Thurs. May (I.); 4th Tues. Oct., Nov., Feb.   Apr. 24, 1920

■   327 **Sincerity**—Queen's Royal, Marine Promenade, New Brighton,
           Wallasey, Merseyside CH45 2JT.
           4th Fri. Jan., March (I.), Nov.   Apr. 7, 1949

    330 **Abraham Green**—M.H., Wellington Rd., Dudley.
           4th Thurs. Jan. (I.); 3rd Thurs. May, Nov.   July 15, 1904

    332 **Greenwich**—Mark Masons' Hall.
           4th Thurs. Sept. (I.); 2nd Thurs. Dec., April   Apr. 27, 1916

C   333 **Kintore**—M.H., Croydon and District Masonic Halls Plc, 73 Oakfield Rd., Croydon.
           3rd Mon. March, May (I.), Nov.   June 24, 1887

    334 **York**— F.M.H., Bateman St., Cambridge.
           3rd Wed. Feb., April (I.); 1st Wed. Dec.   Mar. 15, 1910

K J   339 **Mercia**—Ashfield Ho., Ashby Rd., Burton-on-Trent.
           4th Mon. Jan., March (I.), Nov.   May 18, 1921

ROLL OF ROYAL ARK MARINER LODGES—continued

	340	**Royal Forest of Dean**—M.H., Newham-on-Severn. *4th Thurs. Feb.; 3rd Thurs. May; 4th Thurs. Oct. (I.)*	July 6, 1978
	342	**Chelmer**—M.H., Rainsford Road, Chelmsford CM1 2PZ. *2nd Wed. Jan., April (I.), July, Oct.*	July 3, 1924
K	344	**Nottingham**—M.H., Goldsmith Street, Nottingham. *4th Tues. March; 2nd Wed. May (I.); last Mon. Nov.*	Mar. 15, 1920
K	346	**Tristram**—M.H., Fern Avenue, Jesmond, Newcastle upon Tyne NE2 2RA. *2nd Tues. Jan., April, Sept. (I.)*	Mar. 2, 1939
K	348	**Fidelity and Unanimity**—M.H., Taunton. *2nd Fri. Jan., April (I.), Oct.*	Mar. 4, 1913
J	350	**Emblematic**—M.M.H. *2nd Thurs. Jan.; 4th Thurs. April (I.), Oct.*	Apr. 4, 1945
	351	**St. Anne's**—M.H., Castle Street, Looe, Cornwall PL13 1DD. *2nd Mon. April, Sept., Nov.*	Nov. 3, 2012
K ■	353	**Dove Valley**—M.H., Ashbourne, Derbyshire. *1st Wed. May (I.); 3rd Wed. June; 2nd Fri. Sept.*	Nov. 25, 1995
	354	**Rose and Lily**—F.M.H., Gt. Queen St. *2nd Sat. May, Sept. (I.)*	Oct. 3, 1985
	355	**Royal Savoy**—Halsey Masonic Hall, Cheshunt. *2nd Tue. Oct, Feb., April (I.)*	Apr. 16, 1921
K	356	**Dunelm**—M.H., 36 Old Elvet, Durham DH1 3HN. *2nd Wed. Feb., April, May, Oct. (I.)*	Sept. 7, 1978
	357	**Chiswick**—Mark Masons' Hall. *2nd Wed. Jan. (I.); 1st Tues. June; 1st Fri. Sept.*	June 25, 2002
C	359	**Excelsior**—M.T., Island Rd. South, Garston, Liverpool. *3rd Sat. Jan., March (I.), Nov.*	Dec. 7, 1892
	360	**St. Eilian**—M.H., Holyhead on *4th Wed. Feb.;* M.H., Glanrhos, Amlwch on *4th Wed. April, Sept. (I.), Nov.*	July 24, 1992
	361	**Onslow**—Farmers' and Fletchers' Hall, 3 Cloth St., Smithfield, London EC1A 7LD. *2nd Thurs. March (I.); 1st Tues. July; 3rd Thurs. Nov.*	Apr. 1, 1948
K	362	**Rockcliffe**—F.M.H., Ingham St., South Shields. *3rd Fri. March (I.), May, Sept., Nov.*	Dec. 17, 1923
	363	**Ruspini**—Mark Masons' Hall. *4th Thurs. March; 1st Thurs. Dec. (I.)*	June 1, 1989
C	364	**Gordon**—M.H., Gravesend. *1st Wed. March; 2nd Mon. May (I.), Sept.*	Feb. 2, 1897
	366	**Hertford**—Mayflower Place, Hertingfordbury. *2nd Mon. Feb., June; 1st Mon. Oct. (I.)*	Apr. 1, 1948
KC	367	**Gladsmuir**—M.M.H., London, SW1A 1PL. *4th Tues. Feb. (I.); 1st Mon. June; 4th Tues. Oct.*	Oct. 17, 1894
	368	**Jamaica**—M.T., 45-47 Barbados Ave., Kingston 5. *4th Mon. Jan., April, July (I.); and Oct.*	May 4, 1961
	372	**De La Pole**—M.H., 112 High Street, Sidmouth. *3rd Thurs. Jan., March (I.), June, Oct.*	Sept. 2, 1948
K ■	373	**Tilchestune**—M.H., Elm Ave., Long Eaton. *2nd Thurs. March, Sept., Nov. (I.)*	July 6, 1943
2K	375	**Furness**—M.H., King's Rd., Ulverston. *3rd Fri. Feb. (I.), May, Sept., Nov.*	May 2, 1946

ROLL OF ROYAL ARK MARINER LODGES—*continued*

	376	**Brownrigg**—M.H., Slough. *Last Thurs. Feb., April; 4th Thurs. Nov. (I.)*	Dec. 27, 1889
K	377	**Brentwood**—Hutton M.H., Mount Avenue, Brentwood, Essex CM13 2NS. *4th Mon. Feb., Nov. (I.); 1st Mon. June.*	June 7, 1962
K	379	**St. Martin's**—M.H., Liskeard. *2nd Fri. Jan., March, Sept., Nov.; 3rd Fri. May (I.)*	May 4, 1933
K	380	**Folkestone**—M.H., Windmill St., Hythe. *4th Wed. Jan., March (I.), May, Nov.*	Feb. 5, 1926
KC	383	**St. George**—The Erme M.H., Western Road, Ivybridge, Devon. *2nd Tues. Feb., April, Sept., Nov. (I.)*	May 17, 1907
C	385	**King Solomon**—London Mas. Cen., Clerkenwell Green, E.C.1. *4th Tues. Jan.; 1st Thurs. May, Nov. (I.)*	Feb. 14, 1897
K	387	**St. Oswald**—M.T., Normanby Rd., Scunthorpe. *3rd Thurs. March, April, Oct. (I.)*	Oct. 3, 1963
	390	**Granville**—M.H., Sondes Rd., Deal. *2nd Mon. April (I.); 3rd Mon. Feb., Dec.*	Mar. 8, 1920
	391	**Lewis**—F.M.H., High St., Lewes. *4th Tues. Feb., Sept. (I.); 2nd Tues. May*	July 30, 1919
K	394	**Chorlton**—South Manchester F.M.H., Chorlton-cum-Hardy. *1st Wed. Oct., Dec.; 2nd Mon. April (I.)*	Nov. 6, 1952
	396	**De Tabley**—Queen's Royal, Marine Promenade, New Brighton, Wallasey CH45 2JT. *3rd Wed. Jan., March, Oct. (I.)*	Sept. 3, 1959
KC	399	**Euston**—Mark Masons' Hall. *3rd Fri. Jan. (I.); 3rd Thurs. July.*	Oct. 22, 1890
KC	400	**Matier**—Mark Masons' Hall. *2nd Mon. May (I.); 1st Thurs. Nov.*	May 4, 1889
K	401	**Goddard**—Mas. Centre, The Planks, Swindon SN3 1QP. *2nd Fri. May; 4th Fri. Sept., Nov. (I.)*	July 6, 1978
K ■	403	**Perseverance**—M.H., Mill House, Clayton-le-Moors. *2nd Wed. March (I.), May, Sept., Nov.*	Nov. 23, 1921
K	404	**St. John the Baptist**—M.H., Penzance. *2nd Wed. Jan., March (I.), May, Sept., Nov.*	Jan. 3, 1935
K	405	**Lea**—M.H., Church St., Luton. *1st Thurs. March (I.), Oct.; 3rd Thurs. Nov.*	Jan. 6, 1944
	406	**Scots**—Mark Masons' Hall. *3rd Mon. Feb., Oct. (I.)*	July 7, 1989
K	408	**Hertford Military**—M.H., Severn St., Birmingham. *2nd Thurs. Jan., April (I.), Oct., Nov.*	July 1, 1919
J	409	**Royal Connaught**—Sussex M.C., 25 Queens Road, Brighton BN1 3XA. *4th Mon. March, June (I.), Sept.*	Sept. 5, 1940
	410	**Empress Britannic**—M.M.H. *3rd Thurs. March, June; 2nd Mon. Nov. (I.)*	July 6, 1944 Warrant of Confirmation Mar. 17, 1995
	411	**Ubique**—Mark Masons' Hall. *4th Mon. June; 3rd Thurs. Nov. (I.)*	Dec. 9, 1901
J	413	**St. Nicholas**—M.H., 42 Main Road, Harwich CO12 3LP. *1st Mon. Feb. (I.), April, July, Nov.*	Dec. 4, 1924
K	414	**Mount Ararat**—M.H., Derby Road, Alfreton, Derbys. *1st Mon. March, Oct., Dec.; 4th Wed. May (I.)*	Sept. 6, 1990

ROLL OF ROYAL ARK MARINER LODGES—continued

C J	416	**Royal Oak**—M.H., Sidcup. *2nd Tues. Jan.; 3rd Tues. May (I.), Sept.*	Jan. 27,1987
C	418	**Camden**—Mark Masons' Hall. *3rd Wed. March; 4th Wed. May (I.); 3rd Tues. Oct.*	Feb. 26, 1891
2K	424	**Ashlar**—F.M.H., Park Lane, Johannesburg, *1st Thurs. Feb., June (I.), Oct.*	Dec. 21, 1897
C	425	**Sarnian**—M.T., St. Martin's, Guernsey. *2nd Mon. Feb., April (I.), Oct., Dec.*	May 24, 1897
	427	**St. Denys**—M.R., Watergate, Sleaford. *Last Wed. Feb. (I.), Oct.; 1st Wed. May, Dec.*	Nov. 6, 1930
	428	**Broxbourne**—Halsey M.H., Watford. *1st Sat. Feb.; 3rd Sat. May (I.); 1st Sat. Oct.*	July 1, 1920
K	430	**Charity**—Warwickshire M.T., 2 Stirling Rd., Edgbaston, Birmingham B16 9SB. *3rd Thurs. Jan.; 2nd Wed. March, Nov. (I.)*	May 4, 1979
	431	**Hibernia**—Mark Masons' Hall. *3rd Mon. March; 3rd Thurs. Nov. (I.)*	June 29, 1925
	433	**Britannic**–M.M.H., London. *2nd Tues. April (I.), Oct.; 2nd Fri. Dec.*	Sept. 6, 1979
2K	434	**Stuart**—The Keep, Bedford Rd., Kempston. *3rd Thurs. Feb. (I.), April, Oct.*	Mar. 4, 1937
	435	**Panmure**—Freemasons Hall, Croydon Road, East London. *3rd Tues. March, June; 1st Sat. Sept. (I.)*	July 4, 1985
K J	436	**Mayhew**—F.M.H., Coleman St., Singapore. *4th Tues. Feb., June; 1st Fri. April, Aug.; 1st Thurs. Nov. (I.)*	Dec. 1, 1927
K J	439	**Gloucester**—M.H., Gloucester. *4th Mon. Feb., Oct. (I.); 3rd Tues. May*	Feb. 1, 1962
K	442	**Weyside**—Mas. Centre, Weybourne House, Portsmouth Rd., Guildford. *1st Fri. Feb. (I.), April, Oct.*	Mar. 1, 1934
2KC	443	**Elias de Derham**—M.H., Salisbury SP1 2QD. *4th Mon. Jan., March (I.), Oct., Nov.*	Dec. 14, 1904
KC	444	**Shropshire**—F.M.H., Crewe Street, Shrewsbury. *3rd Fri. March, May (I.), Nov.*	Nov. 30, 1905
2K	445	**St. Swithuns**—M.H. Park View, Crowle. *1st Tues. March; 3rd Tues. June (I.), Oct.*	July 8, 1992
K	448	**Hampton Court**—Cole Court, Twickenham. *3rd Fri. May; 1st Fri. July (I.)*	Mar. 2, 1978
	449	**Mid-Sussex**—Normandy Centre, Denne Rd., Horsham. *1st Mon. March, Nov.; 3rd Wed. May (I.)*	Feb. 2, 1956
J	450	**Sutton Surrey**—M.H., Sutton, Surrey. *2nd Wed. Feb.; 4th Wed. Sept. (I.); 1st Wed. June.*	June 6, 1929
C	451	**Bolingbroke**—M.H., Oakfield Rd., West Croydon. *2nd Sat. May (I.); 3rd Sat. Sept.*	Feb. 9, 1893
	452	**St. Herberts**—M.H., St. John St., Keswick, Cumberland CA12 5AP. *2nd Fri. Jan., April, Sept. (I.)*	Sept. 4, 1969
	453	**Broadwater**—Charmandean Centre, Forest Rd., Worthing. *4th Wed. Jan. (I.), May; 3rd Wed. Sept.*	June 1, 1933
K	454	**Tuscan**—Mark Mason's Hall, London SW1A 1PL. *3rd Mon. June; 1st 5th weekday Oct. (I.)*	July 6, 1972

ROLL OF ROYAL ARK MARINER LODGES—*continued*

K	458	**Ethical**—Mark Masons' Hall, London SW1A 1PL. *3rd Mon. Jan. (I.); 4th Tues. Oct.*	June 4, 1942
	459	**La France**—Mark Masons' Hall, London SW1A 1PL. *3rd Mon. (mornings) April, June, Oct. (I.)*	Nov. 1, 1973
C	461	**George Graveley**—Thurrock M.H., Lenthall Ave., Grays RM17 5AA. *2nd Mon. March (I.), May, July.*	Oct. 10, 1910
K J	462	**Inglewood**—M.H., Portland Place, Penrith CA11 7QN. *4th Tues. Feb., April, Sept. (I.), Nov.*	Oct. 2. 1930
	464	**St. George of Colombo**—Victoria M.T., Colombo 03, Sri Lanka. *1st Mon. March, July, Nov. (I.)*	Oct. 20, 2003
K	467	**West Ham**—M.H., Church Road, Potter St., Harlow CM17 9HD. *1st Thurs. Dec.; 4th Thurs. April (I.), Oct.*	July 23, 1921
	471	**Lilford**—M.R., Thrapston. *2nd Wed. Jan., March (I.), Nov.*	June 4, 1959
2K	473	**Southport**—M.H., Duke St., Southport. *1st Thurs. Feb. (I.), Oct., Dec.*	Jan. 28, 1896
J	474	**Porphyry**—F.M.H., Karachi. *4th Fri. Jan., Feb. (I.), Nov.*	Dec. 27, 1894
	477	**Powys**—M.H., Peterborough. *2nd Fri. Jan., March, Nov.; 1st Fri. Oct. (I.)*	June 1, 1918
K	479	**St. Austin's**—M.H., Warrington WA1 1NB. *3rd Mon. Feb., April; 2nd Mon. Oct. (I.)*	Feb. 7, 1952
K	480	**Wycombe**—M.C., St. Peters St., Marlow, Bucks. *1st Wed. Feb., May, Oct. (I.)*	Oct. 2, 1958
K	481	**Buenos Aires**—Calle Peru 1134, Buenos Aires 1068, Argentina. *3rd Fri. May (I.), July, Sept., Nov.*	Oct. 31, 1922
K	484	**Eastbourne**—M.T., South St., Eastbourne. *3rd Fri. Feb., April; 2nd Wed. Oct. (I.)*	Dec. 6, 1962
KC	487	**Dramatic**—Civil Service Club, Great Scotland Yard, London. *2nd Wed. Jan., April (I.); 3rd Wed. Sept.*	July 1, 1901
KC	489	**United Service**—Mark Masons' Hall. *2nd Tues. Feb. (I.); 3rd Wed. May; 2nd Tues. Nov.*	Aug. 7, 1901
	494	**St. Pancras**—M.M.H., 86 St. James's St., London. *2nd Fri. May, Nov. (I.)*	Mar. 1, 1990
	499	**Star**—M.C., Cole Court, Twickenham. *4th Wed. May (I.); 3rd Thurs. Feb., Oct.*	Oct. 10, 1900
KC ■	501	**Caldene**—M.H., Hebden Bridge. *4th Thurs. March, May, Sept., Nov. (I.)*	Feb. 2, 1904
	502	**Phœnix**—M.T., Glen Cairn, C.P., South Africa. *4th Wed. Jan., April, July; 1st Sat. Nov. (I.)*	Reconstituted 1944 Jan. 3, 1906
K	503	**All Saints**—Derby M.H., 457 Burton Rd. *2nd Fri. Jan., March, May, Nov.*	June 1, 1972
K	504	**Oxford and Cambridge University**—10 Duke St., St. James's, S.W.1. *2nd Thurs. March, Nov. (I.)*	July 7, 1960
	505	**Noel**—M.H., The Crescent, Surbiton. *3rd Mon. March, May (I.), Sept., Nov.*	Dec. 17, 1898
	514	**Ravelin**—F.M.H., Ravelin St., Fort, Bombay. *3rd Thurs. Feb. (I.); 4th Wed. March, July; last working day in Nov.*	Jan. 6, 1913

ROLL OF ROYAL ARK MARINER LODGES—*continued*

		515	**Addington**—Umlazi M.T., Old Main Road, Bellair, Durban, Natal. *3rd Mon. March, May, July, Oct. (I.)*	Dec. 12, 1922
K	J	519	**Windsor Castle**—M.H., Windsor. *3rd Wed. Feb., May, Oct. (I.)*	Apr. 16, 1921
K	J	523	**Wilbraham**—M.H., Kingsway, Widnes, Runcorn WA8 7QH. *3rd Wed. Jan., March (I.), Sept.*	Jan. 20, 1900
	■	525	**Claro**—The Masonic Hall, Deighton Road, Wetherby. *5th Wed. of the Month when occurring (Except Dec) (I.) in Sept, Oct, or Nov.*	May 31, 1997
		527	**Dunmow**—Howard Hall, 36 Bocking End, Braintree, Essex CM7 9AA. *3rd Mon. Feb., Nov. (I.)*	May 1, 1975
K	J	529	**Scarsdale**—M.H., Chesterfield. *4th Fri. Feb., April, Sept., Nov. (I.)*	Jan. 6, 1921
	C	534	**Rose**—Surbiton M.H., 6 The Crescent, Surbiton, Surrey KT6 4BN. *3rd Sat. April (I.); 2nd Wed. June; 1st Sat. Oct.*	Mar. 23, 1904
K	■	535	**Bronté**—The M.H., Mill Hey, Haworth. *3rd Tues. March, May, July (I.), Sept.*	July 1, 1971
		538	**Philanthropic**—New M.C., Hamburg Way, King's Lynn. *3rd Mon. March (I.), Sept., Nov.*	Mar. 27, 1923
K		540	**St. Nicholas**—M.T., Northfield Rd., Ilfracombe. *Last Wed. March (I.), Nov.;* M.H. Trafalgar Lawn, Barnstaple: *Last Wed. Oct. and May.*	Apr. 12, 1922
K		541	**Peace**—M.H., Gaol Square, Stafford. *1st Mon. Feb. (I.); 2nd Fri. Sept.*	Apr. 12, 1919
		542	**Tripp**—M.H., Wellington, Nilgiris, Madras. *4th Mon. April, Oct. (I.);* M.H., Ootacamund, Nilgiris: *4th Mon. Jan., July.*	Sept. 2, 1943
		546	**Hartford**—M.H., Bedlington. *3rd Wed. Feb. (I.), April, June, Oct., Dec.*	Dec. 7, 1944
	J	547	**Blagdon**—M.H., Beaconsfield St., Blyth. *1st Wed. Feb., March, April (I.), Oct. Dec.*	Sept. 5, 1918
		550	**Manica**—M.H., Mutare, Zimbabwe. *1st Thurs. July, Aug., Sept., and the 2nd Sat. after the 1st Thurs. of Oct. (I.)*	Dec. 6, 1956
K		551	**Mizpah**—M.T., Pinelands, Cape Town. *4th Tues. Feb., May, Aug. (I.)*	Nov. 20, 1897
		552	**Adoniram**—M.H., Hope St., Liverpool. *Last day of March (I.), except when that date falls on a weekend when the date shall be the preceding Friday; last Fri. Oct.*	Mar. 3, 1938
		553	**Saint George**—M.H. Garston, Liverpool 19. *2nd Tues. Jan., March (I.), Nov.*	Feb. 5, 1976
K		556	**James Terry**—Halsey M.H., Cheshunt, Herts. *1st Tues. March; Oct.; 2nd Tues. May (I.)*	May 7, 1929
		558	**Israel**—M.C., Pinelands, Cape Town. *1st Mon. Feb., July, Oct.; last week March (I.)*	Jan. 2, 1951
		566	**Biggarsberg Unity**—M.T., Dundee and Vryheid. *2nd Wed. May, Sept., Jan. (Vryheid); 2nd Wed. July, Nov.;* *3rd Sat. March (I.) (Dundee).*	Sept. 7, 1967
K		568	**Regnum**—M.H., 7 South Pallant, Chichester. *4th Tues. Feb., May; 1st Tues. Oct. (I.)*	July 6, 1972

ROLL OF ROYAL ARK MARINER LODGES—continued

569 **Abernethy**—Mark Masons' Hall.
4th Thurs. Jan. (I.); 1st Thurs. April; 2nd Mon. Oct.   Dec. 2, 1953

570 **Grays Thurrock**—Orsett M.H., Essex.
4th Sat. Feb.; 3rd Sat. Dec.; 2nd Wed. April, Nov. (I.)   Dec. 3, 1943

571 **Cerdic**—M.H., Chard.
2nd Wed. March; 4th Wed. May, 1st Thurs. Sept. (I.)   June 6, 1985

573 **Keystone**—M.T., Harare, Zimbabwe.
3rd Thurs. March (I.), June, Sept., Nov.   June 1, 1944

574 **Sao on Kya**—F.M.H., Maymyo, Burma.
3rd Wed. Jan., April (I.), July, Sept., Nov.   Jan. 7, 1937

575 **Stanger**—Victoria County Masonic Hall, Umhlali, S.A.
4th Wed. March, May (I.), July, Sept., Nov.   Feb. 7, 1974

576 **Sphinx**—Mas. Complex, Masonic Street, Port Alfred.
Last Sat. Jan. (I.); 2nd Mon. April, July, Oct.   July 1, 1982

577 **Wicket**—M.M.H.
1st Fri. Feb., Nov. (I.)   Feb. 2, 1996

J   579 **Wairua**—M.H., Kowhai Street, Helensville, New Zealand.
1st Tues. March, June, Sept. (I.), Dec.   Aug. 7, 2010

584 **Manor of Chatham**—M.T., Franklin Rooms, Gillingham.
3rd Wed. March; 1st Thurs. Oct. (I.)   Mar. 4, 1919

585 **Arthur Lewis**—M.T., Courthouse Street, Pontypridd.
2nd Tues. Feb.; 4th Fri. May; 2nd Fri. Nov. (I.)   Feb. 6, 1986

2K   588 *United Service—M.C., Jukskei Ave., The Willows, Pretoria.*
In abeyance Aug. 31, 2010   *July 3, 1924*

C   590 **Athlumney**—Talbot Ho., Stourbridge.
1st Thurs. March, Nov.; 2nd Thurs. Sept. (I.)   July 12, 1912

K   594 **Admiral Beatty**—M.H., Mill Rd., Wellingborough.
2nd Thurs. March, Oct. (I.), Dec.   Mar. 25, 1918

K   ■ 595 **St. Peter's**—M.R., Campbell St., Belper.
Last Tues. Feb., April (I.), Sept.; 2nd Tues. Jan.   Feb. 1, 1962

597 **Stayley**—Oaklands Masonic Club, Mottram Road, Hyde, Cheshire.
last Fri. Feb.; 1st Fri. April Oct. (I.)   May 31, 1916

601 **United Services Lodge of Installed Commanders**—M.C. Ringwood Drive, Pinelands C.P.
2nd Wed. April, (I.), July, Oct.; 4th Wed. Jan.   Feb. 7, 1985

603 **Stradbroke**—M.R., High St., March.
2nd Tues. Feb. (I.), April, Oct., Dec.   Feb. 21, 1914

604 **Duffryn**—M.H., Tredegar.
2nd Mon. Sept., Nov., Feb.; May (I.)   May 7, 1970

K   605 **Bede**—Masonic Hall, Station Rd., Chester le Street.
4th Tues. Feb., March, Sept. (I.), Nov.   May 18, 1921

K   606 **Seymour**—M.R., Leamington Spa.
Last Tues. Jan., March, Sept. (I.), Nov.   May 3, 1920

J   607 **Great Ouse**—M.H., St. Ives, Hunts.
4th Wed. Jan. (I.), Sept., Nov.   Mar. 15, 1922

610 **Chola**—M.T., F.M.H., Cantonement, Trichinopoly, Madras, India.
Last Sat. Feb., May, Aug. (I.), Nov.   Apr. 2, 1953

K J   613 **Itchen**—M.H., Manor Rd., Woolston, Southampton.
2nd Mon. Jan. (I.), March, May, Nov.   May 1, 1918

ROLL OF ROYAL ARK MARINER LODGES—*continued*

K	616	**Carnarvon**—Mark Masons' Hall. *2nd Sat. Feb., June, Oct. (I.)*	Nov. 7, 1929
K	617	**Sir Francis Drake**—M.H., Smallack Drive, Crownhill, Plymouth. *3rd Thurs. Feb., June (I.), Oct.*	Sept. 8, 1994
2K	621	**Boksburg-Cinderella**—Central East Rand Temple, 66 Jubilee Rd., Boksburg. *2nd Mon. Feb., April, Aug.; 3rd Sat. Sept. (I.)*	Nov. 7, 1929
	622	**Warren de Tabley**—The Leicester Warren Hall, Bexton Lane, Knutsford WA16 9BQ. *Last Fri. Jan., March; 4th Mon. Sept. (I.)*	June 5, 1947
	624	**Premier**—Ebute Metta M.H., 22 Odaliki Street, Ebute Metta, Lagos, Nigeria. *4th Wed. Feb., April, Aug., Oct. (I.)*	Mar. 7, 1957
	628	**Silver River**—M.T., Calle Canelones 1429, Montevideo. *1st Thurs. Feb., May, Aug. (I.), Nov.*	Feb. 20, 1946
K	629	**Temperance**—Warwickshire M.T., Clarendon Suites, 2 Stirling Rd., Birmingham B16 9SB. *1st Fri. March, May (I.)*	May 7, 1921
K	630	**Dunckerley**—F.M.H., Park St., Bristol. *2nd Mon. Feb.; 3rd Thurs. May, Sept. (I.)*	Feb. 2, 1989
K	631	**Thornton**—M.H., Church St., Uckfield, E.Sussex. *1st Fri. Feb., May, Nov. (I.)*	June 3, 1976
K	632	**Fitz Hugh**—M.H., Nottingham. *4th Wed. March; 2nd Wed. July; 3rd Wed. Dec. (I.)*	Mar. 4, 1974
2K	633	**Horus**—Mark Masons' Hall. *Last Mon. Jan.; 3rd Mon. May (I.); 2nd Mon. Oct.*	July 7, 1938
	636	**Debenham**—Ashwell House, 167 Verulam Rd., St. Albans, Herts. *1st Thurs. Feb., April, May (I.)*	Nov. 22, 1923
	637	**Phullailce**—F.M.H., Strachan Rd., Karachi. *4th Mon. Jan. (I.), May, Sept.*	Oct. 3, 1963
J	639	**St. Tydfil**—M.H., Merthyr Tydfil. *2nd Tues. Jan., March, May (I.), Sept.*	Oct. 2, 1947
	640	**United Service**—F.M.H., 19 Primrose Rd., Bangalore 25, India. *4th Thurs. Feb., May, Aug. (I.), Nov.*	Dec. 6, 1973
K	641	**Dewsbury**—M.T., Halifax Rd., Dewsbury. *3rd Mon. June (I.), Sept., April.*	Sept. 6, 1973
	642	**Landale Johnston**—F.M.H., 19 Park St., Calcutta. *4th Mon. Feb. (I.), June, Sept; 3rd Mon. Dec.*	May 13, 1920
	644	**Arum**—F.M.H., Jamestown, St. Helena. *4th Tues. March, June, Sept; (I.); 2nd Tues. Dec.*	May 4, 1967
K	646	**Avon**—M.H., Avonmouth, Bristol. *1st Tues. March (I.), June, Nov.*	Jan. 6, 1977
	647	**Guild of Freemen**—London Masonic Centre, Clerkenwell. *1st Thurs. Nov., Mar.; 2nd Thurs. May (I.)*	May 5, 1927
K	648	**Ararat**—F.M.H., Fort, Bombay. *4th Thurs. April, July, Nov., Jan. (I.)*	July 6, 1967
K	650	**St. Bartholomew**—M.T., Wednesbury. *3rd Tues. Jan. (I.), March, Oct.*	June 11, 1918
K ■	651	**Welcome**—M.H., Wellgate, Rotherham, Yorks. *2nd Mon. Jan. (I.), April, June, Oct.*	June 6, 1918
	652	**Alliance**—Mark Masons' Hall. *1st Tues. March; 4th Tues. May; 1st Tues. Nov. (I.)*	June 7, 1951

ROLL OF ROYAL ARK MARINER LODGES—continued

	653	**Capt. Sam B. Aga**—F.M.H., Civil Lines, Nagpur. *2nd Fri. Feb., May, Aug. (I.), Nov.*	Jan. 6, 1976
3K	■ 658	**Pudsey**—M.H., Church Lane, Pudsey, W. Yorks. LS28 7RF. *4th Mon. Jan.; 2nd Mon. June (I.); 3rd Mon. Sept.*	Apr. 10, 1980
K	663	**Perak**—Dewan Freemason, Tiger Lane, Ipoh, Malaysia. *3rd Sat. Jan., April, July, Oct. (I.)*	July 4, 1968
	667	**Moseley**—Moseley M.H., Alcester Rd. South, Birmingham B14 6DT. *1st Mon. March (I.), June, Dec.; 4th Mon. Sept.*	Sept. 7, 1944
	668	**St. Marks**—F.M.H., 9, Exhibition Rd, Pune, India. 411001 *3rd Sat. Feb. (I.), May, Aug; Nov.*	Feb. 21, 1998
	673	**Panch-Ab**—F.M.H., Lahore. *1st Wed. Jan., Feb., Oct., Nov. (I.)*	Feb. 17, 1954
K	674	**Loveland**—M.H., Leigh Rd., Eastleigh. *1st Tues. April, June (I.), Sept.*	Sept. 2, 1971
	679	**Ashoka**—F.M.H., New Delhi, North India. *3rd Mon. May, July; 2nd Tues. Sept. (I.)*	Jan. 6, 1955
	■ 681	**Peace**—Uppermill Masonic Buildings, (Candour Lodge), High Street, Uppermill. *1st 5th Fri. in the 1st (I.), 2nd and 3rd quarters respectively*	Feb. 21, 2009
3K	683	**East Hertfordshire**—M.H., Radlett. *4th Mon. April, Sept.; 4th Mon. June (I.)*	Dec. 4, 1925
	685	**Perseverance**—M.H., York Rd., Kettering. *Last Mon. Jan.; 2nd Mon. March (I.); Last Mon. Oct.*	June 2, 1927
	686	**Lowestoft**—M.H., 101 The Avenue, Lowestoft. *1st Mon. April, Oct. (I.), Dec.*	Feb. 7, 1963
	687	**Mortimer**—M.H., Wymondham. *4th Wed. Feb., April; 1st Thurs. Dec. (I.)*	July 23, 1921
K	689	**Lancastrians**—F.M.H., Bridge St., Manchester. *4th Tues. Feb., April, Nov. (I.)*	Sept. 7, 1944
K	690	**Victory**—M.H., East St., Bridport. *2nd Fri. March, May (I.), Sept., Nov.*	June 1, 1978
J	691	**Morpeth**—M.H., Dacre St., Morpeth. *2nd Wed. Jan., March (I.), Sept., Nov.*	Mar. 3, 1939
K J	696	**Strode**—Queen Victoria M.H., 76 Victoria Rd., St. Budeaux, Plymouth. *1st Thurs. Feb., April (I.), June, Sept.*	Aug. 5, 1920
K	697	**Exmoor**—M.H., Minehead. *4th Fri. Feb.; 2nd Fri. June, Nov. (I.)*	July 6, 1978
K	698	**Machen**—Warwickshire Masonic Peace Memorial Temple, Clarendon Rd., Birmingham. *4th Wed. Jan., May (I.)*	Oct. 13, 1920
J	703	**Hothampton**—Gordon Centre, Canada Grove, Bognor Regis. *2nd Wed. May (I.); 3rd Wed. Jan., Nov.*	Mar. 7, 1946
K	705	**Claughton**—M.T., Clifton Rd., Birkenhead. *3rd Mon. March (I.), Nov.*	Apr. 5, 1973
K	715	**Hipperholme**—M.H., Hipperholme. *4th Fri. Jan., April (I.), Sept.*	Feb. 1, 1924
K	716	**Morecambe**—M.H., 5 Derby St., Morecambe LA4 4BD. *4th Fri. Feb., April, Oct. (I.)*	Feb. 3, 1972
	717	**Shipden**—M.R., Cromer Rd., Sheringham. *2nd Wed. Jan., March, Oct. (I.), Dec.*	May 4, 1933

ROLL OF ROYAL ARK MARINER LODGES—*continued*

K	719	**Yenton**—Yenton Assembly Rooms, Erdington, Birmingham. *3rd Thurs. Jan. (I.); 1st Mon. March, June.*	May 7, 1921
2K	720	**Benoni**—M.T., First Ave., Springs, Gauteng. *1st Mon. March, June, Dec.; 2nd Sat. Sept. (I.)*	June 6, 1946
	721	**P.C. Woo**—Zetland Hall, 1 Kennedy Road, Mid-levels, Hong Kong S.A.R. *1st Wed. Jan., May, Aug., Nov. (I.)*	June 22, 2009
	723	**Four Cardinal Virtues**—M.H., Kinderton St. Middlewich. *3rd Fri. March; 3rd Thur. May (I.), Oct.*	Apr. 5, 1973
	726	**Bentinck**—M.R., 7, Fairbank, Kirkby Lonsdale LA6 2BD. *4th Wed. Feb. Mar, Oct. (I.)*	April 4, 1998
	728	**Royal Colonial Institute**—Mark Masons' Hall. *2nd Fri. March; 3rd Fri. June; 1st Fri. Dec. (I.)*	July 4, 1963
	730	**Thackery**—M.H., Clevedon. *1st Mon. Feb., April, Oct. (I.), Dec.*	Sept. 5, 1946
K	733	**Perseverance**—M.H., Halesowen. *3rd Mon. Feb., May (I.), Oct.*	Nov. 1, 1945
K	735	**Concord**—Athol M.H., Severn St., Birmingham B1 1QG. *1st Fri. March; 3rd Fri. May (I.), Nov.*	Dec. 7, 1978
	738	**The William Crellin Lodge**—M.H., Temple Terrace, Aspatria, Carlisle CA7 3BH. *2nd Thurs. Feb., April (I.), Dec.*	May 30, 1996
K ■	739	**Portsdown**—M.H., Albert Rd., Cosham, Hants. *4th Fri. March, May, Sept., Nov. (I.)*	Oct. 31, 1922
2K J	741	**Golden Harvest Hillbrow Prosperity**—F.M.H., Park Lane, Parktown, Johannesburg. *3rd Fri. Jan. (I.), April, July, Oct.*	July 6, 1944
	742	**Kelvin**—Mark Masons' Hall. *4th Tues. Jan., March (I.); 1st Tues. Nov.*	Feb. 2, 1956
	743	**Howdenshire**—M.H., Selby Rd., Howden. *2nd Mon. Jan. (I.), April, Oct.*	Oct. 5, 1989
K	744	**Central Keystone**—Warwickshire Masonic Peace Memorial Temple, Edgbaston. *1st Thurs. March, Oct. (I.), Dec.*	June 5, 1943
	746	**Santos Patronos**—Calle Peru 1134, (1068) Buenos Aires, Argentina.	Apr. 13, 2000
	747	**Stechford**—M.H., Bordersley Green East, Stechford. *4th Sat. Jan., March (I.), Sept.*	Jan. 6, 1927
2K J	748	**Connaught Army and Navy**—Mark Masons' Hall. *3rd Tues. Feb. (I.); 2nd Wed. July.*	June 3, 1924
	750	**Haven**—M.H., Albion Rd., North Shields. *2nd Mon. Jan., March (I.), Nov.*	June 5, 1980
	751	**Oliver**—F.M.H., London Rd., Leicester. *3rd Mon. Jan., March, Nov. (I.)*	June 4, 1936
K	752	**Steanforde**—Mas. Centre, All Saints' St., Stamford. *Last Wed. Jan., April, Oct. (I.)*	Mar. 6, 1952
K	757	**Vesey**—M.H., Mill St., Sutton Coldfield. *4th Tues. Feb. (I.), Sept.*	Dec. 2, 1976
K	760	**St. Giles**—Maesgwyn Hall, Mold Rd., Wrexham. *Last Tues. Feb., April, Sept., Nov. (I.)*	Sept. 4, 1930
K	761	**Hackworth**—M.H., Middleton Rd., Shildon. *3rd Mon. April (I.), June, Oct., Dec.*	Feb. 29, 2000
	763	**Anglebury**—M.H., Marshall Row, Swanage on *2nd Wed. Feb., April (I.)*; M.H., Howards Lane, Wareham on *2nd Wed. June, Sept.*	April 9, 2003

ROLL OF ROYAL ARK MARINER LODGES—*continued*

K	768	**Abbey**—M.H., York Place, Knaresborough. *5th Fri. in each month when applicable, except Dec. (I.);* *last 5th Fri. in year.*	Sept. 7, 1950
J	772	**Enfield**—Corvino Ristorante Italiano, Beaufort House, 7 Middlesex St., London E1 7AA. *4th Mon. May (I.), July; 1st Wed. Sept.*	Dec. 3, 1926
	773	**Van der Stel**—M.H., Strand, C.P., S. Africa. *1st Wed. May, Aug. (I.), Dec.*	
J	775	**Thomas à Becket**—M.H., Albert Rd., Cosham, Portsmouth. *1st Tues. Feb., June, Oct., Dec. (I.)*	July 4, 1946
K	776	**Rugby**—M.H., Eastfield, Rugby. *3rd Fri. Jan., March, Sept. (I.)*	May 14, 1992
	777	**Mercury**—Brook House, Masonic Centre, Botley, Hants. *2nd Fri. March, May (I.), Nov.*	May 9, 2008
	778	**Barnard Castle**—M.H., Newgate, Barnard Castle. *1st and 2nd 5th Mon. of each year; 3rd Mon. Nov. (I.)*	Oct. 10, 2003
K	783	**Unity**—M.H., Crediton. *4th Thurs. Feb. (I.), June, Oct.*	May 4, 1972
	784	**St. Illtyd**—M.T., Pontyclun, S. Wales. *2nd Thurs. Jan., May, Sept. (I.)*	July 3, 1980
	786	**Sanitarian**—Mark Masons' Hall. *4th Wed. Feb.; 4th Mon. June; 3rd Mon. Sept. (I.)*	July 2, 1964
	788	**Whitley**—M.H., Norham Rd., Whitley Bay. *1st Tues. March (I.), May, Oct.*	Mar. 7, 1957
K	791	**Public Schools**—Mark Masons' Hall. *2nd Wed. Feb. (I.); 1st Wed. June.*	Mar. 7, 1968
	794	**Socrates**—M.H., The Priory, Huntingdon. *2nd Tues. March (I.), Nov.; 1st Tues. Oct.*	May 5, 1938
	796	**Torfaen**—M.H., Pontypool. *1st Fri. March (I.), June, Oct., Dec.*	Feb. 27, 1980
	801	**Vaudeville**—Imperial Hotel, Russel Square, London. *2nd Mon. Jan.; 4th Tues. June; 1st Mon. Oct. (I.)*	Apr. 3, 1930 Warrant of Confirmation Jan. 2007
	802	**Composite**—Mark Masons' Hall. *4th Thurs. April (I.), Sept.; 2nd Thurs. Dec.*	Mar. 30, 2001
	803	**Alexandra**—M.H., Hornsea. *2nd Wed. April, May (I.), Sept.*	Nov. 21, 1994
K	806	**St. Andrew's**—M.H., Castle St., Farnham, Surrey. *4th Thurs. Jan., March, Nov. (I.)*	Jan. 6, 1966
K J	808	**Richmond**—M.H., 6 The Crescent, Surbiton, Surrey. *Last weekday Jan., April (I.); 3rd Mon. June.*	Dec. 1, 1927
K	810	**Worksop**—M.H., Worksop. *2nd Tues. Feb. (I.), Nov.; 2nd Mon. June*	Mar. 1, 1956
	814	**Aurelius**—Colvin Memorial Temple, 7 Holland Road, Clacton-on-Sea CO15 6EG. *2nd Fri. Feb., April (I.), Oct., Dec.*	Sept. 2, 1948
	816	**Rock of Hope**—M.T., Dar-Es-Salaam. *3rd Fri. May, July (I.), Nov.*	June 5, 1998
	820	**Lliedi**—M.H., Harries Ave., Llanelli. *4th Fri. March, Sept. (I.), Dec.*	Sept. 1, 1983

ROLL OF ROYAL ARK MARINER LODGES—*continued*

	821	**Idris**— 2nd Thurs. *March:* M.H., Lleyn Street, Pwllheli; 3rd Tues. *May:* M.H., Mount Street, Bola: 2nd Thurs. *Oct. (I.):* M.H., Water Street, Barmouth:	Oct. 25, 1997
	823	**Cambria**—M.T., Cardiff. *1st Mon. June (I.); 4th Mon. Sept.; 1st Mon. Dec.*	Dec. 6 , 1945
	824	**Weaver**—M.H., York Street, Runcorn. *4th Wed. April, Sept., Nov. (I.)*	Feb. 6, 1930
	828	**King Solomon's Quarries**—M.M.H., London. *4th Thurs. Jan., Nov.; 3rd Thurs. June (I.)*	June 23, 1993
3K	831	**Zetland**—Zetland M.H., Dunheved Rdl., Saltash. *4th Tues. Feb., April, June (I.), Nov.*	Feb. 6, 1969
	834	**Ambresbury**—M.H., 16 High Beech Road, Loughton, Essex IG10 4BL. *4th Fri. Jan., April, Nov. (I.)*	Mar. 6, 1947
K J	835	**Sydenham**—S.E. London M Club, Avenue Rd., SE20 7RT *3rd Sat. Feb. (I.); 1st Sat. April, Oct.*	July 2, 1927
K	836	**Industry and Merit**—F.M.H., Bombay. *3rd Mon. Jan. (I.), April, July, Oct.*	May 7, 1968
	838	**Hawarden**—Farfield Hall, Connah's Quay. *2nd Thurs. May (I.), June; 2nd Fri. Sept.*	July 4, 1974
2K J	839	**Cornwall Legh**—Masonic Guildhall, Wellington Rd., South, Stockport. *3rd Wed. Feb., April, Oct. (I.)*	Dec. 6, 1945
K J	840	**North Shropshire**—St. Marys Hall, Ellesmere. *1st Thurs. Jan.; 3rd Tues. May; 2nd Fri. Oct.*	Mar. 2, 1950
J	841	**Catford**—M.H., Oakley House, Bromley Common, Kent. *1st Wed. April, June, (I.) Dec.*	May 2, 1946
	842	**St. Peter's**—M.H., Woodside, Wigmore, Gillingham. *1st & 2nd fifth Weds. excl. Jan.; 1st fifth Wed. Aug. (I.)*	July 7, 1960
K ■	844	**Dore**—M.H., Dore. *4th Thurs. Feb., April, June, Oct. (I.)*	Sept. 7, 1950
K	845	**Allertonshire**—Masonic Lodge, Picks Lane, Thirsk. *1st Tues. March (I.), May, Sept., Nov.*	Feb. 6, 1958
	847	**Cherwell**—M.H., Banbury. *Last Tues. June (I.); 1st Tues. Nov.*	Apr. 4, 1979
	848	**Kosmos**—M.T., Fanny Ave., Norwood, Johannesburg. *5th Mon. in each month when such days occur except Dec.; 4th Wed. June (I.)*	
	850	**Henham**—M.H., Halesworth, Suffolk. *4th Thurs. March; 3rd Thurs. May, July (I.)*	Feb. 4, 1948
	854	**St. Andrews**—The Masonic Hall, Scott Street, Stanley. *2nd Thurs. March (I.), June, Nov.*	Apr. 14, 2005
	856	**Golden Square**—Mark Masons' Hall. *2nd Wed. April (I.), Oct.; 3rd Wed. Feb.*	July 15, 1932
	857	**Kentish**—Westwood Mas. Centre, Welling, Kent. *1st Tues. March (I.); 4th Tues. Sept.; 1st Tues. Dec.*	May 4, 1944
	858	**Staines**—Staines M.T., Staines. *2nd Fri. March, July, Nov. (I.)*	Sept. 3, 1931
K	860	**Bernard Gilpin**—M.H., Hetton-le-Hole, Durham. *3rd Mon. March, April, Sept. (I.), Oct.*	Jan. 6, 1977

ROLL OF ROYAL ARK MARINER LODGES—*continued*

     861 **Christopher Wren**—Cole Court, London Rd., Twickenham.
           1st Thurs. April; 4th Thurs. Sept. (I.)   June 5, 1930

K   862 **Regis**—The Regis M.H., Halesowen Rd., Warley.
           2nd Thurs. Feb.; 1st Wed. May (I.); 2nd Thurs. Dec.   Jan. 2, 1975

     863 **Jeppestown**—Kensington Hall, Cr. Roberts Ave. & Ivanhoe St.
           4th Mon. Jan., April, July, Oct. (I.)   Oct. 4, 1979

     864 **White Stone**—M.H., Station Road, Chingford, London E4 7AZ.
           4th Mon. April (I.); 3rd Mon. Oct.   June 2, 1955

K   868 **Hyde**—Oaklands M.H., Mottram Road, Cheshire.
           3rd Fri. Jan., Oct.; 3rd Wed. May (I.)   Dec. 2, 1971

     869 **City of London**—Civil Service Club, 13/15 Great Scotland Yard, London SW1A 2HJ.
           4th Mon. Jan., March (I.), Nov.   Dec. 3, 1942

■   872 **Digswell**—The Cloisters, Barrington Road, Letchworth SG6 3TH.
           3rd Wed. March (I.), May; 4th Wed. June   Apr. 6 , 1961

■   875 **Harmony**—M.H., Queen's Rd., Fareham, Hants.
           3rd Fri. Feb., May, Sept. (I.), Nov.   Oct. 1, 1964

     876 **Knole**—M.Ctr., 119a St. John's Road, Sevenoaks, Kent TN13 3PE.
           2nd Fri. March (I.), Oct., Dec.   Sept. 2, 1943

     877 **Sivangnanam**—F.M.H., Trivandrum, India.
           1st Sat. Jan. (I.), April, July, Oct.   Sept. 1, 1988

K ■ 878 **Pontefract**—M.H., Carleton Close, Pontefract.
           2nd Fri. Jan., April, July, Oct. (I.)   Feb. 3, 1955

K   879 **Three Grand Principles**—M.H., Penryn.
           3rd Mon. Jan., March, May, Sept., Nov. (I.)   Apr. 7, 1932

     880 **Semper Fidelis**—M.H., 32 The Esplanade, Fleetwood, Lancashire.
           3rd Wed. Jan., March; Last weekday Oct. (I.)   Sept. 1, 1938

     881 **Ararat**—F.M.H., Sadie Kaplan Ave., Parkview, Bulawayo.
           2nd Mon. March, June (I.), Sept., Dec.   July 7, 1960

     883 **Mill Hill**—Cafe Naz at Corvino, 7 Middlesex Street, London E1 7AA.
           4th Sat. June (I.); 3rd Sat. Dec.   Feb. 4, 1965

     885 **Rising Star**—M.C., van Blerk Ave., Spitskop, Bloemfontein, S. Africa.
           4th Sat. Jan. (I.), April, July; 1st Sat. Oct.   Dec. 4, 1936

K   886 **Oakley**—M.H., Victoria St., Basingstoke.
           1st Thurs. Feb. April (I.), Nov.   Apr. 7, 1949

     890 **Ashington**—M.H., Ashington, Northumberland.
           1st Thurs. March, May (I.), Sept., Nov.   June 5, 1941

     892 **Tower Hamlets**—Mark Masons' Hall.
           2nd Mon. Jan.; 1st Mon. June (I.), Sept.   Dec. 2, 1982

     893 **St. Laurence**—M.H., Redditch.
           2nd Mon. Jan. (I.), March, Nov.   July 4, 1935

K   896 **Clavering**—M.H., Alexandra Road, Gateshead, Durham.
           4th Thurs. Feb., April (I.), June, Aug.   June 3, 1971

K   897 **Barnet Mark Well**—Mark Masons' Hall.
           4th Tues. May; 3rd Mon. Sept.; 1st Tues. Dec. (I.)   Dec. 6, 1979

     898 **Progress**—M.H., Preston.
           4th Wed. Feb. (I.), May, Oct.   Mar. 30, 2011

     900 **Vereeniging**—M.H., Phoenix, Mauritius.
           1st Mon. March, June, Sept. (I.), Dec.   Oct. 3, 1974

ROLL OF ROYAL ARK MARINER LODGES—*continued*

	901	**Kenton**—Harrow District M.C., Northwick Circle, Kenton, Middx. *4th Thurs. March, Nov.; 2nd Thurs. June (I.)*	June 7, 1962
	903	**Prescot**—M.H., High St., Prescot. *2nd Thurs. Jan., March, Nov. (I.)*	Dec. 6, 1951
	906	**Mount Mawenzi**—M.H., Selian, Arusha, Tanzania. *4th Tues. Feb., July, Nov. (I.)*	Aug. 31, 2002
	907	**Vijiyam**—Yaley Residency, Brough Road, Erode-1, Madras, India. *Last Sat. Feb., May (I.), Aug., Nov.*	Jan. 6, 1955
K	908	**Billinge**—M.H., Richmond Terrace, Blackburn. *4th Tues. Feb., May, Nov. (I.)*	Aug. 31, 2002
	909	**Lea Valley**—Halsey Hall, Turners Hill, Cheshunt. *3rd Tues. March; 4th Tues. June, Nov. (I.)*	June 3, 1982
K ■	911	**Keep**—M.R., Conservative Club, Castle St., Clitheroe. *3rd Wed. Jan., April, Sept. (I.), Nov.*	May 7, 1970
	914	**Loyalty**—M.H., Oakfield Rd., Croydon. *1st Fri. March, Oct.; 2nd Fri. June (I.)*	Apr. 3, 1935
K	916	**St. Wulfram's**—M.H., Chambers St., Grantham. *2nd Wed. Jan., March (I.), April, Oct.*	Feb. 6 , 1958
	918	**Rottingdean**—Jerrom Hall, Seaview Rd., Peacehaven, Brighton. *2nd Mon. Feb., May, Nov. (I.)*	Feb. 2, 1961
	920	**Ravenscroft**—M.Ctr., Halsey, Turners Hill, Cheshunt, Herts. *3rd Mon. Feb., (I.), May, Nov.*	Feb. 7, 1980
K	921	**Foundation**—Mark Masons' Hall, London SW1A 1PL. *4th Mon. March, Sept. (I.)*	July 5, 1979
	922	**Wythenshawe**—Masonic Guildhall, Tatton Rd., Sale, Cheshire. *1st Thurs. Feb. (I.), May, Sept.*	Aug. 13, 1917
	923	**Vernon**—M.H., Stourport-on-Severn. *1st Fri. Feb., April; 2nd Mon. Nov. (I.)*	Dec. 4, 1947
K	925	**Moseley**—M.H., Birtley, Co. Durham. *4th Mon. Jan., March, Sept. (I.), Nov.*	Dec. 2, 1948
K J	926	**William Hamilton Underhill**—The Cloisters, Barrington Rd., Letchworth. *2nd Mon. March (I.), Sept., Nov.*	Mar. 6, 1947
	930	**Castle Eden**—Castle Eden M.H., Stockton Road, Castle Eden TS27 4SD. *2nd Fri. May, July, Nov. (I.)*	Nov. 14, 2008
	931	**Headstone**—M.C., Northwick Circle, Harrow, Middx. *4th Mon. Feb.; 2nd Wed. May (I.); 1st Wed. Nov.*	Mar. 4, 1971
	932	**Prudence & Verity**—Mark Masons' Hall. *3rd Mon. Feb., Oct. (I.)*	Nov. 27, 2006
K J	933	**Walsall**—M.H., The Green, Aldridge. *1st Wed. March; 2nd Tues. Oct.; 2nd Wed. April (I.)*	Feb. 2, 1939
	936	**Meridian**—M.M.H., London SW1A 1PL. *4th Wed. Jan. (I.), April; 3rd Wed. Sept.*	Apr. 26, 1995
	937	**Tanjore**—F.M.H., 197 Market Road, Thanjavur 613001, Madras, India. *1st Sat. March, June, Sept. (I.), Dec.*	Sept. 16, 2006
	938	**Nore**—M.T., Cornwell Rd., Whitstable. *3rd Wed. March, May (I.), Sept., Nov.*	June 5, 1943
3K	940	**Galway**—M.H., Welbeck Rd., West Bridgford, Nottingham. *4th Thurs. May (I.); 4th Wed. June, July.*	Feb. 7, 1974

ROLL OF ROYAL ARK MARINER LODGES—*continued*

	944	**Fillebrook**—M.H, Station Road, Chingford, London E4 7AZ. *2nd Wed. March, June (I.); 3rd Thurs. Oct.*	May 2, 1963
K	945	**Crowstone**—Saxon Hall, Aviation Way, Southend-on-Sea, Essex SS2 6UN. *3rd Thurs. Jan., April (I.), Nov.*	Sept. 2, 1948
K	946	**St. Nicholas**—M.H., Main Ridge, Boston. *1st Mon. Feb., April, Oct. (I.), Dec.*	July 6, 1944
K	949	**Constitution**—F.M.H., Bridge St., Manchester. *2nd Tues. Jan., March (I.), Nov.*	Dec. 4, 1986
	950	**Dunraven**—M.T., Bridgend. *1st Thurs. March (I.); 1st Tues. May, Nov.; 4th Tues. Jan.*	Jan. 2, 1964
K	952	**Kenya Blagdon**—M.T., Nairobi. *2nd Thurs. Jan., April (I.), July, Oct.*	Jan. 4, 1962
	953	**City of Chester**—F.M.H., Queen St., Chester. *2nd Fri. Jan., March (I.), Nov.*	Apr. 4, 1974
	955	**Pleydell-Bouverie**—M.H., Godalming. *4th Tues. Jan., April, Oct. (I.)*	Feb. 5, 1941
	957	**Hartismere**—F.M.H., Parkfields, Diss. *1st Tues. April, July, Sept. (I.), Dec.*	Sept. 2, 1954
K	961	**St. Paul's**—M.T., Rua Lisboa, 1120, São Paulo, or at the meeting place of any Lodge of Mark Master Masons governed by the Mark District Grand Lodge of Brazil. *2nd Tues. April, July, Oct.; Last Sat. Nov. (I.)*	Apr. 5, 1951
K	962	**Latimer**—Ashwell House, St. Albans, Herts. *4th Wed. Jan.; 4th Fri. April; 2nd Thurs. June (I.)*	July 6, 1944
	964	**Commemoration**—M.T., Riseley St., Macclesfield. *3rd Mon. Feb., April (I.), Sept.*	Oct. 15, 1919
	965	**Connaught**—F.M.H., Soane St., Ipswich. *3rd Tues. Jan., March, May (I.); 1st Tues. Nov.*	July 1, 1971
2K	966	**Northern Transvaal**—M.H., Voortrekker St., Pietersburg. *4th Sat. March, June (I.), Sept., Nov.*	Apr. 7, 1949
	967	**Yatton**—Yatton M.H., High Street, Yatton. *Last Fri. Feb., May, Oct. (I.)*	Oct. 10, 2011
	968	**Carville**—East M.T., Corbridge Road, Newcastle upon Tyne 6. *1st Fri. Jan., March (I.), Nov.*	June 1, 1939 Warrant of Confirmation Sept. 1, 1998
■	969	**Winchester**—Winchester M.C., Alresford, Winchester. *4th Tues. Jan., March, June, Sept. (I.), Nov.*	July 15, 1989
	971	**Concord**—M.H., Yerbury St., Trowbridge, Wilts. BA14 8DP. *2nd Thurs. March, Sept. (I.), Nov.*	July 3, 1980 Warrant of Confirmation 19 Sept., 2011
3K	972	**Silhill**—M.T., Warwick Road, Knowle, Solihull. *4th Thurs. Jan., March, Nov.; 1st Mon. Oct. (I.)*	Sept. 4, 1947
	974	**James Parsons**—Halsey M.H., Watford. *2nd Wed. Feb. (I.), May, Nov.*	Oct. 1, 1942
K J	975	**Bernard Harvey**—M.C., Slough. *2nd Mon. March, May, Nov. (I.)*	May 31, 1946
	976	**Johan Gutenberg**—M.M.H., London SW1A 1PL. *1st Tues. March; 4th Tues. Sept. (I.)*	June 30, 2005
K J	977	**Eaton**—Moseley M.H., Alcester Rd. South, Kings Heath, Birmingham. *3rd Fri. Feb., April, Oct. (I.)*	June 2, 1960

ROLL OF ROYAL ARK MARINER LODGES—continued

	980	**Marlborough**—M.H., Woodstock, Oxford. *2nd Tues. May (I.); 3rd Wed. March, Nov.*	Jan. 7, 1965
K	981	**Spennymoor**—M.H., Dundas Street, Spennymoor. *4th Mon. Jan., April, Sept., Nov. (I.)*	Sept. 8, 1945
K	984	**Lodge of Harmony**—F.M.H., Faversham. *1st Thurs. Jan., March, May (I.), Dec.*	Mar. 5, 1981
	985	**Cango**—M.T., 45 Marsh Street, Mossel Bay, Western Cape, S. Africa. *1st Sat. March, June, Dec.; Sat following 1st Fri. Sept. (I.)*	Mar. 4, 1965
	986	**All Hallows**—Twickenham District M.C., Cole Court, 150 London Rd., Twickenham, Middx. *3rd Mon. Feb. (I.); 2nd Mon. July; 4th Mon. Oct.*	Apr. 2, 1959
	989	**Northern Heights**—M.H., Grove Road, Sutton. *2nd Thurs. March (I.), Dec.; 3rd Mon. May*	Dec. 1, 2003
	990	**East Lancashire Provincial Grand Officers**—F.M.H., Bridge Street, Manchester M3 3BT. *1st 5th Mon. Jan.–Apr. (I.), Sept.–Nov.*	June 7, 1990
K J	991	**Eleanor Cross**—Halsey M.H., Cheshunt. *4th Sat. Jan. (I.); 3rd Wed. May, Oct.*	Sept. 4, 1947
K	993	**Dartmouth**—M.H., Edward St., West Bromwich. *4th Wed. Jan.; 2nd Tues. May; 4th Tues. Oct. (I.)*	Sept. 2, 1971
	994	**Salford**—Salford M.H., The Crescent, Salford. *3rd Tues. Dec.; 1st Tue. June (I.)*	Sept. 4, 1980
K	995	**Stoneleigh**—Sutton M.H. *2nd Fri. Jan., Sept.; 4th Fri. May (I.)*	Dec. 1, 1949
K	996	**Isma**—Mark Masons' Hall. *4th Tues. Feb.; 1st Wed. May (I.); 3rd Wed. Oct.*	Sept. 7, 1961
K	997	**Pickwick**—Royal National Hotel, 38-51 Bedford Way, London WC1H 0DG. *2nd Thurs. March (I.); 3rd Wed. June; 4th Wed. Sept.*	Oct. 2, 1947
	998	**Boleyn Castle**—Mount Avenue Banqueting Suite, Mount Avenue, Hutton, Brentwood, Essex. *4th Tues. March; 4th Thurs. June; 4th Tues. Oct. (I.)*	June 3, 1971
	999	**Kent Installed Commanders**—M.H., Maidstone. *1st Fri. March (I.), Sept.*	Dec. 5, 1991
K	1000	**Milestone**—Mark Masons' Hall. *1st Thurs. April (I.), Oct.*	Nov. 7, 1968
2K	1001	**University of Manchester**—Freemasons Hall, Bridge Street, Manchester. *2nd Mon. June (I.); 4th Mon. Nov.*	Apr. 7, 1977
	1002	**Leyland**—Wellington Park M.H., Church Road, Leyland, Lancs. *1st Fri. Feb., April; 4th Fri. Sept. (I.)*	Sept. 27, 1996
2K	1004	**Thorne**—M.H., Stonegate, Thorne. *4th Thurs. March, May, Sept., Oct. (I.)*	Nov. 6, 1969
	1008	**St. Peters**—M.H., Castlegate, York. *3rd Thurs. Feb., May, Aug., Nov. (I.)*	July 3, 1992
K	1010	**Rose of York**—F.M.H., Westholme, Stockport Rd., Mossley, Lancs. *2nd Fri. Feb., Sept., Dec. (I.)*	Jan. 2, 1947
K	1012	**Matthew Clarke**—M.T., Clarendon Rd., Hagley Rd., Birmingham, B16 9SB. *3rd Wed. Feb., April (I.), Oct.*	May 3, 1973
K	1013	**Ealing**—M.H., Cole Court, Twickenham. *1st Fri. April (I.), July, Nov.*	Sept. 2, 1971

ROLL OF ROYAL ARK MARINER LODGES—continued

2K	■1014	**Gawthorpe**—M.T., Nelson Square, Burnley. *1st Mon. March, Oct., Dec. (I.)*	Feb. 6, 1947
	1016	**Rivacre**—M.H., 141 Chester Rd., Whitby, Ellesmere Port, Cheshire CH65 6SD. *3rd Wed. Feb., Sept. (I.)*	Apr. 6, 1972
K	1019	**Ormskirk Priory**—M.H., Park Rd., Ormskirk. *2nd Thurs. Feb., Oct. (I.), Dec.*	Feb. 3, 1955
3K	■1024	**Altrincham**—Macclesfield M.H., Oakleigh House, 1 Riseley Street, Macclesfield SK10 1BW. *4th Fri. March, May (I.), Oct.*	Mar. 2, 1950
J	1026	**St. Katherine's**—Fraternity Hall, 288 Eastwood Road North, Southend-on-Sea, Essex SS9 4LT. *4th Sat. Jan., March (I.), Sept., Nov.*	Dec. 5, 1946
	1028	**Carnanton**—M.H., Newquay. *1st Wed. April, May (I.), Sept., Oct., Dec.*	Jan. 7, 1988
	1031	**Maius**—M.H., Grove Road, Risca. *Last Mon. Feb.; 1st Mon. June, Oct. (I.)*	Oct. 24, 1994
K	1032	**Earl of Scarborough**—M.H., Rutland Rd., Skegness. *4th Wed. Jan., March, (I.), Nov.*	Oct. 3, 1963
K	■1035	**Lansdowne**—M.H., Malmesbury, Wilts. SN16 9BU. *1st Mon. April; 2nd Mon. Sept., Nov. (I.)*	June 5, 1975
	1037	**St. John's**—M.R., Water St., Wigton, Cumb. CA7 9AN *3rd Wed. Feb., May, Nov. (I.)*	July 6, 1972
K	1038	**Ashburton**—M.H., Chudley Road, Ashburton. *4th Tues. March, May, June (I.), Oct.*	Oct. 31, 1992
	1039	**Stroud**—M.H., Merrywalks, Stroud, Glos. *Wed. before 2nd Thurs. May (I.), June, July*	Feb. 7, 1991
	1043	**Barry**—M.T., Barry. *2nd Mon. March, May, Sept. (I.)*	Sept. 3, 1970
	1044	**Essex Enthroned Commanders'**—Such venues as the Prov.G.M. may direct. *3rd Tues. March; 2nd Thurs. Sept. (I.)*	Feb. 7, 1952
K	1047	**Cheshunt**—Halsey, M.H., Cheshunt. *3rd Thurs. March; 4th Thurs. June; 1st Thurs. Nov. (I.)*	Feb. 7, 1957
	1046	**Zululand**—Empangeni Masonic Centre, Zululand. *4th Thurs. Feb., April, June (I.), Aug., Oct.*	May 1, 2010
	1049	**Hindhead**—Bordon M.C., High Street, Bordon, Hants. *3rd Thurs. Jan., May, Sept. (I.)*	Mar. 5, 1987
	1050	**Esher**—M.H., Masonic Hall Road, Chertsey. *3rd Mon. Feb., June, Sept. (I.)*	Sept. 3, 1964
	1051	**Rutland**—M.H., Burton Rd., Melton Mowbray. *2nd Wed. Jan.; 3rd Wed. April (I.), Oct.*	Mar. 7, 1963
	1055	**Monument**—Washington M.H., Concord, Washington, Tyne and Wear NE37 2DU. *1st Tues. May (I.), Sept., Dec.*	May 7, 2002
K	1056	**Pymmes Park**—M.H., Maldon Road, Witham, Essex CM8 1HN. *3rd Wed. Oct., April; 2nd Wed. June (I.)*	June 7, 1951
J	1057	**Principality**—M.T., Guildford Crescent, Cardiff. *1st Wed. May (I.); 4th Wed. Oct.*	May 3, 1951
	1058	**Bexhill**—M.H., Wilton Rd., Bexhill-on-Sea. *3rd Mon. Jan. (I.), March; 4th Mon. Oct.*	Apr. 10, 1980
K	■1059	**Manchester Engineers**—F.M.H., Bridge St., Manchester. *1st 5th Fri. Jan., Feb., or March (I.); 1st 5th Fri. Sept., Oct., or Nov.*	Mar. 27, 1998

ROLL OF ROYAL ARK MARINER LODGES—*continued*

	1063	**Middlesex St. David's**—Harrow District M.C., Northwick Park Circle, Kenton, Harrow. *4th Wed. Sept.; 4th Tues. Jan. (I.)*	Apr. 16, 1993
	1064	**Mount Egmont**—F.M.H., Domett St., Waitara, N.Z. *3rd Thurs. March, July, Sept. (I.)*	Sept. 7, 1950
	1068	**Wiclif**—F.M.H., Lutterworth, Leics. *1st Wed. March (I.); 3rd Wed. Sept.; 1st Wed. Dec.*	June 7, 1962
	1071	**Polytechnic**—Mark Masons' Hall. *3rd Tues. April, June; 1st Wed. Oct. (I.)*	Nov. 30, 1993
K	1072	**Birkenhead**—Wallasey Masonic Hall. *2nd Tues. Sept. (I.), Jan.; 1st Tues. April*	Sept. 4, 1947
	1073	**Thanet**—M.T., New Cross St., Margate. *1st Thurs. Feb., March, Nov.; 3rd Thurs. April (I.)*	Mar. 6, 1952
	1074	**Thea Sinensis**—Mark Masons' Hall. *1st Wed. Feb. (I.); 3rd Thurs. April; 4th Thurs. Oct.*	Jan. 7, 1988
K	1076	**Manadon**—M.H., Tavistock Rd., Crownhill, Plymouth. *3rd Mon. Feb., April (I.), June, Oct.*	July 3, 1980
2K	■ 1079	**St. Hiev**—M.H., Charles Street, Bingley, W. Yorks. *3rd Fri. March, May, Sept. (I.)*	Sept. 10, 1994
	1083	**Orpington**—M.H., Bromley, Kent. *1st Wed. Feb., Nov.; 3rd Fri. May (I.)*	Oct. 2, 1975
	1084	**Welchpool**—M.H., Berriew Rd., Welshpool, North Wales. *1st Thurs. Feb., March, Oct. (I.), Nov.*	Sept. 5, 1968
K	1085	**Hantune**—Red House, High Street, Albrighton WV7 3JU. *3rd Mon. Feb., Oct. (I.)*	May 7, 1974
K	1086	**Abbey**—M.H., 3 North Trade Rd., Battle. *4th Mon. Jan.; 1st Mon. April, July, Oct. (I.)*	Mar. 3, 1977
K	1087	**Misbourne**—M.H., Beaconsfield. *3rd Wed. Feb. (I.), June, Oct.*	Sept. 6, 1951
K J	1088	**Afan**—M.T., Forge Rd., Port Talbot. *4th Tues. Jan., April, Sept. (I.)*	May 4, 1978
	1089	**St. Michael's**—M.H., Albany St., Sittingbourne. *4th Thurs. March, May; 2nd Thurs. Nov. (I.)*	July 3, 1952
	1090	**Ashlar**—F.M.H., Plough Lane, Christleton, Chester. *2nd Tues. Jan., March (I.), Nov.*	June 3, 1948
K	■ 1091	**Commemoration**—Corvino's Restaurant (Cafe Naz), 7 Middlesex Street, London E1 7AA. *4th Wed. Oct. (I.); 2nd Fri. Feb.; 4th Wed. May*	Feb. 1, 1990
K	1092	**Tudor**—M.H., Deyncourt Gardens, Upminster RM14 1DF. *1st Tues. March (I.), May; 2nd Tues. Oct.*	Nov. 3, 1966
K	1095	**St. Edward the Martry**—M.H., Shaftesbury. *3rd Fri. Feb. April, June, Oct. (I.)*	Sept. 2, 1954
	1101	**Aorangi**—M.H., Phillip St., Johnsonville, N.Z. *1st Tues. April, June, Aug., Oct. (I.)*	July 3, 1980
	■ 1105	**Mapesbury**—Imperial Hotel, Russell Square, London WC1H 0DG. *2nd Wed. May (I.); 3rd Thurs. July; 1st Thurs. Sept.*	Apr. 29, 1993
K	1109	**King Harold**—Halsey M.H., Cheshunt. *1st Sat. Oct.(I.); 3rd Sat. Dec.*	Sept. 4, 1952
	1110	**Warminster**—M.H., Warminster BA12 9AW. *2nd Tues. Feb., April; 4th Tues. Nov. (I.)*	Oct. 5, 1989

ROLL OF ROYAL ARK MARINER LODGES—*continued*

	1111	**Woodgrange**—Croydon & District M.H., 73 Oakfield Road, Croydon. *2nd Mon. Feb. (I.); 4th Mon. June, 1st Thurs. Oct.*	April 24, 1996
3K	1112	**Elevation**—M.H., Front Street, Burnopfield, Co. Durham. *4th Wed. Feb. (I.), April, June, Oct.*	Apr. 3, 1975
	1114	**Sprig of Acacia**—M.H., Radlett, Herts. *4th Sat. Feb., June (I.); 2nd Sat. Nov.*	Nov. 6, 1951
	1117	**Hampton Parva**—M.H., Church Street, Littlehampton. *3rd Mon. Feb. (I.), April, Oct.*	Feb. 5, 1987
K	1118	**Halcyon**—Mark Masons' Hall. *3rd Thurs. Jan. (I.); 1st Thurs. June; 3rd Thurs. Nov.*	Dec. 6, 1956
	1121	**Hertfordshire Installed Commanders**— Ashwell House, 167 Verulam Rd., St. Albans, Hertfordshire. *2nd Wed. Jan., (I.); 1st Tues. July*	April 4, 1991
	1122	**St. Guthlac**—M.H., Deeping St. James. *3rd Mon. Jan., May, Sept. (I.)*	Aug. 7, 1999
	1123	**Essex Jubilee**—Saxon Hall, Aviation Way, Southend-on-Sea, Essex SS2 6UN. *2nd Fri. Feb., May (I.); 1st Fri. Sept.*	Feb. 7, 1952
	■ 1124	**St. John's Wood**—Mark Masons' Hall. *4th Wed. May, Sept. (I.); 1st Wed. Nov.*	Oct. 29, 1991
	1125	**Neath**—M.T., Neath. *2nd Fri. Jan. (I.); Fri. before 3rd Tues. Oct.*	June 3, 1982
K	1127	**Beaudesart**—Eaton Lodge, Wolseley Rd., Rugeley, Staffs. *2nd Tues. Jan.; 3rd Tues. June (I.); 2nd Tues. Sept.*	Feb. 3, 1955
K	1129	**Wrekin**—M.H., Constitution Hill, Wellington, Telford. *4th Fri. Feb., April (I.), Oct.*	Mar. 1, 1973
	1131	**Camberley**—M.H., Agincourt Hall, London Road, Camberley, Surrey GU15 3JA. *4th Mon. Feb., April (I.), Sept.*	Nov. 5, 1964
	■ 1132	**F.W. Broadbent**—M.H., Francis Street, Farnworth, Bolton, Lancashire BL4 7NG. *2nd Thurs. Jan. (I.); 4th Thurs. June, Aug.*	Apr. 22, 2009
	1135	**St. Egwin**—M.H., Swan Lane, Evesham, Worcs. *1st Mon. Feb.; 2nd Mon. May (I.); 1st Mon. Oct.*	Feb. 4, 1971
	1137	**Wanderers**—M.T., Rua da Constituição, 293 Santos, S.P. Brazil. *4th Wed. March, June (I.), Sept., Nov.*	Aug. 8, 2009
	1138	**Exedra**—M.M.H. *2nd Mon. Jan.; 1st Tues. May (I.); 1st Mon. Oct.*	Aug. 14, 1999
	1141	**Newgate**—East M.T., Headlam St., Newcastle upon Tyne. *1st Mon. March (I.), Sept., Nov.*	Feb. 7, 1952
	1142	**Tuscan Pillar**—M.H., Deyncourt Gardens, Upminster, Essex RM14 1DF. *3rd Fri. Jan., March (I.), Oct.*	Mar. 2, 1967
K	1146	**Ashfield**—M.H., Mansfield. *2nd Mon. April (I.); 1st Mon. June, Aug.*	Apr. 5, 1956
	1150	**South Shropshire**—M.H., Brand Lane, Ludlow. *3rd Wed. Feb.; 4th Wed. May (I.); 3rd Wed. Oct.*	June 7, 1990
	1152	**Minchenden Oak**—Southgate M.C., London. *2nd Wed. March (I.); 3rd Wed. June; 1st Wed. Sept.*	May 31, 1994
	1156	**Guanabara**—M.T., Rua da Matriz No. 76, Rio de Janeiro. *2nd Thurs. May, July, Sept., Nov. (I.)*	June 4, 1953
K	1157	**Crane**—White Lion Hotel, Tenterden, Kent. *2nd Thurs. April, June (I.), Oct.*	Nov. 2, 1972

ROLL OF ROYAL ARK MARINER LODGES—*continued*

	1158 **Sussex Installed Commanders**—Sussex M.C., Queen's Road, Brighton. *4th Thurs. May (I.); Last Wed. Oct.*	May 13, 1992
3K	1159 **True Love and Unity**—M.H., Church Street, Brixham. *1st Tues. March, May (I.), Sept., Dec.*	Sept. 6, 1973
K	1160 **Pro Minimis**—Mark Masons' Hall. *1st Thurs. March, June (I.), Dec.*	July 5, 1962
	1161 **Hexham**—M.H., Westfield Terrace, Hexham. *3rd Fri. March, May, Oct. (I.)*	July 2, 1964
2K	1162 **Wallingford**—M.H., Wallingford, Berks. *Last Fri. March (I.); 1st Fri. Sept.*	Feb. 1, 1973
	1165 **Quator Legati**—M.H., Institute St., Bolton. *2nd Tues. Feb., Oct.; 3rd Mon. May.*	May 30, 1997
	1166 **Wroxham**—M.R., Wroxham. *4th Tues. May (I.), June, July.*	Oct. 4, 1973
K	1167 **Manor of Bensham**—Croydon and District M.H., Oakfield Rd., Croydon. *3rd Fri. March (I.); 2nd Fri. Oct., Dec.*	Oct. 1, 1953
K	1172 **Berkhampstead**—Ashwell House, St. Albans. *3rd Thurs. Feb.; 4th Wed. May; 2nd Wed. Oct. (I.)*	Sept. 4, 1958
	1173 **Flixton**—M.H., Peel Street, Westhoughton, Lancs. BL5 3SP. *2nd Thurs. Jan., May (I.), Sept.*	Apr. 2, 1992
	1183 **Thames**—M.H., Henley-on-Thames. *Last Fri. Jan., May (I.)*	May 7, 1964
2K	1186 **Transvaal Keystone**—Southern M.C., Glensands Ave., Rewlatch, Johannesburg. *1st Sat. Feb. (I.); 1st Tues. April, July, Oct.*	Feb. 2, 1974
K	1187 **St. Winnold**—M.H., Downham Market. *4th Thurs. Sept. (I.); any fifth Thurs. in the months of Sept.-Nov., Jan.-April*	Oct. 5, 1967
K	1188 **Saint Nicholas**—M.H., Bodmin. *2nd Thurs. March, May (I.), Sept., Nov.*	Feb. 1, 1979
K	1189 **Backworth**—M.H., Moor Edge Road, Shiremoor, Northumberland. *2nd Tues. Feb., May (I.), Dec.*	Dec. 4, 1975
	1190 **North Wold**—Harrow District Mas. Centre, Northwick Circle, Kenton, Harrow. *3rd Fri. Feb.; 4th Fri. May, Oct. (I.)*	Nov. 3, 1960
	1195 **Upminster**—M.H., Deyncourt Gardens, Upminster RM14 1DF. *3rd Mon. April, Nov. (I.); 1st Mon. Sept.*	Apr. 6, 1978
	1196 **Hillingdon Heath**—Uxbridge. District M.C., *3rd Wed. Jan. (I.), April; 2nd Wed. Sept.*	July 13, 1994
	1197 **H. A. Mann**—M.H., Sutton. *4th Fri. Feb., Oct.; 4th Thurs. April (I.)*	Nov. 6, 1958
	1198 **Nandi Border**—F.M.H., Eldoret, E. Africa. *2nd Fri. Feb., June, Oct. (I.)*	Mar. 21, 1987
	1201 **South Wales Installed Commanders**—M.T., Coychurch Rd., Bridgend. *4th Sat. Oct. (I.), April.*	July 7, 1988
K	1205 **Air Unity**—Cole Court, London Road, Twickenham. *2nd Mon. Feb., June; 4th Wed. Sept. (I.)*	Apr. 6, 1978
	1210 **Suthburgh**—M.T., North Street, Sudbury, Suffolk. *4th Fri. Jan., March, May (I.); 2nd Fri. Sept.*	June 5, 1975
	1217 **Ghana**—William Galloway Memorial Temple, Liberty Ave., Accra, Ghana. *2nd Fri. April (I.), Oct., Dec.*	June 9, 1995

ROLL OF ROYAL ARK MARINER LODGES—*continued*

1218 **Middlesex Installed Commanders**—Cole Court, 150 London Road, Twickenham.
*2nd fifth Wed. March (I.); 1st fifth weekday Nov.,
(Sat. to be deemed as weekdays).* Oct. 27, 1993

1219 **Surrey Enthroned Commanders**—M.H., Surbiton.
3rd Wed. June (I.); 4th Thurs. Sept. Nov. 5, 1959

K 1220 **Concord**—F.M.H., Rotterdam, The Netherlands.
4th Sat. Jan., April (I.), Oct. July 7, 1966

2K 1222 **Ardwick**—Stanley House, Manchester Rd., Audenshaw, nr. Manchester.
1st 5th Wed. first qtr.; 3rd Mon. May (I.); 1st 5th Wed. last qtr. Apr. 1, 1965

1223 **The Lewis**—M.T., Park Rynie, Natal.
1st Tues. March, June (I.); 2nd Tues. Aug., Nov. Jan. 2, 1969

1225 **Kerala**—F.M.H., Calicut.
4th Sat. Feb., May, Aug., Nov. (I.) July 3, 1986

1227 **London Installed Commanders**—M.M.H. London.
4th Mon. Feb.; Mon. before second Wed. in Sept. Apr. 4, 1991

1228 **Drury Lane**—M.M.H.
2nd Thurs. March; 4th Thurs. May (I.); 3rd Thurs. Oct. Feb. 22, 1996

1229 **Yadavindra**—F.M.H., Shimla-171001, Northern India.
1st Sat. April (I.), June, Aug., Oct. Oct. 2, 1969

1231 **Sir Bevil Granville**—M.H., Bude.
3rd Fri. Feb., April, Sept., Nov. May 1, 1980

1232 **Cornwall**—M.T., Davis Ave., Montego Bay, Jamaica.
4th Mon. May (I.), Nov. Feb. 2, 1984

1233 **Pilgrims**—M.H., Wrotham, Kent.
2nd Thurs. April; 1st Thurs. Sept. Oct. 2, 1975

K 1234 **Hailsham**—M.T., Herstmonceux, Sussex.
2nd Fri. Feb., April (I.), Oct. Sept. 6, 1973

1236 **Bishop's Stortford**—St. Michael's M.H., Springfield Ct.,
Hadham Rd., Bishop's Stortford.
4th Wed. April; 1st Wed. July; 3rd Wed. Sept. (I.) Mar. 2, 1989

1237 **Welcome**—M.H., Grove Rd., Sutton.
3rd Thurs. Jan., April (I.), Nov. Apr. 2, 1964

K 1238 **Tewkesbury Abbey**—M.H., Tewkesbury.
1st Thurs. March, May, Oct. (I.) Sept. 2, 1965

K 1240 **Mercia**—M.H., Pinchbeck Rd., Spalding.
4th Thurs. Feb., April, Oct. (I.) May 2, 1963

1241 **Earl of Courtown**—M.H., St. James Road, East Grinstead.
2nd Mon. May, Nov., March (I.) Feb. 1, 1990

1242 **St. Mary's**—M.H., 14 Lower High St., Thame.
1st Fri. March, June; 2nd Fri. Sept. (I.) July 5, 1984

1243 **The Graftonian**—M.H., Towcester, Northants.
2nd Mon. Feb.; 2nd Tues. April (I.); M.H. Daventry: 1st Tues. Sept. Jan. 6, 1966

1244 **Royal Oak Tree**—Chingford M.C., Station Road, Chingford, London E4 7AZ.
3rd Tues. Feb.; 2nd Tues. May, Oct. (I.) Sept. 7, 1972

1245 **Pulborough**—M.T., Station Road, Pulborough.
1st Tues. Feb.; 3rd Tues. May (I.); 1st Mon. Dec. Nov. 7, 1963

K 1251 **All Saints'**—Southgate Mas. Centre, N14.
3rd Tues. Jan., March (I.), Oct. July 3, 1980

K 1252 **Chingford**—M.H., Station Rd., Chingford, London E4 7AZ.
3rd Fri. March, June, Sept. (I.) May 2, 1963

ROLL OF ROYAL ARK MARINER LODGES—continued

K	1254	**Harpenden**—Ashwell House, St. Albans. *1st Wed. March, May; 3rd Tues. Oct. (I.)*	July 4, 1974
	1256	**Remembrance**—Warwickshire M.T., Edgbaston. *1st Mon. Jan., March, Sept. (I.)*	Nov. 7, 1999
K	1258	**Chandlers Ford**—King's Court Mas. Centre, Chandlers Ford, Hants. *4th Thurs. Feb., April (I.), June, Oct.*	Apr. 4, 1963
	1260	**Teme Valley**—M.R., Church Street, Tenbury Wells, Worcs. *3rd Wed. Jan., April (I.), Sept.*	Apr. 12, 1996
	1261	**Tongariro**—Masonic Lodge Rooms, Church Street, Palmerston North, New Zealand. *2nd Tues. April (I.), June, July, Sept.*	Apr. 9, 2005
K	1264	**Benevolence**—M.H., Bridgeland St. Bideford, Devon. *4th Fri. Jan., March (I.), July; 4th Thurs. Sept.*	July 7, 1977
	1265	**Woodard**—Mark Masons' Hall, London. *4th Tues. March (I.); 3rd Wed. Oct.*	Mar. 23, 2010
	1268	**Coulsdon**—Croydon M.H., Oakfield Road, Croydon Surrey. *2nd Thurs. March (I.); 3rd Thurs. June; 4th Thurs. Oct.*	Oct. 7, 1962
	1277	**Devi Das**—F.M.H., Daon Chandigarh. *3rd Sat. Jan., Feb., March, Sept. (I.)*	Mar. 6, 1969
K	1283	**Jacob Van Lennep**—F.M.H., The Hague, Netherlands. *Last Fri. Jan., April (I.)*	June 6, 1968
K	1285	**Redhill**—Croydon & District M.H., Oakfield Road, Croydon. *2nd Wed. Jan., April, Oct. (I.)*	Feb. 2, 1967
	1287	**Ceredigion**—M.H., Aberaeron, Dyfed. *2nd Tues. March, April; 1st Fri., Sept. (I.)*	Apr. 2, 1981
	1290	**De la Val**—M.H., Seaton Delaval, Whitley Bay NE25 0PT. *Last Fri. Jan., April, Aug. (I.)*	Mar. 6, 1999
K	1291	**Hemel Hempstead**—Ashwell Ho., Verulam Rd., St. Albans. *2nd Wed. Feb. (I.); 2nd Thurs. April, July.*	Sept. 1, 1977
	1298	**Swaziland**—Pim Lorentz Memorial Masonic Hall, Manzini. *3rd Wed. Feb., May, Nov.; 3rd Sat. Aug. (I.)*	June 1, 1967
K	1300	**Turton**—The Last Drop Village, Bromley Cross, Bolton. *3rd Tues. March (I.), Aug., Oct.*	Oct. 6, 1988
	1302	**Austral**—M.T., 13 Tillard Street, Mafikeng, South Africa. *1st Mon. Feb., Aug., Nov.; 1st Sat. May. (I.)*	May. 3, 1997
2K	1303	**Middleton**—Masonic Club, Old Rd., Middleton, Manchester. *1st Wed. April (I.), Oct.*	Sept. 7, 1972
	1304	**George Hargreaves**—Rugeley & District Masonic Centre, Chase Golf Club, Pottal Pool Road, Penkridge, Staffs. ST19 5RN. *3rd Wed. Feb. (I.), April, Oct.*	Oct. 3, 1985
K	1307	**West Bridgford**—F.M.H., W. Bridgford. *4th Tues. Jan., March; 4th Wed. Sept. (I.)*	Feb. 7, 1985
K	1309	**Lodge of Good Report**—F.M.H., Bridge St., Manchester. *1st 5th Wed. in Sept., Oct., Nov., Jan., Feb., March (I.)*	Jan. 1, 1970
	1313	**Friendship from Service**— Mark Masons' Hall, 86 St. James's Street, London SW1A 1PL. *1st Fri. Jan. (I.); 1st Mon. July; 1st Thurs. Sept.*	Sept. 3, 1987
K	1314	**Weald of Surrey**—M.H., Grove Road, Sutton. *2nd Thurs. Jan., April, Oct. (I.)*	Sept. 7, 1978
K	1315	**Elstree and Radlett**—M.H., Rose Walk, Radlett. *2nd Fri. March; 1st Fri. Nov. (I.), June.*	May 6, 1976

ROLL OF ROYAL ARK MARINER LODGES—*continued*

	1316	**The George Parker**—Uxbridge M.C., Hillingdon, Middlesex. *4th Mon. March; 4th Wed. Oct. (I.)*	Dec. 7, 1967
	1317	**Albert Edward**—M.H., Castleton, Gwent. *3rd Wed. April; 2nd Wed. June; 4th Thurs. Nov. (I.)*	Apr. 21, 1993
	1319	**Saxon Shore**—M.H., East Street, Tollesbury, Essex CM9 8QE. *4th Tues. April; 2nd Wed. Nov. (I.).*	July 3, 1969
	1320	**Addiscombe**—M.H., Oakfield Rd., Croydon. *2nd Tues. Feb. (I.); 4th Tues. April; 3rd Tues. Oct.*	Dec. 3, 1970
	1321	**Warlingham**—Nutfield M.C., Redhill. *2nd Mon. May (I.); 1st Mon. Dec., March.*	Mar. 5, 1970
K	1322	**Leigh**—M.H., Ellesmere St., Leigh. *4th Mon. Jan. (I.); 3rd Mon. March, Nov.*	Nov. 7, 1968
	1324	**Zaradatha**—F.M.H., Steenschuur 6, Leiden, The Netherlands. *4th Wed. Jan. (I.), May, Oct.*	Dec. 1, 1988
K	1325	**Leverhulme**—M.T., Clifton Rd., Birkenhead. *3rd Tues. Feb., April,; (I.), Oct.*	July 1, 1971
	1326	**Hundred of Hoo**—M.H., 5 Manor Road, Chatham, Kent ME4 6AG. *1st Wed. Feb.; 2nd Wed. Oct. (I.)*	Mar. 6, 1969
	1330	**Berkshire and Oxfordshire Installed Commanders**— M.C., Goldsmiths Lane, Wallingford, Oxon. *1st Tues. June; 1st Wed. Dec.*	Apr. 25, 1994
K	1332	**Cornish Installed Commanders**— M.H., Redruth or at such other venue within the Province as the W.C. shall direct. *Last weekday Jan. (I.), March, Oct.*	Dec. 4, 1975
	1333	**Wyvern**—M.H., Wivenhoe, Essex. *4th Thurs. Feb., April, Nov. (I.)*	Apr. 30, 2012
	1334	**Bromsgrove**—M.H., Churchfields, Bromsgrove, Worcs. *2nd Fri. July, Sept.; 3rd Fri. May (I.)*	Sept. 3, 1981
2K	1335	**Orkney**—M.T., Gaborone, Republic of Botswana. *3rd Fri. Jan., April, June; 2nd Sat. Nov. (I.)*	Sept. 2, 1971
K	1336	**Gibraltar**—Mark Masons' Hall. *1st Sat. Feb., Nov.; 3rd Sat. June (I.)*	Dec. 2, 1971
	1341	**Ferrers**—M.H., Wellingborough Rd., Rushden. *1st Tues. Feb. (I.); 2nd Tues. May; 4th Tues. Oct.*	June 1, 1972
	1344	**Adon Hiram**—F.M., Hall, Groningen, The Netherlands. *3rd Sat. Sept., Jan., April (I.)*	July 11, 1985
	1346	**Northants, Hunts. and Beds. Installed Commanders**—M.H., Rushden. *2nd Fri. June (I.); 4th Fri. Jan.*	Apr. 2, 1970
K	1347	**Chilwell**—M.H., Chilwell, Nottingham. *4th Fri. March; 2nd Fri. May, June (I.)*	July 4, 1974
	1348	**Caerffili**—M.T., Caerphilly, Mid-Glam. *3rd Fri. May, Sept. (I.), Nov.*	Apr. 2, 1981
	1350	**Grand Union**—M.H., Linslade. *4th Wed. April (I.), Sept., Nov.*	Mar. 7, 1991
K	1352	**Comites Sigillorum**—M.H., Croydon, Surrey. *1st Tues. Feb. (I.); 2nd Tues. May; 1st Tues. Nov.*	Mar. 2, 1972
	1354	**Westwood**—Westwood Mas. Centre, 168 Bellegrove Rd., Welling, Kent. *4th Thurs. Feb., June (I.)*	June 4, 1970

ROLL OF ROYAL ARK MARINER LODGES—continued

	1355 **Campos Salles**—M.T., Rua Lisboa Nr. 1120, São Paulo or at such other venue within the District as the Commander shall direct. *1st Tues. March, June, Sept. (I.), Dec.*	Aug., 21, 2002
K	1356 **Dorking**—Croydon & District M.H., 73 Oakfield Rd., Croydon. *3rd Tues. Feb., April, Oct. (I.)*	Nov. 2, 1974
2K	1358 **Joseph Moffett**—Ashwell House, St. Albans, Herts. *4th Fri. March (I.); 3rd Fri. June, Nov.*	Nov. 1, 1973
	1363 **Piscator**—Royal National Hotel, Bedford Way, Russel Square, London WC1H 0DG. *2nd Fri. Jan.; 4th Fri. April; 4th Thurs. Oct. (I.)*	June 14, 1973
	1365 **Bayons**—M.H., Jameson Bridge St., Market Rasen. *4th Thurs. Feb., April, Nov. (I.)*	Oct. 4, 1979
K	1366 **Craftsmen of Walden**—M.H., Church Street, Saffron Walden CB10 1JW. *1st Tues. May; 2nd Tues. Aug. (I.); 3rd Tues. Oct.*	July 7, 1977
K	1368 **Royal Victoria**—Masonic Building, Bay St., Nassau, Bahamas. *1st Wed. April (I.), Nov.*	Apr. 6, 1972
K	1369 **Integrity**—M.H., Kershaw St., Shaw. *4th Tues. Feb., May, Sept. (I.)*	Apr. 5, 1984
	1373 **Alexander Burnett Brown**—Harrow M.C., Kenton. *4th Fri. May (I.); 3rd Fri. Jan., Sept.*	May 31, 1996
	1374 **Stow-on-the-Wold**—M.H., Church St., Stow-on-the-Wold. *4th Tues. May (I.); 3rd Tues. June, July.*	May 6, 1976
	1376 **Mosam Trajectum**—F.M.H., Kerklaan 7, Roermond, Netherlands. *Last Tues. March, June, Oct. (I.)*	Apr. 6, 1978
	1377 **Porthcawl**—M.T., New Rd., Porthcawl, Mid Glam. *1st Tues. March, May (I.); 2nd Thurs. Oct.*	June 4, 1981
	1378 **Twickenham**—Mas. Centre, Cole Court, Twickenham. *2nd Wed. Feb.; 4th Wed. April (I.); 1st Thurs. Nov.*	May 6, 1976
	1379 **The Lodge of Sympathy**—M.H., Wrotham Rd., Gravesend, Kent. *4th Thurs. Oct. (I.); 2nd Wed. June, Dec.*	July 4, 1974
	1380 **Naze Tower**— Frinton & Walton M.H., Station Road, Kirby Cross, Essex CO13 0LU. *4th Wed. Jan., March, May (I.)*	Jan. 4, 1990
■	1381 **Mossley**—"Westholme", Stockport Rd., Mossley. *1st Thurs. March, May, Oct.*	Apr. 2, 1981
K	1385 **Clanfield**—M.H., Five Heads Rd., Horndean. *2nd Thurs. Jan., March, May (I.), Sept., Nov.*	Dec. 7, 1972
	1386 **Windrush**—M.H., Church Green, Witney. *2nd Fri. Nov., Dec.*	Mar. 5, 1994
■	1389 **University of London**—Mark Masons' Hall. *2nd Thurs. Feb. (I.); 1st Wed. May*	July 2, 1981
2K	1392 **Kenneth Shenton Installed Commanders**— *4th Tues. May:* Rugeley & District M.C., Chase Golf Club, Pottal Pool Road, Penkridge ST19 5RN. *Last weekday Sept.:* F.M.H., Crewe St., Shrewsbury SY1 2HQ.	Mar. 3, 1977
	1393 **Temple of Uxbridge**—Uxbridge M.C., Hercies Rd., Uxbridge. *1st Wed. March; 4th Thurs. Sept. (I.); 2nd Thurs. Dec.*	June 19, 2000
K	1394 **Holywell**—The Lady Augusta M.H., Mostyn, Clwyd. *3rd Mon. May; 1st Mon. Oct., Dec.*	July 7, 1977
	1396 **Ampthill**—M.H., Church St., Ampthill, Beds. *Last Fri. Feb., May, Oct.*	June 5, 1980

ROLL OF ROYAL ARK MARINER LODGES—*continued*

1398 **Old Rectory**—M.H., Henley Rd., Caversham, Reading.
4th Thurs. May; 2nd Thurs. Oct. (I.) May 1, 1975

1399 **Potters Clay**—M.H., Church Road, Potter St, Harlow CM17 9HD.
4th Wed. Feb. (I.), April, Nov. June 5, 1986

K 1400 **Warwickshire Installed Commanders**—
Warwickshire M.T., 1 Clarendon Rd., Edgbaston, Birmingham.
Last weekday Jan. (Sat. excl.); 1st Fri. June. Apr. 10, 1980

1402 **Chandos**—Southgate Mas. Centre.
3rd Mon. Jan., April (I.), Nov. July 7, 1977

K 1404 **Stevenage**—The Cloisters, Barrington Rd., Letchworth.
4th Tues. Jan., Oct.; 3rd Tues. May (I.) May 5, 1977

1407 **Frederick Wheeler**—M.H., Croydon.
1st Thurs. Feb.; 4th Thurs. April (I.), Oct. Oct. 4, 1979

1409 **Worcestershire Installed Commanders**—
Moseley M.H., Kings Heath, Birmingham *on 4th Fri. Jan;*
M.H., Rainbow Hill, Worcester on *3rd Tues. May (I.)* Mar. 3, 2000

1410 **Gild of Good Fellowship**—M.R., The Crescent, Wisbech.
3rd Wed. Feb.; 2nd Wed. May (I.); 3rd Wed. Sept. Mar. 28, 1998

1411 **The Curfew**—M.H., Chertsey.
4th Tues. Feb.; 3rd Thurs. May (I.); 1st Tues. Dec. Dec. 6, 1977

1412 **Millennium Installed Commanders**—M.H., Main Ridge, Boston.
4th Fri. June (I.); 1st Fri. Dec. Mar. 18, 2000

1413 **Mark of Industry**—M.H., Deyncourt Gdns., Upminster RM14 1DF.
2nd Sat. Feb. (I.); 3rd Sat. June; 3rd Sat. Nov. Jan. 29, 1977

1415 **Battlesbridge**—Saxon Hall, Aviation Way, Southend-on-Sea, Essex SS2 6UN.
2nd Tues. Jan.; 3rd Mon. March; 2nd Mon. Nov. (I.) Sept. 24, 1975

1416 **Sir John Jervis**—Ashfield House, 218 Ashby Road, Burton Upon Trent, Staffordshire DE15 0AE.
4th Tues. March, Sept. (I.) Mar. 14, 2009

1417 **The Romney Marsh**—M.H., Dymchurch, Kent.
1st Mon. March, Dec. (I.); 1st Tues. June Dec. 4, 1980

1419 **Lingfield**—Nutfield M.Ctr., Redhill, Surrey.
2nd Fri. Jan.; 1st Fri. April (I.); 3rd Wed. Nov. Oct. 2, 1975
Warrant of Confirmation Jan. 9, 1996

1424 **Melrose**—M.T., Ward Avenue, Mandeville, Jamaica.
1st Wed. Feb., June, Oct. (I.) Oct. 22, 2011

1425 **Malling Abbey**—M.H., West Malling.
4th Mon. Jan.; 1st Mon. June; 1st fifth Thurs. after Aug. (I.) Nov. 26, 1994

K 1426 **St. Editha's**—Masonic Rms., 29 Lichfield St., Tamworth.
3rd Thurs. Jan., Nov. (I.); 1st Thurs. May. Nov. 2, 1978

1427 **Admiral Rous**—M.H., Newmarket.
Last Fri. Feb.; 1st Fri. May (I.) May 7, 1981

1428 **Trinity Lodge of Installed Commanders**—
The Masonic Hall, Trinity Lane, Beverley on *3rd Thurs. June*
The Masonic Hall, 69 Beverley Road, Kingston-upon-Hull on
2nd Thurs. Aug Oct. 31, 1998

K 1429 **Installed Commanders of Reflection**—Such venue as the Commander selects within the Provinces of Gloucestershire, Herefordshire and Bristol
3rd Sat. Feb. (I.), Nov. July 1, 2000

ROLL OF ROYAL ARK MARINER LODGES—*continued*

	1432	**Heinz Ritter Pilgrim**—M.R. Stadtwald Str, 36, 41179 Mönchengladbach, Germany. *1st Tues. May, Nov.; 3rd Tues. Sept.; Last Tues. March (I.)*	Oct. 6, 1977
	1433	**Arewa**—M.T., College Rd., Kaduna, Nigeria. *4th Sat. Feb., May (I.), Nov.*	Sept. 2, 1982
	1434	**Netherlands Installed Commanders**— F.M.H., Rubenslaan 1, Bilthoven, The Netherlands. *5th Sat. in the month, except Jan., June, July, Aug., Dec., public holidays, the day of (or prior to) a recognised religious day (I.) at 1st meeting of the year*	Oct. 29, 1994
	1436	**Portwall**—M.H., Chepstow. *1st Mon. March; last Thurs. April (I.), Sept.; 3rd Fri. Nov.*	Mar. 5, 1981
	1440	**New Sarum**—The Masonic Temple, Bishop Gaul Avenue, Belvedere, Harare, Zimbabwe. *2nd Mon. March, Sept., Dec. (I.)*	Dec. 7, 1989
	1444	**Forest of Waltham**—M.H., Church Road, Potter Street, Harlow, Essex CM17 9HD. *4th Sat. Feb. (I.); 3rd Sat. June, Nov.*	Sept. 4, 1980
	1445	**Neston**—The Hall, Bushell Rd., Neston. *3rd Fri. March (I.), Oct.*	Mar. 4, 1982
K	1446	**Prince Setanta**—M.H., Poulton-le-Fylde. *3rd Mon. Jan., March (I.), Sept., Nov.*	Sept. 6, 1979
	1447	**Monmouthshire Installed Commanders**—M.H., Tredegar. *1st Tues. May, Nov. (I.)*	Nov. 5, 1987
K	1448	**Manor of Bexley**—M.H., Sidcup. *2nd Sat. March, May, Dec. (I.)*	Feb. 5, 1976
	1451	**Maen Clo**—F.M.H., Mostyn St., Llandudno. *5th Mon. March (I.), April, May, Sept., Oct., Nov., when such 5th Mon. occurs.*	Nov. 7, 1991
	1452	**The Ridings Installed Commanders Lodge**—M.H., Malton. *1st Wed. May (I.), June, Sept.*	Mar. 2, 1989
2K	1453	**Christchurch**—M.H., Warren Ave., Christchurch. *4th Tues. Jan. (I.), April, July, Nov.*	Dec. 6, 1979
K	1454	**Stanley**—M.H., Stanley House, Manchester Rd., Audenshaw. *3rd Tues. Jan., Sept. (I.)*	Feb. 2, 1978
	1455	**Sir Frederick Alban**—M.T., St. Helen's Rd., Swansea. *1st Tues. May (I.); 1st Mon. Nov.*	Sept. 3, 1981
2K	1457	**London West Africa**—Mark Masons' Hall. *3rd Fri. March (I.); 2nd Fri. June, Sept.*	Mar. 2, 1978
	1458	**Earl of Euston**—Masonic Rooms, The Green, Eaton Socon. *4th Fri. Feb., Sept. (I.), Nov.*	July 7, 1988
	1460	**Reginald W. Short Installed Commanders Lodge**—M.H., Morris Lane, Devizes SN10 1NU. *4th Wed. May (I.); 1st Mon. Dec.*	Mar. 2, 1989
	1461	**Richard Watts**—St. George Ho., New Rd., Chatham. *5th Tues. of the month except Dec., Installation in 3rd quarter.*	Sept. 4, 1980
K	1462	**All Saints Kings Heath**—Moseley M.H., King's Heath, Birmingham. *1st Thurs. May, Sept. (I.); 2nd Tues. July.*	Nov. 3, 1977
	1463	**Thameside**—M.H. Rectory Road, Orsett, Thurrock RM16 3EH. *1st Thurs. March, Oct.; 2nd Thurs. Dec. (I.)*	June 2, 1977
	1464	**Nottingham Excelsior**—M.H., Goldsmith St., Nottingham. *4th Fri. Feb.; 2nd Tues. July (I.)*	Apr. 5, 1984

ROLL OF ROYAL ARK MARINER LODGES—*continued*

1466 **Cumbria Lodge of Installed Commanders**—M.H., St. John St., Keswick CA12 5AP.
4th Mon. May; Last Sat. Nov. (I.) Mar. 19, 1994

1468 **Cheshire Installed Commanders**—Knutsford M.H.
4th Wed. May (I.), Sept. May 31, 2006

1469 **Gauntlet**—Harrow Mas. Centre, Northwick Circle, Kenton, Harrow.
4th Tues. March, May (I.), Nov. Apr. 5, 1979

1470 **Ilford St. Mary**—Hutton M.H., Mount Avenue, Brentwood, Essex CM13 2NS.
4th Wed. Jan. (I.); 3rd Thurs. May; 1st Wed. Nov. May 1, 1980

1471 **Britannia**—Lessinghaus, Lessingstrasse 3, 33604 Bielefield, Germany.
1st Sat. March (I.); 4th Sat. May; 2nd Sat. Nov. July 6, 1978

K 1473 **Semper Fidelis**—Mark Masons' Hall.
1st Thurs. April; 4th Wed. June; 3rd Wed. Dec. June 1, 1978

1476 **Donyo Sabuk**—F.M.H., Nairobi, Kenya.
3rd Fri. Feb., June (I.), Sept. Dec. 7, 1978

1477 **Branksome**—M.H., Ferncroft Rd., Kinson, Bournemouth.
4th Thurs. Feb. (I.), April, June; 3rd Fri. Nov. May 1, 1980

1480 **Mark of True Friendship**—Southend M.C., Saxon Hall,
Aviation Way, Southend-on-Sea, Essex SS2 6UN.
2nd Wed. March (I.); 4th Wed. May; 1st Wed. Sept. June 1, 1978

1481 **Duddon**—M.H., Cambridge St., Millom LA18 5BD.
4th Fri. May (I.), July, Sept. Jan. 6, 1983

1483 **Triangle Lodge of Installed Commanders**—M.H., Bedlington, or at
such other venue as the P.G.M. shall direct.
2nd Fri. Feb., Sept. (I.); 1st Tues. April Sept. 11, 2004

1488 **Libanon**—F.M.H., Spui 23, Terneuzen, Netherlands.
2nd Sat. Jan., May (I.), Sept. Sept. 2, 1982

1489 **Halsey**—M.H., Jepps Lane, Royston.
4th Thurs. April; 4th Wed. Oct. (I.) Oct. 2, 1980

1490 **Harold W. Richardson**—Sussex M.C., 25 Queens Road, Brighton.
4th Fri. April; 3rd Fri. July (I.); 4th Tues. Oct. July 21, 1995

K 1491 **The Mark of Education**—M.H., Cosham, Portsmouth.
1st Tues. July; 1st Fri. March (I.), Nov. Oct. 9, 1992

K 1492 **Durham Lodge of Installed Commanders**—
M.H., Station Rd., Hetton-le-Hole, Tyne and Wear DH5 9JB.
3rd Thurs. May, Nov. (I.) Mar. 15, 2001

1493 **Jubilee**—M.T., Stopford Road, St. Helier, Jersey.
3rd Mon. March, May, Nov. (I.) Apr. 2, 1992

1494 **The Lord Harris**—M.H., Church Rd., Sidcup, Kent.
3rd Fri. Feb.; 2nd Fri. May, Sept. (I.); 2nd Tues. Dec. Oct. 2, 1980

1498 **The Rose of Minden**—Logenhaus, Logenplatz 2-4, 32052 Herford, Germany.
3rd Tues. Jan.; 1st Wed. July (I.), Nov. Oct. 24, 1980

K 1501 **Signa Bene**—Town Hall, Alcester, Warwickshire.
3rd Wed. Jan.; 3rd Tues. July (I.); 3rd Wed. Nov. May 4, 1989

1502 **Abercrombie**—M.H., Vigie St., Castries, St. Lucia.
4th Thurs. Jan. (I.), April, July, Oct. Feb. 27, 1995

K 1503 **Kidsgrove**—M.H., Liverpool Rd., Kidsgrove, Stoke-on-Trent.
4th Fri. Jan.; 1st Fri. June, Sept. (I.) May 6, 1980

1504 **Ararat**—F.M.H., Zaandam, The Netherlands.
1st Mon. March (I.), Oct.; Fri after 1st Mon. Dec. June 7, 1979

ROLL OF ROYAL ARK MARINER LODGES—continued

1505 **Chevalier**—Royal Masonic School for Girls, Rickmansworth.
1st Tues. Feb.; 2nd Wed. May (I.); 1st Wed. Dec.   Dec. 3, 1982

1507 **Sir John Cotton**—St. Andrew Rooms, Biggleswade, Bedford.
2nd Mon. June, Sept. (I.); 1st Mon. Dec.   May 2, 1912

1510 **Merlaue Weir**—Marlow Mas. Centre, St. Peter St., Marlow, Bucks.
3rd Sat. Jan. (I.), March; 1st Sat. Oct.   June 4, 1981

1515 **Keys of Münster**—A.C.G.L. Centre, Kruppstr 134, 60388, Frankfurt.
Last Sat. Feb. (I.), June, Oct.   Oct. 24, 1980

1516 **Het Sticht**—F.M.H., van Persijnstraat 9, Amersfoort, Netherlands.
1st Mon. April, Oct. (I.)   May 13, 1992

1520 **St. Margaret of Antioch**—Crawley M.H., Ifield, Sussex.
3rd Sat. Feb.; April, Nov. (I.)   Apr. 2, 1981

1521 **Sub-Urban**—Cole Court, 150 London Rd., Twickenham, Middx.
1st Tues. Mar. (I.), June, Oct.   Mar. 1, 1994

1522 **Tarporley**—Portal Premier, Tarporley.
3rd Tues. May (I.); 1st 5th working day Oct.   May 15, 2007

1528 **Cambrensis**—M.T., Guildford St., Cardiff.
2nd Wed. Feb. (I.), Oct.   Mar. 5, 1981

1529 **Ayot**—Ashwell House, St. Albans.
2nd Mon. Nov., March; 2nd Wed. May (I.)   Feb. 2, 1989

1533 **Dinkel**—F.M.H., Dr. Coppestraat 32, Enschede, Netherlands.
4th Fri. Feb., April, Oct. (I.)   Feb. 3, 1983

1535 **De Gorllewin Lodge of Installed Commanders**—M.H., Carmarthen, Dyfed.
2nd Fri. June; 1st Mon. Sept.   June 6, 1991

1536 **Mayflower**—Simpsons Restaurant, Lower Southend Rd., Wickford, Essex.
1st Thurs. Feb. (I.); 1st Fri. May; 3rd Wed. Nov.   July 9, 1994

1538 **Chiltern**—Dunstable Mas. Centre, Cemetery Lane, Dunstable, Beds.
4th Thurs. May, Sept. (I.)   July 2, 1981

1539 **Ridgmont**—M.H., Ridgmont House, Horwich.
2nd Fri. March, Nov.; 2nd Mon. Sept. (I.)   Apr. 3, 1986

1540 **Farne**—F.M.H., Prudhoe Street, Alnwick, Northumberland.
3rd Fri. March (I.), Aug., Nov.   Mar. 20, 1999

1542 **Doric**—Lortzinghaus, An der, Katherinenkirche 3, 49088, Osnabrück.
4th Wed. Jan., April, Oct.; 1st Wed. June (I.)   Apr. 5, 1984

1547 **Thuredrecht**—F.M.H., Munt 9, Dordrecht, Netherlands.
3rd Wed. Nov. (I.), Feb., April.   May 3, 1984

K   1548 **Nailsea**—Nailsea M.H., Nailsea, Somerset.
2nd Wed. Jan., March, Oct. (I.)   July 5, 1990

K   1551 **Stanhope**—M.H., Greenbank, Stanhope.
1st Fri. March, April, Sept. (I.)   Feb. 16, 2000

1552 **Lucayan**—M.T., East Sunrise Highway, Freeport, Grand Bahama Island.
3rd Wed. March, April (I.), Oct.   Jan. 9, 1981

1553 **Turks Island Forth**—M.T., Grand Turk, Turks Island, W.1.
3rd Thurs. March (I.), June, Sept.; 2nd Thurs. Dec.   Nov. 13, 1980

1555 **Friendship and Care**—M.C., Sindlesham, Berkshire.
3rd Fri. Feb. (I.), Oct.   Jan. 7, 1987

1557 **Biggin Hill**—Sevenoaks, M.H., St. Johns Hill, Sevenoaks.
4th Mon. April, Sept. (I.); 2nd Mon. Nov.   June 3, 1982

ROLL OF ROYAL ARK MARINER LODGES—*continued*

1559 **The Friendly**—M.T., 45-47 Barbados Ave., Kingston 5, Jamaica.
2nd Tues. June, Sept. (I.), Dec. July 2, 1981

1564 **Viking**—Southend M.C., Saxon Hall, Aviation Way, Southend-on-Sea, Essex SS2 6UN.
1st Tues. March, June; 3rd Tues. Sept. (I.) Dec. 2, 1982

1565 **Hollandia**—F.M.H., Bilthoven, Netherlands.
4th Fri. Feb.; 3rd Fri. Sept. (I.) Mar. 3, 1988

1568 **Linden Acre**—Wokingham M.H., Reading Rd., Wokingham.
4th Tues. Jan., May (I.) Mar. 1, 1984

1569 **Woodstock**—M.H., Surbiton, 6 The Crescent.
2nd Sat. Feb.; 4th Mon. May (I.); 1st Tues. July Jan. 7, 1988

1572 **Dorset Installed Commanders**—M.H., Victoria Sq., Portland, Dorset.
Such venue as the Commander selects in the Province Feb. 7, 1991

K 1574 **The Harry Wilson**—M.H., Newdegate Place, Nuneaton.
3rd Wed. Feb. (I.); 2nd Mon. March, Nov. Oct. 29, 1994

1575 **Sparrenburg**—FO-Logenhaus, Murhardstr 6, 34119 Kassel, Germany.
2nd Sat. Jan., Sept. (I.); 4th Sat. May May 6, 1982

1576 **Bond of Friendship**—Croydon and District M.H., 73 Oakfield Rd., Croydon.
4th Fri. Nov. (I.); 3rd Fri. Jan.; Last Thurs. May Dec. 5, 2001

1577 **Progress**—Salford Road M.H., 41 The Crescent, Salford.
4th Wed. April (I.), Oct. Apr. 22, 1998

1578 **Harmony**—M.T., Bishop Street, Camperdown.
1st Mon. March (I.), June, Sept., Dec. Jan. 7, 1982

1579 **De Sluitsteen**—F.M.H., Arnhemsestraatweg 360, Velp, The Netherlands.
1st Sat. Feb. (I.), April, Oct. Apr. 2, 1992

1580 **De Keursteen**—F.M.H., Bij de Put 15, Leeuwarden, Holland.
4th Sat. Jan., April (I.), Sept. Feb. 6, 1992

1583 **The Beacon Centenary**—M.H., The Mile, Pocklington.
1st Fri. April, June (I.), Sept. Dec. Feb. 19, 1994

1584 **Oakley**—M.C., Oakley House, Bromley Common, Bromley, Kent.
4th Thurs. Feb.; 2nd Tues. Sept.; 4th Tues. Oct. (I.) May 1, 1986

K 1587 **La Marque d'Alliance**—M.T., Rue Alexandre Colin, 24, 5020 Champion, Belgium.
2nd Sat. March, Oct., Dec. (I.) Feb. 6, 1986

1590 **Cynon Dare**—M.H., Canon Street, Aberdare.
3rd Tues. April, Nov.; 4th Wed. May (I.) June 11, 2003

K 1591 **Cambrian**—M.H., Mostyn Street, Llandudno.
1st Sat. April (I.), Sept. Apr. 4, 1998

1592 **Llynfi Valley**—M.T., Castle Street, Maesteg.
3rd Sat. April, Nov. (I.) Mar. 6, 1998

1596 **Stabroek**—F.M.H., Georgetown, Guyana.
1st Tues. Feb. (I.); 2nd Mon. June; 1st Tues. Nov. Sept. 4, 1986

1600 **Saxony**—Grosse National Mutterloge "Zu Den Drei Weltkugelin"-
3WK-Logenhaus, Heerstr 28, 14052 Berlin.
3rd Sat. Feb., April; Last Sat. Oct. (I.) June 6, 1985

1601 **Den Aks**—M.H. Breda, *4th Tues. March;*
M.H. Eindhoven: *3rd Tues. June; 2nd Tues. Sept. (I.)* June 6, 1985

1602 **Rift Valley**—M.H., Naivasha, Kenya.
3rd Sat. Feb., June (I.), Oct. June 6, 1985

K 1603 **Les Disciples de Salomon**—M.H., Minckelersstraat, 115/B-3000, Leuven, Belgium.
2nd Fri. Feb., May (I.), Oct. Sept. 7, 1989

ROLL OF ROYAL ARK MARINER LODGES—continued

1604 **London East Africa**—M.M.H., London SW1A 1PL.
    4th Sat. Feb. (I.); 3rd Sat. May.   Sept. 6, 1990

1606 **De Cymru**—M.T., Port Talbot on *4th Wed. June;*
    M.T., Caerphilly on *1st Wed. Dec. (I.)*   May 14, 2003

1609 **Sandbach**—Sandbach M.H., The Common, Sandbach, Cheshire CW11 1FJ.
    2nd Tues. Jan. (I.); 4th Wed. May; 1st Mon. Sept.   Jan. 11, 2011

1612 **Tremonia**—Logenhaus der hannoverschen Freimauer, Lemförder Strasse 7, 30169 Hanover.
    3rd Sat. Jan., Nov. (I.); 1st Sat. June   Sept. 6, 1984

K   1613 **Robert Burns**—M.H., The Crescent, Salford.
    4th Mon. Jan., March (I.), Sept., Nov.   Feb. 6, 1986

1614 **Guernsey**—M.C., St. Martins, Guernsey.
    3rd Thurs. March, Nov.; Last weekday (Sat. excepted) Jan. (I.)   Sept. 3, 1994

K   1617 **The Severn**—M.H., Newport, Shropshire.
    1st Fri. April; 2nd Thurs. June; 1st Thurs. Sept. (I.)   Feb. 5, 1988

1618 **Cayman**—Masonic Building, Prospect Park, Grand Cayman, Cayman Islands.
    1st Fri. April (I.), Oct.   May 5, 1999

1623 **Centenary**—Mosely Masonic Hall, Kingsheath, Birmingham.
    3rd Fri. March (I.); 1st Fri. May, July   Mar. 19, 2010

K   1624 **La Marque D'Union**—M.H., Fondation Isi Collin, Rue de Suède, 41/B-1060, Bruxelles, Belgium.
    2nd Sat. Feb.; 2nd Tues. May (I.); 4th Sat. Nov.   June 22, 1994

1628 **Langdon Hills**—M.H., Rectory Rd., Orsett, Thurrock RM16 3EH.
    3rd Wed. April, June, Sept. (I.)   Jan. 7, 1988

1632 **Edwin Perry Morgan**—M.H. Perranporth.
    Last working day in May (I.); 4th Fri. Sept.   Feb. 29, 2000

1634 **Buckinghamshire Installed Commanders**—Beaconsfield M.Ctr., Old School House, Windsor End, Beconsfield.
    3rd Mon. Nov. (I.); 3rd Fri. July at another venue in the Province   Nov. 29, 2010

1636 **Nyanza**—M.H., Kisumu, Kenya.
    2nd Sat. Feb., June, Sept. (I.)   June 7, 1996

1637 **James Jack**—F.M.H., Company Path, Georgetown, Guyana.
    2nd Tues. Feb. (I.), Aug., Nov.   May 28, 2005

1638 **City Livery**—Mark Mason's Hall.
    1st Mon. March; 4th Wed. June (I.); 2nd Wed. Dec.   Mar. 3, 1988

1642 **Ludwig Zum Flammenden Stern**—Bagno-Restaurant, Steinfurt-Burgsteinfurt.
    1st Fri. March, Nov.; 1st Sat. June (I.)   Oct. 27, 1993

1645 **Forest**—Masonic Hall, Rockingham Rd., Corby, Northants.
    1st Thurs. June, Nov., March (I.)   Feb. 7, 1991

K   1646 **Philadelphia**—M.H., Leyland.
    3rd Tues. Sept.; 2nd Mon. Jan. (I.)   Sept. 29, 1999

1647 **Dyffryn Clwyd**—Masonic Buildings, Tower Hill, Denbigh.
    4th Thurs. Sept. (I.), Nov., Feb., April.   May 2, 1991

1652 **Somerset Commanders**—Burnham on Sea M.H.
    4th Sat. Feb. (I.); 2nd Sat. June.   Feb. 25, 1995

1655 **Bowyer**—M.H., Chipping Norton.
    4th Wed. Feb.; 1st Tues. July.   Feb. 8, 1993

1659 **Brackenbury**—M.H., 19 Orwell Road, Felixstowe, Suffolk.
    2nd Thurs. Oct. (I.), Dec.; 4th Thurs. May.   Nov. 11, 1995

ROLL OF ROYAL ARK MARINER LODGES—*continued*

1666 **Bond of Friendship**—Calle 28, Ballivian Cota Cota, La Paz, Bolivia.
1st Mon. March, June, Dec.; 2nd Sat. Aug. (I.) Aug. 19, 1995

1669 **Collingwood**—Guildford M.C., Weybourne House, Portsmouth Road, Guildford.
3rd Fri. Sept.; 4th Fri. Jan. (I.); 3rd Fri. April Feb. 23, 2005

1672 **Accra**—William Galloway Memorial Temple, Liberia Road, Accra, Ghana.
3rd Mon. May, Aug., Nov. (I.) Mar. 19, 2010

2K 1673 **Mark of Enterprise**—M.H., Fondation Isi Collin, Rue de Suède 41/B-1060 Bruxelles, Belgium.
2nd Thurs. March; 1st Sat. June (I.) Aug. 31, 1996

1678 **Wellington**—M.H., Duke Street, Whitehaven CA28 7NZ.
4th Mon. March (I.), June. Feb. 8, 1995

1680 **Edward the Black Prince**—M.H., Tywardreath, Cornwall.
1st Tues. Feb, April, Oct. (I.) Jan. 12, 2008

1682 **The North Kent**—M.H., Wilmington, Kent.
4th Sat. March; 3rd Sat. Aug. (I.), Dec. Dec. 5, 1991

1683 **Barcino**—617 Gran Via Dels Corts Catalanes, Barcelona.
3rd Tues. Oct., Jan., April. Sept. 27, 1993

1685 **Sketty Hall**—M.T., St. Helens Road, Swansea.
1st Wed. March (I.), Nov. Feb. 16, 1995

■ 1687 **Hampshire and Isle of Wight Installed Commanders Lodge**—
M.H., Botley or at such other venue within the Province as the W.Cdr. shall direct.
Penultimate working day (including Sat.) in Jan., May, Sept. (I.) Nov. 8, 2002

1688 **Javea**—M.H., Puerto De Javea, Alicante, Spain.
4th Fri. March, Oct., Nov. (I.) Apr. 29, 1993

1690 **Andulacia**—M.C. (Baja) Edif, Bouganvilla, Avda. Gaviotas, Los Bouches Fuengirola, Spain.
4th Sat. Feb., May (I.), Oct. Nov. 18, 2000

1694 **Friendship Iberia**—Acacia M.C., Cuidad del Cine, 29100 Coin, Spain.
3rd Tues. Feb., May, Oct. (I.) Sept. 12, 1994

1706 **Derbyshire Lodge of Installed Commanders**—
The Masonic Hall, 1 Cambell Street, Belper, Derbyshire DE56 1AP.
3rd Tues. Jan.; 3rd Thurs. June (I.) Mar. 26, 1994

1709 **The Lady of the Lamp**—M.H., Chepstow, Gwent.
1st Fri. Feb. (I.), June, Sept. Sept. 2, 1994

1710 **Scholars in Amity**—Ashwell House, St. Albans or Halsey Hall.
Last day March, Sept., Nov. (I.) Nov. 30, 1994

K 1714 **Ryton**—M.H., Blackhouse Lane, Ryton, Tyne & Wear.
1st Wed. Feb., April, Sept., Nov. (I.) Nov. 19, 1994

1716 **Cornerstone**—F.M.H., Bridge Street, Manchester.
1st Fri. June (I.); 2nd Fri. Dec. June 10, 1994

1722 **Madrid**—M.H. Juan Ramón Jiminez, 6, Madrid.
1st Sat. Feb., May, Sept. May 21, 1994

1723 **Antiqua**—M.H., St. Johns, Antigua, West Indies.
3rd Thurs. Jan., May, Aug., Nov. (I.) Apr. 29, 2004

1725 **Brychan**—M.H., Cerrigcochion Road, Brecon, Powys.
1st Wed. Oct.; 3rd Wed. March; 4th Thurs. May (I.) Feb. 19, 1998

1732 **Haven**—M.H., 1 Kings Rd., Cleethorpes.
1st Thurs. Feb., April (I.), Dec. Mar. 11, 1995

K 1737 **Thomas Arthur Wood**—St. Mary Magdalen Chapel, Guys Cliffe, Warwick.
2nd Mon. Feb., Nov. (I.); 3rd Mon. July. Dec. 20, 1994

ROLL OF ROYAL ARK MARINER LODGES—continued

1738 **Pride of Surrey**—M.H., 9 Grove Road, Sutton, Surrey SM1 1BB.
1st Tues. Jan.; 3rd Thurs. March; 2nd Mon. Sept. (I.)   Mar. 29, 1995

1742 **Sanderstead**—Croydon M.H., Oakfield Road, Croydon.
1st Wed. Oct. (I.); 2nd Thurs. March; 4th Thurs May   Feb 16, 1996

1745 **Orb and Sceptre**—M.H., Sociedad Compás, Calle Toledo 14, Ciudad Quesada, Rojales.
1st Fri. Feb. (I.), April, Oct., Nov.   Oct. 30, 2000

1748 **Euclid**—Mark Mason's Hall.
4th Thurs. Feb.; 1st Wed. June (I.)   Nov. 30, 1999

K   1750 **Devonshire Lodge of Installed Commanders**—M.H., 3 Bossell Road, Buckfastleigh.
2nd Fri. March (I.); 1st Mon. Sept.   March 30, 1996

1753 **Ter Duinen**—Hotel Soll Cress, Koninklijke Baan 225/B-8670 Koksijde, Belgium.
3rd Sat. Jan., May; Last Sat. Aug. (I.)   Jan. 29, 1999

1754 **Lealtad**—Temple "Cyril H. Rees", Calle 8 No. 8084, Calacoto, La Paz, Bolivia.
1st Wed. March, June, Dec.; 2nd Sat. Aug. (I.)   Aug. 14, 1988

1761 **Knock Murton**—M.H., Wath Brow, Trumpet Road, Cleator CA23 3EH.
3rd Mon. Jan., April (I.), Oct.   April 15, 1996

1776 **Seychelles**—M.H., Belombre, Mahe.
1st Wed. April, June (I.), Nov.   Feb. 20, 1997

1777 **Eos**—M.H., Gravesend.
1st Mon. March, June (I.), Nov.   April 27, 1998

1782 **Rope and Anchor**—Logenhaus, Welckerstr 8, 20358 Hamburg.
1st Sat. Feb., April (I.); 4th Sat. Sept.   Oct. 30, 2004

1783 **Ashby-de-la-Zouch**—M.H., Lower Church St., Ashby-de-la-Zouch.
1st Mon. March; 1st Tues April (I.); 4th Tues. Oct.   May 31, 2000

K   1786 **Progress Lodge of Enthroned Commanders**—F.M.H., London Road, Leicester.
3rd Fri. April, Oct. (I.)   Oct. 18, 2002

1787 **East Africa Lodge of Installed Commanders**—F.M.H., Nairobi, Kenya.
2nd Sat. May; 4th Sat. June (I.)   June 27, 1998

1790 **Fraternidad**—
Temple "Cyril H. Rees", Calle 8 No. 8084, Calacoto, La Paz, Bolivia.
1st Tues. March, June, Dec.; 1st Sat. Aug. (I.)   Jan. 8, 2002

1792 **Zum Maurischen Schloss Im See**—Münzhof, Marktplatz 24,
88085 Langenargen/Lake Constance, Germany.
1st Sat. April; 2nd Sat. July; 3rd Sat. Oct. (I.)   Nov. 23, 2002

1794 **Santa Cruz**—GLB Temple, Calle Ayacucho No. 413, Santa Cruz, Bolivia.
1st Tues. March, June, Dec.; 1st Sat. Aug. (I.)   Sept. 11, 2004

1795 **James Webster**—M.C., Queen's Road, Brighton.
2nd Mon. Jan. (I.); 1st Mon. April, July   Jan. 8, 2003

1796 **Hampshire & Isle of Wight Provincial Grand Stewards**—
M.C., Brook House, Brook Lane, Botley, Hampshire.
3rd Mon. Feb., June, Oct. (I.)   Dec. 19, 2001

1798 **Meridies**—M.C., Brook House, Brook LA, Botley, Hampshire.
2nd Mon. Feb. (I.), May, Oct.   Feb. 28, 2003

1799 **Delta**—F.M.H. Beestenmarkt 5, Goes, The Netherlands.
3rd Mon. Feb. (I.), May, Oct.   Dec. 2, 2000

1802 **The Millennium**—M.C. Albany Rd., Sittingbourne, Kent.
1st Sat. Jan. (I.); 3rd Sat. June, Oct.   Jan. 6, 2001

1805 **Cantera Del Oriente**—Calle Ayacucho No. 431, Santa Cruz, Bolivia.
1st Sat. March, June, Aug. (I.), Dec.   Sept. 8, 2012

ROLL OF ROYAL ARK MARINER LODGES—*continued*

1808 **Notts. Installed Commanders**—M.H., Goldsmith Street, Nottingham.
2nd fifth weekday in Jan., May Oct. 20, 2007

1809 **Stanstead Abbots**—M.H., Vantorts Road, Sawbridgeworth, Hertfordshire.
2nd Wed. Feb. (I.), May, Oct. April 29, 2008

1810 **San Juan**—Restaurante Casa Caty, Ctra. Benidorm, Callosa d'En Sarria, Alicante, Spain.
3rd Mon. Feb., April, Oct. (I.) April 4, 2003

1815 **La Ram de Lorraine**—M.T., Rue Nicolas Berger, 66/B-6700 Arlon, Belgium.
1st Wed. April (I.), Sept. Jun. 26, 2004

1817 **Fênix**—M.T., 21 de Abril at Rua Sao Joaquim No. 457, São Paulo, S.P. Brazil.
Last Thurs. Jan., April, July (I.), Oct. Sept. 20, 2012

1819 **Moses Montefiore**—M.T., Rua Artur de Azevedo, 1781, Sao Paulo, SP, Brazil.
1st Mon. March (I.), May, Sept. Nov. Jan. 31, 2011

1822 **Millennium**—Northfield M.H., 641 Bristol Road South, Birmingham B31 2JS.
1st Thurs. Jan.; 2nd Thurs. April (I.) April 4, 2003

1823 **Oliva La Safor**—Restaurante Flor Azahar, Ctra. Albaida, Gandia, Valencia, Spain.
Thurs. after 3rd Tues. Feb., May, Nov. (I.) Sept. 23, 2005

1826 **Tenerife**—M.T., Guaracarumbo Restaurant, Guaza, Tenerife.
4th Wed. Feb., April, Sept. (I.) June 1, 2006

1828 **Royal Prince of Wales**—M.T., 7 Alexandra Street, St. Clair, Port of Spain, Trinidad.
4th Mon. June (I.); 2nd Tues. Aug., Dec. May 7, 2004

1831 **Thomas á Becket**—Charmandean Centre, Worthing.
3rd Wed. Jan., March, May (I.) Sept. 17, 2007

1834 **Charlotte Amalie**—The Masonic Hall, 10 Wimmelskaft Gade, Charlotte Amalie, St. Thomas, U.S. Virgin Islands.
2nd Wed. March (I.), May, Nov. Mar. 2, 2007

1835 **Kypros**—Apollo Rooms, Episkopi, Cyprus.
2nd Fri. Jan. (I.), March, Oct. Oct. 15, 2005

1837 **Cantero**—Meson Aquario, Avenida Centro La Azohia, Murcia, Spain.
3rd Tues. Jan., Feb., March (I.), Nov. May 26, 2011

1838 **Menatschim**—F.M.H., 333 Banbury Road, Oxford.
4th Mon. March (may be held at other venue within Oxfordshire), June (I.) Dec. 16, 2008

1839 **Oak Tree**—Sit Perpetuum Temple, Bisley, Surrey.
2nd Thurs. Jan., April, Sept. (I.) Nov. 29, 2007

1840 **St. James's**—10 Duke Street, London SW1Y 6BS.
1st Mon. Jan. (I.), July Feb. 29, 2012

■ 1843 **The Stuart Parry**—M.H. Ludgershall, Wiltshire.
1st Thurs. March, June, Dec. (I.) Oct. 28, 2010

1846 **Lodge of Enlightenment**—
Harrow M.C. and any other venue within the Province of Middlesex.
2nd Thurs. Oct. (I.); 2nd Thurs. Feb., June Jan. 20, 2005

1847 **The Ship of the Fens**—Masonic Rooms, Ely.
3rd Thurs. June (I.); 4th Thurs. Nov.; 2nd Fri. March May 31, 2008

1848 **Barbados Installed Commanders**—St. George, Barbados.
2nd Tues. March (I.), Sept. May 26, 2005

1850 **Abeokuta**—Lisabi Masonic Hall, Aivetoro Road, Lafenwa, Abeokuta, Nigeria.
3rd Sat. March (I.), July, Oct. April 5, 2008

1852 **Barão de Mauá**—Av. Ricardo Medina Filho, 577, São Paulo, S.P. 05057-100 Brazil.
3rd Thurs. March, Sept. (I.), Nov. June 7, 2008

ROLL OF ROYAL ARK MARINER LODGES—continued

1856 **Mahajan**—Mansfield Bowling Club, Croftdown Road, Highgate, London NW5 1EP.
2nd Mon. March; 1st Wed. May (I.), Nov.   May 6, 2011

1857 **Ditton**—Surbiton Masonic Centre.
2nd Fri. April; 1st Tues. Sept. (I.); 4th Wed. Nov.   Sept. 4, 2007

1863 **Sanct Elmo**—"Casa Viani", 6 & 7 Marsamxett St., Valletta, Malta.
Thurs. before 1st Sat. May, Oct. (I.)   May 9, 2005

1864 **Montserrat**—Barbados.
2nd Sat. March, July (I.), Nov.   May 19, 2008

1865 **Cyril H. Rees Providencia**—
Temple "Cyril H. Rees", Calle 8 No. 8084, Calacoto, La Paz, Bolivia.
3rd Tues. March, June, Aug. (I.); 1st Thurs. Dec.   Mar. 2, 2007

1867 **Quesada Summer**—Sociedad Compas, Ciudad Quesada, Rojales, Alicante.
3rd Mon. June, July, Sept. (I.)   Jan. 27, 2006

1872 **Lim Saywan**—Dewan Freemason, 15 Jalan 18/16, Taman Kanagapuram 46000, Petaling Jaya.
2nd Thurs. March; 3rd Thurs. June (I.); 1st Wed. Nov.   Dec. 12, 2009

1873 **Dominica**—Roseau, Dominica.
3rd Mon. May (I.), Aug., Nov.   May 19, 2008

1874 **Tortola**—M.T., Johnson's Ghut, Tortola, British Virgin Islands.
2nd Fri. Jan, April, Nov. (I.)

1876 **Clifford W. Jeapes**—East Sussex Masonic Centre, Seaview Road, Peacehaven.
1st Thurs. June (I.); 4th Wed. Nov.   June 10, 2010

K ■ 1877 **Mojacar**—Kimrick Restaurant, Mojacar Playa, Almeria, Spain.
2nd Mon. Feb., March, Sept. (I.), Dec.   Dec. 11, 2007

1882 **Ituni**—New Amsterdam, Berbice, Guyana.
3rd Sat. Feb., July, Nov. (I.)   May 15, 2008

K 1886 **Ravensmead and Mandalay**—Oakley House, 358 Bromley Common, Bromley, Kent.
3rd Thurs. Jan.; 2nd Thurs. May; 4th Wed. Sept. (I.)   Dec. 7, 1967

1887 **Taquah**—Tarkwa Masonic Temple, Tarkwa, Ghana.
2nd Sat. Feb., June (I.), Oct.   Mar. 19, 2010

1889 **Equator**—West London Masonic Centre, Churchfield House, Churchfield Road, West Ealing, London W13 9NF.
3rd Fri. Feb., May (I.) Oct.   May 26, 2009

1893 **Premier Siam**—Hilton Phuket Arcadia Resort & Spa, 333 Patak Road, Karon, Phuket 83100, Thailand.
3rd Sat. July; 2nd Sat. Sept., Nov.   July 30, 2012

1894 **Erdemont**—M.H., West Hill, Dartford, Kent DA1 2HJ.
2nd Thurs. Feb., April, Sept.   Oct. 29, 2012

1895 **St. James**—M.M.H., London SW1A 1PL.
4th Thurs. June (I.)   June 30, 2009

1896 **Pico della Mirandola**—Such venues in Rome or other cities in Italy as the Cdr. shall designate.
4th Thurs. March; 2nd Sat. June (I.); 3rd Sat. Nov.   June 18, 2010

1898 **West Sussex Installed Commanders**—
M.H., South Pallant, Chichester, West Sussex PO19 1SY.
2nd Sat. Jan. (I.); 2nd Fri. July   July 19, 2008

1899 **Mayflower**—M.H., Hatton Road, Spilsby PE23 5JZ.
3rd Tues. Feb., April (I.), Oct.   April 17, 2010

1902 **Mount Cardo**—Masonic Ctr., Arrecife, Lanzarote.
Fri. before 2nd Sat. April, Oct. (I.), Dec.   Jan. 28, 2006

1903	New Shores—M.T., Vienna or any other venue in Austria. *3rd Sat. Jan., April; Last Sat. Sept.*	Sept. 24, 2011
■ 1905	Morley—Blenheim House, Batley Field Hill, Batley WF17 0BG. *1st Wed. May, July (I.), Sept. (I.)*	Oct. 13, 2009
1906	The Geoffrey Dicker—F.M.H., Diss, Norfolk IP22 4LE. *Twice a year on days selected by the Provincial Grand Master*	Dec. 14, 2009
1909	Highgate—Imperial Hotel, Russel Square, London WC1B 5BB. *1st Sat. April; 2nd Sat. July (I.), Nov.*	June 7, 2011
1910	The Ark—M.H., Chapel Lane, Alford, Lincs. LN13 9DP. *2nd Fri. July; 3rd Fri. Dec.*	Jan. 14, 2012
1916	Giorgio Vasari—Via Borgunto, 6, 52100 Arezzo, Italy. *4th Thurs. Jan., March, May, Nov.*	June 30, 2012
1918	Mare Centabricum—Bilbao. *4th Sat. in months with 5 Sats.*	Sept. 22, 2012
1933	Entente Cordiale—M.M.H., London SW1A 1PL. *4th Sat. Jan., June; 3rd Sat. Oct. (I.)*	Mar. 10, 2012

SUBSCRIBING GRAND OFFICERS

GRAND OFFICERS
ALPHABETICALLY ARRANGED
PREFIXES

Grand Master .... Most Worshipful
Pro Grand Master .... Most Worshipful

Deputy Grand Master ..... Right Worshipful
Assistant Grand Master .. Right Worshipful
Provincial and District
Grand Masters .... Right Worshipful
Grand Wardens .... Right Worshipful

Grand Overseers .... Very Worshipful
Grand Chaplains .... Very Worshipful
Grand Treasurer .... Very Worshipful
Grand Registrar .... Very Worshipful
President of the
General Board .... Very Worshipful
Grand Secretary .... Very Worshipful
Grand Director of
Ceremonies .... Very Worshipful

All other Grand Officers .... Worshipful

HOLDERS OF R.A.M. GRAND RANK
ALPHABETICALLY ARRANGED
PREFIXES

Grand Master (G.M.) ...... Most Worshipful
Pro Grand Master
(Pro.G.M.) .... Most Worshipful

Deputy Grand Master
(D.G.M.) .... Right Worshipful
Assistant Grand Master
(A.G.M.) .... Right Worshipful
Members of the Grand
Master's Royal Ark Council
(G.M.R.A.C.) .... Right Worshipful
Provincial and District
Grand Masters
(Prov.G.M.)(Dist.G.M.).. Right Worshipful

Holders of Royal Ark Mariner
Grand Rank .... Worshipful

NAME	RANK	YEAR OF APPT.	R.A.M.G.R. YEAR OF APPT.
Abbot, Arthur Edwin	P.G.St.B.	2000	
Ablott, Philip Charles	P.A.G.D.C.	2012	
Abrahams, James Lawrence	P.A.G.D.C.	1998	2003
	P.G.S.D.	2010	
Abrahams, Terence Henry	P.G.St.B.	2006	
Achurch, Frank William	P.A.G.D.C.	1997	2007
	P.G.S.D.	2006	
Ackah, Frank	P.G.St.B.	2005	
	P.G.J.D.	2011	
Ackroyd, David Eamonn	P.G.St.B.	2002	2009
	P.G.J.D.	2010	
Acton, Cyril	P.G.J.D.	2002	
	P.G.J.O.	2012	
Acton, Jack	P.G.St.B.	2007	
Adams, Albert Leslie	G.Stwd.	1990	
Adams, David Nigel	A.G.D.C.	2000	1996
	P.G.S.D.	2002	
	Prov.G.M., Dyfed	2007-2012	
Adams, David Edward Henry, *B.Mus.(Edin.)* *A.R.C.M., F.C.I.E.A.*	A.G.Org.	2005-2007	2006
	G.Org.	2008-2012	
Adams, Dennis Robert	P.G.St.B.	2010	2011
Adams, Hugh Walford	P.G.St.B.	1986	1985
	P.G.J.D.	1996	
Adams, James Munro, *B.E.M.*	P.A.G.D.C.	2002	2004
	P.G.S.D.	2010	

NAME	RANK	YEAR OF APPT.	R.A.M.G.R. YEAR OF APPT.
Adams, John Peter	—		2007
Adams, Malcolm	P.G.St.B.	2009	2010
Adams, Roland Charles	—		2008
Adams, Ronald Hubert	G.Stwd.	1998	
	P.G.J.D.	2003	
Adams, Roy	P.A.G.D.C.	2007	2001
Adams, Terence William	Asst.G.D.C.	1992	1993
	P.G.S.D.	1997	
	P.G.J.O.	2001	
Adamson, Phillip William	—		2011
Addy, Brian	P.A.G.D.C.	1992	2001
	P.G.S.D.	1997	
	G.J.O.	2002	
	P.G.M.O.	2008	
Addy, Benjamin	G.Stwd.	1981	1989
	G.J.D.	1987	GMRAC 2002
	Prov.G.M., Cheshire	1990-2002	
	A.G.M.	2002-2009	
	Dep.G.M.	2010	
	Pro G.M.	2011-2012	
Adedoyin, Adediji, *L.L.B.*	P.G.St.B.	2002	2010
	Dist.G.M., Nigeria	2011	
Adesola, Babajide Akinbode	P.G.St.B.	1995	2002
	P.G.S.D.	2005	
Adkin, Christopher Colin	P.A.G.D.C.	2009	2011
Adler, Anthony John	A.G.D.C.	1995	2001
	P.G.S.D.	2006	
Adrian, William Kenneth	P.A.G.Swd.B.	2007	2006
Adshead, Bryan	G.Stwd.	1987	1991
	Dep.G.D.C.	1991-93	
	P.G.J.O.	1996	
	P.G.M.O.	2002	
	G.J.W.	2003	
Adu, Alexander Kwaku	P.A.G.D.C.	2005	
Aga, Ardeshir Sam	P.G.St.B.	2012	
Ager, Charles Alfred	P.G.St.B.	2007	2009
Agyekum, Taspa Ford	P.A.G.D.C.	2006	
Ainsworth, Keith	P.A.G.D.C.	2010	
Aish, Malcolm Roger	G.Stwd.	1991	2001
	P.G.J.D.	2002	
	P.G.M.O.	2007	
Aistrup, Raymond George	P.A.G.St.B.	1990	
Aitken, Robert	P.A.G.D.C.	1994	1997
Aiyer, Dr. Shankar Krishna	P.A.G.D.C.	2003	2005
	P.G.S.D.	2005	
	P.G.J.O.	2007	
Akwei-Aryee, Uriah Stonewall	P.A.G.D.C.	2010	
Alcoreza Marchetti, David	Dist.G.M., Bolivia	2012	
Aldrich, George Alfred	G.Stwd.	1996	2000
	P.G.J.D.	2003	
Aldridge, Geoffrey John	P.A.G.D.C.	2008	2010
Aleong, David Paul	P.A.G.D.C.	2004	2008
Alexander, David James	G.Stwd.	1997	
	P.G.J.D.	2008	

NAME	RANK	YEAR OF APPT.	R.A.M.G.R. YEAR OF APPT.
Alexander, Geoffrey	P.A.G.D.C.	2012	
Alexander, Ian Douglas Gavin, Q.C.	G.Reg.	1996-00	1996 GMRAC(H.C.)
	P.G.J.W.	2000	
Alexander, John Kenneth	P.A.G.D.C.	1997	2004
Alford, Donald Victor		—	2007
Alfred, His Hon. Joseph Bernard	P.A.G.D.C.	2012	
Ali, Gazanfar Ali Mohammed	P.A.G.D.C.	2006	2004
Alker, Kenneth	P.A.G.Swd.B.	2005	2005
	P.G.J.D.	2011	
Allard, Ralph Derek	P.G.St.B.	2000	1998
	P.G.J.D.	2012	
Allan, David Ian	G.Stwd.	2010	
Allan, James Stewart	P.G.I.G.	2009	
Allan, John James Burgess		—	2010
Allchin, Leslie Arthur		—	1997
Allcock, John Walter	P.G.St.B.	2003	2001
Alldred, David	P.G.St.B.	1997	1990
	P.G.J.D.	2002	
	P.G.S.D.	2004	
	P.G.J.O.	2008	
Allebosch, Felix Emile Pierre Claude Ghislain	P.A.G.Swd.B.	2006	
Allen, Colin Robert	P.G.St.B.	1999	
Allen, Jeremy Peter	P.A.G.D.C.	2007	
Allen, Reginald Arthur	A.G.Swd.B.	2009	
Allen, Richard George	P.G.St.B.	1990	
Allen, Ronald Lynn	P.A.G.D.C.	2008	2010
Alleyne, Noel Orville Arrindell	P.A.G.D.C.	1997	1995
	G.S.D.	2004	
Allinson, Leslie	P.A.G.D.C.	1995	2008
	P.G.S.D.	2002	
	P.G.J.O.	2009	
Allison, Ian William	P.A.G.St.B.	2003	
Allison, Robert Leonard	A.G.D.C.	2005	
Allonby, Revd. David Lionel, O.B.E., J.P.	P.A.G.Chap.	1995	1996
	P.G.S.O.	2005	
Alonso, Sadi Martinez	P.A.G.D.C.	2005	
Alvey, Lt. Alan Verity, R.N.V.R.	G.Stwd.	1986	1986
	Prov.G.M., Bedfordshire	1990	
Amarteifio, Samuel Amos Aduamoa	P.A.G.D.C.	1982	
	P.G.S.D.	1988	
Amato, Louis Alexander Isaac	P.A.G.St.B.	2007	1999
Amon, Donald Lewis	P.G.St.B.	2007	
Ancliffe, Richard, B.E.M.	A.G.St.B.	2002	1990
Anderson, Alan	G.Stwd.	2002	
	P.G.J.D.	2008	
Anderson, Alastair Rankin	P.A.G.D.C.	1994	1996
	P.G.J.D.	2001	
Anderson, Athole John	P.G.St.B.	2011	
Anderson, David	G.Stwd.	1997	2003
	P.G.J.D.	2003	
	P.G.S.D.	2008	
	P.G.J.O.	2010	

NAME	RANK	YEAR OF APPT.	R.A.M.G.R. YEAR OF APPT.
Anderson, Frederick Charles	—	1999	
Anderson, George Alister	—	2008	
Anderson, Jack Clifford	P.G.S.D.	2004	
Anderson, James Gordon Boyd	P.A.G.Swd.B.	2003	2002
	P.G.J.D.	2008	
Anderson, Richard John	P.G.S.D.	2012	
Anderson, Robert Alan	G.Stwd.	1992	
	P.G.J.D.	2000	
Anderson, William Lambert	P.A.G.D.C.	2009	
Anderton, David	G.Stwd.	2007	
	P.G.J.D.	2011	
Anderton, David Raymond	G.St.B.	1999	
Andrew, Robert	P.A.G.D.C.	2012	
Andrew, William Chalmers	P.A.G.St.B.	1991	
Andrews, Dr. John Harold Alan	P.G.St.B.	2004	2009
Andrews, Linton Anthony, *J.P.*	P.A.G.St.B.	2001	2003
	P.G.S.D.	2004	
	P.G.J.O.	2008	
	Dist.G.M., Jamaica & Cayman Islands	2009	
Angell, Nigel Lloyd	P.A.G.D.C.	2011	
Angle, Francis Leonard	—		1998
Annear, John Frank	G.Stwd.	1986	1991
	P.G.J.D.	1991	
	G.J.O.	1997	
Ansell, Dr. Christopher Wilson Guy, *Ph.D., B.Sc.*	P.G.St.B.	2003	2005
	P.G.J.D.	2011	
Ansell, Donald Victor	G.Stwd.	1999	2007
	P.G.S.D.	2007	
Anthony, Clifford Vincent	P.G.St.B	1996	1999
Apperley, Ralph Mannings	A.G.D.C.	2012	
Appleby, John Samuel	P.A.G.D.C.	1980	1975
	P.G.S.D.	1990	
Appleby, Kenneth	P.A.G.D.C.	1998	2005
	P.G.S.D.	2009	
Applewhaite, Lennox Mortimer	—		2006
Apps, William Richard	—		2010
Archer, John Lawrence	P.A.G.D.C.	2007	
Archer, Kenneth Clark	P.A.G.D.C.	2010	
Aris, Alexander Romaan Ivan	P.G.St.B.	1992	
Arkwell, John David	—		1997
Armiger, Leonard	—		2008
Arminson, Roland Colin	P.G.St.B.	1991	2007
	P.G.J.D.	2004	
Armstrong, David	P.A.G.D.C.	1988	
Armstrong, James Derek	P.A.G.D.C.	1994	2007
	P.G.S.D.	2002	
	P.G.J.O.	2010	
Armstrong, James Russell	P.A.G.D.C.	1995	
Armstrong, John	—		1998
Armstrong, Joseph Alan	P.A.G.D.C.	1974	1997
	P.G.S.D.	1987	
	P.G.S.O.	2001	

NAME	RANK	YEAR OF APPT.	R.A.M.G.R. YEAR OF APPT.
Armstrong, Joseph Walton	P.A.G.D.C.	2002	2008
	G.S.D.	2009	
Armstrong, Keith	P.A.G.Swd.B.	2006	
Armstrong, Leonard		—	1997
Armstrong, Richard	P.A.G.Swd.B.	2012	
Armstrong, Raymond	P.G.St.B.	2005	
Arnold, Clive	P.G.St.B.	1997	
	P.G.J.D.	2010	
Arnold, Harry Stephenson	P.A.G.D.C.	1991	1992
	P.G.S.D.	1995	
	Prov.G.M., Bedfordshire	1998-2006	
Arole, Shrikrishna Gopalrao	Dist.G.M., Bombay	2009	2009
Arrowsmith, Ronald Alfred	P.G.St.B.	1978	
	P.G.J.D.	2001	
	P.G.S.O.	2007	
Arul, Chandran	P.A.G.D.C.	2008	2009
	P.G.S.D.	2012	
Asaria, Mansur Mohamedali	P.A.G.D.C.	2004	2005
Ash, Robert	P.A.G.St.B.	2007	2000
Ashbolt, David Frederick	G.Stwd.	2003	2002
	P.G.J.D.	2006	
	P.G.J.O.	2007	
Ashcroft, Barry	P.A.G.D.C.	2010	
Ashcroft, James Paul	P.A.G.D.C.	2007	
Ashcroft, John Wilberforce	P.A.G.D.C.	2012	
Ashcroft, Michael William Norman	P.A.G.D.C.	2010	
Ashenheim, Richard Gordon		—	1997
	P.G.S.D.	1995	
Asher, Richard	P.G.St.B.	2005	2006
Asher, Terence Charles	P.G.St.B.	2007	
Ashley, Cyril William	P.G.St.B.	2011	
Ashman, Gerald Charles	G.Stwd.	1992	1997
	P.G.J.D.	1999	
Ashmore, Graham John		—	1999
Ashton, William John	P.G.St.B.	2012	
Ashton, William Noel	P.A.G.D.C.	1991	1996
	P.G.S.D.	1998	
	P.G.J.O.	2004	
Aspden, Jeremy Broughton	P.G.J.D.	2004	2003
	P.G.J.O.	2008	
Aspinall, Joseph Brian	G.Std.B.	1999	
Aspinall, Ronald	P.A.G.Swd.B.	2003	2007
	P.G.J.D.	2010	
Aspinell, Charles Jonathan, *R.D., J.P.*	P.A.G.D.C.	2008	2009
Aspinwall, David	G.Stwd.	1996	1993
	A.G.D.C.	2003	
	G.S.D.	2010	
Assiamah, Kofi	P.A.G.D.C.	2011	
Astbury, Walter John	A.G.St.B.	2006	
Astfalck, Peter Charles	P.A.G.D.C.	2004	2006
Atkins, Peter Duncan	G.Stwd.	2007	
	G.J.D.	2011	
Atkins, Peter William	P.A.G.D.C.	2010	2008

NAME	RANK	YEAR OF APPT.	R.A.M.G.R. YEAR OF APPT.
Atkinson, Allan Douglas	P.A.G.St.B	1996	2005
	P.G.J.D.	2001	
	P.G.J.O.	2010	
Atkinson, Brian Wickham	P.A.G.St.B.	2001	1995
	P.G.J.D.	2008	
Atkinson, George Robert	P.A.G.Swd.B.	2008	2011
Atkinson, Rodney Frank	P.A.G.D.C.	2012	
Atta-Quayson, John	P.A.G.D.C.	2001	
	P.G.S.D.	2012	
Attfield, Albert William	P.A.G.D.C.	2010	
Attoe, David Michael	P.A.G.D.C.	2011	2008
Attwood, Jeffrey Lawrence	G.Stwd.	2001	
	G.J.D.	2006	
Atwell, Neville Grahame Doorly	P.A.G.D.C.	1997	
Auber, Thomas Frederick, *M.A.*	P.A.G.D.C.	1997	
	P.G.J.D.	2012	
Audin, Alan Harding	P.A.G.D.C.	1995	1996
Audsley, Walter	P.A.G.D.C.	1988	
Auld, Donald	P.G.St.B.	2006	
Auld, Matthew David Edward	P.A.G.St.B.	1997	1999
	G.J.D.	2002	
	P.G.J.O.	2011	
Austin, Anthony Robert	P.A.G.D.C.	2009	2011
Averns, Morris Raymond	G.Stwd.	1987	1992
	G.J.D.	1992	
	P.G.S.D.	1995	
	P.G.J.O.	1997	
	P.G.M.O.	2003	
	P.G.J.W.	2008	
Avery, Revd. Anthony William	P.A.G.Chap.	2001	2011
Avery, Arthur	P.A.G.St.B	1996	2009
Avery, John Charles Mark	P.G.St.B.	1983	1977
	P.G.J.D.	1992	
	P.G.J.O.	2004	
	P.G.M.O.	2012	
Awcock, David Arthur	P.A.G.Swd.B.	2012	2011
Axford, Albert John	P.G.St.B.	2008	
Axford, Col. Arthur, *O.B.E., T.D., D.L.*	G.Stwd.	1977	1981
	P.G.J.D.	1982	
	P.G.J.O.	1987	
	P.G.S.O.	1992	
	G.M.O.	2001	
Aybes, Simon Bernard	P.A.G.Swd.B.	2012	2011
Ayers, Leslie Herbert Thomas	P.A.G.D.C.	1982	1987
Aylwin, Christopher Granville Angus	A.G.Reg.	2011-2012	
Ayling, Ronald George	P.G.St.B.	2003	
Ayre, Anthony John	G.Stwd.	2003	
	P.G.J.D.	2007	
Ayres, Stephen Michael, *J.P.*	G.Stwd.	2002	2003
	P.G.J.D.	2008	
Azu, Robert Barker	P.G.St.B.	2006	
Azzopardi, Joseph Louis	A.G.St.B.	2012	

NAME	RANK	YEAR OF APPT.	R.A.M.G.R. YEAR OF APPT.
Babbage, Ronald	P.G.St.B.	2007	2001
Badjak, Ljuba Milan	P.G.St.B	1996	1994
Baig, Akram	G.Stwd.	2007	2003
	G.J.D.	2011	
Baikie, Peter Tulloch	P.A.G.D.C.	1984	1987
	P.G.S.D.	1990	
	P.G.J.O.	1997	
Bailes, Bryan Alan	P.A.G.D.C.	1999	2002
	P.G.S.D.	2004	
	P.G.J.O.	2010	
Bailey, Charles Arthur	P.A.G.D.C.	2007	2010
Bailey, Derek	P.G.St.B.	1998	1998
Bailey, Donald Ferguson	P.A.G.St.B	1996	
Bailey, George Derek	G.Stwd.	1990	2000
	P.G.J.D.	1995	
Bailey, Ivor John	A.G.D.C.	1987	1993
	P.G.S.D.	1994	
	P.G.J.O.	2008	
Bailey, Michael Robin	P.G.S.D.	2005	
Bailey, Peter Cambria	P.A.G.St.B.	2012	
Bailey, Peter David	P.A.G.D.C.	2009	
Bailey, Peter Harold Edwin, *J.P.*	P.A.G.D.C.	1986	1989
	P.G.J.D.	1995	
	P.G.J.O.	2008	
Bailey, Stephen William	P.G.St.B.	2011	2010
Bailey, Terrence Reginald		—	2010
Baillie, Anthony Thomas	P.A.G.D.C.	1997	2001
	P.G.S.D.	2002	
	P.G.J.O.	2007	
Baillie, Thomas	P.G.St.B.	2009	
Bain, David John	P.A.G.D.C.	2000	
Bain, James Randolph	P.G.S.D.	2006	2005
	G.Insp., Bahamas & Turks	2009	
Bainbridge, John	P.A.G.D.C.	1998	1997
Bajan, Dorab Cawasji	P.A.G.D.C.	2007	
Baker, Anthony James	P.A.G.Swd.B.	2005	
Baker, Bruce	P.A.G.St.B.	2011	2011
Baker, Christopher Robin	P.G.St.B.	2001	
	P.G.J.D.	2012	
Baker, David Edward		—	1995
Baker, Frank	P.A.G.St.B.	1993	
Baker, Frederick	P.A.G.D.C.	1983	
	P.G.S.D.	1990	
Baker, Ian Robert	P.A.G.D.C.	2007	2010
Baker, Ivor Roland	P.A.G.D.C.	1989	1992
Baker, Michael John	G.Stwd.	2011	
Baker, Neil	P.A.G.D.C.	1989	
Baker, Peter Richard Alleyne	P.A.G.D.C.	2002	2004
	G.S.D.	2008	
Baker, Richard Nerod	P.A.G.D.C.	2003	2007
	P.G.S.D.	2009	

NAME	RANK	YEAR OF APPT.	R.A.M.G.R. YEAR OF APPT.
Baker, William Ernest	P.A.G.D.C.	1993	1992
	G.S.D.	1998	
	G.J.O.	2003	
Balderston, William John	G.Stwd.	2003	2004
	P.G.J.D.	2007	
	P.G.J.O.	2012	
Baldwin, Alan	G.Stwd.	2001	
	P.G.J.D.	2006	
Baldwin, Peter Joseph	P.A.G.D.C.	2006	
	P.G.S.D.	2008	
Bale, David William Barrie	P.A.G.D.C.	2005	2010
	P.G.S.D.	2011	
Ball, Graham Richard Lloyd	P.A.G.D.C.	2011	
Ball, John Anthony, *C.B.E.*	P.G.St.B.	1991	1996
	P.G.J.D.	1996	
	P.G.J.O.	2003	
Ball, Peter Maxwell	A.G.D.C.	2004	2000
	G.S.D.	2009	
	Prov.G.M., Nottinghamshire	2012	
Ball, Ronald (Jnr)	P.A.G.Swd.B.	1998	1995
Ballarin, Luiz Alberto	P.A.G.D.C.	2006	2011
Balmer, Revd. Walter Owen	P.A.G.Chap.	1992	1999
	Dep.G.Chap.	1998	
	P.G.J.O.	2004	
Balsom, Peter James	G.Stwd.	1995	2009
	P.G.J.D.	2000	
	P.G.J.O.	2006	
Bamber, Austin Westbury	P.A.G.Swd.B.	2001	2006
	Dep.G.Swd.B.	2010	
Bamford, Eddy	P.A.G.D.C.	2012	
Bampton, Kevin Charles	P.A.G.D.C.	2008	2009
Banbury, Michael James	A.G.D.C.	2006	2005
Banerjee, Shiva Prasad	P.A.G.D.C.	2010	
Banks, David James	P.A.G.D.C.	2003	
Banks, John Lionel	P.A.G.St.B.	2008	
Banks, Nigel Royston	A.G.I.G.	1998	2002
	P.G.J.D.	2004	
	P.G.J.O.	2010	
Banks, Thomas Anthony	P.A.G.St.B.	1994	
	P.G.J.D.	2004	
Bany, Ignace Desire Laval, *M.A.*	P.A.G.Swd.B.	2007	2005
	P.G.J.D.	2012	
Barfoot, Brian John	P.G.St.B.	1997	1996
	P.G.J.D.	2003	
	P.G.J.O.	2008	
Barham, Stanley George	P.G.St.B.	2003	
Barke, Joseph Owen Basil	P.A.G.D.C.	1987	1986
	G.J.O.	1992	
	Prov.G.M., Glos. & Hereford	1996-2004	
Barker, Emilio	P.G.St.B.	2008	
Barker, Gerald Anthony Granville	P.A.G.D.C.	2009	
Barker, Graham Leslie	P.G.J.D.	1994	1994
	P.G.J.O.	2004	

NAME	RANK	YEAR OF APPT.	R.A.M.G.R. YEAR OF APPT.
Barker, Herbert Henness	P.G.St.B	1996	
	P.G.J.D.	2010	
Barker, Jack	P.A.G.D.C.	2005	1998
Barker, Kenneth Neville	P.G.St.B.	2001	1997
Barker, Marion Virgil	G.Stwd.	2000	2002
	P.G.J.D.	2009	
Barker, Roderick John		—	2011
Barkess, Douglas	P.G.St.B.	2001	
Barlow, John	G.Stwd.	1999	
	P.G.J.D.	2004	
Barlow, Sydney John Bruton	P.G.St.B.	1995	2001
	P.G.J.D.	2003	
	P.G.J.O.	2011	
Barnard, Bryan	P.A.G.Swd.B.	2009	
Barnard, William	P.A.G.D.C.	2009	
Barnes, Christopher James	G.Stwd.	1994	2001
	G.J.D.	2003	
	P.G.J.O.	2008	
Barnes, John	P.G.St.B.	2005	
Barnes, Kenneth Henry, *J.P.*	P.G.S.D.	2001	
Barnes, Michael Frederick, *M.Sc., B.Sc.*	P.G.St.B.	1992	1996
	P.G.J.D.	1997	
	Dep.G.Swd.B.	2003	
	P.G.J.O.	2006	
	P.G.M.O.	2012	
Barnes, Robert Collins	P.A.G.D.C.	2010	2011
Barnes, Terence	P.G.St.B.	1990	
Barnett, Desmond	A.G.D.C.	1992	1995
	P.G.J.D.	1995	
	Prov.G.M. Sth. Wales	1996-2008	
Barnett, Raymond Dennis	P.G.St.B.	2006	
Barnfield, Glyn Kenneth	P.G.St.B.	2010	
Barnsdall, Thomas Edward	P.A.G.D.C.	2005	2009
Barnwell, Neville Percival Berkely		—	2010
Baron, Edgar Charles Leonard	G.Stwd.	1983	2001
	P.G.J.D.	1993	
Barr, Derek William	P.G.St.B.	2010	
Barrett, Colin	P.A.G.D.C.	1997	2001
	P.G.S.D.	2002	
	P.G.J.O.	2009	
Barrett, Eric	P.G.St.B.	2008	
Barrett, Ernest Edward		—	2007
Barrington, Nicholas John Fitzcharles Cannington	P.G.S.D.	1995	
Barrow, Dr. Kenrick Orrin Evan	P.G.St.B.	2000	2005
	P.G.J.D.	2008	
Barry, John	P.G.St.B.	1992	1994
Barthorpe, Barry Charles	P.G.St.B.	2006	2007
Bartle, Maurice		—	2005
Bartlett, Gerald John	P.G.St.B.	2009	2005
Bartlett, Peter Edmund Guest	A.G.Swd.B.	2000	
Barton, Brian Frederick	P.A.G.D.C.	2009	2010
Barton, David Francis	P.A.G.D.C.	2011	2010

NAME	RANK	YEAR OF APPT.	R.A.M.G.R. YEAR OF APPT.
Barton, John Edmund	P.A.G.D.C.	2008	2009
Barton, Kelvin Clifford	P.G.St.B.	2010	
Barton, Malcolm Peter Speight	P.A.G.St.B.	2000	
Barton, Richard Anthony	G.Stwd.	1991	1998
	P.G.J.D.	1996	
	P.G.J.O.	2001	
	P.G.S.O.	2012	
Barton, Warner	G.I.G.	2009	
	G.J.D.	2012	
Barwick, Donald Horace	P.G.St.B.	1986	1995
	G.J.D.	1999	
Basche, Philip Arnott	A.G.I.G.	1986	1990
	G.I.G.	1987	
	P.A.G.D.C.	1993	
Basger, Harvey	G.St.B.	1992	
Bashford, Frederick Victor	P.G.St.B.	1993	1993
	P.G.J.O.	2006	
Basnett, George Herbert	G.Stwd.	1983	1986
	P.G.J.D.	1988	
	P.G.J.O.	1995	
Bassett, Albert Henry Arthur	P.A.G.St.B.	2009	
Bassett, Kenneth Charles	G.Stwd.	1997	
	P.G.J.D.	2003	
Bassou, Andre Armand Gabriel	P.A.G.Swd.B.	1989	1994
	P.G.S.D.	1995	
Batcheler, Anthony Charles	P.A.G.D.C.	1991	1995
	P.G.S.D.	1996	
Bateman, Clive Edward	P.G.St.B.	2003	
Bateman, Ronald Alan	P.A.G.Swd.B.	2006	
Bateman, Thomas	P.A.G.D.C.	2001	
Bates, Ronald Thomas	P.A.G.D.C.	1985	1988
	Prov.G.M., Bristol	1988-95	
Bates, Terence Gordon	P.G.St.B.	1998	2000
	P.G.J.D.	2008	
Bathgate, William Thomson	P.G.I.G.	2006	
Bathurst, Roger Barry	P.G.St.B.	2012	2011
Batters, Royce	G.Stwd.	2010	
Batty, Brian Morris	G.Stwd.	1987	1991
	P.G.J.D.	1992	
	P.G.S.D.	1995	
	P.G.J.O.	1997	
	Prov.G.M., West Yorkshire	1999-2007	
Baum, Dennis	P.G.St.B.	1998	1994
	P.G.J.D.	2007	
Bautista, Joseph Henry	A.G.St.B.	2008	
Bavin, Richard	P.G.St.B.	1994	
	P.G.J.D.	2000	
Baxter, Ronald Geoffrey, *M.B.E.*	P.A.G.D.C.	2000	
	P.G.J.D.	2010	
Baxendale, Alan William	P.G.St.B.	2009	2011
Baxter, Arthur	P.A.G.D.C.	2011	
Bayes, Maxwell William	P.A.G.D.C.	2001	2009
	P.G.S.D.	2012	
Bayles, John Reginald	P.G.St.B.	2004	

NAME	RANK	YEAR OF APPT.	R.A.M.G.R. YEAR OF APPT.
Bayley, Dennis Raymond	P.A.G.D.C.	2003	
Bayley, Ian Joseph	P.A.G.D.C.	2007	
Beadle, John Charles William		—	1983
Beal, Henry Walter William	P.G.St.B.	2004	2003
Beales, Frederick Allan Peat	P.A.G.D.C.	2011	
Bealing, Raymond Anthony	P.G.St.B.	1972	1978
	P.A.G.D.C.	1985	
	P.G.S.D.	1994	
Bean, Frederick Colborn		—	2011
Bean, John Kenneth	P.G.J.D.	2003	
Beard, John Michael	A.G.D.C.	1998	
	P.G.S.D.	2009	
Beard, Walter	P.G.St.B.	2005	
Beardmore, Keith Alan	G.Stwd.	2001	2002
	G.J.D.	2006	
	P.G.J.O.	2011	
Beardmore, Kevan Kim William	P.A.G.D.C.	1994	2005
	P.G.S.D.	2001	
	P.G.J.O.	2008	
Beardsley, Duncan Richard	A.G.Swd.B.	2005	2008
Beasley, Ronald William Thomas	P.G.St.B.	2007	2006
Beastall, Gordon Gayler	P.A.G.D.C.	2004	
	P.G.S.D.	2011	
Beattie, Selwyn Smith	P.A.G.D.C.	1993	2005
	G.S.D.	1999	
Beaumont, Andrew Philip	P.A.G.D.C.	2006	2002
Beaumont, Brian	P.G.St.B.	1993	
Beaumont, Keith Robert	P.A.G.D.C.	2011	
Beaven, William John	P.A.G.D.C.	1999	
Beaver, Arthur Donald Cecil	P.G.St.B.	2006	2002
	P.G.J.D.	2012	
Beavers, John Francis	P.A.G.D.C.	1990	1998
	G.S.D.	1995	
	P.G.J.O.	2001	
Beber, Howard André	P.A.G.D.C.	1996	1993
	G.S.D.	2001	
	P.G.J.O.	2011	
Beck, Christopher Roy	P.A.G.D.C.	2006	
	P.G.S.D.	2011	
Beck, Harold Vincent	P.A.G.D.C.	2010	
Becker, Michael		—	2007
Beckerton, Alan	P.A.G.D.C.	2009	
Beckingsale, Andrew Downing	P.A.G.D.C.	1994	1996
	P.G.S.D.	1999	
	P.G.J.O.	2006	
Beddoe, John	P.A.G.D.C.	1998	
	P.G.S.D.	2006	
Beddows, Trevor Edward	P.A.G.D.C.	2007	
Bedells, Richard Neil	P.A.G.D.C.	2010	2010
Bedford, Godfrey	P.A.G.Swd.B.	2007	
Bedford, Roland John	G.Stwd.	1994	1992
	G.J.D.	2000	
	P.G.J.O.	2004	

NAME	RANK	YEAR OF APPT.	R.A.M.G.R. YEAR OF APPT.
Bedding, John Albert	P.G.St.B.	1994	1991
	G.J.D.	2004	
Beddoe, John		—	2003
Beecham, Herbert	P.G.St.B.	1997	1996
Beeching, David Wanstall	P.G.St.B.	1985	1995
	P.G.J.D.	1995	
Beeching, Richard Noel Howard	P.A.G.Swd.B.	2002	
Beedle, Peter	G.Stwd.	2012	
Been, Arthur Allan	P.A.G.D.C.	1993	
Beese, Robert Ian		—	1991
Beesley, Kenneth	G.Stwd.	2006	
	P.G.J.D.	2010	
Beeson, Richard Harry	P.A.G.St.B.	2009	
Behal, Brij	P.A.G.Swd.B.	2000	
Behar, Raphael Nassim	P.G.J.D.	2006	2008
Belcher, Michael Percy	P.G.St.B.	1997	1995
	P.G.J.D.	2004	
Belfitt, William John	P.A.G.Swd.B.	2007	2010
Bell, Clive	P.G.St.B.	2004	
Bell, James Malcolm	P.G.St.B.	2003	
Bell, John	G.Stwd.	2009	2002
	P.G.S.D.	2011	
Bell, John Walton	P.G.I.G.	1998	
	P.G.J.D.	2007	
Bell, Kenneth	G.J.D.	2007	
Bell, Lawrence	P.G.I.G.	2007	
Bell, Malcolm Irving	P.A.G.Swd.B.	2003	2006
	P.G.J.D.	2009	
Bell, Nigel David	P.A.G.Swd.B.	2011	
Bell, Norman	P.A.G.Swd.B.	2005	
Bell, Richard	P.A.G.D.C.	2007	2006
Bell, Robert Stanley	P.A.G.D.C.	1986	2000
Bell, Roger Frederick	P.A.G.Swd.B.	1996	
Bellinger, Brian Charles	P.G.S.D.	2010	
Bellingham, Derrick Walter	P.G.St. B	1996	1996
	P.G.J.D.	2004	
Bellis, Christopher Robin		—	1998
Belsham, Maurice		—	2003
Bence, Thomas How	P.G.St.B.	1997	2001
	P.G.J.D.	2004	
Bendall, Maj. Leonard Charles	P.A.G.D.C.	1996	2002
	P.G.S.D.	2001	
Bendell, Francis Graham	P.A.G.D.C.	2006	
	P.G.J.D.	2011	
Benedict, Antony Visvanadan	P.A.G.D.C.	2008	
Benedict, Jan	P.A.G.D.C.	2001	
Benfield, Thomas Edward	P.A.G.St.B.	2007	2004
Bennett, Beverley Edwin	P.A.G.D.C.	2011	2011
Bennett, Revd. David Edward	P.A.G.Chap.	2000	2002
Bennett, Douglas John		—	1998

NAME	RANK	YEAR OF APPT.	R.A.M.G.R. YEAR OF APPT.
Bennett, Eric Curtis	P.A.G.St.B.	1998	1999
	P.G.J.D.	2005	
	P.G.J.O.	2010	
Bennett, James Frederick		—	2008
Bennett, Jeffery Albert Edward	P.A.G.D.C.	2005	2007
Bennett, Roy, *J.P.*	G.Stwd.	1986	
	P.G.J.D.	1992	
	P.G.J.O.	1999	
Bennett, Philip Harold	P.A.G.D.C.	1996	
	P.G.S.D.	2002	
Bennett, Ronald Edmund William	P.A.G.D.C.	1994	1999
	P.G.S.D.	2011	
Bennett, Samuel Royston		—	2004
Bennett-Rees, David Edward	P.G.St.B.	1999	1995
Bennie, George Robert	P.G.St.B.	1989	1995
	P.G.J.D.	1995	
Bennion, Allan	G.Stwd.	2000	2008
	P.G.J.D.	2005	
Bennison, Roderick	G.Stwd.	1998	2006
	P.G.J.D.	2003	
	P.G.J.O.	2011	
Benoliel, David Max	P.A.G.D.C.	1994	
Bentall, Roger Allen	P.G.St.B	1996	1992
Bentley, David Roger	P.A.G.Swd.B.	2010	
Bentley, Edward		—	2000
Bentley, Ronald Ernest Sydney	P.A.G.Swd.B.	2009	2006
Bentley, William George		—	2008
Beresiner, Yasha	P.A.G.D.C.	1999	2001
Berman, Philip Alan	P.A.G.D.C.	2005	2010
Berridge, Derick	P.A.G.D.C.	2004	
Berrier, Jacques Francis	P.A.G.D.C.	1986	
Berry, Brian Leslie	P.G.St.B.	2007	2010
	P.G.J.D.	2011	
Besanko, Robert John	P.G.St.B	1996	
	P.G.J.D.	2006	
Best, William John	G.Stwd.	1999	
	P.G.J.D.	2006	
Bethune, Ronald David	P.G.St.B.	1991	
Bettles, Clement Ernest		—	2000
Bevan, Brynley	P.A.G.D.C.	1993	1996
	Prov.G.M., Surrey	1996-2004	
Bevan, James Richard	P.A.G.D.C.	1995	2008
	P.G.J.D.	2004	
Beverley, Geoffrey	P.G.St.B.	2010	
Bex, Robin David George	P.G.St.B.	2009	
Bhamgara, Homi Framroze	P.A.G.D.C.	2004	2005
Bharati, Narasimha Gururaj	P.A.G.D.C.	1996	2002
	P.G.S.D.	2006	
Bhardwaj, Hari Krishan	P.A.G.D.C.	2010	
Bhasin, Ved Prakash	P.A.G.St.B.	2001	2004
	P.G.St.B.	2003	
Bibby, David Arnold	P.A.G.Swd.B.	1999	1999

NAME	RANK	YEAR OF APPT.	R.A.M.G.R. YEAR OF APPT.
Bibby, John Alan	G.Stwd.	2009	
	P.G.J.D.	2012	
Bibby, Stanley	P.G.St.B.	2012	
Bickerdike, Frank	P.A.G.St.B.	1988	1979
Bickerton, Andrew David	P.A.G.D.C.	2009	
Bicknell, John Charles	G.Stwd.	2012	
Biddle, Edward Roy	P.A.G.Swd.B.	2005	
Biddle, Robert Christopher	P.A.G.D.C.	2002	2004
Bidwell, William Arthur	P.G.St.B.	2004	
Biel, Roderick Hugh		—	2010
Bielby, Edgar	P.G.St.B.	1993	1999
Bielby, Eric, O.B.E.	P.A.G.St.B.	2007	
Bilding, Leslie Alfred	A.G.D.C.	1997	2000
	P.G.S.D.	2003	
	P.G.J.O.	2008	
Billinge, Barrie Stuart	P.G.St.B	1996	2006
Birch, Colin	P.A.G.St.B.	1998	2004
	P.A.G.D.C.	2012	
Birch, Dr. Geoffrey	P.A.G.D.C.	1978	1988
	P.G.J.O.	1989	
	G.S.O.	1995	
Birch, Geoffrey Harry	G.Stwd.	2001	2007
	P.G.J.D.	2008	
Birch, George Henry Philip	G.Stwd.	1989	1990
	Prov.G.M., West Yorkshire 1994-1999		
Birch, Maurice Askew	P.G.Std.B.	2011	
Bird, Derek Francis	P.A.G.D.C.	1998	
	A.G.Org.	2001	
	P.G.J.D.	2004	
Bird, Geoffrey		—	2009
Bird, Geoffrey Paulin	P.A.G.Swd.B.	2004	
	P.G.J.D.	2010	
Bird, Mark Anthony	P.A.G.Swd.B.	2001	1996
	P.G.J.D.	2008	
Bird, Richard Eynon	P.G.St.B.	1997	
Birdseye, Terence William, J.P.	P.G.St.B.	2006	2005
Bishop, Adrian Thomas Anthony	P.G.St.B.	2007	
Bishop, Roger William	P.A.G.D.C.	2011	
Bishop, Ronald John	P.G.St.B	1996	2011
	P.G.J.D.	2009	
Bissenden, Ernest Charles		—	2008
Bissett, David Roy	P.A.G.St.B.	2008	
Black, Alan Arthur	G.Stwd.	2008	
	P.G.J.D.	2011	
Black, Alan Morrison	P.A.G.D.C.	1984	
	P.G.S.D.	1990	
Black, Douglas Dennis	P.A.G.D.C.	2007	2007
	P.G.S.D.	2012	
Black, MC	P.A.G.D.C.	2007	2006
	P.G.S.D.	2012	
Blackburn, David John	P.A.G.D.C.	2005	2007
	P.G.J.D.	2010	

NAME	RANK	YEAR OF APPT.	R.A.M.G.R. YEAR OF APPT.
Blackburn, Donald	P.A.G.Swd.B.	2001	
	P.G.J.D.	2012	
Blackburn, Kenneth James	P.A.G.D.C.	1991	
	P.G.S.D.	2004	
	P.G.J.O.	2012	
Blackburn, Thomas	P.G.St.B.	1994	2002
	G.Swd.B.	2000	
Blackman, John Christopher	P.G.St.B.	2004	
Blackwood, Michael John	P.A.G.D.C.	2008	2006
Blaiberg, Malcolm	P.G.St.B.	2003	2001
Blair, Lt.Cdr. David Kirkaldy, *R.N.*		—	1985
Blake, Clive William Anthony	P.A.G.St.B.	2012	2011
Blake, David Anthony	P.A.G.D.C.	2004	2005
Blake, James Samuel		—	2008
Blake, Robert Alan	P.A.G.D.C.	2012	
Blake, Roger William	P.A.G.D.C.	2003	2009
	P.G.S.D.	2010	
Blake, Sidney George	P.G.St.B.	2003	
Blakemore, Paul Edward	P.A.G.D.C.	2007	
Blakeney, John Sarginson		—	1994
Blanchard, Brian, *B.Sc.*	P.A.G.St.B.	1996	1994
	P.G.J.D.	2004	
Blanchard, Stephen Eric	P.G.St.B.	2010	
Bland, Henry Horsfall	P.A.G.D.C.	2010	2007
Blankson, Dr. Jo, *Ph.D.*	P.G.St.B.	1999	2001
	P.G.J.D.	2004	
	P.G.J.O.	2010	
Bleackley, David	G.Stwd.	2004	
Bleackley, James Geoffrey	P.G.St.B.	2006	2007
Bleasdale, Keith David	P.A.G.D.C.	1988	
	P.G.S.D.	1999	
	P.G.J.O.	2006	
Blenkinship, David Anthony	A.G.I.G.	2010	
Blevin, John Richmond	P.G.St.B.	2010	
Blewett, Stanley John		—	2001
Blinkhorn, Michael Laxton	P.G.S.D.	2005	
Blinkhorn, Norman	P.G.St.B.	1964	
	P.G.S.D.	1970	
	P.G.J.O.	1980	
Bliss, Norman George	P.A.G.D.C.	2007	
Bloch, Peter John	P.A.G.D.C.	1982	1995
	P.G.S.D.	1990	
	P.G.J.O.	1996	
Blood, Nigel Leonard	P.A.G.Swd.B.	2007	2003
Blount, Donald	P.A.G.D.C.	1998	1992
Bluett, John Victor	P.A.G.D.C.	2009	2001
Blukoo-Allotey, Jacob Amekor Quarshie		—	2010
Blumsom, Derek Roy	P.A.G.St.B.	1999	1997
	P.G.J.D.	2009	
Blyth, Ronald Charles	P.G.St.B	1996	2001
	P.G.J.D.	2005	
Blythe, Michael John		—	2010

NAME	RANK	YEAR OF APPT.	R.A.M.G.R. YEAR OF APPT.
Boak, Christopher David	P.A.G.Swd.B.	2005	2011
	P.G.J.D.	2012	
Board, John Charles	P.A.G.D.C.	2000	2001
	G.S.D.	2008	
	P.G.J.O.	2012	
Boase, Michael James	P.A.G.D.C.	2005	
Bobsin, Alan William	P.G.St.B.	2006	2006
Bodman-Morris, Peter	P.A.G.D.C.	1995	1994
	Dist.G.M., Brazil	1998	
Body, Anthony Shane Trenavin	P.A.G.D.C.	2006	
	G.J.D.	2012	
Boggia, William George	G.St.B.	1995	2000
	P.G.J.D.	2005	
Bollard, Geoffrey Frank	P.A.G.D.C	1996	1997
	P.G.S.D.	2001	
	P.G.S.O.	2005	
Bolton, Christopher John	G.Stwd.	2006	
	P.G.J.D.	2011	
Bolton, Edward George	P.G.St.B.	2007	
Bolton, Hugh Johnston	G.Stwd.	1995	
Bolton, Harold	P.A.G.D.C.	1975	
	P.G.S.D.	1987	
Bolton, John Trevor	G.Stwd.	2011	
Bond, Colin	P.A.G.D.C.	1993	
	P.G.S.D.	1998	
	P.G.J.O.	2005	
Bond, Kenneth William	P.A.G.D.C.	2001	
Bond, Thomas George	P.A.G.D.C.	2007	
Bondy, David Nicholas, *L.L.B.*	P.A.G.Swd.B.	2006	
Bones, John Graham	P.A.G.D.C.	2009	2012
Bonham, George Edward	G.Stwd.	1994	1995
	P.G.S.D.	2005	
	Prov.G.M., Northamptonshire & Huntingdonshire	2006	
Boniface, Alan John	P.G.St.B.	2008	2006
Bonney, Christopher Frank	P.G.St.B.	2000	2004
	P.G.S.D.	2006	
	P.G.J.O.	2011	
Bonomy, Douglas Millegan	P.A.G.D.C.	2010	
Bonomy, John, *O.B.E., J.P.*	G.Stwd.	1986	1995
	G.J.D.	1991	
	G.M.O.	1999	
	P.G.J.W.	2005	
Bonsu, Osei Asamoa		—	2003
Bontoft, Derek Sidney	P.A.G.D.C.	2002	2011
	G.S.D.	2010	
Boocock, John Roderick	P.G.St.B.	2011	
Booij, Sybe Tunnis	P.G.St.B.	2001	2005
	P.G.J.D.	2004	
	Dist.G.M., The Netherlands	2007	
Booker, Roger Leonard	P.A.G.Swd.B.	2006	
Boore, David Charles	A.G.D.C.	2000	2000
Boorman, Christopher Arthur	P.A.G.Swd.B.	2008	2011

NAME	RANK	YEAR OF APPT.	R.A.M.G.R. YEAR OF APPT.
Booth, Eric Whittle	P.A.G.St.B.	1988	
Booth, James Edward	A.G.D.C.	2001	2004
Booth, Leonard William	P.A.G.St.B.	1990	
	P.A.G.D.C.	2002	
Boots, John Anthony Hart, F.R.C.S., F.R.C.O.G.	P.A.G.D.C.	1988	
Boots, Robert William	P.A.G.D.C.	1998	2002
	P.G.S.D.	2008	
Bosemans, Pierre Leon		—	2005
Bosquet, Jean-Claude Frederic Marie	P.A.G.D.C.	2010	
Boston, David Robert	P.G.St.B.	1986	1998
	P.G.J.D.	1991	
	P.G.J.O.	1997	
Bosworth, David Gordon Donald	G.Stwd.	1998	
	P.G.J.D.	2003	
Botell, Eric Francis	P.A.G.D.C.	1978	
	P.G.J.D.	1993	
Botham, Ian	P.G.St.B.	1986	2008
	P.A.G.D.C.	2006	
Bott, Roderick Charles	P.A.G.D.C.	2006	2011
Boughen, Dennis	P.A.G.D.C.	1998	2006
Boughton, Gregory Gordon	P.A.G.D.C.	2009	2005
Boughton, James	G.Stwd.	2009	2008
	P.G.J.D.	2012	
Boughton, Peter Alan	P.A.G.D.C.	2011	
Bougourd, Douglas Roy	P.A.G.Swd.B.	2004	1998
	P.G.J.D.	2010	
Boulton, Ivor John		—	2005
Bourne, Gordon Lionel	P.A.G.D.C.	1974	1976
	G.S.D.	1983	
	P.G.S.O.	1989	
	G.S.W.	1997	1997/98 GMRAC
Bourne, Laurence Eric, J.P.	G.I.G.	2008	
	P.G.S.D.	2010	
	P.G.J.O.	2012	
Bowater, Frank Thorneycroft		—	2008
Bowden, David	P.A.G.D.C.	2012	
Bowen, Dilwyn		—	2008
Bower, David Hemmingway	A.G.D.C.	2007	2006
Bowler, Bruce Ernest William	P.A.G.St.B.	2011	
Bowler, Terrance Albert Dennis	P.A.G.D.C.	1999	1983
	P.G.S.D.	2007	
Bowles, Christopher James, J.P.	P.A.G.D.C.	2006	2007
	G.S.D.	2012	
Bowles, Ralph Perry	P.G.St.B.	1984	
Bowman, John Hartley	P.A.G.Swd.B.	2006	
Bowyer, Richard	G.Stwd.	2009	2007
	P.G.J.D.	2012	
Boyd, Alister	P.A.G.D.C.	1998	1996
Boyd, Edward Rex	P.G.St.B.	2001	2000
	P.G.J.D.	2008	
Bracewell, Dr. Graham Acton	P.A.G.D.C.	1986	1989
	P.G.S.D.	1992	
	P.G.S.O.	2009	

NAME	RANK	YEAR OF APPT.	R.A.M.G.R. YEAR OF APPT.
Brackley, John	A.G.D.C.	1992	1997
	Dep.G.Swd.B.	1998	2005 GMRAC
	A.G.Sec.	2000-2005	
	P.G.S.O.	2002	
	G.Sec.	2005-2012	
	P.G.J.W.	2006	
Brackstone, Stuart Leonard	P.A.G.D.C.	2004	2011
	G.S.D.	2010	
Bradburn, Daniel	P.A.G.D.C.	2007	2005
Bradbury, James Ernest Skidmore	P.G.St.B.	1994	
Braden, Robert Alan	P.A.G.D.C.	1978	1988
	P.G.S.D.	2005	
Brader, Colin Edmund	P.A.G.D.C.	2003	2007
	P.G.S.D.	2011	
Bradley, Allan		—	2001
Bradley, Dennis, *B.E.M.*	G.Stwd.	2012	
Bradley, Roy	P.G.St.B.	2005	
Bradley, Roy Keith	P.G.St.B.	1992	1990
	P.G.S.D.	1995	
	P.G.J.O.	2000	
	Prov.G.M., Northamptonshire & Huntingdonshire	1996 2000	
Bradshaw, Graham Roland	P.A.G.D.C.	2009	
Bragg, William Francis	P.A.G.Swd.B.	2010	
Braham, Michael Edward	P.A.G.D.C.	2010	
Braithwaite, James Nathaniel	P.A.G.St.B.	2004	
Braithwaite, Norman		—	2009
Brailsford, Anthony Bernard	P.A.G.Swd.B.	2008	
Bramford, Edward Walter	P.A.G.D.C.	1989	1994
	G.S.D.	1997	
	Dep.G.D.C.	1998-2000	
	P.G.J.O.	2003	
	P.G.M.O.	2008	
Bramley, Ian	P.A.G.D.C.	2004	
Bramley-Haworth, Nigel Graham	G.Stwd.	2003	2005
	P.G.J.D.	2008	
Branch, Edward Charles	P.G.St.B.	1993	1998
Brannick, Harold	P.A.G.D.C.	1995	1998
	P.G.S.D.	2004	
	P.G.J.O.	2010	
Brar, Tejpal Singh	P.A.G.St.B.	2001	
Brass, Andrew Schoborgh	P.A.G.D.C.	1987	1994
	Dist.G.M., East Africa	1994-2001	
Brassett, Peter George	G.Stwd.	2009	2011
	P.G.J.D.	2012	
Braun, Eric David William		—	2011
Brautigam, James Andrew	P.A.G.Swd.B.	2006	2007
	P.A.G.D.C.	2010	
Bray, John Hamilton		—	1996
Brayford, John Henry	P.A.G.D.C.	1999	
	P.G.S.D.	2006	
	P.G.J.O.	2012	
Brayshaw, Jack	P.A.G.D.C.	1997	2002
Breeze, Alan William Edgar		—	2006

NAME	RANK	YEAR OF APPT.	R.A.M.G.R. YEAR OF APPT.
Breeze, John E., *M.B.E.*	P.A.G.St.B.	1999	
	P.G.J.D.	2007	
Bretherton, Donald	P.A.G.Swd.B.	2005	
Brett-Harris, Gordon Albert Edward	P.A.G.D.C.	1991	1991
	G.S.D.	1996	
	P.G.J.O.	2003	
Brewer, Peter Nigel		—	2008
Brewster, Dr. David Joseph	P.A.G.St.B.	2002	2002
Brewster, Fozlo		—	2007
Brice, William Geoffrey Horace	P.A.G.St.B.	2007	
	P.G.J.D.	2011	
Bricknell, Roger Charles	P.G.St.B.	2005	
Bridger, Ronald James	G.Stwd.	1997	1998
	P.G.J.D.	2004	
Bridges, Andrew Peter Detley	P.G.St.B.	2008	2006
Bridgett, Keith Arthur, *M.A., Ph.D.*	P.G.St.B.	1992	
	P.G.J.D.	2003	
Briggs, Anthony David	G.Stwd.	1996	2009
	G.J.D.	2001	
Briggs, Geoffrey	P.G.St.B.	1995	
Briggs, Thomas Edgar	P.G.J.D.	2003	2005
Brill, Peter James	A.G.St.B.	2009	1997
Brindley, Peter	P.A.G.D.C.	1992	
	P.G.S.D.	1997	
	P.G.J.O.	2006	
Brine, Albert Edward		—	1996
Briney, Martin	A.G.St.B.	2007	
Briney, Stephen Charles	P.A.G.St.B.	2007	2008
Brinkworth, Peter Geoffrey	P.G.St.B.	2008	
Brinton, Roy Vivian	P.A.G.D.C.	1986	1999
	P.G.S.D.	1999	
Bristow, George William	P.A.G.Swd.B.	2005	
Brittan, Reginald Leslie	G.Stwd.	2010	
Broadbent, Eric	P.A.G.D.C.	2001	
Broadhead, David Geoffrey	P.G.St.B.	2012	
Brock, Robert John	P.G.St.B.	2006	2008
Brockie, James Skirving	G.Stwd.	1997	1999
	P.G.S.D.	2007	
Brodrick, Trevor Malcolm Garvin	A.G.D.C.	1997	1997
Brodsky, Michael Leopold Oscar	P.A.G.D.C.	1986	1988
Broeckaert, Dr. Theodore Henri, *I.V.O.*	P.G.I.G.	1999	2002
	P.G.J.D.	2005	
Brooke, John Stuart	P.A.G.St.B.	1999	
	P.G.J.D.	2011	
Brooker, Kenneth William		—	2004
Brookes, Alan William	P.A.G.D.C.	2012	
Brookes, Eric Clive	P.G.St.B.	2000	
Brookes, Howard William	P.A.G.Swd.B.	2007	2005
Brookes, Ian Michael	G.Stwd.	2007	2007
	P.G.J.D.	2011	
Brookes, Laurence Thomas	P.A.G.D.C.	2004	
Brookes, Peter John			2003

NAME	RANK	YEAR OF APPT.	R.A.M.G.R. YEAR OF APPT.
Brooker, Douglas Edward	P.A.G.D.C.	1996	2001
	P.G.S.D.	2002	
Brooker, Kenneth William	P.G.St.B.	2003	2004
Brooks, Albert William Charles	P.A.G.D.C.	1982	1984
Brooks, Eustace Alexander, *M.B.E.*		—	1988
Brooks, Stephen Anthony		—	2008
Brough, Derek	P.G.St.B.	2005	2008
	P.G.J.D.	2011	
Broughton, John Stanley, *J.P.*	P.A.G.D.C.	2006	
	P.G.S.D.	2011	
Brown, Alan		—	2010
Brown, Albert	A.G.St.B.	1988	
Brown, Alexander	P.G.St.B.	2000	2000
Brown, Alfred Martin Jefferson	P.A.G.D.C.	2002	2005
	P.G.S.D.	2007	
	Prov.G.M., Wiltshire	2010	
Brown, Prof. Alfred Norgaard	P.G.St.B.	1994	1995
	P.G.J.D.	1998	
Brown, Rev. Arthur William Stawell	G.Chap.	1973	1974
Brown, Byron John	P.A.G.D.C.	2006	2007
Brown, Christopher Nigel Rupert	G.Swd.B.	2010	2010
Brown, Colin Peter Thomas	P.G.S.D.	2012	
Brown, David	P.G.St.B.	2010	
Brown, David Christopher Herbert	P.A.G.D.C.	1990	1996
	P.G.S.D.	1995	
	P.G.J.O.	2004	
Brown, David James	A.G.I.G.	2005	2007
	P.A.G.D.C.	2011	
Brown, David John	G.Stwd.	1998	1999
	P.G.J.D.	2000	
	P.G.J.O.	2005	
Brown, David Nicholson, *J.P.*	P.A.G.D.C.	2003	
Brown, Edward	G.Stwd.	1994	
Brown, Francis Edward	P.A.G.D.C.	1999	
Brown, Frederick	G.Stwd.	2009	
	P.G.J.D.	2012	
Brown, James George Byfield	G.Stwd.	2001	
Brown, John		—	2004
Brown, Joseph Spencer *Q.P.M*	P.A.G.St.B	1996	
	P.A.G.Swd.B.	2006	
Brown, Kenneth Henry	P.A.G.St.B.	2005	2001
Brown, Max Nicholas	P.G.J.D.	2009	2010
	P.G.S.D.	2012	
	Dist.G.M., South Africa (Western Division)	2012	
Brown, Peter Arthur	P.A.G.D.C.	2012	
Brown, Peter James Hartley	P.A.G.D.C.	2011	
Brown, Robert		—	1993
Brown, Robert Redvers	P.A.G.St.B.	2004	
Brown, Samuel John		—	2010
Brown, Victor Arthur Thorp, *J.P.*	G.Swd.	1996	1998
	P.G.S.D.	2007	
Brown, William Albert	P.A.G.D.C.	2001	2003

NAME	RANK	YEAR OF APPT.	R.A.M.G.R. YEAR OF APPT.
Brown, William Percival Ives	P.A.G.D.C.	1986	1986
	P.G.S.D.	1992	
	P.G.J.O.	2001	
Browne, William Joseph	P.A.G.St.B.	2003	
Brownfield, John William	P.A.G.St.B.	2004	
	P.G.J.D.	2009	
Bruce, Maj. Ian Donald, T.D., D.L.	G.Swd.B.	1994	1995
Brundle, Douglas Philip	G.I.G.	1990	1993
Brunning, Alan Frederick	A.G.D.C.	1991	1990
	P.G.S.D.	1995	
	P.G.J.O.	2000	
	Prov.G.M., Berkshire	2002-2007	
Bruty, Terence Sutherland	P.A.G.Swd.B.	2006	2003
Bryan, Colin	P.A.G.D.C.	1999	1994
	P.G.J.D.	2010	
Bryant, Craig	P.A.G.D.C.	2009	
Bryant, John Robert	P.A.G.D.C.	2011	2010
Bryant, Kevin Jeffrey	P.A.G.D.C.	2011	
Bryant, Kenneth John	P.A.G.D.C.	2005	
Bryen, William James	P.G.S.D.	2005	2007
Buchanan, George William Lewis	P.G.St.B.	2008	2004
Buchanan, John Keith	P.A.G.D.C.	1993	
	P.G.S.D.	2005	
Buchsbaum, Thomas Maria	P.A.G.D.C.	2012	
Buck, Allan James	P.G.St.B.	1990	1992
Buckley, Anthony	P.A.G.St.B.	1992	
Buckley, Harry Brian	P.A.G.D.C.	1997	2005
	P.G.S.D.	2004	
Buckley, Michael Norman	P.A.G.St.B.	1992	1995
	P.G.J.D.	2000	
Budds, Martin Bradford	P.A.G.D.C.	2011	2010
	A.G.Sec.	2012	
Budge, Capt. Peter Reginald	G.Stwd.	1999	2002
	G.Swd.B.	2004	
	P.G.J.O.	2010	
Buffoni, John Peter	P.G.J.D.	1997	2001
	P.G.J.O.	2005	
Bugler, Reginald Arthur Laurie	P.A.G.D.C.	2012	
Bull, Clifford Howard		—	2011
Bull, John Leonard	P.G.St.B.	2001	
Bull, Kenneth William	G.Stwd.	1984	2001
	P.G.J.D.	1989	
	P.G.J.O.	1994	
Bull, Michael Frank	P.A.G.D.C.	2003	2002
	P.G.J.D.	2012	
Bull, Peter Phelps	P.A.G.D.C.	1984	1989
Bullen, James Edward	G.Stwd.	1973	
	P.G.J.D.	1978	
	G.M.O.	1987	
Bullock, Colin Frederick	P.A.G.St.B.	2007	
Bullock, Peter Leonard	P.G.St.B.	2003	2006
	P.G.J.D.	2009	
Bullows, Paul	G.Stwd.	2006	
	P.G.J.D.	2009	

NAME	RANK	YEAR OF APPT.	R.A.M.G.R. YEAR OF APPT.
Bulmer, Joseph, *J.P.*	P.A.G.D.C.	2003	
	P.G.S.D.	2008	
Bundell, Peter Edwin	P.G.St.B.	2011	
Bunn, Edward Robertson	P.A.G.D.C.	1995	1996
	P.G.S.D.	1996	
	P.G.J.O.	2001	
Bunn, John Roger Gordon	G.Stwd.	2001	2002
	P.G.J.D.	2008	
Bunt, Lewis George	P.G.St.B.	1994	1992
	P.G.J.D.	2001	
	P.G.J.O.	2007	
Burdekin, Peter	G.Stwd.	2000	2001
	P.G.J.D.	2003	
	P.G.J.O.	2008	
Burden, David Edward	P.A.G.D.C.	1971	1975
	P.G.S.D.	1989	
Burden, Gerald William	P.A.G.St.B.	1992	
Burden, John	P.G.St.B.	1994	
	P.G.J.D.	2012	
Burger, John Alfred		—	2009
Burgess, Alfred Arthur	P.G.St.B.	1976	
Burgess, Bernard Charles	P.A.G.D.C.	1982	
	P.G.S.D.	2008	
Burgess, David John	P.G.St.B.	2009	
Burgess, James			2003
Burgess, Revd. John Mulholland	Dep.G.Chap.	2003	
Burgheim, Julius-Axel	P.G.St.B.	2011	2007
Burgon, Alexander	P.A.G.St.B.	1989	2002
Burke, Anthony	G.Stwd.	2009	
	P.G.J.D.	2012	
Burke, James Maurice	P.A.G.D.C.	2011	
Burkett, Malcolm	P.A.G.Swd.B.	2011	
Burkill, Arthur Herbert	P.G.St.B.	1973	
Burley, Edgar Llewelyn	P.A.G.D.C.	1988	
Burman, Michael Charles	P.A.G.D.C.	2008	
Burman, Richard Alexander Wallace	P.A.G.D.C.	1982	
	P.G.S.D.	1994	
Burman, Thomas Richard		—	2008
Burmeister, Ronald Alexander	P.A.G.D.C.	1996	
	P.G.J.O.	2006	
Burn, Arthur Alan	P.G.St.B.	2008	2008
Burnell, Brian William		—	2008
Burnett, David Philip	P.A.G.D.C.	2010	2009
Burnikell, Bryan Mortimer	P.G.St.B.	1995	
Burnip, Leslie	P.A.G.D.C.	1985	1999
	P.G.S.D.	1992	
	P.G.J.O.	1997	
Burnip, Robert	G.Stwd.	1996	2008
	G.S.D.	2002	
Burniston, Paul	P.A.G.Swd.B.	2012	
Burns, Kenneth David		—	2008
Burns, Malcolm James		—	2010

NAME	RANK	YEAR OF APPT.	R.A.M.G.R. YEAR OF APPT.
Burns, Wilfred	P.G.St.B.	1997	2006
	P.G.J.D.	2006	
Burrows, David William	P.A.G.D.C.	2011	
Burrows, Peter Harry	P.A.G.Swd.B.	2005	
Burt, Eric Francis	—		1996
Burton, John	P.A.G.D.C.	1994	1985
Burton, Kenneth Howard	P.G.St.B.	1993	
Burton, Michael Edwin	—		2007
Burton, Trevor Charles	—		2011
Bury, Geoffrey Michael	G.Stwd.	2010	
Bussell, John Herbert	P.A.G.D.C.	2006	2007
Buswell, Derek Alfred	P.G.S.D.	2000	2000
	P.G.J.O.	2010	
Butcher, Stanley John	P.A.G.D.C.	2012	
Butcher, Stewart Leslie	G.Stwd.	2011	
Butler, Geoffrey	P.A.G.Swd.B.	2008	2011
Butler, George	P.A.G.D.C.	2008	
Butler, Paul	P.A.G.D.C.	2003	2003
	P.G.S.D.	2008	
Butters, Anthony Charles	P.A.G.D.C.	1991	2009
	P.G.S.D.	1998	
	P.G.J.O.	2007	
Butterworth, Geoffrey	P.A.G.D.C.	1993	1991
Butterworth, Richard John Lanyon	P.A.G.Swd.B.	1998	2000
	P.G.J.D.	2006	
Buxton, Allan Albert	P.A.G.St.B.	2006	
Bye, Phillip Leslie	G.Stwd.	2005	2011
	P.G.J.D.	2008	
Byrne, Ralph	P.A.G.D.C.	2006	
Cain, Col. Rex Martin, O.B.E., D.L.	A.G.Swd.B.	1983	1995
	G.Swd.B.	1986	
Caine, Christopher James	P.A.G.D.C.	2006	2006
Cairns, Stuart	P.A.G.D.C.	2012	
Calcott-James, Revd. Colin Wilfrid	A.G.Chap.	2007-2008	
Calcutt, Brian Anthony	P.A.G.D.C.	2006	2006
Calderley, Denis	P.A.G.D.C.	1985	1993
	P.G.S.D.	1997	
	P.G.J.O.	2005	
Calderwood, Paul Richard	P.G.St.B.	2009	2011
Caldwell, Alexander Muirhead	—		2005
Caldwell, Clarence	P.G.I.G.	2003	1997
Caldwell, James	P.G.St.B.	1996	
Callaghan, Rev. Canon Harry	Dep.G.Chap.	1987-1988	1990
	G.Chap.	1989-1994	
	P.G.S.O.	2000	
Calvert, Alan Buchart	P.G.St.B.	1991	1993
	G.J.D.	1994	
	P.G.J.O.	1999	
Cameron, David William	P.A.G.D.C.	2006	2009
Cameron, Gordon	P.G.St.B.	2004	
Cameron, Ronald	P.A.G.D.C.	2010	

NAME	RANK	YEAR OF APPT.	R.A.M.G.R. YEAR OF APPT.
Camp, Dennis John	P.A.G.D.C.	1986	1981
Campbell, Hartley Tyrrell	A.G.D.C.	1979	1999
Campbell, Iain Peter	P.A.G.D.C.	1999	2002
Campbell, Wallace Ransford	P.A.G.St.B.	2007	2011
	P.G.J.D.	2012	
Camplin, Patrick Alexander	P.G.St.B.	2002	2007
	P.G.J.D.	2009	
Cann, Grahame Lawrence	P.G.St.B.	2007	
Cannon, Revd. Peter Cecil John	P.A.G.Chap.	2000	2008
	P.G.S.O.	2008	
Cantello, William Rowland	P.G.St.B.	1995	
	P.G.J.D.	2005	
Cantrell, Colin	P.A.G.D.C.	2001	2005
	G.Swd.B.	2006	
	P.G.J.O.	2009	
Capes, Frederick Bryan	P.G.St.B.	2001	2004
Caplan, Geoffrey Neil	P.G.St.B.	1998	
Cappin, John Michael	P.A.G.Swd.B.	2010	
Capstick, Herbert Gordon	P.A.G.D.C.	1987	1991
	P.G.S.D.	1994	
	P.G.J.O.	2011	
Carden, Alan	P.G.St.B.	2012	
Cardus, Roy	G.Stwd.	1988	
	P.G.J.D.	2001	
Cardy, Kevin Arthur	—		1989
Caren, William Edward	P.A.G.St.B.	2010	2011
Carey, David Stuart	P.G.St.B.	2008	
Carey, Harold William	P.G.St.B.	1985	
	P.G.J.D.	1994	
Carey, Peter Charles	A.G.St.B.	1999	
Carew-Hunt, Robert Anthony	—		2009
Carley, Stewart Glasgow	G.St.B.	2009	
Carmichael, Keith Stanley, C.B.E.	G.Treasurer	1977-1990	1977
	P.G.J.W.	1984	1977 GMRAC (H.C.)
	P.G.S.W.	1990	
	Pres.Gen.Bd.	1991-2006	
	O.S.M.M.M.	2008	
Carney, Anthony	G.Stwd.	2008	2011
	P.G.J.D.	2011	
Carpenter, David Alan Patrick	—		2011
Carpenter, William Leonard George	P.A.G.St.B.	2009	
Carr, James Michael Butterfield	P.A.G.D.C.	1990	1998
	P.G.S.D.	1997	
Carr, John Bagshaw	P.A.G.D.C.	2008	
Carr, Robert Stratton	P.G.St.B.	2005	2008
Carretero Domenech, Jose	P.G.M.O.	2007	
Carrick, Joseph Leslie	P.G.St.B.	2002	2001
Carroll, Peter Edward	P.A.G.D.C.	2000	
Carroll, Victor	P.A.G.D.C.	2010	2008
Carson, Anthony Edward	P.A.G.St.B.	2011	
Carter, Brian George	G.Stwd.	1999	2006
	P.G.J.D.	2004	

NAME	RANK	YEAR OF APPT.	R.A.M.G.R. YEAR OF APPT.
Carter, Christopher Ernest	A.G.D.C.	1981	1993
	P.G.S.D.	1991	
	P.G.J.O.	2002	
Carter, James Colin	P.A.G.D.C.	2009	
Cartoon, Claude Gerald	P.A.G.D.C.	1985	
	P.G.S.D.	1995	
Cashin, Timothy Paul	P.A.G.D.C.	1999	2004
	P.G.S.D.	2004	
	P.G.J.O.	2009	
Casserly, Alvaro Alonso, *J.P.*	P.A.G.St.B.	1995	1999
	P.A.G.D.C.	2002	
	P.G.S.D.	2010	
Castello, Claud Augustus	P.G.J.D.	1997	
Castle, John Arthur	P.A.G.D.C.	2002	1999
Castle, Peter John Stanfield	P.G.St.B.	2012	
Castle, Roy	P.A.G.D.C.	2006	
Caswell, John Richard	G.Stwd.	2009	2011
Catford, Gordon Vivian	G.Stwd.	1990	1993
	G.S.D.	1995	
	P.G.S.O.	1999	
Cattanach, George Martin		—	2006
Catterall, Geoffrey		—	2011
Caughie, William Agnew	G.Stwd.	2009	2007
	P.G.J.D.	2012	
Caulfield, Edward Charles	P.A.G.D.C.	2005	
Caunter, Martin Bryan	P.A.G.D.C.	2002	
	P.G.S.D.	2012	
Cawston, Roger Edward Sydney	P.G.St.B.	2012	
Chaddock, John Brian	P.G.St.B.	2009	
Chadwick, William Robert Smith	P.A.G.St.B.	1991	
	P.G.J.D.	1996	
Chalfen, Gerald		—	1994
Chalk, Andrew Ralph	P.G.St.B.	1999	2005
Chalkley, Anthony Charles	P.A.G.St.B.	2010	2006
Chalkley, Kenneth Barrington, *M.B.E.*	P.A.G.Swd.B.	2004	
	P.A.G.D.C.	2012	
Chalmers, William Andrew	P.G.St.B.	1999	2001
	G.J.D.	2004	
Chamberlain, Keith	P.G.St.B.	2011	
Chambers, George Edgar	G.Stwd.	1985	1992
	P.G.J.D.	1990	
Chambers, Lt.Col. John Craven	P.G.S.D.	1994	1998
	Dep.G.D.C.	1996-98	
	P.G.J.O.	2001	
	P.G.M.O.	2006	
Champ, Eric Frank Richard	P.A.G.Swd.B.	2005	
Champion, Ivan	P.A.G.D.C.	1995	1992
	P.G.S.D.	2002	
Champion, Cdr. Ronald Albert, *R.N.*	G.S.O.	1996	1999
	G.S.W.	2003	
Chande, Jayantilal Keshauji	P.A.G.D.C.	1980	1990
	P.G.J.O.	1987	
	G.J.W.	1990	
	G.S.W.	2001	

NAME	RANK	YEAR OF APPT.	R.A.M.G.R. YEAR OF APPT.
Chandler, Michael John	P.A.G.D.C.	2008	
Chandramohan, Karunakaran	—		2011
Channing, John Stanley	P.G.St.B.	1992	2010
Chantler, John Roland	P.A.G.D.C.	2006	2007
Chapman, Anthony Ernest Walter	P.A.G.D.C.	1996	2007
	P.G.S.D.	2006	
Chapman, Ivan Herbert Charles	P.A.G.D.C.	2011	2000
Chapman, Michael James	P.A.G.D.C.	2000	2001
	P.G.J.D.	2006	
Chapman, Peter John Lorraine	P.G.S.D.	2008	
Chapman, Philip Frank	—		2010
Chappel, Don	P.G.St.B.	2011	
Chappell, Keith John	P.G.St.B.	2005	2002
	P.G.J.D.	2010	
Chappell, Kenneth Roy	P.A.G.D.C.	2001	
Chappell, Robert Charles	—		2011
Charles, Dr. Robert Henry George, T.D.	P.G.St.B.	2003	
Charlton, Ralph Ian	P.G.St.B.	2010	2011
Charnock, James Sutton	G.Stwd.	1982	1992
	P.G.J.D.	1990	
	P.G.J.O.	1996	
Chaterji, Subroto	Dist.G.M., Bengal.	2009-2012	
Chawner, Kevin	G.S.D.	1991	2000
	P.G.J.O.	2003	
Cheek, Jopseph Gorrell	P.A.G.Swd.B.	2012	
Cheesman, Frederick Kenneth John	—		1982
Cheesman, Peter	P.A.G.D.C.	2010	
Chellappa, Madhavan	P.A.G.D.C.	2001	2003
	P.G.S.D.	2009	
	Dist.G.M., Madras	2011	
Chenery, David Thomas	P.A.G.D.C.	2004	2010
	P.G.J.D.	2009	
Cherry, Robert Denis	P.A.G.D.C.	1990	
Cheveralls, Thomas Albert	A.G.D.C.	1990	1985
Chevin, Sqn.Ldr. Robert William	G.Stwd.	2004	
	P.G.J.D.	2008	
Chhabra, Tirlok Singh	P.A.G.D.C.	2004	
Chick, Alan Brian	P.A.G.D.C.	1999	2000
	P.G.S.D.	2008	
Chilcott, Gerald Desmond	G.Stwd.	2010	
Childs, Colin Henry	P.A.G.St.B.	1989	1995
	P.A.G.D.C.	2003	
	P.G.S.D.	2010	
Childs, James Peter	A.G.D.C.	2007	2011
Chiles, Samuel	P.G.St.B.	1987	
Chilvers, John William	P.A.G.D.C.	2006	
Chimthanawala, Salim Mukhtar Jafarbhai	P.G.St.B.	2011	
Chin, Dr. Chin Por	P.A.G.D.C.	2006	
Chinbuah, Kwasi Ebenezer	P.A.G.D.C.	1997	2002
	P.G.S.D.	2008	
Chinnaswamy, Kasianna Gounder	P.G.J.D.	2010	2008
Chilvers, John William	—		2004
Chockalingam, Rajagopal	P.A.G.D.C.	1994	1993

NAME	RANK	YEAR OF APPT.	R.A.M.G.R. YEAR OF APPT.
Christian, Peter Henry	P.A.G.D.C.	2000	
Chrystie, Robert, *Jnr.*	—		2007
Chuang, Quincy Kwei Lun	P.A.G.D.C.	1987	1996
	P.G.S.D.	2002	
	P.G.J.O.	2007	
	P.G.J.W.	2008	
Chudley, Peter	P.A.G.St.B.	2004	
Chun, Alan David, *M.B.E.*	P.A.G.D.C.	1978	
	P.G.S.D.	1990	
	G.J.W.	1995	1995/96 GMRAC
Chung, Glyn Carlyle	P.G.J.D.	2003	2003
	P.G.J.O.	2008	
Churchill, Barrie Godfrey Brynmor	P.G.St.B.	2011	
Cisotti, Astor Arine	P.A.G.D.C.	2005	
Clabon, Robin Brian	—		2007
Clancy, David Robert	P.G.J.D.	2007	2009
Clancy, Wilfred Leslie	P.A.G.D.C.	1987	
	P.G.J.O.	2009	
Clare, Philip Charles	—		2011
Clare, Raymond Joseph	P.A.G.D.C.	1995	1996
	P.G.S.D.	2001	
	P.G.J.O.	2009	
Clapham, Shane Aubrey Duff	P.A.G.Swd.B.	2012	
Clarembaux, Francis	P.A.G.D.C.	2002	
	P.G.S.D.	2008	
Clark, Barry Charles	G.Stwd.	1997	1999
	P.G.J.D.	2001	
	P.G.J.O.	2006	
Clark, Charles Douglas	P.A.G.Swd.B.	2010	
Clark, Donald Francis	G.Stwd.	1999	
	G.J.D.	2007	
Clark, George	P.A.G.Swd.B.	2008	
Clark, Ian	P.A.G.D.C.	1996	2002
	P.G.S.D.	2002	
	P.G.J.O.	2010	
Clark, Ian Nelson	P.A.G.D.C.	2010	2008
Clark, Keith Maitland	P.A.G.D.C.	2007	
Clark, Michael Trevithick	P.G.St.B.	2008	
Clark, Peter	—		2005
Clark, Robert Nicholas	P.G.St.B.	1995	2006
	P.G.J.D.	2003	
Clark, Roger Winchester	—		2010
Clarke, Alvah Alfred	P.A.G.Swd.B.	2006	2007
Clarke, Barry	P.A.G.D.C.	1984	1986
	G.S.D.	1990	
	P.G.J.O.	1996	
Clarke, Craig Malcolm	P.A.G.D.C.	1987	1981
	P.G.S.D.	1997	
Clarke, Francis William	P.A.G.D.C.	1999	
	P.G.J.D.	2006	
Clarke, Fred	P.A.G.Swd.B.	2011	
Clarke, Glenn Robert	P.A.G.D.C.	2004	2005
Clarke, John	P.A.G.D.C.	2008	
Clarke, John Anthony	A.G.I.G.	1991	1993

NAME	RANK	YEAR OF APPT.	R.A.M.G.R. YEAR OF APPT.
Clarke, John Duncan	P.A.G.D.C.	1997	2004
	P.G.S.D.	2003	
	P.G.J.O.	2012	
Clarke, John Frederick	P.A.G.D.C.	2005	2010
	G.S.D.	2011	
Clarke, Michael John	G.Stwd.	2000	2010
	P.G.J.D.	2005	
	P.G.J.O.	2010	
Clarke, Norman	P.G.St.B.	2010	
Clarke, Paul Anthony	P.G.St.B.	1995	
	P.G.J.D.	2010	
Clarke, Raymond Charles	G.Stwd.	2004	2007
	P.G.J.D.	2008	
	P.G.S.D.	2012	
Clarke, Robert Richard Guy	P.G.S.D.	2007	
Clarke, Roger John	P.A.G.D.C.	2000	1998
	P.G.S.D.	2005	
	P.G.J.O.	2010	
Clarke, Stephen Henry	P.A.G.D.C.	1990	
Clarke, Stanley William Jeffrey	P.A.G.D.C.	1991	1992
	P.G.S.D.	1996	
	P.G.J.O.	2001	
	P.G.M.O.	2005	
Clarke, Thomas Raymond	P.A.G.D.C.	1990	2004
	G.S.D.	1999	
Clarke, Trevor	P.A.G.D.C.	2012	2011
Clarke, William David	P.A.G.D.C.	2012	
Clavier, Anthony James	G.Stwd.	1992	
	P.G.J.D.	1999	
Clay, Brian	P.A.G.Swd.B.	2002	1994
Clay, Derrick	P.A.G.D.C.	2008	
Claydon, Lt.Col. Anthony Venn	G.Stwd.	1998	
	P.G.J.D.	2008	
Clayton, Alan Leo	P.A.G.D.C.	1998	
Clayton, Anthony Kenneth	P.G.St.B.	2012	2011
Clayton, Keith Wallace	P.A.G.D.C.	1983	1983
	P.G.S.D.	1988	
	P.G.J.O.	1997	
	P.G.M.O.	2005	
	P.G.J.W.	2012	
Clayton-Barker, Stephen	P.A.G.D.C.	2004	
Clee, Peter William	P.A.G.D.C.	2000	2001
	P.G.S.D.	2010	
Clemens, Leslie George	P.A.G.Swd.B.	2012	
Clemens, William Frederick	P.G.St.B.	1994	1995
	G.S.D.	2004	
	P.G.J.O.	2011	
Clement, Paul Raymond	A.G.Org.	1989-1999	1995
	P.G.S.D.	1996	
	G.Org.	2000-2007	
	P.G.J.O.	2001	
	Prov.G.M., South Wales	2008	
Clement, Trevor Lindsay	P.G.St.B.	2009	
Clements, Alan William		—	2010

NAME	RANK	YEAR OF APPT.	R.A.M.G.R. YEAR OF APPT.
Clements, John Raymond William	G.Stwd.	2001	2008
	P.G.J.D.	2006	
Clementson, Michael Kevin	G.Stwd.	2010	
Clench, Sidney Francis	P.A.G.D.C.	2008	
Cleven, Alexandre Gaspard Harry	P.A.G.D.C.	2001	2002
	P.G.S.D.	2003	
Clewes, John Tomlinson	P.A.G.D.C.	1972	1977
	G.S.D.	1978	
	G.S.O.	1981	
	P.G.M.O.	1987	
	Prov.G.M., Derbyshire	1989-1998	
Clifford, Carl Stephen	P.A.G.D.C.	1994	1991
	P.G.S.D.	2009	
Clifford, Leonard Arthur James	P.A.G.D.C.	2001	1994
Clingham, Edward David	P.G.S.D.	2006	2008
	Dist.G.M., Zimbabwe	2008-2011	
Clothier, Paul Maurice	P.G.St.B.	1996	
Clough, John Fred	P.A.G.D.C.	2007	2010
	P.G.J.D.	2009	
Clubley, Donald	P.G.St.B.	1997	
Clucas, Alan Harold Qualtrough	G.St.B.	2003	
Clyne, Brian Stewart	P.G.St.B.	2001	
Coad, Kenneth William Alfred	P.A.G.St.B.	2010	
Coates, Clifford		—	2007
Coates, Capt. Hugh Robertson	P.G.J.D.	2003	
Coates, William Arthur	P.G.St.B.	2004	
Cobb, David Bilsland, *C.B.E.*	P.A.G.St.B.	2005	2011
	P.G.J.D.	2011	
Cobham, Stephen Brian	P.G.J.D.	2007	2005
	Dist.G.M., South and East Caribbean	2012	
Coburn, Dennis Roland	A.G.D.C.	1993	2005
	P.G.J.D.	2002	
	P.G.J.O.	2007	
Cochrane, John Stuart	P.G.St.B.	2004	
Cockburn, Roy Lawrence	P.A.G.St.B.	2004	2005
Cockerill, Desmond Frank	P.G.St.B .	1996	
Cockton, Henry Stanley Ronald	P.G.St.B.	1990	
Cody, George Ernest	P.G.St.B.	2008	
Coggon, Peter Brown	P.A.G.Swd.B.	2008	
Cohen, Jack	G.Stwd.	1997	2001
	P.G.J.D.	2002	
	P.G.J.O.	2007	
Cohen, Jerrold George		—	1987
Cohen, Lt.Col. Mordaunt	P.A.G.D.C.	1985	
Cohen, Neil Broadfield	P.G.St.B.	2008	2010
Cohen, Stanley	P.A.G.Chap.	2008	
Coldicott, Raymond George	P.A.G.St.B.	1997	1998
Cole, Bernard Edward	P.A.G.St.B.	1991	
Cole, Cecil Arthur	P.A.G.St.B.	1996	
Cole, Maj. Edward William	G.Stwd.	1994	
Cole, James		—	2007
Cole, Maj. John William Burke	P.G.Swd.B.	1960	

NAME	RANK	YEAR OF APPT.	R.A.M.G.R. YEAR OF APPT.
Cole, Peter Desmond	P.G.S.D.	1997	2005
	P.G.J.O.	2006	
Cole, Peter Robert	G.Stwd.	2008	
	P.G.J.D.	2011	
Cole, Robert Michael	P.A.G.D.C.	1994	2008
	P.G.S.D.	2002	
Colebourne, Denis Gilbey, *T.D.*,	P.A.G.D.C.	1992	1995
	P.G.S.D.	2002	
Coleman, Ronald	P.A.G.St.B.	2004	
Coleman, Roy Charles	P.G.St.B.	2004	
Coles, Peter Thomas	G.Stwd.	2007	2006
	G.J.D.	2010	
Coles, Philip Charles	P.G.St.B.	2012	
Collakis, John	P.A.G.D.C.	2003	2006
	P.G.J.O.	2012	
Collcutt, Keith Edwin	P.A.G.D.C.	2001	1998
	P.G.S.D.	2011	
Collier, Colin Raymond	P.A.G.Swd.B.	2010	
Collin, Revd. Terry	A.G.Chap.	1994	2006
	P.Dep.G.Chap.	2000	
	P.G.Chap.	2008	
Collings, Frederick Charles John	P.G.St.B.	1998	
Collings, Mervyn Brian	P.A.G.St.B.	2012	2008
Collins, Donald	P.A.G.St.B.	2008	
Collins, Philip Major, *J.P.*	P.G.I.G.	2000	2003
	P.G.S.D.	2009	
Collins, Stephen Henry	P.G.St.B.	1988	1999
	P.G.J.D.	1996	
Collinson, Michael John	P.A.G.D.C.	2012	
Collison, John Raymond	A.G.D.C.	2005	2007
Collom, David George	P.A.G.D.C.	2007	
Collyer, Brian Albert	P.A.G.D.C.	2008	
Combes, David Keith	G.Stwd.	2009	2011
Compton, Roy Edwin	P.A.G.Swd.B.	1991	1996
	P.G.J.D.	1996	
	P.G.J.O.	2002	
Compton, Kenneth Vivian		—	1979
Conchie, William Henry	G.Stwd.	1988	1992
	P.G.S.D.	1993	
	Prov.G.M., Cumberland & Westmorland	1995-2003	
Conder, Joseph Herbert Ewart	P.G.St.B.	1994	1996
Condlyffe, Thomas Victor	P.A.G.St.B.	1989	1998
	G.J.D.	1997	
Conn, Michael Peter	P.A.G.D.C.	2010	
Conn, Philip Julian	G.Stwd.	2007	2011
	P.G.J.D.	2011	
Connell, John James	P.G.St.B.	2009	
Connolly, Peter	P.A.G.D.C.	1987	1997
	P.G.S.D.	1994	
	P.G.J.O.	1999	
	G.M.O.	2005	
	Prov.G.M., West Lancashire	2007	

NAME	RANK	YEAR OF APPT.	R.A.M.G.R. YEAR OF APPT.
Connop, Christopher Ronald	P.A.G.D.C.	2009	
Connor, David Harvey	P.A.G.D.C.	2003	
	P.G.S.D.	2009	
Conochie, Dr. Bruce Campbell, *M.B.E.*	P.A.G.D.C.	1984	
Cons, David Peter	P.G.S.D.	2007	
Cook, Francis	A.G.St.B.	2011	
Cook, Harry Shepherd	G.St.B.	1988	1991
	G.J.D.	1995	
	P.G.J.O.	2003	
Cook, Roy Michael	P.G.St.B.	2004	2002
	P.A.G.D.C.	2010	
Cooke, Frank	G.St.B.	2006	
Cooke, H.E. Sir Howard Felix Hanlan, *O.N., G.C.M.G., G.C.V.O., C.D.*	P.A.G.D.C.	1992	2001
	P.G.J.W.	1998	
Cooke, Terence Jeffrey	P.A.G.D.C.	2002	1989
Coombe, Sydney Gerald	P.A.G.D.C.	2010	
Coombes, Barry Frederick George	P.G.St.B.	2010	2009
Cooper, Colin Graham		—	1993
Cooper, Colin Trevor	G.Stwd.	2001	1998
	P.G.J.D.	2008	
Cooper, Frederick George		—	2010
Cooper, Gavin Colvin Hugh		—	2006
Cooper, Geoffrey Mawer	G.S.D.	1983	1996
	P.G.J.O.	1994	
Cooper, Graham	P.A.G.D.C.	2010	
Cooper, Graham Michael	P.A.G.D.C.	2005	2001
Cooper, Jacob Roderick	P.A.G.D.C.	2007	
Cooper, Michael Andrew	P.A.G.D.C.	2002	2004
	P.G.S.D.	2004	
	P.G.S.O.	2009	
	Dist.G.M., Germany	2009	
Cooper, Paul	P.A.G.D.C.	2009	
Cooper, Peter	P.A.G.D.C.	2006	2008
Cooper, Peter John	A.G.I.G.	1998	2000
	G.S.D.	2005	
Cooper, Peter Leslie	P.A.G.St.B.	1995	2008
	P.A.G.D.C.	2007	
Cooper, Samuel	P.G.St.B.	1987	1999
	P.G.J.D.	1996	
Cope, Dennis		—	2007
Cope, Derek Brian	A.G.D.C.	2002	2007
	P.G.S.D.	2007	
Cope Paul Stuart	P.A.G.D.C.	2012	
Copley, Clive	P.A.G.D.C.	2012	
Copley, His Hon. Judge Peter Edward	P.G.St.B.	1991	1997
	P.G.J.D.	1995	
	P.G.J.O.	2012	
Coppin, Alan Edward		—	2000
Coppin, William Edward	P.A.G.D.C.	1993	
Corbett, Gilbert		—	2008
Corbett, Prof. Jozef Jan August	P.G.S.D.	1996	1996
	P.G.J.O.	2007	

NAME	RANK	YEAR OF APPT.	R.A.M.G.R. YEAR OF APPT.
Corcoran, Mark Samuel Livermore	P.A.G.D.C.	2007	2006
	P.G.S.D.	2012	
Corder, Colin William		—	2008
Cordes, Frederick	P.G.St.B.	1988	
Corfield, Robert	G.Stwd.	2001	2006
	P.G.J.D.	2007	
	P.G.J.O.	2012	
Corke, Frank James	P.A.G.D.C.	1993	1992
Cormack, William Mowat	P.G.St.B.	2000	1999
Cornall, Peter Neville		—	2006
Corner, Jim	P.A.G.Swd.B.	2002	
	P.G.S.D.	2007	
Cornish, Peter Ewart	G.Stwd.	1993	2000
	P.G.J.D.	1998	
	P.G.J.O.	2006	
Corry, David Charles	P.A.G.Swd.B.	1998	2011
	P.G.J.D.	2006	
Cory, John Albert	G.Stwd.	1999	2007
	P.G.J.D.	2004	
Cory-Pearce, Richard	G.Stwd.	1997	
Cory-Wright, Kenneth Wade	P.A.G.D.C.	2004	
Cosford, Norman William	P.G.St.B.	1976	
Cotsworth, Anthony Gwilt	P.G.St.B.	2000	
Cottam, Philip	P.A.G.D.C.	1981	
Cotter, Dennis Whitmore	P.A.G.D.C.	2001	2007
	P.G.S.D.	2007	
Cottrell, Roy Ernest	P.A.G.D.C.	2007	
Coulston, Bert Leopold	P.A.G.D.C.	1997	1998
	P.G.S.D.	2007	
Coulthurst, Norman William	G.Stwd.	2005	
	P.G.J.D.	2010	
Coundley, John	P.A.G.D.C.	1998	
Coupe, David Philip	P.A.G.D.C.	2007	2011
	P.G.S.D.	2012	
Coupland, Eric	P.A.G.Swd.B.	2000	
Court, Christopher	P.A.G.St.B.	2012	
Cousins, Arthur	P.G.St.B.	1994	1998
Cousins, Derek George Griffith	P.G.St.B.	1990	
Cousins, Ronald Leslie	G.Stwd.	2003	2001
	P.G.J.D.	2008	
Couto, Benedito Antonio	P.A.G.D.C.	2011	
Coventry, Robert William	P.G.St.B.	2007	
Cover-White, Terence Raymond	P.A.G.D.C.	2010	
Covey, Allan Mark	G.St.B.	1991	
Cowan, Vernon Algernon	P.G.St.B.	1997	
Cowan, Victor Albert	P.A.G.D.C.	2001	2000
Cowburn, Malcolm Stuart	G.Stwd.	1997	1998
	P.G.J.D.	2002	
	P.G.J.O.	2010	
Cowell, Capt. David Moore	P.G.St.B.	2007	
Cowie, Hugh Richard Mervyn		—	2008
Cowin, Roland	P.A.G.D.C.	2008	
Cowley, Maj. Patrick Victor	P.A.G.Swd.B.	1998	

NAME	RANK	YEAR OF APPT.	R.A.M.G.R. YEAR OF APPT.
Cowton, Ernest William	—		1999
Cox, Brian William	P.G.St.B.	2004	
	P.A.G.D.C.	2010	
Cox, Donald Edward	P.G.St.B.	2000	2000
Cox, Ernest John	P.A.G.D.C.	1987	1994
	P.G.S.D.	1995	
Cox, Harry	P.A.G.D.C.	2011	
Cox, Ian Peter	A.G.Swd.B.	2004	2003
	P.G.S.D.	2010	
Cox, Revd. Kenneth	P.A.G.Chap.	2012	
Cox, Kenneth Moore, *J.P.*	P.A.G.D.C.	1994	1986
Cox, Peter Royston	P.G.St.B.	2007	2000
Cox, Ralph	P.A.G.D.C.	1987	
Crabbe, William Kenneth	P.G.St.B.	1992	1994
	P.G.J.D.	2002	
Crabtree, James	P.G.St.B.	1985	
Craddock, Arthur	A.G.I.G.	1970	1972
	A.G.Sec.	1972-1985	
	P.G.J.D.	1974	
	P.G.J.O.	1978	
	Dep.G.Sec.	1986-1992	
	P.G.S.O.	1988	
	G.M.O.	1993	
	P.G.J.W.	2000	
Cradock, Christopher Douglas	P.G.I.G.	1994	1991
	A.G.D.C.	2002	
	P.G.S.D.	2010	
Crago, Michael John	P.A.G.D.C.	2011	2006
Craig, Ralph Maxwell, *J.P.*	G.Stwd.	2007	2008
	P.G.J.D.	2010	
Craigen, Alexander	P.A.G.D.C.	2005	2003
Craigs, Gordon	G.Stwd.	2008	2009
	Prov.G.M., Northumberland	2009	
Crake, Kenneth Frederick	P.A.G.D.C.	1996	
	P.G.S.D.	2009	
Crampton, Lesley John	P.A.G.D.C.	1998	1999
	P.G.S.D.	2006	
	P.G.J.O.	2011	
Cran, Alexander Anthony	P.A.G.D.C.	1991	2000
	G.S.D.	1998	
	P.G.J.O.	2003	
Crane, Edwin Arthur	P.A.G.D.C.	1972	
Crane, Gordon	—		2008
Crane, Thomas Stuart	P.G.St.B.	2012	
Craven, Anthony	P.A.G.D.C.	2000	2004
	G.S.D.	2006	
	P.G.J.O.	2012	
Crawford, Bernard Aloysius Isidore, *A.A.*	P.A.G.D.C.	2005	
Crawford, Sir Frederick William, *Kt.*	P.A.G.D.C.	1996	1997
	G.J.W.	1999	1999 GMRAC
Crawford, John	P.A.G.St.B.	2002	2003
	P.G.J.D.	2008	
Crawford, John Keith	P.A.G.D.C.	2008	
Crawford, Kenneth Seaton	P.A.G.D.C.	1992	

NAME	RANK	YEAR OF APPT.	R.A.M.G.R. YEAR OF APPT.
Crawford, Stanley	P.A.G.D.C.	2010	
Crawshaw, Peter James		—	2011
Crawshay-Jones, Sydney Martin	G.S.D.	1996	2008
	G.J.O.	2008	
Crewes, Kenneth Frank	G.Stwd.	1983	
	G.J.D.	1988	
Crisp, Dennis Clifford	P.A.G.D.C.	1980	1976
	Dist.G.M., River Plate	1983	
Cristens, Willy Francois	P.A.G.D.C.	2007	2006
Crittenden, John Isaac	P.A.G.D.C.	2012	
Crocker, Norman Stephen	P.G.St.B.	1988	
	P.G.J.D.	2000	
Crockford, Ronald Edward	P.A.G.D.C.	2003	2009
Croft, James Peter	P.G.M., Durham	1995	1995
			2008 GMRAC
Croft, Peter Isaac	P.A.G.D.C.	1999	
Crofts, Christopher Noel	P.A.G.D.C.	2006	
Crofts, David Alan	P.A.G.D.C.	2002	2004
	P.G.J.D.	2004	
	P.G.S.D.	2007	
	P.G.J.O.	2008	
Croker, Derek Balsillie	P.A.G.D.C.	1974	
	P.G.S.D.	1982	
Crombie, Michael Seymour Ivor	P.A.G.St.B.	1996	1997
	P.G.J.D.	2005	
Crompton, Jonathan Terence	P.A.G.D.C.	2006	
Crone, Malcolm	P.G.I.G.	2008	
Croney, Arthur William	P.A.G.St.B.	1992	1994
Cronin, Brendan Maxwell	P.G.St.B.	2007	2004
Croome, Roger James	A.G.D.C.	2004	2004
	P.G.J.O.	2010	
Cropley, Herbert	P.A.G.D.C.	1993	2003
	P.G.S.D.	2005	
Cropper, William Joseph	G.Stwd.	2011	
Crosby, George David	P.G.St.B.	1995	1997
	P.G.J.D.	1999	
Crosby, Joseph Edward, B.Sc.	P.A.G.D.C.	2008	2006
Crosby, William Gordon		—	2000
Crosland, Geoffrey Howard	P.G.St.B.	2012	
Cross, Albert Edward	P.A.G.D.C.	2010	
Cross, David John Lauderic	P.G.St.B.	2004	2005
	P.G.J.D.	2010	
Cross, Donald William	P.G.St.B.	2006	
Cross, Melvyn	P.G.St.B.	2011	
Cross, Michael Alan	P.A.G.D.C.	1982	1983
	P.G.S.D.	1989	
	P.G.J.O.	1998	
Cross, Michael Frank	P.A.G.D.C.	2008	
Cross, Philip Allen	A.G.D.C.	1997	2003
Crossan, Frederick John	P.A.G.D.C.	2000	
	P.G.J.D.	2006	
	P.G.S.O.	2012	

NAME	RANK	YEAR OF APPT.	R.A.M.G.R. YEAR OF APPT.
Crossley, Gilbert	P.A.G.D.C.	2004	2010
	G.S.D.	2011	
Crossley, Kenneth Ernest, *J.P.*	P.A.G.D.C.	1998	
Crouch, David	G.Stwd.	1997	
	P.G.J.D.	2008	
Croucher, Roger Henry Harley	A.G.D.C.	1996	1999
	P.G.J.D.	2000	
	P.G.S.D.	2003	
	P.G.S.O.	2005	
	Prov.G.M., Kent	2008	
Crous, Jacobus Gerhardus Durand	P.G.St.B.	2006	
Crow, Robert John	—		2006
Crowle, Raymond Lewis	—		2005
Crown, Frank Joseph	—		2010
Crowther, Gordon Healey	P.A.G.D.C.	1979	1983
	P.G.S.D.	1987	
	P.G.J.O.	1995	
Crummey, Terence Charles James	P.A.G.D.C.	2010	
Crump, Cdr. David Longton, *V.R.D.*	P.A.G.D.C.	1990	2004
	P.G.S.D.	1994	
Cruse, Raymond Henry	P.G.St.B.	2000	
Crutchley, Shaun Barry	P.A.G.D.C.	2007	2008
Cruttenden, William Charles	A.G.I.G.	2002	2005
Cuff, Philip John	—		2011
Cummings, Rudolph Othneil	P.A.G.Swd.B.	2008	2009
Cummins, David Russell, *J.P.*	G.Stwd.	2004	
	G.J.D.	2010	
Curling, Alan Paul	—		2005
Curran, Paul Michael	P.G.S.D.	2010	2010
Currans, Ian Stanley	G.Stwd.	1998	1996
	P.G.J.D.	2004	
Currans, Trevor David	G.St.B.	2002	2000
	P.G.J.D.	2006	
Currie, James Malcolm	P.A.G.D.C.	2000	
	P.G.S.D.	2010	
Currie, Michael John	P.A.G.D.C.	1994	
Currie, Ronald Mcdonald			2001
Curtis, Malcolm Leo	P.A.G.D.C.	1997	1995
	P.G.S.D.	1998	
	P.G.J.O.	2010	
Curtis, Robert Cyril	P.A.G.D.C.	1992	1994
	P.G.S.D.	2003	
Cushing, David Harold	P.A.G.St.B.	2007	
Cusworth, David	P.G.St.B.	2007	2006
Cuthbert, David Stanley	P.A.G.D.C.	2012	
Cuthbert, Peter	P.G.St.B.	2012	
Cuthbertson, Alan	A.G.D.C.	2007	2008
Cuthbertson, Alastair	P.G.St.B.	1993	1999
	P.G.J.D.	2000	
	P.G.J.O.	2010	
Cuthbertson, Malcolm	P.A.G.D.C.	2007	2008
Cutler, His Hon. Judge Keith Charles, *C.B.E.*	Dep.G.Reg.	2005	2005
	G.Reg.	2006-2012	2008 GMRAC
	P.G.J.W.	2011	

NAME	RANK	YEAR OF APPT.	R.A.M.G.R. YEAR OF APPT.
Daane, Arnoldus Gerardus	P.G.St.B.	1994	1998
	P.G.J.D.	2002	
	P.G.J.O.	2010	
Dada, Michael Afolabi	P.A.G.D.C.	2008	
Daff, Trevor	P.G.St.B.	1999	
Dalby, Harry Robert	P.A.G.Swd.B.	2005	
Dalby, The Ven. John Mark Meredith, M.A., Ph.D.	A.G.Chap.	1999	2002
	Dep.G.Chap.	2000	
	G.Chap.	2001-2003	
	P.G.J.W.	2005	
Dale, David Rodney	P.A.G.St.B.	2008	
Dale, Richard John	P.A.G.St.B.	1991	
Daley, John Arthur Patrick	P.G.St.B.	2007	2005
Dalley, John Alfred	G.Stwd.	1997	2001
	P.G.J.D.	2002	
	P.G.J.O.	2008	
Dalrymple, Robert Keith, *B.A.*	P.A.G.D.C.	2002	
	P.G.J.D.	2005	
	P.G.J.O.	2011	
Daly, Gordon Andrew	P.A.G.St.B.	2011	
Daly, William Arthur	—		2011
Dambawinne, Talija Parakrama, *J.P.*	P.A.G.D.C.	2006	2009
	Dist.G.M., Sri Lanka	2012	
Dangoor, Elias Menashi Heskel	P.A.G.D.C.	2007	2006
Daniel, Ian Dalgleish	G.Stwd.	2006	2011
	P.G.J.D.	2010	
Daniel, James Wallace	P.G.J.D.	1989	1999
	P.G.J.O.	1997	
	P.G.J.W.	1999	
	G.S.W.	2007	
Daniel, Michael William	A.G.St.B.	2004	
Daniels, John Michael	P.A.G.D.C.	2008	
Daniels, Maurice			2003
Daniels, Peter Edward	—		2009
Daniels, Russell James	P.A.G.D.C.	2001	
Dankert, Olaf Rudiger	P.G.St.B.	2010	2010
Danks, Alfred Leslie	P.G.St.B.	1991	1984
Dann, Colin	P.A.G.D.C.	2011	
Dann, Stephen Arthur	P.A.G.D.C.	2008	2006
Darby, David Barry	P.A.G.Swd.B.	2005	
Dare, Stephen John	P.A.G.D.C.	2007	
Darkins, Robert Stanley	P.A.G.D.C.	2011	
Darley, Alan Frederick	—		2009
Darne, John Alexander	P.A.G.D.C.	2007	
Dart, Brian Thomas	P.A.G.D.C.	2000	2008
Daruwalla, Rustom Khurshedji	P.A.G.D.C.	2003	2001
Dashwood, Robert James	G.Std.B.	2005	
Dastur, Phil Minno	P.A.G.D.C.	2006	2008
D'Aubney, Robert Edward	P.G.St.B.	2006	
Davenport, Harry Fry	P.A.G.St.B	1993	2002
	P.G.J.D.	1999	
	P.G.J.O.	2006	

NAME	RANK	YEAR OF APPT.	R.A.M.G.R. YEAR OF APPT.
Davenport, Warwick Ross	P.A.G.D.C.	2001	
Davey, Brian	A.G.D.C.	2002	
	P.G.S.D.	2008	
Davey, Donald Harry	P.A.G.D.C.	2005	
Davey, Ernest Parry	P.G.St.B.	1997	
Davey, Frederick George	P.G.St.B.	1986	
	P.G.J.D.	1997	
Davey, John Parry		—	2009
Davey, Michael James	P.A.G.D.C.	1998	1999
	P.G.S.D.	2006	
David, Phillip Gwyn		—	2002
Davidson, Allan	A.G.D.C.	2011	
Davidson, Richard Carruthers, M.B.E.	P.A.G.D.C.	1992	1994
	P.G.S.D.	1998	
	P.G.J.O.	2004	
Davidson, Robert Samuel	P.A.G.D.C.	2002	
	P.G.J.D.	2006	
Davie, Gordon William Sinclair	A.G.D.C.	1989	
Davies, Adrian Frederick Raymond	P.G.S.D.	2007	
Davies, Alan		—	2005
Davies, Alan Kenneth	P.A.G.D.C.	1989	
Davies, Andrew George		—	2009
Davies, Arthur Geoffrey	P.A.G.D.C.	1997	1996
	P.G.S.D.	2003	
	P.G.J.O.	2009	
Davies, Bernard Thomas	P.G.St.B.	2007	
Davies, Brian		—	2010
Davies, Clifford	P.A.G.Swd.B.	2000	2011
	P.G.J.D.	2009	
Davies, David Elwyn	P.G.St.B.	2006	2006
Davies, David Eric Thomas	P.G.St.B.	2002	2000
Davies, David Terence	G.Stwd.	2008	
	P.G.S.D.	2012	
Davies, George	P.A.G.D.C.	1994	1994
	P.G.S.D.	2000	
Davies, Glyn Jackson, J.P.	P.A.G.D.C.	1992	1997
	P.G.J.D.	1995	
	P.G.J.O.	2001	
	P.G.S.O.	2007	
Davies, Graham Stanley		—	1995
Davies, Gwilym Robert, J.P.	P.A.G.Swd.B.	2007	
Davies, Herbert	P.A.G.D.C.	2003	1999
Davies, Horace Clifford		—	2000
Davies, Hywel	P.A.G.D.C.	1997	2000
	G.S.D.	2002	
	P.G.J.O.	2007	
Davies, Ian Lodwick	P.A.G.D.C.	2002	2004
	G.S.D.	2008	
Davies, Ieuan Michael	P.A.G.D.C.	2009	
Davies, Wg.Cdr. John Irfon, C.B.E.	G.Stwd.	1994	1998
	Dep.G.D.C.	1995-1996	
	P.G.J.O.	1998	
	P.G.M.O.	2005	
	G.J.W.	2009	

NAME	RANK	YEAR OF APPT.	R.A.M.G.R. YEAR OF APPT.
Davies, Kenneth	P.A.G.D.C.	2010	
Davies, Leonard	Asst.G.I.G.	1992	2001
	P.A.G.D.C.	1999	
	P.G.J.D.	2005	
	P.G.J.O.	2012	
Davies, Leonard David Henry	P.A.G.Swd.B.	2008	
Davies, Leslie John	G.Stwd.	1991	
Davies, Neil	P.A.G.D.C.	2011	
Davies, Robert Terence		—	2009
Davies, Lt.Col. Ronald Leslie, *O.B.E.*	P.G.St.B.	1993	1995
	P.G.S.D.	1997	
	P.G.J.O.	2002	
Davies, Thomas Ellis	P.G.St.B.	2003	1996
Davies, Revd. Walter Hugh	P.A.G.Chap.	1992	
Davies, William Stuart Vaughan	P.A.G.D.C.	2009	
Davinson, Donald Edward	P.G.S.D.	1997	2005
	P.G.J.O.	2002	
Davis, Cecil Percy		—	2009
Davis, Christopher David	P.A.G.D.C.	2006	2006
	Dep.G.D.C.	2011-2012	
Davis, Christopher Thomas Brooklyn	P.G.St.B.	2012	
Davis, Derek John	P.A.G.D.C.	1991	
	P.G.S.D.	1997	
Davis, George William	P.A.G.D.C.	1994	1999
	P.G.S.D.	2000	
	P.G.J.O.	2011	
Davis, Dr. Harold Barrington	P.G.St.B.	2005	2007
Davis, Herbert Arthur, *J.P.*	P.A.G.D.C.	1988	1987
	P.G.S.D.	1993	
	P.G.S.O.	1997	
	P.G.J.W.	2004	
Davis, John Arthur	P.A.G.Swd.B.	1998	2004
David, John Vincent	P.A.G.D.C.	2005	2011
	P.G.S.D.	2012	
Davis, Keith William Randloph	P.A.G.D.C.	2003	2001
Davis, Lawrence Meredith		—	2011
Davis, Michael	P.G.St.B.	2010	
Davis, Michael Charles	P.A.G.St.B.	2011	2004
Davis, Paul Herbert	P.A.G.D.C.	1984	1968
	G.S.D.	1993	
	P.G.J.O.	1998	
Davis, Ronald Arthur	P.G.St.B.	1995	1993
	P.G.J.D.	2002	
Davis, Richard William	P.G.St.B.	1998	1999
	G.S.D.	2003	
	P.G.J.O.	2007	
	P.G.M.O.	2012	
Davison, Alan Martin	G.S.D.	2004	
Davison, Stephen	P.A.G.D.C.	2011	
Davy, Frederick Leslie	A.G.Swd.B.	2011	
Davy, John	G.Stwd.	1991	2005
	P.G.J.D.	1996	
	P.G.J.O.	2004	

NAME	RANK	YEAR OF APPT.	R.A.M.G.R. YEAR OF APPT.
Davy, Nathan William Foottit	P.G.St.B.	1991	1995
	P.G.J.D.	1997	
Daw, William Stuart	G.Stwd.	1988	2002
	P.G.J.D.	1993	
	P.G.J.O.	2007	
Dawe, Richard John	P.A.G.D.C.	1997	
Dawson, John Clive	P.A.G.D.C.	2004	
Dawson, Peter George	A.G.D.C.	2008	2008
Dawson, William Goode, *T.D., D.L.*	P.G.J.D.	2004	
Day, Alfred John	P.G.J.D.	2000	2000
	P.G.J.O.	2005	
Day, Christopher Richard	P.G.St.B.	2007	
	P.A.G.D.C.	2011	
Deacon, George John	P.A.G.D.C.	2000	2002
	P.G.S.D.	2005	
	P.G.J.O.	2008	
De Alfonso Ortega, Oscar	P.G.J.O.	2010	2010
Dean, John Brian	A.G.I.G.	2000	1997
Dean, Joseph John	—		2009
Dean, Leslie Charles	P.A.G.D.C.	2008	2009
Dearden, John	P.A.G.St.B.	2005	
Dears, Christopher	P.A.G.D.C.	2012	2009
Deaton, Allan	P.A.G.Swd.B.	2000	2009
de Beer, Dion Louis	P.A.G.D.C.	1998	
	P.G.J.O.	2006	
de Beer, Willem Martinus	P.A.G.St.B.	1994	2005
	P.G.J.D.	1995	
	P.G.J.O.	2001	
de Bouvere, Louis	P.G.S.D.	1991	1994
	G.S.W.	1994	1994/95 GMRAC
De Courcey-Cooke, Roger	G.Stwd.	2009	2010
	G.J.D.	2012	
Deeprose, Alan Edgar	P.A.G.Swd.B.	2010	
De Freitas, Gerald John Richard	P.A.G.D.C.	2006	2006
	P.G.S.D.	2011	
Defries, Stephen Louis	P.G.St.B.	1997	
	P.G.J.D.	2003	
de Gruchy, Graham	P.A.G.D.C.	1999	
de Haro, Joseph	P.G.St.B.	1989	1989
	Dist.G.M., Gibraltar	1998-2000	
Deighton, Colin	P.A.G.D.C.	2001	2007
De Jaillon, Hugues Jacques Julien Charles		—	2011
De Joode, Gerard Jan Willem	P.G.St.B.	2012	
Delaney, Damian	P.A.G.Swd.B.	2005	
	P.G.S.D.	2006	
De Lagarde, Edouard Thomas		—	2010
De Lange, Daniel Benjamin	P.A.G.D.C.	1998	1993
	P.G.S.D.	2009	
De Lannoy, Egbert Siegfried Joseph	P.A.G.Swd.B.	2008	2009
	P.G.J.D.	2010	
Delderfield, Christopher Robin	P.G.J.D.	2010	
Delfosse, Jean-Pol	A.G.D.C.	2003	
Deltenre, Guy Edouard Achile Max	P.A.G.Swd.B.	2010	
Delves, Ronald David		—	2000

NAME	RANK	YEAR OF APPT.	R.A.M.G.R. YEAR OF APPT.
De Luca, Allan James	P.A.G.D.C.	2006	2010
De Meza, Louis Sidney	P.G.St.B.	1995	
Dent, Michael George	P.A.G.D.C.	2011	
Denton, John	P.A.G.D.C.	1994	2000
	G.J.O.	2006	
Denton, Douglas	—		2001
Denton, Robert Arthur	P.A.G.D.C.	1995	1994
	P.G.S.D.	2004	
Denyer, Leslie Charles	P.A.G.D.C.	1990	1992
	G.J.D.	2000	
	P.G.J.O.	2007	
Devereux, Charles Geoffrey	P.A.G.Swd.B.	2002	2004
	P.G.Swd.B.	2009	
de Villiers, Jan Hendrik Grey	P.G.St.B.	2000	
Devlin, Jack	G.Stwd.	1984	2001
	P.G.J.D.	1991	
	P.G.J.O.	2004	
Devlin, Robert Stanley	P.A.G.D.C.	2001	
De Vries, Freddy	P.G.St.B.	2007	
de Walder, Peter	P.A.G.D.C.	1994	2000
	P.G.S.D.	2000	
	P.G.J.O.	2004	
Dhadialla, Jagdish Singh	P.A.G.D.C.	2009	2011
Dhanarajan, Samuel	P.A.G.D.C.	1991	
	P.G.J.D.	2009	
Dhas, Arnold Harrison	P.A.G.D.C.	1993	
Dhillon, Avtar Singh	P.G.I.G.	1993	1993
	P.G.St.B.	2005	
Dhuru, Digvijay Mohan	P.G.St.B.	2002	2001
Dias, Gemunu Peiris	P.A.G.D.C.	1980	
	P.G.S.D.	1983	
	P.G.J.O.	1998	
	P.G.M.O.	2002	
Dias, Michael Anthony Sirimal	P.A.G.D.C.	1992	2000
	P.G.S.D.	1995	
	P.G.J.O.	1999	
	Dist.G.M., Sri Lanka	2000-2012	
Dickinson, Reginald	P.A.G.Swd.B.	2001	
	P.G.J.D.	2006	
Dickson, Issac Dua	P.A.G.Swd.B.	2008	
Diggle, Edward	P.A.G.D.C.	1990	
	P.G.J.D.	1998	
Dilloway, Brian Walter Frederick Vaux	P.A.G.Swd.B.	2008	2008
Dimmick, Kenneth Vernon	P.G.I.G.	1995	
Dingvean, Stephen Brian Peter	P.A.G.D.C.	2003	2004
	P.G.S.D.	2011	
Dingwall, Ian	P.A.G.D.C.	2006	
Dinning, Keith	P.A.G.Swd.B.	2003	2011
	P.G.J.D.	2010	
Dinning, Raymond Norman	P.G.I.G.	1996	1999
	P.G.J.D.	2001	
Dinsdale, Carl Philip	P.A.G.D.C.	2006	
Dipple, John Colin	P.G.I.G.	1994	
Disley, Walter	P.G.St.B.	2011	2011

NAME	RANK	YEAR OF APPT.	R.A.M.G.R. YEAR OF APPT.
Divall, William Arthur	G.Stwd.	2003	2007
	P.G.J.D.	2008	
Dixit, Suresh Ramakrisna		—	2011
Dixon, Alan	P.A.G.D.C.	2000	1998
Dixon, Allan Stanley	P.G.St.B.	1992	1990
Dixon, Cecil Francis	P.A.G.D.C.	2004	
Dixon, Rev. Canon David	A.G.Chap.	1990	1992
	Dep.G.Chap.	1993-1996	
	G.Chap.	1997-1999	
	P.G.S.O.	2000	
Dixon, David Buchanan	P.G.St.B.	2010	
Dixon, Jackson	A.G.D.C.	1991	1995
	P.G.S.D.	1996	
	P.G.J.O.	2002	
Dixon, John Eric	P.A.G.St.B.	1999	2009
Dixon, Jonathan Andrew	P.A.G.Swd.B.	2010	
Dixon, Paul George	P.G.St.B.	2005	
Dixon, Robert	P.G.St.B.	2004	2004
	G.J.D.	2011	
Dixon, Simon Campbell William	G.Stwd.	2005	2005
	P.G.J.D.	2006	
	P.G.J.O.	2011	
Dixon, William Turnbull	P.G.St.B.	2000	
Dobbing, Jeffrey Ronald	P.A.G.I.G.	2007	
Dobson, Andrew William	P.A.G.St.B.	2010	
Dobson, David Akrill	P.G.St.B	1996	2000
	P.A.G.D.C.	2006	
Dobson, Leslie	P.G.St.B.	2001	
Dobson, Roy	P.G.St.B.	2002	2011
Dodge, David Sidney	P.G.St.B.	2000	
Dodsley, David Ronald	P.A.G.D.C.	1996	
	P.G.S.D.	2006	
Dodson, Philip Michael	P.A.G.St.B.	2003	
Dodsworth, Wilfrid Trevor	P.G.St.B.	2011	
Doe, Howard Francis		—	2011
Doggett, Anthony George	P.G.I.G.	2009	
Doggett, Richard Hugh	P.A.G.D.C.	1986	1989
	G.Insp., France	1990	
	Dist.G.M., France	1994-1997	
Doherty, Anthony Roger, *G.S.M.*	G.I.G.	1991	1996
	P.A.G.D.C.	1997	
	P.G.S.D.	2002	
Dole, Capt. Trevor Francis	P.A.G.D.C.	2008	2004
Dollery, John George	P.G.St.B.	2011	
Dolphin, Barrie Joseph	P.A.G.D.C.	2010	2008
Dominicus, Adriaan David John		—	2003
Don, Neville Roy Hendrey	P.A.G.Swd.B.	2005	2002
	P.G.J.D.	2010	
Donkin, George	P.A.G.D.C.	1970	
Donnison, Ernest Peter	P.A.G.D.C.	1987	1984
	G.S.D.	1991	
	P.G.J.O.	1996	
	P.G.J.W.	2012	
Dop, Capt. Jan Albert, R.N.A.R. (Rtd.)	P.G.St.B.	2002	2001

NAME	RANK	YEAR OF APPT.	R.A.M.G.R. YEAR OF APPT.
Dore, Charles William	P.G.St.B.	2011	
Dougal, Dereck Malcolm	P.A.G.D.C.	1997	1999
	P.G.J.D.	2004	
Douglas, Alan Reginald	P.A.G.Swd.B.	2012	2004
Douglas, Lewis	P.A.G.D.C.	1999	
	P.G.S.D.	2006	
Douglas, Norman	P.G.St.B.	1990	1989
	P.G.J.D.	1995	
Douglas, Robert James	P.A.G.D.C.	2000	2009
	P.G.S.D.	2012	
Douglas, Trelford Alexander Earl			2003
Dowell, David Keith	P.A.G.D.C.	1994	2001
	P.G.S.D.	1999	
	P.G.J.O.	2005	
Dowell, Peter James	P.A.G.D.C.	2003	2004
	Dep.G.Swd.B.	2008	
Downe, Terence Henry George	P.A.G.D.C.	2010	
Downes, Keith Frederick	P.A.G.D.C.	2001	2010
	G.S.D.	2006	
	P.G.J.O.	2011	
Downes, Kenneth Leonard, *J.P.*	A.G.I.G.	2010	2010
Downie, Alexander	P.G.St.B.	1995	
Downie, Alexander Frank, *M.H.K.*	P.A.G.D.C.	2005	
	P.G.S.D.	2012	
Downie, David Patrick , *M.B.E.*	A.G.I.G.	1999	2003
	P.G.J.D.	2004	
	G.Insp., Isle of Man	2005	
Downie, John Lennox	P.G.S.D.	1997	
	P.G.J.O.	2005	
Downing, Bernard Keith	P.A.G.St.B.	2011	
Doyen, Dominique Marcel Jacques	P.G.S.D.	1994	1994
Doyle, James William	G.Stwd.	2009	2010
	P.G.J.D.	2012	
Doyle, Terrence	G.Stwd.	1999	1999
Drabble, John	P.A.G.Swd.B.	2005	2008
Drage, Colin John Fleming	G.Stwd.	1993	1996
	P.G.S.D.	2003	
	P.G.J.O.	2010	
Drakard, Douglas Frank	P.A.G.St.B.	2012	2006
Drake, John Thorrowgood	P.A.G.D.C.	2006	2005
Drake, The Hon. Sir Maurice, *D.F.C.*	G.Reg.	2001-05	2001 GMRAC (H.C.)
	P.G.J.W.	2003	
Dransfield, Andrew Peter		—	2008
Draper, Philip John	P.G.St.B.	2012	
Dresler, John Henry	G.Stwd.	1961	
	P.G.St.B.	1965	
	P.G.J.D.	1980	
	P.G.J.O.	1990	
Drew, Dr. Christopher Daking Macfarlane	Dep.G.D.C.	1982-84	1982
	P.G.J.O.	1987	
	P.G.M.O.	2002	
Drew, George William		—	1998
Drew, Kenneth James	P.A.G.Swd.B.	2012	2011
Drewett, Edward Jack	P.G.St.B.	2011	2006

NAME	RANK	YEAR OF APPT.	R.A.M.G.R. YEAR OF APPT.
Dribbell, Jack Lodewyk Charles	P.A.G.D.C.	1991	1992
	P.G.S.D.	1997	
	G.M.O.	2002	
Dring, Leslie Felgate	G.S.O.	1999	2005
	G.S.W.	2006	
Drinkwater, Alvine Raymond	P.A.G.D.C.	1999	1999
	P.G.S.D.	2009	
Drinkwater, Eric	G.Stwd.	2004	2007
	G.J.D.	2009	
Driscoll, James Daniel	P.A.G.D.C.	2008	
Driver, Capt. Dara Eruchshaw	P.G.St.B.	2000	
Driver, Vincent John	G.Stwd.	2007	2007
	P.G.J.D.	2010	
	Dep.G.Insp.Wks.	2010-2012	
Druckman, Reuben Leon	P.G.St.B.	1995	2003
	P.G.J.D.	2003	
Drysdale, Thomas			2003
D'Silva, Joseph Janardan	P.A.G.D.C.	2009	2010
D'Souza Kenneth Thomas	G.Stwd.	2012	
Du Boulay, Anthony John Houssemayne	P.G.St.B.	1992	
	P.G.J.O.	2009	
Du-Cann, Edwin John Christian	P.A.G.Swd.B.	2002	
Duck, William	P.A.G.D.C.	2010	
Duckworth, Eric Raymond	A.G.I.G.	1963	
	P.G.I. of Wks.	1968	
	P.G.J.O.	1979	
Duckworth, John Martin	P.G.St.B.	2003	
Duckworth, Peter Ransom	P.G.St.B.	1987	2000
	P.G.J.D.	2000	
	P.G.S.O.	2008	
Duckworth, Simon D'Olier	P.G.St.B.	2007	
Dudley, Terence Edward, *J.P.*	P.G.St.B.	2010	
Duffy, Michael John	G.Stwd.	2004	
Duggan, Harry James	P.A.G.D.C.	2010	2010
Duke, William Raymond		—	2002
Dummer, Timothy Michael	P.A.G.D.C.	2011	
Dumoulin, Henri Paul	P.A.G.St.B.	1996	
Dumont, Jacques Andre	P.A.G.D.C.	1988	1991
	P.G.S.D.	1994	
	P.G.S.O.	1998	
	P.G.J.W.	2003	
Dunbar, Derek Alan		—	2008
Dunford, James George Brian	P.A.G.D.C.	2002	
Dunham, Gregory	P.A.G.Swd.B.	2007	2004
	P.G.J.D.	2012	
Dunleavy, Richard Anthony	P.A.G.D.C.	2008	
Dunn, Alan	P.G.J.O.	2007	
Dunn, Allan	G.Stwd.	1994	
	P.G.J.D.	1999	
Dunn, Hugh Leonard		—	2008
Dunn, Thomas	P.A.G.D.C.	2010	
Dunnico, Clive Rathbone	P.A.G.D.C.	2010	

NAME	RANK	YEAR OF APPT.	R.A.M.G.R. YEAR OF APPT.
Dunster, John Richard	P.A.G.St.B.	1991	1989
	P.G.J.D.	1996	
	P.G.J.O.	2006	
Duperrey, Rene	P.G.St.B.	2005	
	P.G.J.D.	2007	
Du Preez, Stephanus Johannes	—		2008
Duthie, Alasdair Bruce	P.G.St.B, Prov.G.M., S. Africa (Western Division)	1996 ...2001-2006	1998
Duthie, Alistair Stewart	—		2010
Du Toit, Ronald Frederick	P.G.St.B	1986	1996
	P.G.J.D.	1993	
	P.G.J.O.	2001	
Dutt, Trevor Peter, *M.B.B.S., F.R.C.O.G.*	P.G.J.D.	2005	2004
Dutton, John	G.Stwd.	1992	2005
	G.J.D.	1998	
	P.G.J.O.	2006	
Dwyer, William Francis	G.Stwd.	2005	2009
	P.G.J.D.	2008	
Dyer, Maurice John	P.A.G.D.C.	1989	1988
	G.S.D.	2004	
Dyke, Nigel Harry	—		2011
Dyke, Peter Richard	G.Stwd.	1999	2002
	P.G.J.D.	2004	
	P.G.J.O.	2011	
Dykes, Benjamin William	G.Stwd.	2008	2011
	P.G.J.D.	2011	
Eade, Eric George	P.G.St.B.	1992	
	P.G.J.D.	2000	
Eadie, Alan, *M.A.*	A.G.D.C.	1997	1997
	P.G.S.D.	2003	
	P.G.J.O.	2008	
Eales, Stephen William	P.G.St.B.	2001	2010
	P.G.J.D.	2009	
Eardley, William Thomas	P.G.St.B.	2007	
Earl, Stephen John	P.G.St.B.	2010	2011
Earland, Eugene Roderick	P.A.G.D.C.	2009	
Earley, John David	P.A.G.D.C.	2010	
Eastburn, Geoffrey	P.G.St.B.	2011	
Eastman, Andrew John	G.Stwd.	2009	
	P.G.J.D.	2012	
Eastment, John Harvard	—		2005
Easton, John Anthony	P.G.St.B.	2006	2001
Easton, John Harold	P.A.G.D.C.	1992	1994
	P.G.S.D.	1997	
	P.G.J.O.	2001	
	P.G.M.O.	2006	
	P.G.J.W.	2010	
Eaton, John Edward Peter	G.Stwd.	1994	1999
	G.J.D.	1998	
	P.G.J.O.	2002	
Eaton, Ian Alfred	G.Stwd.	2012	2009

NAME	RANK	YEAR OF APPT.	R.A.M.G.R. YEAR OF APPT.
Eaton, Roy Edwin	P.A.G.D.C.	1999	2000
	P.G.S.D.	2004	
	P.G.J.O.	2009	
Edal Behram, Yezdiar Navroji	P.A.G.D.C.	2005	2008
Eden, Anthony Charles	P.G.St.B.	2002	1999
Edgar, George		—	2002
Edgcombe, John Charles	P.A.G.D.C.	2008	
Edge, David Frank	P.A.G.D.C.	1999	2000
Edge, Ian Buxton	P.G.St.B.	2005	
Edmonds, Keith Grahame	P.A.G.D.C.	2007	
Edmonds, W.Cdr. Roland James, *D.F.M.*	G.Stwd.	1986	
	P.G.J.D.	1996	
Edie, George Midmore	P.A.G.St.B.	1999	
Edmondson, John Alfred	G.Stwd.	1984	1988
	P.G.J.D.	1990	
	P.G.J.O.	1995	
	G.J.W.	2002	
Edmunds, Ronald Sidney	P.A.G.D.C.	1991	1998
	P.G.S.D.	2004	
Edwards, Benjamin Marsh	P.A.G.D.C.	2006	2007
	P.G.S.D.	2009	
Edwards, David Michael	P.A.G.D.C.	1999	2002
	P.G.S.D.	2003	
	Prov.G.M., Staffordshire & Shropshire	2007	
Edwards, Edward Francis	P.A.G.D.C.	1996	
Edwards, George Thomas	P.A.G.D.C.	2011	
Edwards, Gerald John Charles	P.A.G.D.C.	2012	
Edwards, James John, *O.B.E.*	P.A.G.D.C.	2007	2004
Edwards, John Barry	P.A.G.D.C.	2012	
Edwards, John Mills	A.G.I.G.	2009	2009
	P.A.G.D.C.	2011	
Edwards, John William	G.Stwd.	1993	
	P.G.J.D.	2001	
	P.G.J.O.	2011	
Edwards, Kenneth	P.A.G.D.C.	1998	
Edwards, Leslie Victor	P.A.G.D.C.	1998	
	P.G.J.D.	2007	
Edwards, Peter George	P.A.G.D.C.	1988	
Edwards, Peter Robert	G.Stwd.	1991	
	P.G.J.D.	1996	
Edwards, Phillip David Watcyn, *J.P.*		—	2010
Edwards, Ronald	P.A.G.St.B.	1999	2000
Edwards, Stuart Ian	G.Stwd.	1999	1997
	P.G.S.D.	2001	2003 GMRAC
	G.Treas.	2004-2012	
	P.G.J.W.	2008	
Edwards, Terence	A.G.D.C.	1998	1998
Edwards, Tony Robert	G.Stwd.	2006	2007
	P.G.J.D.	2009	
Edwards, Victor Edwin	P.A.G.D.C.	1986	
	P.G.S.D.	1995	1996
	P.G.J.O.	2003	
Edwicker, Derek	P.A.G.Swd.B.	2001	1997

NAME	RANK	YEAR OF APPT.	R.A.M.G.R. YEAR OF APPT.
Eeles, David John	—		2009
Egan, Dr. Pritam Singh	P.G.St.B.	2002	
Egdell, William	P.A.G.D.C.	1984	
	P.G.S.D.	1998	
Egenes, Edgar Andrew	P.G.St.B.	1994	2010
	P.G.J.D.	2010	
Eggleton, Jeremy	P.A.G.D.C.	2009	
	P.G.J.D.	2011	
Eglinton, Maurice William	P.G.St.B.	2002	
Elcoat, Brian	P.A.G.D.C.	2012	
Eldridge, John Michael	P.A.G.D.C.	2010	2011
Eley, Christopher Wenham	P.A.G.D.C.	2009	2010
Eley, John Ernest	P.A.G.D.C.	1998	2002
	P.G.S.D.	2001	
	Prov.G.M., Gloucestershire and Herefordshire	2004-2010	
Elgood, Guy David Alsager	A.G.D.C.	2006	2009
	Dep.G.D.C.	2008-2010	
Ellen, Geert	P.G.St.B.	2005	2009
Ellershaw, Robert John, *J.P.*	P.A.G.Swd.B.	2009	2011
Elliot, John Carlyle	P.A.G.D.C.	2005	
Elliott, Arthur Dennis Stephen	P.A.G.D.C.	1996	1996
	P.G.S.D.	2007	
Elliott, Charles Lerway	G.Stwd.	1991	
	P.G.J.D.	1996	
Elliott, Duncan	P.A.G.D.C.	2009	
Ellis, David Edward	P.A.G.St.B.	2012	2007
Ellis, John Henry William	G.Stwd.	2012	2011
Ellis, John Michael	P.A.G.D.C.	1997	
Ellis, Joseph Wynford		—	2008
Ellis, Richard Leonard	P.A.G.D.C.	1997	
	P.G.S.D.	2008	
Ellis Thomas Denzil	P.A.G.D.C.	2010	
Ellis, William Peter	P.A.G.Swd.B.	2009	
Elman, Barry	G.Stwd.	1993	2003
	P.G.J.D.	1998	
	P.G.J.O.	2006	
Elman, Charles		—	2001
Elmes, Kenneth Joseph	P.A.G.D.C.	2012	
Elmont, Peter William	P.A.G.D.C.	2010	
Elmore, Dr. John Anthony	P.A.G.D.C.	2004	2005
	P.G.J.D.	2006	
	P.G.J.O.	2008	
Elmore, Peter George, *J.P.*	G.Stwd.	2006	
	P.G.J.D.	2010	
Else, David Keith	A.G.D.C.	2008	2005
Eltringham, Brian	P.A.G.Swd.B.	1996	
Embley, Colin	P.A.G.D.C.	1999	
Embling, David Robert	P.A.G.D.C.	2002	1998
	P.G.S.D.	2008	
Emerson, Herbert	P.G.St.B.	1999	
Emery, Alan George	P.A.G.D.C.	2000	

NAME	RANK	YEAR OF APPT.	R.A.M.G.R. YEAR OF APPT.
Emmerson, Brian	P.A.G.St.B.	2000	2006
	P.G.J.D.	2009	
Emmerson, David	P.A.G.D.C.	2012	
Emmerson, Herbert Keith	A.G.D.C.	1996	1996
	Prov.G.M., Hertfordshire	1998-2008	
	A.G.M.	2011-2012	
Emmett, Brian	G.Stwd.	1991	1997
	P.G.J.D.	1995	
	P.G.J.O.	2000	
	G.J.W.	2005	
Emmett, Howard Nicholas	P.A.G.D.C.	2011	
Enders, John Henry	P.A.G.D.C.	1984	1995
	P.G.S.D.	1991	
Enever, John William	P.A.G.Swd.B.	2009	
Engineer, Naval Pirojshaw	P.A.G.D.C.	2010	
Engineer, Noshir Kaikhasru	P.G.St.B.	1995	1995
	P.G.J.D.	2005	
England, Christopher John	P.A.G.Swd.B.	2008	2007
England, Harold William Edwin	P.G.St.B.	1977	1985
	P.G.J.D.	1983	
	P.G.J.O.	1989	
Englefield, Alan John	P.G.S.D.	2001	2001
	P.G.S.O.	2003	
English, John		—	2008
Ennever, Brian	P.A.G.D.C.	2011	
	P.G.S.D.	2012	
Enock, David Spencer, *F.C.I.S.*	G.Stwd.	1996	1994
	P.G.J.D.	2001	
Entwisle, David Nicholas	G.St.B.	2011	
Entwistle, Fred Knowles	G.St.B.	1991	
Erlen, Peter Hannes	P.G.St.B.	1996	1997
	P.G.S.D.	2009	
Escott, John	P.A.G.D.C.	1980	
	P.G.S.D.	1984	1987
	P.G.S.O.	1987	
	Prov.G.M., W. Lancs.	1988-1991	
Espag, Anthony Jack		—	2011
Evangelista, Brian	P.A.G.D.C.	2002	2011
	P.G.S.D.	2010	
Evans, Benjamin	P.A.G.D.C.	2011	
Evans, Clive	P.G.St.B.	2012	2007
Evans, Colin	P.A.G.D.C.	2000	
	P.G.S.D.	2005	
Evans, David		—	2008
Evans, David Gerald		—	2002
Evans, Elwyn Barry	P.A.G.D.C.	1997	
	P.G.S.D.	2008	
Evans, Gordon Davies	P.A.G.D.C.	2010	
Evans, John Michael	P.G.St.B.	1999	2004
	G.J.D.	2007	
Evans, John Moelwyn, *J.P.*	P.G.St.B.	2000	
	P.G.J.D.	2008	
Evans, Maurice Myers	P.A.G.D.C.	2006	
	P.G.S.D.	2012	

NAME	RANK	YEAR OF APPT.	R.A.M.G.R. YEAR OF APPT.
Evans, Robert Wilmore	P.G.St.B.	1987	
	G.S.D.	1997	
Evans, Selwyn John	P.A.G.D.C.	1991	
Evans, Teifion Morris	P.A.G.D.C.	2002	2000
Evans, William David Griffith	P.A.G.D.C.	2009	
Evelyn, Stanley	P.A.G.D.C.	2008	
Ewins, Sidney Trevor Rowland	P.A.G.D.C.	1985	1991
	P.G.S.D.	2009	
Eyles, Michael Roger	P.A.G.D.C.	2011	
Fagence, Robin	P.A.G.D.C.	2003	2001
Faint, Wg.Cdr. Michael John	P.G.St.B.	2003	
Fairclough, David Charles Watkin	G.Stwd.	2003	2009
	P.G.J.D.	2008	
Fairclough, Stanley	P.A.G.St.B.	2000	
Fairer, Christopher John	G.Stwd.	2004	2000
Fairer, Dr. John Godfrey, *T.D.*	G.Stwd.	1973	1984
	P.A.G.D.C.	1980	
	P.G.J.O.	1986	
	P.G.S.O.	2007	
Fairer, Richard Hugh	G.Stwd.	1999	1998
Fairfield, Roger Thomas	P.A.G.Swd.B.	2009	2006
Fairhurst, George Brian	G.Stwd.	1995	2006
	P.G.J.D.	2000	
Fairs, Kenneth		—	2010
Fairweather, Keith Thomas	G.Stwd.	2012	2011
Falkner, Michael Arthur	P.A.G.St.B.	2002	2005
	P.G.J.D.	2007	
Fallowfield, Ernest George	P.A.G.D.C.	2010	
Farleigh, Eric Wallace	P.G.St.B.	1989	2002
	P.G.J.D.	1996	
Farlow, Capt. Herbert Charles, *R.M.*	P.G.J.D.	2000	2001
	P.G.J.O.	2004	
Farmer, Donald	P.G.St.B.	2008	
Farmer, Richard William	P.A.G.St.B.	2005	
Farndale, Donald	P.A.G.Swd.B.	2006	
Farook, Mohamed	P.A.G.D.C.	2008	
Farrall, John Henry	P.A.G.D.C.	1994	1995
	P.G.S.D.	1995	
	Prov.G.M. North Wales	1999-2004	
Farrance, Charles William	A.G.Insp. of Works	1985-1986	
	P.G.S.D.	2004	
Farrar, Geoffrey	P.A.G.D.C.	1989	
Farrell, Anthony John	P.G.St.B.	2010	2010
Farrell, Kevin Marshal	P.A.G.D.C.	1992	
	P.G.S.D.	1997	
	P.G.J.O.	2003	
Farrow, Christopher John	G.J.D.	2012	
Farrow, Colin	G.Stwd.	1997	
	P.G.J.D.	2003	
Farrow, Christopher John	P.G.St.B.	2004	2003

NAME	RANK	YEAR OF APPT.	R.A.M.G.R. YEAR OF APPT.
Fathers, John Harry, J.P.	P.A.G.D.C.	1998	
Faulks, Peter Charles	G.Stwd.	2011	
Fawcett, Peter	G.Stwd.	1997	2004
	P.G.J.D.	2003	
Fay, Edward John		—	2009
Feetum, Leonard Paul	G.St.B.	2007	
Feiger, Malcolm Myer	P.A.G.St.B.	2000	2003
Felix, Francis	P.G.J.D.	2000	2008
	P.G.J.O.	2010	
Felix, Michael Finley		—	2008
Fenn, Spencer Thomas Edward	P.A.G.St.B.	1991	1990
	P.G.J.D.	1999	
	P.G.J.O.	2009	
Fennell, Jack Royston		—	1997
Fenton, Stephen Richard Nigel	G.Stwd.	2010	2009
Fenwick, Graham Henry	P.A.G.D.C.	2011	
Ferdinando, David John		—	2009
Ferguson, Keith Berwick	P.A.G.D.C.	2005	2009
Ferguson, Kenneth Arthur, J.P.	G.I.G.	1994	1995
	P.A.G.D.C.	2000	
	P.G.J.O.	2008	
Ferguson, William		—	2002
Fermor, Andrew Patrick Lionel	P.A.G.Swd.B.	2010	
Fernandes, Joao	P.A.G.St.B.	2007	
Ferraz, Claudio Ermel	P.A.G.D.C.	1990	1993
	P.G.J.O.	2009	
Ferres, Ian Wilton	P.G.St.B.	2009	
Ferris, George Leslie	P.G.St.B.	2011	
Ferris, Maurice Peter	P.A.G.Swd.B.	2008	
Ferro, Richard	G.St.B.	1997	1980
	G.J.D.	1983	
	P.G.J.O.	1988	
	G.S.O.	1993	
	P.G.M.O.	2002	
Fewster, Robert Charles	P.A.G.D.C.	1988	1983
	P.G.S.D	1994	
	P.G.J.O.	1999	
	P.G.M.O.	2010	
Ffrench, Aubrey Eugene		—	2008
Fidler, Ronald George	P.A.G.D.C.	1986	1981
Field, David William	P.A.G.D.C.	2005	2004
Field, James John	P.G.St.B.	2004	2000
Fielder, Colin Charles	P.A.G.D.C.	2006	2008
Fielder, Keith Frederick	P.A.G.St.B.	2010	
Fields, Richard Berkeley	P.A.G.D.C.	2001	1999
	P.G.J.O.	2008	
Figov, Justin Gerald	P.G.St.B.	1987	1984
	Dist.G.M., South Africa, (Western Division)	1991-1996	
Findlay, Archibald	P.A.G.D.C.	2011	2007
Finlayson, John Henry	P.A.G.D.C.	1990	1987
	P.G.S.D.	1998	
Finlinson, Gilbert Crellin		—	2010

NAME	RANK	YEAR OF APPT.	R.A.M.G.R. YEAR OF APPT.
Finney, Alan Charles		—	2004
Finney, Geoffrey William	P.A.G.D.C.	1989	1987
	G.S.D.	1994	
	P.G.J.O.	2002	
Firban, Thomas Norman	P.A.G.D.C.	1981	
	P.G.S.D.	1986	
	P.G.J.O.	2007	
Fisher, Anthony Duncan	P.A.G.D.C.	2005	2010
Fisher, David Nicholas	P.A.G.D.C.	2012	
Fisher, John Trollope	P.A.G.D.C.	1988	1992
	P.G.S.D.	1994	
	P.G.J.O.	1999	
	Prov.G.M., Buckinghamshire	2002-2009	
Fisher, Keith Robin		—	2009
Fisher, Ronald Albert	P.G.St.B.	1975	1994
Flaherty, Joseph	P.A.G.Swd.B.	2012	2010
Flamank, Alfred John	P.G.St.B.	1988	1986
	P.G.J.D.	2000	
Fleetwood, John	P.A.G.D.C.	2006	2006
Fleming, John	P.G.J.D.	2003	
	P.G.J.O.	2005	
Fleming, John Bothwell		—	2007
Fleming, William Oliver Rex	P.G.St.B.	2008	
Fletcher, Derek Frank	A.G.St.B.	1991	1994
	P.G.J.D.	1996	
Fletcher, Donald Herbert		—	1999
Fletcher, Frank John	P.A.G.D.C.	2008	
Fletcher, Gordon	P.A.G.D.C.	1995	2001
Fletcher, George Newton, *T.D.*	G.Stwd.	1978	1985
	G.S.D.	1984	
	P.G.J.O.	1990	
	Prov.G.M., Northumberland	1991-1999	
Fletcher, Malcolm Clay	P.A.G.Swd.B.	2007	2006
Flight, Graham Leslie	P.A.G.D.C.	2001	2007
	P.G.S.D.	2009	
Flint, Jack Ernest	P.G.St.B.	2004	
	P.G.S.D.	2009	
Flint, Michael Joseph	P.G.St.B.	2005	2005
	P.G.J.D.	2012	
Flitcroft, Roger William	P.A.G.D.C.	1998	2001
	G.S.D.	2006	
Floodgate, Charles Alexander	P.A.G.D.C.	2003	2003
Florence, Keith Leslie	P.A.G.D.C.	2002	2006
	P.G.S.D.	2009	
Flower, Ronald Frank	P.A.G.D.C.	1995	
	P.G.S.D.	2006	
Flynn, Michael John, *J.P.*	P.G.S.D.	2004	
	G.S.O.	2009	
Foertsch, Heinz	P.A.G.D.C.	1988	1995
Fogarty, Vivian John	A.G.D.C.	2003	2003
Fogden, John Frederick	P.G.St.B.	2007	1998

NAME	RANK	YEAR OF APPT.	R.A.M.G.R. YEAR OF APPT.
Fok, David Alistair	P.A.G.D.C.	2005	
	P.G.S.D.	2008	
Fok, Joseph Paul	P.A.G.D.C.	2008	
Follett, Maurice Hardiman	P.A.G.D.C.	2000	2008
	P.G.S.D.	2010	
Ford, David William Kenneth	P.A.G.D.C.	2005	2006
Ford, Nigel Allen Langley	P.A.G.D.C.	1993	1997
	P.G.J.D.	2003	
Ford, Rex Marchington	P.A.G.St.B.	2008	2011
Ford, Roy William	P.G.St.B.	2009	2011
Ford, Sydney David	P.G.St.B.	2007	
Fordham, Jack Colin	—		1998
Fordyce, Brian Gordon	P.A.G.St.B.	2005	2011
Fordyce, Peter John	P.A.G.D.C.	1999	
Foreman, Bernard Alan	A.G.D.C.	1988	1998
	P.G.S.D.	2002	
Forrest, Malcolm Jeffrey	A.G.Org.	2010	
Forrester, Michael James	P.A.G.D.C.	1994	
Forrester, Roy Hilton	—		1999
Forsey, Maurice Roy	P.A.G.D.C.	2001	2003
Forster, Douglas John	G.Stwd.	2011	
Forster, James Harry	P.G.St.B.	1989	
Forster, James Orman	P.A.G.D.C.	1999	1993
Forster, Peter Watson	P.A.G.Swd.B.	2007	
Forster, Richard	G.Stwd.	2012	2011
Forsyth, John Graham	G.Stwd.	1977	1974
	P.G.J.D.	1982	
	P.G.J.O.	1988	
	P.G.M.O.	1998	
Forsyth, Ronald Alexander	P.A.G.D.C.	2004	2005
Fortune, Patrick Joseph	P.G.St.B.	1992	1994
Foster, Anthony Roy	Dep.G.Swd.B.	2007	2006
Foster, Colin Vaughan	P.A.G.D.C.	1999	1999
	P.G.J.D.	2011	
Foster, Derek Stanley	P.A.G.St.B.	1999	2010
	P.G.J.D.	2009	
Foster, Ian	P.G.St.B.	2012	
Foster, John	P.G.St.B.	2007	
Foster, Michael John	P.G.St.B.	2012	
Foster, Peter Neil	P.A.G.D.C.	1998	
	P.G.J.D.	2008	
Foster, Roger Kenneth	P.A.G.D.C.	2012	
Fotheringham, Peter Ernest Albert	P.A.G.D.C.	1994	1992
Fotinakis, Gerald Roland	P.G.S.D.	2007	
Fountain, Dr. Robert Hugh	P.A.G.D.C.	2000	
	P.G.J.D.	2011	
Fourie, Louis Philip	P.G.St.B.	1990	
	P.G.J.D.	2003	
Fowler, John	P.A.G.St.B.	2002	2010
Fox, Andrew	P.G.St.B.	2011	1998
Fox, David George	P.A.G.D.C.	1999	2002
	P.G.S.D.	2006	
	G.J.O.	2011	

NAME	RANK	YEAR OF APPT.	R.A.M.G.R. YEAR OF APPT.
Fox, Dr. Dennis Henry, *M.B.E.*	G.S.D.	1992	1994
	G.S.O.	1998	
	P.G.J.W.	2010	
Fox, Francis	G.Stwd.	1990	2001
	P.G.J.D.	1996	
Fox, Frederick	P.G.St.B.	2004	
	P.G.J.D.	2012	
Foxcroft, Raymond Cyril	P.A.G.D.C.	2002	
Foxwell, Eric	P.A.G.D.C.	1999	2010
	P.G.J.O.	2011	
Frais, Stephen	P.A.G.D.C.	2005	
Frampton, George Henry	P.A.G.Swd.B.	2005	
Francis, Frederick Arthur	P.A.G.St.B.	1989	1991
	P.G.J.D.	2001	
Francis, Leslie Frederick	G.Stwd.	2012	
Francis, Robert Burns	P.G.St.B.	2007	2005
Francois, Brian Derek	P.G.St.B.	2003	2006
	P.G.J.D.	2012	
Franklin, Charles Walter	P.A.G.Swd.B.	1993	2001
Franklin, Nigel Dennis	P.G.St.B.	2002	2008
Franklin, Peter	P.A.G.D.C.	2012	
Fraser, Colin Eric	P.A.G.D.C.	2004	
Fraser-Platt, George Robert	P.A.G.D.C.	1987	
	P.G.S.D.	1994	
	P.G.J.O.	2006	
Free, Morris Sydney		—	2000
Freedman, Charles, *C.B.*	A.G.D.C.	1976	1992
	P.G.S.D.	1987	
	P.G.J.O.	1992	
Freedman, Philip	P.G.I.G.	2006	2004
Freedman, Steven Derek	G.Stwd.	1999	
	P.G.J.D.	2004	
Freeman, Cecil	P.A.G.D.C.	1987	1990
	P.G.S.D.	1994	
	P.G.J.O.	2002	
Freeman, David Spencer	P.A.G.D.C.	2007	
	P.G.J.D.	2010	
Freeman, Leonard Maurice	P.A.G.D.C.	2009	2002
Freeman, Morris	P.G.St.B.	1999	2011
	P.G.J.D.	2009	
Freeman, Roger Wilfred	P.A.G.Swd.B.	2002	2003
	P.G.J.D.	2008	
Freeman, Walter	P.A.G.D.C.	2003	
Fretten, Raymond George, *B.Sc.*	P.A.G.D.C.	1996	1994
	P.G.S.D.	2002	
	P.G.J.O.	2007	
Friar, Donald	P.A.G.D.C.	1988	1994
	P.G.S.D.	1996	
Fricke, Gernot	P.A.G.Swd.B.	1999	2000
Friday, Robin Anthony		—	2007
Frizell, Ronald Charles Crossfield		—	1996
Froom, Alan Reginald	P.A.G.D.C.	2004	2004
	P.G.S.D.	2011	

NAME	RANK	YEAR OF APPT.	R.A.M.G.R. YEAR OF APPT.
Frost, Brian Walter	P.G.St.B.	1995	1994
	P.G.J.D.	2012	
Frost, Peter	P.A.G.D.C.	2004	2011
	G.Swd.B.	2011	
Frost, Russell Norman	P.G.St.B.	2008	
Frude, Bernard William		—	2001
Fry, Peter Michael		—	2008
Fuchter, Peter Fidelis	P.G.St.B.	1999	2002
	P.G.J.O.	2003	
Fuller, Edward Alexander	P.A.G.D.C.	1999	2001
Fuller, Michael John		—	1982
Fuller, Michael Leslie	P.G.St.B.	2011	
Funnell, Peter Charles	P.A.G.D.C.	2006	
Furber, Robin Edward	G.Swd.B.	2009	2010
Furlong, Brian William	G.Stwd.	1990	1996
	P.G.J.D.	2003	
Furness, Peter	P.A.G.Swd.B	2012	
Gabriel, Leslie William	P.A.G.D.C.	1991	1989
	P.G.S.D.	2001	
Gaby, David Francis	P.A.G.D.C.	1987	
	P.G.S.D.	1999	
Gadd-Claxton, Daniel Lawrence	P.G.J.D.	2007	2007
	P.G.S.D.	2009	
	P.G.J.O.	2011	
Gadsby, Derek Robert		—	1998
Gager, Ian Robert Farquharson	P.A.G.D.C.	2012	
Gain, Martin Thorold, *J.P.*	G.Stwd.	2002	
	P.G.J.D.	2008	
Gait, David Gareth	G.Stwd.	2003	2007
	P.G.J.D.	2008	
Gale, Godfrey	A.G.St.B.	1997	2001
Gallagher, Hugh	P.A.G.D.C.	2008	
Gallear, David Harry	G.Stwd.	2002	2008
	P.G.J.D.	2007	
Galt, Peter Richard	G.Stwd.	1987	1993
	P.G.J.D.	1992	
	P.G.J.O.	1999	
Gambarini, Jose Luiz	P.G.J.D.	2009	2011
Gamble, Graham Bryan	P.A.G.Swd.B.	2011	
Gambrill, Frank Edwin		—	2008
Gan, Richard Ludwik, *B.A., B.Sc., M.Ed.*	G.Stwd.	1992	1993
	A.G.Sec.	1996-2005	
	P.G.S.D.	1997	
	P.G.J.O.	2002	
	Dep.G.Sec.	2005-2009	
	P.G.M.O.	2006	
Gangadeen, Jeremiah Daniel	P.A.G.D.C.	1996	2000
	P.G.S.D.	2001	
	P.G.J.O.	2007	
Gant, John Leslie	P.A.G.D.C.	1985	
Garcia, Stephen	P.A.G.D.C.	2011	2009
Gardener, Michael Trevor	P.G.St.B.	2005	2004

NAME	RANK	YEAR OF APPT.	R.A.M.G.R. YEAR OF APPT.
Gardiner, Frederick William, *C.St.J.*	P.G.J.D.	2004	2001
	P.G.J.O.	2011	
Gardner, Ernest	P.A.G.D.C.	2007	
Gardner, Ronald		—	2007
Gardner, Roy Harold	P.G.St.B.	2000	2001
Garland, James	P.A.G.D.C.	2003	
Garlick, Royston Frederick	P.A.G.D.C.	2002	
Garner, Alfred Edward	P.G.J.D.	1975	2000
	P.G.J.O.	1994	
Garnett, Henry Alan John	G.Stwd.	2006	2008
	P.G.J.D.	2011	
Garratt, Michael John	P.A.G.D.C.	2007	2009
Garratt, Raymond William	P.A.G.D.C.	2008	
Garrett, Robert George	P.A.G.D.C.	1999	2000
	P.G.J.D.	2004	
Garrow, Clarry Alexander	P.A.G.D.C.	2007	2005
Garston, David Alexander	P.A.G.D.C.	2001	2004
	P.G.S.D.	2010	
Garty, Edward Rennie	G.Stwd.	2009	
	G.J.D.	2012	
Garvey, Alan	P.A.G.D.C.	1980	1978
	P.G.S.D.	1985	
	P.G.J.O.	1992	
	P.G.M.O.	2003	
Garwood-Yockney, Gerald William	P.A.G.Swd.B.	2007	2006
Gaskell, Jack Livesley	P.G.I.G	1996	
Gaskill, Roy	G.Stwd.	2007	
Gaston, Jean-Claude	P.G.J.D.	1996	
Gatehouse, Christopher Eric James	P.G.St.B.	2001	2001
Gatherum, Thomas Arthur Terrance	P.A.G.D.C.	2007	
Gaulton, David Eric		—	2010
Gaunt, Geoffrey Albert	P.G.St.B.	2012	
Gazeley, Dennis Gordon	P.A.G.D.C.	1990	1985
	P.G.S.D.	1984	
Gazzard, Simon Thomas	P.A.G.D.C.	2006	
Gee, Ronald David, *T.D.*	P.A.G.D.C.	2000	1999
	P.G.S.D.	2004	
	P.G.J.O.	2010	
Geelhoed, Jacob Johannis	G.Stwd.	2007	
	P.G.J.D.	2010	
Geeson, Roderick Joseph	G.Stwd.	2002	2008
	P.G.J.D.	2007	
Geh, Cheng Lok	P.A.G.D.C.	2007	
Gelling, David George	P.G.S.D.	2006	
Gentry, Gordon Mark, *K.L.J., B.Sc.*	P.G.St.B.	1995	1992
	P.G.S.D.	1989	
	P.G.J.O.	2006	
Genz, Plinio Virgilio	P.G.St.B.	2002	2006
	P.G.S.D.	2003	
	P.G.J.O.	2006	
George, Christopher Francis	P.A.G.St.B.	2009	2009
George, Peter Graham	P.A.G.D.C.	2007	
	P.G.S.D.	2009	
Georgiou, Eleftherios John	P.A.G.D.C.	2010	

NAME	RANK	YEAR OF APPT.	R.A.M.G.R. YEAR OF APPT.
Gerber, Victor Kwame	—		2003
Gerling, Donald Norman, *R.F.D., E.D.*	P.A.G.D.C.	2008	2008
Germain, Keith Lawrence	G.Stwd.	2000	
Gerrards, Hans-Joachim	P.A.G.D.C.	1992	1988
Gerschlowitz, Leon Morris	P.A.G.D.C.	2002	
Gettens, Michael Edward	—		2002
Gibbs, Hugh	P.G.St.B.	2006	
Gibbins, David William	P.G.St.B.	2004	
Gibson, Howard Royston	P.A.G.D.C.	1992	1992
Gibson, John	P.G.St.B.	1996	
Gibson, John Bamborough	G.Stwd.	2010	2011
Gibson, John Barton, *B.E.M.*	P.G.St.B.	1997	1999
	P.G.J.D.	1998	
	P.G.S.D.	2000	
	P.G.J.O.	2005	
	G.M.O.	2010	
Gibson, John Gilbert	P.G.St.B.	2000	
Gibson, Michael James Dehalton	G.Stwd.	2000	2006
	P.G.J.D.	2007	
Gibson, Peter Raymond	P.G.St.B.	1995	
	P.G.J.D.	2005	
Gibson, Rodney Alfred	G.Stwd.	2005	2005
	P.G.J.D.	2008	
Gibson, William Geoffrey	P.A.G.D.C.	2011	
Gibson, William Henry	P.A.G.D.C.	2010	2004
Gibson-Leitch, Allison	P.A.G.D.C.	1995	2004
Giddings, Derek Norman	P.A.G.D.C.	2008	
Giddings, John Charles	P.A.G.D.C.	2009	
Giffen, George	P.G.St.B.	2002	
Gilbert, Anthony James	G.Stwd.	2003	2002
	P.G.J.D.	2007	
Gilbert, Anthony John	A.G.D.C.	1997	2003
	P.G.S.D.	2010	
Gilbert, John Healey	P.G.St.B.	1997	1995
	P.G.J.D.	2004	
	P.G.J.O.	2011	
Gilbert, John Witmore	G.St.B.	1994	
Gilbert, Keith	P.A.G.D.C.	2004	2011
Gilbert, William Douglas	P.A.G.St.B.	1997	
Gilbertson, Brian Francis	P.G.I.G.	2002	2001
Giles, William	P.A.G.D.C.	1995	1994
Gilks, Ronald	G.Stwd.	1996	2009
	P.G.J.O.	2008	
Gill, Gaspar Llewellyn	P.A.G.D.C.	2007	2009
	P.G.S.D.	2012	
Gill, Gilbert Laurence	P.G.St.B.	2009	
Gill, Stephen Courtney Ray		—	2007
Gillanders, Norman John	P.A.G.D.C.	1988	
Gillespie, Philip John	P.G.St.B.	2012	
Gillett, Henry Maesmor John	P.A.G.D.C.	1995	1997
	P.G.S.D.	2002	
	P.G.J.O.	2006	

NAME	RANK	YEAR OF APPT.	R.A.M.G.R. YEAR OF APPT.
Gillhespy, William	P.G.S.D.	1973	1983
	P.G.J.O.	1983	
	Prov.G.M. Durham	1984-1995	
Gillo, Frederick John	P.A.G.D.C.	2002	2007
	P.G.S.D.	2005	
	P.G.S.O.	2010	
Gilmer, James Melrose Vance	P.G.St.B.	2012	
Gilmore, Robert Charles	P.G.St.B.	1963	
	P.G.J.O.	1968	
	P.G.M.O.	1986	
Ginger, Henry John	P.A.G.Swd.B.	2001	2004
Girard-Augry, Pierre	P.G.St.B.	1994	
Gittins, Richard William	A.G.D.C.	2002	2007
Givans, Robert John	P.G.St.B.	1998	2005
Glass, David	P.A.G.D.C.	2003	
Glass, Edward Clive	A.G.Swd.B.	1987	
Glassbrook, George	P.A.G.D.C.	1997	
	P.G.S.D.	2005	
Glazier, Alan	P.G.St.B.	1998	2002
	G.J.D.	2003	
Gleghorn, Thomas		—	2006
Glenister, John Julian		—	2003
Glover, Richard	P.A.G.Swd.B.	2007	2011
Glyn, Philip Charles	P.A.G.D.C.	1985	1998
Goadby, Philip Gerald	P.G.St.B.	1989	
Godfrey, Anton Peter		—	1995
Godfrey-Cass, Douglas Leslie	P.A.G.D.C.	1987	1989
	P.G.S.D.	1994	
	P.G.J.O.	1997	
	P.G.S.O.	2002	
Godwin, Isaac White	P.G.St.B.	2003	1996
Goedbloed, Robert	P.A.G.D.C.	1976	1983
	P.G.S.D.	1983	
	P.G.J.O.	1991	
	P.G.M.O.	2004	
	P.G.J.W.	2012	
Goedhals, Abraham	P.A.G.D.C.	1996	1998
	G.S.D.	2003	
	G.J.O.	2009	
Goff, Gordon Edwin	P.G.St.B.	1994	2007
	P.G.J.D.	2002	
	P.G.J.O.	2007	
	Dist.G.M., South Africa (Eastern)	2007-2012	
Golding, Leslie John Farrell	G.Stwd.	1990	1986
	P.G.J.D.	1999	
Goldsack, Gerald Leslie	P.A.G.D.C.	1996	2011
	P.G.S.D.	2010	
Goldsmith, Alan David	P.A.G.D.C.	1992	1992
	P.G.S.D.	1999	
Goldson, Denis Paul Aylward	P.G.S.D.	1996	1997
	P.G.J.O.	2007	
Goldston, Ralph Russell	P.G.St.B.	1990	1992
	P.G.J.O.	2003	
Goodchild, William Alfred	P.A.G.Swd.B.	2005	2003

NAME	RANK	YEAR OF APPT.	R.A.M.G.R. YEAR OF APPT.
Gooder, Thomas Herbert	P.A.G.D.C.	1987	
Goodfellow, Kenneth Henry	P.A.G.St.B.	1999	2006
Gooding, Cyril Guy		—	1991
Gooding, Gordon Rothwell	P.A.G.D.C.	2006	
Goodman, Geoffrey Alan	P.A.G.D.C.	1990	1992
	P.G.S.D.	1995	
Goodwin, Edwn Bryant	P.G.J.D.	2003	2001
	P.G.J.O.	2007	
Goonetileke, Henry Malin	P.A.G.D.C.	2001	
	P.G.S.D.	2011	
Gopalakrishnan, Rajubettan		—	2009
Gordon, Robert Paterson	P.G.St.B.	2008	2011
Gore, Reginald James	P.G.St.B.	1991	
Gore-Browne, Eric Roy	P.A.G.D.C.	2001	2002
	Prov.G.M., North and East Yorkshire	2004	
Gornall, James	P.A.G.D.C.	1973	
	P.G.S.D.	1983	
Gornall, James Pollock Burnard	P.A.G.D.C.	1973	
Goss, Norman Sydney	P.A.G.Swd.B.	2004	
Gough, Philip	P.A.G.D.C.	2009	
Gough, Rt.Hon. Viscount Shane Hugh Maryon	P.G.J.D.	2002	1999
Gould, Harold, *O.B.E., J.P., D.L.*	P.A.G.D.C.	1992	1991
	P.G.J.D.	1995	
	P.G.J.O.	2002	
	G.S.O.	2006	
Gould, Thomas William James, *J.P.*	P.A.G.D.C.	2000	
	P.G.S.D.	2006	
Gower, Harry	G.Stwd.	1993	1988
Gower, Paul John	P.A.G.D.C.	2009	
Grace, Charles Raymond	P.A.G.D.C.	2010	
Grace, Benjamin William	P.A.G.D.C.	1997	1998
	P.G.S.D.	2009	
Graham, Albert Waide	P.A.G.D.C.	2000	2000
	P.G.J.D.	2005	
Graham, David Andrew	P.A.G.D.C.	1994	
Graham, George	P.A.G.St.B.	1996	
Graham, John	P.G.I.G.	1999	
Graham, Malcolm James		—	2010
Graham, Michael	P.G.St.B.	2008	
Graham, Michael	P.A.G.D.C.	2009	
Graham, Thomas		—	2001
Graham, William Stanley	P.A.G.Swd.B.	2001	
Grahamslaw, William	A.G.St.B.	2008	2005
Grainger, Victor Ernest	P.A.G.D.C.	2003	
Granger, Martin Albert		—	2011
Granger, Richard Brian	P.A.G.D.C.	2005	
Grant, Alexander Angus	P.A.G.D.C.	2000	1998
Grant, Andrew George	P.A.G.D.C.	2007	
Grant, Harold	G.Stwd.	1986	1993
	P.G.J.D.	1995	
	P.G.J.O.	2004	
Grant, Peter William	P.G.St.B.	2008	2010

NAME	RANK	YEAR OF APPT.	R.A.M.G.R. YEAR OF APPT.
Grant, William Forbes	P.G.St.B.	1997	2006
	P.G.J.D.	2008	
Grantham, Gordon Harold	P.G.St.B.	2003	
	P.G.J.D.	2010	
Graves, David Walter	G.Stwd.	1980	1988
	G.J.D.	1987	
Graves, Gordon Nicholson	G.Stwd.	2008	
	P.G.J.D.	2012	
Gray, James Stewart	G.Stwd.	2003	
	P.G.J.D.	2008	
Gray, Ralph Eric	P.A.G.Swd.B.	2009	2003
Gray, Roger Thomas Alfred	P.A.G.Swd.B.	2010	
Gray, Terence William	P.G.St.B.	2007	2009
Gray, Thomas William	P.G.St.B.	2011	
Gray, Trevor Clive	P.A.G.D.C.	2010	
Green, Ashley Norman	P.A.G.D.C.	2005	2008
Green, Challoner Arthur		—	2010
Green, David John	A.G.D.C.	2001	2001
	P.G.S.D.	2006	
	P.G.J.O.	2011	
Green, Garth Ratcliffe	G.Stwd.	2012	
Green, George	P.A.G.St.B.	2005	
Green, Gilbert Harold		—	1986
Green, Gordon George	P.G.St.B.	2007	2009
Green, James Albert	P.A.G.D.C.	2003	2004
	Prov.G.M., Gloucestershire & Herefordshire	2010	
Green, Jeffery Michael	P.A.G.D.C.	2008	
Green, Jeffery Richard		—	2006
Green, Jeffery Robert	P.A.G.D.C.	2003	2006
	P.G.S.D.	2008	
	P.G.J.O.	2011	
Green, John Edwin	G.Stwd.	1991	2001
	P.G.J.D.	2000	
	G.S.O.	2005	
Green, Keith Francis	P.A.G.D.C.	2010	
Green, Norman Kynaston	P.A.G.D.C.	1987	
Green, Peter Sidney	P.A.G.D.C.	2002	2005
	P.G.S.D.	2006	
	P.G.J.O.	2008	
Green, Reginald Henry, *J.P.*	P.A.G.D.C.	2001	2007
	P.G.S.D.	2006	
Green, Maj.Gen. Rudolph George Edward	P.G.S.D.	1997	2001
	P.G.J.O.	2006	
	P.G.J.W.	2008	
Greenacre, Christopher John	P.G.St.B.	2010	
Greene, Anthony Charles	P.A.G.D.C.	2009	
Greenfield, Clive Thomas	A.G.Swd.B.	1995	1999
Greenhalf, Alec William Brenchley	P.G.I.G.	1997	1982
Greenhalgh, David	P.A.G.D.C.	2012	
Greenhalgh, Gordon Mather	G.Stwd.	1992	1994
	P.G.J.D.	1997	
	P.G.J.O.	2002	

NAME	RANK	YEAR OF APPT.	R.A.M.G.R. YEAR OF APPT.
Greenland, David Charles	P.A.G.Swd.B.	2002	2001
	P.G.J.D.	2012	
Greenman, Clement William	P.G.St.B.	2007	
Greenwall, Julian James	G.Stwd.	2010	2006
Greenwood, Alan	G.Stwd.	1995	1998
	P.G.J.D.	2005	
Greenwood, Paul	G.St.B.	2010	
Gregory, Allan Roger	P.A.G.Swd.B.	2010	
Gregory, Edward Sinclair	P.A.G.D.C.	1992	1995
Gregory, Robert Leonard		—	2009
Grenfell, Graham James	P.G.St.B.	2002	2003
Greswell, Anthony Alan	P.A.G.D.C.	2007	
Griffin, Alexander	P.A.G.D.C.	2003	
Griffin, Derek John	A.G.D.C.	2006	2009
	P.G.J.D.	2011	
Griffin, Edgar Vincent	A.G.I.G.	1962	1990
	P.G.St.B.	1984	
	G.J.D.	1992	
	P.G.J.D.	2008	
Griffin, Edward Francis	P.A.G.D.C.	2007	
Griffith, David Michael		—	2005
Griffith, Jack Vaughan	G.Stwd.	1981	1995
	P.G.J.D.	1986	
	P.G.J.O.	1991	
Griffiths, Alan Bevan, *J.P.*	P.A.G.Swd.B.	2011	
Griffiths, Alan Quintus	P.A.G.Swd.B.	2003	
Griffiths, Capt. Antony Raymond	G.Stwd.	1976	1981
	P.G.J.D.	1982	
	P.G.J.O.	2003	
Griffiths, John Middleton	P.A.G.D.C.	2008	
Griffiths, Oliver Denzil	P.A.G.D.C.	2009	2010
Griggs, William Maximillian, *C.B.E.*	P.G.St.B.	1991	
	P.G.J.D.	2008	
Grill, Jacques	P.A.G.D.C.	1995	
Grillage, Michael George Trewartha		—	2005
Grimsey, Gordon Wilfrid	P.G.St.B.	1986	
Grimster, Gordon Frederick	P.G.St.B.	2011	
Grindle, John Gordon	P.G.St.B.	2006	
Grisdale, Harry Stanley	P.A.G.D.C.	1987	1991
Groeger, Steven	P.A.G.D.C.	2011	
Grönmark, Bjarne Gerald	P.A.G.D.C.	1990	1993
Groom, John Derek		—	2007
Groom, William James Lewis	P.A.G.D.C.	1999	2003
	P.G.S.D.	2005	
Grose, Venning Pearce	P.A.G.D.C.	1986	1995
Grosskopff, Rodney Edward	P.A.G.St.B.	1993	2001
	P.G.J.D.	1995	
	P.G.J.O.	2003	
Grout, Noel Alfred Brian	P.A.G.D.C.	1982	1984
	G.S.D.	1987	
	P.G.J.O.	1993	
	P.G.M.O.	2007	

NAME	RANK	YEAR OF APPT.	R.A.M.G.R. YEAR OF APPT.
Grove, Richard Charles	G.Stwd.	2008	
	P.G.J.D.	2011	
Grover, Terence James	P.A.G.D.C.	2004	
Groves, Alan Joseph	P.A.G.D.C.	1996	
Groves, John David	P.A.G.D.C.	2000	
	P.G.S.D.	2003	
Grube, Eugene Ferdinand George	P.A.G.D.C.	1991	
Grummitt, Robert Neville	G.Stwd.	2005	2008
	P.G.S.D.	2009	
Grundmann, Robert Rolf	P.G.St.B.	1995	1997
	P.G.J.D.	2000	
	P.G.S.D.	2005	
	P.G.J.O.	2010	
Gudka, Hansraj Fulchand	P.A.G.D.C.	2008	2009
Gudsell, Peter Brian	P.G.S.D.	2003	
Guest, Michael William	P.G.S.D.	2000	2000
	P.G.S.O.	2005	
	G.J.W.	2011	
Guest, Roger Frank	A.G.D.C.	2008	
Guile, Michael Ian	P.A.G.D.C.	2012	
Guilmant, John Henry	P.A.G.D.C.	1979	
	P.G.S.D.	1984	
Guise, Revd. John Christopher	P.A.G.Chap.	2006	
Guiver, Leonard Albert Charles	P.G.St.B.	2006	
Gunary, William Malcolm Asheton	P.A.G.Swd.B.	1998	1998
	P.G.S.D.	2003	
	P.G.J.O.	2008	
Gunn, Roy Buckingham	P.G.St.B.	1995	
Gunnery, Cedric	Dep.G.D.C.	1976-1978	1984
	P.G.J.O.	1981	
	G.D.C.	1984-1989	1984 GMRAC (H.C.)
	P.G.M.O.	1985	
	P.G.J.W.	1988	
	P.G.S.W.	2005	
Gunning, Peter Arthur	P.G.St.B.	2002	1999
	P.G.J.D.	2011	
Gunning, Philip Harry	G.Stwd.	2012	
Gunther, Norbert Ernst Alfred	P.G.St.B.	2008	
Gurney, David Anthony	P.A.G.D.C.	2007	2005
	P.G.S.D.	2011	
Guthrie, Raymond	P.A.G.D.C.	2003	2004
	P.G.S.D.	2004	
	P.G.S.O.	2008	
Gutteridge, Michael John	P.G.St.B.	1997	1998
	P.G.S.D.	1999	
	P.G.J.O.	2003	
	Prov.G.M., Nottinghamshire	2007-2012	
Gutteridge, Richard Vernon	A.G.D.C.	2005	
	G.S.D.	2011	
Guttridge, Lyn John	P.A.G.D.C.	2002	
	P.G.S.D.	2008	
Guy, Andrew Albert James	P.A.G.St.B.	1991	
Guy, Danny	P.A.G.D.C.	2005	2009
	P.G.S.D.	2011	

NAME	RANK	YEAR OF APPT.	R.A.M.G.R. YEAR OF APPT.
Guy, Stanley Harry	A.G.D.C.	1988	
Gwilliam, Charles Walter	P.A.G.D.C.	2007	
Gwilliam, Gordon Frederick	P.G.St.B.	1998	2006
Gwynn, Col. Charles Morgan, T.D.	P.A.G.D.C.	2012	
Gyesie, Abraham	P.A.G.D.C.	2008	
Hadden, Peter	P.A.G.D.C.	1999	2001
	P.G.S.D.	2004	
Hadler, Clarence Alfred Stuart	P.G.St.B.	2010	
Hadlett, Peter William Thomas	P.A.G.D.C.	2008	2011
Hadley, Clifford William	P.G.St.B.	1994	1997
	G.S.D.	2000	
	P.G.J.O.	2007	
Hadwick, Raymond	P.A.G.St.B.	1997	
	P.G.J.D.	2003	
Haffenden, Bertram James	P.A.G.D.C.	1993	2009
Haggar, David Victor	P.A.G.D.C.	2009	
	P.G.S.D.	2012	
Hagger, William Jack	P.A.G.D.C.	2002	
	P.G.S.D.	2011	
Haggett, Mervyn Terence	P.A.G.Swd.B.	2012	
Hagley, Robin	P.G.St.B.	2003	2010
Haile, Joseph Brook	P.G.St.B.	1989	
	G.J.D.	1998	
Hainsworth, Leslie	P.A.G.St.B.	2012	
Halahan, John Ibrahim Baharum	A.G.I.G.	1994	2008
	G.I.G.	1995	
	P.G.J.D.	2008	
Hale, Dennis	P.A.G.D.C.	1998	
	P.G.J.D.	2011	
Hale, Gerald	P.G.St.B.	1996	
	P.G.J.D.	2002	
Hale, Graham	G.Stwd.	2002	
Hale, John	G.Stwd.	1973	1976
	G.J.D.	1978	1985 GMRAC
	P.G.J.O.	1983	
	Prov.G.M., Cumberland & Westmorland	1984-1990	
	A.G.M.	1990-1993	1990 AGM
	Dep.G.M.	1994-1999	1994 DepGM
	ProG.M.	2000-2010	
Hale, Martyn Ronald	P.A.G.D.C.	2007	
Hale, Sidney	P.G.St.B.	1998	1998
	G.J.D.	2003	
	P.G.J.O.	2009	
Hales, Rodney Stuart	P.A.G.D.C.	2008	2010
Halewood, Alan George		—	2009
Hall, Alan	P.A.G.D.C.	2000	2002
	G.S.D.	2008	
Hall, Brian William	P.A.G.Swd.B.	2008	2011
Hall, Frederick William	P.A.G.D.C.	2006	2009
	P.G.S.D.	2011	
Hall, Geoffrey	P.A.G.Swd.B.	2009	
Hall, Graham Stanley	P.G.St.B.	2011	

NAME	RANK	YEAR OF APPT.	R.A.M.G.R. YEAR OF APPT.
Hall, Kenneth William	P.A.G.St.B.	1977	1990
	P.G.J.D.	1989	
Hall, Michael Youdan	G.Stwd.	2010	
Hall, Oliver Newman	P.G.St.B.	1992	2002
Hall, Raymond Hardy	P.G.St.B.	1995	
Hall, Robert	A.G.I.G.	2007	2009
Hall, Robert Gorton	G.Stwd.	2002	
	P.G.J.D.	2007	
	P.G.J.O.	2012	
Hall, Walter	P.A.G.D.C.	2003	2006
	G.S.D.	2009	
Hall, William Barrington		—	2007
Hall, Youdan John Thomas	P.A.G.D.C.	1997	2000
	P.G.J.D.	2011	
Hallam, Richard Marvin	P.A.G.D.C.	2011	
Hallam, William Ellis		—	2008
Hallberg, Stephen Charles	A.G.Swd.B.	2012	
Halliday, John Christopher		—	2003
Halliday, Thomas Norman	P.G.St.B.	2001	1999
Halls-Dickerson, Peter George	G.Stwd.	1990	1998
	P.G.J.D.	1995	
	Prov.G.M., Middlesex	2001	
Halnan, Patrick John	P.A.G.Swd.B.	2004	
Halsey, Roy William		—	2004
Halstead, Henry	P.G.St.B.	1986	
Hambidge, Gerald Frederick	G.Stwd.	2008	2009
	P.G.J.D.	2011	
Hambleton, Stuart James Howard		—	2011
Hamel, Carl Andre Sydney	P.A.G.D.C.	2004	2002
Hamel-Cooke, Peter Kirk	P.G.St.B.	2006	
Hamill, Revd. Keith Graham		—	2010
Hamilton, David Neil	G.Stwd.	2010	
Hamilton, Huntley		—	2002
Hammond, Dennis Roy	P.A.G.D.C.	2009	2007
	P.G.J.D.	2011	
Hammond, John Aubrey	G.S.D.	1975	1976
	G.J.O.	1980	1991 GMRAC (H.C.)
	Prov.G.M., Staffs. & Shrops.	1987-2002	
Hammond, Peter Dennis	G.St.B.	1980	1984
Hammond, Walter	P.G.St.B.	1993	1996
Hampton, Harold Wilford	P.A.G.D.C.	1994	2003
	P.G.S.D.	2005	
	P.G.J.O.	2012	
Hanchett, John Albert	P.G.I.G.	1996	2010
	P.A.G.D.C.	2003	
Hancock, Ernest Stewart	G.Stwd.	1979	1990
	P.G.J.D.	1984	
	P.G.J.O.	1992	
Hancock, John Norman David	P.A.G.D.C.	2002	
	P.G.J.D.	2012	
Hancock, Robert William	G.Stwd.	2009	2009
	P.G.J.D.	2012	
Hancock, Rodney Stanley	P.A.G.D.C.	2012	

NAME	RANK	YEAR OF APPT.	R.A.M.G.R. YEAR OF APPT.
Hancock, Timothy	P.G.St.B.	2000	2002
	G.J.D.	2009	
Handford, John Richard Henry	G.I.G.	2005	2006
	P.G.J.D.	2008	
Hanford, Gerald Charles	P.A.G.Swd.B.	2004	
Hanfrey, Peter	P.A.G.D.C.	2009	
Hanglin, Marcial	—		1993
Hannabuss, Clifford Arthur	P.A.G.D.C.	2002	
	G.Swd.B.	2007	
	P.G.J.O.	2012	
Hannagan, Lt.Cdr. Angus Patrick Douglas, *R.D.*	P.A.G.D.C.	2009	2010
	A.G.Sec.	2010-2011	
	Dep.G.Sec.	2012	
Hansard, Joseph Roger	P.G.St.B.	2010	
Harborne, Leslie Raymond	P.G.St.B.	1989	1999
	G.J.D.	1995	
	P.G.J.O.	2007	
Harborne, Wg.Cdr. Peter Nigel Isom	P.G.S.D.	2003	2006
	P.G.J.O.	2008	
	Prov.G.M., Buckinghamshire	2009	
Hardaker, Richard Henry	P.A.G.D.C.	2012	
Harden, David George	P.G.I.G.	1997	2002
	P.A.G.D.C.	2009	
Hardiman, Anthony John		—	2011
Harding, Hon. Justice Cornelius Augustine Iashami, *O.R.S.L.*	P.G.J.D.	2009	
Harding, Vernon Richard	P.A.G.D.C.	2009	
Harding, William Henry	P.A.G.D.C.	2012	
Hardman, James Thomas	P.G.St.B.	1999	2001
	G.J.D.	2005	
Hardy, John Bernard	P.A.G.D.C.	1993	1989
	P.G.S.D.	2010	
Hardy, Robert Thomas	P.G.St.B.	1995	
Hargate, Robert John	A.G.D.C.	2012	
Hanfrey, Peter		—	2004
Hanks, David	P.G.St.B.	2008	
Hargreaves, David Ian	P.A.G.D.C.	2012	
Hargreaves, Frederick Ernest	A.G.D.C.	1996	2004
	P.G.S.D.	2002	
	P.G.J.O.	2008	
Hargreaves, John	P.A.G.Swd.B.	2000	2004
Hargreaves, John Arkwright	P.A.G.D.C.	1993	1994
	P.G.J.D.	1995	
	P.G.J.O.	2000	
Hargreaves, Kenneth		—	2008
Hargreaves, Peter	P.A.G.Swd.B.	1999	2002
	P.G.J.D.	2007	
	P.G.J.O.	2012	
Harindran, Col. Ramalingam	P.G.St.B.	2003	
	P.G.S.D.	2007	
Harker, James Edward	P.G.S.D.	1995	1997
	P.G.J.O.	2003	
Harkness, Keith Richard	P.A.G.D.C.	2006	
	P.G.J.D.	2011	

NAME	RANK	YEAR OF APPT.	R.A.M.G.R. YEAR OF APPT.
Harman, Charles Edwin	P.G.St.B.	2009	2008
Harmshaw, John Kay	P.A.G.D.C.	2001	2008
Harries, Dan Robert	P.A.G.D.C.	1993	
Harries, Keith Harding	P.A.G.D.C.	2012	
Harrigan, Wilbur Alister, O.B.E.	P.A.G.D.C.	2004	2010
	P.G.J.D.	2009	
Harriman, Stanley William	P.A.G.D.C.	1988	1985
	G.S.D.	1999	
Harris, Colin Frank	P.A.G.D.C.	2003	2008
	P.G.J.O.	2011	
Harris, Dr. Donald Garvin, O.B.E., J.P.	G.Stwd.	1980	1992
	P.G.J.D.	1994	
	P.G.J.O.	2003	
Harris, Edward George		—	1994
Harris, Frederick Alfred Dennis	P.A.G.D.C.	1997	1995
Harris, Glenwood John	P.A.G.St.B.	2008	
Harris, Ian	P.G.St.B.	1998	1999
	P.A.G.D.C.	2008	
Harris, Ivor Gordon	P.A.G.D.C.	2009	2008
Harris, James	P.G.St.B.	2011	
Harris, John Allan	P.A.G.St.B.	2005	2006
Harris, John Charles Wilfred	P.G.St.B.	2002	2006
	P.A.G.D.C.	2008	
Harris, John Duke	P.G.St.B.	2006	
Harris, Robert	P.A.G.D.C.	2000	2007
Harris, Ronald	P.A.G.D.C.	2003	2006
Harris, Ronald Sparling	P.A.G.D.C.	2001	2004
Harris, Stanley James	G.Stwd.	1993	1996
	P.G.J.D.	1999	
	P.G.J.O.	2012	
Harris, Terence Victor	P.A.G.St.B.	2010	
Harris, William John Walter	P.A.G.D.C.	2008	2003
Harrison, Brian	G.Std.B.	2005	
Harrison, Charles Neville	P.A.G.St.B.	2008	
Harrison, David Walter	P.A.G.D.C.	2001	2000
Harrison, Geoffrey McEwan	P.A.G.Swd.B.	2004	2005
	P.G.S.D.	2010	
Harrison, George Ernest	P.A.G.Swd.B.	2004	2007
Harrison, James Anthony	P.A.G.D.C.	1999	2006
	P.G.S.D.	2005	
	P.G.J.O.	2008	
Harrison, John Brockett	P.G.St.B.	2003	
Harrison, Joseph Raine	P.A.G.St.B.	1995	2001
	P.G.J.D.	2005	
Harrison, Keith Michael	A.G.D.C.	2005	2011
Harrison, Kenneth Alan	P.A.G.D.C.	1995	
	P.G.S.D.	2005	
Harrison, Philip Maxfield	P.A.G.D.C.	2005	2006
	P.G.S.D.	2011	
Harrison, Trevor John, J.P.	G.Stwd.	2001	2000
	P.G.J.D.	2007	
Harry, Revd. Bruce David	A.G.Chap.	2001	2004
	Dep.G.Chap.	2012	

NAME	RANK	YEAR OF APPT.	R.A.M.G.R. YEAR OF APPT.
Harry, Robert Ramsay	P.A.G.D.C.	1995	2006
	P.G.S.D.	2009	
Hart, John	P.A.G.D.C.	2005	2005
Hart, Michael Henry	P.A.G.D.C.	1994	2004
	P.G.S.D.	2005	
Hart, Oliver Nicolas Norwood	P.G.S.D.	2002	2009
Hartburn, Neil Robert	P.G.St.B.	1996	2010
	G.J.D.	2002	
Hartley, Clifford	P.A.G.St.B.	2005	
Hartley, David, F.C.A.	A.G.I.G.	2008	2002
Hartley, Geoffrey	P.A.G.D.C.	1987	1994
	P.G.S.D.	1994	
	P.G.J.O.	2001	
Hartley, Robert Keith	P.A.G.D.C.	2012	
Hartley, Royston George	A.G.D.C.	2011	
Hartley, Stephen Rixon	P.A.G.D.C.	2011	
Hartshorne, Terence John		—	2004
Harvey, Antony David George	P.A.G.D.C.	2007	2011
	G.S.D.	2012	
Harvey, David Gareth	P.A.G.D.C.	2006	
Harvey, John	A.G.D.C.	2004	2009
	P.G.S.D.	2010	
Harvey, Lt.Col. Revd. John William Arthur	G.Stwd.	1995	
	P.G.S.D.	1998	
	Dep.G.Chap.	2005	
	P.G.S.O.	2009	
Harvey, Kenneth Charles	P.A.G.D.C.	2004	
	P.G.S.D.	2010	
Harvey, Oswald Theodore	G.Stwd.	1999	2000
	P.G.J.D.	2008	
Harvey, Robert Charles	P.A.G.D.C.	2008	
Harwood, Alexander James	P.G.St.B.	2002	
Harwood, Kenneth William Charles	P.A.G.St.B.	1992	1989
Harwood, Mark Kenneth	G.Stwd.	2008	
	P.G.S.D.	2011	
Haskins, Christopher Richard	P.A.G.Swd.B.	2010	2009
Haslam, John Brian, *B.Sc.*	P.G.St.B.	1995	1987
	P.G.J.D.	2000	
	P.G.J.O.	2007	
Hasler, Charles Benjamin	P.A.G.D.C.	1982	1981
Hatchett, Thomas Arthur James	P.A.G.St.B.	2008	
Hatherall, Alan George	P.A.G.D.C.	2011	
Hattam, Anthony	P.A.G.D.C.	2012	
Hatton, Christopher Francis	G.Stwd.	2006	
	P.G.J.D.	2009	
Hatton, Maurice	P.A.G.Swd.B.	2011	
Hatton, Nigel Anthony	P.G.St.B.	2003	2000
	P.G.J.D.	2011	
Hatton, Timothy Paul	P.A.G.D.C.	2008	
Haunch, Terence Osborne	A.G.D.C.	1979	
	P.G.S.D.	1989	
Hawes, Richard James	P.A.G.D.C.	2012	
Hawkard, Keith Anthony	G.Stwd.	1993	2002
	P.G.J.D.	1999	

NAME	RANK	YEAR OF APPT.	R.A.M.G.R. YEAR OF APPT.
Hawken, Donald John	P.A.G.D.C.	1993	
Hawken, Peter, *M.B.E.*	P.A.G.Swd.B.	2003	1997
	Prov.G.M., Devonshire	2006	2008 GMRAC
	Dep.Pres. Mark Ex.Comm.	2012	
Hawkes, George, Kenneth	P.G.St.B.	1992	
Hawkey, Christopher John	P.A.G.D.C.	2008	2011
Hawking, Gordon John	P.G.St.B.	2010	2011
Hawkins, Adrian Paul	P.a.G.Swd.B.	2009	2002
Hawkins, Geoffrey William	P.A.G.D.C.	2005	2005
Hawkins, Harold Desmond	P.A.G.St.B.	2005	2002
Hawkins, John Walter	G.Stwd.	1999	1997
	P.G.J.D.	2007	
Haworth, Rex Harman Arthur	P.A.G.D.C.	1976	1993
	P.G.S.D.	1997	
	P.G.J.O.	2005	
Hay, Eric David Arthur	P.G.St.B.	1995	1994
Hay, Hamilton Ian	P.A.G.Swd.B.	2002	2001
Hay, John Stuart	P.A.G.D.C.	1998	1995
Hay, Peter Rossant	Dep.G.Reg.	2008-2009	2008
Haycock, Paul Christopher	P.A.G.St.B.	2012	2004
Hayden, Frederick George James	P.A.G.D.C.	2009	
Hayes, Brian	P.A.G.D.C.	2010	
Hayes, Peter John	P.G.St.B.	2000	2011
Hayford, Eddie	P.G.St.B.	2001	
	P.G.J.D.	2008	
	P.G.S.D.	2012	
Haylett, Geoffrey	P.G.St.B.	1994	
Haylett, Roger Martin	P.A.G.D.C.	2009	
Hayman, John Stafford	P.A.G.Swd.B.	2001	2002
Haynes, William Hugh	P.A.G.D.C.	2012	2011
Haynes, William John Charles	P.G.St.B.	1984	1992
	P.G.J.D.	1994	
Haysey, Dr. Gordon Telford	Dep.G.Swd.B.	1996	2001
	P.G.J.O.	2003	
Hayward, Leonard John, *C.B.E.*	P.A.G.D.C.	1987	1985
	G.S.D.	2001	
	P.G.J.O.	2006	
Hazel, Frederick William	P.A.G.Swd.B.	1998	
Hazell, Albert	P.A.G.St.B.	1999	
Head, Eric John	P.G.St.B.	2011	2003
Head, Ronald	P.A.G.D.C.	2003	
Headdon, Colin Horace, *B.E.M.*	G.Stwd.	1993	1996
	P.G.J.D.	1998	
	P.G.J.O.	2002	
Headey, Ivor Leslie	P.A.G.Swd.B.	2010	
Headworth, Kenneth Raymond	P.A.G.D.C.	1987	
	P.G.S.D.	1996	
Heal, Barry Raymond	P.A.G.Swd.B.	2012	
Heal, John Willis	P.A.G.D.C.	1996	2004
	P.G.S.D.	2009	
Heal, Peter	P.A.G.I.G.	2009	
Heap, Henry Barry		—	2006
Heap, Trevor John Tyson	P.A.G.D.C.	2010	2011

NAME	RANK	YEAR OF APPT.	R.A.M.G.R. YEAR OF APPT.
Heard, Maj. the Rev. Herbert Charles	Dep.G.Chap	1975	
	G.Chap	1977	
Hearn, Alban Henry	P.A.G.Swd.B	1998	2010
	P.G.J.D.	2008	
Heasman, Brian George	P.A.G.Swd.B	1993	1998
	P.G.J.D.	2000	
	P.G.J.O.	2006	
Heaster, Maurice Adrian Sylvester	P.A.G.St.B.	2008	2007
Heath, Eric John	P.A.G.D.C.	1993	
	P.G.S.D.	2006	
Heath, Kenneth George	P.G.St.B.	2002	2009
Heath, Kenneth James	P.A.G.D.C.	2011	
Heath, Raymond	P.A.G.Swd.B	2010	2011
Heaton, Arthur Leslie	P.A.G.D.C.	1999	2006
Heaven, Michael Victor Rhodes	P.A.G.D.C.	2002	2003
Heaviside, Norman Eric	P.G.S.D.	2009	
Hebel, Philip John	P.A.G.D.C.	2006	2007
Heenan, Michael Richard	P.A.G.D.C.	2008	2010
	P.G.S.D.	2011	
Heezen, Robert Conrad Alexander	P.G.St.B.	2010	
Hefford, Anthony Vincent	P.A.G.D.C.	2006	
Helliar, Anthony John	G.Stwd.	2011	
Helliar, Robert	P.A.G.D.C.	2007	2010
Hellyer, Colin David	G.Stwd.	2004	2006
	P.G.J.D.	2007	
	G.S.O.	2012	
Henderson, Arnold James	P.A.G.D.C.	1997	2007
Henderson, Kent William	P.A.G.D.C.	2002	2002
	P.G.S.D.	2008	
	P.G.J.O.	2010	
Henderson, Robert Muir	A.G.D.C.	2009	2011
Henderson, Ronald Pringle	P.A.G.Swd.B	2011	
Henderson, William John Butler, *J.P.*	P.A.G.Swd.B	2000	
Hendey, John Charles	P.A.G.D.C.	1997	
	P.G.St.B.	2004	
Henry, Graham Michael	P.A.G.D.C.	2002	2006
	G.S.D.	2007	
Henshaw, Colin James		—	1995
Henson, Malcolm Stanley	P.A.G.D.C.	2009	
Herbert, Frank Victor	P.A.G.D.C.	1984	1987
Herbert, Graham Trevor	G.Stwd	1996	1998
	Dep.G.D.C.	2001-2003	2008 GMRAC
	P.G.J.O.	2006	
	G.D.C.	2007-2011	
	P.G.J.W.	2010	
Herbert, Michael Edward	P.A.G.D.C.	1987	1989
	Dep.G.D.C.	1992-1994	1997 GMRAC
	Prov.G.M., Leics. & Rutland	1995-2005	
	Pres.Gen.Bd.	2007-2009	
	A.G.M.	2010	
	Dep.G.M.	2011-2012	
Herbert, Stanley George	G.I.G.	1998	
	P.G.S.D.	2005	

NAME	RANK	YEAR OF APPT.	R.A.M.G.R. YEAR OF APPT.
Herman, Michael John	G.I.G.	2004	
	P.G.J.D.	2010	
Herpers, Marcellinus Johannes Hubertus	—		2011
Heshon, Brian Bernard	P.G.St.B.	1988	
Hesketh, Colin	P.A.G.Swd.B.	2008	
Hetherington, Carl William Victor	—		2005
Hetherington, Derek Swinburne	P.A.G.D.C.	1988	1995
	G.S.D.	1999	
Hewgill, Richard George	P.A.G.Swd.B.	1999	2006
	P.G.J.D.	2010	
Hewitt, Ronald Glyn	G.Stwd.	2010	
Heynes, Paul Alfred	P.A.G.St.B.	1988	
Heywood, Beverley John	P.A.G.D.C.	2008	
Heywood, Lawton Croswell	P.G.St.B.	2006	
	P.G.J.D.	2011	
Hick, Anthony Walter Sampson	G.Stwd.	1990	1994
	P.G.S.D.	1994	
	Prov.G.M., Somerset	1997-2004	
Hickinbottom, David James	P.A.G.Swd.B.	2000	2003
	P.G.J.D.	2008	
Hickman, John Charles William	P.G.St.B.	2012	
Hickman-Ashby, Martin James	P.G.St.B.	2011	
Hicks, Gareth Raymond	P.A.G.D.C.	2009	2011
Hicks, Kevin John	P.A.G.D.C.	2001	2006
	P.G.J.D.	2006	
	P.G.J.O.	2011	
Hicks, Trevor Charles	P.A.G.St.B.	2001	1996
	P.G.J.D.	2008	
Hickson, Kenneth	P.G.St.B.	2012	
Hide, Remo	P.A.G.D.C.	2009	2007
Higgins, Jack	—		2011
Higginson, Douglas Allan	P.A.G.D.C.	2009	
Higgs, Gordon Percival	P.A.G.D.C.	1977	1981
	P.G.S.D.	1988	
	P.G.J.O.	1992	
	P.G.S.O.	1999	
	G.Insp., Bahamas & Turks	2006-2009	
	P.G.J.W.	2009	
Higgs, Graham Charles	P.A.G.Swd.B.	2006	
Higham, Cdr. Michael Bernard Shepley, *R.N.*	P.G.J.D.	1980	
	P.G.J.W.	1987	
Higginbotham, Michael John	G.St.B.	2006	
Higson, Shaun	G.Stwd.	2012	
Hilditch, James Robert Guy	P.G.S.D.	2005	2002
	P.G.J.O.	2008	
	Prov.G.M., Oxfordshire	2012	
Hiles, Roland Edmund	P.G.J.D.	1986	1987
	Dist.G.M., S. Africa (E. Div.)	1990-1999	
Hill, Albert Norman	P.A.G.D.C.	1991	1991
Hill, Arthur William George	P.G.St.B.	2004	
Hill, Christopher William		—	2011
Hill, Colin Gordon		—	2005

NAME	RANK	YEAR OF APPT.	R.A.M.G.R. YEAR OF APPT.
Hill, Jack	P.A.G.D.C.	1985	1983
	P.G.S.D.	1994	
	P.G.J.O.	2004	
Hill, Malcolm Lewis		—	1999
Hill, Melvyn Baxter	P.A.G.D.C.	2011	
Hill, Michael Hedley	P.A.G.D.C.	1987	1998
	G.S.D.	1994	
	P.G.J.O.	2002	
Hill, Norman George		—	2008
Hill, Peter Edward		—	2009
Hills, Anthony Bernard Thomas	P.A.G.D.C.	2000	
Hills, Bernard Hugh Frank	P.G.I.G.	1994	1995
	P.A.G.D.C.	1999	
Hills, David George	P.A.G.D.C.	2005	
Hills, John William		—	1999
Hills, Trevor		—	1995
Hilton, Stephen Graham	P.A.G.D.C.	2001	
Hilton, William	P.A.G.Swd.B.	2003	
Hinchliffe, Frank Hulme	G.St.B.	2004	2002
	P.G.J.O.	2011	
Hinchliffe, Gordon Albert	P.A.G.Swd.B.	2009	
Hind, Andrew	G.Stwd.	1982	1994
	P.G.J.D.	1988	
	P.G.J.O.	1995	
Hind, Joseph Alan	P.A.G.Swd.B.	2009	2010
Hind, Col. Robert Keith	Dep.G.Swd.B.	1982	1984
	Dep.G.D.C.	1984-1986	
	G.S.O.	1989	
	G.D.C.	1990-1998	GMRAC(H.C.) 1990/98
	P.G.J.W.	1992	
	P.G.S.W.	1998	
	Prov.G.M., Middlesex	1998-2001	
	O.S.M.M.M.	2002	
Hinder, Gordon Westmoreland	P.G.St.B.	2012	
Hindes, Stephen John	P.A.G.D.C.	2008	2009
Hindle, Graham David	P.G.St.B.	2001	2008
	P.A.G.D.C.	2007	
Hirst, Charles Victor	P.G.St.B.	1994	
Hiscock, Allan James	G.Stwd.	2005	2003
	P.G.J.D.	2008	
Hitchen, George	P.A.G.D.C.	1964	1976
	P.G.J.D.	1970	
	P.G.J.O.	1973	
Hithersay, Brian William		—	2010
Hoadley, Norman Edward	P.A.G.D.C.	1983	1986
	P.G.S.D.	1996	
Hoare, John Michael	P.A.G.D.C.	1987	
	G.S.D.	2005	
Hoare, Kenneth George	P.G.St.B.	2002	2009
Hoath, John Owen	P.A.G.D.C.	2003	2003
	P.G.S.D.	2011	
Hobbs, Brian John	A.G.I.G.	2004	2000
Hobbs, David	P.A.G.D.C.	2004	2000
Hobbs, David Peter Stirling	P.A.G.D.C.	2010	

NAME	RANK	YEAR OF APPT.	R.A.M.G.R. YEAR OF APPT.
Hobbs, Derek		—	1999
Hobson, Anthony Brian	P.A.G.St.B.	2009	
Hobson, Hugh Edwin Henry	P.A.G.D.C.	2010	
Hockin, Cedric William John	P.A.G.St.B.	2001	
Hockin, William John	P.A.G.D.C.	2006	2004
Hocking, Barry Mark	P.A.G.D.C.	1999	1998
	P.G.S.D.	2000	
	P.G.S.O.	2004	
Hockley, Terence James		—	2003
Hodge, His Hon. Judge Rhys Shelley	P.G.S.D.	2004	2009
Hodgetts, Brian		—	2010
Hodgkiss, Bartle	G.Stwd.	1980	
	P.G.J.D.	1985	
Hodgkiss, Stanley Albert	P.A.G.D.C.	2001	
Hodgkinson, William Stanley		—	2010
Hodgson, Douglas	P.G.St.B.	2009	
Hodgson, Keith	P.A.G.D.C.	2004	2007
	P.G.J.D.	2008	
	Prov.G.M., Cumberland and Westmorland	2012	
Hodgson, Raymond Stanley	P.G.St.B.	2005	
Hodgson, Thomas	A.G.D.C.	2011	
Hodkinson, Eli Gordon	P.A.G.D.C.	1987	1983
	P.G.S.D.	1996	
Hodkinson, Wilfred	P.A.G.D.C.	1985	1990
	P.G.S.D.	1990	
	P.G.J.O.	1996	
Hogarth, Henry Desmond	P.A.G.D.C.	1995	1997
	P.G.J.O.	2001	
	G.J.W.	2004	
Hoggard, Keith Leonard	P.A.G.D.C.	2004	2011
Hoggett, Alan	G.Stwd.	1993	1995
	P.G.J.D.	1999	
Holden, Graham	P.A.G.D.C.	2004	2008
Holder, Eric Leslie	P.A.G.D.C.	2006	
Holder, James Paul	P.A.G.St.B.	2012	2011
Holder, Roy William	P.A.G.St.B.	2009	
Holding, Frank	A.G.D.C.	1985	1984
	P.G.S.D.	1992	
	P.G.J.O.	1997	
Holdsworth, Keith George	P.A.G.D.C.	1989	
	P.G.S.D.	1997	
	P.G.J.O.	2003	
Holgate, Michael John Philip	P.A.G.D.C.	2005	
Holiday, Frederick Mark	Prov.G.M., Channel Isles	2000-2005	
Holland, Brian	P.G.St.B.	1996	2000
	P.G.S.D.	2002	
	P.G.J.O.	2007	
Holland, Brian John	G.Stwd.	2011	2007
Holland, Carl Owen	P.G.St.B.	2006	
Holland, David Martin	G.Stwd.	1989	1991
	P.G.J.D.	1995	
	P.G.J.O.	2001	
Holland, Dudley Horace	P.G.St.B.	2005	

NAME	RANK	YEAR OF APPT.	R.A.M.G.R. YEAR OF APPT.
Holland, Frederick Robert Maynard		—	2011
Holland, George Derek...	P.G.St.B.	2007	
Holland, Leslie William...	P.A.G.Swd.B........................	2012	
Holland, Michael Timothy...................................	P.A.G.D.C............................	1997	2000
Holland, Peter Eric	G.Stwd..................................	2008	2009
	G.J.D....................................	2011	
Holland, Ronald Wilber, *M.A.*	A.G.D.C...............................	1984	1987
	P.G.S.D.	1989	
	P.G.J.O.	1994	
	P.G.M.O...............................	2004	
Hollebone, Paul Stephen	G.Stwd..................................	2012	
Holley, Raymond Stanley	P.G.St.B.	2006	2009
Hollier, Michael..	P.A.G.D.C............................	2011	
Hollingsworth, Colin	P.G.St.B.	2012	
Hollingsworth, Justin Andrew	G.Stwd..................................	1991	
	P.G.J.D.................................	2008	
Hollinshead, David Edward................................	A.G.D.C...............................	2008	
Holloway, David Alan	P.A.G.Swd.B........................	2012	
Holloway, Ian Thomas...	P.G.I.G.	2000	
Holman, Arthur Trevor	P.G.St.B.	1992	
	P.G.J.D.................................	1994	
Holmes, Clifford Frederick..................................	P.A.G.Swd.B........................	2012	
Holmes, David Joseph	P.G.St.B.	2007	2003
Holmes, Donald...	P.A.G.Swd.B........................	2002	2007
Holmes, Eric	G.Stwd..................................	2007	
	G.J.D....................................	2010	
Holmes, Frank Ernest	P.A.G.St.B.	2000	
Holmes, Graham John	P.A.G.St.B.	2007	2000
Holmes, Peter Michael		—	1986
Holt, Frank...	P.G.St.B.	1993	
Holt, Mark Robert	P.A.G.D.C............................	2011	2011
Holt, Sir Michael, *C.B.E., M.A., L.L.M., F.C.A.,*	G.Stwd..................................	1976	
	P.G.J.D.................................	1989	
	P.G.J.O.	1995	
Holt, Paul Michael...	P.A.G.D.C............................	2008	2010
Holt, Rodney Samuel..	P.A.G.D.C............................	1995	2000
	P.G.S.D.	2009	
Holt, Stephen John...	G.Stwd..................................	1995	1998
	P.G.J.D.................................	2000	
	P.G.J.O.	2006	
Holt, Vernon..	P.G.St.B.	2000	
Holtam, Vernon...		—	1993
Holtom, John Hector	P.G.St.B.	2001	2004
	A.G.D.C...............................	2006	
	P.G.S.D.	2011	
Holton, Alan Victor..	P.A.G.D.C............................	2011	2011
Holtum, Austin Arthur..	P.G.St.B.	2000	2001
Homer, Michael Lawrence	P.A.G.D.C............................	1983	1980
	P.G.S.D.	1993	
	P.G.J.O.	2000	
	P.G.S.O.	2012	
Hooker, David Carr	P.A.G.D.C............................	1990	1992
	G.S.D...................................	1996	
	Prov.G.M., Warwickshire	2002	

NAME	RANK	YEAR OF APPT.	R.A.M.G.R. YEAR OF APPT.
Hooker, Geoffrey Carr	P.A.G.D.C.	1982	1987
	P.G.S.D.	2000	
	P.G.M.O.	2011	
Hookes, Kenneth Douglas	P.A.G.D.C.	2007	
Hooley, David Frank		—	2009
Hooper, Robert David	G.Stwd.	2001	
	P.G.J.D.	2009	
Hooper, Ronald Charles Aver	P.A.G.D.C.	1990	
	P.G.S.D.	1995	
Hooton, John Michael	A.G.D.C.	1998	2007
	P.G.S.D.	2004	
	P.G.J.O.	2009	
Hope, Robert	P.G.St.B.	2012	
Hope, Ronald Eugene	P.A.G.D.C.	1994	
Hopewell, Anthony	P.A.G.D.C.	2008	
Hopkin, David Victor, *B.Sc.*	P.G.St.B.	2001	2001
	P.G.J.D.	2009	
Hopkin, Cdr. Roy Keith	P.G.J.D.	1996	
Hopkins, David Thomas	P.A.G.St.B.	2011	
Hopkins, Stanley Herbert Ambrose Frank	P.A.G.D.C.	1984	1995
	P.G.S.D.	1995	
	P.G.J.O.	2001	
Hopton, Douglas Taylor	G.Stwd.	2002	2001
	P.G.J.D.	2008	
Hordle, Robert James	P.A.G.D.C.	2008	2010
Hore, Ronald Stewart		—	2009
Horn, Peter John		—	2007
Horne, Keith		—	2011
Horne, Kevin Andrew	P.A.G.D.C.	2012	
Horne, Sibbald Norman	P.A.G.D.C.	2002	
Horne, Thomas John	A.G.D.C.	1988	
Hornsby, William Gordon	P.A.G.D.C.	1990	1999
Horobin, Arthur Richard	P.G.St.B.	2011	
Horrocks, Derek Alan	P.G.St.B.	2009	
Hortis, Graham Sproat	P.G.S.D.	1996	1997
	P.G.J.O.	2002	
Horton, Eric Bernard, *E.R.D., T.D.*	P.G.St.B.	1996	1994
Horton, Raymond Charles	G.Tyler	1990-2003	1993
	P.A.G.D.C.	1992	
	P.G.S.D.	1997	
	P.G.J.O.	2002	
	P.G.M.O.	2004	
Horton, Wilfred Ernest	P.A.G.D.C.	2003	1995
Hosein, Ishmael Azim	P.A.G.D.C.	2009	
Hosgood, David Ewart	P.A.G.D.C.	1999	
Houghton, Dennis	P.A.G.St.B.	1994	
Houghton, John		—	2000
Housham, John Edward James	P.A.G.D.C.	2012	
Houwertjes, Cornelis	P.A.G.D.C.	1990	1995
	P.G.S.D.	1996	
	P.G.J.O.	2003	
How, John Alfred James	G.Stwd.	1988	
	P.G.J.D.	1996	

NAME	RANK	YEAR OF APPT.	R.A.M.G.R. YEAR OF APPT.
Howard, Barrie James	P.A.G.D.C.	2010	
Howard, Desmond	P.A.G.D.C.	1998	
	P.G.S.D.	2006	
Howard, Russell	G.Stwd.	2004	
	P.G.J.D.	2008	
Howell, Gilbert Anthony	P.G.St.B.	2010	
Howell, Michael David	A.G.D.C.	2001	2002
	P.G.S.D.	2006	
Howells, David Graham		—	2003
Howells, Geoffrey Charles	P.A.G.D.C.	2005	
	P.G.S.D.	2012	
Howes, Thomas John	P.A.G.D.C.	1993	2000
	P.G.S.D.	1999	
Howie, Derek James	P.G.St.B.	2010	
Howitt, John Norman George	P.A.G.D.C.	1992	1998
	P.G.S.D.	1999	2004 GMRAC
	P.G.J.O.	2002	
	P.G.J.W.	2009	
	Pres. Mark Ex.Comm.	2012	
Howland, Nolan Robert Hobbs	P.G.St.B.	2011	
Howland, Phillip	G.I.G.	1973	
	P.A.G.D.C.	1983	
Howland, Dr. Roger John	A.G.D.C.	2001	2007
	P.G.S.D.	2006	
Howls, Alan Thomas	P.A.G.D.C.	2006	
Hoy, Philip John	P.G.St.B.	2008	2011
Hoyles, Terence John	P.A.G.D.C.	1990	
Huband, David	P.A.G.D.C.	2005	
Hubbard, Charles Arthur		—	2002
Hubbard, Maj. Charles Bryan		—	2005
Hubber, Geoffrey Wilson	P.A.G.D.C.	1995	1998
	P.G.S.D.	2000	
	P.G.J.O.	2005	
Huckle, Peter George	P.A.G.D.C.	2006	2002
Huddart, Jeffrey Alan	G.Stwd.	2005	2010
	G.J.D.	2010	
Hudson, Issac Douglas		—	1993
Hudson, John Willan	G.Stwd.	2008	2011
	P.G.J.D.	2012	
Hudson, Joseph Thomas Edwin Albert	P.A.G.D.C.	1995	
Hudson, Terence	G.Stwd.	1990	
	G.J.D.	1995	
Hugh, Derek Gordon	G.Stwd.	1991	1998
	P.G.J.D.	2001	
	Dist.G.M., South & East Caribbean	2003-2012	
Hughes, Bryan	A.G.D.C.	2009	
Hughes, Edward Ross	P.G.J.D.	2003	2005
	P.G.S.D.	2006	
	P.G.J.O.	2009	
Hughes, Emyr Rhinallt	P.G.J.D.	2003	
Hughes, Eric Samuel	P.G.St.B.	1995	2003
	P.G.J.D.	2003	
	P.G.J.O.	2009	

NAME	RANK	YEAR OF APPT.	R.A.M.G.R. YEAR OF APPT.
Hughes, Evan Glyn	P.A.G.D.C.	1991	1997
	P.G.S.D.	1997	
	P.G.J.O.	2002	
Hughes, Gareth	P.G.St.B.	2002	2010
	G.J.D.	2008	
Hughes, Glyn	P.A.G.Swd.B.	2011	
Hughes, Idris Limbrick	P.A.G.Swd.B.	2010	
Hughes, Mansel	P.A.G.D.C.	2003	
Hughes, Peter William	A.G.D.C.	2010	2005
Hughes, Thomas Arthur	P.G.St.B.	2005	
Hughes, William John	P.A.G.St.B.	2007	
Hughson, Lyndon William	A.G.D.C.	2010	
Hulks, Keith Stewart	G.I.G.	1992	2000
	P.G.J.D.	2001	
Hull, David Watson	P.G.St.B.	2001	
Humphrey, John	P.G.St.B.	1995	
Humphrey, Paul Baden	P.A.G.D.C.	2007	2009
	P.G.J.D.	2009	
Humphries, Brian William	P.A.G.St.B.	2008	
Humphries, William Samuel	G.Stwd.	2002	
	G.J.D.	2007	
Hunt, Brian	P.A.G.D.C.	1999	
Hunt, Cecil Francis	P.A.G.D.C.	2010	2003
Hunt, David Geoffrey Russell	P.A.G.D.C.	2006	2005
Hunt, Donald Sheard	Dep.G.Swd.B.	1972	1991
Hunter, Frederick Leslie James	P.A.G.Swd.B.	2010	
Hunter, James White	P.G.St.B.	2005	2011
	P.G.J.D.	2009	
	P.G.S.D.	2011	
	P.G.J.O.	2012	
Hunter, Michael Adrian	P.A.G.D.C.	2003	
Huntington, Philip John	P.A.G.D.C.	2012	
Huntley, Alan Whieldon	P.A.G.Swd.B.	2003	
Hurley, John William	P.A.G.D.C.	2005	2010
Hurst, Paul Graham	G.Stwd.	2009	2009
	P.G.J.D.	2012	
Hurworth, Robert Michael	P.A.G.D.C.	2012	2010
Husbands, Ulysses Adolphus Michael	P.A.G.D.C.	2007	2011
Hussey, Dennis Alan	P.G.St.B.	2011	
Hussey, John Patrick	P.A.G.D.C.	1996	1993
Hussey, Raymond Stanley Henry	P.A.G.D.C.	2000	2001
	P.G.J.D.	2003	
	Prov.G.M., Surrey	2004	
Hustler, William Robert	P.G.St.B.	1982	
Hutchings, Hugh Basil	G.Stwd.	1981	
	P.G.J.D.	1991	
Hutchings, Reginald Sidney	P.G.St.B.	1994	
Hutchinson, Colin Herbert	G.S.D.	1997	
Hutchinson, Leslie	P.A.G.D.C.	2012	2010
Hutchinson, Michael John	P.A.G.Swd.B.	2008	
Hutchinson, Thomas Harold	P.A.G.D.C.	1995	
	P.G.S.D.	2004	
Hutchison, Colin	P.A.G.D.C.	2005	

NAME	RANK	YEAR OF APPT.	R.A.M.G.R. YEAR OF APPT.
Hutton, Walter Alan	A.G.I.G.	1997	
Huxtable, Philip Jolyon	G.Stwd.	1996	
	P.G.J.D.	2001	
Hyde, Keith Charles	P.G.St.B.	1993	1999
	P.G.J.D.	1999	
Hyett, Kenneth Edward	P.A.G.St.B.	2008	
Hylton, Dr. George Arthur, *J.P.*	P.G.St.B.	1991	1993
	P.G.S.D.	1995	
	P.G.J.O.	2003	
Hyner, Eric Robert Hubert	P.A.G.Swd.B.	2001	
Ibbetson, Kenneth Thomas	P.A.G.D.C.	2003	2004
Iley, Donald	P.A.G.D.C.	1999	2003
Iliffe, David John	G.Stwd.	2008	
	P.G.J.D.	2011	
Ilott, John	G.Stwd.	1994	1997
	P.G.J.D.	1999	
Ince, George Raymond	P.A.G.D.C.	1992	2001
	P.G.S.D.	2000	
Ince, Kenneth	P.G.St.B.	2003	2005
Infield, Gordon Mark	P.A.G.D.C.	1994	
Ingham, Colin Booth	P.A.G.Swd.B.	2008	2008
Ingham, Peter	P.A.G.Swd.B.	2005	
	P.G.S.D.	2010	
Ingram Clark, Robert Alastair	P.A.G.D.C.	1971	1979
	P.G.M.O.	1977	
	P.G.J.W.	1987	
Ingram, Stuart Andrew Raymond	P.G.St.B.	2004	2007
	P.G.J.D.	2007	
	P.G.J.O.	2012	
Inman, Roger John	P.A.G.Swd.B.	2009	2010
Innes, Colin James	A.G.I.G.	2011	2010
Innes, James Robert	P.A.G.D.C.	2009	2008
Inniss, George Winston	P.G.St.B.	2005	
Irving, Ian Alexander		—	2009
Irving, John Henry	P.A.G.D.C.	1996	
Irwin, Leslie John	P.A.G.D.C.	1987	
	P.G.S.D.	2002	
Isaac, Brian James	P.A.G.Swd.B.	2012	
Isaac, Geoffrey Francis Warwick	P.A.G.D.C.	1996	2001
	P.G.S.D.	2001	
	Prov.G.M., Cornwall	2004	
Ishmael, John	P.A.G.D.C.	2006	
Iveson, John Christopher	P.G.St.B.	1994	
Ivey, William Morgan		—	2008
Ivison, Alan William	P.A.G.D.C.	2012	
Jackman, Leonard John	P.A.G.D.C.	2007	2004
Jackson, Anthony Norman		—	2000

NAME	RANK	YEAR OF APPT.	R.A.M.G.R. YEAR OF APPT.
Jackson, Anthony Woof, *M.B.E., J.P.*	P.A.G.D.C.	1985	1991
	P.G.S.D.	1995	
	P.G.J.O.	2000	
Jackson, Brian Anthony	G.Stwd.	1998	
	P.G.J.D.	2003	
Jackson, David Gilfoy	P.A.G.D.C.	1993	
Jackson, David Richard	P.A.G.D.C.	2000	2001
Jackson, Dr. Frederick Bruce	P.G.St.B.	1984	1997
	P.G.J.D.	1989	
Jackson, Graham Anthony	P.A.G.D.C.	2000	2000
	Dep.G.Swd.B.	2005	
	P.G.J.O.	2009	
Jackson, Gordon Evan	P.A.G.Swd.B.	2003	2009
Jackson, Hedley	A.G.D.C.	1993	1989
	P.G.J.D.	1995	
	P.G.J.O.	2000	
	G.M.O.	2009	
Jackson, John Michael	P.A.G.D.C.	2009	2011
Jackson, Joseph Keith	P.A.G.Swd.B.	2004	
Jackson, Keith Barry	P.A.G.St.B.	1990	1988
	P.G.J.D.	1996	
	P.G.J.O.	2004	
Jackson, Kenneth	P.A.G.St.B.	2012	
Jackson, Luke Arnold		—	2006
Jackson, Robert Cyril	P.A.G.Swd.B.	2009	
Jackson, Sydney Frank	P.G.St.B.	1993	1997
Jackson, Thomas Firth	A.G.St.B.	1990	1999
	P.G.J.D.	1997	
	G.S.O.	2003	
	G.J.W.	2012	
Jacobs, Dr. Franklyn Kenneth Stephen	P.A.G.Swd.B.	2006	
Jacobs, Johannes Jacobus	P.A.G.D.C.	1971	1976
	P.G.S.D.	1987	
	Dist.G.M., South Africa (Cen.Div.)	1987-1992	
Jacobs, Franklyn Kenneth Stephen		—	2006
Jacobs, Mark George	P.A.G.St.B.	1999	2002
Jacobs, Michael John Simon	P.A.G.D.C.	1996	2011
	P.G.S.D.	2001	
	P.G.J.O.	2006	
Jacobs, Stuart Maurice	P.A.G.D.C.	2007	2006
Jacobson, John Charles	G.Stwd.	2005	2006
	P.G.J.D.	2008	
	P.G.S.D.	2010	
	P.G.J.O.	2012	
Jafferji, Nurdin Hassanbhai	P.G.St.B.	2006	
Jago, Dr. Roger Hugh	G.Stwd.	1997	1999
	P.G.J.D.	2000	
	P.G.J.O.	2005	
	P.G.S.O.	2012	
Jain, Ashit Kumar	P.A.G.I.G.	2002	
Jakes, Ronald David	G.Stwd.	2000	2001
	P.G.J.D.	2005	
James, Charles Trevor	P.A.G.D.C.	2012	
James, Colin Mansel	G.Stwd.	1993	

NAME	RANK	YEAR OF APPT.	R.A.M.G.R. YEAR OF APPT.
James, David Ieuan	P.A.G.D.C.	2003	2004
	P.G.S.D.	2005	
	Prov.G.M., Monmouthshire	2006	
James, Dawson Hughes	P.A.G.D.C.	2001	2006
	P.G.S.D.	2008	
James, Ewart Percival	P.G.St.B.	1984	1980
	P.G.J.D.	1989	
	P.G.J.O.	2005	
James, Harris	P.A.G.D.C.	2001	2002
	P.G.S.D.	2006	
James, John Malcolm	P.G.St.B.	2001	2003
James, Kenneth Gwylfa	P.G.St.B.	2005	1996
James, Michael George	P.A.G.D.C.	2008	2004
James, Peter David	P.G.St.B.	2009	
James, Peter Kenneth	P.A.G.Swd.B.	2004	2008
	P.A.G.D.C.	2008	
James, William Alexander	P.G.St.B.	1996	1998
James, William Eric	P.A.G.D.C.	1992	
	P.G.S.D.	2000	
Jameson, William Albert	P.A.G.D.C.	1997	2008
	P.G.J.D.	2009	
Jamieson, Colin Campbell	P.A.G.D.C.	1998	
Jamieson, Douglas John Lindsay	P.A.G.D.C.	1975	2010 RAMGR
	P.G.J.D.	2007	
Jamieson, Leslie Robert	P.G.St.B.	2011	2009
Jamieson, Maurice William		—	2008
Janes, Ronald Thomas	P.A.G.D.C.	2006	
Jarrett, Gilbert Ayodele	P.A.G.D.C.	2010	
Jarrett, Neville Griffith	P.G.St.B.	2007	
	P.G.S.D.	2012	
Jarrett, Roger Edward	P.G.St.B.	2010	
Jarvis, Revd. Eric George	P.A.G.Chap.	1997	1998
Jayakrishnan Nair, Narayanan Nair	P.A.G.D.C.	2004	
Jayaprakash, George		—	2011
Jayne, Eric William	P.A.G.Swd.B.	2009	
Jefferson, Derek		—	2002
Jeffery, Ralph Arthur	P.A.G.D.C.	2003	2001
	P.G.S.D.	2008	
Jeffrey, John Stephenson	P.G.St.B.	1994	2002
Jeffries, Cyril Albert	P.A.G.St.B.	1998	
Jellicoe, Sub-Lt. Clifford Graham, R.N.R.	G.Stwd.	1998	
Jenkins, David Lloyd	P.G.S.D.	2006	
Jenkins, Denis Percy	P.G.I.G	1998	2003
Jenkins, Howard William	P.A.G.D.C.	2011	
Jenkins, Raymond Charles	P.A.G.D.C.	1987	
Jenkins, Lt.Col. Roger John Ellis, T.D.	P.A.G.Swd.B.	2001	2007
	P.G.S.D.	2007	
Jenkins, Trevor Maughan	A.G.D.C.	2011	
Jenkinson, Clifford		—	2009
Jenkinson, David	P.G.St.B.	1995	1996
	P.G.J.D.	2000	
	P.G.J.O.	2010	

NAME	RANK	YEAR OF APPT.	R.A.M.G.R. YEAR OF APPT.
Jenner, Colin Tressider	P.A.G.D.C.	1981	1983
	P.G.S.D.	1989	
	P.G.J.O.	1999	
Jennings, Donald Henry	A.G.D.C.	1984	1986
	P.G.S.D.	1992	
	P.G.J.O.	1997	
Jennings, Duncan Boyd	G.I.G.	2001	2002
	G.J.D.	2006	
Jennings, John David	G.Stwd.	2012	
Jesson, David Kenneth	P.A.G.D.C.	2001	2002
	P.G.J.D.	2006	
	P.G.J.O.	2012	
Jewell, Clifford Charles	P.G.St.B.	2007	
Jewell, Kenneth Ewen	P.A.G.D.C.	1974	
	P.G.S.D.	1988	
Jewell, Maj. William Kenyon	P.A.G.D.C.	2009	
Jewitt, Trevor	G.Stwd.	2001	2006
	P.G.J.D.	2006	
Jiffri, Abdul	P.A.G.D.C.	2006	
	P.G.S.D.	2011	
Johns, Beverley	P.A.G.Swd.B.	2005	
Johns, John Merlin	P.G.St.B.	2006	
Johns, Peter Frederick	A.G.D.C.	2010	
	P.G.J.D.	2012	
Johns, Robert Clifford, *J.P.*	P.A.G.D.C.	1980	1992
	P.G.S.D.	1988	
	P.G.J.O.	1993	
Johnson, Alan Clinton	P.G.St.B.	2005	
Johnson, Allan Ratlidge	P.A.G.D.C.	1987	
Johnson, Arthur Harold, *J.P.*	P.A.G.Swd.B.	2010	
Johnson, Babatunde Adeyemi	P.A.G.D.C.	2008	2008
Johnson, Brian William	P.A.G.D.C.	1991	1994
Johnson, David Kenneth	P.A.G.D.C.	2005	2002
Johnson, David Kenneth	P.A.G.D.C.	2005	2009
Johnson, Douglas Alan Vivian	P.A.G.D.C.	2003	2006
Johnson, Eustace Anthony	G.Stwd.	1988	2001
	P.G.J.D.	1994	
Johnson, Edward Leslie	P.A.G.D.C.	1995	1997
	P.G.S.D.	2000	
Johnson, Edward Samuel Bela	P.G.St.B.	1999	1997
	P.G.J.D.	2005	
Johnson, George Alfred	G.Stwd.	2010	2011
Johnson, Ian Brook	G.Stwd.	2012	
Johnson, Keith Arncliffe	P.A.G.D.C.	2006	
Johnson, Kenneth Ernest	P.A.G.St.B.	2007	
Johnson, Lester Rawlinson Eric	P.A.G.D.C.	2003	
Johnson, Marcus Walter	P.G.St.B.	1996	
Johnson, Trevor	P.A.G.D.C.	1995	1998
Johnston, David Robert	P.A.G.D.C.	1996	
	P.G.S.D.	2002	
	P.G.J.O.	2007	
	Dist.G.M., The Transvaal	2010	
Johnston, Harry	P.A.G.D.C.	2001	
Johnston, John Thomas	P.G.St.B.	1999	2002

NAME	RANK	YEAR OF APPT.	R.A.M.G.R. YEAR OF APPT.
Johnston, Ronald Adam	P.A.G.St.B.	2000	1997
Johnstone, Graham Scott	P.A.G.D.C.	2012	
Johnstone, Neil Hamilton	P.A.G.D.C.	2012	
Johnstone-Smith, Raymond	A.G.D.C.	2010	
Joiner, Lt.Col. Dr. Ian Moir, *F.R.C.O.G.*	G.Stwd.	2001	2003
	P.G.J.D.	2006	
Jolley, Michael Bellian	P.A.G.D.C.	1994	2002
	P.G.S.D.	2003	
Jolley, James		—	2006
Jolley, Michael Bellian	P.G J.O.	2010	
Jolley, Thomas Ainscough	P.G.St.B.	1984	1993
Jolly, Alan	P.A.G.St.B.	1996	
Jones, Alan	P.A.G.D.C.	1998	
	P.G.S.D.	2004	
	P.G.J.O.	2012	
Jones, Alwyn Clwyd	P.A.G.D.C.	1999	2011
	P.G.S.D.	2010	
Jones, Albert Edward Peter	P.A.G.D.C.	1972	1993
	P.G.S.D.	1983	
	P.G.J.O.	1988	
	P.G.S.O.	1998	
	P.G.J.W.	2005	
Jones, Brian Albert Rupert		—	2009
Jones, Donald	P.A.G.D.C.	1994	
Jones, David Owen	A.G.Swd.B.	1993	2003
	P.G.J.D.	1998	
	P.G.J.O.	2011	
Jones, David Stanley	P.A.G.D.C.	2001	2003
Jones, Elfan Walter	P.G.Org.	2011	2006
Jones, Frederick Charles	P.G.St.B.	1990	
Jones, Gareth, *O.B.E.*	G.Stwd.	2009	
	P.G.J.D.	2012	
Jones, Gareth Royston	P.A.G.D.C.	2009	
Jones, George Daniel	G.Stwd.	1995	1998
	P.G.J.D.	2000	
	P.G.J.O.	2006	
Jones, Gordon Ernest	P.A.G.D.C.	1999	
	P.G.S.D.	2008	
Jones, Gordon Howard	P.A.G.D.C.	1987	1991
	Dep.G.Swd.B.	1997	
	P.G.J.O.	2005	
Jones, Hamilton Lewis	P.A.G.D.C.	2011	
Jones, Henry James		—	1990
Jones, Huw	P.A.G.D.C.	2010	2002
Jones, Idris	P.A.G.D.C.	2000	
	P.G.J.D.	2008	
Jones, Ithel Gareth	P.A.G.Swd.B.	2006	2002
Jones, Jack	P.G.St.B.	2006	
Jones, James Daniel	P.A.G.D.C.	1992	2002
Jones, James Llewellyn	P.A.G.D.C.	1998	2001
Jones, Kessick John, *B.A.*	G.Stwd.	1999	2000
	Dep.G.D.C.	2005-2007	
	P.G.J.O.	2010	
	G.D.C.	2012	

NAME	RANK	YEAR OF APPT.	R.A.M.G.R. YEAR OF APPT.
Jones, Martin Alan	P.A.G.Swd.B.	2011	
Jones, Michael Batham	Dep.G.D.C.	1986	1982
	Dep.G.Reg.	1987-2007	1987 GMRAC (H.C.)
	P.G.J.O.	1990	
	P.G.J.W.	1994	
	G.S.W.	2005	
Jones, Norman Reginald	P.A.G.D.C.	2011	
Jones, Owen Glyn	P.A.G.D.C.	2002	
Jones, Richard Andrew	P.G.St.B.	1999	
	P.A.G.D.C.	2006	
Jones, Richard George	P.A.G.Swd.B.	1999	
Jones, Richard Griffith	P.A.G.D.C.	2010	
Jones, Ronald, *J.P.*	G.Stwd.	2001	2009
	P.G.J.D.	2007	
	P.G.S.D.	2008	
	P.G.J.O.	2009	
	Prov.G.M., Dyfed	2012	
Jones, Ronald Alan	P.A.G.Swd.B.	2008	
Jones, Samuel Horton Maurice	G.St.B.	1988	1989
Jones, Steven	P.A.G.D.C.	2009	2010
Jones, Thomas Richard Eirian	P.G.J.D.	2008	2008
Jones, Wilfrid Armory	P.G.St.B.	2000	1998
Jones, William Gwynfor	P.A.G.D.C.	2002	2009
Jordan, Charles Christopher, *M.B.E.*		—	2010
Jordan, James William	P.G.S.D.	2003	2003
	P.G.J.O.	2009	
Jordan, Raymond Leonard	P.G.St.B.	1985	
Joseph, Neville Anthony	P.A.G.D.C.	1987	
	P.G.S.D.	1994	
	P.G.J.O.	2000	
Joseph, Selvanayagam Hyginus Bernard	P.G.St.B.	2006	
Joslin, David Robin	P.A.G.D.C.	2009	2007
Joughin, John William	P.A.G.D.C.	2012	
Joy, John	P.A.G.St.B.	1993	2010
Joyce, David Pickford	P.G.S.D.	2004	2005
	P.G.J.O.	2009	
Judd, John Rodway	A.G.D.C.	1994	1997
	P.G.S.D.	2000	
Judd, Leslie Malcolm	P.G.St.B.	1997	
Juden, Michael John	G.Stwd.	2003	2008
	G.S.D.	2007	
July, Raymond	P.G.St.B.	1996	
Jump, Michael Edward Pearson	G.Stwd.	1982	1991 GMRAC (H.C.)
	P.G.J.D.	1990	
	G. Registrar	1991-1995	
	P.G.J.W.	1994	
	G.S.W.	2000	
Jung, Jan Marie Marcus	P.G.St.B.	2009	2005
Jupe, Harold William	P.A.G.D.C.	2001	1997
	P.G.S.D.	2008	
Just, Ernest	P.A.G.D.C.	1998	2001

NAME	RANK	YEAR OF APPT.	R.A.M.G.R. YEAR OF APPT.
Kalianwala, Byramshaw Jal	P.A.G.D.C.	1985	1993
	P.G.S.D.	1995	
	P.G.J.O.	2007	
Kalsi, Manmohan Singh	P.A.G.St.B.	1994	
	P.A.G.D.C.	2009	
Kandiah, Selvanayagam	—		2009
Kane, Glenis Dare	P.A.G.D.C.	2006	
Kanitsch, Otis Ferdinand	P.A.G.D.C.	1995	1991
Kaplan, Morris	P.G.St.B.	2010	
Karsa, Dr. David Robert	G.Stwd.	2005	
	P.G.J.D.	2010	
Karunakaran Nair, Appukuttan Pillai	P.A.G.D.C.	2009	2008
Kaschula, Gerard Carl Ferdinand	—		2011
Katz, Martin	P.A.G.D.C.	2006	2006
	P.G.S.D.	2011	
Kavanagh, Philip Victor Frederick	P.A.G.Swd.B.	2001	2005
	G.J.D.	2011	
Kavanagh, Trevor Avery	P.G.St.B.	1994	2005
	P.G.J.D.	2009	
Kay, John Lewis	P.A.G.D.C.	2007	2008
Kay, John Stuart	P.A.G.D.C.	2001	2001
	P.G.S.D.	2009	
Kay, Martin John	P.G.St.B.	1996	
Kay, Robert	P.A.G.D.C.	1986	1989
	P.G.S.D.	1993	
Kay, Robert Jervis, *Q.C.*	Dep.G.D.C.	1994-1995	
	P.G.J.O.	1998	
Kaye, Arthur	P.A.G.D.C.	2005	
Kaye, Howard Louis	P.G.St.B.	2007	
Kaye, Nathan	P.A.G.D.C.	1984	
Keast, Kenneth	G.Stwd.	1993	1996
	P.G.J.D.	1998	
	P.G.S.O.	2003	
	P.G.J.W.	2011	
Keats, Louis Maurice	P.G.St.B.	2008	2006
Keeble, Michael David	P.G.St.B.	2001	2003
Keen, Cyril Douglas		—	2009
Keen, George Austin	G.St.B.	1984	1987
Keene, Victor Walter	P.A.G.Swd.B.	2006	
	P.G.J.D.	2011	
Keer, Geoffrey Alan	P.A.G.D.C.	2007	2008
Keery, Samuel James	P.A.G.Swd.B.	2007	2003
Kellet, David	P.A.G.D.C.	2002	1998
	P.G.J.D.	2011	
Kellett, Eric Albert George	P.A.G.D.C.	2008	
Kelly, Andrew	P.A.G.D.C.	2010	
Kelly, Henry Howard		—	2004
Kelly, Joseph Steele, Jnr.	A.G.I.G.	1997	
	P.A.G.D.C.	2002	
Kemp, Allan Ernest	P.A.G.St.B.	1998	2002
	P.G.J.D.	2002	
	P.G.J.O.	2007	

NAME	RANK	YEAR OF APPT.	R.A.M.G.R. YEAR OF APPT.
Kemp, Brian Robert, *M.A.*	P.A.G.St.B.	2000	2001
	P.A.G.D.C.	2002	
	P.G.S.D.	2007	
	P.G.J.O.	2012	
Kemp, Charles Anthony	P.G.St.B.	1991	2000
Kemp, Charles James	P.A.G.Swd.B.	2012	
Kemp, John George	G.Stwd.	1987	2004
	P.G.J.D.	1995	
	P.G.J.O.	2009	
Kendall, Samuel Hedley	P.A.G.D.C.	1992	2004
Kent, H.R.H. Prince Michael of, *G.C.V.O.*	G.S.W.	1981	
	Grand Master	1982-2012	1982 GM GMRAC
Kenward, Ian Joseph	G.Stwd.	2001	2001
	P.G.J.D.	2004	
Kenward, Peter Geoffrey Victor	P.G.St.B.	1997	1999
Kenwood, Gerald Ernest William		—	2009
Kenyon, John Anthony	P.A.G.St.B.	2008	
Kerley, Michael Valentine	P.G.St.B.	2003	
Kernick, John Humphrey	P.A.G.D.C.	2006	
Kerr, William	P.A.G.D.C.	2004	
Kershaw, Alan	P.A.G.St.B.	1994	1995
	P.G.J.D.	2002	
Kershaw, Michael	P.G.St.B.	2001	1995
Kessel, Barry Best	P.A.G.D.C.	1997	2003
	P.G.J.D.	2007	
Ketchell, Peter Robert	P.G.St.B.	2007	2007
Kettleborough, Edward Charles	G.Stwd.	2002	2003
	P.G.J.O.	2007	
Kettlewell, John Charles	P.G.St.B.	2004	
	P.G.S.D.	2009	
Key, Brian Maurice	P.A.G.D.C.	2010	
Key, Maurice	P.A.G.D.C.	1996	2011
	P.G.J.O.	2011	
Keys, John Richard	P.A.G.Swd.B.	2003	2003
Khambatta, Dr. Roeinton Burjor Framji	P.G.J.D.	1988	1991
	Prov.G.M., London	1991-1994	
Khoo, Dr. Boo Khean, *K.M.N., A.M.N.*	P.A.G.D.C.	2001	2007
	P.G.S.D.	2012	
Kibble-Rees, David Charles, *M.A., B.Sc.*	G.Stwd.	2001	1999
	P.G.J.D.	2007	
Kilbourn, Kenneth Cecil	P.A.G.Swd.B.	2011	
Kilburn, Samuel Wilkinson, *O.B.E., J.P.*	P.A.G.D.C.	1984	1993
	P.G.S.D.	1993	
	P.G.J.O.	1999	
Kimmins, Ian James	P.G.St.B.	2000	1994
Kinder, Peter Charles	P.A.G.D.C.	2009	
Kinder, Ross Garnett	G.Stwd.	2008	2010
	P.G.J.D.	2011	
Kindon, Ronald Wilfred	P.A.G.D.C.	2007	
King, Derrick George		—	2007
King, Donald		—	1987
King, Gordon William	P.G.St.B.	2002	2005
	P.A.G.D.C.	2006	
	P.G.S.D.	2010	

NAME	RANK	YEAR OF APPT.	R.A.M.G.R. YEAR OF APPT.
King, John Anthony	P.A.G.D.C.	2004	2005
	P.G.J.O.	2009	
King, Norman	P.A.G.D.C.	1995	
King, Robert, *Q.R.M*	G.St.B	1996	2007
	P.G.J.D.	2005	
Kinghorn, William Gordon	P.A.G.D.C.	1987	
Kingsley, Martin	G.Stwd.	1983	
	P.G.J.D.	1991	
Kingsley-Smith, Clive	G.Stwd.	2012	2009
Kingsman, Barry John	P.A.G.Swd.B	2004	
Kinnersley, Dennis William	P.G.St.B.	2011	2010
Kinsey, David	P.G.I.G.	1982	1994
	P.A.G.D.C.	1988	
	P.G.S.D.	1997	
	P.G.S.O.	2005	
Kinsman, Peter Elliot	P.G.St.B.	2003	2008
Kinton, Douglas Joseph	P.G.St.B.	2009	
Kirby, Anthony John	P.A.G.D.C.	1988	1995
	P.G.S.D.	2003	
	P.G.J.O.	2008	
Kirby, Victor John		—	1987
Kirby, Thomas Stephen Lockwood	P.A.G.D.C.	1998	
Kirilloff, Alexander	P.A.G.D.C.	2005	2006
Kirk, Geoffrey Flather		—	1999
Kirk, Kenneth Stanley	P.A.G.D.C.	2005	
Kirk, Rowland Samuel	A.G.D.C.	1983	1987
	P.G.S.D.	1990	
	P.G.J.O.	1996	
Kirkbride, Barry	P.A.G.D.C.	2002	2002
	P.G.J.D.	2007	
Kirkham, David Henry	P.A.G.St.B.	2002	2007
Kirkwood, James Franklin, *B.E.M.*	P.G.St.B.	2003	
Kirkwood, Robert Greer	P.A.G.St.B.	2004	2009
	P.G.J.D.	2010	
Kirman, John David		—	2007
Kirton, Colin McGregor	P.A.G.Swd.B.	2010	
Kitchen, Trevor Harold	G.Stwd.	1989	1994
	P.G.S.D.	1995	
	P.G.S.O.	2001	
	G.M.O.	2007	
Kitson, James Buller	G.Stwd.	2002	
	P.G.S.D.	2004	
Kitson, Peter	P.A.G.D.C.	1999	
	P.G.S.D.	2006	
Klein, Neville	P.A.G.D.C.	1998	1997
Kleingeld, Karel Erne	P.G.St.B.	1998	1995
	P.G.S.D.	2006	
Knapman, Peter	P.G.St.B.	2005	2004
Knew, John Leonard	G.Stwd.	1994	2006
	P.G.J.D.	2003	
Knight, Arthur James	P.G.St.B.	1990	1994
	P.G.J.D.	1997	
Knight, Lawrence	P.A.G.D.C.	2009	2011
Knight, Nigel Raymond	P.A.G.Swd.B.	2009	

NAME	RANK	YEAR OF APPT.	R.A.M.G.R. YEAR OF APPT.
Knight, Paul Stewart	P.A.G.D.C.	2012	2007
Knight, Roger Mayers	P.G.St.B.	2003	
Knight, Timothy John	P.A.G.Swd.B.	2009	2008
Kniveton, Dr. Bromley Howard	P.G.St.B.	1998	
	P.G.J.D.	2008	
Knox, John, *K.C.L.J.*	G.Stwd.	1994	1997
	G.Swd.B.	2002	
	P.G.J.O.	2007	
Knox, Mark Alexander		—	2008
Knox, Richard John	P.A.G.D.C.	2008	2009
Knutton, Derek Ian	P.G.St.B.	2006	
Kok, Peter Gerard	P.G.St.B.	2007	2008
Konirsch, John	P.G.St.B.	1995	
Kooijman, Bastiaan	P.A.G.D.C.	1996	
Koopman, Johan Peter Justinus Frederik	P.G.St.B.	1997	2002
	G.J.D.	2004	
Kostromin, Paul James	P.G.St.B.	2008	2008
Kothari, Jyandralal Fulchand	P.A.G.D.C.	2007	
Krever, Nicolaas Johannes	P.G.St.B.	2011	
Krieger, Rolf Erich		—	1997
Krisch, Robert	P.A.G.D.C.	2002	1998
Krishnamurthy, Thekalur Venkata Rao		—	2005
Krishnar, Parampathy	P.A.G.D.C.	2010	
Kruisselbrink, Jan Hendrik Willem	P.G.St.B.	1998	
Kruyne, Elizabertus Leendert	P.G.St.B.	2008	2006
Kunhamed, Kummatti Veetil	P.A.G.D.C.	2005	
Kumaran Nair, Govinda Pillai		—	2010
Kwong, Allan Sea Yoon	P.A.G.D.C.	2000	2008
Lacey, John David	G.Stwd.	2005	
	P.G.J.D.	2008	
Lacey, Keith Donald Briance	P.A.G.D.C.	2010	
Lacy, John William	G.St.B.	2007	
Lai, Mun-Wan	P.A.G.D.C.	2005	2011
Laidlaw, Arthur Charles Cranston	P.A.G.D.C.	2006	
Laidlaw, Kenneth, *B.Sc., M.I.E.E., M.I.M.A.R.E.*		—	2004
Laing, Daniel Terrence	P.G.St.B.	2009	
Lakritz, Jack	P.G.St.B.	2011	2011
Lal, Satinder	P.A.G.St.B.	1991	
Lamb, Alan	P.A.G.D.C.	1990	
Lamb, Frank Charles	G.Stwd.	1988	1988
	P.G.J.D.	1993	
	P.G.J.O.	2000	
Lamb, John Kellock	P.G.St.B.	1993	
Lamb, John William	P.A.G.St.B.	2008	
Lambdin, Donald John	P.A.G.D.C.	1986	2000
	P.G.S.D.	1996	
Lambert, Richard Wilson	A.G.Org.	2002	2005
	G.Org.	2003-2005	
Lanceley, Geoffrey William	P.A.G.St.B.	2000	

NAME	RANK	YEAR OF APPT.	R.A.M.G.R. YEAR OF APPT.
Landers, Michael Gordon James	P.A.G.D.C.	2010	
Landmark, Gerhard Michael		—	2006
Lane, Edgar Roger	P.A.G.D.C.	1986	1995
	P.G.J.O.	1998	
Lane, Gerald	P.A.G.D.C.	2011	
Lane, Ivar Edgar		—	2000
Lane, Malcolm Barry	G.Stwd.	1986	
	P.G.J.D.	1994	
Lane, Revd. Malcolm Clifford George, *J.P.*	P.G.St.B.	1999	
	A.G.Chap.	2005	
	Dep.G.Chap.	2009	
Lane, Peter John		—	2004
Langan, Alan Markham	P.A.G.D.C.	2010	2006
Lange, Kaj Jorgen		—	2009
Langelaar, Dick	P.A.G.D.C.	1998	2003
	P.G.J.O.	2007	
Langford, Francis	P.A.G.D.C.	1999	2000
	P.G.S.D.	2009	
Langley, Brian Edward	P.A.G.D.C.	2012	
Langley, David John	P.A.G.D.C.	1996	
Langley, Michael Graham	P.A.G.D.C.	2003	2001
	P.G.J.D.	2012	
Lanham, Alan Ralph	P.A.G.D.C.	2011	
Lannoy, Jean Pascal		—	2001
Lansdowne, Terence Allen		—	2011
Lapham, Raymond George		—	2002
Large, Charles Graeme, *M.B.E., E.D.*	P.A.G.D.C.	1994	1993
	P.G.S.D.	1998	
	P.G.J.O.	2006	
Larkins, Christopher John	P.A.G.D.C.	1988	1988
	P.G.S.D.	2004	
Larkman, Leslie	Asst.G.D.C.	1988	
	P.G.S.D.	1993	
Larner, Percy George	P.G.J.D.	2007	2007
	P.G.J.O.	2012	
Laskey, Charles William	P.G.St.B.	1991	
	P.G.J.D.	2006	
Last, John Derrick	P.A.G.Swd.B.	2001	2001
Lates, Geoffrey Malcolm	P.A.G.D.C.	2003	
Latham, Adrian Lawrence	P.A.G.St.B.	2009	
Latham, Anthony Bruce Mason	P.A.G.St.B.	2004	2006
	P.G.J.D.	2010	
Laurence Thomas Peter	P.G.St.B.	2009	
Lavender, Keith Gwyn	P.A.G.D.C.	2007	
Lavine, Wilbur Theodore	P.A.G.D.C.	2007	
Law, Gordon		—	2011
Lawless, Cecil Bernard	P.A.G.D.C.	1988	1996
	G.S.D.	1997	
Lawson, Lt.Cdr. George Vincent	P.A.G.D.C.	1990	1994
	P.G.S.D.	1997	
	P.G.J.O.	2002	

NAME	RANK	YEAR OF APPT.	R.A.M.G.R. YEAR OF APPT.
Lawson, Michael Howard	P.A.G.D.C.	1988	1989
	P.G.S.D.	1994	
	P.G.J.O.	1997	
	P.G.M.O.	2000	
	P.G.J.W.	2005	
Layton, Roger	A.G.I.G.	2004	
Lazarus, Afeef Assad	P.A.G.D.C.	2000	
	P.G.J.O.	2008	
Lazet, Herbert Gottfried	P.G.St.B.	2006	2010
Lea, David	P.A.G.Swd.B.	2009	
Leach, Dennis Stanley	P.A.G.D.C.	1998	
Leach, Revd. Stephen Windsor	P.A.G.Chap.	2004	2009
Leahy, Stanley	G.Stwd.	1981	
	P.G.J.D.	1992	
Leaman, Gordon	P.G.St.B.	1997	1996
Lean, Allan William	P.G.St.B.	1995	1987
	P.G.J.D.	2004	
Lean, William John	P.A.G.D.C.	1987	1995
	P.G.S.D.	1993	
Leavers, Roy William	G.Stwd.	1998	1999
	G.J.D.	2004	
	P.G.J.O.	2010	
Le Bon, John Frederick	A.G.I.G.	2005	
Le Brun, Frank Raymond	P.A.G.D.C.	1995	1989
	P.G.S.D.	2001	
Lee, Alan Edward		—	2008
Lee, Brian Trevor	P.A.G.Swd.B.	2007	2008
Lee, Colin James	P.G.St.B.	2001	2009
	G.J.D.	2006	
Lee, David Ronald	G.Stwd.	1997	2000
	P.G.J.D.	2001	
	P.G.J.O.	2005	
	P.G.S.O.	2011	
Lee, Douglas William	P.A.G.D.C.	1974	1976
	P.G.S.D.	1988	
Lee, Geoffrey Herbert	G.Stwd.	2009	
	G.J.D.	2012	
Lee, George Stewart, *J.P.*	P.A.G.D.C.	1984	1986
	Prov.G.M., Gloucestershire & Herefordshire	1986-1996	
Lee, Robert John	P.G.St.B.	2008	
Lee, Ronald William	P.G.St.B.	2007	
Lee, Walter Derek	G.Stwd.	1993	2000
	P.G.J.D.	1998	
	P.G.J.O.	2008	
Lee, Wilfred Augustus	P.A.G.D.C.	2011	
Leeman, Edward William	P.A.G.D.C.	2004	2005
Lees, Kenneth Edward	P.A.G.St.B.	1997	2007
Lees, Roy	P.A.G.D.C.	2004	2008
Leeson, Anthony Paul	P.A.G.D.C.	2009	
Le Febvre, Emilein Jean Paul	P.A.G.St.B.	1990	1989
	P.G.J.D.	1997	
Leftley, Malcolm George	P.A.G.D.C.	1994	
Le Garsmeur, Michel Alain	P.A.G.St.B.	1997	

NAME	RANK	YEAR OF APPT.	R.A.M.G.R. YEAR OF APPT.
Leighton, Ronald Ernest	P.A.G.Swd.B	1998	2002
Leitch, William		—	1999
Lendon, Arthur John	P.G.St.B.	1991	2000
	P.G.J.D.	1999	
	P.G.J.O.	2004	
Lennon, Edward	P.G.St.B.	1996	2001
	P.G.J.D.	2007	
Lent, Roger	A.G.St.B.	2003	2002
Leonard, Patrick John		—	2007
Lepper, Charles Francis, *M.A.*		—	2006
Leroy, Michael Jules	P.A.G.D.C.	2012	
Leslie, Robin	A.G.I.G.	1996	
	P.G.J.D.	2003	
Lesser, Leslie Hugh		—	1980
L'Estrange, Revd. Timothy John Nicholas	P.A.G.Chap.	2005	2010
Lever, Philip William Arnold	P.G.St.B.	2006	2000
Lever, David Anthony		—	2006
Levick, Norman Sidney	P.G.St.B.	1997	
Levy, Revd. Elkan David	P.A.G.Chap.	2009	
Lewin-Smith, John Mann	P.A.G.Swd.B	1995	1998
Lewis, Alan Penry	P.G.St.B.	2011	
Lewis, Albert	P.A.G.Swd.B	2004	
Lewis, Albert Kingsley O'Reilly	P.A.G.D.C.	2012	
Lewis, Christopher Gibson	P.A.G.Swd.B	2005	2009
Lewis, Donald Lewis		—	1994
Lewis, Dr. Donald Roy	P.A.G.D.C.	1985	1998
	G.S.D.	1992	
	P.G.J.O.	2001	
Lewis, Howard Andrew	G.Stwd.	2011	
Lewis, Mervyn David Arthur	P.G.St.B.	1992	1997
	P.G.J.D.	2012	
Lewis, Paul Morcombe		—	2007
Lewis, Reginald Arthur		—	2005
Lewis, Robert Charles	P.A.G.D.C.	2001	2002
Lewis, Robert Ronald Elliott	P.G.St.B.	1993	2004
	P.G.J.D.	2005	
Lewis, Thomas Broster	P.A.G.D.C.	2012	
Lewis, Thomas Richard	P.G.St.B.	2012	2011
Lewis, Timothy John	G.Stwd.	1990	1992
	Prov.G.M., London	1994-1996	1997 GMRAC (H.C.)
	G.Sec	1997-2005	
Lewis, Terrance William	P.G.St.B.	1997	
Lewis, Tony Charles Robson		—	2008
Lewis, William Frederick	P.A.G.St.B.	1993	2005
	P.G.J.D.	1999	
Lewis, William Peter	A.G.St.B.	2007	2010
	P.G.J.D.	2012	
Lewis-Barclay, Clive Lucy	G.St.B.	1986	
	P.G.J.D.	1991	
Lewitt, Geoffrey James	P.A.G.St.B.	2010	
Lewry, Raymond John	P.A.G.D.C.	2004	2004
	P.G.S.D.	2008	

NAME	RANK	YEAR OF APPT.	R.A.M.G.R. YEAR OF APPT.
Li, John Kwok Heem, *A.E.*	P.A.G.D.C.	2012	
Lias, Colin Ian	P.A.G.D.C.	2012	
Liddell, Keith	P.A.G.D.C.	2003	2004
	P.G.S.D.	2008	
Liddington, David Harold	P.A.G.D.C.	2009	2004
Lightburn, Peter John	G.J.D.	2009	
Lightfoot, John Edward	P.A.G.D.C.	2002	2007
	P.G.S.D.	2011	
Lihou, Peter Norman	P.G.St.B.	1998	1999
Liles, Naunton Charles William	A.G.Org.	2008-2009	
	Dep.G.Org.	2010-2012	
Lilley, Maurice	P.A.G.St.B.	1992	1998
	P.G.J.D.	1999	
Lilly, Keith Fraser	A.G.I.G.	1982	1986
	G.I.G.	1983	
	P.A.G.D.C.	1988	
	G.S.D.	1993	
	P.G.J.O.	1998	
Limbrick, Harry Bence	P.G.St.B.	2007	2008
Lincoln, Derrick William	P.G.St.B.	1994	2005
	P.G.J.D.	2006	
Lindsay, Most Revd. Hon. Dr. Órland Ugham, *D.D., O.D., O.J.*	P.G.Chap.	2003	2008
Lindsey, Dr. Basil Ivan	P.G.St.B.	2006	
Lines, Adrian Francis	P.A.G.St.B.	1996	1992
Ling, Raymond Walter		—	1997
Ling, Stephen	P.G.St.B.	2005	1996
Lissamer, William George	P.A.G.Swd.B.	2001	
Lister, Anthony Frank	P.A.G.D.C.	2011	2007
Lister, Ian Thomas	P.A.G.D.C.	2011	
Litherland, Geoffrey William	P.G.St.B.	1991	1999
	G.J.D.	1997	
	P.G.J.O.	2003	
Litherland, Thomas	P.A.G.Swd.B.	2001	
Little, Bryan Desmond	P.A.G.D.C.	1996	2002
	P.G.S.D.	2002	
	P.G.J.O.	2007	
	G.M.O.	2012	
Little, Douglas	P.A.G.St.B.	2008	
Littleford, Anthony Terence		—	2011
Littler, David Robert	P.A.G.D.C.	1998	1999
	P.G.S.D.	2006	
Littlewood, Michael John	P.A.G.Swd.B.	2003	
	P.G.J.D.	2008	
Littlewood, Samuel Ronald		—	1997
Livesey, Derek	P.A.G.D.C.	1972	
	P.G.S.D.	1984	
Livesey, William Bullock	P.A.G.St.B.	2007	
Livesley, Eric	G.Stwd.	1984	1993
	P.G.J.D.	1989	
	P.G.J.O.	1995	
Living, Eric Edward	P.G.St.B.	1994	1997
Llewellyn, David Walter, *C.B.E.*	P.G.S.D.	1995	2000
	P.G.J.O.	2001	

NAME	RANK	YEAR OF APPT.	R.A.M.G.R. YEAR OF APPT.
Lloyd, Albert Francis	P.A.G.D.C.	1994	1996
	P.G.S.D.	2003	
Lloyd, Arthur Leslie	P.A.G.St.B.	2002	
Lloyd, Christopher James Bennett	P.A.G.St.B.	2000	2007
	P.G.J.D.	2011	
Lloyd, Ivor Roberts	P.A.G.D.C.	2003	2001
Lloyd, Dr. John Benjamin	P.G.J.D.	1989	1987
	Prov.G.M., Dyfed	1989-2000	1996 GMRAC (H.C.)
Lloyd, Kenneth Harrison	G.Stwd.	1990	
	P.G.J.D.	1996	
Lloyd, Lloyd	G.I.G.	2007	2008
	Dep.G.Reg.	2010-2012	
Lloyd, Peter David	P.G.St.B.	2007	2010
Lloyd-Edwards, Sir Norman	P.G.S.D.	2009	
Lloyd-Williams, David	P.A.G.D.C.	2003	
Lo, Datuk Andrew Vun Bin	P.A.G.D.C.	2012	
Lobb, Brian William	G.Stwd.	1994	1992
	P.G.J.D.	2002	
Lobb, Philip Roy	G.Stwd.	2011	
Loch, Gordon Gilber Han Von		—	2010
Lock, Albert Edward	P.G.St.B.	2011	
Locke, Alan *J.P.*,	G.Stwd.	1996	2006
	P.G.J.D.	2001	
	P.G.J.O.	2007	
Lockett, Gordon Thomas John	P.G.St.B.	1983	1990
	G.J.D.	1988	
	P.G.J.O.	1993	
	P.G.M.O.	2000	
Lockey, Malcolm	P.G.St.B.	1996	1997
	P.G.J.D.	2003	
Lockwood, Peter Arthur	P.A.G.D.C.	2010	
Lockyer, Keith James	P.A.G.D.C.	2005	
Lomas, Barry John		—	2003
Lomas, David	P.A.G.D.C.	2007	2006
Lomas, Thomas, *J.P.*	P.A.G.D.C.	2010	2008
Long, Maj. Alexander	G.Stwd.	1984	
Long, Arnold	P.A.G.D.C.	2002	2002
	P.G.J.O.	2010	
Long, Arthur	P.G.J.D.	2004	
Long, Brian Harold, *B.Sc. (Eng.), J.P.*	P.A.G.D.C.	2003	2011
Long, Edward Harry	P.G.St.B.	2005	2006
Long, Gavin James	P.A.G.D.C.	2006	2011
Long, James Martin, *T.D.*	Dep.G.D.C.	2003-2005	2003
	P.G.J.O.	2008	
Long, John	P.G.St.B.	2001	2004
Long, Michael	P.G.St.B.	2011	2010
Lonsdale, John Richard	P.G.St.B.	2012	
Lonsdale, Joseph Lawrance	P.A.G.Swd.B.	2009	
Loo, Weng Choon	P.A.G.D.C.	2008	2009
Lopez, Charles Dennis	P.A.G.D.C.	2011	
Lord, Keith	P.A.G.St.B.	2004	
Lord, Kenneth	A.G.St.B.	2004	
Lotterman, Reinder		—	2011

NAME	RANK	YEAR OF APPT.	R.A.M.G.R. YEAR OF APPT.
Loughlin, Charles Arthur	P.A.G.D.C.	1976	
Louis, Michael John, *J.P.*	P.G.St.B.	1996	2000
	P.G.J.D.	2000	
	P.G.S.D.	2001	
	P.G.J.O.	2004	
Louw, Petrus Johannes Francois	P.A.G.D.C.	2002	2002
Love, Philip Alexander		—	1999
Lovegrove, Alex Elliot	P.A.G.D.C.	1987	1995
	P.G.S.D.	1993	
Lovett, David George Richmond	A.G.D.C.	1989	1994
	G.S.D.	1997	
	P.G.J.O.	2002	
Low, Richard Leyland	P.G.St.B.	2007	2008
Lowe, Graham Leonard	P.A.G.St.B.	1987	
Lowe, Philip Edward	G.Stwd.	2007	
	G.J.D.	2010	
Lowe, Terence John	P.A.G.Swd.B.	2009	
Lowery, John Henderson, *J.P.*	P.A.G.D.C.	1998	
Lown, Brian William	P.A.G.D.C.	2009	2011
Lown, Dennis Charles Archibald	P.A.G.St.B.	2001	
Lowndes, Peter Geoffrey	Dep.G.D.C.	1987-1989	2004
	P.G.J.O.	1994	2004GMRAC
	G.S.W.	2004	
Lowry, Charles Bowman	P.G.St.B.	2009	
Lucas, George Horace	P.A.G.D.C.	2007	
Luccock, John Brian	P.A.G.St.B.	1991	
	G.J.D.	2000	
Luckett, Roy Henry Frederick	A.G.D.C.	1999	2001
	P.G.S.D.	2011	
Luckman, Reginald Frederick	P.A.G.D.C.	1981	1979
Ludlow, John Marcus		—	1977
Luke, Peter Leslie	P.A.G.Swd.B.	2009	2010
Lunness, John Arthur	P.A.G.Swd.B.	2000	1999
	P.G.J.D.	2008	
Luttrell, John Eric	P.A.G.D.C.	2007	2011
Lye, Raymond John	P.G.J.O.	2009	
Lynch, Anthony George	P.A.G.D.C.	1993	
Lyn-Cook, Evol Washington	P.A.G.D.C.	2012	
Lynn, David George	P.A.G.Swd.B.	2004	2003
	P.G.J.D.	2012	
Lyons-Mound, Geoffrey Frank	P.G.St.B.	2007	2010
	P.G.J.D.	2012	
Mac, Roger Stuart	P.A.G.D.C.	2004	2009
	P.G.S.D.	2009	
	P.G.J.O.	2011	
	Prov.G.M., Warwickshire	2012	
MacAdam, Harry Martin	P.A.G.St.B.	2000	
Macdonald, Christopher John	G.Stwd.	2002	2003
	P.G.J.D.	2004	
Macdonald, Maj. Graham	P.A.G.Swd.B.	2003	2006
Macdonald, John Ian	P.A.G.D.C.	2003	

NAME	RANK	YEAR OF APPT.	R.A.M.G.R. YEAR OF APPT.
MacDonald, Stuart John	P.A.G.D.C.	2011	
Mace, Ronald John	P.G.St.B.	2005	
Mace, Sidney Edwin		—	1988
Macey, David Francis	P.G.S.D.	2011	
Machin, Anthony Glyn	G.Stwd.	2007	2011
	P.G.J.D.	2011	
Machin, Walter	P.A.G.D.C.	1981	1990
	P.G.S.D.	1992	
MacIntyre, Ian David		—	2004
Mack, Errol Noel	P.A.G.D.C.	1996	2003
	P.G.J.O.	2001	
Mackay, Kenneth David	P.G.St.B.	1991	
Mackenzie, Gary Stephen	G.St.B.	2002	
	P.G.J.D.	2010	
Mackenzie, Ian William	P.A.G.St.B.	2005	
MacKenzie, Edward	P.G.St.B.	1995	
Mackenzie, Ian William	P.G.J.D.	2011	2002
Mackinnon, John	P.A.G.D.C.	2009	2011
	P.G.S.D.	2012	
Macklin, Bernard William	P.A.G.D.C.	1996	1998
Mackown, Malcolm William	G.Stwd.	2005	
	P.G.J.D.	2009	
MacLean, Duncan Mactavish	P.A.G.Swd.B.	1999	2000
Macmillan, Gordon Alan	P.G.St.B.	2005	2005
	P.A.G.D.C.	2012	
MacWilliam, V.Revd. Dr. Alexander Gordon	P.A.G.Chap.	2000	
Maddison, Malcolm	P.A.G.D.C.	2011	
Maddy, David John	G.Stwd.	2012	
Madhavan, Krishnan	P.A.G.D.C.	2007	2008
Madhu Sudan, Nakanna	P.A.G.D.C.	2011	
Magee, Terence Sarsfield		—	2011
Magnay, Peter	P.G.J.D.	1998	1998
	Prov.G.M., Northumberland	1999-2009	
Magnus, Donald Isadore	P.A.G.St.B.	2004	
Mahendra, Gnanapragasam Louis	P.A.G.D.C.	2009	
Mahendran, Thuraippah Markandu, P.P.T.	P.A.G.D.C.	2004	2010
Mahy, John Ernest	P.A.G.D.C.	2001	2007
Maidment, Bertram Cary	P.A.G.D.C.	1986	
Main, Frederick Craigie	P.G.St.B.	2002	2008
	G.J.D.	2008	
	P.G.S.D.	2010	
Maison, Joseph Kenneth	P.A.G.D.C.	2005	2005
	P.G.S.D.	2012	
Maitland, James George	P.A.G.St.B.	2003	2011
Majumdar, Arunendra Kumar	P.A.G.St.B.	1993	
Makower, Oliver Alfred Ernest John	A.G.Swd.B.	1982	1996
	G.S.D.	2002	
Malan, Prof. Pierre Edouard	P.G.St.B.	2000	
	P.G.J.D.	2010	
Malcolm, Alan Roy	P.A.G.D.C.	1991	
Malcolm, William	P.A.G.St.B.	2009	

NAME	RANK	YEAR OF APPT.	R.A.M.G.R. YEAR OF APPT.
Mallams, Donald Richard	G.Stwd.	2005	
	P.G.J.D.	2010	
Mallory, Alec Leslie, *J.P., R.I.B.A.*	P.G.St.B.	2002	2009
Maltby, Charles William	P.A.G.D.C.	2010	
Maltby, George		—	2005
Malthouse, Lt.Col. Henry William	Dep.G.Swd.B	1971	1982
	G.S.O.	1986	
	G.S.W.	1996	1996/97 GMRAC
Mamoola, Khaizer Essoofi	P.A.G.D.C.	2009	2003
Manchester, John	P.A.G.D.C.	1998	2000
	P.G.J.D.	2008	
Mander, David John	P.G.St.B.	1997	1999
Mandleberg, Charles John	A.G.D.C.	1987	1988
	P.G.J.D.	1997	
	P.G.M.O.	2005	
	P.G.J.W.	2009	
Mangham, Graham	G.Stwd.	2009	
Mann, Philip Ashley, *T.D.*	Dep.G.Swd.B	1978	
	P.G.J.O.	1993	
Mann, Philip Raymond	P.A.G.St.B.	1997	2003
	P.G.J.D.	2004	
Manners, David	P.A.G.D.C.	1989	
Manomohan, Dr. Madavilakom Padmanabha Pillai	P.A.G.D.C.	2010	
Mansell, Barrie Roy	P.G.J.D.	2009	2009
Manser, Norman Sydney	P.A.G.D.C.	1985	1985
	G.S.D.	1990	
	Prov.G.M., Northants and Hunts.	1995-2000	
Mant, Derrick French	A.G.St.B.	1990	
	P.G.J.D.	1999	
Manuel, Clive Robert	G.Stwd.	2002	
	G.J.D.	2007	
Marcer, Ernesto Alberto	P.G.J.D.	2012	
March, Arthur	P.G.St.B.	1996	1995
March, Frank William	G.Stwd.	1990	1993
	P.G.J.D.	1999	
Marchant, Lt.Cdr. Charles Patrick	P.A.G.D.C.	2007	
Marchant, John Richard	P.A.G.D.C.	1991	1993
	P.G.S.D.	1995	
	P.G.J.O.	2000	
	Dist.G.M., Natal	2004-2009	
Marchant, Michael John	P.G.St.B.	2011	
Marchena, Leroy Lucien	P.A.G.D.C.	2006	
Marcus, David	P.A.G.D.C.	2006	
Marcus, Walter	P.G.J.D.	2006	2006
	P.G.S.D.	2007	
	P.G.J.O.	2008	
Markey, Jack Raymond	P.G.St.B.	2003	
Marks, Byron Donald	P.A.G.D.C.	2007	
Marks, Peter	P.G.St.B.	1988	1997
	G.J.D.	1996	
	P.G.J.O.	2009	
Marland, Henry Hewitt	P.A.G.D.C.	2006	2008

NAME	RANK	YEAR OF APPT.	R.A.M.G.R. YEAR OF APPT.
Marley, Peter Thomas	P.G.St.B.	1995	
Marley, Robert Joseph	P.A.G.D.C.	2004	2004
Marlow, Charles Alan	P.A.G.St.B.	2009	2010
Marlow, Donald Arthur	A.G.St.B.	1986	1986
	P.G.S.D.	2007	
Marlow, Wilfrid John	P.A.G.Swd.B.	2000	1991
Marple, Robert James	P.A.G.D.C.	1996	2003
Marples, Rodney Brian	G.Stwd.	2004	
	P.G.J.D.	2008	
Marr, Peter John	G.Stwd.	1992	2000
	P.G.J.D.	1997	
	P.G.J.O.	2002	
Marrow, Ronald James	P.A.G.D.C.	2011	
Marsh, James		—	2000
Marsh, John David		—	2003
Marsh, Peter Alfred	P.A.G.D.C.	2008	
Marshall, Albert Edward	P.A.G.St.B.	1998	
Marshall, Donald	P.G.St.B.	2007	
Marshall, Frank Ingle		—	1978
Marshall, Maj. Ian Vass Mackay Murray, T.D.	P.A.G.D.C.	2010	
Marshall, John David Glynn	P.G.St.B.	2008	
Marshall, Philip Graham	P.G.St.B.	2002	2007
	P.G.J.D.	2010	
Marshall, Reginald Garnet	P.A.G.D.C.	2009	2008
Marston, Revd. William Thorton	D.G.Chap.	2004	2007
Martin, Alexander Stanley, M.Sc.	P.A.G.D.C.	1997	2004
Martin, Claude Raoul	G.Insp., Belgium	1993	1993
	Dist.G.M., Belgium	1996-2002	
Martin, Colin	P.A.G.St.B.	2009	2002
Martin, David John	P.G.St.B.	2005	1996
Martin, Gordon Macindoe	P.A.G.D.C.	2001	2001
	P.G.S.D.	2009	
Martin, James Anthony	P.G.St.B.	1996	2003
	P.G.J.D.	2008	
Martin, James Edward	P.G.S.D.	2006	2009
	P.G.J.O.	2008	
	Prov.G.M., Channel Islands	2010	
Martin, John Daniel	P.A.G.D.C.	1999	2011
Martin, John David	P.A.G.Swd.B.	1999	2009
	G.J.D.	2004	
	P.G.J.O.	2011	
Martin, John Llewellyn, D.F.C.	A.G.D.C.	1986	
Martin, Kenneth Henry		—	2009
Martin, Leslie Alexander	P.G.J.D.	2002	2003
	P.G.S.D.	2006	
	Dist.G.M., South Africa (Western Division)	2006-2012	
Martin, Peter John	P.A.G.D.C.	2011	
Martin, Robert Ridley	P.A.G.D.C.	1991	
	G.S.D.	1996	
Martin, Ronald Douglas		—	2002

NAME	RANK	YEAR OF APPT.	R.A.M.G.R. YEAR OF APPT.
Martin, Stanley Harry		—	2011
Martinez, Anthony	P.A.G.D.C.	2010	
Martland, Stanley Raymond	G.Stwd.	1993	
	P.G.J.D.	1998	
	P.G.J.O.	2003	
Marton, Reginald John	P.G.St.B.	2007	
Masefield, Graham Jeffrey		—	2011
Mason, Alan James Sullivan	P.G.St.B.	2002	2005
	P.G.J.D.	2010	
Mason, Alastair Geoffrey Donne	G.Stwd.	2002	2006
	P.G.J.D.	2006	
	Dep.G.D.C.	2009-2011	
Mason, Albert	P.A.G.D.C.	1982	
	P.G.S.D.	1991	
	P.G.J.O.	2003	
Mason, Capt. Derek, *A.F.C.*	G.J.D.	1973	
Mason, Douglas John	P.A.G.D.C.	1987	1990
	P.G.S.D.	1994	
	P.G.J.O.	2007	
Mason, Melville Trevor	P.A.G.D.C.	2011	
Mason, Peter	P.G.St.B.	1993	2007
	P.G.J.D.	2001	
Mason, Peter John	P.A.G.D.C.	2004	
Mason, Ronald	P.A.G.D.C.	2005	2006
Mason, Russell John, *C.P.M.*	P.A.G.D.C.	2000	
	P.G.S.D.	2009	
Massey, Alan Ernest		—	2005
Massey, Frank Harry	P.A.G.D.C.	2007	
Massey, John		—	2011
Massey, John Raymond, *O.B.E.*	P.A.G.St.B.	2010	
Masters, Michael George Wenman	Dep.G.D.C.	1990-1992	1990
	P.G.J.O.	1995	1998 GMRAC (H.C.)
	G.D.C.	1998-2006	
	P.G.J.W.	2000	
	G.S.W.	2012	
Matcham, James Edward	P.G.St.B.	2012	
Mather, Dr. James Stephen Boyd, *Ph.D.*	G.Stwd.	1999	2011
	P.G.S.D.	2004	
	G.J.O.	2010	
Mather, Thomas	P.A.G.D.C.	2009	
Mathews, David Thomas		—	2010
Matthews, Barry John		—	2010
Matthews, Christopher Charles	P.G.St.B.	2012	
Matthews, Cyril Arthur Noel	P.G.St.B.	1999	2001
Matthews, Derek Arthur	P.A.G.D.C.	1996	2002
Matthews, Frederick	P.A.G.Swd.B.	2000	1994
	P.G.J.D.	2007	
Matthews, Sqn.Ldr. Frederick Donald, *B.A.*	P.A.G.D.C.	1978	1993
	P.G.S.D.	1984	
	P.G.J.O.	1989	
	P.G.M.O.	1996	
	P.G.J.W.	2010	
Matthews, Joseph		—	1998
Matthews, Keith Morton Lille	P.G.St.B.	2010	2006

NAME	RANK	YEAR OF APPT.	R.A.M.G.R. YEAR OF APPT.
Matthews, Neil Howard, *B.Sc., B.Arch., R.I.B.A.* ...	A.G.D.C.	1998	1998
	G.Insp.Wks.	1998-2012	1998 GMRAC
	P.G.M.O.	2000	
	P.G.J.W.	2005	
Matthews, Stephen James	—		2010
Mattison, Jack Francis Charles	P.G.St.B.	1994	2000
	P.G.J.O.	1999	
	P.G.J.O.	2005	
Maughan, Peter James	P.G.St.B.	2007	
Mauladad, Nazir Ahmed	P.G.St.B.	1990	2001
	P.G.J.D.	1998	
Maultby, John Rollett Leedale	P.A.G.Swd.B.	2011	2008
Maw, Geoffrey William	G.Stwd.	1991	1997
	P.G.J.D.	1996	
Mawson, Peter	—		2010
Mawson, Michael	P.G.St.B.	2010	
Maxfield, Donald James	P.A.G.St.B.	1998	
	P.G.J.D.	2004	
	P.G.J.O.	2009	
Maxwell, Michael Andrew	P.A.G.D.C.	2001	
May, Norman Ernest William	—		2009
May, Stanley Vivian	P.G.St.B.	1986	
Maybury, Terrence Vincent	G.Stwd.	2004	2004
	P.G.J.D.	2009	
Mayer, Kenneth	P.A.G.D.C.	2010	
Mayes, Colin Oliver	P.G.St.B.	1995	2000
	P.G.J.D.	2007	
Mayes, Edward Herbert	P.A.G.St.B.	1997	
Mayes, Wilfred Harold	P.G.St.B.	1980	
	P.G.J.D.	1991	
Mayne, Douglas Henry	P.A.G.D.C.	2009	
Mayne, Harold Edward	P.A.G.D.C.	1978	1989
	G.J.D.	1985	
	P.G.J.O.	1990	
	P.G.M.O.	1996	
Mayoh, Brian William	P.G.St.B.	2012	
Mays, Tony Graham	P.A.G.Swd.B.	2008	2007
McAuliffe, Arthur Gartside		—	1997
McCall, Edward	G.Stwd.	1995	1998
	P.G.J.D.	2000	
	P.G.J.O.	2008	
McClaren, Alexander Sillars	P.G.J.D.	2006	2009
McCord, James Fraser	G.Stwd.	2011	
McCorkindale, Archibald Armour, *O.B.E.*	P.G.St.B.	1995	1999
	P.G.J.O.	1999	
	Dist.G.M., East Africa	2005-2008	
McCormick, Francis	P.A.G.D.C.	1973	1977
	Dist.G.M., Brazil	1977-1981	
McCready, Revd. Kennedy Lemar, *M.A., BSc.*	P.A.G.D.C.	1980	
	P.Dep.G.Chap.	1998	
McCreath, John Richard McConnell	—		2001
McCully, Keith Cedric	P.A.G.D.C.	2011	2010
McDade, James Woodrow	P.A.G.D.C.	2010	2003

NAME	RANK	YEAR OF APPT.	R.A.M.G.R. YEAR OF APPT.
McDarmaid, Robert Ian	P.A.G.D.C.	2007	
McDermott, Lt.Cdr. John Henry		—	2000
McDermott, Norman Hubert	P.A.G.D.C.	2005	2008
	P.G.J.D.	2008	
McDowall, Alexander McAdam	P.A.G.D.C.	1992	1990
	P.G.S.D.	1997	
	P.G.J.O.	2003	
McGann, John	P.A.G.D.C.	2007	2009
McGarel-Groves, Brig. Robin Julian, O.B.E.	P.G.Swd.B.	1967	1987
	P.G.M.O.	2008	
McGeach, Revd. William George	P.A.G.Chap.	2000	
McGeagh, Ernest Alexander	P.A.G.St.B.	2002	
	P.G.J.D.	2007	
McGibbon, Capt. Iain Malcolm, O.B.E.	P.A.G.D.C.	2003	2005
	Dist.G.M., New Zealand	2006	
McGowan, Michael	P.A.G.D.C.	2001	2007
McGown, Robert Young	P.A.G.D.C.	2007	2011
McGrath, Michael George	P.G.St.B.	2005	
McGregor, Duncan	P.G.St.B.	2008	
McHugh, Peter Anthony	P.A.G.D.C.	2008	
McIlwaine, Simon Peter	P.A.G.D.C.	2008	2007
McIntyre, Peter John	A.G.D.C.	2006	2003
McKay, William	P.G.St.B.	1982	1994
	P.G.J.D.	1995	
	P.G.J.O.	2001	
McKee, James Dunlop	P.A.G.D.C.	1996	2002
	P.G.S.D.	2002	
	P.G.S.O.	2006	
McKeeman, James	P.A.G.D.C.	1986	1988
	P.G.S.D.	1995	
	P.G.J.O.	2001	
McKelvie, Ian James	P.A.G.D.C.	1986	
McKenzie, Benjamin Alexander	P.A.G.D.C.	2008	
McLain, John Dunn	G.Stwd.	1998	2006
	G.S.D.	2005	
McLachlan, John		—	2001
McLanaghan, John		—	1993
McLaren, Alexander Sillars	G.Stwd.	2001	2009
McLaren, Dr. Lyndon Edison	P.G.St.B.	1999	2000
McLauchlan, James Kibert		—	1999
McLaughlan, James Ferguson		—	2005
McLaughlin, Neville Paul	P.G.St.B.	1986	
	P.G.J.D.	2000	
McLean, David Bolingbroke	P.A.G.D.C.	1991	1993
	P.G.J.D.	1995	
	P.G.S.D.	1998	
	Prov.G.M., Sussex	2000-2007	
McLean, Donald	P.A.G.Swd.B.	2002	2000
McLean, Fritz Charles	P.A.G.Swd.B.	2001	2002
	P.G.S.D.	2004	
	P.G.J.O.	2008	
McLean, Ronald Henry	P.A.G.D.C.	2010	
McMillan, Robert Alexander	G.Stwd.	2012	

NAME	RANK	YEAR OF APPT.	R.A.M.G.R. YEAR OF APPT.
McNab, Christopher Robert	P.A.G.D.C.	2006	2010
	G.S.D.	2011	
McNally, David Arthur	P.A.G.D.C.	2012	
McNeill, Graham John	P.A.G.D.C.	2008	
McQueen, Duncan	—		2009
McRiner, John David	P.A.G.D.C.	2005	
Meade, Gerard	P.A.G.Swd.B.	2002	2007
	P.G.J.D.	2010	
Meade, Michael	P.G.S.D.	1995	1996
	Prov.G.M., Wiltshire	2002-2010	
Meaden, Peter Arthur	G.Stwd.	1975	
	P.G.J.D.	1999	
Meanwell, Robert Albert	P.A.G.D.C.	2008	
Mear, John William	P.A.G.D.C.	2004	2004
Mecklenburgh, Frederick Rowland	P.A.G.D.C.	1998	1996
Mee, Lionel Broadbent	P.A.G.Swd.B.	2010	2009
Meech, Bruce Albert	P.A.G.D.C.	2002	1998
Meek, Norman Alan	G.Stwd.	2000	
Meeres, Brian	P.G.I.G.	2003	2004
	P.A.G.D.C.	2008	
Meerza, Rodney	P.G.St.B.	2012	
Melber, George Edward	P.G.I.G.	1996	1998
	P.G.J.D.	2001	
	P.G.J.O.	2006	
Melhuish, Albert Edward	G.Stwd.	1989	
	P.G.J.D.	1996	
Melhuish, Dennis Francis	P.G.St.B.	1991	
	G.J.D.	2004	
Mello, David Phenis		—	2000
Melvin, David	P.A.G.D.C.	2005	1993
	P.G.S.D.	2012	
Memory, Dean William	P.G.St.B.	2005	
Mendis, Peter Mohan Ranil Mendis	P.G.St.B.	1995	
	P.G.S.D.	2002	
Menoyo-Garcia, Jose Luis	P.G.St.B.	2011	2011
Mensa-Annan, Rupert Jordan	P.A.G.St.B.	2006	2003
Mensah, Nana Dr. Fredua	P.G.St.B.	1991	1997
	G.Insp., Ghana	1997-2010	
	Dist.G.M., Ghana	2010	
Merchant, Shums	P.G.J.D.	2009	2005
Merry, William Alfred	A.G.D.C.	1986	1996
	P.G.S.D.	1995	
	P.G.J.O.	2002	
Messenger, Peter	P.A.G.D.C.	2006	
Messum, James Leonard	P.G.St.B.	2007	
Messum, Peter Ronald Bunney	P.A.G.D.C.	2007	2010
Meynell, Colin John	P.A.G.Chap.	2003	
Middleton, Stewart Charles Lambert	P.A.G.D.C.	2002	2004
	G.S.D.	2010	

NAME	RANK	YEAR OF APPT.	R.A.M.G.R. YEAR OF APPT.
Mighall, Simon Andrew, *B.Sc.*	A.G.D.C.	1999	2002
	A.G.Sec.	2007-2009	
	P.G.S.D.	2008	
	Dep.G.Sec	2010-2011	
	P.G.J.O.	2010	
	P.G.M.O.	2012	
Mignotte, Ernest Mortimer	P.A.G.St.B.	2006	
Milburn, Lance	G.I.G.	2012	
Milburn, Norman Dunkeld	P.A.G.Swd.B.	1998	2000
	G.J.D.	2002	
	G.J.O.	2012	
Milburn, Ronald	P.A.G.D.C.	2012	
Miles, Brian	P.A.G.D.C.	2005	2005
	Dep.G.Tyler	2008-2011	
	P.G.S.D.	2010	
Miles, John Stockley, *J.P.*	P.A.G.D.C.	2000	2005
Miles, Peter Donald	P.A.G.D.C.	2005	2009
Milford, Sir Clive Reginald	P.A.G.St.B.	2010	
Milgate, Frederick Arthur	P.A.G.D.C.	1995	2003
	P.G.J.D.	2012	
Millard, Stanley Francis	G.Stwd.	1991	2003
	P.G.J.D.	2002	
Miller, Alan	G.Stwd.	1994	1997
	P.G.J.D.	1999	
Miller, David John McCulloch	P.A.G.D.C.	2011	
Miller, David Walter	G.Stwd.	2011	
Miller, James Thomson	P.G.S.D.	1996	2001
Miller, Revd. Robert Anthony	P.Dep.G.Chap.	2001	1983
Miller, William	P.A.G.D.C.	2009	
Miller, William Paul		—	2009
Millings, Leonard John	P.A.G.D.C.	2010	2010
Mills, Edward Walter Thomas	G.Stwd.	2005	
	P.G.J.D.	2008	
Mills, Graham	A.G.D.C.	2005	2004
	P.G.S.D.	2007	
Mills, Jack	P.A.G.D.C.	1992	
Mills, Maurice		—	2005
Mills, Lt.Col. Stephen Eaton	P.G.St.B.	2001	2002
	P.G.S.D.	2003	
	P.G.J.O.	2009	
Millson, Robert Joseph		—	2005
Milne-Leith, David Hendry Allan	P.A.G.D.C.	2000	1998
	P.G.S.D.	2007	
Milner, Bryan Crampton		—	2000
Milner, Paul Anthony	P.A.G.D.C.	2009	2001
Milward, Ian Clive	P.A.G.D.C.	1990	
Minchin, Frederick Reginald	P.G.St.B.	2007	
Minett, Graham John	G.Stwd.	2012	
Minns, Michael John	P.A.G.D.C.	2009	
Minshaw, John William Michael	A.G.D.C.	1999	2001
Misselke, Eric Franz Hans	P.G.St.B.	1999	1995
Mitchell, Beresford Charles	Dist.G.M., New Zealand Sth. Island	1988-1995	1990

NAME	RANK	YEAR OF APPT.	R.A.M.G.R. YEAR OF APPT.
Mitchell, Christopher John	P.A.G.Swd.B.	2006	2009
Mitchell, John Wallace		—	2001
Mitchell, Leonard Michael	G.Stwd.	2006	2008
	G.J.D.	2009	
Mitchell, Lynne Forbes	P.A.G.D.C.	2010	
Mitchell, Peter John	P.A.G.D.C.	1990	
Mitchell, Peter Silvanus	P.A.G.D.C.	2007	2001
Mitchell, Robert Simon Curtis	G.Stwd.	1999	2005
	P.G.J.D.	2004	
	P.G.J.O.	2011	
Mitchell, Stanley Frederick		—	1988
Mitchell, Sidney James		—	1991
Mitchell-Fyffe, Andrew	P.G.St.B.	1995	1996
Mitchinson, Graham John	P.A.G.St.B.	2007	
Mitchinson, John Brian	P.A.G.D.C.	2006	
	P.G.S.D.	2012	
Mitchinson, Robert Thomas Hardiker		—	2005
Mitten, Martin Francis	P.G.St.B.	1998	2007
	G.J.D.	2005	
Mock, Eric George Sanders	P.G.S.D.	2009	
Mogford, David Martin	P.A.G.D.C.	2004	2002
	P.G.S.D.	2010	
Moiser, Frank Victor	P.G.St.B.	1996	
Moles, Anthony Clive	P.G.St.B.	1989	1985
	P.G.S.D.	1994	
	P.G.J.O.	1999	
Moles, Phillip Nicholas, *J.P.*	G.Stwd.	2012	2002
Molland, George Kenneth	P.A.G.St.B.	1997	2006
	P.G.J.D.	2006	
Molver, Errol Neal	P.A.G.D.C.	2011	
Molyneux, Brian, *J.P.*	P.A.G.D.C.	2002	
	G.S.D.	2008	
Monk, Alan Frederick Alexander, *J.P.*	A.G.I.G.	2003	2009
Monks, Eric Frances	P.A.G.D.C.	1995	1994
	P.G.J.O.	2010	
Monplaisir, Kenneth Allan Patrick, *O.B.E., Q.C.*	P.A.G.Swd.B.	1995	2005
	P.G.S.D.	2006	
Moody, Peter Lawrence	P.A.G.D.C.	1982	
Moore, Alan David	P.G.St.B.	2006	2005
Moore, Anthony Francis, *M.B.E.*	P.G.J.D.	1996	1998
	P.G.J.O.	2003	
	P.G.S.O.	2012	
Moore, Brian Alec Charles	G.Stwd.	1990	1991
	P.G.J.D.	2008	
Moore, Bernard Garnet	P.G.St.B.	1998	1998
	P.G.J.D.	2007	
Moore, Christopher Lintern	G.Stwd.	2011	
	P.G.J.D.	2012	
Moore, Dennis Frank	P.G.St.B.	2002	1995
Moore, Duncan John	P.A.G.D.C.	2000	2003
	G.S.D.	2007	
Moore, George William	P.A.G.Swd.B.	2001	2007
Moore, Jack Edward		—	2005

NAME	RANK	YEAR OF APPT.	R.A.M.G.R. YEAR OF APPT.
Moore, John Herbert Vincent	A.G.D.C.	2010	
Moore, Leonard Colin	P.G.St.B.	1998	
	P.G.J.D.	2006	
Moore, Rodney	G.Stwd.	1999	
	P.G.J.D.	2004	
Moore, William John	G.Stwd.	1991	1995
	P.G.J.D.	1997	
Moores, Noel Sydney	P.A.G.D.C.	1971	1971
	P.G.J.D.	1979	
Moorse, Stuart Neil	P.A.G.D.C.	2006	2002
Moralee, John Young	P.A.G.D.C.	2009	2006
Morby, Anthony Roger	P.A.G.D.C.	2000	2002
	P.G.J.D.	2004	
	P.G.J.O.	2008	
Moreland, Malcolm Christopher	P.A.G.D.C.	1989	1995
	P.G.S.D.	1994	
	P.G.S.O.	2001	
Moreton, Aubrey Peter Thomas	P.A.G.St.B.	1994	
Morey, John Walter	P.G.St.B.	2000	
	P.G.J.D.	2008	
Morgan, David Glanville	P.G.St.B.	1989	
Morgan, David Neil	G.St.B.	2012	
Morgan, Evan Edmund	P.G.St.B.	1997	
Morgan, Ifor Selwyn		—	2000
Morgan, Jeffrey Paul	P.G.S.D.	2010	2009
Morgan, John	P.A.G.D.C.	2003	2010
	P.G.S.D.	2010	
Morgan, John Graham, *R.C.C., T.D., J.P.*	P.A.G.D.C.	2007	
	P.G.S.D.	2012	
Morgan, Jonathan Lloyd Conwy	G.Stwd.	2001	2003
	P.G.J.D.	2007	
Morgan, Leslie Sydney	P.A.G.Swd.B.	2004	
	P.G.J.D.	2012	
Morgan, Rev. Dr. Michael	P.A.G.Chap.	1984	1988
	Prov.G.M., Hants. and I.O.W.	1988-1997	1990 GMRAC (H.C.)
Morgan, Terence David	P.A.G.Swd.B.	2009	2006
Morison, Raymond Marshfield	P.G.St.B.	1993	1995
	P.G.J.D.	2006	
Morley, David Roy	P.G.St.B.	1995	
	P.G.J.D.	2000	
Morley, James Bramley	G.Stwd.	1978	1983
	P.A.G.D.C.	1984	
	G.S.D.	1988	
	Prov.G.M., West Yorks.	1989-1994	
Morley, Richard Stanley	P.A.G.D.C.	2008	
Morley, William	P.A.G.D.C.	2003	2002
Morley, William Henry	P.G.J.D.	2010	2003
Morrell, Anthony	P.A.G.St.B.	2003	
	P.G.J.D.	2010	
Morris, Alfred	P.G.St.B.	1985	2008
	P.G.J.D.	2006	
Morris, Alfred Leonard	P.G.St.B.	2000	1986
	P.G.J.D.	2011	

NAME	RANK	YEAR OF APPT.	R.A.M.G.R. YEAR OF APPT.
Morris, Allan David, J.P.	P.A.G.D.C.	1988	1992
	G.S.D.	1999	
	P.G.J.O.	2009	
Morris, Andrew Timothy	P.G.S.D.	2005	2005
	P.G.J.O.	2008	
Morris, Anthony	P.G.S.D.	1995	1995
	P.G.J.O.	2000	
	Prov.G.M., Leicestershire & Rutland	2005	
Morris, Cyril	P.A.G.D.C.	2000	2005
	P.G.J.D.	2010	
Morris, David Benjamin	G.Stwd.	2002	2002
	P.G.J.D.	2008	
Morris, David John Miles	P.A.G.D.C.	2006	2005
Morris, Donald James	P.G.St.B.	1998	1999
Morris, George Edward	P.A.G.D.C.	2002	2002
Morris, John Albert, J.P.		—	2006
Morris, John Edward	G.Stwd.	1994	1999
	P.G.J.D.	2000	
Morris, Kenneth Graham		—	2011
Morris, William Andrew	P.G.St.B.	2011	
Morrisey, Patrick Norman	P.A.G.St.B.	2007	
Morrison, Nolan	G.J.D.	2008	
Morrow, Robert Anthony Henry	P.A.G.D.C.	1999	1998
	P.G.S.O.	2003	
	P.G.J.W.	2004	
Mortimore, Alan Wilson	P.A.G.D.C.	2008	
Mortley, Peter		—	1993
Morton, Michael	P.A.G.D.C.	1996	
Morzaria, Kurtikumar Chotalal	P.A.G.D.C.	2012	2010
Moses, David	P.A.G.D.C.	2010	
Moss, Ernest Frederick Robert	P.G.S.D.	2010	
Moss, Frank Trevor Alfred	P.A.G.D.C.	2012	
Moss, Richard Samuel	P.A.G.D.C.	2001	2008
	G.S.D.	2007	
	P.G.J.O.	2012	
Moth, Roy	P.A.G.D.C.	2008	
Motley, Charles Osburn	Dep.G.D.C.	1988-1990	
	P.G.J.O.	1997	
Mould, Herman Auguste	P.A.G.D.C.	1998	2001
	P.G.J.D.	2008	
Moulson, John	P.A.G.D.C.	2002	
	G.S.D.	2009	
Moulton, Frederick Kenneth	P.A.G.D.C.	1998	1992
Mountford, John Ernest	P.G.I.G.	2003	
Moxey, Colin	A.G.Swd.B.	1991	1997
	P.G.J.D.	1997	
	P.G.J.O.	2002	
Moxley, Derek Straker, J.P.	G.Stwd.	1973	1973
	P.G.J.O.	1977	
Moxom, Nigel Charles	P.G.St.B.	2002	2004
	P.G.J.D.	2009	
Moy, David	P.A.G.D.C.	1997	2003
Moye, Roger Alan		—	2009

NAME	RANK	YEAR OF APPT.	R.A.M.G.R. YEAR OF APPT.
Moyes, James McDougal	P.G.St.B.	1995	2000
	P.G.J.D.	2001	
Moyle, Anthony Raymond, *J.P.*	G.Stwd.	1996	1995
	G.J.D.	2001	
	P.G.S.D.	2010	
Moyse, James Albert	P.A.G.D.C.	1979	1975
	P.G.S.D.	1992	
Mueller, Carl Lynn	—		2003
Mugford, William Douglas	P.G.St.B.	1985	
Muir, Brian Fraser	A.G.I.G.	2008	2002
Mullally, Maj. Michael, *T.D., F.C.I.S., F.C.I.*	A.G.D.C.	1993	1999
	P.G.S.D.	2000	
	P.G.J.O.	2006	
Mullan, Capt. Edwin Frederick	P.A.G.D.C.	1992	1998
	G.S.D.	2004	
	G.S.O.	2010	
Mullard, Harry	P.A.G.St.B.	2010	
Muller, Robert Judah August	P.G.St.B.	1996	1999
Müller, Wilhelm Christo	P.A.G.D.C.	1995	1996
	Dist.G.M., South Africa Eastern Division	1999	
Muller, Ward Ingersol	P.A.G.D.C.	1989	
	P.G.J.D.	2000	
Mullins, William	P.A.G.D.C.	2007	
Mumford, Nigel	P.A.G.D.C.	1997	
	P.G.J.D.	2007	
Munday, Eric Alec	P.A.G.Swd.B.	1987	
	P.G.J.D.	1997	
Munday, Eric Alfred	P.G.St.B.	1968	1983
	P.G.S.D.	1987	
Munday, Gary Christopher		—	2011
Munday, James	P.A.G.St.B.	2012	
Munday, James Gordon	P.A.G.St.B.	1998	
Munday, Jonathan Eric Lewis	P.G.St.B.	2007	
Munday, Robert Leslie	G.St.B.	1998	2000
	Dep.G.Swd.B.	2002	
	Dist.G.M., Spain	2007	
Munford, Ian Ross	P.A.G.St.B.	1991	2000
	P.G.J.D.	1996	
	P.G.J.O.	2006	
Munro, Eric Percival, *M.B.E.*	P.A.G.D.C.	2010	
Munro, James Ian	G.Stwd.	2008	2010
	P.G.J.D.	2011	
Murdoch, Geoffrey		—	2002
Murdoch, Ian Walter	P.A.G.Swd.B.	2008	
Murgatroyd, Ernest Arthur	P.A.G.D.C.	2003	
Murgett, Cecil Reginald	A.G.St.B.	1987	
Murley, James Edwin	P.A.G.St.B.	2007	2010
Murphy, Alan Christopher	P.A.G.St.B.	2012	
Murphy, Brian Arthur	G.Stwd.	1978	
	G.S.D.	1985	
Murphy, Michael John	P.G.I.G.	2000	2001
	P.A.G.D.C.	2007	
	P.G.S.D.	2012	

NAME	RANK	YEAR OF APPT.	R.A.M.G.R. YEAR OF APPT.
Murray, Alan Sholto	G.J.D.	1989	
Murray, Jack	P.A.G.D.C.	1993	2006
	P.G.S.D.	1998	
Murray, Leslie William	P.G.St.B.	1999	
	P.G.S.D.	2008	
Murray, Peter John Anthony	P.A.G.Swd.B.	2008	2011
Murray, Reginald Victor	P.A.G.D.C.	1988	1985
Murtagh, Ronald Joseph		—	2011
Murzell, Nicholas John	Dep.G.D.C.	1999-2002	1999
	P.G.J.O.	2004	
	P.G.M.O.	2009	
Muston, Paul Howard	G.Stwd.	2006	2007
	P.G.J.D.	2009	
Mylan, James Leonard	P.G.St.B.	1984	
	P.G.J.D.	1994	
Nadler, Joseph	P.A.G.Swd.B.	2002	
Nagarajan, Viswanathan	P.G.St.B.	1995	2000
	P.G.S.D.	2000	
	P.G.J.O.	2005	
	Dist.G.M., Northern India	2008	
Nairn, Ian Douglas	G.Stwd.	2006	
	G.J.D.	2010	
Nakhoda, Hatim Fidahusein	P.A.G.D.C.	2004	
Nall, Robert James	P.A.G.Swd.B.	2010	2001
Nanot, Jean-Louis	A.G.Swd.B.	1990	
Nanton, Leslie Eustace Bindon	P.A.G.D.C.	2005	2006
Narayanaswamy, Puducode Ramakrishna	P.A.G.D.C.	1995	
Narayanan, Mathur Srinivas Iyer, *B.Sc.*	P.G.St.B.	1992	2002
	P.G.J.D.	1997	
Narayanan, Sermadevi Venkatasubramania		—	1989
Narayanan, Viswanathan	P.A.G.D.C.	2006	
Narayanan Nair, Jayakrishnan Nair		—	2003
Narey, Colin	P.A.G.D.C.	2011	
Narey, Trevor	P.G.St.B.	1999	2008
	P.G.J.D.	2007	
Nash, David John	G.Stwd.	2011	
Nash, Geoffrey Ivor	P.G.St.B.	1992	2001
	G.J.D.	1997	
	P.G.J.O.	2002	
Nash, William George	P.A.G.D.C.	1974	1980
	P.G.S.D.	1982	
Nasmith, Robert Greenwood		—	2009
Nayar, Damodaran Asan Gopalakrishnan	P.A.G.D.C.	2012	
Nayar, Harish Kumar	P.G.I.G.	2002	
Nayar, Kishore	P.G.St.B.	2005	2006
	P.A.G.D.C.	2011	
Naylor, Alan Keith	P.A.G.D.C.	2012	
Neate, Graham David	P.A.G.D.C.	2004	
Negandhi, Damodar Bhagwandas	P.A.G.D.C.	2005	

NAME	RANK	YEAR OF APPT.	R.A.M.G.R. YEAR OF APPT.
Neil, Samuel James	G.Stwd.	2002	
	P.G.J.D.	2008	
Neilson, David		—	1990
Nelson, David Brian	G.Stwd.	1995	1997
	G.J.D.	2000	
	Prov.G.M., Somerset	2004	
Nelson, Ian Sinclair	P.A.G.St.B.	1998	
Nelson, Peter John	P.A.G.Swd.B.	2006	2004
Nelson, Thomas Arnold	P.A.G.D.C.	1987	1992
	P.G.S.D.	1995	
	P.G.J.O.	2008	
Nethercott, Roy William	P.G.St.B.	2007	2002
Nettleship, Robert John	P.A.G.D.C.	2009	
Nettleton-Hammond, Roger Benjamin	P.G.St.B.	2012	2009
Neve, Ian Andrew	P.A.G.D.C.	1993	1988
	P.G.S.D.	2009	
Nevell, Leonard Arthur	P.A.G.D.C.	1981	1995
	G.S.D.	1990	
	P.G.J.O.	1996	
Neville, Roy Norman	G.Stwd.	2006	2011
	P.G.J.D.	2009	
Neville, Terence Rodney	P.A.G.D.C.	2008	
Nevin, Leslie	P.G.St.B.	2012	
Newbould, Roy Sharpe	P.G.St.B.	2004	2008
Newell, David Leonard Henry		—	1994
Newell, George Frederick	P.A.G.D.C.	2002	
	P.G.J.O.	2005	
Newlands, William Campbell	P.A.G.Swd.B.	1992	1993
	P.G.J.D.	2005	
Newman, James Henry	P.A.G.D.C.	2012	
Newman, Royston James	P.A.G.D.C.	2009	2011
Newmarch, Michael George Leuchars	P.A.G.St.B.	2006	2005
Newnham, Denis	A.G.St.B.	1988	2000
	P.G.J.D.	1998	
Newsome, Reginald Arnold	G.Stwd.	2000	1999
	P.G.J.D.	2004	
	P.G.J.O.	2010	
Newson-Smith, Grevile Robin	P.A.G.D.C.	2011	
Newth, Michael John	P.A.G.D.C.	1991	1996
	P.G.S.D.	1999	
	P.G.J.O.	2004	
	P.G.M.O.	2011	
Newton, Gerald	P.A.G.St.B.	2009	
Newton, Graham	P.A.G.D.C.	2007	
Newton, Leonard	P.A.G.D.C.	2004	2000
Newton, Percy	P.A.G.D.C.	1983	
Newton, Robert Gibb	P.A.G.D.C.	2012	
Nichol, Thomas David	P.A.G.Swd.B.	2002	
Nicholas, David John	P.A.G.St.B.	2005	2010
Nicholl, Terence James	P.G.I.G.	2003	
	P.A.G.D.C.	2010	
Nicholls, Wg.Cdr. John Hamilton	P.G.St.B.	1995	2007
Nichols, George	P.A.G.D.C.	1993	
	P.G.S.D.	2009	

NAME	RANK	YEAR OF APPT.	R.A.M.G.R. YEAR OF APPT.
Nicholson, John Anthony	P.A.G.Swd.B.	2010	
Nicholson, Terrance	P.A.G.Swd.B.	1999	1993
Nicol, Ian Murray	P.A.G.St.B.	2000	
	P.G.J.D.	2008	
Nida, Edgar Jacob	P.G.St.B.	2003	2004
Nilgiria, Ferhad Jamshed	P.A.G.D.C.	2007	2007
	P.G.J.O.	2011	
Nixon, Carl Mervyn	P.A.G.D.C.	2011	2005
Nixon, Kirkland Hencliffe	P.A.G.D.C.	2012	
Noakes, Peter Edward	P.G.St.B.	1990	1989
Noble, Christopher	A.G.D.C.	1999	2003
Noel, Dr. Pierre Raoul Francis	P.A.G.D.C.	1990	1994
	P.G.S.O.	1999	
Noorbhai, Bashir	P.G.J.D.	2001	2003
	P.G.S.D.	2010	
Norbury, David	G.Stwd.	2005	
	P.G.J.D.	2010	
Norman, Frank Arthur Langlands	P.A.G.Swd.B.	2004	2011
	P.A.G.D.C.	2012	
Norman, Hugh		—	1993
Norman, Paul Anthony	G.I.G.	2006	
	P.G.J.D.	2009	
	Prov.G.M., East Anglia	2010	
Norris, Anthony		—	2008
Norris, John Harold	P.G.St.B.	1976	2002
	P.G.S.D.	1981	
	P.G.J.O.	1990	
North, Derek George	P.A.G.St.B.	2011	
Northampton, The Most Hon.The Marquess of	P.G.S.W.	2006	
Northbrook, Winston Ernest	P.G.St.B.	2006	
Northcott, Donald Henry	P.G.St.B.	2000	
Northover, John Stuart	P.G.St.B.	1992	1997
	P.G.J.D.	1999	
	P.G.J.O.	2008	
Northway, William Job	P.A.G.D.C.	1988	1998
Norwood, William	P.A.G.St.B.	1998	2005
Notley, Ivan Hugh	P.A.G.D.C.	2000	2003
	P.G.S.D.	2006	
	G.M.O.	2011	
Notley, Malcolm Anthony Leslie	P.A.G.Swd.B.	2002	
Nunn, George Michael	G.St.B.	1990	1997
	P.G.J.D.	2005	
Nunn, Kenneth William		—	2007
Nunn, Roland Sydney	G.Stwd.	1997	1996
	P.A.G.D.C.	2007	
Nurse, Patrick Roy	P.A.G.D.C.	2000	
	P.G.S.D.	2009	
Nuttall, Anthony Horrobin	G.Stwd.	1996	1995
	P.G.J.D.	2001	
Nuttall, James Robert Lewis	P.G.I.G.	1999	1995
Nye, John Maurice	P.A.G.D.C.	2009	
Nye, Stanley Edward Norman	P.A.G.D.C.	1999	2001

NAME	RANK	YEAR OF APPT.	R.A.M.G.R. YEAR OF APPT.
O'Brien, Daniel Anthony		—	2008
O'Brien, Hugh Allison	P.A.G.D.C.	2009	
O'Brien, Ivor Ethelbert	P.A.G.D.C.	2009	
O'Hagan, Jonathan De Villiers		—	2008
O'Hanlon, Dennis Brian	P.A.G.D.C.	1989	
O'Leary, David James	P.A.G.D.C.	2000	2003
O'Leary, John Kenyon	P.A.G.St.B.	1997	1993
	P.G.J.D.	2004	
O'Neill, Arthur		—	2005
O'Reilly, Bernard	P.A.G.Swd.B.	2003	1999
O'Shaughnessy, Kevin Myles Patrick	P.A.G.D.C.	2012	
O'Sullivan, Anthony John	P.G.St.B.	1995	1998
O'Sullivan, Garrett	P.G.St.B.	1979	
O'Sullivan, Gavin Thomas	G.Stwd.	2007	2010
	P.G.J.D.	2010	
O'Sullivan, Lawrence	P.G.St.B.	2009	2002
O'Toole, Michael	G.Stwd.	2004	
	P.G.J.D.	2011	
Oakes, John Trevor	P.A.G.D.C.	1996	2000
Oakes, Norman Basil	P.A.G.D.C.	2001	
	P.G.S.D.	2009	
Oakley, Austin Peter		—	2004
Oakley-Smith, John, *J.P.*	P.G.St.B.	1997	2001
	P.G.J.D.	2003	
	P.G.S.D.	2005	
	P.G.J.W.	2008	
Oates, Hilton	P.A.G.D.C.	2010	2009
Oatham, Albert Leonard	P.G.St.B.	2010	
Oats, Michael William Charles	P.A.G.Swd.B.	2012	
Oatway, Albert	P.A.G.Swd.B.	1999	
Obadiah, Abraham Joseph	P.A.G.D.C.	1997	2002
	G.S.D.	2006	
Odams, Alan		—	2003
Ogden, Bryan Russell	P.G.J.D.	2001	2001
	Prov.G.M., Cheshire	2002	
Ogden, John Edward	G.Stwd.	2003	
	P.G.J.D.	2008	
Oldfield, Alan	G.Stwd.	2009	
	P.G.J.D.	2012	
Oliver, Derek Franklin	P.A.G.D.C.	2010	
Oliver, Jack		—	1993
Oliver, James		—	2010
Oliver, John Henry	P.G.St.B.	1993	2003
Oliver, Michael John	P.G.St.B.	1999	2009
	P.G.J.D.	2009	
Olliver, Richard John	A.G.D.C.	2008	
Olszewski, Jan Alexander	P.A.G.Swd.B.	2010	
Olver, Richard Noel		—	2005
Ong, Hean Tat	P.A.G.D.C.	1998	1999
	P.G.S.D.	2004	
	P.G.J.O.	2011	
Ong, Richard Guan Seng	P.A.G.D.C.	2006	2009
Ong, Sing Kwee	P.A.G.D.C.	2012	

NAME	RANK	YEAR OF APPT.	R.A.M.G.R. YEAR OF APPT.
Onslow, Dennis	P.G.St.B.	1997	2002
	P.G.J.D.	2004	
Opie, Nicholas Leo		—	2007
Orchard, Cyril Francis John	P.A.G.D.C.	2009	
Organ, Raymond John	P.A.G.D.C.	2002	2007
	P.G.S.D.	2009	
Ormerod, Malcolm	P.G.St.B.	2010	
Orr, Malcolm Edward		—	2009
Orton, Phillip George	G.Stwd.	2001	2000
	Dep.G.Swd.B.	2006	
Osborn, Robin Osborn	P.A.G.D.C.	1987	2000
	P.G.S.D.	1995	
	P.G.S.O.	2000	
	P.G.J.W.	2007	
Osborne, George Sidney		—	1998
Osborne, Haydn	P.A.G.Swd.B.	2009	
Osborne, Thomas Edward	P.A.G.D.C.	1998	
Osborne, Winston		—	2005
Osgathorp, Michael James Herbert	P.A.G.Swd.B.	2003	2010
Oshowole, Maj. Abiudun Alfred, *J.P.*	P.G.St.B.	2001	
Ostwind, Paul		—	2003
Ostwind, Paul Louis	P.A.G.Swd.B.	2004	
	P.G.J.D.	2011	
Oughton, Peter	P.G.I.G.	1998	2001
Ovenden, Dennis Edwin	P.G.St.B.	1995	
Overton, John Leslie	P.G.St.B.	2010	
Overy, Stephen Geoffrey	G.Stwd.	2009	
	P.G.J.D.	2012	
Ovington, Derrick	P.A.G.D.C.	1980	
	P.G.S.D.	1994	
Owen, Dr. Alan John	P.A.G.D.C.	1983	
Owen, Brian Harold	A.G.I.G.	2012	
Owen, Denys John Chant	P.A.G.D.C.	1992	
Owen, Evan Kenneth	P.A.G.D.C.	1997	
Owen, Eric Wyn	P.G.St.B.	1997	
	P.G.J.D.	2007	
Owen, Frank Harkness	P.G.St.B.	1999	1995
	P.G.S.D.	2009	
Owen, Gwynant, *M.B.E.*	P.G.St.B.	2000	
Owen, John William Henry	P.A.G.D.C.	2002	
Owen, Richard Byron	P.G.St.B.	2005	
Owen, Robert Peter	P.A.G.St.B.	1997	2000
	P.G.J.D.	2002	
	P.G.J.O.	2007	
Owen, Thomas Joseph	P.G.I.G.	2006	2005
Owen, William	P.A.G.St.B.	2011	
Owens, Barrie	P.A.G.D.C.	2005	2008
	G.S.D.	2010	
Owens, Henry Edward	P.A.G.D.C.	2005	2010
Padam, Mohan Singh	P.G.St.B.	2007	
Padberg, Hermann Heinrich	P.G.St.B.	2001	1995

NAME	RANK	YEAR OF APPT.	R.A.M.G.R. YEAR OF APPT.
Page, Bryan Frank	P.A.G.D.C.	1988	1983
	P.G.S.D.	1994	
	P.G.J.O.	2005	
Page, David Asbrey	P.G.St.B.	1992	
Page, Ewan Stafford	A.G.D.C.	1988	1988
	Prov.G.M., Berks. & Oxon	1988-1994	1997 GMRAC
	Prov.G.M., Berkshire	1994-2002	
Page, Gerald		—	2009
Page, Samuel Ivor	P.A.G.D.C.	2011	
Page, Thomas Stanley		—	1988
Page, Col. Walter Fountain, *M.C., T.D.*	G.Sw.B.	1985	1988
Paige, Ian Evald	P.A.G.D.C.	2002	2006
	P.G.S.D.	2007	
Pain, Michael Kenneth	P.G.St.B.	2007	2002
Painter, Douglas Arnold	P.G.St.B.	1996	2001
Palmer, Geoffrey Vincent	P.G.St.B.	2005	
Palmer, Harold George	P.G.St.B.	1988	1997
	P.G.J.D.	2002	
Pam, Stephen Henry	P.A.G.St.B.	2010	2006
Pandelai, Arvind		—	2008
Pankhurst, Keith Frederick	P.G.St.B.	2011	
Pape, Alan	P.A.G.St.B.	2006	
Parab, Aroon Kumar Sadanand		—	2008
Pardoe, Ronald Thomas	P.G.St.B.	1994	
Park, Thomas Parr	P.G.St.B.	1992	2003
	P.G.J.D.	2000	
Parker, Alan Egerton	P.A.G.D.C.	2004	
Parker, Alan Patrick	P.A.G.D.C.	1990	1993
	G.S.D.	1995	
	P.G.S.O.	2000	
Parker, Anthony Clifford	P.A.G.D.C.	2002	
	P.G.S.D.	2007	
Parker, David Eric	P.A.G.D.C.	2006	
Parker, David Fishwick	P.A.G.D.C.	2008	
Parker, Ivan Keith	G.Stwd.	2000	1997
	P.G.J.D.	2007	
Parker, John Robert	P.A.G.D.C.	2004	2010
Parker, Owen Desmond	P.G.St.B.	2007	2004
Parker, Richard	P.A.G.D.C.	2000	2005
	P.G.J.O.	2005	
Parker, Roger Trevor	G.Stwd.	2000	2005
	P.G.J.D.	2006	
Parkes, Brian Ernest	P.A.G.D.C.	2011	
Parkes, Douglas James	G.Stwd.	1994	1998
	P.G.J.D.	2004	
Parkes Bowen, Dr. Malcolm David Marston	Dep.G.Swd.B.	2000	2009
	P.G.J.O.	2009	
Parkin, Brian Arnold	P.A.G.St.B.	2000	
Parkin, David James	P.A.G.Swd.B.	2000	2003
Parkin, James Hodgson	G.Stwd.	1996	
	G.S.D.	2001	
Parkin, Ramon Philip	P.G.St.B.	2011	

NAME	RANK	YEAR OF APPT.	R.A.M.G.R. YEAR OF APPT.
Parkins, Brian James	G.Stwd.	2008	
Parkins, Brian James Michael	P.G.J.D.	2011	
Parkins, Calwyn Kirwan Onslo Bonner	P.A.G.St.B.	2005	
	P.G.J.D.	2012	
Parlour, Peter Gordon	P.A.G.D.C.	2003	
Parnell, David Peter Lewarne		—	2004
Parr, Frederick Charles	P.A.G.D.C.	2009	
Parrington, Ronald Frank Clayton	P.G.S.D.	1967	
Parrish, Barrie James	P.G.St.B.	2006	
Parrish, Eric Lionel	P.A.G.D.C.	1996	1992
Parrish, Geoffrey John	G.Stwd.	2006	2005
	P.G.J.D.	2010	
Parrott, Hugh	P.A.G.D.C.	2007	
Parry, Neville Hurst	G.Stwd.	2004	
	P.G.J.D.	2009	
Parsons, Frank Frederick	P.G.St.B.	2005	
Parsons, Frederick Stephen		—	2007
Parsons, Henry Harold	P.G.St.B.	1969	1992
	P.G.J.O.	1998	
Parsons, Robert Spencer	P.A.G.D.C.	1993	1994
	G.S.D.	1998	
	P.G.J.O.	2011	
Partington, Brian		—	2011
Partington, John Russell	A.G.St.B.	2009	
Partridge, Roy	P.A.G.D.C.	2010	
Parvin, Trevor Edward	P.A.G.D.C.	2009	2009
Pascho, David Frederick	G.Stwd.	1994	1996
	P.G.J.D.	1998	
	P.G.J.O.	2004	
Pascoe, Colin Ernest	P.A.G.D.C.	2009	2005
Pascoe, Harry	P.G.St.B.	1982	1983
	P.G.J.D.	1989	
Pascoe, Norman Douglas	P.G.S.D.	1989	
Pashley, Revd. Howard Thomas	A.G.D.C.	1999	2007
	P.Dep.G.Chap.	2007	
Pate, Bernard George	P.A.G.St.B.	2001	2000
Pate, Francis William	P.A.G.D.C.	1999	1999
Patel, Achyutkumar Chandubai	P.A.G.D.C.	2001	1999
	P.G.S.D.	2012	
Patel, Bhagwanji Makan	P.A.G.D.C.	2004	2006
	P.G.J.D.	2009	
Patel, Capt. Firoz Manecksha	P.A.G.D.C.	1998	2006
	P.G.S.D.	2006	
Patel, Ghanshyam Maganbhai	G.Stwd.	2010	
	P.G.S.D.	2012	
Patel, Hasmukh Jashbhai	P.G.J.D.	1998	1998
	P.G.S.D.	2001	
	P.G.J.O.	2006	
Patel, Mukeshkumar Manubhai		—	2009
Patel, Praful Kumar Chimanbhai	P.G.St.B.	2002	
	P.G.J.D.	2009	
Patel, Rajnikant Ashabhai	P.G.St.B.	2000	2003
	P.G.J.D.	2005	

NAME	RANK	YEAR OF APPT.	R.A.M.G.R. YEAR OF APPT.
Patel, Rutton Munchershaw Hormusji	P.A.G.D.C.	1993	1996
	P.G.J.D.	2003	
Patel, Shirish Pranlal	P.A.G.St.B.	2011	
Patel, Uddayan	G.Stwd.	2008	
	P.G.J.D.	2011	
Paternoster, John Roger	P.A.G.D.C.	2011	2011
Paterson, Paul Phillip	P.A.G.D.C.	2002	2004
	Dep.G.D.C.	2004-2006	
	P.G.J.O.	2009	
Paterson, Robert	—		1999
Paterson, Robert John	P.A.G.Swd.B.	2008	2003
Patey, William Leonard	P.A.G.D.C.	2010	
Patience, Donald	P.A.G.Swd.B.	2007	2007
Patnick, Edward Keith	G.Stwd.	1998	2006
	G.S.D.	2004	
	P.G.J.O.	2010	
Patrick, Philip James	P.A.G.D.C.	1997	2009
	P.G.S.D.	2002	
	P.G.J.O.	2008	
Patrick, William Desmond	P.A.G.D.C.	1995	1996
	G.Insp, Western Atlantic	1997-2005	
	P.G.J.W.	2004	
Pattison, Sidney	P.A.G.D.C.	1999	
Pattison, Tony Robert	P.A.G.St.B.	2005	2002
Pattni, Chhotalal Damji	G.Stwd.	2011	
Patton, Maj. Michael Anthony	P.A.G.D.C.	2001	2004
	G.S.D.	2006	
Paul, John Neil	P.G.St.B.	2007	
Pausey, Kenneth John	P.A.G.D.C.	1974	1975
	P.G.J.O.	1979	1988 GMRAC (H.C.)
	Prov.G.M., Bucks.	1982-2002	
Pawsey, Hubert Sydney	P.G.St.B.	1985	
	P.G.J.D.	1992	
Payen, James Etienne	P.G.St.B.	2012	
Payne, Hadyn Jack	P.A.G.St.B.	2003	2000
Payne, John Bryan	—		2000
Payne, Jonathan Richard	P.A.G.St.B.	2011	2005
Payne, Noel Kenneth	G.Stwd.	1978	1998
	P.G.J.D.	1995	
	P.G.J.O.	2006	
Payne, Richard Charles Arthur	G.Stwd.	1997	
	P.G.J.D.	2008	
Payne-Jeremiah, Revd. Dr. William Desmond	P.G.St.B.	1997	1999
	P.G.J.D.	2003	
	Dep.G.Chap.	2006	
	P.G.J.O.	2009	
Peabody, David John	P.A.G.Swd.B.	2001	
Peachey, Keith Brian	P.G.St.B.	1999	
Peacock, Douglas Raymond	P.A.G.D.C.	2009	2007
Peacock, Graham John	—		2005
Peake, George	P.G.S.D.	2004	
Pearce, Adrian Francis	A.G.St.B.	2012	
Pearce, Brian Arthur	—		2006

NAME	RANK	YEAR OF APPT.	R.A.M.G.R. YEAR OF APPT.
Pearce, John Hedley Tyrrell	P.A.G.D.C.	1984	1990
	P.G.S.D.	1996	
Pearce, Michael George	P.G.St.B.	2011	2009
Pearce, William Raymond	P.G.St.B.	2010	
Pearson, Arthur John	G.Stwd.	2008	2010
	P.G.J.D.	2012	
Pearson, James Victor	A.G.St.B.	2000	
	P.G.J.D.	2008	
Pearson, John Reginald	P.A.G.D.C.	2005	2002
Pearson, Keith	P.G.St.B.	2001	2001
	P.A.G.D.C.	2007	
Peck, David John	P.A.G.St.B.	2007	2011
Peck, Derek Edward		—	2000
Peck, Raymond	P.G.St.B.	2002	2002
	P.G.J.D.	2011	
Peddie, John Stewart	P.A.G.D.C.	1987	1990
	G.S.D.	1992	
Peel, Adrian Timothy	P.A.G.Swd.B.	2011	
Peeters, Geeraart Adrianus Siegfried Ma	P.G.S.D.	2011	
Pegg, Michael George	P.G.St.B.	2006	
Peirce, Frederick Ernest William	P.A.G.D.C.	1971	1974
	P.G.J.D.	1987	
	P.G.J.O.	1993	
Pell, Walter Anthony		—	2004
Pelotier, Jacques	P.A.G.St.B.	1997	
Pelser, George	P.A.G.D.C.	2003	1998
Penfold, Peter Lyndon	P.A.G.Swd.B.	2008	2011
Pengelly, Christopher John	G.Stwd.	2007	
	P.G.J.D.	2010	
Pengelly, David William	P.A.G.D.C.	2004	
Pengelly, Philip John	P.A.G.D.C.	1994	1996
	G.S.D.	1999	
	P.G.J.O.	2004	
Penn, Gordon Geoffrey	P.G.St.B.	2002	
Penn, Nigel William	G.Stwd.	2006	2006
	Dep.G.D.C.	2007-2009	
	P.G.J.O.	2012	
Penny, Clifford John	P.A.G.D.C.	2005	2006
Penny, Leslie Alan	P.A.G.D.C.	1997	
	P.G.S.D.	2010	
Penny, Raymond Douglas Mawson	G.Stwd.	1992	
	P.G.J.D.	1997	
	P.G.J.O.	2008	
Pepperrell, Brian Arthur	A.G.D.C.	1988	1987
	Dep.G.D.C.	1993-95	
	P.G.J.O.	1998	
	P.G.M.O.	2005	
Percival, Anthony Charles	P.G.St.B.	2005	2005
Percival, Barrie Owen	P.A.G.D.C.	2004	
	P.G.S.D.	2009	
Percival, Donald Geoffrey	P.A.G.St.B.	1992	1993
	P.G.J.D.	2002	
Perera, Milroy Sherwin	P.A.G.D.C.	1997	
	P.G.J.O.	2008	

NAME	RANK	YEAR OF APPT.	R.A.M.G.R. YEAR OF APPT.
Peres, Revd. Dr. Jacques-Noel	P.A.G.Chap.	1996	
Perkins, David John	P.A.G.D.C.	2008	2005
Perkins, Geoffrey		—	2009
Perkins, Graham Laurence	P.G.St.B.	2007	
Perkins, Kenneth	P.G.St.B.	1991	
Perkins, Norton Benjamin		—	2009
Perks, Kenneth Gordon Thomas	P.A.G.St.B.	2002	2002
Perks, Roger John	G.Stwd.	2010	2011
Perry, Allan Barry	P.A.G.D.C.	1997	2001
Perry, Maurice Christopher John	P.G.St.B.	1996	
Perry, Ronald Leonard	P.G.St.B.	1989	
	P.G.J.D.	1998	
Perry, Stuart Riches	P.G.St.B.	2000	
	P.G.J.D.	2008	
Persaud, Doodnauth	P.A.G.D.C.	2004	2003
	P.G.S.D.	2011	
Pescod, Michael John	P.A.G.D.C.	2010	
Peters, Frederik Dirk	P.A.G.D.C.	1990	1993
	P.G.S.D.	1995	
	Dist.G.M., Netherlands	1998-2007	
Peters, James Stuart	G.Stwd.	1985	1990
	P.G.J.D.	1991	
	P.G.J.O.	1997	
	P.G.M.O.	2004	
	P.G.J.W.	2008	
Peters, John Newland	P.A.G.D.C.	2010	2011
Peters, William John	P.A.G.Swd.B.	2010	2008
Pethig, Neil Alexander	P.A.G.D.C.	2000	
	P.G.S.D.	2003	
Petit, Georges Edward Alexander	Dist.G.M., Bolivia	2000-2012	2000
Petrie, David Mowat	P.A.G.D.C.	1994	
	P.G.J.D.	2009	
Petrie, Kenneth Parkin	P.A.G.D.C.	1991	1997
	P.G.S.D.	2000	
Pettit, Norman Frederick		—	2006
Petty, Michael Davis		—	2005
Pewter, Barry Richard	P.A.G.Swd.B.	2011	2008
Pharo, Peter Edward, T.D.	P.A.G.D.C.	1993	1996
	G.S.D.	2000	
Pheasant, Colin George	P.G.St.B.	2009	
Phillimore, Frank Kenneth George	P.A.G.D.C.	2005	2001
Phillimore, John Henry	P.A.G.D.C.	1991	1996
	P.G.S.D.	1997	
	P.G.J.O.	2005	
Phillimore, Reynold Victor	G.St.B.	2000	2003
	P.G.J.D.	2005	
Phillip, John David	P.G.St.B.	1987	
Phillips, Bernard Richard	P.A.G.D.C.	2009	
Phillips, Dr. Brent Elliot Vincent Augustus	P.A.G.D.C.	2004	2004
	P.G.J.D.	2010	
Phillips, David William	P.A.G.D.C.	2012	
Phillips, Douglas Richard		—	2007

NAME	RANK	YEAR OF APPT.	R.A.M.G.R. YEAR OF APPT.
Phillips, Ivor Richard	A.G.Swd.B.	2006	
Phillips, John Anthony		—	2009
Phillips, John David	P.G.St.B.	1999	2007
	P.G.J.D.	2006	
Phillips, John Francis	P.A.G.D.C.	2012	
Phillips, John Thomas Henry	P.A.G.St.B.	2011	2010
Phillips, Neil	P.A.G.D.C.	2008	
Phillips, Paul		—	2011
Phillips, Peter	P.A.G.D.C.	2007	2004
Phillips, Richard Elgin	P.A.G.D.C.	1999	1996
Phillips, William Brocklebank	P.A.G.D.C.	1997	
	P.G.J.D.	2009	
Phillips, Wynford Luther	P.A.G.D.C.	2000	
Philp, Clifford John		—	2009
Philpot, Henry Michael	P.A.G.D.C.	2011	2009
Philpott, Christopher Harold	A.G.D.C.	1994	1986
Pick, Harold Arthur		—	1996
Pickard, Philip Clifford	G.Stwd.	2005	2008
	P.G.J.D.	2008	
Pickering, Gerald Ledger, J.P.	P.A.G.Swd.B.	1998	2005
	G.S.D.	2005	
Pickles, William Robert	P.G.St.B.	2007	
Picton, David John	P.A.G.D.C.	1996	
	G.S.D.	2003	
	P.G.J.O.	2007	
Piczenik, David James	G.Stwd.	1992	1996
	P.G.J.D.	1998	
	P.G.J.O.	2008	
Piedrahita, Francisco Casiano	P.A.G.D.C.	2009	
Pienaar, Johannes Nicholaas Willem	P.A.G.D.C.	1989	1999
	P.G.J.D.	2003	
Pienaar, Matthys Machiel	P.G.St.B.	2003	2010
	P.G.J.D.	2011	
Piercy, John Lewis Huteson	P.A.G.D.C.	1995	1987
Pierson, Linford Ainsworth	P.G.St.B.	2008	
Piggford, Frederick	P.A.G.St.B.	1998	
Piggins, Arthur	P.A.G.Swd.B.	2001	2004
	P.G.J.O.	2011	
Piggott, Keith		—	2005
Pigott, Jack	P.A.G.Swd.B.	2004	
Pike, Michael John		—	2008
Pike, Robert William John	P.G.St.B.	2006	
Pilkington, Revd. Charles George Willink	P.A.G.Chap.	1995	2006
Pilling, Derek Lenfesty	P.A.G.D.C.	2006	2007
	P.G.S.D.	2012	
Pindar, Jack Smith	P.A.G.D.C.	2003	
Pinder, Hartis Eugene	P.A.G.D.C.	2006	2005
Pinfield, Michael David	G.Stwd.	2011	
Pinker, Norman James	P.A.G.D.C.	1986	
Pinkerton, David Scott	G.Stwd.	2007	
	P.G.J.D.	2010	
Pinkett, Edwad George	P.A.G.D.C.	2009	

NAME	RANK	YEAR OF APPT.	R.A.M.G.R. YEAR OF APPT.
Pinney, Laurence Frank	P.G.InspWks.	1974	
Pinnock, John Dudley	A.G.D.C.	2012	
Pipe, Maxwell Charles	P.A.G.D.C.	2011	
Piper, Harry Norman	P.A.G.D.C.	1991	
Pitchford, Kenneth	P.A.G.Swd.B.	2011	
Pither, Eric	P.A.G.D.C.	1982	
Pittaway, John Kenneth	P.G.S.D.	1998	1999
	P.G.J.O.	2003	
Pitto, Frederick William	P.A.G.St.B.	2008	
Place, Robert William	P.A.G.D.C.	1990	
	P.G.S.D.	1998	
Plaistowe, Eric Gordon	P.G.I.G.	1992	1991
	G.J.D.	1997	
	P.G.J.O.	2002	
Planner, Brian Charles		—	2010
Platt, John Kenneth		—	2006
Platt, Paul Edward	P.A.G.D.C.	2010	2011
Platten, David Barry		—	2011
Platts, John Douglas Arthur	G.Stwd.	1995	1997
	P.G.J.D.	1999	
	P.G.J.O.	2004	
	Prov.G.M., Bristol	2009	
Playford, Antony John	P.A.G.St.B.	2012	
Pluckrose, Anthony		—	2009
Pointon, Terrence Madew	P.A.G.D.C.	2001	2010
	P.G.S.D.	2007	
Polkinghorne, Edwin Russell	P.A.G.D.C.	1999	2003
	P.G.J.O.	2006	
Pollard, Harold Farrar	P.A.G.D.C.	1991	
Pollard, John Lewis	P.A.G.D.C.	2008	
Pollexfen, Vernon James	P.G.St.B.	1987	2002
Pomfret, James Edward	P.G.St.B.	2000	1997
Pond, Stanley Victor	P.A.G.D.C.	1993	1998
Ponnaiya, Selvaraj	P.A.G.D.C.	2010	
Ponting, Michael Frederick	A.G.Insp.Wks.	1990-1991	1995
Pool, Stephen Ronald	P.G.St.B.	2000	
Poole, Alexander Francis John	P.A.G.St.B.	2009	
Poole, Michael James	G.Stwd.	1999	2004
	P.G.J.D.	2006	
	G.S.O.	2011	
Poole, Peter Norman	P.G.St.B.	2003	
Pooley, Arthur Edward	P.A.G.D.C.	2001	
Poologasingam, Subramaniam	P.A.G.D.C.	2011	
Poot, Frank Cornelis Johannes	G.St.B.	2010	
Pope, John Rodney	P.A.G.D.C.	2011	
Pope, Peter Charles		—	2010
Portbury, James	P.A.G.D.C.	2001	
Porter, Alan Roy	P.A.G.D.C.	1997	2000
	G.S.D.	2003	
Porter, Philip Joseph	P.A.G.D.C.	2002	2003
	P.G.S.D.	2008	
Porter, Michael William	P.A.G.D.C.	2007	

NAME	RANK	YEAR OF APPT.	R.A.M.G.R. YEAR OF APPT.
Porter, Capt. Walter David	G.Stwd.	1999	2000
	P.G.J.D.	2004	
Porter, Walter David	P.G.J.O.	2011	
Porter, William John	P.A.G.D.C.	2011	
Porter, William Keith	P.A.G.Swd.B.	2001	
Porwal, Narendra Shankarlal	P.A.G.D.C.	1991	1999
	P.G.S.B.	1997	
	P.G.J.O.	2005	
Postlethwaite, Jack	P.G.St.B.	1997	
Postlethwaite, James Stephenson	P.A.G.D.C.	2006	
Potter, Graham	P.A.G.Swd.B.	2012	2004
Potter, Ian Dalton	P.G.St.B.	2012	
Potter, Nigel Hewitt	P.A.G.D.C.	1996	2002
	P.G.S.D.	2001	
	G.J.O.	2007	
Potts, Frederick, *M.B.E.*	P.G.St.B.	1994	2001
Potts, Robert John	A.G.D.C.	2008	2007
	P.G.J.D.	2010	
Potts, William David	P.G.St.B.	1980	
	G.J.D.	1988	
Poultney, Henry John	P.A.G.D.C.	2001	
Poulton, William Michael	P.A.G.Swd.B.	2001	
Pouncey, Herman	P.A.G.Swd.B.	2002	
Poupart, Jean Baptiste	P.G.J.D.	1994	1995
Powell, Alfred Charles	P.A.G.D.C.	1992	2004
	P.G.S.D.	2002	
Powell, Allan Edgar	P.A.G.D.C.	2001	2004
	P.G.J.O.	2007	
Powell, David Anthony	P.A.G.D.C.	2005	
	P.G.S.D.	2009	
Powell, David Richard	P.A.G.D.C.	2010	2011
Powell, David Sydney	P.A.G.D.C.	2005	
Powell, Frank Lucas	G.Stwd.	2006	2011
	P.G.J.D.	2009	
Powell, John Allen	P.A.G.D.C.	2008	
Powell, John Anthony Roy		—	2009
Powell, John David	P.G.St.B.	2008	
Powell, Thomas Henry	P.G.St.B.	1985	
	G.J.D.	1993	
Poxon, Robert	P.A.G.D.C.	1994	2002
	G.S.D.	2000	2008 GMRAC
	Prov.G.M., Derbyshire	2003	
Poynter, Anthony Robert	P.G.St.B.	2007	2005
Pradhan, Pradhakar Shivram	P.G.St.B.	2001	2004
Pratt, Alfred John Peter	P.A.G.St.B.	2005	
Pratt, Anthony Alvin Rigby	P.G.St.B.	2002	2008
Pratt, David Stephen	P.A.G.D.C.	1991	1996
	P.G.S.D.	1999	
	P.G.J.O.	2010	
Pratt, William John Thomas	G.Stwd.	2011	
Prax, Geoffrey Ian	G.Stwd.	2000	2001
	P.G.S.D.	2004	
	P.G.J.O.	2008	

NAME	RANK	YEAR OF APPT.	R.A.M.G.R. YEAR OF APPT.
Preece, Lindsay	G.Stwd.	1996	1997
	P.G.J.D.	2002	
Preedy, Lt.Cdr. Timothy George, *R.N.*	P.A.G.D.C.	1985	1977
Prescott, Mark Gabriel	P.G.St.B.	2008	2009
Preston, Alexander George	A.G.D.C.	2006	2007
Preston, Revd. David Francis	A.G.Chap.	2003	
Preston, Kenneth Stuart	G.Stwd.	2003	2010
	P.G.J.D.	2008	
Preston, Peter Oliver		—	1999
Preston, Ronald William	P.A.G.Swd.B.	2006	2003
Pretsell, William	P.A.G.D.C.	2010	
Prevett, Brian James	P.A.G.Swd.B.	2008	2007
Price, Brian William	P.A.G.D.C.	1994	2001
	P.G.S.D.	2003	
	P.G.S.O.	2012	
Price, Colin	P.A.G.Swd.B.	1999	1996
Price, Chesney Alexander	P.A.G.St.B.	2000	2004
	P.G.J.D.	2006	
Price, David John	P.A.G.St.B.	1998	2003
	P.G.J.D.	2003	
Price Edward John Staite	G.Stwd.	2010	2011
Price, Edwin	P.A.G.D.C.	2011	
Price, Michael John, *C.B.E.*	P.G.S.D.	2005	
Price, Norman Thomas George	P.G.St.B.	1989	
	P.G.J.D.	2003	
Price, Richard Brian Ward	P.G.S.D.	2006	
Prideaux, Colin Antony	P.A.G.D.C.	2010	
Priestley, Brian Ben	P.G.St.B.	2002	2005
Priestley, Donald	A.G.D.C.	2002	1999
	P.G.S.D.	2010	
Prince, Henry	P.A.G.D.C.	1982	
	P.G.S.D.	1989	
Pring, John	P.A.G.Swd.B.	1998	2006
	P.G.J.D.	2005	
Pringle, Gp.Capt. Herbert John	P.A.G.D.C.	1990	1993
Pringle, Michael	P.A.G.D.C.	1987	1994
Prior, Bernard Lionel	P.A.G.St.B.	1999	2005
	P.G.J.D.	2010	
Pritchard, Glyn	P.G.St.B.	1993	
	G.J.D.	2000	
Pritchard, Robert James	P.A.G.D.C.	1996	1992
Pritt, Colin		—	1999
Prizeman, John Herbert	P.G.J.D.	2004	2004
	P.G.J.O.	2006	
	Prov.G.M., Hampshire & Isle of Wight	2007	
Probert, Kenneth	P.A.G.D.C.	2012	
Probert, Cdr. Peter Frank	P.G.St.B.	2010	
Procter, Brian Henry	P.A.G.D.C.	2010	2010
Procter, Keith	P.A.G.St.B.	2002	
Proudley, John Raymond		—	2008
Pugh, Christopher	P.G.St.B.	2007	

NAME	RANK	YEAR OF APPT.	R.A.M.G.R. YEAR OF APPT.
Pugh, Colin George	P.A.G.D.C.	1990	1989
	P.G.J.D.	2000	
	P.G.J.O.	2009	
Pugh, David Lloyd	A.G.D.C.	2009	
Pugh, Michael Arthur, A.E., M.B.B.S., F.R.C.S., F.R.C.O.S.	P.G.St.B.	2002	1998
	P.G.J.D.	2007	
Pullin, Arthur William	P.A.G.St.B.	1992	
	P.G.J.D.	2004	
Pullin, Stanley Clive	P.A.G.D.C.	2004	2006
Pulman, William Marcel Hugh	P.A.G.D.C.	2006	2011
Punt, David George, O.B.E.	P.G.S.D.	2012	2003
Purcell, David Eric	G.Stwd.	2007	2006
	P.G.J.D.	2010	
Purdie, David Charles	G.Stwd.	2010	
Purdon, Leon Hamilton	P.G.St.B.	1992	
Purdy, Phillip Reginald Robert		—	2009
Purkis, Raymond John	P.A.G.D.C.	1989	1985
	P.G.S.D.	1995	
	P.G.J.O.	2000	
Purkiss, Dennis Charles	P.A.G.D.C.	1995	1996
Purnell, Frederick Arthur	A.G.D.C.	2000	
Purnell-Edwards, Patrick	P.A.G.D.C.	2010	
Purser, George Robert Gavin	G.Swd.B.	1991	1998
	G.J.W.	1998	1998 GMRAC
	A.G.M.	2000-2001	
	Dep.G.M.	2002-2009	
Purslow, Michael Gordon	P.A.G.D.C.	1990	
Purssell, Roy Antony Baynton	P.G.St.B.	2000	2004
Punt, David George	A.G.D.C.	2005	
Puttrell, Richard Boswell	A.G.D.C.	2009	2010
Pyke, Godfrey Bennett		—	2003
Pymer, Reginald	P.A.G.D.C.	2003	
Quansah, Kow Abaka	P.A.G.D.C.	1997	
	P.G.S.D.	2005	
	P.G.J.O.	2010	
Quant, Stephen Peter	P.G.St.B.	2002	
Quickmire, Douglas	P.G.St.B.	2006	
Quinn, George William	P.A.G.D.C.	2000	2000
	P.G.S.D.	2008	
Quinn, Roger Paul	P.A.G.St.B.	2012	
Quinn, Thomas	P.A.G.D.C.	2012	
Race, Russell John	P.G.S.D.	2004	2003
	G.S.W.	2009	
Rackliff, Alfred Edward	P.A.G.D.C.	1962	1987
	P.G.S.D.	2001	
	P.G.J.O.	2009	
Rademan, Frederick John	P.A.G.D.C.	1988	2005
	P.G.S.D.	2002	
	P.G.J.O.	2007	

NAME	RANK	YEAR OF APPT.	R.A.M.G.R. YEAR OF APPT.
Radford, Alan William..	P.A.G.D.C............................	2005	2007
	G.S.D....................................	2010	
Radford, William Alan..	P.A.G.St.B.	2004	2006
	P.G.J.D................................	2011	
Radia, Sudhirchandra Govindji	P.G.St.B.	2007	2003
Radmore, Christopher David.................................	A.G.Swd.B.	2003	2005
	P.A.G.D.C.............................	2006	
	Prov.G.M., Hertfordshire	2008	
Rae, Everard William Duncombe.........................	P.A.G.D.C.............................	1998	
Rainford, Robert Francis	P.A.G.D.C............................	2010	
Raison, Ian Arthur	—		2009
Rajan, Thomas Soundra..	P.G.St.B.	1982	
	P.G.J.D.................................	1996	
Rajdev, Mahendra Bhagwanji	P.G.St.B.	2006	2004
Ramachandra, Dato Dr. Nadarajan........................	P.A.G.D.C.............................	2008	2010
Ramond, Gerard Joseph Rene	P.G.S.D.	1994	
Ramsay, David Keith..	P.A.G.D.C.............................	2008	2010
	G.S.D....................................	2012	
Ramsay-Smith, Ramsay Howard..........................	—		2005
Ramsden, Arthur..	A.G.D.C................................	1985	1991
	P.G.S.D.	1990	
Ramsden, Graham	P.A.G.D.C.............................	1997	
	P.G.S.D.	2008	
Ramsden, Prof. William Arthur, *Q.C.*	P.A.G.St.B.	1997	1997
Ranauta, Ajit Singh...	P.A.G.Swd.B........................	2002	
Ranauta, Harcharan Singh	P.A.G.St.B.	2002	
Randall, Herbert Benjamin	P.G.St.B.	1983	1980
	P.G.J.D.................................	1998	
Randle, Richard	P.A.G.Swd.B........................	2012	
Rangachari, Gopaladesikachari	P.A.G.D.C.............................	1998	2006
	P.G.J.D.................................	2004	
Ranganathan, Govindaraja......................................	P.A.G.D.C.............................	2003	2001
	P.G.J.D.................................	2011	
Rankin, Frank Alexander..	P.A.G.D.C.............................	1997	2002
	P.G.S.D.	2004	
	P.G.J.O.	2009	
Ransom, Martin John..	P.G.St.B.	2006	
Ransom, Ralph Dementri	—		2011
Ratcliffe, Neil Thomas	P.G.St.B.	2004	
Rathnam, Dr. Tanjore Amirthalingam Kanaga	P.A.G.D.C.............................	2002	
	P.G.J.D.................................	2003	
Rau, Henry Carlos	P.A.G.D.C.............................	2006	
Raven, Graham	G.Stwd..................................	2012	
Raven, James William	P.A.G.St.B.	1989	1989
	P.G.J.D.................................	1997	
	P.G.J.O.	2006	
Ravindran, Kunniraman Kurup	P.A.G.D.C.............................	2008	2005
Rawcliffe, Stanley	G.Stwd..................................	2007	
	P.G.J.D.................................	2010	
Rawlings, Robin Ian	P.G.St.B.	1985	1991
	P.G.J.D.................................	1991	
	Dist.G.M., South East Asia 1998-2003		

NAME	RANK	YEAR OF APPT.	R.A.M.G.R. YEAR OF APPT.
Rawlings, Ronald Richard	G.Stwd.	2009	
	P.G.J.D.	2012	
Rawlins, David John Frederick	G.Stwd.	1982	1984
	G.J.D.	1985	
	P.G.J.O.	1995	
	P.G.M.O.	2007	
	Prov.G.M., Warwickshire	2007-2012	
Rawlinson, John Michael	P.A.G.D.C.	1992	2000
	P.G.S.D.	2001	
Rayfield, Wg.Cdr. Gordon	P.A.G.D.C.	2000	2001
Raymont, James William John	P.A.G.St.B.	2001	1999
	P.G.J.D.	2010	
Rayner, Raymond Leonard	P.G.St.B.	2004	2005
Rea, David Wallis	G.J.D.	1994	1995
	P.G.J.O.	2005	
Read, John Lawrence Ward	A.G.D.C.	1994	1999
Read, Kenneth Albert		—	1997
Reader, Hon.Maj. Reginald Frank	P.A.G.D.C.	1984	1987
	Prov.G.M., Leics. & Rutland	1988-1995	
Reading, David George	G.I.G.	2010	
	G.J.D.	2011	
Rebeiro, Henry Gonsalves		—	2004
Reddyhoff, Ernest Wilfred	P.G.St.B.	2001	
Redfern, Kenneth Alan		—	2009
Redman, Graham Frederick	P.A.G.D.C.	1989	1992
	Dep.G.Swd.B.	1994	
	G.Swd.B.	1997	
	P.G.S.O.	2004	
Redman-Brown, Geoffrey Michael	G.Stwd.	1977	1980
	Dep.G.D.C.	1980-1982	1983 GMRAC
	G.S.W.	1986	1986 GMRAC (H.C.)
	Prov.G.M., Oxfordshire	1994-2004	
Redpath, William John	G.Stwd.	1987	1989
	P.G.J.D.	1992	
	P.G.J.O.	1997	
Reed, Douglas		—	2006
Reed, Nicolas Andrew	P.A.G.D.C.	2004	
	P.G.J.O.	2008	
Reed, Raymond Walter	P.G.St.B.	2010	2006
Reed, Wilfrid Edward	A.G.I.G.	1991	1990
	P.A.G.D.C.	1998	
	P.G.S.D.	2006	
Reedman, Victor Malcolm	P.G.St.B.	2000	2000
Rees, Maurice Llewellyn Thomas	P.A.G.D.C.	2007	2010
Rees, Royden	G.Stwd.	2006	
	P.G.J.D.	2009	
Rees, Thomas John	P.A.G.Swd.B.	1991	1996
	P.G.J.D.	1998	
	P.G.J.O.	2003	
Reeve, Brian Douglas	P.G.St.B.	2008	
Reeve, John Whittington	P.A.G.D.C.	1982	1983
	P.G.S.D.	2005	
Reeve, Mark Steven	P.A.G.Swd.B.	2010	2010
Reeves, Robert	P.G.St.B.	2004	

NAME	RANK	YEAR OF APPT.	R.A.M.G.R. YEAR OF APPT.
Reiach, Norman James	P.A.G.D.C.	2008	2011
Reid, James	P.A.G.D.C.	2012	2003
Reid, Lt. Col. Robert,	P.A.G.D.C.	2005	2006
Reid, William Donald	P.G.I.G.	1992	2004
	P.G.J.D.	2006	
Reilly, Edward Peter	P.A.G.D.C.	1999	2009
	P.G.S.D.	2010	
Relf, Richard John		—	2003
Rennie, William Law	G.Stwd.	2007	2008
Renshaw, Gwiylm Thomas		—	2005
Renshaw, John Herbert	P.A.G.D.C.	2003	
Renshaw, Joseph Donald		—	1990
Rhode, George Peter	P.A.G.D.C.	2004	2009
Rhodes, David Keith	P.A.G.St.B.	2003	1994
Rhodes, John Barry		—	1992
Rhodes, Jeffrey Charles	P.A.G.D.C.	1995	2010
	P.G.S.D.	2001	
Rhodes, Stanley James	P.G.St.B.	2002	1994
Ribi, Peter Ernst	A.G.D.C.	1991	1995
	P.G.S.D.	1996	
	P.G.S.O.	2000	
	P.G.S.W.	2007	
Ribi, Peter John	G.Stwd.	2008	
	P.G.J.D.	2011	
Rice, John George	P.G.St.B.	1994	2004
	P.G.J.D.	2011	
Rice, Richard (Jnr.)	P.A.G.D.C.	1993	1992
	P.G.J.D.	1995	
	Dist.G.M., South Africa (Central)	2002-2007	
Rice, Robert David	G.Stwd.	2005	2007
	P.G.S.D.	2009	
Rich, Arthur Francis	P.A.G.D.C.	1988	1985
	P.G.S.D.	2000	
Rich, George	P.G.I.G.	1995	
Richards, Colin	G.Stwd.	1998	2006
	G.J.D.	2003	
	P.G.J.O.	2008	
Richards, George Leslie, *B.A.*	P.G.St.B.	1992	2003
	P.G.J.D.	2011	
Richards, Dr. John Desmond Morgan, *M.D., F.R.C.P.*	G.Stwd.	1999	2003
	P.G.J.D.	2007	
Richards, Michael Arthur	G.Stwd.	1986	1987
	G.J.D.	1991	
	P.G.J.O.	1996	
	G.M.O.	2008	
Richards, Timothy Raymond Roper	P.G.S.D.	2001	2007
	G.M.O.	2006	
Richardson, Anthony Fleetwood	P.A.G.D.C.	1995	2003
	P.G.S.D.	2007	
Richardson, Alan Stanley		—	1997
Richardson, David Barrie	P.A.G.D.C.	2004	2006
	P.G.S.D.	2012	

NAME	RANK	YEAR OF APPT.	R.A.M.G.R. YEAR OF APPT.
Richardson, Donald Kennedy	G.J.D.	1975	1981
	P.G.J.O.	1984	
Richardson, Douglas John		—	2002
Richardson, Fred	A.G.D.C.	2000	2003
	P.G.J.D.	2004	
	P.G.J.O.	2008	
Richardson, Gordon Mark	P.A.G.St.B.	2009	
Richardson, Roger Francis	G.Stwd.	2003	2006
	P.G.J.D.	2007	
	P.G.J.O.	2012	
Richardson, Roy Clifford	P.A.G.Swd.B.	2011	
Richardson, William	P.A.G.D.C.	1999	2002
	P.G.S.D.	2010	
Riches, Robert Ward		—	2011
Richmond, Roger Francis	G.St.B.	2009	
Ricketts, Mickael Reuben Cawkwell	P.G.St.B.	2010	
Riddell, Sydney John	P.G.St.B.	1990	
Ridge, Gerald Walter Gillan	P.A.G.D.C.	2008	2008
	P.G.S.D.	2009	
	P.G.J.O.	2011	
Ridge, Jeremy Austen	P.A.G.D.C.	1999	2000
	P.G.J.D.	2008	
Ridge, John George	P.G.St.B.	2004	
	P.G.S.D.	2012	
Ridler, Brian	P.A.G.D.C.	2007	2006
	G.S.D.	2012	
Ridley, Timothy John	P.G.St.B.	2011	
Ridley, William Mark	P.A.G.D.C.	1994	2004
	P.G.J.D.	2003	
Riedlsperger, Johann	G.Stwd.	1998	
	P.G.J.D.	2003	
Riley, Lawrence Melvyn	P.A.G.St.B.	2000	2001
	P.G.J.D.	2009	
Riley, Nigel Frederic	G.Stwd.	1985	1996
	G.J.D.	1990	
Rink, Paul James Ernest, O.B.E.	P.G.S.D.	2009	
Ritchter-Addo, James Bannerman	P.A.G.D.C.	1989	
	P.G.S.D.	1998	
Rivers, Leon Gerald	P.A.G.D.C.	1983	1987
	P.G.J.O.	1987	
	Dist.G.M., Zimbabwe	1990-1995	
Rivers, Michael Gerald	P.A.G.D.C.	1994	
	P.G.J.D.	2001	
Rix, Peter Frederick	P.G.St.B.	1985	
Roach, David John	P.A.G.D.C.	2005	2006
Roake, Brian Stanley	G.Stwd.	2006	2004
	P.G.J.D.	2009	
Roalfe, Michael Henry	G.S.D.	2003	2005
	P.G.M.O.	2007	
Roan, Rev. Canon William Forster	A.G.Chap.	2000	2003
	Dep.G.Chap.	2001	
	G.Chap.	2007-2011	
	P.G.J.W.	2011	
Roast, Peter Richard	G.Stwd.	1993	1999
	P.G.J.D.	2000	

NAME	RANK	YEAR OF APPT.	R.A.M.G.R. YEAR OF APPT.
Robbens, Stuart Victor	G.Stwd.	2005	
	G.J.D.	2008	
Roberson, Thomas Benjamin	P.A.G.D.C.	1978	
	G.S.D.	1990	
	P.G.J.O.	1999	
Robert, Jean Pierre	P.A.G.D.C.	2000	1999
	G.S.D.	2007	
	P.G.J.O.	2012	
Roberts, Alan	P.A.G.D.C.	2008	
Roberts, Arthur		—	1996
Roberts, His Ex. Dr. Carl Bertrand	P.A.G.D.C.	2007	
Roberts, David Glyn	P.G.St.B.	1994	1995
	P.A.G.Swd.B.	1999	
	P.G.J.D.	2007	
Roberts, Derek Norman	P.G.I.G.	2002	2009
	P.A.G.D.C.	2007	
	P.G.J.D.	2009	
	P.G.J.O.	2012	
Roberts, Dr. Ernest Forbes	P.A.G.D.C.	1992	1989
Roberts, Graham Philip Melville	P.G.St.B.	2008	2009
Roberts, Henry	P.G.St.B.	1995	
Roberts, Howard	P.G.St.B.	2004	
	P.G.J.D.	2011	
Roberts, Jonathan	A.G.D.C.	2012	
Roberts, Jonathan Charles	P.A.G.D.C.	2005	2005
	A.G.Sec.	2010-2012	
	P.G.S.D.	2010	
Roberts, Keith Philip	P.A.G.D.C.	2008	2008
Roberts, Norman Stuart	P.A.G.St.B.	2009	
Roberts, Norwell Lionel, Q.P.M.	P.A.G.Swd.B.	2008	2010
Roberts, Reginald David Roy	P.A.G.D.C.	1991	1999
	G.J.D.	2005	
Roberts, Richard Brian	Dep.G.Swd.B.	2009	2006
Roberts, Roger John Stanley	P.G.St.B.	2002	
Roberts, Rowland	P.A.G.D.C.	1997	1993
Roberts, Thomas Alan	P.A.G.D.C.	2009	
Roberts, Thomas Ellis	A.G.St.B.	2000	2003
Robertson, John Errington Ross	G.Stwd.	2002	2009
	P.G.J.D.	2008	
Robertson, John Richard Straun, J.P.	P.A.G.St.B.	2000	2009
	P.G.S.D.	2008	
Robertson, Cdr. Kenneth Norman	G.St.B.	1990	
	P.G.J.D.	1996	
	P.G.J.O.	2004	
Robins, Cdr. Cecil Edward, O.B.E.	P.A.G.D.C.	2002	2002
	P.G.S.D.	2008	
	P.G.J.O.	2010	
Robinson, Lt.Cdr. Arthur	P.A.G.D.C.	2000	
Robinson, Arthur	P.A.G.St.B.	2007	
	P.G.J.D.	2012	
Robinson, Basil Anthony	P.A.G.D.C.	2011	
Robinson, Bryan Walter	P.G.St.B.	1974	1979

NAME	RANK	YEAR OF APPT.	R.A.M.G.R. YEAR OF APPT.
Robinson, Cyril	P.G.St.B.	1994	2004
	P.G.J.D.	1999	
	P.G.J.O.	2007	
Robinson, Christopher	P.G.St.B.	2000	1996
Robinson, David Richardson	P.A.G.D.C.	2009	2011
Robinson, John Joseph	P.G.St.B.	2009	
Robinson, John Peter	P.A.G.D.C.	1995	
Robinson, John Ridley	P.A.G.D.C.	1997	
Robinson, Keith	P.A.G.D.C.	2007	
Robinson, Keith Douglas	P.A.G.D.C.	1993	
	P.G.S.D.	2001	
Robinson, Keith Ollerton	P.A.G.D.C.	2008	2003
Robinson, Keith Stanley		—	2007
Robinson, Kenneth James	A.G.D.C.	2012	
Robinson, Michael Arthur	G.Stwd.	1998	
	P.G.J.D.	2004	
	P.G.J.O.	2010	
Robinson, Peter	P.G.I.G.	2006	
Robinson, Sydney Mcdonald	P.A.G.Swd.B.	2007	
Robinson, William Henry		—	2007
Robson, John	G.Stwd.	2000	2003
	G.J.D.	2006	
Robson, John George	P.A.G.St.B.	1999	
	P.G.J.D.	2007	
Robson, Keith	P.G.St.B.	1999	2003
	P.G.J.D.	2004	
Robson, Malcolm	P.A.G.D.C.	2004	2004
	G.S.D.	2012	
Rockliffe, Eric	P.G.St.B.	2004	
Rodda, William Victor Edward	P.A.G.D.C.	1997	2005
Roddick, Norman James		—	1998
Roden, Kenneth Richard	P.A.G.St.B.	1998	1997
Rodger, George	P.A.G.D.C.	1999	2001
	P.G.S.D.	2004	
	P.G.J.O.	2010	
Rodger, Jock Halliday	P.A.G.D.C.	2003	2005
Rodgers, Wg.Cdr. John Brian, M.Sc., F.C.A., C.Eng.	G.Stwd.	2002	2010
	P.G.S.D.	2007	
Rodrigues, Carl Andrew	P.G.St.B.	2001	2002
Rodrigues, Wagner Tadeu	P.A.G.D.C.	2009	2005
Rodriguez Porrua, Rafael	P.G.J.D.	2011	
Roebuck, Terence Edward	P.G.St.B.	2012	
Roeschlaub, Revd. Robert Friedrich	A.G.Chap.	2004	
	Dep.G.Chap.	2010	
Roff, Limbury Michael Poulton	G.Stwd.	1998	1999
	G.S.D.	2002	
	P.G.J.O.	2007	
Rogers, Barry Woodward	P.A.G.D.C.	2011	
Rogers, David		—	2002
Rogers, David George	P.A.G.St.B.	2005	
Rogers, David Thomas	P.A.G.St.B.	2007	
Rogers, James Francis	P.A.G.Swd.B.	2012	

NAME	RANK	YEAR OF APPT.	R.A.M.G.R. YEAR OF APPT.
Rogers, Keith Henry	—		2011
Rogers, William Harold	G.Stwd.	2011	
Roland, Harvey Andrew	P.A.G.D.C.	2008	2010
Rolfe, Kenneth Bradley	P.A.G.St.B.	1991	1998
	G.J.D.	1996	
	P.G.J.O.	2003	
Rollin, Peter Hamilton	P.A.G.D.C.	1984	1987
	P.G.S.D.	1988	
	P.G.J.O.	1994	
	Prov.G.M., East Anglia	1998-2010	GMRAC 2002
	Pres.Gen.Bd.	2010-2011	
	Pres.Gen.Bd. at M.M.H.	2012	
Rollins, Kenneth Oswald Hubert	P.A.G.D.C.	2005	2004
Ronan, John Edward	P.G.St.B.	2008	
Ronan, Michael Joseph	P.A.G.D.C.	2007	
Rondel, Kenneth Michael	P.G.S.D.	2012	
Rondel, Philip John	P.G.St.B.	1997	
Roney, Albert William	G.Stwd.	1991	1996
	P.G.J.D.	1996	
Ronson, Ian	P.A.G.D.C.	2009	
Rooke, Gerald Percival	P.A.G.D.C.	1983	
	P.G.S.D.	1990	
	P.G.J.O.	2001	
Rooke, His Hon. Judge Giles Hugh	P.G.S.D.	2004	
Rooke, Raymond	P.A.G.D.C.	1993	1996
	P.G.J.D.	1996	
	P.G.J.O.	2002	
Roper, David Julian	P.G.I.G.	2001	
	P.G.S.O.	2009	
Roper-Hall, Michael John	P.G.St.B.	1998	
Rose, David Stewart	P.G.St.B.	2007	2009
Rosenberg, Cyril	P.G.St.B.	1994	1987
Ross, Andrew Howard	G.Stwd.	2007	
	P.G.J.D.	2011	
Ross, Desmond	G.I.G.	2003	
	P.G.J.D.	2009	
Ross, Hector Munro	P.A.G.D.C.	2003	
Ross, Johnston Montgomery	P.A.G.D.C.	2008	
Ross, Kenneth Montgomery	P.A.G.D.C.	2008	
Ross, Peter Mark	P.A.G.D.C.	1999	2004
	P.G.J.D.	2004	
	P.G.J.O.	2009	
Ross, Trevor John	P.G.St.B.	1997	1999
	P.G.J.D.	2003	
Rosser, Alfred David John	P.A.G.D.C.	2002	
	P.G.S.D.	2009	
Rosson, John Bladon	G.Stwd.	2005	2007
	P.G.J.D.	2010	
Rothburn, Aubrey	G.St.B.	1997	
	P.G.J.D.	2004	
Rothman, Leon Bernard	—		2010
Round, Trevor Charles	P.A.G.St.B.	1995	1994
Rouse, William Robin	P.A.G.D.C.	2006	1996
	P.G.J.D.	2010	

NAME	RANK	YEAR OF APPT.	R.A.M.G.R. YEAR OF APPT.
Routledge, Alfred	P.A.G.D.C.	1993	1993
	P.G.S.D.	1996	
	P.G.S.O.	2001	
Routlede, Richard Gibson, *R.V.M.*	P.A.G.D.C.	2007	1998
Rowberry, Michael William		—	2005
Rowbottom, John		—	2010
Rowe, John Albert		—	2008
Rowell, Thomas Gordon	P.A.G.D.C.	1996	2005
Rowden, Robert Henry		—	1999
Rowland, John	A.G.I.G.	2009	
Rowland, William Arthur	P.G.St.B.	2000	1997
Rowlands, David Gwynfryn		—	2010
Rowlandson, Norman	P.A.G.D.C.	2009	
Rowley, Clifford Ernest		—	2011
Roworth, Peter Guy	P.A.G.D.C.	2004	
	P.G.S.D.	2009	
Roy, Terry Lewis	P.A.G.D.C.	2007	2006
Rubie-Todd, Peter Ernest	G.Stwd.	2003	2003
	Dep.G.D.C.	2006-2008	
	P.G.J.O.	2011	
Rubin, Justice (Ret.) Mohideen Pierre Haja	Dist.G.M., Singapore	2012	
Rucker, David	P.G.I.G.	1998	1999
	P.A.G.D.C.	2004	
	P.G.S.D.	2012	
Rudd, Gordon William		—	1998
Rudd, John Kenneth	G.Stwd.	1995	
	P.G.J.D.	2011	
Ruderman, Brian Alec	P.A.G.D.C.	2012	
Rullmann, Jan Hendrik Woodrow	P.A.G.D.C.	1988	1989
Rumble, Roger John	P.A.G.St.B.	2007	
Rumbold, Robert George	G.Stwd.	2003	2006
	P.G.S.D.	2007	
Rundlett, John Philip	A.G.D.C.	1989	1994
	P.G.S.D.	1998	
Ruparelia, Gautam Karsandas	P.G.St.B.	2007	
Rushton, Peter John	G.Stwd.	2009	
Russell, David	P.A.G.D.C.	2003	2004
	P.G.S.D.	2011	
Russell, David		—	2007
Russell, Ernest James Lansdowne	P.G.St.B.	1992	2005
	P.G.J.D.	1999	
Russell, Gerrit Phillip		—	2004
Russell, Henry William	P.A.G.D.C.	1986	
	P.G.S.D.	2008	
Russell, John Bell, *O.B.E.*	P.A.G.D.C.	2000	
Russell, Peter John	P.A.G.St.B.	2001	
Russell, Robert Giles	G.Stwd.	1982	1989
	G.J.D.	1986	
	Prov.G.M., Warwickshire	1990-2002	
Rutter, Thomas	P.A.G.D.C.	1985	

NAME	RANK	YEAR OF APPT.	R.A.M.G.R. YEAR OF APPT.
Ryan, Alfred Henry	P.G.St.B.	1992	2001
	P.G.J.O.	2002	
	Dist.G.M., Gibraltar	2007	
Ryan, Colin Hugh	G.Stwd.	1997	
	G.J.D.	2002	
Ryding, Kenneth	P.G.St.B.	2011	
Rydings, Ernest Hector	P.A.G.D.C.	1990	
Rymer, Eric John	G.Stwd.	2008	2011
	Dep.G.D.C.	2010-2012	
Rynsard, John Gilbert Frederick	P.A.G.D.C.	1986	1991
	P.G.S.D.	1993	
Sacre, James Frederick	P.G.St.B.	1997	1993
Sadler, Frederick James		—	2003
Sager, Brian Albert	G.Stwd.	2006	2003
	P.G.J.D.	2010	
Saggers, Alan Leonard		—	2000
Sagoo, Jagjit Singh		—	2005
Saint, John Leonard	P.G.J.D.	2008	
Sait, Dr. Joonissait Mohamed Ismail	P.A.G.D.C.	2012	
Sale, Martin Jeffrey	P.A.G.D.C.	2003	2001
	P.G.S.D.	2008	
Salkeld, Richard	P.A.G.D.C.	1995	
Salt, Peter Gerrard	P.A.G.D.C.	2010	
Salton, David Keith	P.A.G.D.C.	2012	2007
Salussolia, Elidio	P.G.St.B.	1981	
	P.G.J.D.	1988	
Samuels, District Judge Seymour Martin	P.A.G.D.C.	1988	1989
	P.G.S.D.	1994	
	P.G.J.O.	2000	
San, Aaron	G.Stwd.	2008	
Sanda Palacios, Eusebio	P.A.G.I.G.	2006	
Sandbach, Richard Stainton Edward	Dep.G.Reg.	1975-1984	1975
	P.G.M.O.	1977	1976 GMRAC (H.C.)
	G.S.W.	1985	1985 GMRAC (H.C.)
Sander, Ivor Findlay	P.A.G.D.C.	1988	1992
	Dist.G.M., Transvaal	1992-2002	
Sanders, Dr. Michael Keith	P.A.G.D.C.	1997	1997
	P.G.S.D.	2007	
Sanders, Robert John	P.G.St.B.	2002	
Sanderson, Donald		—	2002
Sanderson, Douglas Graham	P.A.G.D.C.	2005	2011
Sanderson, Francis Maxwell	P.G.St.B.	1995	2011
	P.G.J.D.	2002	
Sanderson, Robert	P.A.G.D.C.	2005	2011
Sandiford, Basil Roy Eric	P.A.G.D.C.	2004	2008
Sandler, Merton	P.A.G.D.C.	2011	
Sands, Peter James	A.G.D.C.	1996	1996
	G.S.D.	2002	
	Prov.G.M., Berkshire	2007	
Sanger-Davies, Michael Joseph	P.G.St.B.	2009	2006

NAME	RANK	YEAR OF APPT.	R.A.M.G.R. YEAR OF APPT.
Sankey, Ronald Brian	P.G.St.B.	1997	2001
	P.G.J.D.	2012	
Sapsford, Glen Francis	P.A.G.D.C.	2003	2000
	P.G.J.D.	2007	
Sargeant, John Peter	A.G.D.C.	1971	1981
	P.G.S.D.	1995	
Sargent, Roger Wallace	A.G.I.G.	2006	
	P.A.G.D.C.	2012	
Sarre, Brian Anthony	P.A.G.D.C.	2011	
Saunders, Dennis Brian	P.A.G.D.C.	1995	1988
	G.Swd.B.	2001	
Saunders, Edward Peter	P.A.G.D.C.	1991	
	P.G.S.D.	2005	
Saunders, John Arthur	—		1999
Saunders, Mark Richard	P.A.G.Swd.B.	2010	
Saunders, Peter	P.A.G.D.C.	1994	
Savage, Douglas Frederick	P.G.St.B.	2001	2002
Savage, George Samuel	P.A.G.D.C.	2009	
Savage, Walter Norman	P.G.I.G.	1993	
	P.A.G.D.C.	1999	
Sawyer, David Malcolm	P.G.St.B.	2010	
Sawyers, Herbert Thomas	P.A.G.D.C.	1989	1991
	P.A.G.D.C.	1997	
	P.G.J.O.	2005	
Saxon, Kenneth James	P.A.G.Swd.B.	2011	2011
Saxon, Michael Damian	P.A.G.D.C.	2007	2009
Saxton, Peter	P.A.G.D.C.	2006	
	P.G.S.D.	2012	
Sayani, Noorali Rashid	P.A.G.D.C.	1999	2001
Sayer, Philip John	P.A.G.D.C.	2009	
Saywack, Donald Thomas	P.A.G.D.C.	1996	1997
	G.Insp., Guyana	1997	
Schaefer, Wolfgang	P.A.G.Swd.B.	2005	2008
	P.G.S.D.	2011	
Schmidt-Zorner, Eduard	P.A.G.Swd.B.	2006	2005
Schofield, Derek	P.A.G.D.C.	1988	1980
	G.S.D.	1993	
	P.G.J.O.	1998	
	P.G.M.O.	2005	
Schofield, Frederick	P.A.G.D.C.	1989	
Schofield, Keith Partington	P.G.St.B.	1994	1998
	P.G.J.D.	1999	2008 GMRAC
	P.G.S.D.	2001	
	Prov.G.M., East Lancashire	2003	
Schofield, William	P.A.G.D.C.	1993	
Scholtz, Roland Ivan	P.G.St.B.	1992	
Schran, Günther Caspar	P.A.G.D.C.	1994	2004
	P.G.J.D.	2001	
Schultink, Robert	P.A.G.D.C.	1989	1994
	G.J.W.	1994	1994/95 GMRAC
Schultz, Bernard Hermann	P.A.G.D.C.	1987	1993
	P.G.J.O.	2002	
Schuttensack, Albert		—	2009

NAME	RANK	YEAR OF APPT.	R.A.M.G.R. YEAR OF APPT.
Schwab, Werner Maria	P.G.St.B.	1999	2005
	G.J.D.	2005	
Scobie, Peter Ralph	P.A.G.Swd.B.	2000	
	P.G.J.D.	2010	
Scoffield, Brian Philip	P.G.St.B.	2003	2002
Scoins, Dr. Hubert Ian		—	1997
Scorer, Robert Strickland	G.Stwd.	1990	1998
	P.G.J.D.	1995	
	Dep.G.D.C.	1996-1997	
	P.G.J.O.	2000	
Scorer, Trevor	P.A.G.St.B.	2006	
Scott, Allan Cameron	P.A.G.D.C.	2008	
Scott, Frederick	P.A.G.D.C.	2012	
Scott, James McDonald	P.G.St.B.	1998	1988
Scott, John Arthur	P.A.G.D.C.	1999	2003
	P.G.S.D.	2004	
	P.G.J.O.	2010	
Scott, John Gaitskell	P.A.G.D.C.	2000	
Scott, John Teasdale	P.A.G.D.C.	2005	2005
Scott, Lawrence Stewart	P.A.G.Swd.B.	2012	
Scott, Thomas Robson	P.A.G.St.B.	2011	
Scott-Darling, Stuart	P.G.St.B.	2004	2004
Scott-Moncrief, Dr. Nigel Francis John	Dep.G.D.C.	2002-2004	2002
	P.G.J.O.	2007	
	P.G.M.O.	2012	
Screen, Ian Christopher	P.A.G.D.C.	1999	2003
	P.G.S.D.	2010	
Screen, Roger Charles	P.G.St.B.	2007	
Scriven, John Cooke	P.G.St.B.	2007	
Scull, Colin Albert, *J.P.*	P.A.G.D.C.	1998	
Sealey, Gerald Anthony	P.A.G.St.B.	2009	
Seaman, Andrew William	P.G.St.B.	2010	
Seaman, Derek		—	2004
Searle, David Harold	P.G.St.B.	1993	
Searle, Norman Percy Walter	G.Stwd.	1998	
Searle, Richard James	P.A.G.I.G.	2009	
Sears, Alan	A.G.Org.	2003	
Searson, John	P.G.St.B.	2000	2011
	P.A.G.D.C.	2010	
Seaward, Ernest Harold Matthew, *I.S.O., J.P.*	P.A.G.D.C.	1988	2003
	G.S.D.	1994	
	P.G.J.O.	2000	
Seddon, Stephen Graham	P.A.G.D.C.	1988	1999
	P.G.S.D.	1998	
Seddon, William Richard	A.G.D.C.	1993	1995
	P.G.S.D.	2000	
	P.G.J.O.	2006	
Seeley, Clive Victor	P.A.G.D.C.	2005	
Seeley, Leslie Vernon	P.G.St.B.	1987	2001
	P.G.J.D.	1994	
Seeley, Raymond Michael Scott	P.A.G.D.C.	2011	
Seeman, Graham David	P.A.G.Swd.B.	2008	
Seidu, Mahama	P.A.G.D.C.	2010	

NAME	RANK	YEAR OF APPT.	R.A.M.G.R. YEAR OF APPT.
Selby, John Richard	P.G.St.B.	2000	2005
	P.G.J.D.	2010	
Sellers, David Robinson	G.Stwd.	2000	2002
	P.G.J.D.	2005	
	P.G.S.D.	2011	
Selvanayagam, Kandiah	P.A.G.D.C.	2003	
Seret, Michel		—	2009
Serjeant, Anthony Keith	P.A.G.D.C.	2000	1995
Sermon, John Sylvester	P.A.G.D.C.	1992	2003
	P.G.S.D.	2004	
Sengupta, Asok	P.A.G.D.C.	2006	
Seret, Michel	P.A.G.D.C.	2006	
Sethi, Greh Bhushan	P.A.G.D.C.	2009	
Setterfield, Gordon Frederick	P.A.G.D.C.	2007	
Severin, Norman Frederick	P.A.G.D.C.	2006	2004
Seward, Percy	P.A.G.Swd.B.	2006	
Seymour, Derek Andrew Romaine	P.G.St.B.	1997	
Seymour, Peter Leith		—	2010
Seymour-Hamilton, Wyndham	A.G.D.C.	2001	2003
Shaftoe, Francis Allan	G.St.B.	2011	
Shah, The Hon. Mr. Justice Amritlal Bhagwanji, S.S.	P.G.S.D.	1998	1998
	Dist.G.M., East Africa	2001	
Shah, Amritlal Zaverchand	P.A.G.St.B.	2011	
Shah, Anil Amritlal	P.G.St.B.	2001	2004
	P.G.J.D.	2008	
Shah, Bhupendra Motichand	P.A.G.D.C.	2009	2011
Shah, Surenara Kumar	P.G.St.B.	1992	1999
	P.G.J.D.	1998	
Shah, Thakershi Tejshi	P.G.St.B.	1990	1989
	P.G.J.D.	1995	
	P.G.S.D.	2000	
	P.G.J.O.	2004	
Shah, Vijay Motichand	P.A.G.St.B.	2012	
Shailer, Derek Anthony	P.A.G.Swd.B.	2006	
	P.G.J.D.	2011	
Shannon, Rt. Hon. The Earl of	G.S.W.	1967	1971
	Prov.G.M., Surrey	1971-1981	
Sharma, Mani Ram	P.A.G.D.C.	2007	
Sharma, Dr. Sominder Prakash	P.G.St.B.	2012	
Sharman, Charles Reginald	P.G.St.B.	2011	2008
Sharp, Christopher	P.A.G.D.C.	2009	
Sharp, Alexander Chalmers	P.A.G.D.C.	1995	
	P.G.S.D.	2001	
	P.G.J.O.	2009	
Sharp, Frank Edward	P.A.G.D.C.	2002	2008
Sharp, Hayden Maurice	Dep.G.D.C.	1985-1987	
	P.G.J.O.	1991	
Sharp, John Leonard	P.G.J.D.	2012	2009
Sharp, John Leonard Ephraim	P.A.G.D.C.	2002	2000
	P.G.St.B.	2007	
Sharp, Keith Leslie	P.A.G.D.C.	1995	2001
	P.G.S.D.	2003	
	P.G.J.O.	2008	

NAME	RANK	YEAR OF APPT.	R.A.M.G.R. YEAR OF APPT.
Sharples, Trevor	P.A.G.St.B.	2011	
Sharpley, James William	G.Stwd.	2002	2005
	P.G.J.D.	2007	
Sharpley, William Frederick	P.A.G.D.C.	1989	1992
	P.A.G.D.C.	1997	
Shaw, Adrian		—	2011
Shaw, David William	P.A.G.D.C.	2011	
Shaw, Frank Jeremy	P.G.St.B.	1997	1999
	P.G.J.D.	2002	
	P.G.J.O.	2007	
	Prov.G.M., Dorset	2008	
Shaw, John	P.A.G.St.B.	2007	
Shaw, Michael John	P.G.St.B.	2012	
Shaw, Richard Ernest	P.A.G.St.B.	2006	
Shaw, Ronald Walter	P.G.St.B.	1994	1994
	P.G.J.D.	2009	
Sheern, Terence Douglas	P.A.G.D.C.	2009	
Sheldon, Richard Sirr	P.A.G.D.C.	1979	
Sheldon, William John	A.G.D.C.	2009	
Shelley, Frank Reginald	P.A.G.D.C.	1985	1995
	P.G.S.D.	1990	
	P.G.J.O.	1998	
	P.G.M.O.	2011	
Shelley, John Bernard, O.B.E.	P.A.G.St.B.	2005	
Shepherd, Paul Leslie	G.Stwd.	2011	
Shepherd, Paul Sheridan	P.A.G.D.C.	2003	
	G.S.D.	2009	
Sheppard, Geoffrey		—	2010
Sheppardson, Anthony	P.A.G.D.C.	1985	1989
	P.G.S.D.	1991	
	P.G.J.O.	1996	
	G.S.O.	2008	
Sherlock, William Alec Brown	G.St.B.	2012	2007
Sherman, Barry	P.A.G.D.C.	2002	2002
	P.G.S.D.	2012	
Sherriff, Ian Gary John		—	2003
Sherwin, Philip	P.A.G.D.C.	1998	2000
	P.G.S.D.	2004	
	Dist.G.M., East Africa	2008	
Shields, Daniel	P.A.G.D.C.	2009	
Shingler, Paul Wayne	P.A.G.Swd.B.	2012	
Shirley, Ian George	P.G.St.B.	2000	
Shivdas, Pathiyan Kevungal		—	1990
Shiveral, Charles Hill	P.A.G.D.C.	2011	2010
Shorey, Louis William		—	2005
Shorrock, Dennis Roland	P.A.G.D.C.	1992	2000
	P.G.S.D.	1998	
	P.G.J.O.	2003	
Shorrock, William Stephen	P.A.G.Swd.B.	2010	2007
Short, Brian	A.G.D.C.	2011	
Short, Douglas Peter	G.Stwd.	2010	
Shorto, Robert John	P.G.St.B.	1983	1981
Showell, Edward Frederick	P.G.St.B.	2004	1989

NAME	RANK	YEAR OF APPT.	R.A.M.G.R. YEAR OF APPT.
Showler, Wilfred		—	2006
Shugrue, Leslie George	P.A.G.Org.	1999	2006
	P.G.J.D.	2004	
Shuttleworth, Ivor Stephen	P.A.G.D.C.	1989	1993
	P.G.S.D.	1995	
	P.G.J.O.	1999	
	Prov.G.M., Dyfed	2001-2007	
Sidey, Reginald Maurice	P.A.G.D.C.	2002	
Siew, Hon Hoong	P.A.G.D.C.	2011	
Sigsworth, Brian Frank	G.Stwd.	2003	2009
	P.G.J.D.	2008	
Sillett, Robert David Taylor, *M.A., L.C.P.*	P.A.G.D.C.	1986	1990
	G.S.D.	2011	
Silva, Frank	P.G.I.G.	1993	
	P.G.S.D.	2006	
Silvers, Ernest Leonard	P.G.St.B.	1974	
Silvester, Eric George	P.A.G.I.G.	1997	
Simkins, Peter Alfred	G.Stwd.	1988	1993
	P.G.J.D.	2009	
Simm, Stanley	P.A.G.Swd.B.	1996	1998
	P.G.J.D.	2001	
	P.G.J.O.	2006	
Simmons, Edward Hubert Lancelot	P.A.G.D.C.	2008	2009
Simmons, Peter Leonard	P.G.S.D.	2007	2007
	P.G.J.O.	2010	
Simmons, Walter Ernest	P.A.G.D.C.	1993	2001
	P.G.S.D.	2004	
	P.G.S.O.	2009	
Simms, John Stanley	P.A.G.D.C.	1984	1987
	P.G.J.D.	1998	
Simons, John Railton	P.A.G.Chap.	2008	2008
Simons, Simon	P.A.G.St.B.	2006	
Simpson, Alan	P.A.G.St.B.	2006	
Simpson, Bryan Joseph	P.A.G.D.C.	2006	
	P.G.J.D.	2011	
Simpson, Charles	P.G.St.B.	1980	1993
	P.G.J.D.	1986	
Simpson, George Thomas	P.A.G.D.C.	2002	2006
Simpson, Michael Birt	P.A.G.D.C.	2011	
Simpson, Ronald Charles	G.St.B.	2001	
Sinclair, Hon. Dossel Owen, *O.D., J.P.*	P.G.J.D.	2004	2005
Singh, Dato' Balwant, *J.P., D.I.M.P.*	P.A.G.D.C.	1996	2006
	P.G.J.D.	2006	
Singh, Bhagwan Balaji	P.A.G.D.C.	2003	2004
	Dist.G.M., Madras	2004-2011	
Singh, Hardev	P.A.G.D.C.	2007	
Singh, Nirmal		—	2009
Singh, Dr. Santokh	P.A.G.D.C.	2004	2011
Siritunga, Lalith Henry Gunawardena	P.A.G.D.C.	1998	2004
	P.G.S.D.	2000	
	P.G.S.O.	2005	
Sivell, Gerald Wyndham	G.Stwd.	1987	1998
	P.G.J.D.	1993	

NAME	RANK	YEAR OF APPT.	R.A.M.G.R. YEAR OF APPT.
Skelly, Murdoch McLean, *I.S.O.*	P.G.J.D.	1997	1996
	P.G.J.O.	2003	
Skidmore, Ernest Roy	P.A.G.D.C.	2010	
Skilleter, David Cecil, *J.P.*	P.G.St.B.	2011	2011
Skinner, Brian Stanley	P.G.St.B.	2010	
Skinner, Ronald	P.A.G.D.C.	2010	
Skyrme, Michael Edward	P.A.G.D.C.	1983	
	P.G.S.D.	1996	
Slack, John Somerset	P.A.G.D.C.	2003	
Slade, Richard James	P.G.St.B.	1995	2000
	P.G.S.D.	2000	
	Prov.G.M., Oxfordshire	2004-2012	
Slaney, Arnold Keith	P.G.St.B.	2003	
Slater, Malcolm Ernest	A.G.D.C.	1995	2001
	P.G.S.D.	2001	
	P.G.J.O.	2005	
	G.J.W.	2008	
Slater, William	P.A.G.Swd.B.	2007	2008
Slater, William Edward	P.A.G.St.B.	2002	2006
Slaughter, Gerald Barton	P.G.St.B.	1999	2002
Slaughter, Royston Arthur	A.G.D.C.	1990	1994
	P.G.S.D.	1996	
	P.G.J.O.	2002	
	P.G.S.O.	2009	
Sleeman, Frederick John	P.A.G.D.C.	2000	2005
	P.G.J.D.	2011	
Sleep, David George	P.A.G.D.C.	2004	
Sleigh, Trevor Thomas	—		2011
Sloper, Thomas Gilbert	P.G.St.B.	2003	2004
Smailes, Peter William	P.A.G.D.C.	1997	
Smal, Daniel Richard Jean Julien	P.A.G.Swd.B.	2005	2008
Small, Alan James	P.A.G.D.C.	2006	
Small, Kenneth Gilbert		—	1994
Smallwood, Norman Brian		—	2008
Smart, Alec James		—	2008
Smart, Alistair Maclean	P.G.St.B.	2009	
Smart, George Ernest	P.A.G.Chap.	2008	
Smart, John Robert Kennedy	P.A.G.D.C.	1978	2001
	P.G.S.D.	1994	
	P.G.J.O.	2004	
Smart, Owen Frederick Thomas	P.G.St.B.	1985	1986
	P.G.J.D.	2003	
	P.G.J.O.	2010	
Smee, Alan Arthur John	A.G.D.C.	2006	2007
	G.S.D.	2011	
Smee, John Frederick	P.A.G.D.C.	1999	1996
	P.G.S.D.	2007	
Smeeton, Herbert Fisher	G.St.B.	1985	
	G.J.D.	1990	
	P.G.J.O.	1995	
Smeets, Rene	P.A.G.D.C.	2011	
Smerdon, Ronald Andrew	A.G.I.G.	2007	
	P.G.J.D.	2012	
Smiles, John Iddon	P.A.G.St.B.	2008	

NAME	RANK	YEAR OF APPT.	R.A.M.G.R. YEAR OF APPT.
Smillie, Edward		—	2005
Smit, Bartel	P.A.G.D.C.	1987	1989
	P.G.S.D.	1992	
	P.G.J.O.	1997	
	P.G.S.O.	2012	
Smith, Alan, *C.B.E.*	G.Stwd.	1998	2008
	P.G.J.D.	2004	
	P.G.J.O.	2012	
Smith, Alan Edge	P.G.St.B.	1990	1989
	P.G.J.D.	1996	
	P.G.J.O.	2012	
Smith, Alan Eli	P.A.G.D.C.	1999	2005
	P.G.S.D.	2004	
	P.G.J.O.	2010	
Smith, Alan Hodgson	P.G.St.B.	1989	2000
	P.G.J.D.	2000	
Smith, Alan Keith	P.G.St.B.	2012	
Smith, Albert Percival	P.A.G.D.C.	2002	
	P.G.S.D.	2010	
Smith, Bernard Edward	P.G.St.B.	2003	1999
	P.G.J.D.	2012	
Smith, Brian	P.A.G.D.C.	2006	
Smith, Brian Richard Carey		—	2002
Smith, Christopher Martin	P.G.S.D	1999	1998
	P.G.J.O.	2003	
	Prov.G.M., Bedfordshire	2007	
Smith, Claude Nigel Willie	A.G.St.B.	2010	
Smith, David Arthur	A.G.Swd.B.	2008	2009
Smith, David	G.Stwd.	1990	1996
	P.G.J.D.	1996	
	P.G.J.O.	2004	
Smith, David William		—	2005
Smith, Degary Nicholas		—	2001
Smith, Derek	G.Stwd.	1998	2003
	P.G.J.D.	2003	
Smith, Derek William Hayter	P.G.I.G.	1999	
Smith, Don Mitchell	P.A.G.D.C.	2002	2007
Smith, Duncan	P.A.G.D.C.	2008	
Smith, Edward Laurence Joseph	P.G.St.B.	1990	1988
	P.G.S.D.	2008	
Smith, Edward Richard		—	2001
Smith, Edwin Wilson	P.G.I.G.	1995	1982
Smith, Frank George Hood	P.A.G.Swd.B.	2010	
Smith, Frederick Alfred	P.A.G.St.B.	1993	2000
	P.G.J.D.	2002	
Smith, Frederick Arthur	G.Stwd.	1986	1991
	P.G.S.D.	1990	
	P.G.J.O.	1995	
	P.G.J.W.	2012	
Smith, Garry	A.G.I.G.	1995	2007
	P.A.G.D.C.	2000	
Smith, Geoffrey George	P.G.St.B.	1996	2004
	P.G.J.D.	2004	
Smith, George Desmond		—	2007

NAME	RANK	YEAR OF APPT.	R.A.M.G.R. YEAR OF APPT.
Smith, Gerald	G.Stwd.	2012	2006
Smith, Gordon Walkerley, *J.P.*	P.A.G.D.C.	1989	1993
	Prov.G.M., Lincolnshire	1993-2006	2003 GMRAC (H.C.)
Smith, Dr. Gregory Roger	G.Stwd.	2010	
Smith, Graham	G.Stwd.	1991	1994
	P.G.J.D.	1996	
	P.G.J.O.	2004	
Smith, Graham	P.A.G.D.C.	2004	
Smith, Graham Marshall	P.A.G.D.C.	2006	2010
Smith, Howard Brian	Dep.G.Swd.B.	1995	
	G.J.W.	2000	
Smith, Ian Christopher Marshall	P.A.G.D.C.	2001	2004
	P.G.S.D.	2007	
Smith, Ian Peter	—		2008
Smith, Ivan Falconer	P.G.St.B.	1999	1997
	P.G.J.D.	2006	
Smith, Jack Naylor	P.A.G.D.C.	1986	1982
Smith, James George	—		2004
Smith, John Benjamin	P.A.G.D.C.	2012	2011
Smith, John Hartley	G.Stwd.	2011	
Smith, Kenneth Arthur Clive	A.G.D.C.	2003	2008
Smith, Langford Bernard	P.A.G.D.C.	1991	
Smith, Marcus David	—		2008
Smith, Martin Howard	P.G.St.B.	2003	
Smith, Mervyn Thomas	G.Stwd.	1996	2002
	P.G.J.D.	2002	
	P.G.J.O.	2007	
Smith, Michael Anthony	P.A.G.D.C.	2005	
Smith, Michael John	P.A.G.D.C.	2008	
Smith, Montague Peter	P.A.G.St.B.	2012	
Smith, Nigel David	—		2009
Smith, Nicholas Patrick	P.G.J.D.	1996	2007
Smith, Peter John	Dist.G.M., Belgium	2002-2012	2002
Smith, Peter John	P.A.G.D.C.	1988	
	P.G.S.D.	1992	
	P.G.J.O.	1998	
Smith, Peter Roy	P.A.G.D.C.	2001	
Smith, Philip James	P.A.G.D.C.	2009	
Smith, Raymond John	G.Stwd.	1993	1996
	P.G.J.D.	1995	2004 GMRAC
	P.G.J.O.	2005	
	Prov.G.M., London	2007-2011	
	Pres.Mark Ben.Fund.	2012	
Smith, Roger William	—		2007
Smith, Ronald Stanley	G.D.C.	1991	1994
	P.G.S.D.	1994	
	Prov.G.M., Bristol	1995-2002	
Smith, Royden Matthew	P.A.G.D.C.	2002	2005
Smith, Stanley	P.G.St.B.	2006	2005
Smith, Stanley Reginald	P.G.St.B.	1993	2000
	P.G.J.D.	1998	
	P.G.J.O.	2004	
Smith, Sydney George	P.A.G.D.C.	2009	

NAME	RANK	YEAR OF APPT.	R.A.M.G.R. YEAR OF APPT.
Smith, Sydney John	P.A.G.D.C.	2012	
Smith, Terence Thomas	P.G.St.B.	2007	
Smith, Trevor James	G.Stwd.	2001	2003
	P.G.J.D.	2003	
Smith, Victor Frank David	G.I.G.	1989	1985
	P.A.G.D.C.	1996	
	P.G.S.D.	2002	
	P.G.J.O.	2006	
Smith, Walter Jack	P.A.G.D.C.	2009	
Smith, William Gordon	P.A.G.D.C.	2005	2005
Snaith, Raymond Gregory	P.A.G.D.C.	2008	
Snape, David Michael	P.A.G.D.C.	2000	2009
Snape, Graham Paul	A.G.D.C.	1999	
	P.G.S.D.	2005	
	P.G.J.O.	2010	
Snel, Frans Willem Jacobus Johannes, *M.A.*		—	1995
Snook, Anthony Guy	P.A.G.D.C.	1998	
	P.G.S.D.	2003	
Snowball, Revd. Michael Sydney	A.G.Chap.	2002	2008
	Dep.G.Chap.	2007-2008	
Snowball, Robert Bowley	P.A.G.D.C.	1998	2004
	P.G.S.D.	2003	
	P.G.J.O.	2010	
Sole, Bernard William	G.Stwd.	2004	2003
	G.J.D.	2008	
Solves, Milton	P.A.G.D.C.	1993	2008
	P.G.J.D.	2012	
Somaia, Vrajlal Vallabhdas	P.G.St.B.	2005	
Sommerin, Harald John	P.A.G.D.C.	2007	2009
	P.G.J.D.	2012	
Soper, Donald Eric	P.G.J.D.	1979	1985
	P.G.J.O.	1988	
	P.G.M.O.	2003	
Soriano Carrillo, Jesus	P.G.S.D.	1998	
Soulsby, Gerald Gill		—	2011
Soulsby, The Right Honourable, The Lord	P.G.S.D	1999	
Soulsby, Willan Michael	P.A.G.D.C.	2002	
	P.G.J.D.	2011	
Southgate, Derek William	G.Stwd.	2001	1998
	P.G.J.D.	2008	
Southwell, Lt.Col. Gerald	G.Stwd.	2001	2005
	P.G.J.D.	2007	
Southworth, Michael	G.Stwd.	2000	2008
	P.G.J.D.	2005	
Spain, Keith	P.A.G.St.B.	1996	2000
Sparks, David	G.Stwd.	1995	1994
	P.G.J.D.	2000	
	G.J.O.	2005	
Spavin, Roy	P.A.G.D.C.	2001	1997
Speake, Donald Henry	G.Stwd.	2000	2003
	P.G.J.D.	2006	
Speechley, Francis James	P.A.G.D.C.	1987	
	P.G.S.D.	1994	
Speed, Richard Alan Patrick	G.Stwd.	2004	
	P.G.J.D.	2008	

NAME	RANK	YEAR OF APPT.	R.A.M.G.R. YEAR OF APPT.
Spence, Jonathan	G.Swd.B.	2008	2008
	G.S.W.	2010	
Spencer, Albert	P.A.G.D.C.	1992	1993
	P.G.J.D.	2001	
	Dist.G.M., Transvaal	2002-2010	
Spencer, Andrew John	P.G.St.B.	2000	2001
	P.A.G.D.C.	2008	
Spencer, Francis Charles	Dep.G.D.C.	2000-2002	2000
	Prov.G.M., Worcestershire	2004	
Spencer, Geoffrey Frederick	P.A.G.D.C.	2009	2010
Spencer, George Herbert	P.A.G.D.C.	1992	
	P.G.S.D.	1995	
Spencer, Ivor Roy	P.A.G.Swd.B.	2009	
Spencer, Michael	P.A.G.D.C.	2000	
	P.G.S.D.	2010	
Spencer, Michael George	G.Stwd.	1995	1995
	Dep.G.D.C.	1997-1999	
	P.G.J.O.	2002	
	Prov.G.M., Essex	2007	
Spevak, Anton	G.Stwd.	1997	1994
	P.G.S.D.	2003	
Spicer, Michael Anthony	P.G.St.B.	2005	2002
Spiers, Neville Alan	P.G.St.B.	2005	2003
Spilsbury, Robert John	P.G.St.B.	2007	2004
Spilsted, William Derek	P.G.I.G.	2008	2010
Spires, Colin Frederick	G.Stwd.	1985	1987
	G.J.D.	1996	
Spivey, David Ralph	P.A.G.Swd.B.	2011	
Spofforth, Ian James Richard	G.Treas.	1991-2003	1990
	P.G.J.W.	1997	1991 GMRAC (HC)
	P.G.S.W.	2004	
Sprackling, Cecil John	G.Stwd.	1989	1998
	P.G.J.D.	1997	
	P.G.J.O.	2002	
Sprason, Ronald Edward		—	2008
Spring, Dan	P.G.St.B.	2007	
Springthorpe, Kenneth	P.A.G.D.C.	2008	
Spurgeon, Jeremy	P.G.St.B.	2000	
Spurr, Colin Luke Edmondson	P.A.G.Swd.B.	2003	
Squeglia, Vincenzo Enzo	P.A.G.St.B.	2001	
Squelch, Denis Herbert		—	2004
Squire, Stanley Claude	G.Stwd.	2000	2005
	P.G.J.D.	2005	
St. Clair-Daniel, Hon. Wilfred, *C.B.E.*	P.A.G.D.C.	1984	2001
	P.G.S.D.	1991	
Stacey, Robert Sidney	P.A.G.St.B.	2009	
Staines, Rodney	A.G.D.C.	1995	1997
	P.G.S.D.	2012	
Stainthorpe, John Bryan	P.A.G.D.C.	2004	2000
Stallwood, Robert Wallace		—	1988
Stancer, Charles Frederick	P.A.G.D.C.	1995	1993
Stannard, Peter John		—	1997
Stansbie, Brian Leonard		—	1994

NAME	RANK	YEAR OF APPT.	R.A.M.G.R. YEAR OF APPT.
Stanworth, Robert Procter	P.A.G.D.C.	1986	1990
	G.S.D.	1992	
	P.G.J.O.	1999	
Stapleton, Aubrey Cecil		—	2005
Stapley, Brian Frederick George, M.A., F.C.A.	G.I.G.	1993	1998
	P.A.G.D.C.	2004	
	P.G.J.O.	2011	
Starck, Michael	P.G.St.B.	2005	
	P.A.G.D.C.	2006	
Starkey, Frank Austin, C.Eng., M.I.E.E.	P.A.G.D.C.	1992	1991
	P.G.S.D.	1997	
	G.S.O.	2001	
	P.G.M.O.	2006	
Starling, Leonard Stanley	P.A.G.D.C.	2011	
Starnes, Christopher Francis	A.G.I.G.	1977	1980
	G.I.G.	1978	
	P.A.G.D.C.	1982	
	A.G.Sec.	1986-1999	
	P.G.J.O.	1988	
	P.G.S.O.	1995	
	P.G.M.O.	2000	
Starr, Edward Murray	A.G.D.C.	2003	2010
	P.G.S.D.	2009	
Starritt, David Raynor	P.A.G.D.C.	2012	
Statham, John Frederick	P.A.G.D.C.	2012	
Statter, Hubert	P.G.J.D.	1974	1977
	P.G.J.O.	1983	
Stayt, Michael John	P.A.G.Swd.B.	2000	1997
Stead, Peter	P.A.G.D.C.	2008	
Steel, David Llewellyn	P.G.St.B.	2006	
Steele, Geoffrey Walter		—	2007
Steele, Revd. Keith Atkinson	P.A.G.Chap.	1998	2006
	P.G.J.O.	2010	
Steele, Norman Edwin	P.G.J.D.	2000	2005
Steele, William Lemmon	P.A.G.D.C.	1997	1995
Steele, William	P.G.St.B.	1990	1999
Steenkamp, Reginald	P.A.G.D.C.	1995	
Steer, Michael Charles	P.A.G.D.C.	1997	2010
	P.G.S.D.	2009	
Steggall, Malcolm Ronald	P.G.St.B.	1997	1993
	P.G.J.D.	2008	
Steggles, James	P.A.G.D.C.	2002	2007
	G.S.D.	2007	
	P.G.J.O.	2011	
	Prov.G.M., West Yorkshire..	2012	
Stephens, Anthony William Player	P.G.St.B.	2005	
Stephens, Brian	P.G.St.B.	1982	1999
	P.G.J.D.	1991	
	P.G.J.O.	1998	
Stephens, John Arthur	P.A.G.D.C.	2011	2005
Stephens, Peter George	P.A.G.D.C.	2007	2011
	P.G.J.D.	2011	
Stephens, Peter Maurice	Asst.G.St.B.	1991	
Stephenson, Raymond		—	2007

NAME	RANK	YEAR OF APPT.	R.A.M.G.R. YEAR OF APPT.
Steven, Ernest Robert	P.A.G.D.C.	1994	1995
	P.G.S.D.	1995	
	Dist.G.M., River Plate	1995-2009	
Stevens, Michael David	A.G.St.B.	2006	
	P.G.J.D.	2011	
Stevens, Terence Roy	P.G.St.B.	2007	2006
Stevens, Walter Leslie James	P.A.G.D.C.	1975	1986
	P.G.S.D.	1990	
Stevenson, Iain Alexander	G.Stwd.	1999	
Stevenson-Hamilton, Angus John Delano, Q.P.M., C.P.M.	P.A.G.D.C.	2002	2006
	Dist.G.M., Hong Kong	2007	
Stewart, Alan Edgar	P.A.G.D.C.	1978	1975
	G.S.O.	1984	
	P.G.M.O.	1989	
	G.Insp., I.O. Man	1994-2005	
	P.G.J.W.	2009	
Stewart, Charles	G.Stwd.	1980	1987
	P.G.S.D.	1985	
	P.G.J.O.	1992	
Stewart, Frederick	P.A.G.D.C.	1999	2006
	P.G.S.D.	2010	
Stewart, William Dalglish	P.A.G.Swd.B.	2000	
Still, Edward George	P.G.St.B.	1998	
Stirland, Fred	G.I.G	1997	2009
	P.G.J.D.	2007	
Stivens, John	—		1998
Stock, Francis Joseph	P.G.J.D.	2000	2003
	P.G.J.O.	2007	
Stockdale, David Robert	P.A.G.D.C.	2002	2006
	P.G.S.D.	2011	
Stockford, Philip	P.A.G.St.B.	2009	
Stockting, Peter John	—		2007
Stockwell, Bernard William Charles	P.A.G.D.C.	1989	
Stoddard, Robert William	—		2011
Stone, Geoffrey Vincent	P.A.G.D.C.	1997	2000
	P.G.S.D.	2005	
Stone, Howard Victor	P.G.St.B.	2007	2009
Stone, Raymond Victor	P.A.G.St.B.	2007	
Stone, Richard Ian	P.G.St.B.	2007	
Stonely, John	G.Stwd.	1995	1996
	P.G.J.D.	2005	
	P.G.J.O.	2011	
Stones, George	P.G.St.B.	2004	
Stonley, Henry Gerald	P.A.G.D.C.	1969	1971
	P.G.S.D.	1976	
	P.G.J.O.	1987	
Stooke, Kenneth Vivian	—		2010
Storey, Edward Joseph	P.A.G.St.B.	2001	
Storey, Neville Andrew	P.A.G.D.C.	2005	2009
Storr, Terence Alfred	P.A.G.D.C.	2005	
Stow, Gordon William Alfred	A.G.St.B.	1993	2009
	P.G.J.D.	1999	

NAME	RANK	YEAR OF APPT.	R.A.M.G.R. YEAR OF APPT.
Strain, William George	P.A.G.D.C.	1998	2004
	G.S.D.	2003	
	P.G.J.O.	2008	
Stratford, Carl Edgar Joseph		—	2011
Straw, Terence Ronald	P.A.G.D.C.	2011	
Strickland, Ian Geoffrey Peter	P.G.St.B.	2012	
Stringer, Herbert William	G.Stwd.	1996	1995
	P.G.J.D.	2002	
Stringer, Lester John		—	2007
Stringer, Vivian James	P.A.G.St.B.	1997	2001
	P.G.S.D.	2002	
	P.G.S.O.	2005	
Stringer, William Anthony	P.A.G.St.B.	2004	2007
	P.G.J.D.	2010	
Stringfellow, Norman Alexander	P.A.G.D.C.	1993	
	P.G.S.D.	2000	
Strong, Joseph Glaister	P.A.G.D.C.	2001	2005
	P.G.J.D.	2006	
	P.G.J.O.	2010	
Strover, Wyndham Alfred	P.A.G.D.C.	1997	
	P.G.S.D.	2006	
Strudwick, James Augustine		—	2006
Stubbs, Charles David	P.G.St.B.	2005	2001
Stuck, Desmond Ainsley	P.A.G.D.C.	2000	
Sturt, Clifford Mark	P.G.St.B.	2010	2011
Sud, Inderjit Singh	P.A.G.D.C.	1994	
	P.G.Swd.B.	2002	
Suddick, Raymond	G.Stwd.	2006	
	P.G.J.D.	2009	
Sugden, Phillip Garth		—	2001
Suggate, Stanley Charles Henry		—	1997
Sullivan, Patrick Daniel	P.G.St.B.	2010	
Sumaria, Ashwinkumar Ratilal	P.G.St.B.	2011	
Summers, William	P.A.G.D.C.	1993	1994
	P.G.S.D.	1998	
	P.G.J.O.	2005	
Sundararaj, Dr. David Visvasam Baskar	P.A.G.D.C.	2005	2008
	P.G.J.D.	2006	
Sundaresan, Santhanagopala	P.A.G.D.C.	2011	2009
Sunderland, Gordon Trevor	P.G.St.B.	1994	2001
	P.G.J.D.	2003	
Sunderland, Peter	P.A.G.D.C.	1994	2008
	P.G.S.D.	2001	
Sunderland, Raymond		—	1987
Surtees, William Mitchenson	P.A.G.D.C.	2008	
Sussman, Julian Bernard	P.A.G.D.C.	1989	1991
	P.G.S.D.	1995	
	Dist.G.M., South Africa (Cen. Div.)	1997-2002	
Sutcliffe, Paul Malcolm	P.A.G.St.B.	2000	1999
	P.G.J.D.	2007	
Sutherland, David Frank	P.G.St.B.	1985	
	P.G.J.D.	1994	
Suttie, Frank	P.A.G.St.B.	1988	

NAME	RANK	YEAR OF APPT.	R.A.M.G.R. YEAR OF APPT.
Sutton, Anthony William	P.G.St.B.	2002	2006
	P.G.J.D.	2009	
Sutton, Richard Cresswell	P.A.G.D.C.	2008	2010
Swain, Robert Guy	P.G.St.B.	1999	
Swainson, William Alan	P.G.St.B.	2002	
Swallow, Joseph William	P.G.I.G.	1999	
Swan, John Edward	P.A.G.D.C.	1991	1992
Swan, Owen	P.A.G.Chap.	2008	
Sweeney, Andrew Christopher	G.Stwd.	2003	2002
	G.J.D.	2009	
Swift, William	P.G.St.B.	1995	1997
	P.G.J.D.	1999	
	P.G.J.O.	2005	
Swinburne, James	P.A.G.D.C.	2001	2000
	P.G.S.D.	2009	
Swinnerton, Peter Richard	P.A.G.D.C.	1994	1997
Sykes, Alan William	P.G.J.D.	2003	2002
	P.G.J.O.	2008	
Sykes, James Desmond	P.A.G.D.C.	1996	2002
	P.G.J.D.	2011	
Sykes, Trevor	P.G.St.B.	2001	
	P.G.J.D.	2012	
Sylvester, John Edward Knight, *B.A.*	P.A.G.Chap.	2000	2002
	P.Dep.G.Chap.	2006	
Syrdahl, Thom Erik	P.A.G.D.C.	2012	
Tachie-Menson, Angus Clarence		—	2010
Taiga, Moses Oghenerume	P.G.S.D.	2012	
Tait, Thomas	P.G.St.B.	1991	1991
	G.J.D.	2005	
Talbot, John Beverley	G.Stwd.	2005	
	P.G.J.D.	2009	
Talbot, Peter	P.A.G.D.C.	2004	2011
	P.G.S.D.	2010	
	Prov.G.M., North Wales	2012	
Talbot, Raymond	P.A.G.D.C.	1994	2007
	P.G.S.D.	2001	
	P.G.J.O.	2009	
Tallon, Anthony John	P.G.St.B.	1992	1996
	P.G.J.D.	1998	
	P.G.J.O.	2004	
Tamlin, John Louis Francis	P.A.G.D.C.	2005	
Tan, Kenneth Kok Oon	P.A.G.D.C.	1984	1991
	Dist.G.M., Hong Kong	1991-1996	
Tan, Kim Seng	P.A.G.D.C.	1995	2001
Tan, Tock Yong	P.A.G.D.C.	1989	1989
	P.G.S.D.	1998	
	P.G.J.O.	2010	
Tanna, Biharilal Keshavji	P.A.G.D.C.	1996	2002
	P.G.J.D.	2004	
	P.G.J.O.	2010	
Tanna, Hashwant Karsandas	P.A.G.St.B.	2010	
Tappin, Reginald	P.A.G.D.C.	2000	

NAME	RANK	YEAR OF APPT.	R.A.M.G.R. YEAR OF APPT.
Tarbuck, Frank Aubrey		—	2010
Taylor, Albert Arthur	P.A.G.D.C.	1992	1991
	P.G.S.D.	1999	
	P.G.J.O.	2006	
Taylor, Alfred James	G.Stwd.	2004	2008
	P.G.J.D.	2007	
Taylor, Anthony	P.A.G.D.C.	2011	
Taylor, Anthony Stuart	P.A.G.D.C.	1999	2002
Taylor, Brian	P.G.St.B.	1998	2005
Taylor, Colin	P.A.G.St.B.	2004	2009
	A.G.D.C.	2011	
Taylor, Douglas Ronald	P.A.G.Swd.B.	2012	
Taylor, Gary Douglas	P.A.G.D.C.	2010	
Taylor, Gayton Cusley	G.S.D.	1979	1984
	G.J.W.	1984	1984/5 GMRAC
Taylor, Geoffrey Ian	P.A.G.D.C.	1998	
Taylor, Harold	G.Stwd.	1998	2009
	A.G.D.C.	2003	
	P.G.J.D.	2007	
Taylor, Ian Hamilton	A.G.D.C.	2007	
Taylor, Dr. John	G.Stwd.	2000	
	P.A.G.D.C.	2003	
	P.G.S.D.	2010	
Taylor, John	P.G.J.D.	2003	2011
Taylor, John Randall	P.A.G.St.B.	2002	
Taylor, Keith Llewelyn	P.A.G.Swd.B.	2004	
	P.G.J.D.	2011	
Taylor, Kenneth Earl	P.A.G.D.C.	2005	2007
Taylor, Kenneth Summers	G.I.G.	2002	
	P.G.J.D.	2009	
Taylor, Kevin Henry	G.Stwd.	2008	2010
	P.G.J.D.	2011	
Taylor, Michael George	P.A.G.D.C.	2006	2009
Taylor, Percy Guy	P.G.St.B.	2011	
Taylor, Peter Alexander	A.G.Swd.B.	1999	2006
Taylor, Peter Allan		—	2010
Taylor, Peter Michael	P.A.G.D.C.	2004	
	P.G.S.D.	2010	
Taylor, Philip Keats	P.A.G.Swd.B.	2009	
Taylor, Raymond Owen John	P.G.St.B.	1988	2007
	P.G.J.D.	2000	
Taylor, Roderick Gordon	G.Stwd.	2007	
	P.G.J.D.	2011	
Taylor, Roger Martin	P.A.G.D.C.	2008	
Taylor, Thomas Richardson	G.Stwd.	1986	1990
	P.G.J.D.	1992	
	P.G.J.O.	1999	
Taylor, Whilston Davis	P.G.J.D.	1982	1981
	Dist.G.M., Jamaica & Caymen Islands	1990-2009	
Taylor, William Albert James	P.G.St.B.	2009	2007
Taylor, William John	P.A.G.D.C.	1994	1996
	P.G.J.D.	2001	

NAME	RANK	YEAR OF APPT.	R.A.M.G.R. YEAR OF APPT.
Tedder, Gerald Leon	P.G.M.O.	2004	
	G.S.W.	2008	
Temple, John Howard	P.G.I.G.	1992	
	P.G.J.D.	2009	
Tennant, Laurence Francis	—		2008
Terry, Michael Carl	—		2002
Tester, Rex Cecil	P.A.G.D.C.	2009	
Tewson, John Leslie	A.G.St.B.	1992	1998
Thatcher, Michael Francis	A.G.I. of Wks.	1989	2008
	P.G.J.D.	2001	
Theivanthiran, Sinnathamby	P.A.G.D.C.	2008	
Theodossiou, Theodosios Socratous	P.G.S.D.	2006	2008
	P.G.S.O.	2010	
	Dist.G.M., Cyprus	2010	
Thetford, Derrick	P.A.G.Swd.B.	2005	2006
Thiagarajah, Cecil	P.A.G.D.C.	2011	2011
Thoday, Simon Andrew	G.Stwd.	2004	2006
	P.G.J.D.	2007	
Thomas, Alan Ford	P.G.St.B.	1996	1997
	P.G.J.D.	2001	
Thomas, Alan Rosser	G.Stwd.	2000	2007
	P.G.J.D.	2005	
	P.G.J.O.	2011	
Thomas, Alun Martin	P.G.St.B.	2008	
Thomas, Brian Francis	G.Stwd.	2003	
	P.G.J.D.	2007	
Thomas, Brian Robinson	P.A.G.St.B.	2009	
Thomas, Byron Lloyd	P.A.G.D.C.	2005	
Thomas, Clive	P.G.St.B.	2003	2010
Thomas, David Brian	P.A.G.Chap.	2008	
Thomas, David William	P.G.St.B.	1998	1992
	P.G.J.D.	2007	
Thomas, Derek	A.G.D.C.	2004	2006
	P.G.S.D.	2010	
	P.G.J.O.	2012	
Thomas, Euan Norman	—		2003
Thomas, Francis Vivian	P.G.St.B.	1995	1998
Thomas, Frank Neil	P.A.G.St.B.	2010	
Thomas, Ian Hanbury William	P.G.St.B.	2010	
Thomas, James Derek	P.A.G.D.C.	2001	2001
	P.G.J.D.	2011	
Thomas, John	P.A.G.D.C.	2002	1997
Thomas, John Ewart Weeks	G.Stwd.	2002	
Thomas, John William	P.A.G.St.B.	2009	
Thomas, Kenneth Lloyd	—		2004
Thomas, Michael John Glynn	P.A.G.Swd.B.	2009	
Thomas, Paul Henry	P.G.St.B.	2007	2002
Thomas, Ronald	P.A.G.Swd.B.	2009	2002
Thomas, Ronald James Pearson	P.G.St.B.	1994	
Thomas, Terence James	P.A.G.D.C.	2003	2005
Thomas, Dr. Vivian, *J.P.*	A.G.Chap.	2011-2012	
Thomas, William Edward	G.Stwd.	2006	
	P.G.J.D.	2009	

NAME	RANK	YEAR OF APPT.	R.A.M.G.R. YEAR OF APPT.
Thomas, William Geofrey Howard	P.A.G.St.B.	2010	
Thomason, Eric Middleton	G.Stwd.	1988	2000
	P.G.J.D.	1994	
	P.G.J.O.	2001	
Thompson, Barrie Whiticker	P.G.St.B.	2003	2007
	P.G.J.D.	2012	
Thompson, Brian	P.A.G.Swd.B.	2007	2005
Thompson, Brian Stephen	P.G.St.B.	1993	1991
Thompson, Colin Michael	P.A.G.D.C.	2009	
Thompson, David Hedley	G.Stwd.	1995	1998
	P.G.J.D.	2000	
	P.G.J.O.	2005	
Thompson, Edward Theodore	P.A.G.Swd.B.	2012	
Thompson, Frank Michael Noel	P.A.G.D.C.	2012	
Thompson, John Victor	P.A.G.Swd.B.	1999	
Thompson, Kenneth George	P.A.G.D.C.	1997	1993
	P.G.S.D.	2003	
	P.G.J.O.	2011	
Thompson, Malcolm Hayes	Dep.G.Stwd.B.	1988	1991
	Prov.G.M., South Wales	1991-1996	
Thompson, Peter Andrew	P.G.I.G.	2000	
Thompson, Peter Haggerty	P.G.St.B.	2002	
Thompson, Sydney Winton		—	1997
Thompson, William Augustus John	G.Stwd.	1998	2000
	P.G.J.D.	2003	
Thompson, William Philip	P.G.S.D.	2007	2009
	Dist.G.M., River Plate	2009	
Thomson, Andrew	P.A.G.Swd.B.	1998	1998
Thomson, Rev. Clarke Edward Leighton, T.D., M.A.	P.G.Chap.	1974	1975
	G.Chap.	1975-1981	
	Prov.G.M., Middlesex	1984	
Thomson, Hugh Robert	P.A.G.D.C.	2011	
Thomson, Keith	P.A.G.D.C.	2002	
	P.G.S.D.	2010	
Thomson, Lloyd Reginald	P.A.G.D.C.	1989	
	P.G.S.D.	2005	
Thomson, Nigel	P.G.I.G.	2003	2002
	P.A.G.D.C.	2012	
Thomson, Ronald Bell		—	2003
Thomson, Thomas, C.P.M., M.A.	G.Tyler	2004-2012	2004
	P.A.G.D.C.	2005	
	P.G.S.D.	2010	
Thorn, Herbert Leonard		—	2005
Thorne, Col. Sir Neil Gordon, O.B.E., T.D., D.L.	P.G.S.D.	2003	2007
Thorne, Rex Francis, O.B.E.	Dep.G.Swd.B.	2004	
Thornton, Ralph Maurice	P.A.G.St.B.	2010	
Thorpe, Ian James	P.A.G.D.C.	2012	
Thorpe, James Irving		—	1993
Thorson, Ole	P.G.St.B.	2009	
Thurgood, Arthur John	A.G.D.C.	1984	1986
	P.G.S.D.	1933	
Thurlow, George Edwin	P.A.G.D.C.	1991	

NAME	RANK	YEAR OF APPT.	R.A.M.G.R. YEAR OF APPT.
Thurston, Colin William	P.A.G.D.C.	1993	2001
	P.G.S.D.	2009	
Tibbles, Henry Sibbon	G.Stwd.	1987	
Tickle, Trevor Cyril Kenneth	P.A.G.D.C.	1995	
	G.S.D.	2001	
	P.G.J.O.	2007	
Tiddy, Patrick John		—	2009
Tidmarsh, Roy John Eric	P.A.G.D.C.	2007	
Tierney, Brian Gerald, *M.B.E.*	G.Stwd.	1984	1987
	P.G.J.D.	1989	
	P.G.J.O.	1994	
	G.S.O.	2007	
Tiffin, David	P.A.G.Swd.B.	2006	2009
Tilbury, Derek Rowland	P.A.G.D.C.	2009	
Tile, Robert James Railstone	P.A.G.D.C.	1985	1991
	P.G.J.O.	1994	
Tiler, Joseph John	P.A.G.Swd.B.	1989	1998
	G.J.D.	1996	
	P.G.J.O.	2002	
	P.G.M.O.	2011	
Tilley, George	P.G.St.B.	2008	2009
Tilling, Dr. Keith John	G.Stwd.	1993	1998
	P.G.J.D.	1999	
	P.G.J.O.	2006	
Tindall, Christopher Norman	P.A.G.D.C.	2005	
	P.G.S.D.	2010	
Tindall, Geoffrey Brian	P.G.S.D.	2012	
Tink, David Walter	P.A.G.St.B.	2006	
Tinkler, Lawrence	P.A.G.D.C.	2009	2007
Tod, Michael Campbell Ross	P.G.St.B.	1997	1995
Todd, Charles Brian	P.A.G.D.C.	1998	
	P.G.S.D.	2004	
Todd, Robert		—	2011
Todd, William Leonard	P.A.G.D.C.	2006	2002
Toft, Kenneth Edward	P.A.G.D.C.	2000	
Toh, Tony Chong Weng	P.A.G.D.C.	2001	
Toler, Philip Albert	G.Stwd.	1993	2000
	P.G.S.D.	2002	
Tomkinson, Alan George	P.G.St.B.	2005	
Tomlin, John	P.A.G.D.C.	2005	2007
Tomlinson, Bill	P.A.G.D.C.	2006	
Tomlinson, Leonard Joseph	P.A.G.D.C.	2005	
Tonkin, Frank	G.Stwd.	1981	1980
	G.S.D.	1984	
	G.S.O.	1987	
	Prov.G.M., Cornwall	1992-2004	
Toon, Richard Henry	G.St.B.	1997	2001
	P.G.J.D.	2007	
Topliss, Victor Barry	P.A.G.D.C.	2008	2007
Topping, John Alfred	P.A.G.D.C.	1992	1994
Torrance, Archibald Iain	G.Stwd.	2010	2011
Torres, Peter Basil	G.Stwd.	1996	1999
	P.G.J.D.	2001	
	P.G.J.O.	2007	

NAME	RANK	YEAR OF APPT.	R.A.M.G.R. YEAR OF APPT.
Tossell, Reginald John	G.Stwd.	2005	2011
	P.G.J.D.	2009	
Towersey, Frederick Robert	P.A.G.D.C.	1992	1997
	P.G.S.D.	2006	
	P.G.J.W.	2010	
Town, Frederick William	P.G.St.B.	2007	2008
Townsend, Alan Edwin, *M.B.E.*	P.A.G.Swd.B.	2011	2010
Townsend, John Michael	P.A.G.D.C.	2007	
Townsend, Paul Stephen	—		2003
Trafford, Donald William	P.A.G.D.C.	2000	1994
Travers, Barry Worthing	P.A.G.D.C.	2002	2005
	G.S.D.	2009	
Traves, Arthur Alan	P.A.G.D.C.	1998	1998
Treacy, James Michael	P.A.G.D.C.	2007	2005
Tremaine, David Edmund	P.A.G.Swd.B.	2006	2010
Trend, Thomas Frederick William	P.A.G.D.C.	1983	1984
	P.G.S.D.	1989	
	P.G.J.O.	1999	
Tretiakov, Jorge Juan	P.A.G.Swd.B.	2004	
Trew, Bernard Henry Francis	P.G.St.B.	1988	1994
	P.G.J.D.	2000	
	P.G.J.O.	2009	
Trew, Gordon Alexander	G.Stwd.	2005	2007
	P.G.J.D.	2008	
	P.G.J.O.	2011	
Trigger, Francis John	A.G.St.B.	2010	
Trist, Terence Albert	—		1993
Trodd, Eric, *K.L.J.*	P.A.G.Swd.B.	2011	2006
Trollope, Rex	P.A.G.D.C.	2011	2007
Trott, John Edmund, *O.St.J.*	G.St.B.	1979	
	G.Tyler.	1981-1989	
	P.G.J.D.	1985	
	P.G.J.O.	1989	
	P.G.S.O.	2002	
Trott, Keith Hardwick	P.A.G.D.C.	1990	2001
	P.G.S.D.	1996	
	P.G.J.O.	2010	
Trumble, David John Charles	P.A.G.D.C.	2005	2006
	P.G.S.D.	2010	
Truswell, James Bennett	G.Stwd.	1999	2002
	P.G.S.D.	2004	
	Prov.G.M., West Yorkshire..2007-2012		
Tryner, Ernest William	P.G.I.G.	1997	2000
	P.A.G.D.C.	2007	
Tsoi, Hak Chiu Herman	P.A.G.Swd.B.	2009	
Tsoi, Herbert Hak Kong	P.A.G.D.C.	2004	
	P.G.S.D.	2011	
Tuck, Sidney Edward Ernest	P.A.G.D.C.	1996	1997
	P.G.S.D.	2011	
Tucker, David	P.A.G.D.C.	2001	2003
	P.G.S.D.	2007	
Tucker, Denis	P.A.G.D.C.	2011	
Tucker, William Duncan Alister, *O.B.E., J.P.*	P.A.G.D.C.	1981	
Tuckett, Kenneth William John	P.G.St.B.	1990	

NAME	RANK	YEAR OF APPT.	R.A.M.G.R. YEAR OF APPT.
Tuffey, Ronald	P.A.G.D.C.	2009	2010
Tulip, James Thomas	P.G.St.B.	1993	1989
Tulip, Kenneth	P.G.I.G.	2003	
Tulip, Reginald	P.A.G.St.B.	2010	
Tunbridge, Colin Paul	P.G.St.B.	1999	2001
	P.G.J.D.	2004	
	P.G.J.O.	2010	
Tunbridge, Edwin Richard John	P.A.G.Swd.B.	2012	
Tunstall, Maurice	P.A.G.D.C.	2004	2009
	P.G.J.D.	2011	
Turnbull, Michael David Patterson	P.A.G.D.C.	2001	2003
Turner, Edward Valentine	P.G.St.B.	1995	
Turner, James William, *E.R.D.*	P.A.G.D.C.	1998	2000
	P.G.S.O.	2003	
Turner, Keith Howard, *T.D.*	P.A.G.D.C.	1998	2001
	P.G.S.D.	2001	
	P.G.J.O.	2008	
Turner, Maurice John	P.G.St.B.	1987	1989
Turner, Peter Frood	P.A.G.D.C.	2000	2001
	P.G.S.D.	2012	
Turner, Roy	P.A.G.D.C.	1985	1985
	G.S.D.	1991	
Turner, Stanley		—	2011
Turner, Terence Norman Paul	P.A.G.D.C.	2000	2002
	G.S.D.	2006	
	P.G.J.O.	2011	
Turpin, Wg.Cdr. Richard Herbert, *O.B.E.*	P.A.G.D.C.	2004	2009
	P.G.S.D.	2007	
	P.G.J.O.	2008	
Tuthill, Robert Gregory	A.G.D.C.	1998	2000
	P.G.S.D.	2005	
Twitchen, Kenneth Geoffrey	P.A.G.D.C.	1987	1987
	P.G.S.D.	1994	
Tyacke, Brian Richard		—	1998
Tynan, Ivor Bryan	G.St.B.	2004	
	P.G.J.D.	2011	
Tysoe, Clifford Harry	P.A.G.D.C.	1992	2007
	P.G.S.D.	1997	
Tyson, Reginald Barie	P.A.G.St.B.	1996	1990
	P.G.J.D.	2002	
Tyson, William Desmond	G.Stwd.	1987	1988
	P.G.J.D.	1992	
Underby, George Vincent	P.A.G.D.C.	1985	
Underhill, Norman Boyce	A.G.D.C.	1977	1979
	P.G.S.D.	1982	
	P.G.J.O.	1987	
Underwood, Anthony Roy	P.G.St.B.	2010	
Underwood, Douglas Jonah	A.G.D.C.	1994	1993
Unwin, Roger John	P.A.G.D.C.	2009	
Upton, Derek Arthur	P.G.S.D.	2011	
Upton, Robert Harry, *J.P.*	G.Stwd.	2004	2006
	P.G.J.D.	2008	

NAME	RANK	YEAR OF APPT.	R.A.M.G.R. YEAR OF APPT.
Urwin, Edward Taylor	P.A.G.D.C.	1988	1995
	P.G.S.D.	1994	
	G.J.O.	1999	
	P.G.M.O.	2005	
Usher, Matthew Swinburn	P.A.G.St.B.	2000	
Utting, David Charles	P.G.St.B.	1996	1997
	P.G.J.D.	2004	
Vaid, Bomi Ardeshir	P.G.St.B.	2004	2006
Vaillant, Paul		—	2007
Vakil, Ardeshir Sarosh	P.A.G.D.C.	2008	2009
Valentine, Alan John	G.Stwd.	2006	
	P.G.J.D.	2009	
Valere, Clarence Courtney Philerman	P.A.G.D.C.	2010	
Vallipuram, Reginald Balasingam	P.A.G.D.C.	2011	
Vallis, Cyril Ley		—	1973
van Aartsen, Antonie Peter	P.G.St.B.	2007	2006
van Beek, Hendrick Frans	P.A.G.D.C.	1991	1997
	P.G.S.D.	1996	
	G.J.O.	2000	
van Bentveld, Dirk	P.A.G.St.B.	2001	1996
van den Berg, Pieter	P.G.J.D.	2012	
van der Beek, Anthony Theodoor	P.G.St.B.	2010	
van der Burgh, Andries Johannes	P.A.G.D.C.	2008	2009
van der Heiden, Edward Arnold		—	2009
van der Merwe, Phillip Anthony	P.A.G.St.B.	2006	
van der Plaat, Johannes Bertus	P.G.St.B.	2011	2006
van der Zel, Jacobus Nicolaas	P.G.St.B.	2004	1999
van Engen, Ronald Evering	P.A.G.D.C.	1996	
van Greunen, Henry	P.A.G.D.C.	—	1995
	P.G.S.D.	2003	
	P.G.J.O.	2008	
Vanhinsbergh, Steven Matthew	G.Stwd.	2010	
van Loggerenberg, Adolf Johannes Phillipus	P.A.G.D.C.	1989	
van Putten, Cornelis	P.G.St.B.	2005	2004
	P.G.J.D.	2008	
van Wijk, Herman	P.A.G.St.B.	2007	
	P.G.J.D.	2012	
Varcoe, Brian Richard	P.A.G.D.C.	1992	1992
Vardon-Odonkor, Charles	P.A.G.D.C.	2006	
Varley, Arthur Steven	G.I.G.	2011	
Varma, Dr. Koyikal Karthikeya	P.A.G.D.C.	2002	2004
	P.G.S.D.	2006	
	P.G.J.O.	2008	
Varma, Ramavarma Ravi		—	2006
Vasishta, Dr. Narender	P.G.S.D.	1998	
Vatcher, Edward Peter Guy	P.A.G.D.C.	2006	
Vaughan, Alan John	P.A.G.D.C.	1995	1999
	G.S.D.	2001	
	P.G.J.O.	2007	
	P.G.M.O.	2012	
Vaughan, David William Andrew	P.A.G.D.C.	2008	

NAME	RANK	YEAR OF APPT.	R.A.M.G.R. YEAR OF APPT.
Vaughan, Peter Reginald	P.A.G.D.C.	2002	2010
	P.G.S.D.	2010	
	P.G.J.O.	2012	
Vaughan, Robert Christopher	P.G.S.D.	2006	
Vause, John Edward	P.A.G.D.C.	2010	
Veal, John Henry	P.A.G.D.C.	2001	1997
	P.G.J.D.	2007	
Veale, David Donald		—	2010
Veening, Jan Albert	P.G.St.B.	1998	
	P.G.J.D.	2000	
Venkatachalam, Kumarappa	P.G.J.D.	2009	2009
Venkatasubramanian, Vellore Venkatachala	P.G.St.B.	1977	1998
	P.G.J.O.	1996	
	P.G.J.W.	2006	
Venkat Ramana, Kalavakolanu	P.A.G.D.C.	2009	
Venker, Willem	P.G.St.B.	2009	2010
Venn, Maj. Ronald Francis	G.Stwd.	2007	2008
	P.G.J.D.	2009	
Venn, William Dennis George	P.A.G.D.C.	1988	
	P.G.S.D.	1998	
Vennel, Coimbatore Narasimhalu		—	1997
Venning, Tom William Dawe	P.G.I.G.	1995	1998
Venzi, Fabio	Dist.G.M., Italy	2010	
Verbist, Jean	P.A.G.D.C.	2001	2002
	P.G.J.D.	2003	
	P.G.J.O.	2008	
	Dist.G.M., Belgium	2012	
Verduyn, Micheal Noel Russell	G.Stwd	1987	1983
	P.G.J.D.	1994	
	P.G.J.O.	2005	
Vergette, Robin	G.Stwd.	2000	
	P.G.J.D.	2007	
Verhelst, Roland Georges Jules	P.G.St.B.	2004	
Verlander, Roger William	P.G.St.B.	2002	
Verney, His Hon. Judge Sir Lawrence, *T.D., D.L.*	G.Treasurer	1968	1968/9 GMRAC
Vernon, Barrie	P.G.St.B.	2006	2004
	P.G.J.D.	2012	
Vernon, Denis	P.G.St.B.	1990	
	P.G.J.D.	2011	
Vialet, Frederick Clarence, *Jr.*	P.A.G.D.C.	2007	2008
Vick, Derrick John	P.G.St.B.	2004	
Vickers, Brian Anthony	G.Stwd.	1987	1989
	P.G.J.D.	1992	
	P.G.S.O.	1997	
	P.G.M.O.	2002	
	P.G.J.W.	2011	
Vickery, Anthony David	P.G.St.B.	2010	2008
Vieira, Luiz Herculano	P.A.G.D.C.	2011	
Viggers, David George	P.A.G.D.C.	2003	2001
Vince, Martin William	P.A.G.Swd.B.	2003	2007
Vincent, George Henry	A.G.I.G.	1975	1983
	G.I.G.	1977	
	P.A.G.D.C	1982	
	P.G.S.D.	1990	
	P.G.J.O.	1999	

NAME	RANK	YEAR OF APPT.	R.A.M.G.R. YEAR OF APPT.
Vinecor, Warren Benjamin		—	2007
Vines, Brian Anthony	P.G.St.B.	2007	
Violet, Peter Richard Albert	P.G.St.B.	1999	1999
Visser, Anthonie Marius	P.A.G.Swd.B.	2007	
Visser, Philippus		—	2008
Voice, Noel Reginald	P.G.St.B.	2008	
Voigt, David Russell	P.G.St.B.	2001	
Vollans, David Edwin	P.G.St.B.	2006	
Von Gerard, John Keith		—	2003
von Hoff, John, Baron	A.G.Swd.B	1986	2009
	G.Swd.B	1987	
	A.G.Sec.	2009	
	P.G.J.O.	2009	
	P.G.M.O.	2010	
von der Heyde, Helmut, H.S.	P.A.G.D.C.	2000	1999
Vooght, John Michael	P.G.St.B.	2012	2009
Vos, Drs Johannes	P.A.G.D.C.	1995	1997
	P.G.S.D.	2001	
	P.G.J.O.	2009	
Vosloo, Deon Talbot	P.G.St.B.	2000	1999
Vosloo, Francois Hewitt	P.G.St.B.	2010	2012
	Dist.G.M., South Africa (Eastern)	2012	
Vousden, Peter Edward		—	1984
Voysey, Frederick William	P.G.St.B.	2007	2003
Vyas, Bakul Harshadray		—	2008
Vyas, Hemant Harshadray		—	2008
Wacey, Roger Frederick		—	2011
Waddingham, Harry	P.A.G.St.B.	2007	
Wade, Raymond	P.A.G.D.C.	2011	2011
Wade, Roland John	G.Stwd	1987	1988
	P.G.J.D.	1992	
	P.G.S.D.	1995	
	P.G.J.O.	1997	
	Prov.G.M., Kent	2003-2008	
Wadsworth, Peter	P.A.G.D.C.	1981	
	G.S.D.	1986	
Wagstaff, James William	P.A.G.D.C.	1998	2003
Wainwright, Alan William	P.A.G.D.C.	2000	2000
	P.G.J.D.	2005	
	P.G.S.D.	2007	
	P.G.J.O.	2009	
Wainwright, George Frederick	G.Stwd.	2010	
Wainwright, John Raymond	P.G.St.B.	2005	2007
	P.G.J.D.	2011	
Waite, Albert	P.G.St.B.	2006	2010
Waite, Terence Henry		—	2008
Waites, Ernest William	P.A.G.D.C.	2008	
Wake, Jeremy Philip	G.Stwd.	2011	
Wake, John Anthony		—	1994
Wakely, Eric Leonard John	G.Stwd.	1992	1996

NAME	RANK	YEAR OF APPT.	R.A.M.G.R. YEAR OF APPT.
Wakely-Smith, Sidney Rex	P.A.G.D.C.	1987	1994
	P.G.S.D.	1993	
	P.G.J.O.	1999	
Wakem, Francis, *Q.P.M.*	G.Stwd.	1997	
	G.J.D.	2003	
	P.G.S.O.	2010	
Walder, Graham Robert	P.A.G.D.C.	2010	2010
Waldron, Brian Thomas	P.A.G.Swd.B;	2009	
Waldron, Paul	P.A.G.D.C.	2011	
Waley, Simon Francis Norman	P.G.S.D.	1995	2000
	P.G.J.O.	2001	
	G.J.W.	2006	
Walford, Royston George	A.G.I.G.	2011	
Walker, Alan Royle	P.A.G.D.C.	1982	1984
	P.G.S.D.	1990	
Walker, David	P.A.G.Swd.B.	2010	2009
Walker, David Eric John	A.G.I.G.	2001	2004
	P.A.G.D.C.	2008	
Walker, Frank Brian	P.A.G.D.C.	1996	2003
	P.G.J.D.	2003	
Walker, Frederick Alan	G.Stwd.	2008	
	P.G.J.D.	2011	
Walker, Gordon	P.G.St.B.	2000	
Walker, Ian Hamilton	P.A.G.D.C.	2001	
Walker, Ian Stuart	P.G.St.B.	2005	
Walker, John	P.A.G.D.C.	2007	2000
Walker, Michael Richard Hinchliffe	P.G.St.B.	2008	
Walker, Michael Robert	G.Stwd.	2008	
	P.G.J.D.	2011	
Walker, Neil Harley	P.A.G.D.C.	2000	2000
Walker, Richard Alan Lewis		—	1987
Walker, Richard Malcolm	P.A.G.D.C.	2009	2011
	P.G.S.D.	2012	
Walker, Ronald Murray		—	2001
Walker, Revd. Trevor John	A.G.Chap.	2006	2007
	Prov.G.M., Lincolnshire	2007	
Walker, Revd. Canon Walter Stanley	P.A.G.Chap.	2001	
Walkerdine, Bryan	P.A.G.D.C.	1994	2006
	P.G.S.D.	2004	
Walker-Sherriff, John Dennis		—	2010
Wall, David	P.A.G.D.C.	2004	2009
	P.G.S.D.	2011	
Wall, Geoffrey	P.A.G.D.C.	1987	
	P.G.S.D.	1995	
	P.G.J.O.	2003	
Wall, Ian Duncan		—	2000
Wallace, John Speirs	G.Stwd.	1987	1994
	P.G.S.D.	1992	
	G.S.O.	1997	
	P.G.J.W.	2011	
Wallace, Capt. John Vyvyan, *F.C.M.S.*	P.A.G.D.C.	2004	2005
	P.G.S.D.	2010	
Wallace, William John	P.A.G.St.B.	1995	2004
	P.G.J.D.	2000	

NAME	RANK	YEAR OF APPT.	R.A.M.G.R. YEAR OF APPT.
Wallis, David Arthur Orlando	G.Stwd.	1980	
	P.G.J.D.	1988	
	P.G.J.O.	2010	
Wallis, Richard Henry Wilson	P.A.G.D.C.	1996	1997
	P.G.S.D.	2003	
	P.G.J.O.	2009	
Wallis, Richard Victor, *J.P.*	P.G.S.D.	1995	1999
	G.M.O.	2003	2010 GMRAC
	G.J.W.	2010	
Walls, Dr. Archibald George	P.G.St.B.	2007	
Wallwork, Barrington Barton	G.Stwd.	1993	2002
	P.G.J.D.	1998	
	P.G.J.O.	2009	
Walsh, Derek Francis	A.G.St.B.	1996	1996
Walsh, Nidrel James	P.G.St.B.	2011	
Walsh, Patrick Joseph	P.A.G.Swd.B.	2012	2010
Walsh, Thomas Aubrey	P.A.G.St.B.	1989	
Walt, Guy	P.G.St.B.	1993	
Walter, Leonard Arthur		—	2004
Walters, Dr. John Roebuck, *Ph.D*	P.A.G.Swd.B.	2000	2008
	P.G.J.D.	2008	
Walters, Raymond Edward Roy	P.A.G.St.B.	2003	2001
	P.G.J.D.	2012	
Walton, David	G.Stwd.	1992	2005
	P.G.J.D.	1997	
	P.G.J.O.	2005	
Walton, Frank William		—	1999
Walton, Ian Stretton	P.A.G.St.B.	2002	1998
Warburton, James William	P.A.G.D.C.	2005	
Warburton, John	A.G.Org.	2004	
	P.A.G.D.C.	2009	
Ward, Alan Arthur	P.A.G.Swd.B.	2007	
Ward, Alexander Edward	P.G.St.B.	2008	2006
Ward, John		—	2010
Ward, Michael Leonard		—	2010
Ward, Peter	P.A.G.Swd.B.	2009	
Ward, Peter Frank Thomas	G.Stwd.	1972	1972
	P.G.J.D.	1977	
	P.G.J.O.	1989	
	P.G.M.O.	2011	
Ward, Selwyn Eric	P.A.G.D.C.	2006	2011
Ward, Terence Desmond	P.A.G.Swd.B.	2005	2006
	P.G.S.D.	2007	
	P.G.J.O.	2011	
Ward, Thomas Lindsay	A.G.I.G.	2001	2008
	P.A.G.D.C.	2011	
Ward, William Thomas	P.G.St.B.	1981	
	P.G.J.D.	1990	
Wardle, Stephen Edgar	P.A.G.D.C.	1999	2010
	P.G.S.D.	2009	
Ware, Robert George	P.A.G.Swd.B.	2007	
Ware, Harry Richard Alex	P.G.St.B.	2004	

NAME	RANK	YEAR OF APPT.	R.A.M.G.R. YEAR OF APPT.
Wareham, Brian Clifford	G.Stwd.	1993	1996
	P.G.J.D.	1998	
	P.G.J.O.	2003	
	Prov.G.M., Sussex	2007-2012	
Warham, John	P.G.St.B.	1999	2000
	P.G.S.D.	2009	
Warmsley, Frank Leslie	P.G.St.B.	1987	1996
Warn, George Ian	P.G.St.B.	1992	1998
	P.G.J.D.	2000	
	P.G.J.O.	2007	
Warneford, Derek	P.G.J.D.	1999	1999
	P.G.J.O.	2005	
Warner, Peter David	P.G.St.B.	2009	2010
Warr, Roger	P.A.G.St.B.	2002	
Warrell, Leslie Albert	P.A.G.St.B.	2003	2000
	P.G.J.D.	2010	
Warren, David Leonard	P.A.G.D.C.	2012	
Warren, John Warwick	G.Stwd.	2004	2011
	P.G.J.D.	2009	
Warrington, Geoffrey	P.G.St.B.	1997	
Warwick, Steven John	G.St.B.	1994	1994
	P.G.J.D.	2001	
	P.G.J.O.	2012	
Warwick, Walter	P.A.G.D.C.	2003	2009
	P.G.J.O.	2009	
Waspe, Anthony John	G.Stwd.	2003	2004
	P.G.J.D.	2007	
	P.G.J.O.	2012	
Wassell, Ian John Harry	—		2005
Waterfall, Phillip Burdett	P.A.G.D.C.	1994	2005
	G.S.D.	2002	
	P.G.J.O.	2007	
Waterman, Michael James	P.A.G.St.B.	2009	
Waters, David Stewart	—		2007
Waters, Keith Roger Duncan	G.Stwd.	1997	2002
	G.J.D.	2003	
	P.G.J.O.	2009	
Watkin, Michael Arthur	P.A.G.D.C.	2012	
Watkin, Peter Gordon	A.G.D.C.	2009	
Watkins, Alan Ronald	P.A.G.Swd.B.	2012	
Watkinson, Geoffrey Thomas	P.G.St.B.	2008	
Watkinson, Peter Neil	P.A.G.D.C.	1983	1991
Watkinson, Roger John	P.A.G.D.C.	1988	
	P.G.S.D.	1996	
Watkinson, Stanley James	P.A.G.D.C.	1990	
Watson, Bruce Irving	Dist.G.M., Zimbabwe	2011	
Watson, Colin	P.A.G.D.C.	1997	
Watson, Harry Mortimer, *B.Sc., F.R.I.C.S.*	P.A.G.Swd.B.	2006	
Watson, John	P.A.G.D.C.	1988	1995
	P.G.J.D.	2003	
Watson, John Edward	P.A.G.St.B.	1997	2007
Watson, John Willis	P.A.G.D.C.	2001	
Watson, Maurice John	—		1999
Watson, Peter James	A.G.St.B.	1999	

NAME	RANK	YEAR OF APPT.	R.A.M.G.R. YEAR OF APPT.
Watson, Robert Taylor	P.A.G.D.C.	2008	
Watson, Thomas Youell	P.G.St.B.	2000	
Wattison, Brian Frederick	G.S.D.	2008	1996
Watton, Christopher Robert	G.Stwd.	1992	1996
	P.G.S.D.	1995	
	P.G.J.O.	2000	
	Prov.G.M., Dorset	2001-2008	
Watts, Douglas Gordon	G.Stwd.	2004	
	P.G.J.D.	2007	
Watts, John Dereke	P.G.St.B.	1999	
	P.G.J.D.	2010	
Watts, Michael John	P.A.G.Swd.B.	2003	2006
Watts, William John	P.G.St.B.	2009	2004
Waudby, Philip Richard	P.A.G.D.C.	2010	2007
Wayne, Bernard	P.G.St.B.	1995	1993
	P.G.J.D.	2001	
Wearne, Harold	P.G.St.B.	1998	2002
	P.G.J.D.	2003	
	P.G.S.D.	2009	
Webb, Alfred Andrew	P.A.G.St.B.	2007	
Webb, Brian Richard John	P.A.G.Swd.B.	2007	
Webb, Clive Richard	P.A.G.Swd.B.	2010	
Webb, Dennis Brookes	P.A.G.D.C.	1999	
Webb, Graham Anthony	P.G.St.B.	1994	2003
	P.G.J.D.	2009	
Webb, Harold William Charles	P.A.G.D.C.	2012	
Webb, John Michael	A.G.D.C.	1986	1986
	P.G.S.D.	1994	
	P.G.J.O.	2001	
	G.J.W.	2007	
Webb, Jack Alfred	P.A.G.St.B.	1994	2000
	G.J.D.	2001	
Webb, Thomas Vallance	P.G.S.D.	2004	
Webber, Christopher Evan	P.A.G.D.C.	2000	
Webber, David Alan	G.Stwd.	2004	1999
	P.G.J.D.	2009	
Webber, Peter John		—	1999
Webber, Roy Harold	P.G.St.B.	1982	1995
	G.J.D.	1987	
	P.G.J.O.	1996	
Webster, Geoffrey Scruton	P.A.G.Swd.B.	2006	2008
Webster, Ian Fraser	G.Stwd.	2002	
	P.G.J.D.	2008	
Webster, Neil	A.G.I.G.	2012	2008
Webster, Ronald	P.G.St.B.	1981	1986
	P.G.J.D.	1986	
	P.G.J.O.	1991	
Webster, Terence Gordon		—	1994
Weed, Arthur Walter	G.Stwd.	2005	2011
	P.G.J.D.	2008	
Weedon, Richard Alan	P.A.G.Swd.B.	2012	2006
Weekes, Paul David Charles		—	2008
Weeks, Norman Thomas Stowell	P.G.St.B.	2001	
Weetch, Joseph Albert	P.G.St.B.	2002	2001

NAME	RANK	YEAR OF APPT.	R.A.M.G.R. YEAR OF APPT.
Welch, Joseph Charles	P.A.G.Swd.B.	2010	
Welle Donker, Jan Frederik	P.G.St.B.	2012	
Wellings, Peter James	G.Stwd.	2006	2006
	P.G.J.D.	2010	
Wellings, Trevor Frederick, *F.S.C.A.*	G.Stwd.	1991	1988
	P.G.J.D.	2003	
Wellington, Ian	P.G.St.B.	2008	
Wells, David Dermont	P.A.G.D.C.	1992	1981
Wells, Harry	A.G.Insp. of Wks.	1987-1988	1995
	A.G.Insp. of Wks.	1993-2012	
	P.G.J.O.	1998	
Welsh, Matthew Alan	P.A.G.Swd.B.	2001	
Welsh, Stephen William Mark	P.A.G.St.B.	2011	
Wensley, Simon Mark	A.G.St.B.	2011	
Wessels, Pieter Johannes	P.A.G.D.C.	2010	2008
Wesson, Charley	P.G.St.B.	2009	
West, Jack Edward	P.G.St.B.	1994	
West, John Edward	P.A.G.St.B.	2002	
West, Neville	P.A.G.D.C.	1996	
	P.G.S.D.	2011	
West, Raymond James		—	2010
West, Terrence	P.G.St.B.	1994	2005
	P.G.J.D.	2001	
Westbury-Jones, Timothy John	P.G.St.B.	2009	
Westley, Marshall Gordon	P.G.St.B.	2011	
Weston, Graham	G.Stwd.	1995	1998
	P.G.S.D.	1999	
	P.G.J.O.	2003	
Weston, Paul Frederick	P.A.G.D.C.	2005	2011
Westwood, Patrick David Murray	P.A.G.D.C.	2012	
Westwood, Robert Edgar	P.G.St.B.	1994	1996
Wetherell, Brian Edward		—	2005
Whale, Geoffrey Edward	A.G.D.C.	2000	1998
	G.Swd.B.	2005	
	P.G.J.O.	2011	
Wheatcroft, Edwin John Peter	P.A.G.D.C.	2000	
Wheatley, Albert James Stanley	P.A.G.D.C.	1994	2000
	P.G.S.D.	2000	
Wheatley, Keith Gardiner Kenneth	P.A.G.D.C.	1990	1991
	P.G.S.D.	1996	
	P.G.J.O.	2003	
	P.G.S.O.	2011	
Wheeler, Anthony George	P.G.St.B.	2010	
Wheeler, Dennis Wolfgang	P.G.St.B.	2006	
Wheeler, Fredrick Henry	P.G.St.B.	2006	2003
Wheeler, Ralph John	A.G.D.C.	1990	1993
	G.S.D.	1995	
	P.G.J.O.	2004	
Whelan, Shane Maurice	G.Stwd.	2010	2009
Whelan-Whitfield, John Norman	P.G.St.B.	2002	2005
	P.G.J.D.	2008	
While, Ernest Samuel	P.G.St.B.	2004	2001
Whitaker, Jonathan Charles, *J.P.*	P.A.G.D.C.	2010	2009

NAME	RANK	YEAR OF APPT.	R.A.M.G.R. YEAR OF APPT.
White, Brian Orpeth	A.G.D.C.	2007	
White, Brian Thomas	P.A.G.D.C.	2000	2001
	P.G.S.D.	2007	
White, Bruce	P.A.G.D.C.	2012	
White, Christopher Robin	P.A.G.St.B.	2011	
White, David Christopher	A.G.D.C.	2010	2008
White, David Grant	P.A.G.St.B.	2012	
White, Jack William Francis	—		2000
White, Michael Brian	G.Stwd.	2000	
	P.G.J.D.	2006	
White, Robert Cecil John	P.A.G.D.C.	2000	2000
White, Robin Leonard Woolford	P.A.G.D.C.	1998	2000
	P.G.S.D.	2004	
White, Stanley Victor	P.A.G.D.C.	2004	2003
White, Stephen Nigel	P.G.St.B.	2012	
White, Thomas Barrett	P.A.G.Swd.B.	2011	
White, Wallace Ernest	—		2000
Whitfield, John	A.G.St.B.	2005	
Whitehead, Edward Peter	P.A.G.D.C.	2002	2003
Whitehead, John	P.A.G.D.C.	2000	1992
	P.G.S.D.	2011	
Whiteley, Jeffrey William	G.Stwd.	2011	
Whiteman, Geoffrey	P.A.G.St.B.	1997	2003
	P.G.J.D.	2007	
Whiteman, Leslie James	—		1998
Whitfield, John	P.G.J.D.	2011	
Whiting, Spencer Rowland, *D.S.O.*	Dist.G.M., Transvaal	1987-1992	1987
Whitlock, Michael Anthony	P.A.G.Swd.B.	2012	
Whitmore, Paul Reginald	P.A.G.D.C.	2006	2008
Whitney, John	P.A.G.D.C.	2008	
Whitney, William Arthur	P.G.St.B.	2002	2002
Whittall, Frederick Michael Armstrong	G.Stwd.	1999	1995
Whittall, William Joseph	G.J.D.	1977	1978
	P.G.J.O.	1984	
	P.G.M.O.	2008	
Whittle, Alfred	P.A.G.D.C.	2004	
Whittle, Leonard George	P.G.St.B.	1981	1991
Whitton, Frank Olav	P.A.G.D.C.	2000	
Whitton, Leslie William		—	2011
Whitworth, James	P.A.G.D.C.	1995	
Wibberley, Edmund		—	2005
Wibberley, Robert Edward	P.G.St.B.	2000	2005
	G.S.D.	2005	
Wickens, Michael John	P.G.St.B.	2005	
	P.A.G.D.C.	2011	
Wicker, Jack Lewis, *O.B.E.*	P.G.St.B.	1996	
Wickramapala, Angulugaha Gamage Berty, *J.P.*	P.A.G.D.C.	2001	
Wickstead, John Horace	P.A.G.D.C.	1982	1989
	P.G.J.O.	1987	1993 GMRAC (H.C.)
	Prov.G.M., Devonshire	1991-2000	
Wiegratz, Siegfried Carl Waldemar	P.A.G.D.C.	2005	2004

NAME	RANK	YEAR OF APPT.	R.A.M.G.R. YEAR OF APPT.
Wiffen, Alan George	G.Stwd.	2000	2010
	P.G.J.D.	2007	
Wigger, Bernard Herbert Roy	P.G.St.B.	2003	2010
Wiggins, Michael John	P.A.G.D.C.	1987	1994
	P.G.S.D.	1992	
	P.G.J.O.	2001	
Wiggins, William Geoffrey Denison		—	2008
Wijewarden, Diyal	P.A.G.D.C.	2000	
Wilburn, Dennis Edgar, *J.P.*	G.Stwd.	1976	
	G.J.D.	1981	
	P.G.J.O.	1989	
Wild, David Nicholas	P.A.G.St.B.	2010	
Wild, Kenneth Clarence	P.A.G.D.C.	1977	1973
Wilde, Robert David	P.A.G.D.C.	2011	
Wilding, David Michael	P.A.G.D.C.	2010	
Wileman, Richard John	P.A.G.Swd.B.	2005	2004
Wiles, Gordon Alan	P.G.St.B.	2005	
	P.G.J.D.	2011	
Wiles, Peter James	P.G.St.B.	2006	2005
Wilford, Geoffrey	P.A.G.D.C.	2011	
Wilford, Keith William	P.A.G.D.C.	2001	2000
	P.G.S.D.	2008	
Wilford, Stanley George	P.G.J.D.	1975	1973
	P.G.J.O.	1981	
Wilkins, David John	P.G.St.B.	2004	
Wilkins, Ivor Vivian		—	2011
Wilkins, Keith Henry David	P.G.St.B.	2004	
Wilkinson, John Robert, *O.B.E.*	P.A.G.D.C.	1981	
	G.S.D.	1996	
Wilkinson, Nigel	P.A.G.D.C.	2011	
Wilkinson, Raymond George	P.A.G.Swd.B.	2003	2008
	P.G.J.D.	2011	
Wilkinson, Robert	P.G.St.B.	1981	
	P.G.J.D.	1994	
Wilkinson, Ross Stanley		—	2006
Wilkinson, Stuart Michael	P.A.G.D.C.	2012	
Wilkinson, Thomas Dodd	P.G.St.B.	1990	
	P.G.J.D.	1999	
	P.G.J.O.	2005	
Wilkinson, Thomas Edwin	P.A.G.D.C.	2011	
Willans, Keith	P.A.G.D.C.	2001	2004
	P.G.S.D.	2007	
	P.G.J.O.	2008	
Willcock, David John William	G.Swd.B.	2012	
Williams, Alun	A.G.I.G.	2006	2006
	P.A.G.D.C.	2010	
Williams, Anthony, *J.P.*	P.A.G.D.C.	2000	
Williams, Anthony Frederick		—	2011
Williams, Barry Arthur	P.A.G.Swd.B.	2001	2009
	P.A.G.D.C.	2012	
Williams, Barry Keith	P.G.St.B.	1999	2001
	P.G.J.D.	2006	
Williams, Ben Trevor	P.A.G.D.C.	2005	2011

NAME	RANK	YEAR OF APPT.	R.A.M.G.R. YEAR OF APPT.
Williams, Brian	P.A.G.D.C.	2010	
Williams, Colin	P.G.St.B.	1999	2003
	P.G.J.D.	2007	
Williams, Christopher	G.Stwd.	2005	
	G.J.D.	2009	
Williams, Cyril Topham	P.A.G.D.C.	2006	
Williams, David Ivor	G.Stwd.	1982	1992
	P.G.J.D.	1989	
	P.G.J.O.	1994	
	Prov.G.M., London	1997-2007	
Williams, Dennis John	P.A.G.D.C.	1999	2007
	P.G.S.D.	2009	
Williams, Edward	P.G.St.B.	1993	1999
	P.G.J.D.	2000	
Williams, Eldred Samuel	P.A.G.St.B.	1996	
	P.G.J.D.	2003	
Williams, Eric Graver	G.Stwd.	2007	2010
	P.G.J.D.	2010	
Williams, Eric Stanley	P.A.G.D.C.	2012	
Williams, Francis Maurice	P.A.G.D.C.	2005	
Williams, Frank Terry	P.A.G.Swd.B.	2007	
Williams, Gary Reginald	P.A.G.D.C.	2007	
Williams, Graham Paget	P.A.G.D.C.	2008	2008
Williams, Graham Roy	G.Stwd.	2009	
Williams, Revd. Gwynfor	Dep.G.Chap.	2011	
	G.Chap.	2012	
Williams, Gwynfor David		—	2005
Williams, Iwan	P.A.G.D.C.	2012	
Williams, Jeffrey David	P.A.G.D.C.	2005	
Williams, John	P.G.I.G.	2004	1991
Williams, John Ernest Terence	P.A.G.Swd.B.	2012	
Williams, Keith Warren		—	2011
Williams, Maldwyn Glynda	A.G.St.B.	2005	
Williams, Nicholas David		—	2005
Williams, Paul Alan	P.A.G.D.C.	2003	
Williams, Paul Michael, *O.B.E., C.St.J., D.L.*	G.Stwd.	2012	
Williams, Peter David	P.A.G.St.B.	1991	1995
	G.J.D.	1996	
	P.G.J.O.	2001	
Williams, Peter Glyn	G.Stwd.	1983	1985
	G.Sec.	1986-1996	1986 GMRAC (H.C.)
	P.G.J.W.	1988	
	P.G.S.W.	1997	
Williams, Phillip Austin	P.A.G.D.C.	2007	
Williams, Phillip Verdun	P.A.G.D.C.	2012	
Williams, Reginald Leonard	P.G.St.B.	1984	
Williams, Robert Edward Lloyd	P.G.St.B.	2001	
Williams, Robert Hywel Wyn	G.Stwd.	1981	
	P.G.J.D.	1987	
Williams, Robert John	P.G.St.B.	1990	1985
Williams, Robert Michael	P.G.St.B.	1996	2011
	P.G.J.D.	2012	

NAME	RANK	YEAR OF APPT.	R.A.M.G.R. YEAR OF APPT.
Williams, Ryan Andrew	P.A.G.D.C.	2008	2009
	Dep.G.D.C.	2012	
Williams, Ronald Leslie		—	2009
Williams, Terwyn Alun	P.A.G.D.C.	2011	
Williams, Thomas Gareth	P.A.G.D.C.	1995	1998
	P.G.S.D.	2001	
	Prov.G.M., North Wales	2004-2012	
Williams, Vivian John	P.A.G.D.C.	2011	
Williams, Vyvian John	P.A.G.D.C.	2011	
Williamson, Barry James	P.A.G.D.C.	1993	1991
	P.G.S.D.	2012	
Williamson, David Kenneth	G.S.W.	2002	2002
			2007 GMRAC (H.C.)
Williamson, John McKay	P.A.G.D.C.	1994	
Williamson, Kenneth	P.A.G.St.B.	2001	2006
	P.G.J.D.	2008	
Williamson, Leslie Frederick	P.A.G.D.C.	2005	2010
	P.G.J.D.	2010	
Williamson, William Joseph	P.G.St.B.	2004	
Willis, Bernard	P.G.St.B.	2010	2009
Willis, James	P.A.G.D.C.	2011	2010
Willmot, Frank Stanley	P.A.G.St.B.	2007	
Willmott, David Malcolm	P.A.G.D.C.	2000	2002
	P.G.S.D.	2005	
Willoughby, Stephen John Henry	G.Stwd.	2011	
	P.G.S.D.	2012	
Wills, Brian Bernard	P.A.G.D.C.	1993	1997
	G.S.D.	1998	
	P.G.J.O.	2003	
Wills, David John	P.A.G.D.C.	2009	
Wills, Philip	A.G.D.C.	2012	
Wilshaw, Peter		—	2005
Wilson, Andrew		—	1996
Wilson, Charles Martin	A.G.D.C.	2000	2005
	P.G.J.D.	2006	
	P.G.J.O.	2008	
	Prov.G.M., Sussex	2012	
Wilson, David George	P.A.G.St.B.	2008	
Wilson, Prof. Denovan Keith	P.A.G.D.C.	1998	1999
	P.G.S.D.	1999	
	P.G.J.O.	2001	
Wilson, Francis Donald	P.G.J.D.	1989	
Wilson, Ian Francis Evelyn		—	1975
Wilson, John	A.G.St.B.	2001	
Wilson, John Anthony		—	2009
Wilson, John Barrie	G.St.B.	1998	2004
	P.G.J.D.	2009	
Wilson, John Gilbert, F.C.A.	P.A.G.D.C.	1996	1998
	P.G.J.O.	2006	
Wilson, Joseph Graeme	P.A.G.D.C.	2011	
Wilson, Keith Richard		—	2004
Wilson, Martin John	P.A.G.D.C.	2008	

NAME	RANK	YEAR OF APPT.	R.A.M.G.R. YEAR OF APPT.
Wilson, Mervyn Frank	P.A.G.D.C.	1993	2001
	P.G.S.D.	1999	
	P.G.J.O.	2005	
	P.G.M.O.	2012	
Wilson, Michael	P.A.G.D.C.	2004	2003
Wilson, Ralph	P.G.St.B.	1983	1981
	P.G.J.D.	1990	
	P.G.J.O.	2001	
Wilson, Robin Keith	P.G.S.D.	2012	
Wilson, Reginald	P.G.I.G.	2005	
Wilson, Richard Filmer	P.G.St.B.	2011	
Wilson, Ronald	A.G.St.B	1997	1993
Wilson, Ronald Albert	P.A.G.D.C.	1986	1992
Wilson, William Peter		—	2007
Wilton, Derek Edward	P.G.St.B.	2007	
	Dep.G.Swd.B.	2012	
Wilton, Royston Albert	P.A.G.Swd.B.	2002	
	P.G.J.D.	2009	
Wincott, Raymond Arthur		—	2004
Winder, John	P.A.G.St.B.	2012	
Windsor, Raymond Powdrill	P.A.G.Swd.B.	1998	2004
	P.G.J.D.	2008	
Winfield, Gerald	P.A.G.St.B.	2000	2011
Winfield, John Carter	P.G.St.B.	2008	
Winstanley, David, *J.P.*	P.G.St.B.	1998	
	P.G.J.D.	2006	
Winston, John Wentworth	P.G.St.B.	2011	
Winter, John	P.A.G.St.B.	2009	2010
Winterbottom, Michael John	P.A.G.D.C.	2011	
Winterflood, Robert John	P.A.G.D.C.	2010	
Wintersgill, Derek Matthew	P.A.G.D.C.	1994	1996
	P.G.S.D.	2004	
Wintersgill, Keith Andrew		—	2005
Wischhussen, Victor Edmund		—	1992
Wisden, Victor Alan	P.G.St.B.	2000	2008
	P.G.J.D.	2008	
Wise, Hillier Bernard Alexander	G.Stwd.	1982	1984
	P.G.J.D.	1987	
	P.G.J.O.	2010	
Wise, James	P.A.G.D.C.	1996	1995
	P.G.S.D.	2002	
Wise, Peter John	G.Stwd.	1995	1996
	P.G.J.D.	2000	
	P.G.J.O.	2005	
Wise, Robert Malcolm	P.G.St.B.	2010	
Withers, John William Kenneth		—	1997
Withey, Dr. David Roger	A.G.Swd.B.	2002	2007
	P.G.J.D.	2009	
Withey, John Anthony	P.A.G.D.C.	2001	
Withnell, James	P.A.G.D.C.	1991	
	P.G.S.D.	2011	
Witteridge, Henry James Louis	P.A.G.D.C.	1997	
Witts, Garry David	P.A.G.D.C.	2012	2007

NAME	RANK	YEAR OF APPT.	R.A.M.G.R. YEAR OF APPT.
Wolfe, Hon. Mr. Justice Lensley Hugh, *O.J.*	P.G.St.B.	2003	2010
	P.G.J.D.	2011	
Wolstencroft, Ian	P.G.St.B.	1996	2007
	P.G.J.D.	2002	
	P.G.J.O.	2009	
Wolstenholme, Stanley, *I.S.M.*	P.A.G.D.C.	2002	
Wong, Bing Lai	P.A.G.D.C.	1995	1999
	P.G.S.D.	2008	
Wong, Edmund Yee-Wah	P.A.G.D.C.	2010	2009
Wong, Peter Hong Yuen, *O.B.E., J.P.*	P.A.G.D.C.	1998	
	P.G.S.D.	2010	
Wonnacott, Ernest John	P.A.G.Swd.B.	1999	1999
	P.G.J.D.	2007	
Wonnacott, James Alan		—	2010
Wood, Alaric Waldo	P.G.J.O.	1976	1973
	P.G.M.O.	2012	
Wood, Andrew Neville, *J.P.*	P.A.G.D.C.	2011	
Wood, Christopher Peter	P.A.G.St.B.	2008	
Wood, Colin James	P.A.G.St.B.	1992	1995
Wood, Derek		—	2007
Wood, Derek Charles		—	2003
Wood, Douglas	P.A.G.D.C.	2009	
Wood, George Robert	P.A.G.D.C.	1989	1991
	P.G.S.D.	2012	
Wood, Guion	P.A.G.St.B.	2001	2007
Wood, John	P.G.St.B.	2011	
Wood, Stephen Newton	P.A.G.D.C.	2010	
Wood, Terence Stanley	P.A.G.D.C.	2001	2002
	P.G.S.D.	2007	
Wood, William Kenneth	A.G.Swd.B.	2010	
Wood-Griffiths, Thomas Brian	P.G.St.B.	1992	1980
	P.G.J.D.	2002	
Woodall, Brian	P.A.G.D.C.	1999	2002
	G.S.D.	2005	
Woodall, John	P.A.G.D.C.	1991	1986
	P.G.S.D.	1998	
Woodbridge, Martin Christopher		—	2010
Woodburn, Ernest Henry	P.A.G.D.C.	1989	
Woodcock, Alan Arthur	P.A.G.D.C.	2000	
Woodcock, Colin Robert	P.A.G.D.C.	2009	2008
Woodcock, Graham Henry	P.A.G.D.C.	2009	2008
Woodcock, Michael	P.G.S.D.	2011	
Woodcock, Michael Edwin	P.A.G.St.B.	2011	2004
Woodcock, Peter	P.G.St.B.	1998	
Woodcock, Robert Peter	P.A.G.D.C.	2007	
Wood-Griffiths, Thomas Brian	P.G.J.O.	2011	
Woodhouse, Ivor Claude		—	2009
Woodhouse, Nigel Robert John	P.G.St.B.	1994	1991
	Dist.G.M., Germany	1994-2009	
Woodhouse, John Derrick	P.A.G.D.C.	1995	
Woodhouse, Langton	P.A.G.D.C.	2010	
Woodhouse, Leslie	P.A.G.Swd.B.	2012	2010

NAME	RANK	YEAR OF APPT.	R.A.M.G.R. YEAR OF APPT.
Woodings, David Francis	P.A.G.D.C.	2007	2007
Woodman, Brian Sidney	P.A.G.St.B	1999	1996
Woodrow, John Charles	Dist.G.M., Brazil	2005	
Woods, Digby Ralph	G.Swd.B.	2003	
Woods, George	P.G.St.B.	1996	
Woods, Walter Ernest Gordon	P.A.G.D.C.	1982	
	P.G.S.D.	1988	
	P.G.J.O.	1999	
Woodward, Andrew Joseph	P.A.G.D.C.	2011	
Woodward, Basil Rex	G.Stwd.	1985	
	P.G.J.D.	1992	
	P.G.J.O.	2005	
Woodward, Brian Peter	P.A.G.D.C.	2007	2010
Woodward, Colin	G.Stwd.	1991	1998
	P.G.S.D.	1996	
	Prov.G.M., Worcestershire	1998-2005	
Woodward, Charles Edward	A.G.D.C.	1985	1989
	G.Swd.B.	1993	
	P.G.J.O.	2003	
Woodward, Harold	P.A.G.Swd.B.	2009	
Woodward, Neil Thomas	G.Stwd.	2003	2002
	P.G.J.D.	2007	
Woodward, Dr. Robert John	G.Stwd.	1996	1995
	P.G.J.D.	2002	
Woolgrove, Francis George	P.A.G.D.C.	1996	1993
	P.G.S.D.	1997	
	G.J.O.	2004	
Woolley, David Geoffrey	P.G.St.B.	2000	1999
	P.G.J.D.	2007	
Woolmer, Robert Jesse	P.A.G.St.B.	2001	1996
	P.G.J.D.	2008	
Woolnough, David Edwin	G.Stwd.	1995	2000
	G.S.D.	2000	
Woolway, John	P.A.G.Swd.B.	2004	
Wooton, George Robert Arthur	P.G.St.B.	1991	1988
Worby, Peter Edward	A.G.Chap.	2009	
Wordingham, Alexander	P.G.St.B.	2007	
Workman, David William	P.G.St.B.	2012	
Workman, Frank Thomas		—	2002
Worthy, Ronald Thomas Arthur	P.G.St.B.	1995	
Wotton, Christopher George Hider	P.A.G.D.C	2012	
Wragg, William	P.G.I.G.	2002	1999
Wreford, Peter Eric		—	2009
Wren, Brian John	P.A.G.D.C.	1999	1999
	P.G.S.D.	2007	
Wreyford, John Frederick	G.Stwd.	1994	
	P.G.J.D.	1999	
Wright, Alan John	P.G.St.B.	2011	2004
Wright, Anthony Leonard	G.I.G.	2000	2001
	G.J.D.	2006	
Wright, Barry William	P.G.St.B.	2010	
Wright, Beverley Vine	P.G.St.B.	2001	
Wright, Brian George		—	2009

NAME	RANK	YEAR OF APPT.	R.A.M.G.R. YEAR OF APPT.
Wright, Colin Penty	G.S.O.	2004	2006
	G.J.W.	2007	
Wright, Lt.Col.Charles Thomas Orme Alford	P.A.G.D.C.	1999	
	P.G.S.D.	2010	
Wright, David Alexander	P.A.G.D.C.	2007	2003
	G.S.D.	2012	
Wright, Revd. Derek Anthony	A.G.Chap.	1998	2010
	Dep.G.Chap.	1999	
	G.Chap.	2000	
Wright, Howard	P.A.G.Swd.B.	2008	
Wright, James Kenneth	P.A.G.St.B.	2006	
Wright, Maj. James Stephen, *T.D.*	P.A.G.D.C.	2000	2004
	P.G.S.D.	2005	
Wright, John Alan	A.G.D.C.	1985	1984
	Dep.G.D.C.	1988	GMRAC 2000
	P.G.J.O.	1991	
	Prov.G.M. Essex	1997-2007	
Wright, Dr. John Lawson William, *R.D., F.R.C.S.*	P.G.J.D.	1997	1998
	P.G.J.O.	2002	GMRAC 2002
	P.G.J.W.	2005	
	Dep.Pres.Gen.Bd. at MMH.	2009-2012	
	G.S.W.	2011	
Wright, Keith		—	2007
Wright, Terence William		—	2011
Wright, William Edmund	P.G.St.B.	1995	
Wyatt, Dennis Charles	P.A.G.D.C.	2001	1999
Wyatt, Trevor George, *M.Sc.*	G.Stwd.	2003	
	G.J.D.	2008	
Wybron, Norman Francis	P.A.G.Swd.B.	2007	
Wyss, Jean-Pierre	P.A.G.D.C.	2008	2009
Yalden, Michael Edward	P.A.G.Swd.B.	2003	2006
	Dep.G.Swd.B.	2011	
Yan, Dr. Poh Lok	P.A.G.D.C.	1999	2000
	P.G.S.D.	2008	
	P.G.J.O.	2010	
Yarinakis, Anthony	P.G.St.B.	1997	2000
	P.G.J.D.	2004	
	P.G.J.O.	2012	
Yarnell, Norman Alfred	P.G.St.B.	2008	
Yates, Gordon	G.Stwd.	1994	1996
	P.G.J.D.	2000	
Yernault, Maurice	P.A.G.D.C.	2011	
Yellowlees, Andrew Nicholas	P.A.G.D.C.	2001	
Yeoh, Datuk Dr. Poh Hong, *P.J.N.*	P.G.S.D.	2004	2006
Yorke, Desmond Philip	P.A.G.D.C.	1998	
Youell, Arthur Christopher	P.A.G.Chap.	2010	
Young, Charles Allen	P.A.G.D.C.	1997	2002
Young, Ernest	P.G.St.B.	1990	
Young, James Annand Mclean	G.Stwd.	2010	
Young, Keith	P.A.G.D.C.	2009	
Young, Laurence James	A.G.Swd.B.	2007	2004
Young, Rene Hamel	P.A.G.D.C.	1992	

NAME	RANK	YEAR OF APPT.	R.A.M.G.R. YEAR OF APPT.
Young, William	P.A.G.D.C.	2012	
Youngson, David Thoms	P.A.G.Chap.	2012	
Zain, Tuan Sabeer, *B.B.M., P.P.A., P.B.M., P.B.S.*	P.A.G.D.C.	1981	1979
	P.G.S.D.	1986	
	P.G.S.O.	1992	
	P.G.M.O.	2001	
Zammit, Hector		—	2001
Zanelli, Leo John	G.Stwd.	1996	
	P.G.J.D.	2005	
Zannou, Dr. Fidel	P.G.St.B.	1995	1996
	P.G.J.D.	1997	
Zavad, David	P.G.St.B.	2004	2003
	P.G.J.D.	2006	
	Dist.G.M., Natal	2009	
Zeitz, Klaus Rudolph Hans		—	2001
Zimon, Alan Raymond		—	2011
Zografos, George	P.G.St.B.	2008	2006
Zonhoven, Wilhelmus	P.A.G.D.C.	1982	1984
	P.G.S.D.	1989	
	P.G.J.O.	1995	

MARK ACTIVE OFFICERS

President of the General Board at Mark Masons' Hall
Rollin, Peter Hamilton 2012

Grand Senior Warden
Malthouse, Lt.Col. Henry William 1996
Bourne, Gordon Lionel 1997
Jump, Michael Edward Pearson..2000
Chande, Jayantilal Keshaji..2001
Williamson, David Kenneth..2002
Champion, Ronald Albert 2003
Lowndes, Peter Geoffrey 2004
Jones, Michael Batham 2005
Dring, Leslie Felgate...2006
Daniel, James Wallace 2007
Tedder, Gerald Leon..2008
Race, Russel John 2009
Spence, Jonathan...2010
Wright, Dr. John Lawson William, *R.D., F.R.C.S.*..2011
Masters, Michael George Wenman...2012

Grand Junior Warden
Chun, Alan David..1995
Crawford, Sir Frederick William 1999
Smith, Howard Brian 2000
Edmondson, John Alfred...2002
Adshead, Bryan...2003
Hogarth, Henry Desmond 2004
Emmett, Brian 2005
Waley, Simon Francis Norman 2006
Wright, Colin Penty 2007
Slater, Malcolm Ernest..2008
Davies, Wg.Cdr. John Irfon, *C.B.E.*..2009
Wallis, Richard Victor, *J.P.*..2010
Guest, Michael William 2011
Jackson, Thomas Firth 2012

Grand Inspector
Downie, David Patrick, *M.B.E.* 2005
Bain, James Randolph...2009

Grand Master Overseer
Axford, Col. Arthur, *O.B.E., T.D., D.L.*..2001
Dribbell, Jack Lodewyk Charles..2002
Richards, Timothy Raymond Roper 2006
Kitchen, Trevor Harold 2007
Richards, Michael Arthur..2008
Jackson, Hedley 2009
Gibson, John Barton, *B.E.M.* 2010
Notley, Ivan Hugh...2011
Little, Bryan Desmond..2012

Grand Senior Overseer
Birch, Geoffrey 1995
Wright, Colin Penty 2004
Green, John Edwin 2005
Gould, Harold, *O.B.E.*..2006

Tierney, Brian Gerald, *M.B.E.* 2007
Sheppardson, Anthony 2008
Flynn, Michael John, *J.P.* 2009
Mullan, Capt. Eidwin Frederick 2010
Poole, Michael James 2011
Hellyer, Colin David 2012

Grand Junior Overseer
Annear, John Frank 1997
Van Beek, Hendrik Frans 2000
Baker, William Ernest 2003
Woolgrove, Francis George 2004
Sparks, David 2005
Denton, John 2006
Potter, Nigel Hewitt 2007
Crawshay-Jones, Sydney Martin, *M.R.C.V.S.* 2008
Goedhals, Abraham 2009
Mather, Dr. James Stephen Boyd, *Ph.D.* 2010
Fox, David George 2011
Milburn, Norman Dunkeld 2012

Grand Chaplain
Wright, Revd. Derek Anthony 2000
Williams, Revd. Gwynfor 2012

Grand Treasurer
Edwards, Stuart Ian 2004

Grand Registrar
Cutler, His Hon. Judge Keith Charles, *C.B.E.* 2006

President of the Mark Benevolent Fund
Smith, Raymond John 2012

President of the Mark Executive Committee
Howitt, John Norman George 2012

Grand Secretary
Brackley, John 2005

Grand Director of Ceremonies
Jones, Kessick John 2012

Grand Inspector of Works
Matthews, Neil Howard, *B.Sc., B.Arch., R.I.B.A.* 1998

Grand Sword Bearer
Blackburn, Thomas 2000
Saunders, Dennis Brian 2001
Woods, Digby Ralph 2003
Furber, Robin Edward 2009
Brown, Christopher Nigel Rupert 2010
Frost, Peter 2011
Willcock, David John William 2012

Deputy President of the General Board
Wright, Dr. John Lawson William, *R.D., F.R.C.S.* 2009

Deputy Grand Chaplain

Burgess, Revd. John Mulholland	2003
Marston, Revd. William Thornton	2004
Snowball, Revd. Michael Sydney	2007
Lane, Revd. Malcolm Clifford George, *J.P.*	2009
Roeschlaub, Revd. Robert Friedrich	2010
Harry, Revd. Bruce David	2012

Deputy Grand Registrar

Hay, Peter Rossant	2008
Lloyd, Lloyd	2010

Deputy President of the Mark Benevolent Fund

Deputy President of the Mark Executive Committee

Hawken, Peter, *M.B.E.*	2012

Deputy Grand Secretary

Hannagan, Lt.Cdr. Angus Patrick Douglas, *R.D.*	2012

Deputy Grand Director of Ceremonies

Elgood, Guy David Alsager	2008
Mason, Alastair Geoffrey Donne	2009
Rymer, Eric John	2010
Davis, Christopher David	2011
Williams, Ryan Andew	2012

Deputy Grand Inspector of Works

Driver, Vincent John	2010

Deputy Grand Sword Bearer

Thorne, Rex Francis, *O.B.E.*	2004
Orton, Phillip George	2006
Foster, Anthony Roy	2007
Dowell, Peter James	2008
Roberts, Richard Brian	2009
Bamber, Austin Westbury	2010
Yalden, Michael Edward	2011
Wilton, Derek Edward	2012

Grand Senior Deacon

Martin, Robert Ridley	1996
Wilkinson, John Robert, *O.B.E.*	1996
Hutchinson, Colin Herbert	1997
Lawless, Cecil Bernard	1997
Evans, Robert Wilmore	1997
Hetherington, Derek Swinburn	1999
Beattie, Selwyn Smith	1999
Clarke, Thomas Raymond	1999
Harriman, Stanley William	1999
Pharo, Peter Edward, *T.D.*	2000
Woolnough, David Edwin	2000
Parkin, James Hodgson	2001
Burnip, Robert	2002
Makower, Oliver Alfred Ernest John	2002
Porter, Alan Roy	2003
Alleyne, Noel Orville Arrindell	2004
Davison, Alan Martin	2004

Dyer, Maurice John 2004
Cooper, Peter John 2005
Hoare, John Michael 2005
McLain, John Dunn 2005
Pickering, Gerald Ledger, *J.P.* 2005
Wibberley, Robert Edward 2005
Woodall, Brian 2005
Flitcroft, Roger William 2006
Obadiah, Abraham Joseph 2006
Patton, Michael Anthony 2006
Henry, Graham Michael 2007
Juden, Michael John 2007
Moore, Duncan John 2007
Baker, Peter Richard Alleyne 2008
Davies, Ian Lodwick 2008
Hall, Alan 2008
Molyneux, Brian, *J.P.* 2008
Wattison, Brian Frederick 2008
Armstrong, Joseph Walton 2009
Hall, Walter 2009
Moulson, John 2009
Shepherd, Paul Sheridan 2009
Travers, Barry Worthing 2009
Aspinwall, David 2010
Bontoft, Derek Sidney 2010
Brackstone, Stuart Leonard 2010
Middleton, Stewart Charles Lambert 2010
Owens, Barrie 2010
Radford, Alan William 2010
Clarke, John Frederick 2011
Crossley, Gilbert 2011
Gutteride, Richard Vernon 2011
Christopher Robert McNab 2011
Sillett, Robert David Taylor, *M.A., L.C.P.* 2011
Smee, Alan Arthur John 2011
Bowles, Christopher James, *J.P.* 2012
Harvey, Antony David George 2012
Ramsay, David Keith 2012
Ridler, Brian 2012
Robson, Malcolm 2012
Wright, David Alexander 2012

Grand Junior Deacon

Hudson, Terrance 1995
Spires, Colin Frederick 1996
Condlyffe, Thomas Victor 1997
Haile, Joseph Brooks 1998
Barwick, Donald Horace 1999
Pritchard, Glyn 2000
Luccock, John Brian 2000
Briggs, Anthony David 2001
Webb, Jack Alfred 2001
Hartburn, Neil Robert 2002
Ryan, Colin Hugh 2002
Barnes, Christopher James 2003
Glazier, Alan 2003
Richards, Colin 2003
Bedding, John Albert 2004

Chalmers, William Andrew 2004
Koopman, Johan Peter Justinus Frederick 2004
Melhuish, Dennis Francis 2004
Hardman, James Thomas 2005
Mitten, Martin Francis 2005
Roberts, Reginald David Roy 2005
Schwab, Werner Maria, *L.L.M.* 2005
Tait, Thomas, *J.P.* 2005
Attwood, Jeffrey Lawrence 2006
Lee, Colin James 2006
Robson, John 2006
Wright, Anthony Leonard 2006
Bell, Kenneth 2007
Clark, Donald Francis 2007
Evans, John Michael 2007
Humphries, William Samuel 2007
Manuel, Clive Robert 2007
Hughes, Gareth 2008
Morrison, Nolan 2008
Robbens, Stuart Victor 2008
Sole, Bernard William 2008
Wyatt, Trevor George 2008
Drinkwater, Eric 2009
Hancock, Timothy 2009
Lightburn, Peter John 2009
Mitchell, Leonard Michael 2009
Sweeney, Andrew Christopher 2009
Williams, Christopher 2009
Coles, Peter Thomas 2010
Cummins, David Russell, *J.P.* 2010
Holmes, Eric 2010
Huddart, Jeffrey Alan 2010
Lowe, Phillip Edward 2010
Nairn, Ian Douglas 2010
Atkins, Peter Duncan 2011
Baig, Akram 2011
Dixon, Robert 2011
Holland, Peter Eric 2011
Kavanagh, Philip Victor Frederick 2011
Reading, David George 2011
Barton, Warner 2012
Body, Anthony Shane Trenavin 2012
De Courcey-Cooke, Roger 2012
Farrow, Christopher John 2012
Garty, Edward Rennie 2012
Lee, Geoffrey Herbert 2012

Assistant Grand Chaplain

Preston, Revd. David Francis 2003
Calcott-James, Revd. Colin Wilfrid 2007
Worby, Peter Edward 2009
Thomas, Dr. Vivian, *J.P.* 2011

Assistant Grand Secretary

Roberts, Jonathan Charles 2010
Budds, Martin Bradford 2012

Assistant Grand Registrar
Alwin, Christopher Granville Angus 2011

Assistant Grand Director of Ceremonies
Brook-Partridge, Bernard..1995
Cross, Philip Allen 1997
Brodrick, Trevor Malcolm Garvin 1997
Edwards, Terance 1998
Minshaw, John William Michael 1999
Noble, Christopher..1999
Boore, David Charles..2000
Purnell, Frederick Arthur 2000
Booth, James Edward..2001
Seymour-Hamilton, Wyndham 2001
Gittins, Richard William...2002
Fogarty, Vivian John 2003
Smith, Kenneth Arthur Clive 2003
Allison, Robert Leonard..2005
Collison, John Raymond...2005
Harrison, Keith Michael..2005
Banbury, Michael James 2006
McIntyre, Peter John...2006
Preston, Alexander George 2006
Bower, David Hemmingway...2007
Childs, James Peter...2007
Cuthbertson, Alan..2007
Taylor, Ian Hamilton 2007
White, Brian Orpeth..2007
Dawson, Peter George 2008
Else, David Keith..2008
Guest, Roger Frank 2008
Hollinshead, David Edward..2008
Olliver, Richard John 2008
Henderson, Robert Muir 2009
Hughes, Bryan...2009
Pugh, David Lloyd..2009
Puttrell, Richard Boswell 2009
Sheldon, William John..2009
Watkin, Peter Gordon..2009
Hughes, Peter William 2010
Hughson, Lyndon William..2010
Johnstone-Smith, Raymond 2010
Moore, John Herbert Vincent..2010
White, David Christopher...2010
Davidson, Allan...2011
Hartley, Royston George...2011
Hodgson, Thomas..2011
Jenkins, Trevor Maughan..2011
Short, Brian 2011
Taylor, Colin..2011
Apperley, Ralph Mannings 2012
Hargate, Robert John 2012
Pinnock, John Dudley 2012
Roberts, Jonathan 2012
Robinson, Kenneth James...2012
Wills, Philip...2012

Assistant Grand Inspector of Works
Wells, Harry 1993

Assistant Grand Sword Bearer
Taylor, Peter Alexander...1999
Bartlett, Peter Edmund Guest 2000
Beardsley, Duncan Richard...2005
Phillips, Ivor Richard 2006
Young, Laurence James 2007
Smith, David Arthur..2008
Allen, Reginald Arthur..2009
Wood, William Kenneth..2010
Davy, Frederick Leslie 2011
Hallberg, Stephen Charles 2012

Grand Librarian

Grand Organist
Adams, David Edward Henry, *B.Mus.(Edin.), A.R.C.M., F.C.I.E.A.* 2008

Grand Standard Bearer
Crook, James...1995
Aspinall, Joseph Brian 1999
Simpson, Ronald Charles..2001
Clucas, Alan Harold Qualtrough...2003
Dashwood, Sir Richard James, *Bt.*..2005
Harrison, Brian..2005
Cooke, Frank...2006
Higginbotham, Michael John..2006
Feetum, Leonard Paul 2007
Lacey, John William..2007
Roberts, Graham Philip Melville 2008
Voice, Noel Reginald 2008
Carley, Stewart Glasgow...2009
Richmond, Roger Francis 2009
Greenwood, Paul...2010
Poot, Frank Cornelis Johannes..2010
Entwisle, David Nicholas..2011
Shaftoe, Francis Allan...2011
Morgan, David Neil 2012
Sherlock, William Alec Brown 2012

Deputy Grand Organist
Liles, Naunton Charles William..2010

Assistant Grand Standard Bearer
Walsh, Derek Francis 1996
Gale, Godfrey..1997
Wilson, Ronald..1997
Watson, Peter James..1999
Carey, Peter Charles..1999
Roberts, Tom Ellis...2000
Pearson, James Victor 2000
Callesen, Uwe 2001
Wilson, John..2001
Ancliffe, Maj. Richard, *B.E.M.*...2002
Lent, Roger..2003
Daniel, Michael William 2004

Lord, Kenneth 2004
Williams, Maldwyn Glyndwr 2005
Astbury, Walter John 2006
Briney, Martin 2007
Grahamslaw, William 2008
Bautista, Joseph Henry, *M.B.E.* 2008
Brill, Peter James 2009
Partington, John Russell 2009
Smith, Claude Nigel Willie 2010
Trigger, Francis John 2010
Cook, Francis 2011
Wensley, Simon Mark 2011
Azzopardi, Joseph Louis 2012
Pearce, Revd. Adrian Francis 2012

Assistant Grand Organist
Sears, Alan 2003
Forrest, Malcolm Jeffrey 2010

Grand Inner Guard
Halahan, John Ibrahim Baharam 1995
Varley, Arthur Steven 2011
Milburn, Lance 2012

Assistant Grand Inner Guard
Hutton, Walter Alan 1997
Dean, John Brian 2000
Cruttenden, William Charles 2002
Monk, Alan Frederick Alexander 2003
Hobbs, Brian John 2004
Layton, Roger 2004
Le Bon, John Frederick 2005
Brown, David James 2005
Hall, Robert 2007
Hartley, David 2008
Muir, Brian Fraser 2008
Roland, John 2009
Blenkinship, David Anthony 2010
Downes, Kenneth Leonard, *J.P.* 2010
Innes, Colin James 2011
Walford, Royston George 2011
Owen, Brian Harold 2012
Webster, Neil 2012

Grand Stewards
Wakely, Eric Leonard John 1992
James, Colin Mansel 1993
Bolton, Hugh Johnston 1995
Cory-Pearce, Richard 1997
Doyle, Terrence 1999
Fairer, Richard Hugh 1999
Whittall, Frederick Michael Armstrong 1999
Meek, Norman Alan 2000
Brown, James George Byfield 2001
Bleackley, David 2004
Gaskill, Roy 2007
Hunter, Paul Edward 2007
Rennie, William Law 2007

San, Aaron	2008
Caswell, John Richard	2009
Combes, David Keith	2009
Hurst, Paul Graham	2009
Mangham, Graham	2009
Rushton, Peter John	2009
Williams, Graham Roy	2009
Allan, David Ian	2010
Batters, Royce	2010
Brittan, Reginald Leslie	2010
Bury, Geoffrey Michael	2010
Chilcott, Gerald Desmond	2010
Clementson, Michael Kevin	2010
Fenton, Stephen Richard Nigel	2010
Gibson, John Bamborough	2010
Greenwall, Julian James	2010
Hall, Michael Youdan	2010
Hamilton, David Neil	2010
Hewitt, Ronald Glyn	2010
Johnson, George Alfred	2010
Perks, Roger John	2010
Price, Edward John Staite	2010
Purdie, David Charles	2010
Short, Douglas Peter	2010
Smith, Dr. Gregory Roger	2010
Torrance, Archibald Iain	2010
Vanhinsbergh, Steven Matthew	2010
Wainwright, George Frederick	2010
Whelan, Shane Maurice	2010
Young, James Annand Mclean	2010
Baker, Michael John	2011
Barnwell, Neville Percival Berkely	2011
Bolton, John Trevor	2011
Butcher, Stewart Leslie	2011
Cropper, William Joseph	2011
Faulks, Peter Charles	2011
Forster, Douglas John	2011
Helliar, Anthony John	2011
Holland, Brian John	2011
Lewis, Howard Andrew	2011
Lobb, Philip Roy	2011
McCord, James Fraser	2011
Miller, David Walter	2011
Nash, David John	2011
Pattni, Chhotalal Damji	2011
Pinfield, Michael David	2011
Pratt, William John Thomas	2011
Rogers, William Harold	2011
Shepherd, Paul Leslie	2011
Smith, John Hartley	2011
Wake, Jeremy Philip	2011
Whiteley, Jeffrey William	2011
Beedle, Peter	2012
Bicknell, John Charles	2012
Bradley, Dennis, *B.E.M.*	2012
D'Souza, Kenneth Thomas	2012
Eaton, Ian Alfred	2012
Ellis, John Henry William	2012

Fairweather, Keith Thomas 2012
Forster, Richard 2012
Francis, Leslie Frederick 2012
Green, Garth Ratcliffe 2012
Gunning, Philip Harry 2012
Higson, Shaun 2012
Hollebone, Paul Stephen 2012
Jennings, John David 2012
Johnson, Ian Brook 2012
Kingsley-Smith, Clive 2012
Maddy, David John 2012
McMillan, Robert Alexander 2012
Minett, Graham John 2012
Moles, Phillip Nicholas, *J.P.* 2012
Raven, Graham 2012
Smith, Gerald 2012
Williams, Paul Michael, *O.B.E., C.St.J., D.L.* 2012

Grand Tyler

Thomson, Thomas, *C.P.M., M.A.* 2004

Deputy Grand Tyler

Succession of Grand Masters, Pro Grand Masters, Deputy Grand Masters, Assistant Grand Masters, Provincial and District Grand Masters, since the formation of the Grand Lodge of Mark Master Masons in June, 1856.

Names in italics signify Past Grand Rank

Year of Appt. / Year of Death

Grand Masters

Year of Appt.		Year of Death
1856	The 2nd Lord Leigh, *P.C.*	1905
1860	The 4th Earl of Carnarvon, *P.C., D.L., F.R.S.*	1890
1863	Viscount Holmesdale (in 1886 The 3rd Earl Amherst, *K.J.St.J.*)	1910
1866	William Wither Bramston Beach, *P.C.*	1901
1869	The Revd. George Raymond Portal, *M.A.*, (in 1881 Canon Portal)	1889
1873	Earl Percy, *P.C.* (in 1899 The 7th Duke of Northumberland, *K.G.*)	1918
1875	The 3rd Earl of Limerick, *K.P., P.C.*	1896
1878	The 2nd Lord Skelmersdale, *P.C.* (in 1880 The 1st Earl of Lathom, *G.C.B.*)	1898
1881	The 5th Lord Henniker, *V.D., F.S.A.*	1902
1884	The 9th Earl of Kintore, *K.T., G.C.M.G., P.C.*	1930
1886	H.R.H. The Prince of Wales, *K.G.* (in 1901 H.M. King Edward VII)	1910
1901	H.R.H. The 1st Duke of Connaught and Strathern, *K.G.*	1942
1939	H.R.H. The 1st Duke of Kent, *K.G.*	1942
1943	The 3rd Earl of Stradbroke, *K.C.M.G., C.B., C.V.O., C.B.E., V.D., T.D.*	1947
1948	Brig.-Gen. William Harry Verelst Darrell, *C.B., C.M.G., D.S.O.*	1954
1954	The 5th Lord Harris, *C.B.E., M.C., D.L., K.St.J.*	1984
1973	The 4th Earl of Stradbroke, *K.St.J.*	1983
1982	H.R.H. Prince Michael of Kent, *G.C.V.O.*	—

Past Grand Masters

1881	H.R.H. The 1st Duke of Albany, *K.G.*	1884
1883	H.R.H. The Prince of Wales, *K.G.* (in 1901 H.M. King Edward VII)	1910
1891	H.R.H. The 1st Duke of Connaught and Strathern, *K.G.*	1942
1937	H.M. King George VI	1952

Pro Grand Masters

1886	The 9th Earl of Kintore, *K.T., G.C.M.G., P.C.*	1930
1887	The 2nd Lord Egerton of Tatton (in 1897 The Earl Egerton of Tatton)	1909
1890	The 6th Marquess of Hertford, *C.B., T.D.*	1912
1893	Earl of Euston, *D.L.*	1912
1913-		
1943	The 3rd Earl of Stradbroke, *K.C.M.G., C.B., C.V.O., V.D., T.D.*	1947
1982	The 4th Earl of Stradbroke, *K.St.J.*	1983
1983	Dr. Gilmore Leonard Colenso Colenso-Jones	1990
1986	The 4th Lord Swansea, *D.L., C.St.J.*	2005
2000	John Hale	—
2011	Benjamin Addy	—

Deputy Grand Masters

1856	The 2nd Lord Methuen	1891
1857	The 4th Earl of Carnarvon, *P.C., D.L., F.R.S.*	1890
1860	Viscount Holmesdale (in 1886 The 3rd Earl Amherst, *K.J.St.J.*)	1910
1863	William Wither Bramston Beach, *P.C.*	1901
1866	The Revd. George Raymond Portal, *M.A.* (in 1881 Canon Portal)	1889
1869	Sir Edmund A. H. Lechmere, *3rd Bt., K.St.J.*	1899
1870	Earl Percy, *P.C.* (in 1889 The 7th Duke of Northumberland, *K.G.*)	1918
1872	The 3rd Earl of Limerick, *K.P., P.C.*	1896
1875	William Romaine Callender, *Jnr.*	1876
1876	The 2nd Lord Skelmersdale, *P.C.* (in 1880 The 1st Earl of Lathom, *G.C.B.*)	1898
1878	The 5th Earl of Donoughmore, *K.C.M.G.*	1900
1880	The 5th Lord Henniker, *V.D., F.S.A.*	1902
1881	The 9th Earl of Kintore, *K.T., G.C.M.G., P.C.*	1930
1881	The Hon. Wilbraham Egerton (in 1883 The 2nd Lord Egerton of Tatton) (in 1897 The Earl Egerton of Tatton)	1909
1887	The 6th Marquess of Hertford, *C.B., T.D.*	1912
1890	Earl of Euston, *D.L.*	1912
1893	Viscount Dungarvan (in 1904 The 10th Earl of Cork and Orrery, *D.L.*)	1925
1900	The Hon. Alan de Tatton Egerton (in 1909 The 3rd Lord Egerton of Tatton)	1920

DEPUTY GRAND MASTERS—continued

Year of Appt.		Year of Death
1905	The 6th Earl of Donoughmore, *K.P., P.C.*	1948
1909	The 2nd Earl of Lathom, *K.G.St.J.*	1910
1910	The 3rd Earl of Stradbroke, *K.C.M.G., C.B., C.V.O., C.B.E., V.D., T.D.*	1947
1913	Richard Loveland Loveland, *K.C.*	1923
1920	Sir Richard Vassar Vassar-Smith, *Bt.*	1922
1922	The 2nd Lord Aldenham, *F.S.A.*	1936
1936	Rev. Canon Frederick Halsey, *M.A.*	1952
1952	The 5th Lord Harris, *C.B.E., M.C., D.L., K.St.J.*	1984
1954	Maj. Robert Lindsay Loyd, *O.B.E., M.C.*	1977
1967	The 4th Earl of Stradbroke, *K.St.J.*	1983
1973	Col. Edwin Perry Morgan, *M.B.E., T.D., J.P.*	1980
1979	Dr. Gilmore Leonard Colenso Colenso-Jones	1990
1983	The 4th Lord Swansea, *D.L., C.St.J.*	2005
1986	Col. Geoffrey Seymour Hamilton Dicker, *C.B.E., T.D., D.L.*	2009
1994	John Hale	—
2000	Edward Kenneth Smart	2007
2002	George Robert Gavin Purser	—
2010	Benjamin Addy	—
2011	Michael Edward Herbert	—

Assistant Grand Masters

1973 | Dr. Gilmore Leonard Colenso Colenso-Jones | 1990
1979 | The 4th Lord Swansea, *D.L., C.St.J.* | 2005
1983 | Col. Geoffrey Seymour Hamilton Dicker, *C.B.E., T.D., D.L.* | 2009
1986 | Thomas Were Howard, *O.B.E., J.P.* | 1997
1990 | John Hale | —
1994 | Edward Kenneth Smart | 2007
2000 | George Robert Gavin Purser | —
2002 | Benjamin Addy | —
2010 | Michael Edward Herbert | —
2011 | Herbert Keith Emmerson | —

Provincial Grand Masters

BEDFORDSHIRE

1985 | Jack Maurice Mayes | 2005
1990 | Alan Verity Alvey | —
1998 | Harry Stephenson Arnold | —
2007 | Christopher Martin Smith | —

BERKS AND HANTS (UNTIL 1873)

1857 | Rt. Hon. William Wither Bramston Beach | 1901

BERKSHIRE AND OXFORDSHIRE (UNTIL 1994)

1879 | The 7th Earl of Jersey, *G.C.B., G.C.M.G., P.C.* | 1915
1889 | The 11th Viscount Valentia, *K.C.V.O., C.B., T.D.* | 1927
1927 | Rev. Canon Fitzwilliam John Carter Gillmore, *T.D., M.A.* | 1934
1934 | Maj. Robert Lindsay Loyd, *O.B.E., M.C.* | 1977
1955 | William Conrad Costin, *O.B.E., M.C.* | 1970
1971 | Wilfred Bathurst Coxeter | 1982
1980 | Dr. Oliver Charles Wilkinson | 1987
1987 | Dr. Robert Amos Griffiths | 1988
1988 | Dr. Ewan Stafford Page | 2007

BERKSHIRE

1994 | Dr. Ewan Stafford Page | —
2002 | Alan Frederick Brunning | —
2007 | Peter James Sands | —

BRISTOL

1875 | William Augustus Frederick Powell | 1906
1906 | Col. Jas. Roger Bramble, *F.S.A.* | 1908
1910 | Arthur Cecil Powell | 1949
1949 | Maj. Ernest John Dunscombe | 1963
1960 | Philip William Hort | 1978

PROVINCIAL GRAND MASTERS—continued

Year of Appt.		Year of Death
1975	Eric Goodwin Simmonds, *M.B.E.*	1989
1988	Ronald Thomas Bates	—
1995	Ronald Stanley Smith	—
2002	Norman William Cavvell	2009
2009	John Douglas Arthur Platts	—

BUCKINGHAMSHIRE

1882	Revd. John Studholme Brownrigg, *M.A.* (in 1906 Dean of Bocking)	1930
1930	Revd. Bernard William Harvey, *M.A.*	1948
1948	The 7th Earl of Courtown, *O.B.E., D.L.*	1957
1956	Capt. Robert George Edmund Whitney, *M.B.E.*	1966
1966	Richard Francis Cartwright	1982
1982	Kenneth John Pausey	—
2002	John Trollope Fisher	—
2009	Peter Nigel Isom Harborne	—

CHANNEL ISLANDS

1989	Dennis George Perrin	2010
1994	John Alan Spencer	2002
2000	Frederick Mark Holiday	—
2005	Paul Edmund Archibald Carré	2010
2010	James Edward Martin	—

CHESHIRE AND NORTH WALES (UNTIL 1880)

1872	The Hon. Wilbraham Egerton (in 1883 The 2nd Lord Egerton of Tatton) (in 1897 The Earl Egerton of Tatton)	1909

CHESHIRE
1872 *(until 1880)* as "Cheshire and North Wales"

1880	The Hon. Wilbraham Egerton (in 1883 The 2nd Lord Egerton of Tatton) (in 1897 The Earl Egerton of Tatton)	1909
1893	The Hon. Alan de Tatton Egerton (in 1909 The 3rd Lord Egerton of Tatton)	1920
1919	Col. Hubert Cornwall Legh	1926
1925	Maj. Cuthbert Leicester-Warren, *D.L.*	1954
1935	George Leigh, *O.B.E.*	1948
1945	Rev. Dr. Miles Weight Myres, *F.S.A.*	1957
1957	Frederick John Lees	1969
1969	Lt.Col. John Leighton Byrne Leicester-Warren, *T.D., V.L.*	1975
1974	John Lyne Nuttall	1986
1980	Charles Victor Vinten-Fenton, *M.Sc.*	1997
1990	Benjamin Addy	—
2002	Bryan Russell Ogden	—

CORNWALL

1867	Sir Frederick Martin Williams, *Bt.*	1878
1879	Col. John Whitehead Peard	1880
1881	Sir Charles Brune Graves-Swale, *Bt.*	1903
1898	The 4th Earl of Halsbury, *P.C., F.R.S., F.S.A.*	1921
1923	Sir Philip Colville-Smith, *C.V.O.*	1937
1938	Col. Edward Neynoe Willyams, *D.S.O., D.L.*	1964
1956	Col. Edwin Perry Morgan, *M.B.E., T.D., J.P.*	1979
1973	John Edward Price	1983
1980	Lt.Cdr. Terence Christian Arnold Waghorn, *R.N.*	1992
1992	Frank Tonkin	—
2004	Geoffrey Francis Warwick Isaac	—

CUMBERLAND AND WESTMORLAND

1872	Earl of Bective, *M.P.*	1938
1894	Lord Henry Cavendish-Bentinck, *T.D.*	1934
1932	George Aitchison, *M.B.E.*	1941
1943	Joseph Barron, *M.B.E.*	1949
1949	Richard Morton Rigg	1951
1951	Ernest Craig Dunlop, *M.B., F.R.C.S.*	1957
1956	George Albert Marley	1966
1967	John James Bainbridge	1974
1974	Haydn Moore	1984

PROVINCIAL GRAND MASTERS—continued

Year of Appt.		Year of Death
1984	John Hale	—
1990	Arthur French Sewell	2000
1995	William Henry Conchie	2012
2003	Kenneth Graham	2007
2007	William Kenneth Wilson	2012
2012	Keith Hodgson	—

DERBYSHIRE
1858 *(until 1894)* as "Leicestershire, Northamptonshire, Derbyshire and Rutlandshire"

1894	Abraham Woodiwiss	1912
1912	The 9th Duke of Devonshire, *K.G., G.C.M.G., G.C.V.O., P.C., D.L., F.R.S.*	1938
1938	The 10th Duke of Devonshire, *K.G., M.B.E., T.D.*	1950
1949	Thomas Harrison Thorpe	1957
1953	Edward Boot	1953
1953	Capt. John Spencer, *D.S.O., M.B.E., M.M.*	1980
1974	Dr. Reginald Lathom Brown	1990
1979	Eric Horton	1998
1989	John Tomlinson Clewes	—
1998	Thomas William Bailey, *Q.P.M.*	2007
2003	Robert Poxon	—

DEVONSHIRE

1857	Revd. John Huyshe, *M.A.*	1880
1873	Lt.Col. John Tanner Davy	1887
1890	The Hon. Sir Henry Stafford Northcote, *Bt., C.B.* (in 1900 The Lord Northcote, *G.C.M.G., G.C.I.E., P.C.*)	1911
1904	Maj. George Sydney Strode Strode, *O.B.E., D.L.*	1950
1943	Col. Charles Beechey Spencer, *O.B.E., T.D.*	1967
1966	Col. Frederick Wynford Dewhurst	1979
1975	Henry Edgar Eland Holladay	2007
1991	Dr. John Horace Wickstead	—
2000	David Iwan John Owen	2007
2006	Peter Hawken	—

DORSET

1879	Montague John Guest	1909
1882	Revd. William Mortimer Heath, *M.A.*	1917
1894	Col. William Ernest Brymer	1909
1909	The 9th Earl of Shaftesbury, *K.P., G.C.V.O., C.B.E., P.C.*	1961
1915	Col. William Watts, *K.C.B., V.D.*	1922
1923	Charles Henry Watts Parkinson	1927
1927	Capt. George Habgood	1946
1937	Robert Russ Conway	1950
1946	Capt. Angus Valdimar Hambro	1958
1953	Charles Henry James Kaile	1964
1964	Edwin Arthur Winzar	1982
1973	Harold Frederick Joy	1996
1978	Kenneth Valentyne Cross, *J.P.*	2007
1994	Raymond Osborne	2006
2001	Christopher Robert Watton	—
2008	Frank Jeremy Shaw	—

DURHAM
1870 *(until 1920)* as "Northumberland and Durham"

1920	The 6th Lord Ravensworth, *D.L.*	1932
1932	William Todd	1938
1938	Robert Wilkin Ernest Dixon	1959
1959	Col. Frederick Walton, *M.C., D.L.*	1969
1969	John MacMurray, *M.C.*	1982
1975	Colin Victor Armitage, *O.B.E., J.P.*	1984
1984	William Gillhespy	2012
1995	James Peter Croft	—

DYFED
1870 *(until 1989)* as "South Wales"

1989	Dr. John Benjamin Lloyd	—

PROVINCIAL GRAND MASTERS—*continued*

Year of Appt.		Year of Death
2001	Ivor Stephen Shuttleworth	—
2007	David Nigel Adams	—
2012	Ronald Jones	—
	EAST ANGLIA	
1883	The 5th Lord Henniker, *V.D., F.S.A.*	1902
1904	The 3rd Earl of Stradbroke, *K.C.M.G., C.B., C.V.O., C.B.E., V.D., T.D.*	1947
1948	The 4th Earl of Stradbroke, *K.St.J.*	1983
1972	Lt.Col. Walter John Short	1979
1977	Col. Geoffrey Seymour Hamilton Dicker, *C.B.E., T.D., D.L.*	2009
1984	Ronald William Chitty	1999
1990	Peter Rolfe Churchyard	2010
1998	Peter Hamilton Rollin	—
2010	Paul Anthony Norman	—
	EAST LANCASHIRE 1870 *(until 1910)* as "Lancashire"	
1910	The 17th Earl of Derby, *K.G., G.C.B., G.C.V.O., T.D., P.C.*	1948
1948	Rev. Canon Thomas Whitehead Taylor, *M.A.*	1961
1961	Thomas Sharples Barlow	1970
1969	Arnold Moreton	1981
1979	George Farnworth Nuttall	1986
1983	George Gray	2006
1993	Fred Kemp	2011
2003	Keith Partington Schofield	—
	ESSEX	
1899	The 5th Earl of Warwick and Earl Brooke of Warwick Castle, *D.L.*	1924
1924	Col. Arthur John Hanslip Ward, *M.B.E., V.D., D.L.*	1938
1938	Maj. Arthur John Oakley Turner, *T.D.*	1960
1958	Percy Victor Faning	1971
1971	Leonard Enos Kirk	1986
1978	Thomas Were Howard, *O.B.E., J.P.*	1997
1986	Norman Thomas Clarke	2000
1992	John William Deal	1997
1996	Roger John Emery	1997
1997	John Alan Wright	—
2007	Michael George Spencer	—
	GLOUCESTER (UNTIL 1988)	
1879	Rev. Charles Raikes Davey	1885
1885	John Walker	1889
	GLOUCESTER AND HEREFORDSHIRE	
1888	Baron Chas. Conrad Adolphus de Boils de Ferrières	1908
1891	Sir Richard Vassar Vassar-Smith, *Bt.*	1922
1923	John Waghorne	1936
1936	Capt. Francis Kenelm Foster, *O.B.E.*	1950
1950	Charles Kingsley Gregory	1955
1956	Percy Harold Creese	1964
1964	Lt.Col. John Thomas Tait	1968
1968	James Hughes, *O.B.E.*	1983
1983	Douglas Edwin Stratford Beckingsale	1991
1986	George Stewart Lee, *J.P.*	—
1996	Joseph Owen Basil Barke	—
2004	John Ernest Eley	—
2010	James Albert Green	—
	HAMPSHIRE AND ISLE OF WIGHT	
1873	Rev. Canon George Raymond Portal	1889
1889	Rt. Hon. William Wither Bramston Beach	1901
1900	R. Loveland Loveland, *K.C.*	1923
1913	Rev. Frederick Bethune Norman Norman Lee	1921
1921	Col. Sir Arthur Richard Holbrook, *K.B.E., V.D., D.L.*	1946
1946	Col. George Nowers Dyer, *C.B.E., D.S.O.*	1955

PROVINCIAL GRAND MASTERS—continued

Year of Appt.		Year of Death
1955	George Walter Hector Young, *O.B.E.*	1968
1963	Richmond Rudolph Hawkins Hammond, *O.B.E.*	1964
1964	Rev. Canon George Turner Waldegrave, *M.B.E., M.A.*	1966
1966	Maj. John Hall Barlow	1980
1972	John Horace Mitchener	2000
1988	The Rev. Dr. Michael Morgan	—
1997	Nigel John Buckingham	2008
2007	John Herbert Prizeman	—

HERTFORDSHIRE

1885	Sir (Thomas) Frederick Halsey, *1st Bt., P.C.*	1927
1924	Charles Edward Keyser, *F.S.A.*	1929
1929	William Hamilton Underhill	1932
1933	Rev. Canon Frederick Halsey, *M.A.*	1952
1951	Rev. Joseph Moffett, *O.B.E., D.D.*	1962
1962	Arthur Steane Baker	1968
1968	Dr. David Glynwyn Robert Bonnell	1972
1972	Richard James Hammond	1985
1980	Arthur William Potter Fawcett, *M.B.E., T.D.*	1988
1988	Dennis William Charles Thomas	2007
1998	Herbert Keith Emmerson	—
2008	Christopher David Radmore	—

KENT

1857	Charles Purton Cooper	1873
1872	Rev. George Wilson Sicklemore, *M.A.*	1878
1879	Rev. Thomas Robinson, *M.A.*	1895
1896	Viscount Dungarvan (in 1904 The 10th Earl of Cork and Orrery, *D.L.*)	1925
1908	The 2nd Lord Aldenham, *F.S.A.*	1936
1936	The 5th Lord Harris, *C.B.E., M.C., D.L., K.St.J.*	1984
1956	Sir Eric Studd, *Bt., O.B.E.*	1975
1975	Frederick William Friday	1978
1978	Guy Patrick Rudgard, *J.P.*	1995
1986	Ronald Byers de Gray	2005
2003	Roland John Wade	—
2008	Roger Henry Harley Croucher	—

LANCASHIRE (UNTIL 1910)

1870	William Romaine Callender, Jnr.	1876
1876	The 2nd Lord Skelmersdale, *P.C.* (in 1880 The 1st Earl of Lathom, *G.C.B.*)	1898
1899	The 2nd Earl of Lathom, *K.G.St.J.*	1910

LEICESTERSHIRE, NORTHAMPTONSHIRE, DERBYSHIRE AND RUTLANDSHIRE (UNTIL 1894)

1858	William Kelly, F.S.A.	1894

LEICESTERSHIRE AND RUTLAND

1858 *(until 1894)* as "Leicestershire, Northamptonshire, Derbyshire and Rutlandshire"

1894	Earl of Euston, *D.L.*	1912
1912	Maj. William Jesse Freer, *V.D., D.L., F.S.A.*	1932
1932	Lt.Col. Sir Charles Frederick Oliver, *T.D., D.L.*	1939
1939	George William Hunt	1954
1954	Albert Ernest Bambury	1969
1966	John Eric Foister	1999
1988	Reginald Frank Reader	—
1995	Michael Edward Herbert	—
2005	Anthony Morris	—

LINCOLNSHIRE

1874	John Sutcliffe	1878
1880	Charles Harrison, *M.D.*	1924
1883	Jack Sutcliffe	1931
1892	The 4th Earl of Yarborough, *K.G., P.C., F.S.A., K.G.St.J.*	1936
1905	The 2nd Lord Heneage, *O.B.E.*	1954
1954	Frederick George Melville Stennett	1973
1973	Fred Hallam Holmes	1982

PROVINCIAL GRAND MASTERS—*continued*

Year of Appt.		Year of Death
1980	Raymond Leonard Ringrose	2012
1990	Walter Patton	1993
1993	Gordon Walkerley Smith, *J.P.*	—
2007	Trevor John Walker	—

LONDON

1990	Henry de Lerisson Cazenove	1991
1991	Dr. Roeinton Burjor Framji Khambatta	—
1994	Timothy John Lewis	—
1996	David Ivor Williams	—
2007	Raymond John Smith	—
2011	David Frederick Ashbolt	—

MIDDLESEX AND SURREY (UNTIL 1892)

1870	Col. Sir Francis Burdett, *Bt.*	1892

MIDDLESEX
1870 *(until 1892)* as "Middlesex and Surrey"

1892	Lt.Col. Arthur Bott Cook	1899
1899	Sir Reginald Hanson, *Bt.*	1905
1905	Harry Robert Graham	1933
1927	Alexander Burnett Brown	1948
1931	H.R.H. The Duke of York, *K.G.* (afterwards H.M. King George VI)	1952
1937	Arthur Lionel Fitzroy Cook	1955
1953	Fenn Kidson, *C.B.E.*	1965
1963	George Parker	1969
1967	Geoffrey Trevor Burnett Brown	1982
1978	Reginald Gordon Read, *O.B.E.*	1983
1984	Rev.Preb. Clarke Edward Leighton Thomson, *T.D., M.A.*	—
1994	Norman Victor Todd	2004
1998	Col. Robert Keith Hind	—
2001	Peter George Halls-Dickerson	—

MONMOUTHSHIRE

1876	Lorenzo Augustus Homfray	1903
1885	Capt. Samuel George Homfray	1894
1896	John Owen Marsh	1923
1924	Frederick Stanley Williams May	1951
1951	Benjamin Balfour de Witt Gibbs, *M.C.*	1972
1972	Owen Idris Lloyd-Owen	1991
1985	David Arthur Thomas	1995
1990	Frederick Mansel Gabb	2011
1996	Brian Charles Cull	2009
2006	David Ieuan James	—

NORTHAMPTON, HUNTINGDON AND BEDFORD (UNTIL 1984)

1894	Earl of Euston, *D.L.*	1912
1912	Lord Lilford	1945
1939	Charles Herbert Perram, *M.D.*	1957
1956	Maj. Leslie Phipps Dorman, *T.D.*	1971
1963	Charles Samuel Messinger	1970
1971	Norman Harry Rolfe	1984

NORTHAMPTONSHIRE AND HUNTINGDONSHIRE

1985	John Charles Bennett	2007
1995	Norman Sidney Manser	—
2000	Roy Keith Bradley	—
2006	George Edward Bonham	—

NORTH AND EAST YORKSHIRE

1881	John Woodall Woodall	1905
1888	Lord Bolton	1922
1919	Lt.Col. Miles John Stapylton, *O.B.E.*	1931
1932	Alfred Procter	1933
1933	Llewellyn Kitchen	1948

Year of PROVINCIAL GRAND MASTERS—*continued* *Year of*
Appt. *Death*

1948	Sir William Henry Crosthwaite	1968
1968	John Owen Place	1997
1987	George Alfred Cooper	2003
2004	Eric Roy Gore-Brown	—

NORTHUMBERLAND
1870 *(until 1920)* as "Northumberland and Durham"

1920	Col. Charles Warren Napier-Clavering	1931
1932	Brig.Gen. William Henry Sitwell, *C.B., D.S.O.*	1932
1933	Rev. Percy Thomas Lee, *M.A.*	1948
1943	James Colvin Watson	1955
1955	Arthur Terence Howell	1973
1972	James Rendell Bartlett	1994
1982	Charles Henry Arthur Brown	1991
1991	George Newton Fletcher, *T.D.*	—
1999	Peter Magnay	—
2009	Gordon Craigs	—

NORTHUMBERLAND AND DURHAM (UNTIL 1920)

1870	Earl Percy, *P.C.* (in 1899 The 7th Duke of Northumberland, *K.G.*)	1918
1873	The Revd. Canon Henry Baker Tristram, *D.D., F.R.S.*	1906
1906	Col. William Mathvin Angus, *C.B., V.D.*	1935
1909	James Cartmell Ridley	1915
1911	Col. Charles Warren Napier-Clavering	1931

NORTH WALES
1872 *(until 1880)* as "Cheshire and North Wales"

1880	William Bulkley Hughes	1881
1882	Col. Sir Charles Hughes-Hunter, *Bt., D.L.*	1907
1909	Sir William Bulkley Hughes Hughes-Hunter, *Bt.*	1951
1952	Alvin Langdon Coburn	1966
1966	Eric Johnson	1981
1974	Maj. Philip Arundale, *T.D.*	1992
1979	Fred Butterworth	2005
1990	John Clarke Whittaker	1994
1995	Eric Thomas	2001
1999	John Henry Farrall	—
2004	Thomas Gareth Williams	—
2012	Peter Talbot	—

NOTTINGHAMSHIRE

1883	John Watson	1889
1889	Lt.Col. William Newton	1899
1889	His Honour Judge William Masterman, *D.C.L.*	1903
1903	Richard Fitzhugh	1918
1919	John Tricks Spalding	1924
1924	Rev. Edward St. John Morse	1941
1941	Charles Wright Gowthorpe	1949
1948	Francis Henry Starling	1953
1951	Maj. Edward Harold Spalding, *T.D.*	1955
1955	Harry White, *O.B.E.*	1975
1973	Arthur Morley Custance	1999
1990	Harvey William Housley	2010
1998	Ronald Geoffrey Bradley	2009
2007	Michael John Gutteridge	—
2012	Peter Maxwell Ball	—

OXFORDSHIRE
(until 1994) as "Berkshire and Oxfordshire"

1994	Geoffrey Michael Redman-Brown	—
2004	Richard James Slade	—
2012	James Robert Guy Hilditch	—

SOMERSET

| 1858 | The 4th Earl of Carnarvon, *P.C., D.L., F.R.S.* | 1890 |

Year of
Appt.

PROVINCIAL GRAND MASTERS—*continued*

Year of
Death

1879	Gen. Henry Edward Doherty, *C.B.*	1885
1881	Richard Charles Else	1905
1903	Col. William Long, *C.M.G., D.L.*	1926
1926	George Norman, *M.R.C.S.*	1938
1939	Alfred Leonard Fuller, *F.R.C.S.*	1941
1942	Percival Birkett Rigg, *F.R.I.B.A.*	1949
1949	Thomas Walter Robert Procter	1964
1955	Herbert Leonard Fuller, *F.R.C.S.*	1966
1967	Harry George Bascombe Catford	1984
1976	John James Webber, *M.C.*	2006
1986	David Palmer	2006
1997	Anthony Walter Sampson Hick	—
2004	David Brian Nelson	—

SOUTH WALES

1870	Theodore Mansel Talbot	1876
1881	Sir Pryse Pryse, *Bt.*	1906
1899	Col. Sir Edward Stock Hill, *K.C.B.*	1902
1904	Robert Lock	1921
1921	Col. The 6th Lord Kensington, *C.M.G., D.S.O., T.D.*	1938
1938	John McGregor, *M.D.*	1949
1950	Sir Frederick John Alban, *C.B.E.*	1965
1963	Thomas William Hughes	1968
1968	Wilfrid Baden Porter	1979
1979	Norman Alexander Morgan	1983
1983	Stanley Bernard Roberts	2011
1991	Malcolm Hayes Thompson	2004
1996	Desmond Barnett	—
2008	Paul Raymond Clement	—

STAFFORDSHIRE (UNTIL 1900)
1878 *(until 1882)* as "Warwickshire and Staffordshire"

1882	Col. Foster Gough, *LL.D.*	1892
1885	Col. George Singleton Tudor, *V.D.*	1899

STAFFORDSHIRE AND SHROPSHIRE
1878 *(until 1882)* as "Warwickshire and Staffordshire"

1901	Josiah Francis Pepper	1907
1907	Col. George Walton Walker	1918
1919	Rowland George Venables	1920
1922	Maj.Gen. Sir John Emerson Wharton Headlam, *K.B.E., C.B., D.S.O., D.L.*	1946
1931	Harry Richardson, *O.B.E.*	1945
1945	Harold Arthur Jowett, *M.C.*	1948
1948	Robert Bradley Mummery	1964
1964	Joseph Armstrong Whittall	1970
1970	Noel John Edward Boardman	1987
1987	John Aubrey Hammond	—
2002	Frederick Arthur Cotton	2009
2007	David Michael Edwards	—

SURREY
1870 *(until 1892)* as "Middlesex and Surrey"

1857	George Beauchamp Cole	1886
1892	Col. Gerrard Noel Money, *C.B.*	1895
1895	The 4th Earl of Onslow, *G.C.M.G., P.C.*	1911
1912	The 5th Earl of Onslow, *G.B.E., P.C., D.L., F.S.A., F.Z.S., F.R.Hist.S.*	1945
1927	Sir George Anthony King	1928
1928	The 5th Lord Harris, *C.B.E., M.C., D.L. K.St.J.*	1986
1934	Col. The Hon. Stuart Pleydell-Bouverie, *D.S.O., O.B.E., T.D.*	1947
1947	Lt.Col. Harry Ainsley Mann, *O.B.E., M.C.*	1962
1962	Frederick Thomas Buckerfield Wheeler	1970
1967	John Leslie Jeffree, *M.B.E.*	1970
1971	The 9th Earl of Shannon, *F.R.S.A.*	—
1981	Rev. Neville Barker Cryer, *M.A.*	—

PROVINCIAL GRAND MASTERS—*continued*

Year of Appt.		Year of Death
1991	Leslie Reginald Austin	2000
1996	Brynley Bevan	—
2004	Raymond Stanley Henry Hussey	—

SUSSEX

1874	Sir John Cordy Burrows	1876
1876	John Mackie Cunningham, *M.D.*	1878
1880	Thomas Trollope, *M.D.*	1905
1883	Col. Lord Arthur William Hill, *P.C.*	1931
1889	Gerard Ford	1889
1890	H.R.H. The 1st Duke of Connaught and Strathearn, *K.G.*	1942
1901	Very Revd. Edward Reid Currie, *D.D. (Dean of Battle)*	1921
1910	Maj. Robert Lawrence Thornton, *C.B.E., D.L.*	1947
1923	Sir Charles O'Brien Harding	1929
1929	Henry Gervis, *M.B.*	1941
1938	Sir Reginald Arthur Spence	1961
1957	Revd. Charles Herbert Mosse, *M.A.*	1970
1970	Harold William Richardson	1975
1975	Clifford William Henry Jeapes	1997
1991	James William Albert Webster	2002
2000	David Bolingbroke McLean	—
2007	Brian Clifford Wareham	—
2012	Charles Martin Wilson	—

WALES, SOUTH-WESTERN DIVISION

1857	Revd. Edmund Stanley Stanley	18—

WARWICKSHIRE AND STAFFORDSHIRE (UNTIL 1882)

1878	Revd. William Kirkpatrick Riland Bedford, *M.A.*	1905

WARWICKSHIRE
1876 *(until 1882)* as "Warwickshire and Staffordshire"

1882	Lord Brooke (in 1893 The 5th Earl of Warwick and Earl Brooke of Warwick Castle, *D.L.*)	1924
1886	The 6th Marquess of Hertford, *C.B., T.D.*	1912
1912	The 5th Earl of Warwick and Earl Brooke of Warwick Castle, *D.L.*	1924
1919	Col. Zaccheus Walker, *V.D.*	1930
1931	Matthew Herbert Clarke	1944
1944	Percy Howard Jackson	1952
1952	David Geoffrey Price	1969
1966	Edward Samuel Jacobs	1970
1970	Leslie George Seymour, *J.P.*	1976
1976	Ronald Charles Gardner	2001
1990	Robert Giles Russell	—
2002	David Carr Hooker	—
2007	David John Frederick Rawlins	—
2012	Roger Stuart Mac	—

WEST LANCASHIRE
1870 *(until 1910)* as "Lancashire"

1910	The Hon. Sir Arthur Stanley, *G.B.E., C.B., C.V.O., D.L.* (in 1944 *G.C.V.O.*)	1947
1920	George Adams Harradon	1935
1935	Maj. Allan Maitland Pooley, *T.D.*	1946
1947	Shepherd Eastwood	1973
1967	Col. James Munroe Gornall, *T.D., D.L.*	1973
1973	Sir Kenneth Maxwell Stoddart, *K.C.V.O., A.E., D.L., LL.D., J.P.*	2008
1983	Gp.Capt. James Reginald Leggate, *D.S.O.*	1999
1988	John Escott	—
1991	Dr. Brian Bennett Ratcliffe	1992
1993	Anthony Walton	2007
2007	Peter Connolly	—

WEST YORKSHIRE

1871	Thomas Perkinton	1877
1877	John Wordsworth	1883
1883	Charles Letch Mason	1907

PROVINCIAL GRAND MASTERS—*continued*

Year of Appt.		Year of Death
1904	Frederick Cleeves	1925
1925	Sir William Henry Clarke	1930
1929	The 6th Earl of Harewood, *K.G., G.C.V.O., D.S.O., T.D.*	1947
1944	Edwin Herbert Middlebrook	1951
1948	Albert Frost	1957
1954	Capt. Ralph Gibbs	1962
1959	Carl Whitehead	1990
1989	James Bramley Morley	—
1994	George Henry Philip Birch	—
1999	Brian Morris Batty	—
2007	James Bennett Truswell	—
2012	James Steggles	—

WILTSHIRE

1892	The 5th Earl of Radnor, *P.C.*	1900
1901	Revd. Canon Frederick William Macdonald, *M.A.*	1928
1924	Maj.Gen. Thomas Charles Pleydell Calley, *C.B., C.B.E., M.V.O.*	1932
1932	Revd. Hugh Effingham Tilney-Basset, *M.A.*	1950
1946	Douglas Charles Adey Morrison	1948
1949	Harry Charles Preater	1968
1968	Reginald William Short, *J.P.*	1973
1973	Lt.Col. Revd. Giles Royds Brocklebank, *D.S.O., M.C.*	1978
1978	Donald Henry Andrews	2007
1988	Geoffrey William Edward Short	1996
1995	Ivan Stuart Parry	2009
2002	Michael Meade	—
2010	Alfred Martin Jefferson Brown	—

WORCESTERSHIRE

1884	Sir Augustus Frederick Godson, *M.A.*	1906
1906	The 2nd and last Lord Athlumney and Meredyth	1929
1919	William Thomas Page	1933
1934	Charles David Eaton	1946
1946	Richard Mason Hadley	1950
1950	Vernon William Grosvenor, *C.B.E., LL.B.*	1961
1960	William Samuel Burton	1968
1969	Frank Clifford	1984
1981	Gregory Evan Rackstraw	1992
1986	Revd. Canon Albert Webb	2008
1993	Dr. John Henry Huby Oliver	2002
1998	Colin Woodward	—
2005	Francis Charles Spencer	—

District Grand Masters
THE ARGENTINE REPUBLIC (UNTIL 1974): NOW RIVER PLATE

1908	Francis Hepburn Chevalier Boutell	1937
1920	Joseph Joddrell Dowson	1929
1929	Eustace Lauriston Conder	1935
1935	William Cowlishaw	1954
1946	Gibson Richard Mawson	1952
1952	Lawrence Charles Harriss	1974
1959	William Graham Carr	1987
1971	Douglas Murison	1990

AUCKLAND, NEW ZEALAND (UNTIL 1967)

1882	Henry Greesmith Wade	1900
1886	Frederick William Edmund Dawson	1900
1901	Sir Alfred Seymour Bankart, *M.B.E.*	1933
1934	Charles Herbert Jenkins	1965
1940	George Howard Plummer	1953
1944	Daniel Boys Patterson	1962
1952	Henry Brooke Villiers Townshend	1967

DISTRICT GRAND MASTERS—continued

Year of Appt.   Year of Death

AUSTRALIA (NEW SOUTH WALES) (UNTIL 1890)
1887   Norman Selfe 1911

AUSTRALIA (QUEENSLAND) (UNTIL 1950)
1897   Harry Courtenay Luck 1934
1927   Alexander Corrie 1941
1930   William Henry Greenfield 1941
1943   Alfred Thornton Pollard 1953

AUSTRALIA (SOUTH)
1857   Benjamin Arthur Kent 1865

AUSTRALIA (TASMANIA)
1883   George Talmage .... 18—
1898   Hon. Charles Ellis Davies 1921

AUSTRALIA (VICTORIA)
1873   Henry Wallace Lowry 1891
1891   Charles Roper Martin 1910
1909   Frederic Sidney Jermaine-Lilham, M.R.C.S., L.R.C.P. 1936

BELGIUM (FORMERLY A GROUP)
1996   Claude Raoul Martin .... —
2002   Peter John Smith .... —
2012   Jean Verbist .... —

BENGAL
(INCORPORATED INTO MADRAS – 2012)
1865   Hugh David Sandeman 1910
1875   Henry Hover Locke 1886
1878   Hon. Sir Thoby Prinse, K.C.I.E. 1914
1881   Lt.Col. Anthony Stewart 1886
1884   Lt.Col. Sir George Benjamin Wolseley, G.C.B. 1921
1888   Brig.Gen. George Edward Langham Somerset Sanford, C.B. 1901
1891   H.H. the Maharajah of Kuch Behar, G.C.I.E. 1911
1894   Hon. Sir John Edge, K.C. 1911
1897   Maj.Gen. Arthur Godolphin Yeatman-Biggs, C.B. 1898
1898   Hon. Mr. Justice Sir William Robert Burkitt, C.S. 1908
1909   Hon. Chief Justice Sir John Stanley, K.C.I.E., C.B.E., K.C. 1932
1912   Col. Sir William Arthur Dring, K.C.I.E. 1912
1913   The 1st and last Lord Carmichael, G.C.S.I., G.C.I.E., K.C.M.G. 1926
1917   David Landale Johnston 1950
1924   Charles David Stewart 1940
1927   Henry Rivers Nevill, C.I.E., O.B.E., V.D. 1940
1930   Sir Eric Studd, Bt., O.B.E. 1975
1937   Charles Carey Morgan 1956
1940   Archibald Barr Pollock 1955
1952   Shyam Kinkor Ghosh 1962
1957   Frank Carlile Kidd 1964
1959   Durga Prasad, M.B. 1968
1965   Arthur John Patel 1973
1973   Revd. Paul Aiyaiyengar Krishnaswami, M.A. 1976
1977   Archibald Prince Edwards 1994
1995   Leonard Osborne Harold de Silva 2003
1999   Denzil Alfred Hilt 2010
2003   Banshi Badan Dutt 2012
2009   Subroto Chaterji ....

BOLIVIA
2000   George Edward Alexander Petit .... —
2012   David Alcoreza Marchetti .... —

BOMBAY
1864   James Gibbs, C.S.I., C.I.E. 1886
1870   James Percy Leith 1906
1873   Edward Tyrrell Leith 1888

DISTRICT GRAND MASTERS—continued

Year of Appt.		Year of Death
1877	Theodore Cooke, *C.I.E., LL.D.*	1911
1881	James William Smith	1900
1887	Hon. Henry James Parsons	1922
1896	The 2nd Lord Sandhurst, *G.C.S.I., G.C.I.E.* (in 1917 The 1st Viscount Sandhurst, *G.C.V.O., P.C.*)	1921
1900	Hon. Sir Lawrence Hugh Jenkins, *K.C.I.E.*	1928
1909	William Alban Haig-Brown	1945
1924	Sir Reginald Arthur Spence	1961
1934	William Arthur Charles Bromham, *O.B.E.*	1944
1941	Sorab Rustomji Davar	1949
1949	Revd. Canon Charles Arnold Bolton	1970
1958	Tom Livesay Foxcroft	1974
1961	Boman Rustomji Mullaferoze	1980
1964	Dennis Maxwell Palmer	1982
1967	Albert MacMull	1971
1972	Phiroz Shapoorji Sethna	1997
1984	Capt. Sam Behram Aga	2002
1992	Causie Kaikhosroo Maarfatia	2008
2009	Shrikrishna Gopalrao Arole	—

BRAZIL

1953	Ernest Cunningham, *C.B.E.*	1966
1960	David Dickson Burnett	1978
1966	Frank Craymer Toogood	1976
1974	Alick Stuart Beck, *O.B.E.*	1983
1977	Francis McCormick	—
1987	Frank Gerald Hillman Toogood	1998
1991	George Joseph Ian Rutherford, *O.B.E.*	2010
1998	Peter Bodman-Morris	—
2005	John Charles Woodrow	—

BURMA

1870	Maj. Harvey Tuckett Duncan, *C.S.I.*	1900
1884	Revd. John Fairclough	1897
1888	George Francis Travers Drapes	1901
1891	Hon. Judge Donald Grant MacLeod	1898
1899	James Copley Moyle	1909
1907	Lt.Col. Henry Wilson Iles	1920
1916	Arthur Blake	N.S.
1929	Nasarwanjee Nowrojee Parakh, *M.D.*	1935
1935	William Henry Chance	1972
1950	Maurice Bower Padgett	1960
1960	Ruston Sorab Sacklat	1966
1967	Louk Choon Foung	1979
1975	Chan Seng Hwet	1981
1980	Ko Ko Gyi	—

CANADA (MONTREAL)

1883	Hon. William Bagley	1888

CENTRAL AFRICA (UNTIL 1970)

1966	James William Johns	1986

CEYLON (UNTIL 1975)

1959	Charles Melville Jennings	1978
1964	Alexander Edward Butler	1983

CHINA

1857	Samuel Rawson	1893

CYPRUS

2010	Theodosious Socratous Theodossiou	—

EAST AFRICA

1978	Alexander Smith	1983

DISTRICT GRAND MASTERS—continued

Year of Appt.		Year of Death
1984	George Newsom Wade	2005
1994	Andrew Schoborgh Brass	—
2001	The Hon. Mr. Justice Amritlal Bhagwanji Shah, S.S.	—
2005	Archibald Armour McCorkindale	—
2008	Philip Sherwin	—

FINLAND (CONSTITUTED G.LODGE OF M.M.M. OF FINLAND–JULY 1971)

1957	Arvo Aalto	—
1970	Gustav Nikolai Lavanti (Dep.Dist. G.M.-in-charge)	—

FRANCE (CONSTITUTED G.L.M.M.M. OF FRANCE – MAY 1997)

1994	Richard Hugh Doggett	—

GERMANY (WEST GERMANY UNTIL 1992)

1992	Dr. Keith William Harry Fenwick	2011
1994	Nigel Robert John Woodhouse	—
2009	Michael Andrew Cooper	—

GIBRALTAR

1884	Hon. Chief Justice Sir Henry James Burford Burford-Hancock, *C.M.G.*	1895
1899	Charles Hammerton	1903
1908	Maj. Thomas Francis Cooper	1933
1920	Eng. Rear-Admiral Lindsay James Stephens, *C.B.E.*	1958
1924	Lt.Col. William Francis Ellis, *C.M.G., O.B.E.*	1953
1954	Judge Henry Hume Barne	1960
1960	Anthony Mena	1982
1980	Francis Joseph Borg	1993
1993	Menase James Massias	1997
1998	Joseph De Haro	—
2001	Stanley Alfred Ward	2007
2007	Alfred Henry Ryan	—

GHANA (FORMERLY A GROUP)

2010	Nana Dr. Freduah Mensah	—

HONG KONG

1964	Alfred John Butcher	1996
1972	Brook Antony Bernacchi, *O.B.E., Q.C., J.P.*	1996
1981	Hon. Pak Chuen Woo, *C.B.E., J.P.*	2008
1991	Kenneth Kok Oon Tan	—
1996	Paul Fok Hin-Fai	2009
2007	Angus John Delano Stevenson-Hamilton	—

HONG KONG AND SOUTH CHINA (UNTIL 1964)

1925	Hon. Percy Hobson Holyoak	1926
1926	James Maitland McHutchon	1965
1930	Charles William Jeffries, *F.R.A.S.*	1941
1941	Alfred Morris	1945
1947	Maj. Thomas George Stokes	1958
1950	William James Geall	1961
1954	Maurice Jean Baptiste Montargis	1960
1959	William Leslie Ernest Miller	1985
1962	Alfred John Butcher	1996

ITALY

2010	Fabio Venzi	—

JAMAICA AND CAYMAN ISLANDS
(FORMERLY JAMAICA. RENAMED IN 2009)

1877	Robert Hamilton, *M.D.*	1880
1889	Maj. John Charles Macglashan, *C.M.G.*	1898
1897	William Andrews	1898
1899	Emmanuel Xavier Leon	1915
1912	Edward Jordan Andrews	1919
1916	Hon. Sir John Pringle, *K.C.M.G.*	1923

DISTRICT GRAND MASTERS—*continued*

Year of Appt.		Year of Death
1924	Sir Henry Isaac Close Brown, *Q.C.*	1962
1958	Percy Lyons Abraham	1967
1963	Audley Louis Evans	1971
1972	Noel Joslyn Fraser, *O.B.E.*	1989
1977	Rudolph Tarchous Cousins	1988
1990	Whilston Davis Taylor, *O.D., J.P.*	—
2009	Linton Anthony Andrews, *J.P.*	—

MADRAS

1870	Col. Alexander John Greenlaw	1870
1882	Maj.-Gen. Robert Henry Cunliffe	1903
1886	Lt.Col. Sir George Montgomery John Moore	1911
1902	Hon. Mr. Henry Alexander Sim, *C.I.E.*	1928
1906	Hon. Mr. Gabriel Stokes, *K.C.S.I.*	1920
1909	Sir Murray Hammick, *K.C.S.I., C.I.E.*	1936
1914	William Taylor Mitchell	1917
1919	Llewellyn Eddison Buckley, *C.S.I.*	1945
1922	Sir Archibald Young Gipps Campbell, *K.C.I.E., C.S.I., C.B.E., V.D.*	1957
1934	Sir George Townsend Boag, *K.C.I.E., C.S.I.*	1969
1946	The Hon. Sir Muthiah David Devadoss	1955
1955	Rao Bahadur Penagapany Sundara Sivangnana Mudaliar	1962
1959	Diwan Bahadur Churya Kunhi Raman	1968
1968	Lt.Col. Gurdayal Singh Gill, *C.I.E., O.B.E.*	1982
1982	Shabdai Samuel Koder	1994
1988	Churya Rajaraman	2005
2000	Surianarayanan Chellappa	2004
2004	Bhagwan Balaji Singh	—
2011	Madhavan Chellappa	—

MADRAS AND BRITISH BURMA (UNTIL 1870)

1865	Col. Alexander John Greenlaw	1870

MALAYA (UNTIL 1967)

1917	Hon. Frederick Mitchell Elliot	1949
1924	Thomas Oswald Mayhew	1933
1933	George William Arthur Trimmer	1972
1938	Baldwyn Lowick	1955
1954	Edward Gilbert Holiday	1978
1965	Leslie Rayner	1966
1966	Dr. Ivan Gilbert Hardinge	1977

MEDITERRANEAN (UNTIL 1972)

1881	Alexander Meyrick Broadly	1916
1882	Chevalier Edward Rosenbusch	1898
1888	Col. Marmaduke Ramsay	1893
1893	Admiral Sir Albert Hastings Markham, *K.C.B.*	1918
1897	Gen. Sir John Fletcher Owen, *K.C.B.*	1924
1902	Col. Henry Thomas Hughes-Hallet	1909
1925	Lt.Col. Sir Arthur Henry McMahon, *G.C.M.B., G.C.V.O., K.C.I.E., C.S.I.*	1949
1950	Brig. Charles Esmond de Wolff, *C.B., C.B.E., LL.B.*	1986

NATAL

1883	Robert Isaac Finnemore	1906
1895	Thomas Cook	1908
1907	Lt.Col. Henry Buxton Browne	1912
1913	Charles William Perks Douglas-de-Fenzi	1927
1916	Frederic Charles Loney	1930
1925	John Hutton Atkinson	1946
1931	Thomas James Harding	1954
1935	Edward Richard Rawlinson	1961
1941	Marcus Lewis	1961
1958	Andrew Egenes	1970
1969	Robin Thomas Flack	1978
1978	Bernard Albert Armitage, *M.D., F.R.C.S.*	1993

DISTRICT GRAND MASTERS—continued

Year of Appt.		Year of Death
1983	Frank Ernest Auslebrook	1996
1987	Arthur George Richardson	2001
1992	John Wolton Gray	2003
2004	John Richard Marchant	—
2009	David Zavad	—

NETHERLANDS

1972	Henri Anton van den Akker	2005
1987	Dr. Cornelius Johannes Hagen	1997
1998	Frederik Dirk Peters	—
2007	Sybe Tunnis Booij	—

NEW ZEALAND
(FORMERLY NORTH AND SOUTH ISLANDS)

2002	Surg.Cdr. Roger Harman Weeks, *V.R.D.*	2005
2006	Capt. Iain Malcolm McGibbon, *O.B.E.*	—

NEW ZEALAND, NORTH ISLAND (UNTIL 2002)

1967	Reginald Thomas Hookham	1969
1969	John Leslie Bernard Morris	1977
1974	Edward Henry Kibblewhite Watson	1974
1974	Clive Ackland Frater	1984
1979	Richard Restless Reeves	1984
1984	Michael Andrew Allan	2003
1989	Roland Warren Somerville	2010
1999	Surg.Cdr. Roger Harman Weeks, *V.R.D.*	2005

NEW ZEALAND, SOUTH ISLAND (UNTIL 2002)

1880	Thomas Sherlock Graham	1918
1903	Charles Dillworth Fox	1932
1921	William Isaac Bolam	1934
1927	Jesse Steer	1945
1932	John Jacobs	1962
1938	Frederick Arthur Kitchingham, *O.B.E.*	1967
1945	Samuel Lawn, *M.B.E.*	1963
1955	Henry Laurence Keenan	1975
1966	Edward William Pickford	1989
1974	Oswald Henry Jackson, *J.P.*	1985
1986	Francis Joseph Gray	1987
1988	Beresford Charles Mitchell	—
1995	Konstantin Dimitry Sharapoff	—
1998	John Gordon Goldsworthy	2008

NEW ZEALAND, WESTLAND (SOUTH ISLAND) (UNTIL 1904)

1882	John Bevan	1911

NIGERIA

2011	Adediji Adedoyin	—

NORTH AFRICA (UNTIL 1953)

1882	Thomas Fellowes Reade	1884
1897	His Excellency Idris Bey Ragheb	1931
1906	Sir Francis Reginald Wingate, *Bt., G.C.B., G.C.V.O., G.B.E., K.C.M.G., D.S.O.*	1953
1920	John Langley, *C.B.E.*	1945
1932	Frank Frederick Maeers, *O.B.E.*	1970
1939	William Henry Perkins	1965
1950	John Edmund Moss Brunskill	1975

NORTHERN INDIA

1953	Hira Lal	1959
1960	Rai Bahadur Hari Nath Khanna	1961
1961	Sardar Bahadur Khazan Singh	1975
1975	Col. George Benjamin	1989
1977	Col. H.H. Raja Sir Harindar Singh Brarbans Bahadur of Faridkot, *K.C.S.I., O.S.M.*	1990

DISTRICT GRAND MASTERS—continued

Year of Appt.		Year of Death
1992	Abinash Chand Jain	—
1997	Col. Bawa Gurvachan Singh	2009
2008	Viswanathan Nagarajan	—

PAKISTAN

1967	Herman Marcus Selzer	—
1971	Kabir Ahmad Sheikh	—

PUNJAB (UNTIL 1967)

1894	Edwin Woodhall Parker	1919
1897	Col. Charles Francis Massay	1915
1899	Col. James Greaves Kelly, *C.B., A.D.C.*	1923
1902	Rev. Henry James Spence-Gray	1950
1906	Lt.Col. Arthur Grey, *C.I.E.*	1924
1909	Lt.Col. Sir Arthur Henry McMahon, *G.C.M.G., G.C.V.O., K.C.I.E., C.S.I.*	1949
1915	Surg.Gen. Hon. Sir Charles Pardey Lukis, *K.C.S.I.*	1917
1919	Col. Richard Heard	1950
1924	Lt.Col. Gerard Irving Davys, *O.B.E., M.D.*	1953
1928	Herbert Leonard Offley Garrett	1941
1936	The Rt. Rev. Bishop George Dunsford Barne, *C.I.E., O.B.E., V.D., M.A.*	1954
1949	Lt.Gen. Sir Ross Cairns McCay, *K.B.E., C.B., D.S.O.*	1969
1953	Henry Joseph Pearson, *O.B.E.*	1961
1961	Herman Marcus Selzer, *M.D.*	—

RHODESIA (UNTIL 1966 AND AGAIN FROM 1970 TO 1980)

1956	Ferdinand Farrant Duckworth	1963
1963	James William Johns	1986

RIVER PLATE (1908 UNTIL 1974 AS THE ARGENTINE REPUBLIC)

1971	Douglas Murison	1990
1983	Dennis Clifford Crisp	—
1995	Ernest Robert Steven	—
2009	William Philip Thompson	—

SINGAPORE

2012	Justice (Ret.) Mohideen Pierre Haja Rubin	—

SOUTH AFRICA

1876	Hon. Richard William Hoskins Giddy	1886

SOUTH AFRICA (CENTRAL DIVISION) (INCORPORATED WITH THE TRANSVAAL 2007)

1950	Charles Arthur Budd	1960
1960	Oliver Winterburn	1996
1971	Samuel Harry Wilks	1979
1979	Joseph de Wahl	1988
1983	Jan Hendrik van der Riet	1997
1987	Johannes Jacobus Jacobs	—
1992	Ronald Arthur Charles Jennings, *D.F.M.*	1999
1997	Julian Bernard Sussman	—
2002	Richard Rice	—

SOUTH AFRICA (EASTERN DIVISION)

1891	Charles J. Egan, *M.D.*	1909
1909	Charles Arthur Carter	1926
1913	Alan Bell Gordon	1924
1925	Rev. Chancellor Cyrill John Wyche	1945
1932	Maj. Eric Bolingbroke Walker, *M.B.E., M.C.*	1950
1943	Hugh Richard Whiting	1949
1947	Laurence Frederick Monaghan	1973
1958	David Kirk Philip	1978
1968	John Ernest Marchant Lashmar	1988
1979	Dennis Wilfred Lake	1985
1984	Noel William Timberlake	1993
1990	Roland Edmund Hiles	—
1999	Wilhelm Christo Muller	—
2006	Robin Anthony Page	2007

DISTRICT GRAND MASTERS—continued

Year of Appt.		Year of Death
2008	Gordon Edwin Goff	—
2012	Francois Hewitt Vosloo	—

SOUTH AFRICA (TRANSVAAL) (UNTIL 1987)

1902	George Richards	1911
1911	Charles Aburrow	1932
1918	Joseph Waldie Peirson, K.C.	1924
1924	Harry Robert Harding	1928
1928	Reginald Shaw Rigg	1963
1931	Wilfred Henry Hulbert	1958
1936	Henry Britten	1954
1939	James Vincent Stanton	1952
1944	John Thomson Kay	1947
1947	Percival John King	1953
1953	Herbert Isaac Cohen	1967
1960	James Alexander Bremner	1981
1972	Frank Topham	1997

SOUTH AFRICA (WESTERN DIVISION)

1894	Capel Jenner Hogg	19—
1904	Col. William Standford, D.S.O., M.V.O.	1926
1926	Thomas Nathaniel Cranstoun-Day	1967
1938	Walter Hudson	1951
1944	Walter Frederick Weeden	1954
1951	Robert Fontaine Lawton	1967
1956	John Blackwell Layton	1972
1961	Arthur Raymond Gale	1962
1962	Samuel Cohen	1979
1969	Marcus Austin Thomson	1989
1974	William Edward Key	1992
1979	Leonard Frank Songhurst	1999
1986	Robin Peter Schell	2008
1991	Justin Gerald Figov	—
1996	Alexander Schell	2004
2001	Alasdair Bruce Duthie	—
2006	Leslie Alexander Martin	—
2012	Max Nicholas Brown	—

SOUTH AND EAST CARIBBEAN

2003	Derek Gordon Hugh	—
2012	Stephen Brian Cobham	—

SOUTH EAST ASIA
(Constituted the Grand Lodge of M.M.M. of South East Asia – July 2012)

1967	Dr. Ivan Gilbert Hardinge	1977
1975	Alexander John Wilton	1982
1977	Joseph William Yee Eu	2007
1998	Robin Ian Rawlings	—
2003	Kok Cheong Cheah	—

SPAIN (FORMERLY A GROUP)

1996	Ian Leslie Hutchinson	—
2007	Robert Leslie Munday	—

SRI LANKA (1959 UNTIL 1975 AS CEYLON)

1976	Dadabhoy Nusserwanjee Jilla	1996
1983	Lankanatha Asoka Goonewardene	2003
1991	Duleep Nissanka Daluwatte	—
2000	Michael Anthony Sirimal Dias	—
2012	Talija Parakrama Dambawinne, J.P.	—

THE TRANSVAAL (FORMERLY SOUTH AFRICA, TRANSVAAL)
(INCORPORATED SOUTH AFRICA (CENTRAL DIVISION) 2007)

1987	Spencer Rowland Whiting, D.S.O.	2004

GRAND INSPECTORS

Year of Appt.		Year of Death
1992	Ivor Findlay Sander	—
2002	Albert Spencer	—
2010	David Robert Johnston	—

Tunis and Malta (until 1881)

1879	Alexander Meyrick Broadley	1916

West Germany (until 1992)

1980	James George Chapman	2002
1985	Wg.Cdr. William Alfred Spencer, *R.A.F.*	2000

West Indian Islands

1891	Col. John Elliott, *C.B., C.M.G.*	1911
1895	John Locke	1918

Zimbabwe

1963	James William Johns	1986
1983	Richard Lewin	2002
1990	Leon Gerald Rivers	—
1996	Michael Godfrey Carless	2009
2002	John George Kane	2012
2008	Edward David Clingham	—
2011	Bruce Irving Watson	—

Bahamas and Turks

2006	Gordon Percival Higgs	—
2009	James Randolph Bain	—

Belgium (until 1996)

1993	Claude Raoul Martin	—

France (until 1994)

1990	Richard Hugh Doggett	—

Ghana (until 2010)

1997	Nana Dr. Fredua Mensah	—

Guyana (until 2003)

1997	Donald Thomas Saywack	—

Isle of Man

1994	Alan Edgar Stewart	—
2005	David Patrick Downie, *M.B.E.*	—

Spain (until 1996)

1994	Ian Leslie Hutchinson	—

Western Atlantic (until 2005)

1997	William Desmond Patrick	—

ORDERS ADMINISTERED FROM MARK MASONS' HALL

Great Priory of the Temple
2012-2013
Most Eminent and Supreme Grand Master:
Timothy John Lewis, G.C.T.
The Very High and Right Eminent Great Seneschal:
Malcolm Ernest Slater, G.C.T.
Great Vice-Chancellor:
R.E.Kt. John Brackley, G.C.T.

The Great Priory of the Temple meets on the 3rd Wednesday in May.

Great Priory of Malta
2011-2012
Great Prior:
R.E.Kt. Edwin Bryant Goodwin
Great Sub-Prior:
V.E.Kt. Raymond Rooke
Great Vice-Chancellor:
R.E.Kt. John Brackley, G.C.M.

The Great Priory of Malta meets on the 3rd Tuesday in November.

Grand Imperial Conclave of the Red Cross of Constantine
2012-2013
Grand Sovereign:
M.Ill.Kt. Richard Victor Wallis, *J.P.*, G.C.C.
Deputy Grand Sovereign:
R.Ill. and Em.Kt. Alexander Michael Jones, *J.P.*, G.C.C.
Grand Eusebius:
R.Ill. and Ven.Kt. Dr. The Revd. Charles Peter Bernard Blackwell-Smyth
Grand Recorder:
R.Ill.Kt. John Brackley, G.C.C.

Grand Imperial Conclave meets on the 1st Tuesday in July.

Grand Council of Royal and Select Masters
2012-2013

Grand Master:
M.Ill.Comp. John Alan Wright

Deputy Grand Master:
R.Ill.Comp. Kessick John Jones

Grand Principal Conductor of the Work:
R.Ill.Comp. Michael George Spencer

Grand Recorder:
R.Ill.Comp. John Brackley, P.G.P.C.W.

Grand Council meets on the 3rd Tuesday in April.

Grand Council of the Order of the Allied Masonic Degrees
2012-2013

Grand Master:
M.W.Bro. Thomas Firth Jackson

Deputy Grand Master:
R.W.Bro. Lt.Col. John Craven Chambers

Grand Secretary:
R.W.Bro. John Brackley, P.G.S.W.

Grand Council meets on the 4th Tuesday in October.

Grand Conclave of the Order of the Secret Monitor
2012-2013

Grand Supreme Ruler:
M.Wy.Bro. Michael William Guest

Deputy Grand Supreme Ruler:
R.Wy.Bro. Brian William Price

Assistant Grand Supreme Ruler:
R.Wy.Bro. Madhavan Chellappa

Grand Recorder:
R.Wy.Bro. John Brackley, P.G.Chan.

Grand Conclave meets on the 2nd Thursday in November.

Grand Senatus of the Order of the Scarlet Cord
2012-2013

Grand Summus:
M.Dist.Comp. Andrew Christopher Sweeney
Deputy Grand Summus:
R.Dist.Comp. Barry Clarke
Assistant Grand Summus:
R.Dist.Comp. Ian Stanley Currans
Grand Recorder:
R.Dist.Comp. John Brackley, P.G.Chan.

Grand Senatus meets on the 1st Thursday in May.

Grand Priory of the Knights Beneficient of the Holy City
2012-2013

Grand Master:
M.E. & Revd.Kt. Michael Edward Herbert, G.C.H.C.
Grand Prior and Deputy Grand Master:
R.Revd.Kt. Philip Major Collins, *J.P.*, G.C.H.C.
Grand Chancellor:
R.Revd.Kt. Comp. John Brackley, G.C.H.C.

Grand Priory meets on the 2nd Thursday in September.

ROYAL ORDER OF SCOTLAND

Provincial Grand Lodge of London and Metropolitan Counties
2011-2012

Provincial Grand Master:
Bro. Nigel John Francis Scott-Moncrieff
Deputy Provincial Grand Master:
Bro. James Martin Long
Substitute Provincial Grand Master:
Bro. Charles Ward Parshall
Provincial Grand Secretary:
Bro. John Brackley

Provincial Grand Lodge meets at Mark Masons' Hall,
86 St. James's Street, London, SW1A 1PL
on the 4th Friday in November.

REPRESENTATIVES

AT Grand Lodge of Mark Master Masons of England and Wales and its Districts and Lodges Overseas		FROM Grand Lodge of Mark Master Masons of England and Wales and its Districts and Lodges Overseas
M.W.Bro. John Hale, P.Pro G.M.	Grand Lodge of Scotland	R.W.Bro. Rt. Hon. The Earl of Elgin and Kincardine, K.T., *D.L., J.P.,* *LL.D., M.A.,* G.S.W.
(In Abeyance)	Grand Lodge of Iran	(In Abeyance)
M.W.Bro. John Hale, P.Pro G.M.	Sup.G.R.A. Chapter of Scotland	M.E.Comp. Rt. Hon. The Earl of Elgin and Kincardine, K.T., *D.L., J.P., LL.D., M.A.,* G.S.W. First Grand Principal
M.W.Bro. John Hale, P.Pro G.M.	Sup.G.R.A. Chapter of Ireland	M.E.Comp. Michael J. Ward
	Sup.G.R.A. Chapter of New Zealand	M.W.Bro. T.W. Griffiths, Grand Master
R.W.Bro. Peter Glyn Williams, P.G.S.W.	Sup.G.R.A. Chapter of the State of Israel	M.E.Comp. Israel John Herman
R.W.Bro. Timothy John Lewis, P.Prov.G.M.	Sup.G.R.A. Chapter of Quebec	W.Bro. Edward Peter Guy Vatcher, P.A.G.D.C.
R.W.Bro. Peter Glyn Williams, P.G.S.W.	United Grand Lodge of Mark Master Masons of Victoria	M.W.Bro. Bruce E. Bartrop Past Grand Master
	Grand Lodge of Mark Master Masons of South Australia & Northern Territory	M.W.Bro. David Crawford, P.G.M.
	Grand Chapter of Royal Arch Masons in Virginia	R.E.Comp. Gordon Hector Sprigg, *Jr.*
M.W.Bro. John Hale, P.Pro G.M.	Grand Chapter of Royal Arch Masons of New Brunswick	M.E.Comp. Robert J. Melanson, Past First Grand Principal
R.W.Bro. Michael George Wenman Masters, P.G.J.W.	Grand Chapter of Royal Arch Masons of Delaware	E.Comp. Albert H. Westerside
Vacant	United Supreme Grand Chapter of Mark & Royal Arch Masons of N.S.W. & A.C.T.	M.E.Comp. Emlyn Norman Garland Past 1st Grand Principal and Grand Master
R.W.Bro. George Robert Gavin Purser, P.Dep.G.M.	Grand Lodge of Mark Master Masons of Queensland	R.W.Bro. Garry Kevin Fenton, Dep.G.M.
R.W.Bro. Keith Stanley Carmichael, *C.B.E.,* P.G.S.W., O.S.M.M.M.	Grand Lodge of Mark Master Masons of Finland	M.W.Bro. Martti Asumaa, G.M.

REPRESENTATIVES—*(continued)*

FROM	AT	
R.W.Bro. Timothy John Lewis, P.Prov.G.M.	The Danish Order of Freemasons Grand Lodge of Denmark	R.W.Bro. Jens Ernst Lassen
M.W.Bro. John Hale, P.Pro G.M.	Grand Chapter of Royal Arch Masons of Arkansas	E.Comp. Jess N. Bonds, III
R.W.Bro. Timothy John Lewis, P.Prov.G.M.	Grand Royal Arch Chapter of Nova Scotia	Vacant
R.W.Bro. Ian James Richard Spofforth, P.G.S.W.	Grand Royal Arch Chapter of California	E.Comp. His Honour Judge Marcus J. Anwyl-Davies, *Q.C.*
R.W.Bro. Ian Douglas Gavin Alexander, *Q.C.*, P.G.J.W.	Grand Chapter of Royal Arch Masons of Connecticut	Comp. Russell A. Schiebel
R.W.Bro. Col. Robert Keith Hind, P.Prov.G.M., O.S.M.M.M.	Grand Lodge of Mark Master Masons of Switzerland	R.W.Bro. Peter Ernest Ribi, Grand Master
M.W.Bro. John Hale, P.Pro G.M.	Grand Chapter of Royal Arch Masons of Saskatchewan	R.E.Comp. Lou Lintick
R.W.Bro. Timothy John Lewis, P.Prov.G.M.	Grand Chapter of Royal Arch Masons of Ohio	R.E.Comp. Jean W. Justus, Jr.
Vacant	Grand Chapter of Royal Arch Masons of Kansas	E.Comp. Richard A. Wortman
R.W.Bro. Michael Edward Herbert, Dep.G.M.	Grand Chapter of Royal Arch Masons of Maine	Comp. Howard C. Weymouth
	Grand Chapter of Royal Arch Masons of Washington	M.E.Comp. Louis E. Bartrand
	The Norwegian Order of Freemasons Grand Lodge of Norway	R.W.Bro. Bjorn Olav Bergholtz, K.C.R.C.

Grand Lodges of Mark Master Masons, Grand Royal Arch Chapters, and Craft Lodges in amity and addresses of the Grand Secretaries

EUROPE
Grand Lodge of Mark Master Masons

Estonia
Toomas Tonise, *(Deputy Grand Secretary)*, Foreign Relations
G.L.M.M.M. of Estonia, P.O. Box 3992, 10509 Tallinn, Estonia   2009

Finland
Kaj. H. Lindstrom
Kasarmikatu 16D, 00130 Helsinki, Finland
Email: office@suurloosi.fi   1971

Greece
Anastassios Albanis
P.O. Box 261 44, GR 100 22 Athens, Greece
Tel: +30210 3811684 Fax: +30210 3300649
Email: info@markandmariner.gr   2010

Switzerland
Jean-Pierre Moirandat
Chemin Pra-Forny 296, CH-1091 Aran, Villette/Lavaux, Switzerland
Tel: 0041 (0)21 799 34 96
Email: rainbowgolfing@sunrise.ch   1996

Grand Royal Arch Chapter

Ireland
D. Barry Lyons
F.M.H. 17, Molesworth Street, Dublin, 2
Email: office@freemason.ie

Germany
Robert C. Simpson
Hauptstr 1c, 66978 Clausen, Germany

Scotland (Chapter)
G. J. Smith
Royal Arch Chambers, 23 St. John Street, Edinburgh EH8 8DG

Craft Grand Lodge

The Danish Order of Freemasons Grand Lodge of Denmark
Jens. E. Lassen
P.O. Box 2563, Blegdamsvej 23, Dk – 2100 Copenhagen, Denmark

Norway
Arne Hilmar Andresen, Head of Office of Foreign Affairs
The Norwegian Order of Freemasons, Grand Lodge of Norway,
P.O. Box 506, Sentrum N-0105 Oslo, Norway   2009

Scotland (Craft)
David M. Begg, *C.A.*
F.M.H., 96 George St., Edinburgh EH2 3DH
Tel: 0131 225 5577

Sweden
Grand Lodge of Sweden
Grand Chancellor: Karl-Erik Ericsson
Nybrokajen 7, SE-111 48, Stockholm, Sweden

OCEANIA
Grand Lodge of Mark Master Masons

Queensland
Cliff Isted
P.O. Box 15024, City East Qld 4002, Australia   1932

GRAND ROYAL ARCH CHAPTERS, ETC.—*continued*

South Australia and Northern Territory
Malcolm Colegate
Box 19, Rundle Mall, Adelaide SA 5000, Australia
Tel: 8223 1633. Email: glsa@freemasonrysaust.org.au   1906

Victoria
George C. Kerr
300 Albert Street, East Melbourne VIC 3002, Australia
Tel: 9419 2288   1901

Grand Royal Arch Chapter

United Supreme Grand Chapter of Mark and R.A. Masons, New South Wales and A.C.T.
John S. Williams
23-25 New Canterbury Road, Petersham, 2049, New South Wales, Australia
Tel: 02 9569 5699, Fax: 02 9569 6227

New Zealand
A.N. French
P.O. Box No. 38-224, Howick, Auckland 1730

Western Australia
W.D. Carr
P.O. Box No. 6002, Hay Street, East Perth, WA 6892, Australia
Tel: 09 325 7751, Fax: 09 325 7751

NORTH AMERICA
Grand Royal Arch Chapter

CANADA
Alberta, Marvyn R. Rogers, P.O. Box 1124, Athabasca, AB, Canada T9S 2A9

British Columbia and The Yukon
E.D. Wilson
35188 Spencer Street, Abbotsford, British Columbia, Canada V3G 2E3
Tel: 604 854 3446

Ontario
Melvyn J. Duke
253-3060 Constitutional Bvd., Mississauga, Ontario, Canada L4Y 3X8

Manitoba
Stan J. Payne
Box 69003, Tuxedo Park, P.O., 2025 Croydon Ave, Winnipeg, Canada R3P 2G9

New Brunswick
Robert M. Johnston
26 Clarwood Drive, Quispamsis, New Brunswick, Canada, E2E 4K4
Tel: (506) 847 4108. Email: grandramnb@gmail.com

Nova Scotia
Lawrin. C. Armstrong
R.R. 4, Shubenacadie, N.S., Canada, B0N 2H0

Quebec
Charles André Bräun
2295 rue Saint-Marc, Montreal, Québec, Canada H3H 2G9

Saskatchewan
Lorne Kingston
159 Weaver Cres., Swift Current, Saskatchewan, Canada S9H 4B8

U.S.A.
General Grand Chapter, United States of America
John F. Kirby
P.O. Box 489, Danville, KY 40422-0489

Alabama
Hiram O. Williams, *Jr.*
P.O. Box 100333, Birmingham, AL. 35210-0333

GRAND ROYAL ARCH CHAPTERS, ETC.—*continued*

Alaska
David A. Hunt
Box 100641, Anchorage 99510, Alaska

Arizona
David G. Stankow
345 W. Monroe Street, Phoenix 85003-1617

Arkansas
Homer F. Chamness
P.O. Box 24, Fort Smith, Arkansas 72902-0024
Tel: 501 494 7535

California
Kenneth G. Hope
801 Elm Ave, Long Beach 90813-4414

Colorado
Gerald A. Ford
Masonic Temple, 1614 Welton St. Denver 80202

Connecticut
Charles B. Fowler, *Jnr*.
525 Stillwater, Windsor CT06095-3842

Delaware
Mark E. Irwin
317 Kalorma Road, Sykesville MD21784

Dist. of Columbia
Urban T. Peters
11713N Marlton Avenue, Upper Marlboro MD20772

Florida
William Robert Young
400-C Julia Street, Titusville, Florida 32796

Georgia
Ted H. Hendon
Masonic Temple, 811 Mulberry St., Macon 31298-5099

Hawaii
Revd. J.B. Connell
1227 Makiki St., Honolulu, 96814

Idaho
David A. Grindle
P.O. Box 332, Meridian ID 83680 0332, U.S.A.

Illinois
Edward E. Derry
P.O. Box 227, Washington IL. 61571-0227

Indiana
Marion K. Crum
6954 Georgetown Road, Nashville, Indiana 47448-8584

Iowa
Robert J. Seiler
812 14th Place, Camanche, Iowa 52730-1204
Email: seiler837@q.com

Kansas
Thomas J. Owen
Box 1217, Topeka KS 66601-1217

Kentucky
John F. Kirby
P.O. Box 489, 517 Dogwood Drive, Danville, 40422-0489

Louisiana
Huston F. Boothe
41325 South Preston Drive, Hammond LA 70403-7243

GRAND ROYAL ARCH CHAPTERS, ETC.—*continued*

Maine
Robert D. Chaput
190 Mosher Road, Gorham, Maine 04038, U.S.A.

Maryland
William G. Gulley
4180 Hills Market Road, Felton DE19943

Massachusetts
John B. McCulloch
20 Old Ford Road, Weymouth, MA 02189

Michigan
Ralph W. Raiford, Jr.
3330 Alpine Drive, Ann Arbor, Michigan 48108

Minnesota
Dexter C. Pehle
P.O. Box 11, 230 South 1st Street, Suite 110, Virginia MN 55792-0011
Tel: 001 218 741 2629. Email: mnram@earthlink.net, Email2: mnyrcm@earthlink.net

Mississippi
Fred F. Bean
P.O. Box 1030, Meridian, M.S. 39302-1030

Missouri
Frederick A Troxel, *Jr.*
2102 NE Colonnade Ave., Blue Springs, MO 64029-9697
Tel: 816 224 4940, Fax: 816 224 4934. Email: gyr@moyorkrite.org

Montana
Bradford L. Huffman
Grand York Rite Bodies of Montana 1923, 10th Avenue, South, Great Falls, Montana 59405

Nebraska
Jay H. Speck
11902 Elm Street, Suite 6D, Omaha 68144-4362

Nevada
Russel M. Wilde
2321 Meadowbrook Lane, Carson City 89701

New Hampshire
Robert L. Sutherland Jr.
280 Bayside Road, Greenland, USA 03840-2146

New Jersey
Ernest E. Fricks
26 Windmill Drive, Clementon, N.J. 08021-5821

New Mexico
Allen L. Bruner
P.O. Box 66059, Albuquerque, NM 87193-6059
Tel: 505 792 2748. Email: nmgyr@comcast.net

New York
Charles J. Reilly
14 West Jackson Avenue, Middletown 10940-4210

North Carolina
Robert A. Schafer
P.O. Box 17212, Raleigh, North Carolina 27619

North Dakota
Merle L. Huhner
P.O. Box 9544, Fargo 58106-9544

Ohio
Dale G. Ray
Alexander Commons Suite, 401, 564 West Tucarawas Ave., Barberton, Ohio
Tel: 330 753 3672, Fax: 330 753 3673

Oklahoma
Ralph K. Harris
16305 101st East Avenue, Tulsa 74128-4630

GRAND ROYAL ARCH CHAPTERS, ETC.—*continued*

Oregon
Dalvin L. Hollaway
P.O. Box 767, Canyonville, OR 97417

Pennsylvania
Roy E. Cook
M.T., 1 N. Broad St., Philadelphia, 19107

Rhode Island & Providence Plantations
R.J. Stearns
111 Pettis Drive, Warwick, RI 02886

South Carolina
Johnnie T. Morris
P.O. Box 7463, Columbia S.C. 29202

South Dakota
Richard C. Geib
609 Wayside Drive, Rapid City, S.D. 57702

Tennessee
L.A. Hill, Sr.
P.O. Box 24216, Nashville, Tennesse

Texas
Orville L. O'Neill
Box 296, Waco, Texas 76703-0296

Utah
Owen C. Orton
4200 South 4900 West, West Valley City, 84120-4823

Vermont
Donald C. Brown
1232 Herbet Road, Williamstown, 05679

Virginia
Howard F. Coleman
4101 Nine Mile Road, Richmond, Virginia 23223-4999

Washington
Jeffery S. Bartow
P.O. Box 1539, Ellensburg, WA 98926 U.S.A.
Email: jbartow@kvalley.com

West Virginia
J. W. Vandall
1135 McClung Ave., Barboursville 25501

Wisconsin
Milton F. Gregory
123 Globe Heights Drive, Racine, WI 53406

Wyoming
Kenneth S. Watts
506 West Park Ave., Riverton, Wyoming 82501

SOUTH AMERICA
Grand Lodge of Mark Master Masons

Brazil
Claudio Ermel Ferraz
Rua Celso Mantouani 235, Parque do Castelo, São Paulo Sp, Brazil 04803 240   2004

REST OF THE WORLD
Grand Lodge of Mark Master Masons

India
Grand Secretary: B. Kamakoti
Freemasons' Hall, Janpath, New Delhi 110001, India
Tel: 11 2332 1949/1956

South East Asia
Cecil Thiagarajah
Dewan Freemason, 15 Jalan 18/16 Taman Kanagapuram, 460 00 Petaling, Jaya, Malaysia

Togo
P. Edji, *Grand Secretary*
Grand Lodge of Togo, B.P. 1634, Lome, Togo

Grand Royal Arch Chapter

Israel
Chanan Adelaar
P.O. Box 33698, Tel Aviv 61336, Israel

South Africa
Andrew M. Arthur
Grand Lodge Centre, 75 13th Street, Orange Grove 2192, Johannesburg, South Africa
Tel: 27 11 640 1324

Craft Grand Lodge

Iran
Ahmad Aliabadi
P.O. Box 11-1777, Tehran, Iran (in Abeyance)

"DAUGHTER" GRAND LODGES OF M.M.M.

IN ORDER OF PRECEDENCE

United Grand Lodge, M.M.M., Victoria	1901
Grand Lodge, M.M.M., South Australia and Northern Territory	1906
Grand Lodge, M.M.M., Queensland	1932
Grand Lodge, M.M.M., Finland	1971
Grand Lodge, M.M.M., Switzerland	1996
Grand Lodge, M.M.M., France *(Recognition withdrawn March 2012)*	*1997*
Grand Lodge, M.M.M., Brazil	2004
Grand Lodge, M.M.M., South East Asia	2012

GRAND MASTER'S LODGES OF INSTRUCTION FOR MARK MASTER MASONS AND ROYAL ARK MARINERS

Meetings are held at Mark Masons' Hall, 86 St. James's Street, London, SW1A 1PL in September to April inclusive. Details of meetings can be obtained from the Secretary, W.Bro. C. Lloyd: Tel: 01702 588676; Email: c.j.b.lloyd@btinternet.com.
The Annual Festival of the Lodges of Instruction will be held on Tuesday, 23rd April, 2013 at M.M.H.

Chairman:
V.W.Bro. K.J. Jones, P.G.J.O., G.D.C., G.M.R.A.C.
Preceptor:
V.W.Bro. D.F. Pascho, P.G.J.O., R.A.M.G.R.
Assistant Preceptor:
W.Bro. T. Quinn, P.A.G.D.C., Pr.R.A.M.G.R.
Secretary:
W.Bro. C.J.B. Lloyd, P.G.J.D., R.A.M.G.R.
Assistant Secretary and Treasurer:
W.Bro. C.W. Whorne, Prov.G.S.D., Pr.R.A.M.G.R.
Festival Secretary:
W.Bro. M.I. Guile, P.A.G.D.C., Pr.R.A.M.G.R.
Members:
W.Bro. J.H. Bussell, P.A.G.D.C., R.A.M.G.R.
V.W.Bro. G.A. Trew, P.G.J.O., R.A.M.G.R.

CALENDAR for 2012-13 SEASON

Sept. 3rd	1615 R.A.M. Installation* 1700 R.A.M. Elevation 1800 Mark Advancement	Jan. 14th	1615 R.A.M. Installation* 1700 R.A.M. Elevation 1800 Mark Advancement
Sept. 17th	1615 Mark Installation* 1700 Mark Advancement 1830 R.A.M. Elevation	Jan. 21st	1615 Mark Installation* 1700 Mark Advancement 1830 R.A.M. Elevation
Oct. 1st	1615 R.A.M. Installation* 1700 R.A.M. Elevation 1800 Mark Advancement	Feb. 4th	1615 R.A.M. Installation* 1700 R.A.M. Elevation 1800 Mark Advancement
Oct. 15th	1615 Mark Installation* 1700 Mark Advancement 1830 R.A.M. Elevation	Feb. 18th	1615 Mark Installation* 1700 Mark Advancement 1830 R.A.M. Elevation
Nov. 5th	1615 R.A.M. Installation* 1700 R.A.M. Elevation 1800 Mark Advancement	Mar. 4th	1615 R.A.M. Installation* 1700 R.A.M. Elevation 1800 Mark Advancement
Nov. 19th	1615 Mark Installation* 1700 Mark Advancement 1830 R.A.M. Elevation	Mar. 18th	**Festival Rehearsal** 1645 R.A.M. Elevation 1800 Mark Advancement
Dec. 3rd	1615 R.A.M. Installation* 1700 R.A.M. Elevation 1800 Mark Advancement	April 8th	**Festival Rehearsal** 1645 R.A.M. Elevation 1800 Mark Advancement
Dec. 17th	1615 Mark Installation* 1700 Mark Advancement 1830 R.A.M. Elevation	April 22nd April 23rd	**Festival Rehearsal** 1645 R.A.M. Elevation 1800 Mark Advancement **Annual Festival** **Warwickshire****

*For Installed Commanders or Masters as appropriate.
**Times T.B.C.

MARK BENEVOLENT FUND

The One Hundred and Forty-Fifth Annual Festival
will be held on SATURDAY 21st SEPTEMBER, 2013 at Norwich
Chairman:
R.W.Bro. PAUL ANTHONY NORMAN
Provincial Grand Master for East Anglia

GENERAL SUMMARY

This Fund was founded in the year 1868 for the purpose of rendering assistance to Mark Master masons in distress, their widows and children.

Since the establishment of the Fund, a sum of £6,101,523 has been distributed in relief. Grants during the year ended 31st December, 2011, amounted to £305,844 comprising of £242,095 ordinary grants and £63,750 in emergency grants.

FESTIVAL STEWARDSHIP, 2013

Every Brother or Lady accepting the office of Steward is called upon to pay a fee to "The Steward's Fund", *which is entirely distinct from the Mark Benevolent Fund, and is applied for the purpose of defraying the expenses connected with the Annual Festival. On payment of the Steward's Fee each Steward is furnished with a Steward's Badge, which is specially designed for each Festival.*

FEES

Brethren or Ladies subscribing a minimum donation of £50.00 may act as Stewards by paying a Steward's Fee.

A charge of £10.00 is made if a Stewards Badge or Bar is required.

Stewards of the year who wish to attend the Festival may do so on payment of an additional luncheon or dining charge which is determined annually.

Stewards of the year may invite Ladies as guests on payment of the additional charge.

Patrons (although not serving as a Steward of the year) may attend the Festival in company with a Lady on payment of the normal luncheon or dining charge.

CHARITY JEWELS

A Mark Benevolent Fund Charity Jewel will be presented free of charge to individuals and to Lodges which qualify as Vice-Patrons, Patrons, Grand Patrons. The following procedures shall apply —

(a) On qualification as a Life Subscriber (£50) or Life Governor (£100) the donor will be sent the appropriate collarette and offered a Charity Jewel free of charge.

(b) On qualification as a Vice-Patron (£250.00) the donor will be sent the appropriate collarette and offered a Charity Jewel free of charge.

(c) On qualification as a Patron (£500.00) the donor will be sent a Patron's collarette and offered a Charity Jewel free of charge, if he has not been offered one under (b) above.

(d) Lodges may qualify as Patrons and Vice-Patrons by contributing not less than £50.00 or £25.00 respectively for each subscribing member.

(e) On qualification as a Vice-Patron, a Lodge will be sent a Vice-Patron's collarette and a Jewel free of charge. The Master should be invited to wear the collarette and jewel as a mark of distinction.

(f) On qualification as a Patron, a Lodge will be sent a Patron's collarette and, if it has not had a Charity Jewel under (e) above, a jewel free of charge — similarly to be worn by the Master as a mark of distinction.

(g) On qualification as a Grand Patron (£1,000) the donor or Lodge will be sent the distinctive collarette and jewel, which will be presented by the Provincial Grand Master.

(h) On qualification for the Grand Patron Gold Award (Individual donor: £2,500; Lodges and Provinces at Grand Patron level: £2,500 or £5,000 respectively) the donor or Lodge or Province will be presented with the Gold Award Collarette and Jewel.

Applications should be made to the Hon. Secretary, Mark Masons' Hall, 86 St. James's Street, London, SW1A 1PL.

FORTHCOMING FESTIVALS

PROVINCES

2013 EAST ANGLIA	2017 BERKSHIRE	2021 EAST LANCASHIRE
2014 BUCKINGHAMSHIRE	2018 LINCOLNSHIRE	2022 OXFORDSHIRE
2015 WORCESTERSHIRE	2019 SUSSEX	2023 SURREY
2016 DEVONSHIRE	2020 KENT	

NOTICES

1. GRAND LODGE SUMMONS
   Secretaries of Lodges are required to forward a copy of the summons to W.M.s and to all other Brothers who wish to attend the meetings of Mark Grand Lodge and the Annual Assembly of the Ancient and Honourable Fraternity of Royal Ark Mariners.

2. CONSTITUTIONS & REGULATIONS/YEAR BOOK
   The Secretary of each Lodge will receive one copy of the Yearbook, incorporating the Constitutions and Regulations, for which a payment of £12.00 must be included on the Annual Return form, as at 31st August 2012. Further copies may be obtained on application to Mark Masons Hall Ltd.

3. G.L.M.M.M. WEBSITE
   To keep up to date with events in all Orders administered from Mark Masons' Hall go to www.glmmm.com

4. CHARITIES WEBSITE
   Brethren are advised of the new website with information an all the Masonic Charities administered from Mark Masons' Hall. Information and downloadable forms are available at:
   http://www.markbenevolence.org.uk

5. PUBLICATIONS AND REGALIA
   Publications and Regalia for all Orders may be purchased by Brethren from Mark Masons Hall Ltd: Tel: 020 7747 1191 (shop) or email: regalia@mmh.org.uk
   Shop opening hours: 11am-5pm daily.
   Online sales are also available at our Online Shop: http://shop.mmh.org.uk

Please notify the Year Book editor of any errors, or amendments for this publication.
Email: yearbook@mmh.org.uk

Mark Masons Hall Ltd

86 St. James's Street,
London SW1A 1PL

Suppliers of Regalia
& Books for all Orders

Tel: 020 7747 1191

Email: regalia@mmh.org.uk
Web-shop: shop.mmh.org.uk

Provincial Grand Lodge of London
and the Metropolitan Counties

The Carvery at 86

Superb restaurant offering a fine selection of Hors d'Ouvres, hand carved roast meats, sumptuous choice of desserts from the trolley and an extensive selection of wines.

12.00pm until 3.00pm Monday to Friday

Where you belong

86 St James offers flexible event packages at affordable prices. Ladies Nights' special package, meetings, lunches, receptions

A Place to Meet

Our Lounge Bar is open for Masons & their guests. Enjoy our real ales, lunchtime menu and a great atmosphere.

Contact the Hospitality Team for more details
Reservations and Enquiries: 020 7747 1185
Email to: info@86stjames.com

Rewards

The 86 St James Membership Card aims to reward the most important clientele there is - the regular guest. We value your custom and want to reward you with exclusive discounts and seasonal offers. Additionally we will automatically include you in our monthly prize draw where 3 lucky members will have the chance to win a 3 course Carvery Meal for 2.

What are the permanent members' benefits?

Currently there is a 20% discount in the Carvery Restaurant, a 10% discount on all items at the Regalia Shop and a 10% discount at the Bar after 8.30pm. Plus, there will be many other benefits for members designed to reward you for your continuous custom.

GRAND LODGE OF MARK MASTER
MASONS OF ENGLAND AND WALES
AND ITS DISTRICTS AND LODGES
OVERSEAS

CONSTITUTIONS

AND

REGULATIONS

FOR THE GOVERNMENT OF

The Order of Mark Master Masons

AND

The Degree of The Ancient and Honourable
Fraternity of Royal Ark Mariner

2012

CONSTITUTIONS and REGULATIONS
FOR THE GOVERNMENT OF THE ORDER OF THE GRAND LODGE OF MARK MASTER MASONS OF ENGLAND AND WALES AND ITS DISTRICTS AND LODGES OVERSEAS

Thirty-first Impression, incorporating all approved amendments to June 2012

DUTY

As a citizen every Mark Mason has a Duty to maintain and uphold the law of the land in which he resides. As a Mark Master Mason he also has a Duty to uphold the integrity and good repute of the Order.

SECTION I

GRAND LODGE

1. The Order shall be governed by a body styled "THE GRAND LODGE OF MARK MASTER MASONS OF ENGLAND AND WALES AND ITS DISTRICTS AND LODGES OVERSEAS", consisting of the brethren listed in Regulation 4(i) below, which body is hereinafter referred to as "GRAND LODGE".

2. Grand Lodge possesses supreme authority, and alone has the inherent power of enacting laws and regulations for the government of the Order, and of altering, repealing, and abrogating them, always taking care that the antient Landmarks be preserved.

3. (i) Grand Lodge has also the power of investigating, regulating and deciding all matters relative to the Order, and all administrative matters relating to the administration of Orders governed from Mark Masons' Hall, and alone possesses the authority for erasing Lodges save that the Mark Executive Committee alone shall have the power to expel a Brother on recommendation under Rule 60(ii) or on appeal under Rule 66.

(ii) In all cases of expulsion by the United Grand Lodge of England, the Supreme Grand Chapter of England or under the constitution of any Sovereign Grand Lodge recognised by Grand Lodge including the Degree of The Ancient and Honourable Fraternity of Royal Ark Mariner with whom Grand Lodge is in amity of a Brother who is a member of the Order of Mark Master Masons he shall ipso facto be expelled from that Order.

(iii) In the case of the general suspension of a Brother under any of the jurisdictions named in (ii) above, being a member of the Order of Mark Master Masons he shall ipso facto be suspended from the Order for a like period and on like terms unless the Mark Executive Committee shall otherwise direct.

(iv) Permanent exclusion of a Royal Ark Mariner from a Royal Ark Mariner Lodge shall take effect as permanent exclusion from the Mark Master Masons Lodge attached to the former.

(v) A resignation by a Brother from the United Grand Lodge of England under Rule 277A of the Book of Constitutions shall take effect as a resignation from the Orders of Mark Master Masons and The Ancient and Honourable Fraternity of Royal Ark Mariners.

4. (i) The precedence of members of Grand Lodge shall be as follows:

1. The Grand Master
2. Pro Grand Master
3. Past Grand Masters
4. Past Pro Grand Masters
5. Deputy Grand Master
6. Past Deputy Grand Masters
7. Assistant Grand Master
8. Past Assistant Grand Masters
9. Provincial and District Grand Masters
10. Past Provincial and District Grand Masters
11. President of the General Board at Mark Masons' Hall
12. Past Presidents of the General Board at Mark Masons' Hall
13. Grand Senior Warden
14. Past Grand Senior Wardens
15. Grand Junior Warden
16. Past Grand Junior Wardens
17. Grand Inspectors
18. Past Grand Inspectors
19. Grand Master Overseer
20. Past Grand Master Overseer

GRAND LODGE

21. Grand Senior Overseer
22. Past Grand Senior Overseers
22. Grand Junior Overseer
23. Past Grand Junior Overseers
24. Grand Chaplain
25. Past Grand Chaplains
26. Grand Treasurer
27. Past Grand Treasurers
28. Grand Registrar
29. Past Grand Registrars
30. President of the Mark Benevolent Fund.
31. Past Presidents of the Mark Benevolent Fund.
32. President of the Mark Executive Committee
33. Past Presidents of the Mark Executive Committee
34. Grand Secretary
35. Past Grand Secretaries
36. Grand Director of Ceremonies
37. Past Grand Directors of Ceremonies
38. Grand Inspector of Works
39. Past Grand Inspectors of Works
40. Grand Sword Bearer
41. Past Grand Sword Bearers
42. Deputy President of the General Board at Mark Masons' Hall
43. Past Deputy Presidents of the General Board at Mark Masons' Hall
44. Deputy Grand Chaplain
45. Past Deputy Grand Chaplain
46. Deputy Grand Registrar
47. Past Deputy Grand Registrars
48. Deputy President of the Mark Benevolent Fund
49. Past Deputy Presidents of the Mark Benevolent Fund
50. Deputy President of the Mark Executive Committee
51. Past Deputy Presidents of the Mark Executive Committee
52. Deputy Grand Secretary
53. Past Deputy Grand Secretaries
54. Deputy Grand Director of Ceremonies
55. Past Deputy Grand Directors of Ceremonies
56. Deputy Grand Inspector of Works
57. Past Deputy Grand Inspectors of Works
58. Deputy Grand Sword Bearer
59. Past Deputy Grand Sword Bearers
60. Grand Senior Deacons
61. Past Grand Senior Deacons
62. Grand Junior Deacons
63. Past Grand Junior Deacons
64. Assistant Grand Chaplain
65. Past Assistant Grand Chaplains
66. Assistant Grand Registrar
67. Past Assistant Grand Registrars
68. Assistant Grand Secretaries
69. Past Assistant Grand Secretaries
70. Assistant Grand Directors of Ceremonies
71. Past Assistant Grand Directors of Ceremonies
72. Assistant Grand Inspector of Works
73. Past Assistant Grand Inspectors of Works
74. Assistant Grand Sword Bearer
75. Past Assistant Grand Sword Bearers
76. Grand Librarian
77. Past Grand Librarians

GRAND LODGE

78. Grand Organist
79. Past Grand Organists
80. Grand Standard Bearers
81. Past Grand Standard Bearers
82. Assistant Grand Standard Bearers
83. Past Assistant Grand Standard Bearers
84. Assistant Grand Organist
85. Past Assistant Grand Organists
86. Grand Inner Guard
87. Past Grand Inner Guards
88. Assistant Grand Inner Guards
89. Past Assistant Grand Inner Guards
90. Grand Stewards
91. Past Grand Stewards
92. Grand Tyler
93. Past Grand Tylers
94. Deputy Grand Tyler
95. Past Deputy Grand Tylers
96. Masters, Past Masters who are qualified under Rule5, Wardens and Overseers of Private Lodges.

(ii) Officers of the Grand Lodge, holding or having held identical active or past ranks, take rank amongst themselves in order of appointment, provided that Officers of the year take precedence of those holding corresponding past rank.

(iii) Casual vacancies may be filled by the Grand Master.

5. (i) Every Brother regularly elected and installed as Master of a Lodge, who has filled the office for the period from one regular date of installation to the next, or who is deemed under these Rules to have filled such office for that period, shall so long as he continues to be a subscribing member of a Lodge be a member of Grand Lodge, but if for twelve months he has ceased to be a subscribing member of a Lodge, he shall no longer be a member of Grand Lodge, nor can he regain the right of membership of Grand Lodge as a Past Master until he has again become a subscribing member of a Lodge.

(ii) A Brother who resigns from all his Mark Lodges, or only holds Honorary Membership of a Mark Lodge shall be entitled to retain the style and title of his Grand, Provincial or District Rank but shall not be entitled to vote on any matter.

6. (i) The Grand Master, Pro Grand Master, Past Grand Masters, and Past Pro Grand Masters, are entitled to the appellation of "Most Worshipful" (M.W.). The prefix of "Right Worshipful" (R.W.) is accorded to and should be used only by the Deputy Grand Master and Past Deputy Grand Masters, Assistant Grand Master and Past Assistant Grand Masters, Present and Past Provincial and District Grand Masters, Present and Past Presidents of the General Board at Mark Masons' Hall, and Present and Past Grand Wardens of Grand Lodge. The prefix of "Very Worshipful" (V.W.) should be used only by Present and Past Grand Inspectors, Present and Past Grand Overseers, Present and Past Grand Chaplains, Present and Past Grand Treasurers, Present and Past Grand Registrars, President and Past Presidents of the Mark Benevolent Fund, President and Past Presidents of the Mark Executive Committee, Present and Past Grand Secretaries, Present and Past Grand Directors of Ceremonies, and no others. The title or address of "Worshipful" (W.) is to be used by the rest of the Present and Past Grand Officers of Grand Lodge, and by the Present and Past Masters of Lodges, and all other members should be styled or designated as "Brother" only. The prefix "Worshipful" (W.) is also accorded to Masters and Past Masters of Lodges or Chapters of any recognised Constitution.

(ii) Salutes shall be;

Most Worshipful Brethren	11
Present and Past Deputy Grand Masters	9
Present and Past Assistant Grand Masters	9
Other Right Worshipful Brethren	7
Very Worshipful Brethren	5
Other Present and Past Grand Officers	3
Present and Past Provincial,or District and Overseas Officers	3

Present and Past Deputy and Assistant Provincial or District Grand Masters shall be entitled as such to 5, only within their own Provinces or Districts. The Senior Officer shall be saluted, all other salutations being at his discretion.

GRAND LODGE

(iii) No Brother when acting in a higher office may receive a salute other than that to which he is personally entitled.

7. (i) Three regular Grand Lodges shall be holden in each year, on the Tuesday next before the second Wednesday in the months of March, June and September. The Grand Master may summon an additional regular meeting of Grand Lodge to be holden on the second Tuesday in the month of December. Provided that if such regular day of meeting be proclaimed as a public holiday, or if for any reason it should be impracticable or inconvenient to hold the meeting on such day, the Grand Master may direct that the meeting shall be held on some other day in the month of March, June and September as the case may be.

(ii) Such Grand Lodges shall normally be held in London, but, should the Grand Master think fit, one of such Lodges may be held in the Provinces.

8. The Grand Master, or, in his absence, the Pro Grand Master, or, in his absence, the Deputy Grand Master, or in his absence, the Assistant Grand Master, or in their absence, the two Grand Wardens, may summon special Grand Lodges whenever the good of the Order shall, in their opinion, require it. The summons for a special meeting of Grand Lodge shall state the purpose for which it is convened, and no other business shall be entered on at such meeting.

9. (i) All matters of business to be brought under the consideration of Grand Lodge shall be made known previously to the Mark Executive Committee, that through it all the representatives of Lodges may be apprised of such business, and be prepared to decide thereon. A member of Grand Lodge other than a member of the Mark Executive Committee intending to submit a proposition for its consideration shall state in writing the nature of his intended motion or business, which statement shall be laid before the Mark Executive Committee on the third Thursday in January and the first Thursday in April or July.

(ii) No other matter shall be discussed in Grand Lodge without the express permission of the Grand Master.

10. The General Board or the Mark Executive Committee may direct that any notice of motion, memorial, petition or other matter which in its judgment is unseemly, irregular, or not within the cognizance of Grand Lodge, shall be omitted from the list of business to be brought before Grand Lodge. In such case the Brother who gave such notice of motion, or put forward such memorial, petition or other matter, shall be informed of his right to submit to the Grand Master a statement in writing relating thereto.

11. Copies of the Agenda for each meeting of Grand Lodge, together with the minutes of the proceedings of the preceding meeting of Grand Lodge, shall be sent to all Grand Officers, present and past, who are subscribing members of a Lodge, and two copies shall be sent to the Secretary of each Lodge, of which one shall be for the use of the Master. Copies of the Agenda shall also be available for other members of Grand Lodge attending the meetings thereof. Copies of the Agenda and minutes shall also be sent to any other member of the Order who shall register his address for this purpose, and pay in advance such sum for life subscription or such sum per annum as Grand Lodge may from time to time approve. Transmission by electronic means will be deemed an acceptable means of delivery without the requirement for a Brother to give prior permission.

12. If at any meeting of Grand Lodge the Grand Master be absent, Grand Lodge shall be ruled by the Pro Grand Master, or, in his absence, by the Deputy Grand Master, or in his absence, by the Assistant Grand Master, or in his absence, by the member of Grand Lodge present who shall be senior in rank according to the table of precedence contained in Rule 4.

13. Grand Lodge is declared to be opened in ample form when the Grand Master or Pro Grand Master presides, in due form when a Past Grand Master or Past Pro Grand Master or the Deputy or Assistant presides, at other times in form, yet always with the same authority.

14. (i) Grand Lodge being opened, the minutes of the last regular meeting, and of any intervening Grand Lodge shall be read and respectively put for confirmation. Minutes which have been previously circulated may be taken as read unless specifically called for. Reports and communications considered at a previous meeting need not be read in extenso, unless specially called for.

(ii) Communications from the Grand Master shall first be considered, to be followed by reports from the General Board and its Committees, after which the remaining business shall be proceeded with.

(iii) Notices of motions, memorials and petitions shall be considered in the order in which they are received unless the Grand Master shall otherwise direct, and, if renewed by the General Board, or the Mark Executive Committee, shall stand on the paper of business in precedence to all subsequent notices, and shall, so long as renewed, maintain such precedence until they have been considered by Grand Lodge, or otherwise disposed of. Such notices cannot be withdrawn without the consent of Grand Lodge or the General Board.

GRAND LODGE

15. If it shall appear to the Grand Master that any proposed resolution contains anything contrary to the antient Landmarks of the Order, he may refuse to permit the same to be discussed.

16. The consideration of any business before Grand Lodge may, if the Grand Master or Presiding Officer so directs, be adjourned to the next regular meeting of Grand Lodge or to a special meeting to be convened for that purpose.

17. Questions under discussion in Grand Lodge shall ordinarily be decided by show of hands, and the Grand Master or the Presiding Officer shall then declare the motion carried or lost, provided that, if after such declaration a division is demanded by twenty-five or more Brethren, the Ayes shall go to the North and the Noes to the South of Grand Lodge. The numbers shall be ascertained by the Grand Director of Ceremonies.

18. Whenever the Grand Master shall call to order, there shall be general silence.

19. Every speaker shall rise, addressing himself to the Grand Master. He shall not be interrupted, except on a point of order, or unless the Grand Master shall call him to order and in any event shall not speak for more than five (5) minutes.

20. If a member shall have been twice called to order and be guilty of a third offence at the same meeting, or if he shall behave in a manner disrespectful to the Chair or unbecoming a Mason, the Grand Master may command him to quit Grand Lodge during the remainder of such meeting.

21. The proposer of an original motion shall have the right of reply, but no other Brother shall speak twice to the same question, unless by permission. This rule shall not apply to the Grand Registrar or Deputy Grand Registrar, the President or Deputy-President of the General Board, the President or Deputy President of the Mark Executive Committee, or the Grand Secretary.

22. Mark Master Masons of any recognised Constitution, not members of Grand Lodge, may, by permission of the Grand Master, be present as visitors, but shall not speak to any question without leave of the Grand Master, or be permitted to vote. Such Brethren must retire from Grand Lodge if called on by the Grand Master to do so.

23. (i) Save as herein specially provided the General Board shall have control and management of all the property of Grand Lodge. The moneys of Grand Lodge and the Consolidated Account shall be paid to the current account thereof and all investments shall be made in the names of Trustees (being not less than two nor more than four in number) who shall be elected by Grand Lodge and hold office during the pleasure of Grand Lodge. The right to appoint Trustees is vested in Grand Lodge. A Trustee and his estate shall be kept fully indemnified by Grand Lodge in respect of any losses occasioned to the property and assets of Grand Lodge otherwise than as a result of his wilful neglect default or fraud. A nominee company which is a Trust Corporation registered in England and Wales may be appointed by such Trustees to act on their behalf for the purchase holding and sale of the investments of Grand Lodge.

(ii) The accounts of Grand Lodge shall be audited annually by a professional firm of Chartered Accountants which must be registered Auditors, be presented to Grand Lodge in March and be available for inspection in the office of Grand Lodge, and a copy shall be sent to every Private Lodge.

(iii) The auditors shall be elected by Grand Lodge annually and shall hold office during the pleasure of Grand Lodge.

(iv) Nothing in this Rule shall affect the Fund of Benevolence referred to in Rules 165 et seq.

SECTION II
SOVEREIGN GRAND LODGE

24. It shall be lawful for any group of at least three Lodges situate Overseas to make representations to the Grand Master, in the case of Lodges in a District or an Inspectorate, through the District Grand Master or Grand Inspector, as to the desirability of forming a Sovereign Grand Lodge of which such Lodges shall form part, and the Grand Master may grant dispensation to such Lodges, and to any other Lodges which in his opinion might conveniently be grouped with such Lodges in forming a Sovereign Grand Lodge, to consider, either separately or by joint meetings, the desirability of its formation, and thereafter, should he think fit, he may, with the assent of Grand Lodge, give permission for the formation of a Sovereign Grand Lodge and grant recognition to such Sovereign Grand Lodge when formed. Provided always that, save as provided in Rule 25, no Sovereign Grand Lodge shall be recognised as having jurisdiction over any Lodges in a District without the assent of the District Grand Lodge, or as having jurisdiction over any Lodge which has not expressed its desire to be transferred to its jurisdiction when formed. The Grand Master may give such directions as he may think fit for the ascertainment of the wishes of District Grand Lodges or individual Lodges in these matters, and as to the conditions of transfer.

25. After the recognition of a Sovereign Grand Lodge no Warrant shall be granted for the formation of any Lodge within its territory without the assent of such Sovereign Grand Lodge, but this shall not prevent the issue of a Warrant for the formation of a Royal Ark Mariner Lodge to be attached to a Lodge remaining under the jurisdiction of Grand Lodge.

26. It shall also be lawful for a Lodge to express to the Grand Master, in the case of a Lodge in a District or an Inspectorate through the District Grand Master or Grand Inspector, its desire to be transferred to the jurisdiction of an existing Sovereign Grand Lodge, within or near to whose territory it is situate, and the Grand Master, should he think fit may, with the assent of Grand Lodge, give directions for such transfer.

SECTION III

GRAND OFFICERS
GRAND MASTER

27. The Grand Master shall be nominated at the Grand Lodge in September, elected at the Grand Lodge in March, and installed at the Grand Lodge in June.

PRO GRAND MASTER

28. The Grand Master, if a Prince of the Blood Royal, may appoint a Pro Grand Master, who shall in all respects rank as Grand Master.

29. (i) Should the Grand Master die or resign during his Mastership, the Pro Grand Master or Deputy Grand Master, or the Assistant Grand Master, or in their absence the Senior Grand Officer available shall assume the duties and powers of Grand Master and shall summon a meeting of Grand Lodge to elect a Grand Master.

(ii) The Grand Master elect shall at once assume the duties and powers of Grand Master and shall be installed at the next regular meeting of Grand Lodge, or at a special Grand Lodge, as he may desire.

DEPUTY GRAND MASTER

30. The Deputy Grand Master shall be appointed annually by the Grand Master on the day of his installation, and shall possess all the powers and privileges of the Grand Master or Pro Grand Master in their absence.

ASSISTANT GRAND MASTER

31. The Assistant Grand Master shall be appointed annually by the Grand Master on the day of his installation and in the absence of the Grand Master, the Pro Grand Master and the Deputy Grand Master, shall possess all the powers and privileges of the Grand Master.

32. (i) Upon the annual installation of the Grand Master he may appoint the following Grand Officers, who shall thereupon be invested in antient form:-

President of the General Board at Mark Masons' Hall
Grand Senior Warden
Grand Junior Warden
Grand Master Overseer
Grand Senior Overseer
Grand Junior Overseer
Grand Chaplain
Grand Registrar
President of the Mark Benevolent Fund
President of the Mark Executive Committee
Grand Director of Ceremonies
Grand Inspector of Works
Grand Sword Bearer
Deputy President of the General Board at Mark Masons' Hall
Deputy Grand Chaplain
Deputy Grand Registrar
Deputy President of the Mark Benevolent Fund
Deputy President of the Mark Executive Committee
Three Deputy Grand Directors of Ceremonies
Deputy Grand Inspector of Works
Deputy Grand Sword Bearer
Six Grand Senior Deacons
Six Grand Junior Deacons
Assistant Grand Chaplain
Assistant Grand Registrar
Six Assistant Grand Directors of Ceremonies
Assistant Grand Inspector of Works
Assistant Grand Sword Bearer
Grand Organist
Two Grand Standard Bearers
Two Assistant Grand Standard Bearers
Assistant Grand Organist

GRAND OFFICERS

Grand Inner Guard
Two Assistant Grand Inner Guards
Twenty-four Grand Stewards.

(ii) A Deputy Grand Secretary, two Assistant Grand Secretaries, a Grand Librarian and a Deputy Grand Tyler may also be appointed.

(iii) If a Grand Officer is absent from a meeting of Grand Lodge, the Grand Master may appoint any member of Grand Lodge to act in his place.

(iv) Grand Officers must be installed Masters; provided that the Grand Master may from time to time appoint Brethren of eminence and distinction, whether so qualified or not, to such Past Grand rank as he may deem advisable.

(v) A Brother shall not hold more than one office in Grand Lodge at one and the same time, save that a Provincial or District Grand Master may hold one other office.

(vi) Casual vacancies may be filled by the Grand Master at any time and at any meeting of Grand Lodge, a Provincial or District Grand Lodge, or a Regular Mark Lodge.

33. The Grand Master is empowered to confer on Brethren who have rendered special service to The Mark Degree a distinction to be known as: "The Order of Service to Mark Masonry"

34. (i) The Grand Treasurer shall be nominated at Grand Lodge in September, elected in March, and invested at Grand Lodge in June.

(ii) The election of the Grand Treasurer shall be by ballot, and be conducted in a similar manner to that of the elected members of the Mark Executive Committee.

35. The Grand Secretary shall be appointed by the Grand Master, and shall hold office without reappointment during the pleasure of Grand Lodge.

36. The Grand Tyler shall be appointed by the Grand Master, and shall hold office during his pleasure.

37. The Grand Master may require any of the Grand Officers of the year to attend him when visiting Provincial or District Grand Lodges or private Lodges.

38. The Grand Registrar shall affix, or may authorise the Grand Secretary to affix, the Seal of Grand Lodge to all patents, warrants, certificates, and other documents issued by the authority of Grand Lodge, as well as to such as the Grand Master, in conformity with the established laws and regulations of the Order, may direct. He shall superintend the records of Grand Lodge, and take care that all documents be issued in due form. He shall also keep, or cause to be kept, a record of the Marks of all Brethren registered in the books of Grand Lodge.

39. (i) The Grand Secretary shall sign certificates, issue summonses for all meetings of Grand Lodge, and of the General Board and its Committees, and attend and take minutes thereof, receive returns from the several Lodges, and enter them in the books of Grand Lodge, receive fees and contributions payable by Lodges or Brethren, and pay or cause the same to be paid to the Consolidated Account of Grand Lodge; transmit to all Lodges accounts of the proceedings of the meetings of Grand Lodge, and all papers and documents which may be ordered by the Grand Master, Grand Lodge, or the General Board; receive all petitions, memorials, etc., and submit them to the Grand Master or other proper authority; attend upon the Grand Master with any books or papers he may require; and generally do all such things as heretofore have been done or ought to be done by a Grand Secretary. Under the authority of the Grand Registrar, he shall affix the Seal of Grand Lodge to patents, warrants, certificates or other documents. He shall also have the care of the Seal, regalia, clothing, insignia and jewels of Grand Lodge. The Grand Secretary shall have the power to delegate all or part of his duties to a Chief Executive Officer.

(ii) Applications to the Grand Master concerning Masonic business shall be made through the Grand Secretary.

40. The Grand Inspector of Works shall advise the General Board when requested on any matter connected with building and work. He shall furnish reports on the state of repair of the properties of Grand Lodge when requested.

41. The Grand Director of Ceremonies shall have the arrangement and direction of all processions and ceremonies of Grand Lodge, and shall preside over all Brethren summoned to assist under Rules 37 and 44 or otherwise.

42. The Grand Inner Guard shall attend every meeting of Grand Lodge, preserve order within the porch, and see that none be admitted except those properly clothed.

43. The Grand Tyler shall attend all regular meetings of Grand Lodge, and act under the instructions of

GRAND OFFICERS

the Grand Director of Ceremonies.

44. (i) Twenty-four Grand Stewards shall be annually appointed by the Grand Master. Once in each year an invitation to nominate an Installed Master to be appointed Grand Steward will be sent to 24 Provincial Grand Lodges by the Grand Secretary for submission to the Grand Master for approval as a Grand Steward for that year.

(ii) The Grand Stewards shall be responsible for the regulation of the Grand Festival to be held after the Grand Lodge in June and shall so arrange that no expenses thereof shall fall on the funds of Grand Lodge. They shall also when directed attend in the porch of Grand Lodge for the purpose of assisting the Grand Director of Ceremonies.

45. The name, residence, and qualification of a Brother recommended as a Grand Steward shall be transmitted to the Grand Secretary by the last day of February in each year.

46. Should a Lodge or Provincial Grand Lodge fail to make a nomination by the prescribed date, or should a Brother nominated decline to serve, or be incapable of discharging the duties of a Grand Steward, or fail to receive the approval of the Grand Master, the right of nomination shall vest in the Grand Master.

47. The Grand Stewards shall have the exclusive privilege of becoming members of the Grand Stewards' Lodge, subject to its by-laws and regulations.

48. Should the Grand Master be dissatisfied with the conduct of any Grand Officer he may refer the subject of the complaint to the Mark Executive Committee, and should the Committee report that the complaint is well founded, he may displace such Grand Officer and appoint another, or in the case of a Past Grand Officer he may deprive him of his rank and privileges.

SECTION IV
GENERAL BOARD AT MARK MASONS' HALL

49. (i) The General Board shall consist of the President of the General Board, Grand Treasurer, Grand Registrar, President of the Mark Benevolent Fund, President of the Mark Executive Committee, Grand Secretary, Grand Inspector of Works, the Grand Masters for the time being of all Orders administered from Mark Masons' Hall provided their membership is greater than two thousand five hundred (2,500) subscribing members, the Deputy President of the General Board, and the Chairman of the Foreign Relations Committee, all of whom shall be Masters or Past Masters of Lodges, such members being appointed as by the Grand Master at the June meeting of Grand Lodge. Vacancies on the Board may be filled as directed by the Grand Master.

(ii) Each of the appointed members shall hold the appointment during the Grand Master's pleasure.

(iii) The Grand Master, Pro Grand Master, Deputy Grand Master and Assistant Grand Master are entitled to receive all agendas, minutes and other papers sent to the members of the General Board and are entitled to attend and speak at meetings of the General Board but will not be eligible to vote. Electronic transmission of these documents is permissible provided the recipient has given prior permission for this method of transmission.

(iv) A member of the General Board at Mark Masons' Hall shall, provided he is a holder of Grand Rank in the Ancient and Honourable Fraternity of Royal Ark Mariners, wear a collarette consisting of a rainbow ribbon one inch and a quarter in width worn close round the neck with a winged globe, having gold wings, suspended therefrom. (Plate No. 31 RAM Regulations)

50. (i) The regular meetings of the Board shall be held on the first Thursday in the months of April, July, October and the third Thursday in January. The Grand Master or the President may from time to time direct that:

(a) the date for holding of a regular meeting of the Board be changed to a date not more than seven days before or after the date hereinbefore prescribed and in such event notice in writing shall be given to all members of the Board not later than fourteen days before the regular date or the changed date (whichever shall be the earlier);

(b) a special meeting of the Board be convened and in such event not less than fourteen days notice in writing thereof shall be given to all members of the Board and such notice shall specify the business to be transacted at such special meeting. The meetings of the Board shall be at such hour as the President shall direct.

(c) In all cases a document may be delivered electronically to a Brother provided that the Brother has previously agreed to accept delivery by electronic means.

(ii) Should the President be absent the Deputy President shall preside and if both be absent the Board shall name one of its members to preside.

51. Three members shall constitute a Board except when considering Masonic complaints, disputes or matters of discipline when acting as an Appeal Court, when five members must be present. Where such consideration affects a member of the Board or a Lodge to which he belongs, such member shall withdraw while the Board deliberates.

52. Except as otherwise expressly directed by resolution of Grand Lodge or by these Rules the Board shall have the control and regulation of all the business of Grand Lodge, and in particular the Board:

(a) Shall have the direction of everything relating to the buildings, furniture, and other property of Grand Lodge.

(b) Shall have control of the finances of the Consolidated Account, examine all demands thereon, and authorise payment of the same.

(c) Shall appoint, control and dismiss all clerks and other employees of Grand Lodge, and shall regulate all salaries.

(d) Shall conduct the correspondence between Grand Lodge and its subordinate Lodges and Brethren. Communications with other Sovereign Grand Lodges or Chapters, or with Lodges, Chapters or Brethren of recognised Constitutions, shall be conducted by the Grand Secretary under the direction of the Grand Master, and be reported to the Board and the Mark Executive Committee.

(e) The Board may delegate all or any of its functions to the Grand Secretary.

53. The Board shall make a report to Grand Lodge at each regular meeting, which shall set out any proposals for the good of the Order, and any other matters which in the opinion of the Board should be communicated to Grand Lodge, and shall include a summary of payments made from the Mark Benevolent Fund, granted since the date of the last report. Copies of such report shall be distributed as provided in Rule 11.

GENERAL BOARD AT MARK MASONS' HALL

54. The Board may appoint Committees for such purposes it may deem proper, but no such Committee shall have any executive powers unless they are expressly given to them by resolution of the Board.

(i) In particular the Board shall create a Mark Executive Committee. The Mark Executive Committee shall consist of the Grand Master, Deputy Grand Master, Assistant Grand Master, President of the General Board at Mark Masons' Hall, President of the Executive Committee (Chair), Grand Registrar, Grand Treasurer, Grand Secretary, Grand Director of Ceremonies, Deputy President of the Mark Executive Committee, two serving Provincial Grand Masters elected by ballot at the June Investiture meeting of Grand Lodge, two serving Provincial Grand Masters nominated by the Grand Master. A casual vacancy amongst the members shall be filled by appointment by the Grand Master.

(ii) In the absence of the President of the Mark Executive Committee the Deputy President will preside. In the event that the President and Deputy President are absent then the highest ranking voting Brother will preside. The Brother presiding shall, in the event of equality of votes, have a casting vote.

(iii) The Executive Committee shall meet four times per year on on such days as shall be determined by its President.

(iv) A special meeting may be convened by the Grand Master or the President at seven days' notice.

(v) Each of the elected or nominated members may be appointed for a period of up to five years, and may be re-elected or re-nominated for a similar period of up to five years, but at all times hold the appointment at the pleasure of the Grand Master.

(vi) An elected or nominated member who has served two consecutive terms of five years shall not be eligible for a further period of election or nomination until twelve months after the ending of his second term of office.

(vii) Four members shall constitute a quorum except when considering Masonic complaints, disputes or matters of discipline, when five members must be present.

(viii) The Executive Committee shall make a report to the General Board at each regular meeting.

(ix) The Terms of Reference of the Mark Executive Committee are as follows:

(a) To approve and submit to the Communication of the Grand Lodge for ratification, proposed amendments to the Statutes or rituals of the Grand Lodge. Where a change in the Constitutions could affect the other Orders the change shall be agreed by the General Board.

(b) To consider the agendas of the Meetings of Grand Lodge.

(c) To ensure that its members respect their duties, in particular that of confidentiality, and to sanction any breaches of the rules.

(d) To hear and determine all subjects of Masonic complaint or irregularity respecting Lodges or individual Brethren. The Mark Executive Committee may chose to remit the matter to a Disciplinary Committee empowered to act on behalf of the Mark Executive Committee.

(e) To determine applications for Bi-Centenary, Centenary, and Jubilee Warrants, Jubilee jewel designs, Lodge Banners, charity jewel designs, and all items of regalia.

(f) To approve the exceptional appointment of an Assistant Provincial / District Grand Master for a Province / District not entitled to appoint such Officer under Rule 71(iii) of the Constitutions and Regulations

(g) To approve changes of name of Lodges and the amalgamation of Lodges

(h) To recommend to the General Board the Constitution of a new Province or District.

(i) To note the appointment of all Provincial / District Grand Masters

(j) The Executive Committee shall make a report to the Grand Lodge of Mark Master Masons, which shall set out any proposals for the good of the Order and any other matters which in the opinion of the Executive Committee should be communicated to the Grand Lodge. Copies of this report should be included in the agenda for the June Investiture meeting.

(k) Official Communications from the Executive Committee shall be made in writing and may be in electronic format provided the recipients have previously agreed to this method of transmission.

(l) All transactions and resolutions of the Executive Committee shall be duly recorded in a Minute book

GENERAL BOARD AT MARK MASONS' HALL

55. (i) Recommendations, petitions and representations to the Board or any of its Committees can only be received in writing and signed by the Brother or other person addressing the Board.

(ii) Official communications from the Board shall be made in writing.

56. All transactions and resolutions of the Board shall be duly recorded in the minute book.

COMPLAINTS, IRREGULARITIES, DISPUTES AND APPEALS

57. (i) A Provincial or District Grand Master shall hear and determine all subjects of Masonic complaint or irregularity respecting Lodges or individual Brethren within his Province or District. He shall send to the Grand Secretary a report, stating the complaint or alleged irregularity, and any circumstances relevant thereto, and his decision thereon.

(ii) The Mark Executive Committee shall have the same Powers in regard to all subjects of complaint or irregularity, (a) respecting Lodges or Brethren not within a Province or District; (b) relating to returns to Grand Lodge or payments in respect of such returns.

(iii) A Provincial or District Grand Master or the Mark Executive Committee may in any such case admonish or suspend an offending Lodge, or an Officer or member thereof, or an offending Brother, subject to an appeal to the Appeal Court.

(iv) Notwithstanding the reporting of matters under Rule 58 it is the duty of a Provincial or District Grand Master to report to the Grand Secretary each custodial sentence (immediate or suspended) and any sentence in respect of dishonesty, violence, or moral turpitude imposed by any civil power, whether in the United Kingdom or elsewhere, on a member of a Lodge within his Province or District. And it is his duty to report to the Grand Secretary other conduct which is likely to bring the Order into disrepute.

58. A Brother sentenced by any civil power whether in the United Kingdom or elsewhere to a custodial sentence (immediate or suspended) or any sentence in respect of an offence of dishonesty, violence or moral turpitude shall report the same within 28 days to the Master of his Lodge and the Provincial or District Grand Secretary, or, if he be Unattached, to the Grand Secretary.

59. (i) Subject to the provisions of Rule 57 the Mark Executive Committee may for just cause suspend any Lodge, or may suspend any Brother from any or all of his activities within the Order, and a Provincial or District Grand Master may suspend any Lodge within his jurisdiction, or any Brother within such jurisdiction from any or all activities within the Order in such Province or District. Suspension may be for a definite or indefinite period and may include terms appropriate to the case.

(ii) If a Lodge is suspended it shall remain liable for payment of all dues in respect of its members to Grand Lodge and to a Provincial or District Grand Lodge, and each member shall pay a sum necessary to cover payment for his dues and a proportional part of any other expenses incurred by the Lodge, and notwithstanding such suspension the Officers of the Lodge shall take any steps necessary for the payment of dues and other necessary expenses of the Lodge and the collection of contributions from its members, and the making of any necessary returns. During the period of suspension no member or Officer shall be entitled to any privilege of the Order by virtue of membership of such Lodge.

(iii) If a Brother is suspended he shall nevertheless remain liable for payment of subscriptions to all Lodges of which he is a member, as well as any other sums due to such Lodges, but shall have the right to resign from any or all of such Lodges.

60. (i) If a Provincial or District Grand Master, the Mark Executive Committee, or the General Board should be of the opinion that the conduct of a Lodge has been of such a character as to merit erasure, he or they shall either with or without imposing any other penalty, refer the matter to Grand Lodge with a recommendation that the Lodge be erased. In all such cases the Master and Wardens of the Lodge shall be given due notice by the Grand Secretary to appear before Grand Lodge or submit a written statement to show cause why Grand Lodge should not act on such recommendation, before any resolution is moved for the erasure of the Lodge.

(ii) If a Provincial or District Grand Master or the Mark Executive Committee should be of the opinion that the conduct of a Brother has been of such a character as to merit expulsion, he or they shall either with or without imposing any other penalty, refer the matter to a Disciplinary Committee as defined in the Mark Executive Committee terms of reference, with a recommendation that the Brother be expelled from the order.

(iii) Provided always that Grand Lodge shall have power to order erasure, even if no such recommendation has been made, but unless a representative of the Lodge is present the question of erasure shall be adjourned to a subsequent meeting of Grand Lodge and the Master and Wardens of the Lodge be given notice to show cause why an order should not be made for erasure.

GENERAL BOARD AT MARK MASONS' HALL

(iv) A Provincial or District Grand Master or the Grand Secretary or the Disciplinary Committee may recommend to the Mark Executive Committee that a Brother be invited to resign from the Order. The Mark Executive Committee after receiving such a recommendation or on its own motion may direct that the Brother in question be invited to resign from the Order.

(v) (a) If the Mark Executive Committee direct that a Brother be invited to resign from the Order the Grand Secretary shall notify the Brother in writing.

(b) Such resignation shall be in writing signed by the Brother concerned and shall be delivered to the Grand Secretary not later than 28 days after delivery to the Brother of the notice of invitation to resign (or within such longer period as the Grand Secretary may allow).

(c) The resignation shall specifically refer to Rule 60(iv) and shall be accompanied by the Brother's Grand Lodge Certificate.

(d) If the Brother so requests in his resignation the Grand Secretary (subject to any conditions imposed by him) may waive delivery of such Certificate.

(e) The Grand Secretary shall forthwith notify the resignation to the Secretary of each Lodge of which the Brother was a member. Where applicable such notification shall be made to the relevant Provincial or District Grand Master.

(f) If the Brother so invited to resign shall fail to comply with any requirement of or any condition imposed under this Rule the invitation to resign shall thereby be withdrawn and the Grand Secretary shall refer the matter to the Disciplinary Committee for further consideration.

61. (i) It is acknowledged that, notwithstanding the obligations of a Freemason are lifetime obligations, circumstances may arise when a Brother wishes to resign voluntarily from the Order of Mark Master Masons (and the Degree of the Ancient and Honourable Fraternity of Royal Ark Mariners). If such arises, a Brother may apply to the Grand Secretary, indicating his wish to resign, naming all the Lodges in the Order and the Ancient and Honourable Fraternity of which he is a member, and fully stating his reasons for wishing to resign and enclosing his Grand Lodge Certificate(s). Upon receipt of any such request, it will be placed before the Grand Master who shall have the sole and absolute discretion to accept or reject any such request. If any such request is granted, the same shall take effect from the date of receipt by the Grand Secretary. The Grand Secretary shall notify the Brother within 30 days as to whether or not his request has been granted.

(ii) If a Brother has resigned under (i) above, he may at any time thereafter apply to the Grand Secretary with a request that his resignation be rescinded and the Grand Master may rescind the same on such terms and conditions as he thinks fit. If the Grand Master rescinds the Brother's resignation, he shall immediately be restored to the rank and position he held immediately before his resignation, provided that he shall not be restored to a rank above that of Past Master unless the Grand Master specifically orders.

(iii) Any request by a Brother to resign or to rescind his resignation under this Rule and any response by the Grand Secretary on behalf of the Grand Master must be in writing and contain a specific reference to this Rule.

62. (i) The Mark Executive Committee may summon the Officers of a Lodge to attend and produce the Warrant, books, papers and accounts thereof, and to answer questions relative to its affairs, or a Brother to attend and produce his Certificate and to answer questions regarding his conduct, and a Provincial or District Grand Master shall have similar powers with regard to a Lodge or Brother within his Province or District. Provided that if by reason of distance or other sufficient cause personal attendance would impose great difficulty, it shall suffice if the Lodge or Brother send the documents required, and answer in writing questions put by the Mark Executive Committee or the Provincial or District Grand Master.

(ii) If the summons be not complied with, and no sufficient reason given for non-compliance, the Lodge or its Officers, or the Brother, may be suspended, and the proceedings reported to Grand Lodge.

63. (i) Should any Masonic question, dispute, or difference arise which cannot be settled between the parties thereto, any party may apply in writing for its determination:

(a) If such question, dispute or difference arises in a place not within a Province or District, to the Grand Secretary who shall lay the matter before the Mark Executive Committee.

(b) If such question arises in a Province or District, to the Provincial or District Grand Secretary who shall lay the matter before the Provincial or District Grand Master.

(ii) The decision of the Mark Executive Committee or of a Provincial or District Grand Master shall be binding on all parties, subject to an appeal to the Appeal Court.

(iii) In any such case a Provincial or District Grand Master shall send to the Grand Secretary a report showing the nature of the question, dispute or difference, with any circumstances relevant thereto, and his decision thereon.

GENERAL BOARD AT MARK MASONS' HALL

64. Notwithstanding any provisions in Rules 57 and 63 the Grand Master may direct that any matter shall be determined by Grand Lodge, the Disciplinary Committee or by a named Provincial or District Grand Master, or by the Mark Executive Committee, or by a special Tribunal appointed by him with such powers as he may deem appropriate, and there shall be no appeal against such direction.

65. In any matter arising under Rules 57 to 63 the competent Authority, before arriving at a decision, shall give all parties due opportunity of being heard or of submitting written statements and giving or adducing relevant evidence, provided that, if in the opinion of such Authority harm may arise from delay, it may temporarily suspend a Lodge or Brother, or require a Lodge or Brother to do or abstain from doing any specified act or acts pending the hearing and decision of the matter, but in any such case a report of such action and the reason therefore shall be made forthwith to the Grand Secretary.

66. (i) Any Lodge or Brother feeling aggrieved by the decision of a Provincial or District Grand Master, the Mark Executive Committee, or any other Body or Authority in the Order whatsoever, may appeal against such a decision within twenty-one days to the Appeal Court. The appeal must be made in writing, specifying the particular grievance complained of and the grounds of appeal, and be transmitted, together with all documentary evidence, including any report of oral evidence, to the Grand Secretary accompanied by a certificate that notices and copies of the appeal have been sent by the appellant to the Authority against whose decision the appeal is made, and also to the opposite party, and on the hearing of the appeal the proof of the service of the notices and the copies of appeal shall, unless admitted, be upon the appellant. Such notices shall be considered duly served if proved to have been sent by registered letter or recorded delivery to the last known address of the Brother or Brethren concerned or to the Secretary of the Lodge, or as may be directed under Rule 160. No appeal can be received unless couched in proper and respectful language.

(ii) Any other party affected may, and if so directed by the General Board shall, submit a like statement with copies of any additional evidence which such a party may wish to advance, and the appellant may submit a statement in reply. No evidence shall be adduced by a party other than that given before the Authority appealed from without the leave of the Appeal Court.

(iii) (a) The Appeal Court shall be constituted from a panel of twelve members. Six of the members shall be appointed annually by the Grand Master at the June meeting of Grand Lodge. The remaining six members shall be elected at the June meeting of Grand Lodge. At the first elections two of the six members shall serve for three years, two of the six members shall serve for two years and the remaining two of the six members shall serve for one year. Subject to the foregoing the elected members shall serve for three years. Any elected member shall be eligible for re-election. One of the appointed members shall be designated by the Grand Master to be President of the Appeal Court. Members of the General Board shall not be eligible for appointment or election to membership of the Appeal Court.

(b) The Grand Master is empowered to make an appointment in the event of a vacancy occurring.

(c) A quorum of the Appeal Court shall be three, at least one of whom shall be legally qualified. In the event of equality the presiding member for the time being shall have a second or casting vote. In the event of an emergency the quorum may be reduced to not less than two members one of whom shall be legally qualified.

(d) The President of the Appeal Court, after consultation with the Grand Secretary, shall decide the time and place of each appeal and reference and the constitution of the Court.

(e) In so far as these Rules do not provide, the Appeal Court shall decide the procedure to be adopted for each appeal and reference.

(f) For the purpose of these Rules the Appeal Court is a 'competent authority' and an 'authority'

(g) On any Appeal the Appeal Court may confirm or reverse or vary the decision by increasing or reducing the penalty and in relation to a Brother may make a recommendation that the Brother be invited to resign under Rule 60(iv) or may pronounce the expulsion of a Brother, and in relation to a Lodge may make a recommendation to Grand Lodge under Rule 60(i) that a Lodge be erased.

(h) On any reference under Rule 48 or Rule 63 the Appeal Court may make such an order or report as may be just.

(j) The decision of the Appeal Court shall be final save that Grand Lodge alone shall have the power to erase.

(k) Should the circumstances so warrant the Appeal Court may impose such penalty or penalties as it may think fit on any other party affected under Rule 66(ii).

GENERAL BOARD AT MARK MASONS' HALL

(l) Orders of suspension and exclusion shall continue pending appeal unless the Appeal Court shall otherwise direct.

(m) Any decision to suspend or expel a Brother from any Order administered by Mark Masons' Hall will ipso facto apply to all of the other Orders so administered.

(iv) If by reason of distance or other sufficient cause it is not practicable for a Brother or the Officers of a Lodge concerned in any complaint, appeal, or reference to attend at the consideration thereof, it shall be in order for the Brother of the Lodge to request a member of Grand Lodge to represent his or its interests at such consideration but there shall be no obligation on that member to comply with such request.

67. In the case of any complaint, charge, dispute or appeal the Authority charged with its decision may give any directions as to interlocutory matters, and may also extend the time for doing any act, or excuse compliance with any requirement in these Rules, if in its opinion no injustice will be caused thereby.

68. Grand Lodge, the Mark Executive Committee, or a Provincial or District Grand Master, may appoint a Committee consisting of one or more Brethren to investigate and report on any matter which may come before them respectively, and may adopt and act on such report wholly or in part. A Committee appointed by a Provincial or District Grand Master shall consist of a Brother or Brothers of his Province or District unless in any case the Grand Master may be pleased to direct otherwise, but a Committee appointed by the Mark Executive Committee need not consist of, or include, a member or members of that Board.

SECTION V

PROVINCIAL AND DISTRICT GRAND MASTERS, AND PROVINCIAL AND DISTRICT GRAND LODGES

69. The Grand Master has power to constitute any specified area in England, Wales or the islands adjacent thereto a Province, and to constitute any specified area Overseas a District, and to create a Provincial or District Grand Lodge having jurisdiction within such areas, and to combine, divide, or re-arrange Provinces or Districts or direct that a Province or District shall cease to exist. The Grand Master may direct that an existing Lodge under the jurisdiction of Mark Grand Lodge shall form part of an existing Province or District, or may direct that a Lodge or Lodges in a Province or District shall cease to form part of such Province or District.

70. (i) A Provincial or District Grand Master shall be appointed by the Grand Master by Patent to hold office during his pleasure. He must be qualified as an Installed Master of a regular Lodge and must also be a subscribing member of a Lodge in the Province or District. By such Patent he shall be granted powers and jurisdiction similar to those possessed by the Grand Master, but only within his Province or District, except as in these rules may be otherwise provided, but shall not assume such powers and jurisdiction until he has been invested and installed. He shall be invested and installed at the next regular Provincial or District Grand Lodge, or at a special Provincial or District Grand Lodge summoned for that purpose, and after installation shall in his Province or District take precedence over all save the Grand Master, Pro Grand Master or Deputy or Assistant Grand Master, and past holders of these offices.

(ii) All applications to the Grand Master or the General Board by Lodges or Brethren in a Province or District shall be made through the Provincial or District Grand Master or his nominee.

71. (i) To ensure the regular performance of the duties of his office, a Provincial or District Grand Master may by Patent appoint a Deputy, to hold office during his pleasure, who must be qualified as an Installed Master of a regular Lodge and must also be a subscribing member of a Lodge in the Province or District, to execute all the functions of the office in his name.

(ii) In his Province or District the Deputy shall rank immediately after the Provincial or District Grand Master.

(iii) For each complete forty Lodges in a Province or District, whether of Mark Master Masons or Royal Ark Mariners, the Provincial or District Grand Master may also appoint an Assistant Provincial or Assistant District Grand Master, to hold office during his pleasure, who in the Province or District shall rank immediately after the Deputy Provincial or Deputy District Grand Master. Each such Assistant Provincial or Assistant District Grand Master must be qualified as an Installed Master of a regular Lodge and must also be a subscribing member of a Lodge in the Province or District.

(iv) Provided that in any District, if it shall appear to the Grand Master that the area of the District, the means of communication, or other sufficient reason renders such a provision desirable, he may authorise the District Grand Master to appoint such a number of Assistant District Grand Masters as he may direct without regard to the limitation hereinbefore stated.

(v) In the case of Unattached Lodges Overseas not under the jurisdiction of a District Grand Master, the Grand Master shall have the power to form them, or any or any one of them, into a group or groups, and to confer upon a Brother or Brethren appointed by him such jurisdiction as he may think fit in respect of any such group, or of any such Unattached Overseas Lodges. The Grand Master shall, at any time, and from time to time, have the power to alter such groups, to extend or limit such jurisdiction, and to remove any Brother in his place. A Brother while holding such appointment shall be styled Grand Inspector and, may be appointed at the Grand Master's pleasure.

72. The Provincial or District Grand Master must transmit, in writing, the name and place of abode of his Deputy and Assistants, to all the Lodges of his Province or District, and also to the Grand Secretary for registration, within one month of the appointment.

73. (i) In the event of the death, resignation, removal or suspension of a Provincial or District Grand Master, the Deputy Provincial or Deputy District Grand Master or the Assistant Provincial or Assistant District Grand Master shall act in his place until another Brother has been appointed and installed as Provincial or District Grand Master or the suspension removed, and shall be designated by the title of his office with the addition of the words "in charge".

(ii) If at any time the Provincial or District Grand Master be not available, the Deputy Provincial or Deputy District Grand Master or the Assistant Provincial or Assistant District Grand Master shall exercise his functions subject to any directions he may give.

PROVINCIAL AND DISTRICT GRAND MASTERS, AND PROVINCIAL AND DISTRICT GRAND LODGES

(iii) If there shall be no Deputy Provincial or Deputy District Grand Master, or Assistant Provincial or Assistant District Grand Master, or if they be not available, the senior Grand Officer in the Province, and then available, shall act as is directed above.

74. A Provincial or District Grand Lodge consists of the Provincial or District Grand Master with the Provincial or District Grand Officers present or past, and the Masters, Wardens and Overseers of every Lodge in the Province or District, together with Masters of Lodges, and Past Masters qualified under Rule 5, who are subscribing members of Lodges in the Province or District.

75. (i) A Provincial or District Grand Master shall hold an annual Provincial or District Grand Lodge, at which the appointment of the Provincial or District Grand Officers shall be made, and shall also hold such other meetings of the Provincial or District Grand Lodge as he shall consider necessary. All such meetings shall be held within the Province or District, unless a dispensation is granted by the Grand Master.

(ii) Should a Provincial or District Grand Officer be absent from any such meeting, the Provincial or District Grand Master may direct any member of the Provincial or District Grand Lodge to act in his place.

76. (i) Should the Provincial or District Grand Master be absent, the Provincial or District Grand Lodge shall be ruled by his Deputy or Assistant, or failing him by such member of the Lodge (being an Installed Master) as the Provincial or District Grand Master may designate.

(ii) When a Provincial or District Grand Master presides, Provincial or District Grand Lodge is to be declared open in due form; if the Deputy or any other Brother presides, in form only, yet always with the same authority.

77. (i) A Provincial or District Grand Master is empowered to appoint annually the following Provincial or District Grand Officers, all of whom must be Subscribing members of a Lodge in his Province or District:—

(a) In the case of a Province or District containing 10 or less Lodges, a Senior and Junior Warden, a Master, Senior and Junior Overseer, a Chaplain, a Registrar, a Secretary, a Director of Ceremonies, an Almoner, a Charity Steward, an Inspector of Works, a Sword Bearer, a Deputy Chaplain, a Deputy Secretary, a Deputy Director of Ceremonies, one Senior and one Junior Deacon, an Assistant Chaplain, an Organist, a Standard Bearer, an Inner Guard, not more than four Stewards, and a Tyler.

(b) In the case of a Province or District containing more than 10 and less than 21 Lodges, a Senior and Junior Warden, a Master, Senior and Junior Overseer, a Chaplain, a Registrar, a Secretary, a Director of Ceremonies, an Almoner, a Charity Steward, an Inspector of Works, a Sword Bearer, a Deputy Chaplain, a Deputy Secretary, a Deputy Director of Ceremonies, one Senior and one Junior Deacon, an Assistant Chaplain, an Assistant Director of Ceremonies, an Organist, a Standard Bearer, an Inner Guard, not more than four Stewards, and a Tyler.

(c) In the case of a Province or District containing more than 20 and less than 35 Lodges, a Senior and Junior Warden, a Master, Senior and Junior Overseer, a Chaplain, a Registrar, a Secretary, a Director of Ceremonies, an Almoner, a Charity Steward, an Inspector of Works, a Sword Bearer, a Deputy Chaplain, a Deputy Secretary, a Deputy Director of Ceremonies, two Senior and two Junior Deacons, an Assistant Chaplain, (except that in a Province or District having 40 or more Lodges whether of Mark Master Masons or Royal Ark Mariners, an Assistant Secretary may also be appointed), two Assistant Directors of Ceremonies, an Organist, a Standard Bearer, an Inner Guard, not more than four Stewards, and a Tyler.

(d) In the case of a Province or District containing more than 35 and less than 56 Lodges, a Senior and Junior Warden, a Master, Senior and Junior Overseer, a Chaplain, a Registrar, a Secretary, a Director of Ceremonies, an Almoner, a Charity Steward, an Inspector of Works, a Sword Bearer, a Deputy Chaplain, a Deputy Secretary, a Deputy Director of Ceremonies, three Senior and three Junior Deacons, an Assistant Chaplain, an Assistant Secretary, four Assistant Directors of Ceremonies, an Organist, a Standard Bearer, an Inner Guard, not more than four Stewards and a Tyler.

(e) In the case of a Province or District containing more than 55 and less than 78 Lodges, a Senior and Junior Warden, a Master, Senior and Junior Overseer, a Chaplain, a Registrar, a Secretary, a Director of Ceremonies, an Almoner, a Charity Steward, an Inspector of Works, a Sword Bearer, a Deputy Chaplain, a Deputy Secretary, a Deputy Director of Ceremonies, a Deputy Sword Bearer, four Senior and four Junior Deacons, an Assistant Chaplain, an Assistant

PROVINCIAL AND DISTRICT GRAND MASTERS, AND PROVINCIAL AND DISTRICT GRAND LODGES

Secretary, six Assistant Directors of Ceremonies, an Organist, a Standard Bearer, an Assistant Standard Bearer, an Inner Guard not more than six Stewards, and a Tyler.

(f) In the case of a Province or District containing 78 or more Lodges, a Senior and Junior Warden, a Master, Senior and Junior Overseer, a Chaplain, a Registrar, a Secretary, a Director of Ceremonies, an Almoner, two Charity Stewards, an Inspector of Works, a Sword Bearer, a Deputy Chaplain, a Deputy Secretary, a Deputy Director of Ceremonies, a Deputy Sword Bearer, six Senior and six Junior Deacons, two Assistant Chaplains, two Assistant Secretaries, eight Assistant Directors of Ceremonies, an Organist, two Standard Bearers, two Assistant Standard Bearers, a Deputy Organist, an Inner Guard, two Assistant Inner Guards, not more than eight Stewards and a Tyler.

(ii) the Provincial or District Grand Officers shall be annually appointed in the Provincial or District Grand Lodges, and such Officers whenever practicable shall be then invested, together with the Provincial or District Grand Treasurer.

(iii) A Brother shall not hold more than one office in the same Provincial or District Grand Lodge at the same time.

(iv) In every Province or District having less than seven Lodges the Provincial or District Grand Master is empowered to confer on any Brother who is a member of a Lodge within his Province or District and who has rendered service of distinction and merit to Mark Masonry, the rank of a Past Provincial or Past District Grand Officer not higher than that of Past Provincial or Past District Grand Sword Bearer, unless he be a Clerk in Holy Orders appointed as Provincial or District Grand Chaplain, Deputy Provincial or District Grand Chaplain or Assistant Provincial or District Grand Chaplain, but no Provincial or District Grand Master shall have power in any one year to confer such rank upon more than one Brother.

(v) In every Province or District numbering seven or more Lodges the Provincial or District Grand Master is empowered to confer on any Brother who is a member of a Lodge within his Province or District and who has rendered service to Mark Masonry, the rank of a Past Provincial or Past District Grand Officer, except that of a Past Deputy Provincial or Past Deputy District Grand Master or Past Assistant Provincial or Past Assistant District Grand Master, but no Provincial or District Grand Master shall have power in any one year to confer such rank upon more than two Brethren for every complete seven Lodges in his Province or District.

(vi) Promotion of a Brother already holding Provincial or District Grand Rank, Present or Past, to a higher rank in the same Province or District shall not count as conferment of past rank for the purposes of this limitation.

(vii) Every Brother upon whom such rank shall have been conferred shall be entitled to wear his clothing as a Provincial or District Grand Officer at all meetings of the Order.

(viii) A return showing all appointments, conferments of Past Rank, and promotions shall be sent to the Grand Secretary, immediately after such appointments are made.

78. In addition to the entitlement under Reg. 77 a Provincial or District Grand Master may at his discretion appoint to Past Provincial or Past District Grand Rank, Officers (Present or Past) of other Provincial or District Grand Lodges or holders of London or Overseas Mark Grand Rank, who have become members of Lodges within his Province or District.

79. A Brother cannot be appointed a Provincial or District Grand Warden unless he be the Master or a Past Master of a Lodge; nor a Provincial or District Grand Overseer unless he be a Warden or Past Warden of a Lodge. These limitations shall apply also to the conferment of the corresponding Past Rank.

80. Provincial and District Grand Officers, present and past, take precedence amongst themselves in similar order to Grand Officers holding or having held corresponding ranks as provided by Regulation 4, except that Past Provincial and District Grand Masters take precedence in their own Provinces and Districts after Deputy Provincial and District Grand Masters and, where appointed by authority of Regulation 71(iii), after Assistant Provincial and District Grand Masters.

81. With the exception of Provincial or District Grand Masters, or those Deputy Provincial or Deputy District Grand Masters, present or past being Officers of Grand Lodge, Provincial or District Grand Officers can claim precedence as such only within their Province or District.

PROVINCIAL AND DISTRICT GRAND MASTERS, AND PROVINCIAL AND DISTRICT GRAND LODGES

82. A Provincial or District Grand Master shall have a like power to remove a Provincial or District Grand Officer or to deprive a Past Provincial or Past District Grand Officer of his rank, as is vested in the Grand Master by Rule 48 in respect of Officers of Grand Lodge, but no such action shall be taken without the approval of the Grand Master.

83. Should a Provincial or District Grand Officer die, resign, be removed or become incapable of performing the duties of his office by reason of absence or any other cause, the Provincial or District Grand Master may forthwith appoint another Brother to fill the office for the remainder of the year. On completion of the year, such officer shall rank as a Past Provincial or Past District Grand Officer. An Officer so appointed may, if the Provincial or District Grand Master so direct, be invested in a private Lodge, and a similar direction may be given in the case of a Brother appointed as Deputy Provincial or Deputy District Grand Master, or of any Officer unable to attend for investiture at the meeting of Provincial or District Grand Lodge.

84. A Provincial or District Grand Lodge has the power of framing by-laws, provided that they are not contrary to, or inconsistent with, the laws and regulations of Grand Lodge. Such by-laws shall not be valid until approved by the Mark Executive Committee.

85. Minutes of the proceedings of a Provincial or District Grand Lodge shall be entered in a book, which shall be produced by the Provincial or District Grand Master for the inspection of the Grand Master or the Mark Executive Committee whenever required.

86. A Provincial or District Grand Lodge may appoint one or more Committees in such manner and with such powers as the by-laws may provide.

87. (i) A Provincial or District Grand Lodge may direct payments (exclusive of the contributions payable to Grand Lodge) to be made by Provincial or District Grand Officers on first appointment to Present or Past Rank or on promotion, and also by Lodges in the Province or District, for the establishment of a local fund for general purposes, but the payments required from Lodges shall not exceed 40% of the similar fees payable to Grand Lodge.

(ii) Such annual dues for every subscribing member on the Roll of Grand Lodge during any part of the year as the Provincial or District Grand Lodge may prescribe provided that the amount levied does not exceed 40% of the Annual Dues payable to Grand Lodge.

(iii) Any of the fees or dues set out above may be altered by resolution of Provincial or District Grand Lodge, provided that notice of such resolution shall have been given at the preceding meeting.

(iv) District Grand Lodges may require payments of like fees and dues. They may, however, require larger fees or dues but only with the previous approval of the Mark Executive Committee.

(v) In every case the regulations enforcing such fees and dues must be approved by the Mark Executive Committee.

88. The Provincial or District Grand Lodge shall annually elect a Provincial or District Grand Treasurer who shall receive all monies due to, or held for, the Provincial or District Grand Lodge and shall without undue delay deposit the same in an account in the name of the Provincial or District Grand Lodge at a bank to be approved by resolution of the Provincial or District Grand Lodge. The Provincial or District Grand Treasurer shall regularly enter a complete record of all monies passing through his hands in the proper books of account, which shall be the property of the Provincial or District Grand Lodge and which, together with all Provincial or District funds and property in his possession, shall be transferred to his successor upon investiture. He shall prepare a statement of accounts annually, to be presented at the Annual Meeting of the Provincial or District Grand Lodge duly audited by an auditor or auditors (who shall be elected annually by the Provincial or District Grand Lodge) and, following the approval and adoption of the audited statement of accounts by the Provincial or District Grand Lodge, a copy thereof shall be transmitted to each Lodge within the Province or District, and three copies thereof transmitted to the Grand Secretary. The same procedure of annual accounts audit and presentation to the Provincial or District Grand Lodge shall, mutatis mutandis, be followed in relation to any other funds maintained by or in connection with the Provincial or District Grand Lodge (whether by the Treasurer, Charity Steward, or other Officer) and whether relating to General or Charitable purposes or otherwise.

89. (i) In the case of unattached Lodges Overseas not under a District Grand Master, the Grand Master shall have the power to form them, or any one of them into a group or groups styled Inspectorate, and to confer upon a Brother or Brethren appointed by him such jurisdiction as he may think fit in respect of any such group, or of any such Unattached Overseas Lodges. The Grand Master shall, at any time, and from time to time, have the power to alter such groups, to extend or limit such jurisdiction, and to remove any Brother in his place. A

PROVINCIAL AND DISTRICT GRAND MASTERS, AND PROVINCIAL AND DISTRICT GRAND LODGES

Brother while holding such appointment shall be styled Grand Inspector and, in the first instance may be appointed for such term at the Grand Master's pleasure.

(ii) A Grand Inspector is empowered to appoint annually the following Inspectorate Officers, all of whom must be subscribing members of a Lodge in his Inspectorate:- An Inspectorate Secretary and an Inspectorate Director of Ceremonies

OVERSEAS MARK GRAND RANK

90. The Grand Master has power to confer the Rank designated Overseas Mark Grand Rank on Past Masters of Overseas Lodges not under a District, who have rendered long and meritorious service to the Order and are members of Grand Lodge in accordance with Regulation 5. The holders of such Rank are entitled to wear the regalia prescribed in these Regulations at all meetings of Grand Lodge, Provincial and District Grand Lodges and Private Lodges, but can claim precedence by virtue of their rank only in Overseas Lodges not under a District.

SECTION VI

PRIVATE LODGES

91. (i) Every application for a Warrant to hold a new Lodge must be by petition to the Grand Master. In all cases the petition must be signed by at least three Mark Master Masons regularly registered under the Constitution of the Grand Lodge (who shall be the Master and Wardens). Each signatory must specify the Lodges or, if such signatory is not registered under Grand Lodge, the Lodges or Chapters working the Mark Ritual under a recognised Constitution, of which he is or has been a member, and must produce clearance certificates from each such Lodge or Chapter, if still in existence, for transmission to the Grand Secretary, unless the Grand Master or the Provincial or District Grand Master excuses such production in any particular case. Petitioners who are not registered under Grand Lodge must also apply for a certificate, which will be issued on payment of the prescribed joining fee. The petition must be recommended by the Master and Wardens of a regular Lodge and be transmitted to the Grand Secretary. In the case of a Lodge in a Province or District, the petition and certificates are to be sent to the Provincial or District Grand Master or his Deputy or his Assistant, who is to forward such petition, with his recommendation or opinion thereon, to the Grand Secretary for the decision of the Grand Master. It shall be within the power of the Grand Master to waive such of the foregoing requirements as the Grand Master shall think fit.

(ii) The following is the form of petition:

To the Most Worshipful Grand Master of the Grand Lodge of Mark Master Masons of England and Wales and its Districts and Lodges Overseas. "We, the undersigned, being regularly registered Mark Master Masons of the Lodges mentioned against our respective names, pray for a Warrant of Constitution, empowering us to meet as a regular Lodge of Mark Master Masons under the title of .... at .... on the .... in the months of .... and there to discharge the duties of the Order in a constitutional manner, according to the forms of the Order and the regulations of Grand Lodge; and we have nominated and do recommend Brother (A.B.) to be the first Master, Brother (C.D.) to be the first Senior Warden, and Brother (E.F.) to be the first Junior Warden of the said Lodge. The prayer of this petition being granted, we promise strict obedience to the commands of the Grand Master and to the Laws and Regulations of Grand Lodge."

(iii) The first Officers of a Lodge cannot be altered except by special sanction of the Grand Master.

92. In order to avoid irregularities, every new Lodge shall be consecrated according to antient usage, by the Grand Master or his Deputy or Assistant, or other Grand Officer or Master or Past Master of a Lodge acting as Deputy pro tempore. A Lodge shall not be acknowledged, nor its Officers admitted as such into Grand Lodge or Provincial or District Grand Lodge, nor shall any of its members as such be entitled to the benefits of the Fund of Benevolence or other privileges of the Order, unless it has been regularly constituted and consecrated. Provided always that nothing in this Rule shall interfere with the prerogative of a Provincial or District Grand Master, or his Deputy or Assistant, or an Installed Master whom he shall designate, to consecrate a Lodge in his Province or District.

93. Lodges rank in precedence for all purposes (including precedence in a Province or District) in order of their numbers as registered in the books of Grand Lodge. The Grand Master's Lodge, the Grand Stewards' Lodge, and certain Time Immemorial Lodges, shall not have a number but shall be placed at the head of all other Lodges. Every Lodge shall also bear a name, which shall not be changed without the permission of the Grand Master.

94. (i) Save as hereinafter provided a Lodge cannot meet without its Warrant of Constitution, specially entrusted to the Master at his installation, who shall be responsible for its safe custody, and who shall produce it at every meeting of the Lodge. Such Warrant remains the property of the Grand Master and shall be surrendered to him on the dissolution of the Lodge, and it cannot in any circumstances be transferred. No endorsements or other marking shall be made on a Warrant.

(ii) Should a Warrant be lost, destroyed or improperly withheld from those lawfully entitled to hold and use the same, or withheld by competent Masonic authority, the Lodge must suspend its meetings until a new Warrant or Warrant of Confirmation has been applied for and granted by the Grand Master in such terms or on such conditions as he may think proper, or until the Warrant be found or restored. Provided that the Grand Master, Pro Grand Master, Deputy or Assistant Grand Master, but no other authority, may grant a dispensation to a Lodge to meet without its Warrant on such occasions, and subject to such conditions, as the dispensation may provide.

PRIVATE LODGES

95. If a Warrant is lost, destroyed, improperly withheld, or so injured as to be wholly or in part illegible, a Warrant of Confirmation may be issued by the Grand Master bearing the date of the original Warrant or such later date as the Grand Master may think proper. Should the original Warrant subsequently be found or restored, the Warrant of Confirmation shall be surrendered unless the Grand Master otherwise directs.

96. (i) The regular Officers of the Lodge are the Master, two Wardens, three Overseers, Treasurer, Registrar of Marks, Secretary, two Deacons, Inner Guard and Tyler.

(ii) The Master may also appoint any of the following additional officers, a Chaplain, a Director of Ceremonies, an Almoner, a Charity Steward, an Assistant Secretary, an Assistant Director of Ceremonies, an Organist and one or more Stewards.

(iii) Save by dispensation from the Grand Master, or in a Province or District, from the Provincial or District Grand Master, no Brother shall hold more than one regular office, but a Brother may hold one of the additional offices together with a regular office.

(iv) As among the Officers of the Lodge, the order of precedence shall be as follows: Master, Senior Warden, Junior Warden, Master Overseer, Senior Overseer, Junior Overseer, Chaplain, Treasurer, Registrar of Marks, Secretary, Director of Ceremonies, Almoner, Charity Steward, Senior Deacon, Junior Deacon, Assistant Secretary, Assistant Director of Ceremonies, Organist, Inner Guard, Stewards, Tyler.

(v) The Immediate Past Master as such is not an Officer of the Lodge but shall take precedence immediately after the Junior Warden. In the event of the death or absence of the Immediate Past Master, the Senior Past Master of the Lodge present shall act in his place.

97. (i) Every Lodge shall annually, at the regular meeting next before the day named in its by-laws for the installation, elect its Master by ballot. If there is only one nomination and if no other member duly qualified shall have indicated to the Secretary that he wishes to be considered and if no member present calls for a ballot then it shall be permissible for the Master to declare the election in favour of the nominated member; provided that the election shall not be so declared unless notice of the intention so to do and the identity of the sole Brother nominated shall have been given on the summons convening the meeting at which the election is to take place. The Brother so elected, if he be able, willing and qualified to serve as Master, shall be regularly installed in the Chair at the next meeting according to antient usage. A Master elect shall not assume the Master's Chair until he has been regularly installed. The Master shall be presented with a current copy of The Constitutions and Regulations.

(ii) No Brother shall be installed as Master, except by special dispensation from the Grand Master, unless at the date of installation:

(a) he shall have served, or be deemed to have served the office of Master or of Senior Warden or of Junior Warden in a regular Lodge of Mark Master Masons for one complete year, that is to say from one installation meeting till the next;

(b) he shall also have been installed as Master of a regular Craft Lodge of Freemasons except when he has previously served as Master of a Lodge of Mark Master Masons;

(iii) Service as Master or Warden shall date from the time of installation as a Master or of investiture as a Warden.

(iv) Petitions for such dispensations, setting forth fully the matters thought to justify the grant of a dispensation, must, in a Province or District, be forwarded through the Provincial or District Grand Master to the Grand Secretary and in other cases direct to the Grand Secretary together with the appropriate fee.

98. Every Master elect, before being installed, shall solemnly pledge himself to preserve the Landmarks of the Order, to observe its antient usages and established customs, and the Constitutions and Regulations, and to enforce them strictly within his own Lodge.

99. The Master is responsible for the due observance of the by-laws of the Lodge over which he presides, a copy of which shall be presented to him on his installation.

100. If not less than seven days before the date of the regular installation meeting the Master elect should die, or become disqualified or incapacitated, or send to the Master or Secretary a notice in writing of his intention not to accept the office of Master, or if he shall not, at least seven days before such date, have obtained any dispensation necessary for his installation, notice shall be sent to each member of the Lodge stating the fact, and stating also that on the said date the Brethren will again proceed to elect a Master, who, if then present and willing and qualified to serve, shall be immediately installed and shall forthwith appoint and invest the Officers. If the Brother so elected is not present, or if he is not eligible under Rule 97 without a dispensation, the

PRIVATE LODGES

installation shall be postponed and the provisions of Rule 102 shall apply, but if he is not able or willing to accept the office of Master then the outgoing Master shall continue as Master till the next regular installation meeting, and shall appoint and invest the Officers, either forthwith or at a regular or emergency meeting to be held within five weeks, and Wardens appointed and invested at such meeting shall at the date of the next installation meeting be deemed to have filled their offices for one year.

101. If less than seven days before the date of the regular installation meeting the Master elect should die, or become disqualified or incapacitated, or send to the Master or Secretary a notice in writing of his intention not to accept the office of Master, the outgoing Master shall continue as Master till the next regular installation meeting, and shall appoint and invest the Officers as provided in Rule 100.

102. If the Master elect (though ready and willing to act as such) is not present at the regular installation meeting, the installation shall be postponed to a regular or emergency meeting, to be held within five weeks of the regular day of installation. Should the Master elect be also absent from such meeting the outgoing Master shall continue as Master till the next regular installation meeting and shall forthwith appoint and invest the Officers. A Master installed, or a Warden appointed and invested at such a meeting, shall at the date of the next regular installation meeting be deemed to have filled his office for one year.

103. Should the outgoing Master be absent from the regular installation meeting or a meeting held under the provisions of Rules 100 to 102, or should the outgoing Master so request, the Immediate Past Master, or failing him the Senior Past Master of the Lodge present, or an Installed Master selected by the outgoing Master shall act in his place.

104. Should circumstances arise with regard to the election or installation of a Master, or as to the appointment or investiture of an Officer, which are not covered by the provisions of Rules 97 and 100 to 103, or which render doubtful the procedure to be adopted under those provisions, the Lodge, or the Master thereof, may ask for a direction from the Grand Master or in a Province or District the Provincial or District Grand Master as to the procedure to be followed. There shall be no appeal against any such direction, nor shall any question be subsequently raised, as to the regularity of anything done according to such direction.

105. (i) If in any Lodge it should become impracticable to hold the election or installation meeting upon the day named in the by-laws for that purpose, the Grand Master, or in a Province or District the Provincial or District Grand Master, may grant a dispensation for the holding of such meetings, or either of them, upon a day which, in the absence of special circumstances, shall be not more than fourteen days before or after that fixed by the by-laws, which day shall for all purposes be deemed the regular day of meeting.

(ii) in every case of such dispensation being granted by a Provincial or District Grand Master, a report shall be forwarded to the Grand Secretary forthwith.

106. Should a Prince of the Blood, a Peer of the Realm, or the Governor of a Colony, the Grand Master or Pro Grand Master honour a private Lodge by accepting the office of Master, he may appoint a Deputy Master, who shall be regularly installed and entitled, when in office, to all the privileges of actual Master and, after he has served his period of office, to those of a Past Master.

107. A Brother shall not be Master of more than one Lodge at the same time, nor shall he continue as Master of the same Lodge for more than two years consecutively, without a dispensation from the Grand Master: provided that this Rule shall not apply to an outgoing Master continuing in office under the provisions of Rule 100, 101 or 102, or to a Master entitled to appoint a Deputy Master under Rule 106, but it shall apply to such Deputy Master as if he were the Master of the Lodge.

108. (i) The Treasurer shall be elected annually by ballot on the regular day of election of the Master and in the same manner.

(ii) The Tyler shall be chosen by show of hands on the same day provided that a Lodge may by resolution decide that a member of the Lodge shall act as Tyler without remuneration, and in such case the Tyler shall be appointed by the Master and shall have the same status as other regular Officers of the Lodge. Should the Treasurer or the Tyler be disabled from discharging his duties through absence, ill-health or other special cause the Master may appoint any subscribing member of the Lodge or in the case of the Tyler any other Brother to act for him so long, during the remainder of the year, as he is so disabled.

109. (i) After his installation the Master shall appoint the Officers, other than those elected, and invest all Officers present. All Officers other than the Tyler must be subscribing members of the Lodge.

(ii) Should a vacancy occur in any office (including that of Treasurer or Tyler) the Master may appoint a Brother to serve in such office for the remainder of the year.

PRIVATE LODGES

110. (i) Should the Master be dissatisfied with the conduct of any Officer, he may submit a complaint to a meeting of the Lodge. The summons for such meeting shall state that a complaint against an Officer will be considered, but neither the name of the Officer nor the nature of the complaint shall be mentioned in such summons. Notice in writing shall be given to the Officer in question at least fourteen days before the date of such meeting of the exact nature of the complaint against him which is to be considered at such meeting.

(ii) If a resolution is moved and seconded that the Officer be removed, a ballot shall be taken, after all not entitled to vote have withdrawn, and if two-thirds of the members present vote in favour of the resolution, the Officer shall be removed and the Master shall appoint another member in his place. The Officer against whom the complaint is made shall have the right to vote in the ballot.

(iii) A Tyler (not a member of the Lodge) may be removed for a sufficient cause by the majority of the Brethren present and voting at a regular meeting of the Lodge; provided that fourteen day's notice in writing shall have been given to him of the complaint against him and he shall be entitled to submit a statement in writing relating thereto.

(iv) All Visitors and Honorary Members of the Lodge should withdraw during the consideration of any such complaint, unless their presence is necessary for such consideration.

111. If the Master of a Lodge is deemed unfit to perform his duties for a single meeting of the Lodge then the Lodge may resolve that he be barred from taking the chair for that meeting.

112. If the Master of a Lodge fails to carry out his duties of his office, or brings the Lodge and / or Mark Masonry into disrepute by virtue of his conduct, then the Lodge may apply to the Mark Executive Committee through the Provincial or District Grand Master to have him removed from Office. If a resolution is moved and seconded by the members of the Lodge that the Master be removed, a ballot shall be taken, after all not entitled to vote have withdrawn, and if two-thirds of the members present vote in favour of the resolution then application to the Mark Executive Committee for his removal may be made.

113. If the Master die, be removed, or be rendered incapable of discharging the duties of his office, the Senior Warden, or in the absence of the Senior Warden the Junior Warden, or in the absence of both Wardens, the Immediate Past Master, or in his absence the Senior Past Master of the Lodge, shall direct the Lodge to be summoned until the next installation of Master.

114. In the Master's absence, the Immediate Past Master, or if he be absent the Senior Past Master of the Lodge present, or if a Past Master of the Lodge be not present, then the Senior Past Master present who is a subscribing member in the Lodge, shall take the chair. If no Past Master who is a member of the Lodge be present, then the Senior Warden, or in his absence the Junior Warden, shall rule the Lodge. When a Warden rules the Lodge, he shall not occupy the Master's chair, nor can advancements take place unless the chair is occupied by an Installed Master.

115. (i) Every Lodge has the power of framing bylaws for its government provided that they are not inconsistent with the Constitutions and Regulations. The by-laws must be submitted to the Mark Executive Committee – in Provinces or Districts through the Provincial or District Grand Master – for the approval of the Committee, and when approved a fair copy must be sent to the Grand Secretary for registration.

(ii) No alteration of, or addition to, the by-laws of a Lodge shall be made unless notice of a motion for such alteration or addition be given at a meeting of the Lodge, and the summons for the next meeting, which shall be circulated at least seven days before the date of such meeting, contain or be accompanied by a copy of such alteration or addition. If such alteration or addition is approved by a simple majority, with or without amendment, at such meeting, the by-laws as amended shall forthwith be submitted to the Mark Executive Committee as above, and if approved they shall thereupon become of force without need for confirmation at a subsequent meeting, unless the existing by-laws require such confirmation or the Mark Executive Committee directs that they shall be submitted for confirmation.

(iii) Should the new by-laws as passed by the Lodge differ from the copy on, or sent with, the summons, the Mark Executive Committee may, if it think fit, require the by-laws to be submitted for confirmation to a further meeting of the Lodge.

(iv) By-laws, or any alteration thereof, which have been approved by the Mark Executive Committee, shall be deemed for all purposes to be valid and to have been validly enacted and no question of any irregularity in procedure shall thereafter be raised. Provided that if it shall thereafter appear to the Mark Executive Committee that, by reason of changes in the Constitutions and Regulations or other cause, the by-laws of a Lodge contain anything inconsistent therewith, the Mark Executive Committee may withdraw its approval and require the Lodge, whether or not it be a Province or District, to amend its by-laws to bring them into harmony with the Constitutions and Regulations.

PRIVATE LODGES

116. The regular dates and place of meeting, the date of the installation meeting and the date on which the annual subscription becomes due shall be specified in the by-laws. The by-laws may also provide that the Secretary shall be excused payment of subscription in recognition of his services, in which case all dues in respect of his membership shall be defrayed from the funds of the Lodge; that one or two adverse votes shall serve to exclude a candidate; that a member whose subscription is in arrears for a specified period (which shall not be less than six months) shall not be eligible for appointment or election to office, or be entitled to attend the banquet; and that a member whose subscription is in arrear for one year, may be excluded by resolution of the Lodge.

117. A Lodge shall determine the amount of the annual subscription and of the fees to be paid to the Lodge by candidates for advancement, joining or rejoining, by resolution in open Lodge from time to time, after notice on the summons for any meeting.

118. Every Brother on admission as a member of a Lodge shall be supplied with a printed copy of the by-laws and his acceptance thereof shall be deemed a submission thereto. Electronic transmission of these by-laws is permissible provided the recipient has previously consented to receiving them in this manner.

119. The Grand Master may, at the request of a Provincial or District Grand Master, grant permission to a Lodge belonging to his Province or District to meet in any other Province or District provided that both Provincial or District Grand Masters are in agreement.

120. The Grand Master, or a Provincial or District Grand Master, may by dispensation authorise a Lodge to hold a specified meeting or meetings at a specified place other than its ordinary place of meeting. Should the specified place be within the jurisdiction of an Authority other than the Authority granting the dispensation, a further dispensation shall be required from the Authority within whose jurisdiction the specified place may lie.

121. A permanent alteration of the regular dates or place of meeting of a Lodge can only be effected by an amendment of its by-laws under the provisions of Rule 115, provided that a change of place of meeting of a Lodge in a Province or District to a place without such Province or District shall not be made without the special leave of the Grand Master.

122. (i) No meeting shall be held on a Sunday or on Good Friday or Christmas Day. Should the specified date of a regular meeting fall on one of these days, or on the Thursday or Saturday before Easter, the meeting may be held on such day not more than 14 days before or after the regular day, as the Master may determine, which day shall for all purposes be deemed the regular day of meeting.

(ii) Should the specified date of a regular meeting fall on a public holiday then the meeting may be held either upon that day, provided it be not a prohibited day, or not more than 14 days before or after the regular day, as the Master may determine, which day shall for all purposes be deemed the regular day of meeting.

(iii) If in any Lodge it should become impracticable or inconvenient to hold the regular meeting upon the day named in the by-laws for that purpose, the Grand Master, and in a Province or District the Provincial or District Grand Master, may grant a dispensation for the holding of such meeting upon a day which, in the absence of special circumstances, shall not be more than fourteen days before or after that fixed by the by-laws, which day shall for all purposes be deemed the regular day of meeting.

123. No regular meeting of a Lodge may be cancelled, or held otherwise than at the prescribed place and on the prescribed day, except as otherwise provided in these Rules, and not more than one meeting may be held on one day. No meeting of a Lodge may be adjourned, but consideration of any matter of business may by resolution be postponed for consideration at a later meeting.

124. A Lodge of Emergency may only be called by order of the Master, or, in his absence, the Senior Warden, or, in his absence, the Junior Warden. The business to be transacted at such Lodge shall be stated in the summons, and no other business shall be transacted.

125. No Lodge shall be opened unless three Brethren are present in addition to a Tyler, and no business shall be transacted at a meeting unless at least three members of that Lodge are present, but an entry of the meeting shall be made in the minute book. Any items of business on the agenda for such meeting, other than the election or installation of a Master, may be considered at the next meeting of the Lodge. If the meeting in question be the election or installation meeting a special report shall be made to the Grand Master, or the Provincial or District Grand Master, and his direction taken as to the course to be pursued.

126. (i) A Lodge shall keep a minute book in which the Secretary shall regularly enter a record of all business transacted or considered at each meeting of the Lodge, and in particular the names of Brethren advanced or elected for advancement, or elected as joining or rejoining members, at any meeting, with the names of their proposers and seconders, and all particulars required for the purpose of returns under Rule 127.

PRIVATE LODGES

(ii) The names of all members present at each meeting of the Lodge, together with those of all visiting Brethren, with their Lodges and rank in the Order, shall also be entered in the minute book. An attendance register may be used to record the names of those Brethren present provided it is referenced in the minutes of the meeting.

(iii) Minutes can only be confirmed at a regular meeting of the Lodge.

127. (i) Every Lodge shall keep a register of its members and of their Marks, and once in each year, before the 30th September, transmit to the Grand Secretary on the prescribed form details of the subscribing membership of the Lodge and of changes in membership during the preceding twelve-months period ending on 31st August. With such return shall be transmitted the Annual Dues payable by the Lodge in respect of every brother who has been a subscribing member of the Lodge, as shown in the records of Grand Lodge, during any part of the preceding twelve-months period, whether or not such member shall be in arrears.

(ii) This list shall also show the names of all Brethren who have ceased to be subscribing members of the Lodge during such year, stating whether by reason of death, resignation, exclusion, or election to Honorary Membership.

(iii) Each Lodge shall also, immediately after any Brother has become a member of such Lodge, make a return together with the appropriate fee to the Grand Secretary showing the names, Mark, address, profession or occupation of such Brother, and also in the case of a Brother who has been advanced, the name and number of at least one regular Craft Lodge of Freemasons of which he is a subscribing member or an honorary member or a serving Brother, or in the case of a joining member the number of some regular Lodge of which he is or has been a member or, if he has never been a member of a regular Lodge, then the name and number of some Lodge or Chapter working the Mark Ritual under a recognised Constitution to which he belongs or has belonged.

(iv) No Brother elected as a joining or rejoining member of a Lodge shall be shown on any return until he shall have paid the fee for joining or rejoining.

128. (i) Lodges in Provinces or Districts shall, in addition to the returns to be made to the Grand Secretary, make similar returns to the Provincial or District Grand Secretary and transmit therewith all monies payable to the Provincial or District Grand Lodge.

(ii) In a District the returns and fees for Grand Lodge required by Rule 164, and also any other monies due to Grand Lodge, may, if the Grand Master so direct, be sent or paid to the District Grand Master, who shall transmit the same to the Grand Secretary.

129. (i) Every Lodge shall annually, immediately after the installation of the Master, make a return to the Grand Secretary of the Master, Past Masters, Wardens, and Overseers, and all members who claim to be entitled to attend Grand Lodge as Grand Officers, or as Past Masters having served the office of Master in some other regular Lodge, specifying the Lodge in which each has served the office of Master.

(ii) In Provinces and Districts similar returns shall also be made to the Provincial or District Grand Secretaries, which return shall also include the names of any Brethren not being Past Masters who claim to be entitled to attend Provincial or District Grand Lodge as Provincial or District Grand Officers.

130. (i) Should a Lodge fail to make any returns or payments to Grand Lodge for the space of six months after the same are due, the Mark Executive Committee may admonish, fine, or suspend such Lodge, or any Officer or member thereof responsible for the default, or may recommend that such Lodge be erased or such Officer or member be expelled from the Order.

(ii) A Provincial or District Grand Master shall have such like powers in case of failure to make returns or payments to a Provincial or District Grand Lodge.

131. Should a Brother be deprived of the privileges of the Order through the neglect of a Lodge in not making the necessary returns, and remitting the fees to Grand Lodge, he shall, on producing the required proof to competent authority, be entitled to all such privileges, and the offending Lodge shall be reported to the Mark Executive Committee and rigorously proceeded against for its default.

132. (i) All moneys due to, or held for, the Lodge shall be paid or remitted to the Treasurer direct, who shall without undue delay deposit the same in an account in the name of the Lodge at a bank to be approved by resolution of the Lodge. The Bank account shall have a minimum of three signatories. The Treasurer shall make such payments as are duly authorised, or have been sanctioned by the Lodge. All cheques must bear the signature of the Treasurer and (unless the Lodge resolved to the contrary) of at least one other member authorised by the Lodge. The Treasurer shall regularly enter a complete record of all moneys passing through his hands in the proper books of account, which shall be the property of the Lodge, and which, together with all Lodge funds and property in his possession, shall be transferred to his successor upon investiture. He shall prepare a statement

PRIVATE LODGES

of accounts annually, at a date to be determined by the members, showing the exact financial position of the Lodge, which statement shall be verified and audited by two auditors elected annually in accordance with Rule 132(ii). Copies of the accounts and of the certificate signed by the auditors that all balances have been checked and that the accounts have been duly audited shall be sent to all members of the Lodge with the summons convening the meeting at which they are to be considered and, following the approval and adoption of the audited statement of accounts by the Lodge three copies thereof shall be transmitted to the Provincial or District Grand Secretary or, in the case of Lodges Abroad not under Districts, to the Grand Secretary. The books of accounts shall be produced for inspection in open Lodge at such meetings, and on any other occasion if required by a resolution of the Lodge. The same procedure of annual accounts, audit and presentation to members or the Lodge shall, mutatis mutandis, be followed in relation to any other funds maintained by or in connection with the Lodge (whether by the Treasurer or by a Charity Steward or other Officer) and whether relating to General or Charitable purposes or otherwise.

(ii) The Lodge shall each year at the Installation Meeting elect two subscribing members of the Lodge (other than the Treasurer Worshipful Master, Wardens, and the Secretary) to act as auditors.

(iii) The audit of the statement of accounts shall be carried out by the auditors in accordance with Instructions issued from time to time by the Mark Executive Committee.

133. A Lodge may appoint one or more Committees for the purpose of considering and reporting to the Lodge on any matters connected with the management of its affairs, or the suitability of candidates proposed for advancement or joining, but no such Committee shall have any executive powers unless the same have been conferred on it by resolution of the Lodge.

134. (i) When any Master Mason or Brother of the Order is a candidate for membership of a Lodge the following particulars shall be sent to all members of the Lodge seven clear days before the meeting at which he is to come up for election: In all cases the:

(a) Full name
(b) Date of Birth
(c) Place or places of abode
(d) Name and number of Craft Lodge
(e) Names of Proposer and Seconder*
(f) Date of the proposal in open Lodge

*both of whom must be subscribing members of the Lodge or Honorary Members who are Past Masters of the Lodge. All Lodges in Provinces or Districts shall send to the Provincial or District Grand Secretary a copy of the Summons for every regular and emergency meeting of the Lodge at the same time as it is issued to the members. All Lodges designated Unattached or Lodges Abroad not under Districts shall send to the Grand Secretary a copy of the Summons for every regular and emergency meeting at the same time as they are issued to the members.

(ii) In the case of a candidate for advancement there shall also be shown his rank in the Craft and the name and number of at least one regular Craft Lodge of Freemasons of which he is a subscribing member or an honorary member or a serving Brother. No Master Mason shall be advanced in a Lodge, other than that in which he has been proposed and elected without the special dispensation of the Grand Master.

(iii) In the case of a candidate for joining there shall be shown his rank in the Order and the name and number of some regular Lodge of which he is or has been a member, or if he has never been a member of a regular Lodge then the name and number of a Lodge or Chapter working the Mark Ritual under some recognised Constitution, to which he belongs or has belonged.

(iv) A Brother shall not be accepted as a candidate for advancement or for joining or re-joining unless he has been proposed and seconded in open Lodge at a meeting prior to that at which he comes up for election or a notice that he is to be proposed and seconded has been circulated to all members at least 14 days prior to the meeting at which he is due to join, rejoin or be advanced. Such notice must in all cases contain the details of the candidate and the names of the proposer and seconder as listed in Rule 134(i), with the exception of the date of the proposal in open Lodge.

135. (i) A candidate for advancement shall produce his Grand Lodge Certificate as a Master Mason or a Certificate from the Secretary of the Lodge in which he was raised, and a candidate for joining a Lodge shall produce his Certificate as a Mark Master Mason. Should such Certificate in the first case be from a body other than the United Grand Lodge of England, or in the second case from a body other than Grand Lodge, the Secretary of the Lodge shall, before the ballot is taken, satisfy himself that the body granting the Certificate is

PRIVATE LODGES

recognised by the United Grand Lodge of England, or by Grand Lodge, as the case may be, and in case of doubt shall make any necessary inquiries of the Grand Secretary, or the Provincial or District Grand Secretary.

(ii) A candidate for joining or re-joining from this Constitution shall also produce to the Secretary a Clearance Certificate from every regular Mark Lodge of which he is or has been a member, provided that such Lodge is still working, in which case a certificate from the Grand Secretary shall be substituted.

136. (i) A candidate for advancement, or a candidate for joining not already registered on the books of Grand Lodge, shall before the ballot is taken sign the following declaration:

To the Master, Wardens, Overseers and Members of the .... Lodge of Mark Master Masons, No. .... I, ..., do declare that should I be admitted as a member of the above Lodge, I hereby solemnly pledge myself to maintain and uphold the supremacy of the Grand Lodge of Mark Master Masons of England and Wales and its Districts and Lodges Overseas – to pay strict obedience to its Constitutions and Laws – and to conform to all the antient usages and established customs of the Order. I further solemnly promise to submit to, and observe, the by-laws of the Lodge from time to time made for its government. Witness my hand, this .... day of .... Witness ....

(ii) A candidate for joining or re-joining who is already registered in the books of Grand Lodge, shall before the ballot is taken sign the following declaration:

To the Master, Wardens, Overseers and Members of the .... Lodge of Mark Master Masons, No. .... I, ..., do declare that should I be admitted a Member of the above Lodge I will submit to and observe the by-laws of the Lodge from time to time made for its government. Witness my hand, this. .... day of .... Witness ....

(iii) In either case the signature of the candidate should be witnessed or certified by a Member of the Lodge.

(iv) These declarations must be carefully preserved by the Lodge.

137. If, on a ballot, three adverse votes shall appear against a candidate for advancement, joining, or rejoining, he shall not be admitted. Every private Lodge has the power to diminish this number by its bylaws: provided that if less than five members vote when the ballot is taken, a single adverse vote shall exclude.

138. (i) Should a candidate elected for advancement not attend for advancement within one year, his election shall be void, as shall be the election of a Brother as a joining or rejoining member if he shall not have paid the requisite fee within one year of his election.

(ii) For the purpose of this rule "a year" shall mean the period from the meeting at which the candidate was elected, up to and including the corresponding meeting of the Lodge in the next year. Should the election be at an emergency meeting, the year shall commence to run from the succeeding regular meeting.

139. (i) A Brother who has done good service to a Lodge or to the Order may be elected an Honorary Member of a Lodge. His name must be proposed and seconded in open Lodge and must appear on the summons for the following meeting at which he must be balloted for, and three adverse votes shall exclude. Should the Brother be a member of the Lodge concerned, acceptance by him of Honorary Membership shall be deemed notice of immediate resignation.

(ii) An Honorary Member may attend the Lodge as such, but he shall not hold any office therein, or vote, or propose or second any resolution, provided that if he is a Past Master of the Lodge he may propose or second a candidate.

(iii) An Honorary Member shall pay no subscription, but shall remain liable for any arrears of subscription at the date of his election as an Honorary Member. No dues shall be payable by the Lodge in respect of an Honorary Member for any period after the date of his election as such, nor shall his name be shown on any return save in respect of dues accrued before that date, or as required by Rule 127.

140. (i) A Master Mason may by dispensation from the Grand Master be advanced by a Lodge for which he is to act as Tyler without payment of any fee except the prescribed fee for registration and issue of a certificate, which fee shall not be payable in the case of a Master Mason who has been previously obligated as a Serving Brother. Such advancement shall not constitute the Brother a member of the Lodge, but shall give him the status of an unattached Brother, and he may be elected as a joining member of any Lodge on the usual conditions. A Brother so advanced may act as Tyler of any Lodge.

(ii) No dues shall be payable by a Lodge in respect of a Tyler who is not a member of such Lodge.

PRIVATE LODGES

141. (i) A Brother on advancement, or a Brother joining from another Constitution, shall be presented with a current copy of Constitutions and Regulations and a Certificate of registration in the Books of Grand Lodge, for which Certificate and registration the Lodge shall pay to Grand Lodge the prescribed fee. A Brother to whom a Grand Lodge Certificate is granted must sign his name in the margin thereof, or it will not be valid.

(ii) A Brother's Grand Lodge Certificate should be presented to him in open Lodge, and the fact entered on the minutes, but, in cases where this cannot conveniently be done, the Certificate shall be sent to him by registered post, or by recorded delivery, and the Secretary shall report the fact at the next regular meeting of the Lodge so that it be duly recorded.

(iii) The Grand Secretary may supply to a District Grand Master Certificates bearing the seal of Grand Lodge and signed by the Grand Secretary, which Certificates, after signature by the District Grand Secretary, may be issued to Brethren advanced in Lodges in that District. The District Grand Master shall make a return to the Grand Secretary, showing to whom such Certificates were issued and remit to him the fees for the same.

(iv) Should a Certificate be lost or destroyed, of which satisfactory proof must be adduced, the Grand Secretary may issue a duplicate on payment of the prescribed fee.

142. A Brother may give notice of resignation of his membership either in open Lodge or by letter to the Secretary, and such notice, unless withdrawn, shall take effect as from date on which it is communicated to the Lodge, unless the notice itself states some other date in the current Lodge year. A notice by letter may be withdrawn prior to its communication to the Lodge, and if when notice of resignation is communicated to the Lodge, whether by the member or the Secretary, the Lodge pass a resolution asking for its withdrawal, it may be withdrawn at or before the next regular meeting of the Lodge. Provided that if notice has been served on a member under Rule 144 that a complaint against him will be considered by the Lodge, no subsequent notice of resignation shall (a) take effect until after the date of the meeting called for the consideration of the complaint; (b) prevent the Lodge from considering the complaint and, if thought fit, passing a resolution for the permanent exclusion of the member; (c) be withdrawn unless the Lodge at such meeting passes a resolution asking for its withdrawal.

143. Should a Brother behave in such a manner as to disturb the harmony of the meeting of a Lodge, he shall be formally admonished by the Master. Should he persist in his irregular conduct, he shall be punished by exclusion for the remainder of the meeting, and the case may be reported to higher Masonic authority.

144. (i) A Lodge may, by resolution passed as hereinafter set forth, exclude a member permanently from its membership for sufficient cause provided that a notice has been served on such member that a complaint has been made against him, with full particulars of the complaint, and that such complaint will be considered at a meeting at which he may attend and be heard, or at which any written statement by him will be considered. Such notice shall be served upon the member concerned not less than fourteen days before the date of such meeting, and notice shall be served on all other members of the Lodge not less than seven days before such date, that at such meeting a complaint against a Brother will be considered, but no mention shall be made of the name of the Brother or the nature of the complaint. The notices shall be considered as duly served if sent to the last known address of each member but in the case of the member against whom the complaint is made the notice shall be sent by registered letter or by recorded delivery, the envelope being plainly marked on the outside "Private and Confidential". The provisions of Rule 160 shall apply to the service of such notice.

(ii) If at such meeting, after the member concerned has been heard if present, or any written statement by him read, and any relevant evidence which may be offered has also been heard or read, a resolution is duly proposed and seconded that the member against whom the complaint has been made shall be permanently excluded from the Lodge, such resolution shall be voted upon by ballot, after all present not entitled to vote have withdrawn, the power of exclusion cannot be exercised unless two-thirds of the members present at the ballot vote in favour of the resolution. The member against whom the complaint is made shall be entitled to vote.

(iii) All Visitors or Honorary Members of the Lodge should withdraw during the consideration of the complaint unless their presence is necessary for the purpose of such consideration.

(iv) Every resolution so passed by a Lodge within a Province or District shall be reported forthwith to the Provincial or District Grand Master who shall, after making such enquiries as he may think fit, confirm such resolution or annul the same and order the reinstatement of the excluded Brother. In either case he shall communicate his decision to the Lodge and to such Brother, either of whom may within six weeks from the date of the decision, or within such further time as the Provincial or District Grand Master may think fit to allow, apply to him to vary such decision. The Provincial or District Grand Master shall consider such application and decide thereon after hearing the parties and/or giving them an opportunity to make such

PRIVATE LODGES

statements in writing and to furnish such evidence as they may think fit and such decision shall be final and binding on all parties subject only to an appeal to Grand Lodge. Every such decision shall be reported forthwith to the Grand Secretary. If a Lodge is not within a Province or District the above provisions shall apply with the substitution of the Mark Executive Committee for the Provincial or District Grand Master.

(v) Any Lodge failing to comply with an order for the re-instatement of a member may be suspended by the Provincial or District Grand Master or the Board for such period as may be thought fit, or the matter may be reported to the Grand Lodge with a recommendation that the Lodge be erased.

(vi) Where re-instatement of a Brother is ordered, he shall resume his former position in the Lodge, and the Lodge shall have no claim against him for subscriptions for any period during any part of which he has been excluded, but the Lodge shall pay all dues for such period, and for any purpose connected with the Fund of Benevolence the Brother shall be deemed to have paid his subscriptions during such period.

145. (i) Should a member be two years in arrears, he shall thereupon cease to be a member of the Lodge, and can only become a member again by regular proposition and ballot according to Rules 134 to 138. This Rule shall apply also where the by-laws provide that a member shall be excluded if he is in arrears for a shorter period than two years. If the by-laws provide that in such case he may be excluded, then the Lodge may at any time when a member is in arrears for the stated period, exclude him by resolution, and no prior notice to the members of the Lodge of such resolution shall be necessary. In all cases where a member may become liable to exclusion under this rule it shall be the duty of the Secretary of the Lodge to send to him, at least fourteen days before the date when he may become liable to exclusion, a letter by registered post or by recorded delivery, plainly marked "Private and Confidential" warning him that unless the arrears or a sufficient part thereof, are paid by such date he will be, or may be, excluded, and unless that has been done the Brother may apply to the Provincial or District Grand Master or the Mark Executive Committee, who may, notwithstanding anything in these Rules or the by-laws, order that the Brother be reinstated on payment of all arrears.

(ii) Provided also that in time of war the Grand Master may direct that subscriptions shall be excused, or arrears remitted, in the case of a Brother who is on active service, or a prisoner of war, or in enemy occupied country. Such direction may be given either as to individual Brethren or as to classes of Brethren.

(iii) No dues shall be payable by a Lodge in respect of Brethren whose subscriptions are so excused and where arrears are remitted dues paid in respect of the periods to which such arrears relate shall be refunded to the Lodge.

146. The Secretary of a Lodge shall (a) if so required by a member grant a certificate stating that he is a member and whether or not he is indebted to the Lodge; (b) if so required by an ex-member grant a certificate stating the circumstances of the termination of his membership, whether at the date of such termination he was indebted to the Lodge, and if so whether such indebtedness has since been discharged. Any such certificate shall be dated, and either handed to the Brother or sent by registered post or by recorded delivery in an envelope plainly marked "Private and Confidential". Such certificate may be transmitted electronically provided the recipient has previously agreed to this method of transmission. No other form of certificate shall be given by a Lodge or any Officer thereof.

147. (i) Should the Grand Master, Pro Grand Master, Deputy Grand Master or Assistant Grand Master visit a private Lodge or Provincial or District Grand Lodge, he shall have the right to preside and direct the Grand Wardens and Grand Overseers if present to occupy the Wardens' and Overseers' chairs.

(ii) A Provincial or District Grand Master or his Deputy or his Assistant shall have a like right when visiting a Lodge in his Province or District.

(iii) The Grand Master and the Mark Executive Committee respectively shall have the right to depute one or more Grand Officers to visit a private Lodge, or a Provincial or District Grand Lodge, who shall have the right to attend the Lodge and speak therein.

(iv) A Provincial or District Grand Master shall have the right to depute one or more Provincial or District Grand Officers to visit a private Lodge in his Province or District who shall have the right to attend the Lodge and speak therein.

148. (i) A visitor to a Lodge shall give the name and number of some Lodge (which may be a Lodge or Royal Arch Chapter working the Mark Ritual under any recognised Constitution) of which he is a subscribing member, or if he is not a subscribing member of any such Lodge or Chapter, shall describe himself as "unattached". An unattached Brother may not visit the same Lodge on more than one occasion in any one year.

(ii) A visitor shall not be admitted into a Lodge unless he be vouched for by one of the Brethren present, or shall have produced his certificate, and, after due examination, shall have proved himself a Mark Master Mason. Should any doubt arise as to the regularity of his advancement, he shall not be admitted.

PRIVATE LODGES

(iii) It is within the power of the Master of every Lodge to refuse admission to any visitor whose presence he has reason to believe will disturb the harmony of the Lodge.

(iv) A visitor, during his presence in the Lodge, is subject to its by-laws, and cannot address the Lodge, save by permission, and he shall withdraw from the Lodge should the Master so direct.

149. If any Lodge shall pledge its jewels or furniture or any part thereof, or permit or suffer any charge or lien to be created or to arise thereon, it shall become liable to suspension or erasure.

150. (i) No Lodge of Instruction or the like shall be held except under the sanction of a regular Lodge, which shall be answerable for its proceedings and mode of working, nor, in cases where members of more than one Lodge are admitted to such Lodge, except with the licence of the Grand Master, or in a Province or District with the licence of the Provincial or District Grand Master, who may, if he think fit, withdraw such licence. In all cases the proposed place of meeting shall be reported to the Grand Secretary or the Provincial or District Grand Secretary.

(ii) If a Lodge, which has given its sanction for a Lodge of Instruction being held, shall see fit, it may, at any regular meeting, withdraw that sanction by a resolution of the Lodge, to be communicated to the Lodge of Instruction, provided notice of the intention to withdraw the sanction be inserted in the summons for that meeting.

(iii) Minutes of Lodges of Instruction shall be kept recording the names of all Brethren present at each meeting and of Brethren appointed to hold office. Such minutes shall be produced when called for by the Grand Master, the Provincial or District Grand Master, the Mark Executive Committee, or the Lodge granting the sanction.

(iv) Whenever a Lodge of Instruction ceases to exist, the books, papers, and other documents become the property of, and must be handed to, the Lodge under whose sanction it worked, or to the Grand Secretary on behalf of the Grand Master. The other property of a Lodge of Instruction shall be disposed of in such a manner as its members shall determine and Rule 156 shall apply to property in the possession of, or under the control of, Officers of the Lodge of Instruction by virtue of their office.

151. (i) A proposal for the surrender of the Warrant of a Lodge must be set out, with the names of the proposer and seconder, in a summons dispatched to members not less than fourteen days before the date of the meeting at which such proposal is to be considered. If such resolution is carried by a majority of those voting, a report of the proceedings shall be forwarded to the Grand Master, in a Province or District through the Provincial or District Grand Master, and the Grand Master shall decide whether he will accept the surrender of the Warrant, or whether the Lodge shall continue, and if so under any and what conditions. Provided that members unable to attend the meeting may by letter inform the Secretary of the Lodge whether they support or oppose the proposal for the surrender of the Warrant, and any such letters shall be forwarded to the Grand Master with the above mentioned report.

(ii) Should the number of members of a Lodge at any time become less than three the Lodge shall cease to meet save by dispensation from the Grand Master, and after the expiration of six months the Lodge shall become extinct and be erased unless the Grand Master otherwise directs.

(iii) Should a Lodge fail to meet for one year, it shall be liable to be erased.

152. (i) Should two or more Lodges pass resolutions desiring amalgamation the Grand Master may give effect to such desire, either by granting a new Warrant (which may be ante-dated to a date not earlier than that of the earliest Warrant of the Lodges concerned) or by directing that certain of the Lodges shall cease to exist and that their members shall (if they so desire) automatically become members of the surviving Lodge on such conditions as he may think fit. The Grand Master may give directions as to change of the name or number of a Lodge, disposal of Lodge property, and any other matter incidental to such amalgamation.

(ii) The provision of Rule 151 shall apply to resolutions for amalgamation.

153. Upon the dissolution of a Lodge, the Warrant, together with all the books and papers relating to the affairs of the Lodge, must be delivered up to the Grand Master. Its other property shall be disposed of as the Lodge may, prior to its dissolution, have resolved, or in default of or subject to any such resolution, as the Grand Master may direct. A Warrant cannot in any circumstances be transferred.

154. (i) A Lodge which has completed one hundred years of uninterrupted existence shall be entitled to receive a centenary warrant, provided that at least one meeting of the Lodge shall have been held, or deemed to have been held, in each of the one hundred years of its uninterrupted existence.

(ii) A Lodge which has completed one hundred and fifty years of uninterrupted existence shall be entitled to receive a sesqui-centenary warrant, provided that at least one meeting of the Lodge shall have been held, or deemed to have been held, in each of the one hundred and fifty years of its uninterrupted existence.

PRIVATE LODGES

(iii) An application for the grant of a centenary or sesqui-centenary warrant may be submitted to the Mark Executive Committee for approval by the Grand Master not more than six months before the date on which the period of uninterrupted existence shall have been completed.

(iv) The fee for a centenary warrant shall be as prescribed in Rule 164.

(v) Every subscribing member of a Lodge to which a centenary warrant has been granted may wear a commemorative centenary jewel of the design prescribed by Rule 178.

155. (i) A Lodge which has completed fifty years of uninterrupted existence may be authorised to wear a commemorative jubilee jewel of the design prescribed by Rule 179, provided that at least one meeting of the Lodge shall have been held, or deemed to have been held, in each of the fifty years of its uninterrupted existence.

(ii) An application for permission to wear a jubilee jewel may be submitted to the Mark Executive Committee for approval by the Grand Master not more than six months before the date on which the fifty years of uninterrupted existence shall have been completed.

(iii) Every subscribing member of a Lodge which has been granted permission to wear a jubilee jewel shall be entitled to wear that jewel.

SECTION VII

GENERAL RULES

156. (i) The property of Grand Lodge, a Provincial or District Grand Lodge, or any private Lodge, not vested in special trustees, shall be held as set out below in trust for the members of the respective Lodges.

(ii) In the case of Grand Lodge by the President and Deputy President of the General Board.

(iii) In the case of a Provincial or District Grand Lodge by the Provincial or District Grand Master and Deputy Provincial or District Grand Master.

(iv) In the case of a Private Lodge by the Master and Wardens, unless the by-laws otherwise provide.

(v) Documents or other property in the possession or under the control of a Brother by virtue of his office in a Lodge shall be delivered to his successor in such office, or as the Master may direct. In case of dissolution of a Lodge such documents or other property shall be delivered to such person as the Lodge by resolution or, failing such resolution, as the Grand Master may direct.

157. No Lodge, or Board or Committee appointed by a Lodge or body of the Order, shall have power to pledge the credit of any Brother, nor shall it have power to pledge the funds of the body appointing it except in so far as such body has given such power expressly.

158. Any body within the Order may, by resolution, require its minute books, books of account, or any other documents relating to its property or affairs which are in the custody or control of any of its Officers or members as such, to be produced for its inspection.

159. Where in these Constitutions and Regulations anything is to be done within a fixed number of days or weeks from the happening of any event, e.g., the receipt of a notice or the giving of a decision, the day on which such event happens shall not be counted. Where a notice is to be given a fixed number of days before a meeting, neither the day of posting the notice, nor the day of the meeting, shall be counted.

160. (i) Summonses, notices or other documents may be served by letter addressed to a Brother at his last known address, or when directed to a Lodge or the Master or Wardens of a Lodge by being addressed to the Secretary.

(ii) In cases where service by these means may be difficult or impracticable the Grand Secretary or a Provincial or District Grand Master may give directions as to the method of service or if he think fit, give direction that services of any such summonses, notices or other documents be dispensed with.

(iii) Documents so addressed and dispatched shall be deemed to have been duly served.

(iv) Documents may be served by electronic means provided the Brother receiving them has given prior agreement to receiving documents in electronic format.

161. The following rules shall apply, save as may herein be otherwise expressly provided, to the conduct of business in Grand Lodge, a Provincial or District Grand Lodge, a Private Lodge, or any Board, Committee, or Tribunal:

(i) The Presiding Officer shall have control of the business of the meeting, and shall decide in what order the items shall be taken, and the order in which the Brethren shall speak. He may call any Brother to order, and such Brother shall obey his direction. He may call on the meeting to indicate by show of hands whether a vote on any item shall be taken without further discussion, and he may similarly call on the meeting to decide whether the consideration or further consideration of any items shall be adjourned to a future occasion. He may also decide whether a matter not on the Summons or Agenda shall be considered, unless the Constitutions, or the by-laws, or the rules of the Committee or Board, forbid the consideration of such matter at such meeting, or its consideration without notice.

(ii) The decision of the Presiding Officer shall be final as to the number voting on any matter, and as to whether a vote, whether by ballot or otherwise, shall be taken again. When votes are equal the Presiding Officer shall have a second or casting vote.

(iii) Every resolution or amendment to a resolution must be proposed and seconded, and the names of the proposer and seconder entered in the minutes. This shall apply to resolutions or amendments moved from the Chair. The Presiding Officer may rule when a proposed amendment is proper to be considered as such, or when it should be the subject of a separate resolution. When several amendments have been proposed he may decide in what order they should be taken.

(iv) Should the Presiding Officer consider that any item on the Agenda, or any proposed resolution or amendment, is improper in its nature, or couched in an offensive or improper manner, or not within the competence of the meeting, he may so rule, but any Brother may challenge such ruling and require that the opinion of the meeting shall be taken by show of hands as to whether the matter in question shall be considered.

GENERAL RULES

(v) Where a Brother presides over a meeting in the absence of the Master, President, or Chairman, he shall possess all the powers with regard to the business of the meeting of the Brother who would normally preside.

162. A Brother shall not appear clothed in any of the jewels, collars, or badges of the Order at any place or public resort, procession, funeral or ball, unless the Grand Master or Provincial or District Grand Master shall have previously given a dispensation.

163. No Brother shall publish the proceedings or take any photograph of any Lodge, or of any other body of the Order, without the leave of the Grand Master, or of the Provincial or District Grand Master, but this prohibition shall not apply to publication to a superior Authority in the Order, or for any purpose authorised by these rules.

SECTION VIII
SCHEDULE OF FEES AND CONTRIBUTIONS

164. Fees to Grand Lodge. Fees shall be payable to Grand Lodge in respect of:

    a. Warrants of Constitution and Confirmation, Centenary and Sesqui-Centenary Warrants.

    b. Patents for Provincial and District Grand Masters.

    c. The Registration of:
        (i)   A Brother on Advancement.
        (ii) A Joining Brother.
        (iii) A Founder member of a new Lodge.

    d. Dispensations.

    e. Duplicate replacement or amended Grand Lodge Certificates.

    f. Fees of Honour:
        (i)   A Grand Officer, present and past, on first appointment.

        (ii) On promotion to an Office or rank for which a higher fee is appropriate, the fee payable shall be the difference between the fee for the former rank at the current rate and that due for the higher rank irrespective of the date of the original appointment.

        (iii) On appointment to Overseas Mark Grand Rank. They shall be such amounts as shall be determined by resolution of Grand Lodge at the March Communication to take effect from 1st September following that Communication.

Annual Dues

The Annual Dues and Fees payable by each Lodge for each year ending 31st August in respect of every Brother who has been a subscribing member of that Lodge, as shown in the records of Grand Lodge, during any part of that year are due on 31st August of that year. They shall be such amounts as shall be determined by resolution of Grand Lodge at the March Communication to take effect from 1st September following that Communication.

Levy

Grand Lodge may, providing notice of such intent appears on the Summons for the meeting, determine by resolution that a levy shall be payable to Grand Lodge by each Lodge in respect of every Brother who is at the time of such resolution a subscribing member of that Lodge. The levy shall be in such an amount, and paid on such date as shall be determined by the resolution of Grand Lodge. The General Board shall have power to vary any or all of the Dues and Fees payable by Lodges overseas.

Value Added Tax at the Standard Rate is payable on all Fees and Dues payable to Grand Lodge by all Brethren resident in the UK and the European Union.

SECTION IX
THE MARK BENEVOLENT FUND

165. The name of the Charity shall be the Mark Benevolent Fund hereinafter in these Regulations referred to as "The Fund".

166. The Fund is supported by contributions received for the charitable purposes of the Order.

167. The Fund shall be administered in accordance with the provisions of a Trust Deed dated the 13th day of September 2011 and made by:-
- (a) Geoffrey Michael Redman-Brown;
- (b) Raymond John Smith;
- (c) John Lawson William Wright;
- (d) Michael Howard Lawson;

the terms of which are set out in Annex A to these Regulations, and which Trust Deed was approved by Grand Lodge on the said 13th day of September 2011.

SECTION X
INTERPRETATION, AMENDMENT AND COMING INTO FORCE OF RULES

168. In these Rules, unless the context otherwise requires:

"Board" shall mean the General Board;

"Brother" shall mean a Mark Master Mason;

"Lodge" or "regular Lodge" a Lodge of Mark Master Masons on the Register of Grand Lodge;

"Past Master" a Past Master of a Lodge on such Register;

"Prescribed fee" a fee set out in Rule 87 or Rule 164 or such further or other fee as Grand Lodge may from time to time prescribe;

"Recognised Constitution" a Supreme Grand Lodge or Grand Chapter of an Order working the Mark Ritual which shall have been accorded recognition by Grand Lodge;

"Subscribing Member" a member of a Lodge liable to pay a subscription, or a Secretary excused from paying a subscription by the by-laws in return for his services;

"Regular Craft Lodge of Freemasons" a private Lodge under the jurisdiction of the United Grand Lodge of England, or under the jurisdiction of any Grand Lodge which is recognised by the United Grand Lodge of England.

In all cases a document may be delivered electronically to a Brother provided that the Brother has previously agreed to accept delivery by electronic means.

169. (i) No additions to, or amendment of, these Constitutions and Regulations shall be made unless notice of such proposal has been sent out in the summons for the next regular meeting of Grand Lodge and the proposal considered and approved at such meeting. If it be desired to move an amendment to such a proposal notice in writing shall be given to the General Board seven clear days before the next regular meeting of Grand Lodge. If the terms of the proposal appear in the minutes of the summons it shall not be necessary to set them out in extenso in the agenda of subsequent summonses, except in respect of any item covered by the original proposal which has been amended.

(ii) Provided that if the meeting at which new Rules should be considered or confirmed coincides with the Grand Festival, such consideration or confirmation may be adjourned to the next meeting.

170. These Rules shall come into force on the 12th June 2012 and from that date shall replace and supersede any previous Rules. Provided that nothing in these Rules shall render invalid any act done before such date in accordance with the Rules then in force.

171. All matters affecting the government of the Order not expressly or impliedly provided for in these Regulations shall be determined according to the Constitutions for the time being in force of the United Grand Lodge of Antient Free and Accepted Masons of England which shall be applied mutatis mutandis so far as applicable to the Order of Mark Master Masons.

SECTION XI
REGALIA, CLOTHING, INSIGNIA, AND JEWELS

172. (i) The following clothing and insignia shall be worn by members of the Order:

Grand Master and Pro Grand Master — The Compasses extended to 45°, with a segment of a circle at the points, and the Arms of Grand Lodge on a Quatrefoil.

They are also entitled to wear a distinguishing badge round the neck pendent to a white ribbon 1/2 inch broad edged with gold lace, consisting of a keystone within a circle, the whole in enamel and bearing the legend "Lapis reprobatus caput anguli".

Deputy Grand Master — The Compasses and Square with a Keystone on a Quatrefoil. (Plate No. 3)

Assistant Grand Master — As for Deputy Grand Master with the word "Assistant" engraved on a bar across the lower part of the Jewel. (Plate No. 3)

(ii) The following Jewels should be gold or gilt, surrounded by a Quatrefoil chased with rose leaves and hyssop, with a mallet and chisel in satire at base:

President of the General Board — The Shield of Grand Lodge. (Plate No. 10)

Grand Senior Warden — The Level. (Plate No. 4)

Grand Junior Warden — The Plumb and Axe. (Plate No. 5)

Grand Inspector — Compasses on a gold plate, representing a Keystone with Lewis. (Plate No. 41)

Grand Overseer — The Keystone surmounted by All-seeing eye. (Plate No. 6)

Grand Chaplain — An open Book. (Plate No. 7)

Grand Treasurer — Two Keys in saltire. (Plate No. 8)

Grand Registrar — A Scroll with Seal of Grand Lodge attached. (Plate No. 9)

President of the Mark Benevolent Fund — The Shield of Grand Lodge with "Benevolence" engraved on a bar above the Shield. (Plate No. 10)

President of the Mark Executive Committee — The Shield of Grand Lodge with "Executive" engraved on a bar above the Shield. (Plate No. 10)

Grand Secretary — Two Pens in saltire with wreath. (Plate No. 11)

Grand Director of Ceremonies — Two Wands in saltire with wreath. (Plate No. 12)

Grand Inspector of Work — Semi-circular Protractor. (Plate No. 13)

Grand Sword Bearer — Two Swords in saltire. (Plate No. 14)

Deputy President of the Board — The Shield of Grand Lodge with the word "Deputy" engraved on a bar below the shield. (Plate No. 10)

Deputy Grand Chaplain — An open Book with "Deputy" engraved on a bar on the Quatrefoil above the Book. (Plate No. 7)

Deputy Grand Registrar — A Scroll with Seal of Grand Lodge attached, engraved with the word "Deputy" on top of Scroll. (Plate No. 9)

Deputy President of the Mark Benevolent Fund — The Shield of Grand Lodge with "Benevolence" engraved on a bar above the Shield, and the word "Deputy" on a bar below the Shield. (Plate No. 10)

Deputy President of the Mark Executive Committee — The shield of Grand Lodge with "Executive" engraved on a bar above the shield and the word "Deputy" on a bar below the Shield. (Plate No. 10)

Deputy Grand Secretary — Two Pens in saltire with wreath engraved "Deputy" on a bar across upper part of Pens. (Plate No. 11)

Deputy Grand Director of Ceremonies — Two Wands in saltire engraved "Deputy" on a bar across upper part of Wands. (Plate No. 15)

REGALIA

Deputy Grand Inspector of Works	Semi-circular Protractor with the world "Deputy" engraved above the Protractor. (Plate No. 13)
Deputy Grand Sword Bearer	Two Swords in saltire engraved "Deputy" on a bar above centre of blades. (Plate No. 14)
Grand Deacon	A Mercury. (Plate No. 16)
Assistant Grand Chaplain	An open Book with "Assistant" engraved on a bar on the Quatrefoil below the Book. (Plate No. 7)
Assistant Grand Registrar	A Scroll with Seal of Grand Lodge attached, engraved with the world "Assistant" on the bottom of the scroll. (Plate No. 9)
Assistant Grand Secretaries	Two Pens in saltire without wreath, engraved "Assistant" on a bar below centre of pens. (Plate No. 11)
Assistant Grand Director of Ceremonies	Two Wands in saltire engraved "Assistant" on a bar across lower part of Wand. (Plate No. 15)
Assistant Grand Inspector of Works	Semi-circular Protractor with the word "Assistant" engraved on a bar on the Quartrefoil below the Protractor. (Plate No. 13)
Assistant Grand Sword Bearer	Two Swords in saltire engraved "Assistant" on a bar across hilts of Swords. (Plate No. 14)
Grand Librarian	A Lamp. (Plate No. 17)
Grand Organist	A Lyre. (Plate No. 18)
Grand Standard Bearer	Standard of Grand Lodge and the Standard of the Grand Master for the time being in saltire. (Plate No. 19)
Assistant Grand Standard Bearer	Standard of Grand Lodge and and the Standard of the Grand Master for the time being, in saltire engraved "Assistant" on a bar across lower part of Staves. (Plate No. 19)
Assistant Grand Organist	A Lyre with the word "Assistant" engraved on the Quatrefoil below the Lyre. (Plate No. 18)
Grand Inner Guard	Two Mallets in saltire. (Plate No. 20)
Assistant Grand Inner Guard	Two Mallets in Saltire engraved "Assistant" on a bar below centre of Mallets. (Plate No. 20)
Grand Steward	A Cornucopia. (Plate No. 21)
Grand Tyler	A Sword. (Plate No. 22)
Deputy Grand Tyler	A Sword engraved "Deputy" on a bar below the sword. (Plate No. 22)

(iii) The Jewels described as under, will not have the Emblem surrounded by a Quatrefoil but will be enclosed in a Circle containing the name of the Province or District:

Provincial or District Grand Master	Square and Compasses on a gold plate, representing a Keystone with Lewis. (Plate No. 23)
Deputy Provincial or Deputy District Grand Master	A Square on a gold plate, representing a Keystone with Lewis. (Plate No. 24)
Assistant Provincial or Assistant District Grand Master	The same as above, but with the word "Assistant" on a bar across lower part of Keystone. (Plate No. 24)

(iv) Other Provincial and District Grand Officers may wear Jewels similar to those worn by Officers of Grand Lodge, but with the Emblem surrounded by a circle, with the name of the Province or District inscribed on the circle. The emblem of the Jewel worn by a Provincial or District Grand Charity Steward shall be a Heart. The emblem of the Jewel worn by a Provincial or District Grand Almoner shall be a SCRIP-PURSE upon which is a heart.

REGALIA
PAST RANKS

173. (i)

Past Grand Master and Past Pro Grand Master	The Compasses extended to 45°, with a segment of a circle at the points and a Keystone with Lewis between the arms of the Compasses.
Past Deputy Grand Master	The Compasses and Square, with a Keystone between the arms of the former.
Past Assistant Grand Master	As for Past Deputy Grand Master with the word "Assistant" engraved on a bar across the lower part of the Jewel.
Past Provincial or Past District Grand Master	The Square and Compasses, on a gold plate, representing a Keystone with Lewis, with a Keystone suspended from the Compasses, on a blue enamel oval, surrounded by a red enamel garter containing the name of the Province or District in gold.
Past Provincial or Past District Deputy/ Assistant Grand Master	A Jewel to be suspended from a collarette $1^{1}/_{2}$ inches wide in the colours of the Order. The jewel will be based on Past Provincial/ District Grand Officer jewel but $^{3}/_{4}$ size.

(ii) Other Past Grand Officers may wear the Emblem of their respective Offices on a blue enamel oval, surrounded by a red enamel garter containing the words "Grand Lodge of Mark Master Masons" in gold.

(iii) Other Past Provincial or Past District Grand Officers may wear jewels similar to those worn by Past Grand Officers of Grand Lodge, but with the name of the Province or District inscribed in gold letters on the red enamel garter.

(iv) Holders of Overseas Mark Grand Rank may wear Jewels identical to those of Past Provincial or Past District Grand Officers, except that the word OVERSEAS, shall be inscribed in gold letters on the red enamel garter and that the emblem shall be identical in design to the Jewel of a Past Master (see Regulation 189(i)).

174. (i)

Master	The Square.
Past Master	The Keystone suspended from a Square.
Senior Warden	The Level.
Junior Warden	The Plumb and Axe.
Overseer	All-seeing Eye.
Chaplain	An open Book.
Treasurer	Two Keys in saltire.
Registrar of Marks	A Scroll.
Secretary	Two Pens in saltire.
Director of Ceremonies	Two Wands in saltire.
Almoner	A Scrip-Purse upon which is a Heart.
Charity Steward	A Heart.
Deacon	A Mercury.*
Assistant Secretary	Two Pens in saltire surmounted by a bar bearing the word "Assistant".
Assistant Director of Ceremonies	Two Wands in saltire bearing the word "Assistant", on a bar below the centre.
Organist	A Lyre.
Inner Guard	Mallet and Chisel.
Steward	A Cornucopia.
Tyler	A Sword.

*This is not compulsory for Lodges established prior to 1886.

REGALIA

(ii) These Jewels shall be in silver, on a plate representing a Keystone not exceeding three inches in length, with the name and number of the Lodge engraved thereon.

(iii) Members of Lodges (T.I. or otherwise) desirous of wearing a distinctive Jewel, must obtain the permission of the Grand Master, on the recommendation of the Mark Executive Committee.

JEWEL OF THE ORDER

175. A Keystone of mother-of-pearl, or white cornelian, with silver Lewis, suspended by a silver bar to a light blue and crimson ribbon, one inch wide. On the obverse is engraved the mark of the Brother, within an equilateral triangle, surrounded by a double circle bearing the Hebrew characters הכאשלשמי.. On the reverse a double circle, bearing the letters H. T. W. S. S. T. K. S. Officers of Grand Lodge and Provincial or District Grand Lodges shall suspend the jewel, if worn, by a dark blue and crimson ribbon, with gold or gilt Lewis, and gold or gilt bars.

CHARITY JEWEL

176. (i) A Charity Jewel shall be presented to every Brother who may serve as Steward at the Festival, which is held annually, and contribute a minimum donation of £50 to the Funds. Every additional Stewardship shall entitle the Brother to a Bar.

(ii) The Jewel shall be worn as a breast jewel and be suspended from a ribbon $1^{1}/_{4}$ inches wide, of $^{5}/_{8}$ inches dark blue centre with $^{5}/_{16}$ inches border of maroon. A Vice-Patron may wear the Jewel suspended around the neck from a ribbon $1^{1}/_{4}$ inches wide of 1 inch maroon centre with $^{1}/_{8}$ inch border of light blue. A Patron may wear the Jewel in a similar manner to a Vice-Patron with gold embroidery of the prescribed pattern and depth on the ribbon. A Grand Patron shall wear a skeletal lozenge shaped jewel suspended around the neck from $1^{1}/_{2}$ inches wide tricolour ribbon of maroon, white and light blue each of $^{1}/_{2}$ inches width with maroon being on the outside. A Grand Patron Gold Award may wear the skeletal lozenge jewel in a similar manner to the Grand Patron with gold embroidery of the prescribed pattern and depth of the ribbon.

KEYSTONE JEWEL *(Individuals)*

177. (i) Donors of £100 or more to the 150th Anniversary Keystone Fund, plus the cost of the Jewel and 150th Anniversary Button are entitled to wear a small breast jewel suspended from a ribbon of Grand Lodge colour, viz.: – dark blue edged with crimson with the 150th Anniversary Button attached in the centre of the ribbon. (Plate No. 30)

(ii) Masters of those Lodges which have qualified for the Jewel may wear the large jewel suspended from a collarette of the ribbon of the Order and the 150th Anniversary Button attached at the apex on all occasions during the period of their office. Commanders of Royal Ark Mariner Lodges which have qualified may wear the jewel suspended from a collarette of rainbow ribbon. The qualifications for any Lodge or its equivalent in another Masonic Body recognised as supporting the New Premises Fund are as set out in the Schedule hereto: (Plate No. 30a)

The Individual and Lodge jewels may be purchased in metal or silver gilt versions at current market prices: Metal Jewel; Silver Gilt Jewel; 150th Button

SCHEDULE

Lodge Amount per subscribing member of total membership per Grand Lodge records at date of passing 150th Anniversary Keystone Resolution

A. Mark and Royal Ark Mariner Lodges £25 per subscribing member
B. Provinces £10 per member in the Province
C. Districts & Inspectorates Overseas £5 per member in the District or Inspectorate

178. (i) A centenary jewel shall be a keystone of white enamel on which shall be an equilateral triangle within a double circle bearing on a blue background the Hebrew characters הכאשלשמי. with gold or gilt Lewis, surmounted by a gold or gilt Quatrefoil. (Plate No. 28)

(ii) A centenary jewel shall be worn as a breast jewel suspended by a ribbon one inch and a quarter in width of Grand Lodge colour, viz: – dark blue edged with crimson.

(iii) The ribbon of the jewel shall be attached to a bar brooch of gold or gilt, on the bar of which shall appear in blue lettering the name and number of the Lodge.

(iv) A scroll of gold or gilt on which shall appear in blue lettering the word "Centenary", shall be attached to the centre of the ribbon.

(v) The dates signifying the one hundred years of uninterrupted existence (e.g., 1868 – 1968) shall be in gold or gilt upon the crimson within the Quartrefoil.

REGALIA

179. (i) A jubilee jewel shall be a keystone of mother of pearl, or white cornelian on which shall be, in the appropriate colours, the arms of Grand Lodge or the badge of the Lodge, as required, within a double circle bearing on a blue background the name and number of the Lodge. The Lewis shall be of gold or gilt. (Plate No. 29)

(ii) A jubilee jewel shall be worn as a breast jewel suspended by a ribbon one inch and a quarter in width of Grand Lodge colours, viz:—dark blue edged with crimson.

(iii) The ribbon of the jewel shall be attached to a bar brooch of gold or gilt on the bar of which shall appear the word "Jubilee".

(iv) The dates signifying the fifty years of uninterrupted existence (e.g., 1918—1968) shall be in gold or gilt upon the keystone.

180. (i) A sesqui-centenary jewel shall be a keystone of mother of pearl, or white cornelian on which shall be, in the appropriate colours, the arms of Grand Lodge or the badge of the Lodge, as required, within a double circle bearing on a blue background the name and number of the Lodge. The Lewis shall be of gold or gilt. (Plate No. 29)

(ii) A sesqui-centenary jewel shall be worn as a breast jewel suspended by a ribbon one inch and a quarter in width of Grand Lodge colours, viz: – dark blue edged with crimson.

(iii) The ribbon of the jewel shall be attached to a bar brooch of gold or gilt on the bar of which shall appear the word "Sesqui-Centenary".

(iv) The dates signifying the one hundred and fifty years of uninterrupted existence (e.g., 1856 – 2006) shall be in gold or gilt upon the keystone.

181. In Grand Lodge or when appearing in their official capacities, or when the Grand Master so directs or a Provincial or District Grand Master so desires, Grand Officers shall wear chains of gold or metal gilt (Plate No. 38), and on other occasions collars of ribbon as specified in Rule 196. On all such occasions as are mentioned in this regulation, chains will be worn with full dress aprons.

182. (i) In Grand Lodge and in Provincial or District Grand Lodges, or when officially present at any Lodge in their respective Provinces or Districts, Provincial or District Grand Masters may wear chains of gold or metal gilt (Plate Nos. 39 or 40), and on other occasions collars of ribbon only, as specified for Officers of Grand Lodge.

(ii) In Grand Lodge and in Provincial or District Grand Lodges, or when officially present at any Lodge in their respective Provinces or Districts, Deputy and Assistant Provincial or District Grand Masters may wear chains of gold or metal gilt (Plate Nos. 39 or 40), and on other occasions collars of ribbon only, as specified for Officers of Grand Lodge, if Grand Officers, otherwise collars of ribbon only specified for Officers of Provincial or District Grand Lodge.

(iii) On all such occasions as are mentioned in this regulation, chains will be worn with full dress aprons.

183. (i) The full dress collars for Grand Officers, Present and Past, shall be of ribbon four inches broad, dark blue in the centre with one inch of crimson on each edge, embroidered with rose leaves and hyssop in gold, with edging of gold lace on each side. (Plate No. 27)

(ii) Undress collars for Grand Officers, Present and Past, shall be of similar ribbon, but without embroidery or edging, and with a vertical strip of gold braid enclosing a gold button.

184. Collars of Provincial or District Grand Officers shall be similar to the undress collars of Grand Officers but shall have a narrow edging of gold braid on each side with or without a fringe.

185. Collars of Holders of Overseas Mark Grand Rank shall be identical to those of Provincial or District Grand Officers.

186. (i) Officers of a Private Lodge (in their own Lodge) shall wear collars four inches broad, light blue in the centre, with one inch of crimson on each edge.

(ii) "Past Masters of Private Lodges shall wear on all occasions collars four inches broad, light blue in the centre with one inch of crimson on each edge, with a continuous line of silver braid a quarter of an inch wide in the centre."

(iii) A Master installed in any other recognised Constitution is entitled to the prefix 'Worshipful' but if he is a subscribing member of a Lodge under this Constitution he is not entitled to wear a Past Master's Collar until he has qualified as such by being installed as Master of a Lodge of Mark Master Masons in this Constitution.

REGALIA
APRONS

187. (i) Present and Past Grand Masters, Pro Grand Masters, Deputy Grand Masters, and Assistant Grand Masters, shall wear aprons of white kid, sixteen inches wide, fourteen inches deep, square at the bottom, bearing the Keystone and lined with dark blue, edged with ribbon four inches wide, dark blue in the centre, crimson on the edges, ornamented with embroidery and an edging of gold lace and bullion fringe. The aprons of Present and Past Deputy Grand Masters and Assistant Grand Masters shall have the word "DEPUTY" or the word "ASSISTANT", as appropriate, placed in small Roman Capitals on a bar below the Keystone.

(ii) The undress apron shall be as above described but without embroidery, edging or fringe.

188. (i) Present and Past Provincial or District Grand Masters shall wear similar aprons. In the centre shall be the Keystone with the name of the Province or District on a bar above surrounded by a wreath of rose leaves and hyssop in gold, to which shall be added three levels in gold.

(ii) Deputy and Assistant Provincial or District Grand Masters will wear the apron bearing the insignia of their Grand Rank.

189. (i) The full dress apron of other Grand Officers, Present and Past, shall be similar to the above but without embroidery, with edging of gold lace and narrow bullion fringe. In the centre shall be the emblem of the office surrounded by a wreath of rose leaves and hyssop in gold, to which shall be added three levels in gold in the case of a Master or Past Master of any recognised Constitution.

(ii) The undress apron shall be as above described but without the edging or fringe. The emblem, wreath, and levels shall be in dark blue, or dark blue and crimson, in place of gold.

(iii) In the case of the aprons, both full-dress and undress, of Grand Overseers, the word "MASTER", or the word "SENIOR", or the word "JUNIOR", as appropriate, shall be placed in small Roman capitals immediately above the emblem of office and inside the wreath.

(iv) In the case of the aprons, both full-dress and undress, of Grand Deacons, the word "SENIOR" or the word "JUNIOR", as appropriate, shall be placed in small Roman capitals immediately above the emblem of office and inside the wreath.

Grand Deacons may in all cases have the Emblem in gold.

190. The aprons of Provincial or District Grand Officers, Present and Past, shall be as described for Grand Officers with the following variations, viz.: – the emblem shall not be surrounded by a wreath, but shall be enclosed on a garter or circle in which shall be inserted the name of the Province or District: the emblem, garter, or circle may be in gold, or dark blue: if they are in gold the apron shall have a plain gold fringe. The emblem on the Apron of a Provincial or District Grand Charity Steward shall be a Heart. Provincial or District Grand Deacons, may in all cases have the emblem in gold.

191. The aprons of Holders' of Overseas Mark Grand Rank shall be identical to those of Provincial or District Grand Officers, except that the word OVERSEAS, shall be inscribed in the garter or circle and that the emblem shall be identical in design to the Jewel of a Past Master (see Regulation 174(i)).

192. Members of Private Lodges shall wear aprons of the same dimensions, with crimson lining and a ribbon two inches wide, and three rosettes, the colours of the ribbon and rosettes light blue in centre and crimson at each edge. Officers and Past Officers of Lodges may have the emblems of their office in silver or light blue in the centre of the apron.

193. The Masters and Past Masters of Lodges of any recognised Constitution shall wear in the place of three rosettes on the apron perpendicular lines upon horizontal lines, forming three several sets of two right angles; the length of the horizontal lines to be two and a half inches each, and of the perpendicular lines one inch each, these emblems to be of silver, half an inch broad, or of ribbon of the order.

GAUNTLETS

194. In private Lodges in which gauntlets of light blue and crimson silk with silver embroidery have been worn in the past, they may continue to be worn. (Plates illustrating the Jewels, etc., will be found at the end of the Constitutions and Regulations).

SECTION XII

REGULATIONS FOR THE GOVERNMENT OF THE DEGREE OF THE ANCIENT AND HONOURABLE FRATERNITY OF ROYAL ARK MARINER

Thirty-first Impression, incorporating all approved amendments to June 2012

1. (i) The Annual Assembly of the Ancient and Honourable Fraternity of Royal Ark Mariners shall be holden in each year, on the second Tuesday in the month of December, provided that if such regular day of the meeting be proclaimed as a Public Holiday or if for any reason it should be impracticable or inconvenient to hold the meeting on such day, the Grand Master may direct that the meeting shall be held on some other day in the month of December as the case may be.

(ii) Such Annual Assemblies shall normally be held in London but, should the Grand Master think fit, such Annual Assemblies may be held in the Provinces.

2. The Degree of The Ancient and Honourable Fraternity of Royal Ark Mariner shall be conferred only upon a Mark Master Mason. Candidates from recognised Constitutions not registered in the Books of Grand Lodge must sign a declaration of submission in the form set out in Regulation 19.

3. The Degree of The Ancient and Honourable Fraternity of Royal Ark Mariner is governed by the Most Worshipful Grand Master for the time being, with the advice of a Board to be called the Grand Master's Royal Ark Council. The Grand Master, the Pro Grand Master, Deputy Grand Master and Assistant Grand Master must have been Obligated as Royal Ark Mariners and be Installed Commanders of a Lodge of Royal Ark Mariners prior to their Installation or Appointment.

4. (i) The Grand Master's Royal Ark Council shall consist of those members of the Mark Executive Committee who are holders of Grand Rank in the Ancient and Honourable Fraternity of Royal Ark Mariner and other brethren similarly qualified, appointed by the Grand Master during his pleasure. Members of the General Board at Mark Masons' Hall who are members of the Ancient and Honourable Fraternity of Royal Ark Mariner shall be non-voting members of the Grand Master's Royal Ark Council.

(ii) The Grand Master's Royal Ark Council shall meet on such days as shall be determined by the President.

(iii) The President of the Mark Executive Committee of the Order of Mark Master Masons, if qualified under Regulation 4(i) above, shall act as chairman of meetings of the Grand Master's Royal Ark Council; in the absence of the President of the Mark Executive Committee, the chair shall be taken by the Deputy President of the Mark Executive Committee, if similarly qualified. If both the President and the Deputy President of the Mark Executive Committee are absent from a meeting of the Grand Master's Royal Ark Council, the Council shall elect a member to act as chairman at such meeting. If neither the President nor the Deputy President of the Mark Executive Committee is qualified under Regulation 4(i) above, the Council shall elect annually a member to act as chairman of meetings of the Council for the ensuing year.

(iv) Any member of the Grand Master's Royal Ark Council who has served for three consecutive years, shall on retirement from the Council be entitled to retain the style and dignity of Grand Master's Royal Ark Council (Honoris Causa) but it shall not of itself entitle him to attend meetings of the Council.

5. (i) The Grand Master's Royal Ark Council shall possess power and authority over the Degree of The Ancient and Honourable Fraternity of Royal Ark Mariner similar to those of the Mark Executive Committee over the Order of Mark Master Masons. It shall also exercise powers similar to those exercised by Grand Lodge in respect of hearing appeals from other Authority; in dealing with questions of erasure and expulsion; in amendment of these Regulations and approval of alterations in the fees prescribed by Regulation 23; and in all other matters where the Grand Master may so direct.

(ii) Provincial and District Grand Masters, their Deputies and Assistants (who shall have been Obligated as Royal Ark Mariners and be Installed Commanders of a Lodge of Royal Ark Mariners prior to their Installation or Investiture) shall have the same powers over Royal Ark Mariner Lodges and their Provinces or Districts as they have over Mark Lodges.

6. (i) The Grand Master may confer the rank designated Grand Rank of the Ancient and Honourable Fraternity of Royal Ark Mariner on Past Commanders who have rendered meritorious service in the Royal Ark Mariner Degree.

(ii) The holders of such rank shall wear at all Mark and Royal Ark Mariner Lodge meetings the distinctive regalia prescribed under Rule 30.

(iii) A fee of honour as laid down in Rule 23 shall be payable by each Past Commander upon whom Grand Rank of the Ancient and Honourable Fraternity of Royal Ark Mariner is conferred.

ROYAL ARK MARINER

(iv) The Grand Master may once a year confer the rank designated Overseas Grand Rank of the Ancient and Honourable Fraternity of Royal Ark Mariner on Past Commanders of Overseas Royal Ark Mariner Lodges not under a District, and who are subscribing members thereof. The holders of such rank shall be entitled to wear at all Mark and Royal Ark Mariner Lodge meetings the distinctive regalia prescribed under Rule 20 and, on appointment, shall pay the fee of honour laid down in Rule 23.

(v) The Grand Master may confer the rank designated GMRAC (honoris causa) of the Ancient and Honourable Fraternity of Royal Ark Mariner on holders of RAM Grand Rank who have rendered meritorious service in the Royal Ark Mariner Degree, which brethren will wear the regalia specified in Rule 30(ii).

7. (i) In every Province or District of Mark Master Masons the Provincial or District Grand Master may once a year confer on Past Commanders all of whom shall be subscribing members of a Royal Ark Mariner Lodge in the Province or District, the rank designated Provincial or District Grand Rank of the Ancient and Honourable Fraternity of Royal Ark Mariner as appropriate.

(ii) No Provincial or District Grand Master shall have power in any one year to confer such rank upon more than two Past Commanders for every complete three Royal Ark Mariner Lodges in his Province or District.

(iii) The holders of such rank shall wear at all Mark and Royal Ark Mariner Lodge meetings the distinctive regalia prescribed under Rule 30.

(iv) A Provincial or District Grand Lodge may direct that a Fee of Honour not exceeding forty percent (40%) of the Fee of Honour payable in respect of Royal Ark Mariner Grand Rank shall be payable to Provincial or District Grand Lodge funds by Past Commanders upon whom Provincial or District Grand Rank of the Ancient and Honourable Fraternity of Royal Ark Mariner, as appropriate, is conferred.

8. The Grand Master, Pro Grand Master, Past Grand Masters and Past Pro Grand Masters are entitled to the appellation of "Most Worshipful" (M.W.). The prefix of "Right Worshipful" (R.W.) shall be accorded to and shall only be used by the Deputy Grand Master and Past Deputy Grand Masters, Assistant Grand Master and Past Assistant Grand Masters, members of the Grand Master's Royal Ark Council including those Honoris Causa, and present and past Provincial and District Grand Masters. The title or address of "Worshipful" (W.) is to be used by all other holders of Grand Rank, Provincial, District or Overseas Grand Rank of the Ancient and Honourable Fraternity of Royal Ark Mariner and by the Present and Past Commanders of Royal Ark Mariner Lodges. All other members shall be styled or designated as "Brother" only.

9. (i) The precedence of members of the Grand Master's Royal Ark Council, including those Honoris Causa, Provincial and District Grand Masters, shall be as follows:

1. The Grand Master
2. Pro Grand Master
3. Past Grand Master
4. Past Pro Grand Masters
5. Deputy Grand Master
6. Past Deputy Grand Masters
7. Assistant Grand Master
8. Past Assistant Grand Masters
9. Members of the Grand Master's Royal Ark Council
10. G.M.R.A.C. Honoris Causa
11. Provincial and District Grand Masters
12. Past Provincial and District Grand Masters save that in a Province or District, only the Grand Master, Pro Grand Master, Deputy Grand Master, and the Assistant Grand Master and past holders of those offices, shall have precedence over the Provincial or District Grand Master, and the Deputy and Assistant Provincial or District Grand Masters.

(ii) Holders of Grand Rank in the Ancient and Honourable Fraternity of Royal Ark Mariner shall take precedence amongst themselves in order of appointment.

(iii) Holders of Provincial, District, and Overseas Grand Rank of the Ancient and Honourable Fraternity of Royal Ark Mariner, also those appointed to London Royal Ark Mariner Grand Rank prior to the Constituting of the Provincial Grand Lodge of London shall take precedence amongst themselves in order of appointment.

ROYAL ARK MARINER

10. Salutes shall be: Most Worshipful Brethren..11
Present and Past Deputy Grand Masters..9
Present and Past Assistant Grand Masters..9
Other Right Worshipful Brethren..7
Holders of Royal Ark Mariner Grand Rank...3
Holders of Provincial, District and Overseas Royal Mariner Grand Rank..........3

Present and Past Deputy and Assistant Provincial or District Grand Masters shall be entitled as such to 5, only within their own Provinces or Districts. The Senior Officer shall be saluted, all other salutations being at his discretion.

11. Every application for a Warrant to hold a new Lodge must be by petition to the Grand Master's Royal Ark Council, signed by at least three Royal Ark Mariners registered under the Regulations for the Government of the Degree of the Ancient and Honourable Fraternity of Royal Ark Mariners and its Districts and Lodges Overseas (who shall be the first Commander and Wardens), and specifying the Royal Ark Mariner Lodges to which they belong, or formerly belonged. The petition must be recommended by the Mark Lodge to which it is proposed that the Lodge of Royal Ark Mariners shall be attached, and be transmitted to the Grand Secretary. In the case of a Lodge in a Province, District, or Inspectorate, the petition is to be sent to the Provincial or District Grand Master, or Grand Inspector who is to forward it with his recommendation or opinion thereon to the Grand Secretary for the decision of the Grand Master's Royal Ark Council. It shall be within the power of the Grand Master to waive such of the foregoing requirements as the Grand Master shall think fit.

12. The following is the form of petition:

To the President and Members of the Grand Master's Royal Ark Council. We, the undersigned, being regularly registered Royal Ark Mariners of the Lodges mentioned against our respective names, pray for a Warrant of Constitution, empowering us to meet as a regular Lodge of Royal Ark Mariners under the title of .... at .... and to be attached to the .... Lodge of Mark Master Masons No. .... on the .... of ...., and there to discharge the duties of the Degree in a constitutional manner, according to the forms of the Degree and the regulations of the Grand Master's Royal Ark Council; and we have nominated, and do recommend Brother .... to be the first Commander, Brother .... to be the first Senior Warden, and Brother .... to be the first Junior Warden of the said Lodge. The prayer of this petition being granted, we promise strict obedience to the commands of the Grand Master, and the Laws and Regulations of the Degree. At a meeting of the .... Lodge of Mark Master Masons, No. ...., held on .... it was resolved that the consent of that Lodge be given to the above petition. Signed on behalf of the Lodge, ... Master.

13. (i) The regular officers of the Lodge are the Commander, Senior Warden, Junior Warden, Treasurer, Scribe, Senior Deacon, Junior Deacon, Guardian and Warder.

(ii) The Commander may also appoint as additional Officers a Chaplain, a Director of Ceremonies, an Almoner, a Charity Steward, an Assistant Scribe, an Assistant Director of Ceremonies, an Organist and Stewards.

(iii) As among the Officers of the Lodge, the order of precedence shall be as follows: Senior Warden, Junior Warden, Chaplain, Treasurer, Scribe, Director of Ceremonies, Almoner, Charity Steward, Senior Deacon, Junior Deacon, Assistant Scribe, Assistant Director of Ceremonies, Organist, Guardian, Stewards, Warder.

14. Every Lodge shall annually, at the regular meeting next before the day named in its by-laws for the installation, elect its Commander and Treasurer by ballot. If there is only one nomination and if no other member duly qualified shall have indicated to the Scribe that he wishes to be considered and if no member present calls for a ballot then it shall be permissible for the Commander to declare the election in favour of the nominated member, provided that the election shall not be so declared unless notice of the intention so to do and the identity of the sole Brother nominated shall have been given on the summons convening the meeting at which the election is to take place. No Brother shall be installed as Commander, except by special dispensation from the Grand Master, unless at the date of Installation: he shall have deemed to have served the office of Senior Warden or of Junior Warden in a regular Lodge of Royal Ark Mariners for one complete year, that is to say from one installation meeting to the next; he shall also be installed as Master of a Lodge of Mark Master Masons. The Brother so elected, if he be able, willing and qualified to serve as Commander, shall be regularly installed in the Chair at the next meeting according to antient usage. A Commander elect shall not assume the Commander's Chair until he has been regularly installed. The Commander shall be presented with a current copy of the Constitutions and Regulations.

ROYAL ARK MARINER

15. (i) Every Royal Ark Mariner Lodge shall be attached to a Warranted Lodge of Mark Master Masons and shall, unless the Grand Master otherwise directs, bear the name and number and enjoy the precedence of the Lodge to which it is attached. Should the Lodge to which it is attached be suspended or erased the Grand Master may give directions for its attachment to some other Lodge.

(ii) A Royal Ark Mariner Lodge may also be transferred from one Mark Master Masons' Lodge to another at its own request, subject to the concurrence of the Lodges concerned and the approval of the Grand Master. Where the Royal Ark Mariner Lodge is situated in a Province, District, or Inspectorate the application for such approval shall be transmitted through the Provincial, District or Inspectorate Grand Secretary.

(iii) The Royal Ark Mariner Lodge shall in all such cases take the name and number of the Lodge to which it is transferred unless the Grand Master shall otherwise direct.

(iv) Not more than one Royal Ark Mariner Lodge may be attached to any one Lodge of Mark Master Masons at the same time.

16. A Royal Ark Mariner Lodge shall keep a minute book, cash book, and roll of members, separate from those of the Mark Lodge to which it is attached. A separate fee shall be charged for conferring the Degree, and each Royal Ark Mariner Lodge shall procure for every Brother taking the Degree therein a Certificate from the Grand Lodge of Mark Master Masons, to be paid for by the Lodge at the same time.

17. Lodges of Royal Ark Mariners shall not be convened by the same summons which is issued for Mark Lodge meetings, and they shall have a separate and distinct set of Officers from those of the Mark Lodge to which they are attached, there being nothing to prevent the same Brethren from being Officers in both.

18. (i) When any Brother Mark Master Mason or Brother of the Order is a Candidate for membership of a Lodge the following particulars shall be sent to all members of the Lodge seven clear days before the meeting at which he is to come up for election: In all cases the:

    (a) Full name
    (b) Date of Birth
    (c) Place or places of abode
    (d) Name and number of Mark Lodge
    (e) Name of Proposer and Seconder*
    (f) Date of the proposal in open Lodge
    *both of whom must be Subscribing Members (or Honorary Members who are Past Commanders of the Lodge).

(ii) A Candidate for Election or Joining shall produce his Grand Lodge Certificate as a Mark Master Mason or a Certificate from the Secretary of the Lodge in which he was Advanced. Should such Certificates be from a Body other than the Grand Lodge of Mark Master Masons of England and Wales and its Districts and Lodges Overseas, the Secretary of the Lodge shall, before the ballot is taken, satisfy himself that the Body granting the Certificates is recognised by the United Grand Lodge of England or by Grand Lodge, as the case may be, and in case of doubt shall make any necessary inquiries of the Grand Secretary or the Provincial or District Grand Secretary.

(iii) If on a ballot three adverse votes shall appear against a Candidate for Election, Joining or Re-Joining, he shall not be Admitted. Every private Lodge has the power to diminish this number by its By-Laws; provided that if less than five members vote when the ballot is taken, a single adverse vote shall exclude.

(iv) Should a Candidate elected for Elevation not attend for Elevation within one year, his election shall be void, as shall be the election of a Brother as a Joining or Re-Joining member if he shall not have paid the requisite fee within one year of his election.

(v) For the purpose of this rule "a year" shall mean the period from the meeting at which the Candidate was elected up to and including the corresponding meeting of the Lodge in the following year. Should the election be at an emergency meeting, the year shall commence to run from the succeeding regular meeting.

(vi) Every Royal Ark Mariner Lodge shall make an immediate return to the Grand Secretary of the members elevated there in or joining the Lodge and at the same time transmit the fee for each member so elevated or joining. Royal Ark Mariner Lodges in a Province or District shall also make a similar return to the Provincial or District Grand Secretary and transmit the proper fees therewith.

19. (i) A candidate for elevation or a candidate for joining not already registered as a Royal Ark Mariner in the books of Grand Lodge, shall before the ballot is taken sign the following declaration:—

To the Commander, Wardens and members of the .... Lodge of Royal Ark Mariners No. .... I, ... do declare that should I be admitted as a member of the above Lodge, I hereby solemnly pledge myself to maintain and uphold the supremacy of the Most

ROYAL ARK MARINER

Worshipful Grand Master of the Grand Lodge of Mark Master Masons of England and Wales and its Districts and Lodges Overseas and of the Degree of the Ancient and Honourable Fraternity of Royal Ark Mariner, and to pay strict obedience to the Regulations for the government of the Degree of the Ancient and Honourable Fraternity of Royal Ark Mariner and to conform to all the antient usages and established customs of the Degree. I further solemnly promise to submit to, and observe, the by-laws of the Lodge from time to time made for its government. Witness my hand, this .... day of .... Witness ....

(ii) A candidate for joining or rejoining who is already registered as a Royal Ark Mariner in the books of Grand Lodge, shall before the ballot is taken sign the following declaration:—

To the Commander, Wardens and members of the .... Lodge of Royal Ark Mariners No. ...., I, ... do declare that should I be admitted as a member of the above Lodge I will submit to and observe the by-laws of the Lodge from time to time made for its government. Witness my hand, this .... day of .... Witness ....

(iii) In either case the signature of the candidate shall be witnessed or certified by a member of the Lodge.

(iv) These declarations must be carefully preserved by the Lodge.

20. (i) Every Royal Ark Mariner Lodge shall keep a register of its members and once in each year, before 30th September, transmit to the Grand Secretary on the prescribed form details of the subscribing membership of the Lodge, and of changes in membership, during the preceding twelve months period ending on 31st August. With such return shall be transmitted the Annual dues payable by the Lodge in respect of every Brother who has been a subscribing member of the Lodge, as shown in the records of Grand Lodge, during any part of the preceding twelve months period, whether or not such member shall be in arrears. In addition, a return showing the names of the Commander, Senior Warden and Junior Warden shall be transmitted to the Grand Secretary on the prescribed form immediately after the installation meeting of the Lodge.

(ii) Royal Ark Mariner Lodges in a Province or District shall render at the same times a copy of the above-mentioned returns to the Provincial or District Grand Secretary and transmit therewith any monies payable to the Provincial or District Grand Lodge.

21. (i) The Grand Master's Royal Ark Council shall possess power and authority over the Degree of the Ancient and Honourable Fraternity of Royal Ark Mariner similar to those of the Mark Executive Committee over the Order of Mark Master Masons. It shall also exercise powers similar to those exercised by Grand Lodge in dealing with questions of erasure; in amendment of these regulations of alterations in the fees prescribed by Regulation 16; and in all other matters where the Grand Master may direct. The Appeal Court alone shall have the power to expel a Brother.

(ii) Every Royal Ark Mariner Lodge has the power of framing by-laws for its government, provided that they are not inconsistent with the Regulations of the Grand Master's Royal Ark Council, or the Rules of Grand Lodge. The provisions of Rules 115 to 118 of the Constitutions and Regulations shall apply to such by-laws.

(iii) A Lodge shall have the same powers over its members as that of a Lodge of Mark Master Masons.

(iv) Expulsion of a Brother from the Order of Mark Master Masons or by the United Grand Lodge of England, the Supreme Grand Chapter of England or under the constitution of any Sovereign Grand Lodge recognised by Grand Lodge, the Grand Master's Royal Ark Council or other Masonic Order with whom the Council or other Masonic Order with whom the Council is in amity shall ipso facto take effect as expulsion from the Degree of the Ancient and Honourable Fraternity of Royal Ark Mariner.

(v) Suspension of a Brother by or from any of the Orders in (iv) above shall ipso facto take effect as suspension from the degree of the Ancient and Honourable Fraternity of Royal Ark Mariner for a like period and on like terms unless the Grand Master's Royal Ark Council shall otherwise direct.

22. Save as in these Regulations expressly provided the constitutions and Regulations of Grand Lodge (including the procedure for voluntary resignation) shall, mutatis mutandis, apply to the government of and discipline within the Royal Ark Mariner Degree as well as to the Duties to be observed by the Brethren of the Degree.

SCHEDULE OF FEES

23. Fees to the Grand Lodge of Mark Master Masons. Fees shall be payable to the Grand Lodge of Mark Master Masons in respect of:

a. Warrants of Constitution and Confirmation and Centenary Warrants

ROYAL ARK MARINER

  b. On the Registration of:
      (i)   A Brother on Elevation.
      (ii) A Joining Brother.
      (iii) A Founder member of a new Lodge.
  c   Dispensations.
  d. Duplicate replacement or amended Grand Lodge Certificates.
  e. Fees of Honour:
      (i) On appointment to Grand Rank in the Ancient and Honourable Fraternity of Royal Ark Mariner.
      (ii) On appointment to Overseas Grand Rank in the Ancient and Honourable Fraternity of Royal Ark Mariner.

They shall be such amounts as shall be determined by resolution of Grand Lodge of Mark Master Masons at the March Communication to take effect from 1st September following that Communication.

Annual Dues - The Annual Dues and Fees payable by each Lodge for each year ending 31st August in respect of every Brother who has been a subscribing member of that Lodge, as shown in the records of Grand Lodge, during any part of that year are due on 31st August of that year. They shall be such amounts as shall be determined by resolution of the Grand Lodge of Mark Master Masons at the March Communication to take effect from 1st September following that Communication. The Grand Master's Royal Ark Council shall have power to vary any or all of the Dues and Fees payable by Lodges overseas. Value Added Tax at the Standard Rate is payable on all Fees and Dues to Grand Lodge by all Brethren resident in the UK and the European Union.

24.   **FEES TO BE PAID TO PROVINCIAL OR DISTRICT GRAND LODGES**

A Provincial or District Grand Lodge may direct payments to be made to Provincial or District Grand Lodge funds by Lodges within the Province or District, for the under mentioned items, provided that the sums to be charged shall be stated in the Provincial or District by-laws and in no case shall exceed 40% of those similarly charged by Grand Lodge.

      (i)   Registration of a new Lodge or removal of a Warrant
      (ii)   For each candidate Elevated
      (iii) For each joining member
      (iv) Registration of by-laws or amendments of by-laws
      (v)   Dispensations other than those which can only be granted by the Grand Master

REGALIA, JEWELS, AND INSIGNIA

25. (i)   The jewel which every registered Royal Ark Mariner is entitled to wear, is a segmental plate, representing a rainbow, suspended from which is a Dove, with an olive branch in its mouth, hanging from a rainbow ribbon being the colours of the Degree, one inch and a quarter in width, suspended from a bar brooch (Plate No. 35). The name of the Royal Ark Mariner Lodge may be inscribed on the bar, and the number of the Lodge may be inscribed on an oval plate fastened on the ribbon. A Past Commander may also wear the letter N inside a triangle pendent from a similar ribbon. Subject to the provisions of this Rule the metal work of the jewel shall be silver or white metal.

      (ii)   The metal work of the jewel worn by a member of the Grand Master's Royal Ark Council, or by a holder of Royal Ark Mariner Grand Rank, or by a Royal Ark Mariner, who was a Commander or Past Commander and also a Present or Past Officer in the Grand Lodge of Mark Master Masons, shall be gold or gilt.

26. (i)   A centenary jewel shall be a green equilateral triangle on a white enamel Quatrefoil with a gold edge. On the apex of the triangle in gold, the letters "G", "L" and "M". At the angles of the triangle in gold, the letters "N", "J" and "S". In the triangle a gold Rainbow above which is the all seeing eye and below a dove. On the base of the triangle an Ark on Water. (Plate No. 36)

      (ii)   A centenary jewel shall be worn as a breast jewel suspended by a rainbow ribbon one inch and a quarter in width.

      (iii) The ribbon of the jewel shall be attached to a bar brooch of gold or gilt, on the bar of which shall appear in green lettering the name and number of the Lodge.

      (iv) A bar, of gold or gilt, on which shall appear in green lettering the word "Centenary" shall be attached immediately below the bar brooch of the jewel.

ROYAL ARK MARINER

(v) The dates signifying the one hundred years of uninterrupted existence (e.g., 1868-1968) shall be in gold or gilt upon the white within the Quatrefoil.

27. (i) A jubilee jewel shall be an equilateral triangle of white enamel on which shall be, in the appropriate colours, the arms of Grand Lodge, surmounted on a green background. (Plate No. 37)

(ii) A Jubilee Jewel shall be worn as a breast jewel suspended by a rainbow ribbon one inch and a quarter in width.

(iii) The ribbon of the jewel shall be attached to a bar brooch of gold or gilt, on the bar of which shall appear in green lettering the dates signifying the fifty years of uninterrupted existence (e.g., 1918-1968).

(iv) The name and number of the Lodge shall appear in green lettering on the white enamel of the equilateral triangle.

28. (i) The Apron is of white kid, with segmental flap, bordered with rainbow ribbon, one inch and a quarter in width with three rosettes.

(ii) The Apron of a Commander is as above, but with three triangles of silver or white metal, or embroidered in silver, instead of rosettes. Triangles will be of gold or gilt when worn by a member of the Grand Master's Royal Ark Council or by a holder of Royal Ark Mariner Grand Rank.

COLLARS

29. (i) A Lodge should provide collars for the use of its officers which shall be of rainbow ribbon four inches broad, with silver button and cord, and jewels of silver or white metal, showing the following emblems which, with the exception of the Deacon's, are enclosed in a triangle, viz.:

Commander	An Ark.
Past Commander	The Letter N.
Senior Warden	The Letter J.
Junior Warden	The Letter S.
Chaplain	An open Book.
Treasurer	A Key.
Scribe	Pens in Saltire.
Director of Ceremonies	Wands in Saltire.
Almoner	A Script Purse on which is a Heart.
Charity Steward	A Heart.
Senior Deacon	A Triangle.
Junior Deacon	A Triangle.
Assistant Scribe	Pens in Saltire bearing the word "Assistant" on a bar across the lower part of the pens.
Assistant Director of Ceremonies	Wands in saltire bearing the word "Assistant" on a bar across the lower part of the wands.
Organist	A Lyre.
Guardian	Axes in saltire.
Steward	A Cornucopia.
Warder	An Axe.

(ii) A Past Commander shall wear a collar similar to that of a Commander from which shall be suspended a Past Commander's jewel bearing the letter N inside a triangle, all of silver or white metal, provided that a member of the Grand Master's Royal Ark Council, or a holder of Grand Rank in the Ancient and Honourable Fraternity of Royal Ark Mariner, or a Royal Ark Mariner who on the 12th day of March 1968 was a Commander or Past Commander and also a Present or Past Officer in the Grand Lodge of Mark Master Masons, shall be entitled to wear a collar and jewel similar to that of a Past Commander but with gold button and braid on the collar and the jewel of gold or gilt.

(iii) The Grand Master, the Pro, Deputy, and Assistant Grand Master, also Provincial and District Grand Masters, and their Deputy and Assistant Provincial and District Grand Masters, shall all wear the Collar Jewel of their respective offices in the Degree of Mark Master Masons.

30. (i) A member of the General Board at Mark Masons' Hall shall, provided he is a holder of Grand Rank in the Ancient and Honourable Fraternity of Royal Ark Mariners, wear a collarette consisting of a rainbow ribbon one inch and a quarter in width worn close round the neck with a winged globe, having gold wings, suspended therefrom. (Plate No. 31) This collarette and jewel remains the property of Grand Lodge.

ROYAL ARK MARINER

(ii) A member of the Grand Master's Royal Ark Council and members of the Council Honoris Causa, shall wear a collarette consisting of a rainbow ribbon one inch and a quarter in width worn close round the neck with a winged globe, having gold wings, suspended therefrom. (Plate No. 31) Members of the Grand Master's Royal Ark Council and members Honoris Causa shall be permitted to wear the winged globe with gold wings. This collarette and jewel remains the property of Grand Lodge.

(iii) A holder of Royal Ark Mariner Grand Rank shall wear a collarette consisting of a rainbow ribbon one inch and a quarter in width, with a gold cord and button affixed vertically across the apex, worn close round the neck and under the points of the shirt collar, with an Ark superimposed on a triangle in gold suspended therefrom. (Plate No. 32)

(iv) A holder of Provincial, District or Overseas Grand Rank of the Ancient and Honourable Fraternity of Royal Ark Mariner shall wear a collarette consisting of a rainbow ribbon one inch and a quarter in width, worn close round the neck and under the points of the shirt collar, with an Ark superimposed on a triangle in silver or white metal suspended therefrom.

Dated 2011

Annex A - Trust Deed

THE GRAND LODGE OF MARK MASTER MASONS'
FUND OF BENEVOLENCE
CHARITY NUMBER: 207610
TRUST DEED

as amended and restated by a resolution of the Trustees dated 13th September 2011 and approved by Grand Lodge on the same date

William Sturges LLP
Burwood House
14-16 Caxton Street
London SW1H 0QY
Tel: 0207 873 1000
Fax: 0207 873 1010

DECLARATION OF TRUST

Date: 2011.

Parties

GEOFFREY MICHAEL REDMAN-BROWN, RAYMOND JOHN SMITH, JOHN LAWSON WILLIAM WRIGHT and MICHAEL HOWARD LAWSON all c/o 86 St James's Street, London SW1A 1PL ("the existing Trustees" who together with the future trustees of this deed are referred to as "the Trustees")

Background

The Trustees are the Trustees of the Grand Lodge of Mark Master Masons Fund of Benevolence (Charity No 207610) and hold the sum of £12,547,571 (as of 31st August 2011) on the trusts declared in this deed and it is contemplated that further money or assets may be paid or transferred to the Trustees upon the same trusts.

Now this deed witnesses as follows:

1 **Definitions**

In this deed the following words and phrases have the following meanings unless the context other requires:-

1.1	"**the Act**"	The Charities Act 1993 including any statutory modification or re-enactment thereof (including the provisions of the Charities Act 2006) for the time being in force;
1.2.	"**Assistant Grand Master**"	Any Assistant Grand Master appointed by the Grand Master;
1.3.	"**The Board**"	The General Board of the Order as defined by the Constitution;
1.4.	"**Brother**"	A Mark Master Mason;
1.5	"**the Charity**"	The charitable trust constituted by this deed;
1.6.	"**Clause**"	A clause of this Deed;
1.7	"**the Commission**"	The Charity Commission for England and Wales;
1.8	"**Constitution**"	The Constitutions and Regulations for the Government of the Order of Mark Master Masons;
1.9.	"**Dependant**"	Any person who is considered by the Trustees to be a dependant of a Freemason or deceased or former Freemason and subject to the Rules and Regulations;
1.10.	"**Deputy Grand Master**"	The person who is appointed Deputy Grand Master by the Grand Master;
1.11.	"**Deputy Grand President**"	The person who is the Pro Grand Master of the Grand Lodge or if there is no Pro Grand Master then the Deputy Grand Master of Grand Lodge;

1.12	**"Ex Officio Officer"**	The persons referred to in Clause 14 hereof;
1.13.	**"Deputy President"**	The person who is appointed Deputy President of the Charity by the Grand President;
1.14.	**"District"**	A Masonic District under the jurisdiction of Grand Lodge;
1.15.	**"Financial Expert"**	An individual, company or firm who is authorised to give investment advice under the Financial Services and Markets Act 2000 (or any statutory modification or re enactment thereof);
1.16	**"Freemason"**	A Freemason or Freemasons who have at any time been advanced into or joined a Lodge;
1.17	**"the Fund"** or **"the Fund of Benevolence"**	The property of the Charity;
1.18	**"Grand Festival"**	The Annual Grand Festival of Mark Master Masons;
1.19	**"Grand Lodge"**	The Grand Lodge of Mark Master Masons of England and Wales and its Districts and Lodges Overseas;
1.20	**"Grand Master"**	The person who from time to time is the Grand Master of Grand Lodge;
1.21	**"Grand President"**	The person who is the Grand Master for the time being;
1.22	**"Lodge"** or **"regular Lodge"**	Lodge of Mark Master Masons which is or has been under the jurisdiction of Grand Lodge;
1.23	**"Mark Master Mason"**	A Freemason who is or has been a member of a Lodge;
1.24	**"the Objects"**	The objects of the Charity set out in Clause 3;
1.25	**"Order"**	The Order of Mark Master Masons under the Grand Lodge;
1.26.	**"The President"**	The Brother who is appointed President of the Charity by the Grand President;
1.27	**"Pro Grand Master"**	Any Pro Grand Master from time to time appointed by the Grand Master;
1.28.	**"Province"**	A Masonic Province under the jurisdiction of Grand Lodge;
1.29.	**"Provincial Grand Lodge"**	A Provincial Grand Lodge formed from time to time in relation to any specified area in England and Wales which has been declared a Province by the Grand Master;
1.30	**"Provincial Grand Master"**	A Grand Master of a Provincial Grand Lodge from time to time appointed by the Grand Master;
1.31	**"Regulations"**	The Regulations of the Constitution;
1.32	**"Rule"**	Any rule made pursuant to Clause 10 of this deed;
1.33	**"The Secretary"**	Any person appointed by the Trustees in accordance with the provisions of this deed to perform the duties of Secretary of the Charity;
1.34	**"Subscribing Member"**	A member of a Lodge liable to pay a subscription, or a Secretary or Tyler of a Lodge excused from paying a subscription by the by-laws of a Lodge in return for his services;
1.35	**"Treasurer"**	The Treasurer of the Charity appointed by the Trustees in accordance with the provisions of this deed;
1.36	**"Trustee"**	A Trustee of this Charity;
1.37	**"Vice Grand President"**	"Vice Grand President" The person who is (in order of seniority) the Deputy Grand Master of Grand Lodge (where there is a Pro Grand Master for the time being of Grand Lodge) and all Assistant Grand Masters of Grand Lodge.

2. **Name**

The Charity and the Fund of Benevolence shall hereafter be administered and managed by the Trustees under the name of The Mark Benevolent Fund (registered charity number 207610) or such other name or names as Grand Lodge shall from time to time decide.

3. **Objects**

The Trustees shall hold the Fund of Benevolence and its income upon trust to apply them subject to the provisions of the Regulations for:

   3.1 such exclusively charitable purposes as may be determined from time to time by the Trustees, who in reaching that determination shall seek and consider the views of the Grand Lodge; and

   3.2 the relief of need, hardship and distress amongst Mark Masters Masons, their families or other dependant, and/or amongst retired employees of the Grand Lodge in such manner as they shall from time to time determine.

4. **Trustees**

   4.1. Until otherwise determined by a resolution of the Grand Lodge the number of Trustees shall be not less than nine nor more than twelve and shall be:-

   4.1.1. The President;

   4.1.2. The Deputy President;

   4.1.3. The President of the Board;

   4.1.4. Three Provincial Grand Masters elected by Grand Lodge at the Annual Investiture and who shall serve for three years and can be re-elected not more than for a further period of three years; and

   4.1.5. Three Mark Master Masons who shall be appointed by the Grand President to serve at his pleasure.

   4.2. The Trustees may co-opt up to three further Trustees to serve for up to three years from the date of their appointment but who may be co-opted thereafter for not more than a further period of three years.

   4.3. Any Trustee who ceases to be a Mark Master Mason shall immediately cease to be a Trustee.

   4.4. The Grand President may fill any vacancy created by death, resignation or any other cause whatsoever and new Trustees so appointed shall hold office until the next date for appointment of Trustees when they shall be eligible for reappointment for the same period as if they were being appointed for the first time.

5. **Powers**

In furtherance of the Objects but not otherwise the Trustees may exercise any of the following powers:

   5.1 to make grants to any individual, group, organisation or institution;

   5.2 to provide and assist in the provision of money, materials or other help;

   5.3 to organise and assist in the provision of conferences, courses of instruction, exhibitions, lectures and other educational activities;

   5.4 to publish and distribute books, pamphlets, reports, leaflets, journals, films, tapes and instructional matter on any media;

   5.5 to promote, encourage, carry out or commission research, surveys, studies or other work, making the useful results available;

   5.6 to provide or procure the provision of counselling and guidance;

   5.7 to provide or procure the provision of advice;

   5.8 alone or with other organisations to seek to influence public opinion and make representations to and to seek to influence governmental bodies and institutions regarding the development and implementation of policies provided that all such activities shall be conducted on the basis of well-founded reasoned argument and shall in all other respects be confined to those which an English and Welsh charity may properly undertake;

   5.9 to enter into contracts to provide services to or on behalf of other bodies;

   5.10 to acquire or rent any property of any kind and any rights or privileges in and over property and to construct, maintain, alter and equip any buildings or facilities;

   5.11 subject to any consent required by law, to dispose of or to deal with all or any part of the property comprised in the Fund with or without payment and subject to such conditions as the Trustees think fit;

5.12 subject to any consent required by law, to borrow or raise money for any purpose including for the purposes of investment or of raising funds, and to charge the whole or any part of the fund with repayment of money so borrowed or raised;

5.13 to set aside funds for special purposes or as reserves against future expenditure;

5.14 to invest the Fund and its income anywhere in the world in the purchase of or at interest upon the security of such stocks, funds, shares, securities or other investments or property of whatsoever nature and wheresoever situate (including without limitation any property not within the word "investment" as strictly construed) and whether involving liability or not (whether for investment purposes or in the course of carrying out the Objects) as the Trustees shall in their absolute discretion think fit to the extent that the Trustees shall have the same full unrestricted powers of varying and transferring investments and layout of monies in all respects as if they were absolutely entitled thereto beneficially;

5.15 to arrange for any property comprised in the Fund to be held in the name of a nominee (being a corporate body registered or having an established place of business in England and Wales) acting under the control of the Trustees or under the control of a Financial Expert acting under the Trustees' instructions and to pay any reasonable fee required;

5.16 to deposit documents and physical assets comprised in the Fund with any corporate body registered or having an established place of business in England and Wales as custodian and to pay any reasonable fee required;

5.17 to lend money and give credit to, take security for such loans or credit and guarantee or give security for the performance of contracts by any person or company;

5.18 to open and operate bank accounts and other facilities for banking and to draw, accept, endorse, issue or execute promissory notes, bills of exchange, cheques and other instruments;

5.19 subject to the restriction in Clause 5.21 to raise funds by way of subscription donation or otherwise;

5.20 to accept (or disclaim) gifts of money and any other property;

5.21 to trade in the course of carrying out the Objects and carry on any other trade which is not expected to give rise to taxable profits;

5.22 to incorporate subsidiary companies to carry on any trade or to assist or act as agents for the Charity;

5.23 subject to Clause 7:

    5.23.1 to engage and pay employees consultants and professional or other advisers; and

    5.23.2 to make reasonable provision for the payment of pensions and other retirement benefits to or on behalf of employees or former employees and their spouses and dependants;

5.24 to appoint and constitute such advisory committees as the Trustees may think fit;

5.25 to establish and support or aid in the establishment and support of any other organisations and to subscribe, lend or guarantee money or property for charitable purposes;

5.26 to amalgamate with or acquire or undertake all or any of the property, liabilities and engagements of any body having objects wholly or in part similar to those of the Charity;

5.27 to co-operate with charities, voluntary bodies, statutory authorities and other bodies and to exchange information and advice with them;

5.28 to pay out of the Fund the costs of forming and registering the Charity;

5.29 to insure the property of the Charity against any foreseeable risk and take out other insurance policies as are considered necessary by the Trustees to protect the Charity;

5.30. To pay any premium in respect of any indemnity insurance to cover the liability of the Trustees (or any Trustee) which by virtue of any rule of law would otherwise attach to them in respect of any negligence default breach of trust or breach of duty of which they may be guilty in relation to the Charity provided that any such insurance shall not extend to any claim arising from any act or omission which the Trustees (or any Trustee) knew to be a breach of trust or breach of duty or which was committed by the Trustees (or any Trustee) in reckless disregard of whether it was a breach of trust or breach of duty or not and provided also that any such insurance shall not extend to the costs of an unsuccessful defence to a criminal prosecution brought against the Trustees (or any Trustee) in its or their capacity as the Trustees or Trustee of the Charity;

5.31 during the period of 21 years from the date hereof or during such longer period as may for the time being be allowed by law to accumulate the whole or any part or parts of the income of the Fund by investing the same and the resulting income in any investments authorised by clause 5.14 and adding such accumulations to the Fund; and

5.32 to do all such other lawful things as shall further the Objects.

6. **Power to Delegate**

6.1 The Trustees may delegate any of their powers or functions to committees consisting of two or more persons appointed by them but at least one member of every committee must be a Trustee and all proceedings of committees must be reported promptly to the Trustees.

6.2 The Trustees may delegate day to day management of the affairs of the Charity to any person including any organisation whether established by the Trustees or by or with any other charities or voluntary bodies.

6.3 The Trustees may delegate the management of investment to a Financial Expert provided that:-

6.3.1 the investment policy is set down in writing for the Financial Expert by the Trustees;

6.3.2 every transaction is reported promptly to the Trustees;

6.3.3 the performance of the investments is reviewed regularly by the Trustees;

6.3.4. the Trustees are entitled to cancel the delegation arrangement at any time;

6.3.5 the investment policy and the delegation arrangements are reviewed at least once a year;

6.3.6. all payments due to the Financial Expert are on a scale or at a level which is agreed in advance are notified promptly to the Trustees on receipt; and

6.4. the Financial Expert may not do anything outside the powers of the Trustees.

7. **Benefits to Trustees and Conflict of Interest**

7.1 No Trustee may buy goods or services from the Charity, or sell goods or services to the Charity, or receive remuneration, or receive any other financial benefit from the Charity or from any trading company owned by the Charity, except in accordance with this deed or with the prior written approval of the Charity Commission and any conditions it prescribes.

7.2. A Trustee (as defined in Clause 7.8) may receive a financial benefit or other assistance from the Charity if he or she satisfies the criteria for receiving benefits or assistance set out in Clause 7.3 and subject to compliance with Clause 7.5.

7.3.

7.3.1. The Trustees may employ, or enter into a contract for the supply of goods or services with, one of their number. Before doing so, the Trustees must be satisfied that it is in the best interests of the Charity to employ, or contract with, that Trustee rather than someone who has no connection with the Charity. In reaching that decision, they must balance the advantage of employing a Trustee against the disadvantages of doing so (especially the loss of the Trustee's services as a result of dealing with the Trustee's conflict of interest as required by Clause 7.3). The remuneration or other sums paid to the Trustee must not exceed an amount that is reasonable in all the circumstances. The Trustees must record the reason for their decision in their minute book.

7.3.2. The Trustees may pay all the usual professional charges for business done by any Trustee who is a Solicitor Accountant or other person engaged in the profession or by any Partner of his or hers when instructed by the Charity to act in a professional capacity on its behalf.

7.3.3 A Trustee must be absent from the part of any meeting at which his or her employment or remuneration, or any other matter concerning the contract, are discussed. He or she must also be absent from the part of any meeting at which his or her performance in that employment, or his or her performance of the contract, is considered. He or she must not vote on any matter relating to his employment or the contract and must not be counted when calculating whether a quorum of Trustees is present at the meeting.

7.4 At no time may a majority of the Trustees benefit under Clause 7.3 hereof.

7.5. Without prejudice to Clause 7.3 whenever a Trustee has a personal interest in a matter to be discussed at a meeting, and whenever a Trustee has an interest in another organisation whose interests are reasonably likely to conflict with those of the Charity in relation to a matter to be discussed at a meeting (a "conflict of interests"), he or she must:

  7.5.1. declare an interest before discussion on the matter begins;
  7.5.2. withdraw from that part of the meeting unless expressly invited to remain;
  7.5.3. in the case of personal interests not to be counted in the quorum for that part of the meeting; and
  7.5.4. in the case of personal interests withdraw during the vote and have no vote on the matter.
7.6. For the purposes of Clause 7.5 a Trustee shall not be considered to have a personal interest or a conflict of interests by virtue of membership of the Order or any other Masonic body unless that Trustee is also a member of the governing body of the Order or such other body.
7.7 This Clause 7 applies to a firm or company of which a Trustee is:
  7.7.1 a partner;
  7.7.2. an employee;
  7.7.3. a consultant;
  7.7.4. a director; or
  7.7.5. a shareholder, unless the shares of the company are listed on a recognised stock exchange and the Trustee holds less than 1% the issued capital, as it applies to a Trustee personally.
7.8
  7.8.1. "Charity" shall include any company in which the Charity
    (a) holds more than 50% of the shares; or
    (b) controls more than 50% of the voting rights attached to the Shares; or
    (c) has the right to appoint one or more directors of the company.
  7.8.2. "Trustee" shall include:-
    (a) any child, parent, grandchild, grandparent, brother, sister, spouse or civil partner of Trustee or any person living with the Trustee as his or her partner or
    (b) the spouse or civil partner of any person falling within paragraph
  7.8.1 above or
    (c) a person carrying on business in partnership with the Trustee or with any person falling within sub- paragraph (a) and (b) above.
7.9. The Trustees may be paid all reasonable travelling hotel and other expenses properly incurred by them in connection with their attendance at meetings of trustees or committees of trustees or General Meetings or Festivals or otherwise in connection with the discharge of their duties but shall otherwise be paid no remuneration.

8. **The Fund**

 8.1 How supported

The Fund is supported by contributions received for the charitable purposes of the Order.

 8.2 Banking account

  8.2.1 Such contributions shall be paid to bankers appointed by the Trustees to an account to be called "THE MARK BENEVOLENT FUND" or such other name as the Trustees shall with the prior approval of the Grand President from time to time determine.

 8.3 Indemnity

A Trustee and his estate shall be kept fully indemnified from the Fund in respect of any losses occasioned to the property and assets of the Fund otherwise than as a result of his wilful neglect default or fraud.

 8.4. Nominee Company

A nominee company which is a Trust Corporation registered in the United Kingdom or a holding company registered in the United Kingdom acting under the control of the Trustees may be appointed by the Trustees elected under this Clause to act on their behalf for the purchase holding and sale of the investments of the Fund.

 8.5 Accounts

The accounts of the Charity shall be audited annually by a professional firm of Chartered Accountants which must be registered auditors and be presented to Grand Lodge for approval in March of each year and be available for inspection in the office of Grand Lodge, and a copy shall be sent to every Lodge.

9. **Qualification of Donors**

9.1 Qualification of Donors

	Brethren	Ladies
Life Subscriber	50	25
Life Governor	100	50
Vice-Patron	250	125
Patron	500	250
Grand Patron	1000	500
Grand Patron Gold Award	2500	1250

9.1.2. Brethren, Ladies and Lewises, who have attained a qualification prior to 30th August, 1993 shall remain entitled to such qualification.

9.1.3 Lodges which at the time of application have contributed to the Fund not less than £50 or £25 for every subscribing member may qualify as Patrons or Vice-Patrons respectively. After Patron status they may qualify for Grand Patron on contributing a further £1,000 to the Fund. After Grand Patron status they may qualify for Grand Patron Gold Award on contributing a further £2,500 to the Fund. Lodges which have attained a qualification prior to 30th August, 1993 shall remain entitled to such qualification.

9.1.4. Provinces or Districts which at the time of application shall have contributed £100 or £50 for every subscribing member within the Province or District may qualify as Patrons or Vice-Patrons respectively. After Patron status they may qualify for Grand Patron if all their Lodges have Grand Patron status and on contributing a further £2,000 to the Fund. After Grand Patron status they may qualify for Grand Patron Gold Award if all their Lodges have Grand Patron Gold Award status and on contributing a further £5,000 to the Fund.

9.1.5 Permanent privileges may be acquired by Ladies on payment of half the amounts.

9.1.6 Donations less than £10 received in any one year from a donor shall be credited to a nominated Lodge. This also applies to amounts of less than £20 received from a Lodge.

9.1.7 The qualifications may be varied from time to time by a resolution of the Grand Lodge.

9.1.8 The contribution payable to advance to a higher level of qualification shall be the difference between the contribution required for the former level at the prevailing rate and that required for the new level irrespective of the date of qualification.

9.2 **Application of the Fund**

The Fund shall be applied to the charitable purposes herein mentioned subject always to such approvals or consents as may for the time being be prescribed by law or in this deed. With the sanction of Grand Lodge any moneys in the Fund may be used to purchase real property or leasehold property having (unless otherwise authorised by the Charity Commissioners) not less than 20 years of the term unexpired at the date of purchase and to improve the same for use either for letting as a whole or in parts or to provide offices for the administration of the Fund or partly for letting and partly to provide such offices and the use of such offices may with the sanction of the Trustees be shared with other bodies or persons on proper terms (including with the Order or any of its Trustees or Committees). Any moneys in such Fund not immediately required for such purposes may be invested in such stocks shares property and chattels of what nature and wheresoever situate (and whether or not producing income) as the Trustees shall determine as if they were the absolute beneficial owners thereof subject nevertheless to such consents (if any) as may for the time being be required by law, but the interests and dividends on, and proceeds of, such investments (including any rents arising from such real or leasehold property so far as not required for its maintenance repair and improvement) shall be applied in the manner aforesaid. The allocation of the said Fund to these several purposes shall, save as herein otherwise provided be at the discretion of the Trustees provided that the Trustees may allocate such amount as it may deem necessary and proper towards the expenses of collection and administration of the Fund.

9.3 **Administration**

Grants and relief from the Fund shall be administered by the Trustees or by Grand Lodge on the Trustees' recommendation. The Trustees shall report to Grand Lodge the totals of grants and relief provided.

10. **Rules**

The Trustees may make Rules regulating all matters affecting the operation and conduct of the Charity and the Fund so far as the same do not conflict with the provisions of the Constitution and Regulations of the Order or this Trust Deed including the selection of and the criteria for grants to and the assistance of beneficiaries and all procedural financial and administrative matters.

11. **Proceedings of the Trustees**

11.1. The quorum necessary for the transaction of business of the Trustees shall be four Trustees. Questions arising at any meeting shall be decided by a majority of votes. In the case of an equality of votes the President shall have a second or casting vote.

11.2. Unless otherwise resolved by the Trustees the Trustees shall meet at least three times each year. Ex Officio Officers shall be given notice (in a manner agreed between them and the Trustees from time to time) setting out the proposed business to be transacted and may attend meetings of the Trustees save that the Ex Officio Officers shall not be entitled to vote at any such meeting.

11.3. The President (or in his absence the Deputy President) shall be entitled to be Chairman of all meetings of the Trustees at which he shall be present provided that the Ex Officio Officers (or any one of them) may appoint a person to preside in the place of the President for the purpose of that Meeting. If there be no President or Deputy President present or if at any Meeting they are unwilling to do so or are not present within five minutes after the time appointed for holding the meeting the Trustees present shall choose one of their number to be Chairman of that meeting save that if the President or failing him the Deputy President shall arrive he may assume the Chair of the meeting.

11.4 The President may, and on the request of three Trustees shall, at any time call a meeting of the Trustees. An Ex Officio Officer may also call a meeting of the Trustees at any time.

11.5 The Trustees may take a decision without a meeting by indicating their views to each other by any means, including electronic means. Such a decision shall require the unanimous consent of the Trustees and may, but need not, take the form of a resolution in writing, copies of which have been signed by each consenting Trustee or to which each consenting Trustee has otherwise indicated agreement in writing, whether sent or supplied in electronic form or otherwise.

12. **Secretary**

The Trustees may appoint a Secretary for such term at such remuneration (if not a Trustee) and upon such conditions as they may think fit and any Secretary so appointed may be removed by the Trustees.

13. **Treasurer**

The Trustees shall appoint a Treasurer from time to time, who may be a Trustee, and may from time to time remove such person and appoint someone in his place.

14. **Ex Officio Officers**

The Grand President, the Deputy Grand President and any Vice Grand President shall be Ex Officio Officers of the Charity. They shall have the right to attend all meetings and, in order of seniority, preside thereat, and shall be entitled to receive all notices and papers, but they shall not be entitled to vote.

15. **Amendment of Trust Deed**

15.1. No additions to, or amendment of this deed shall be made unless notice of such proposal as approved by a resolution of the Trustees has been sent out in the summons for the next regular meeting of Grand Lodge and the proposal considered and approved at such meeting. If it be desired to move an amendment to such a proposal notice in writing shall be given to the General Board of Grand Lodge seven clear days before the next regular meeting of Grand Lodge or such shorter period as the Presiding Officer of Grand Lodge shall permit. If the terms of the proposal appear in the minutes of the summons it shall not be necessary to set them out in extenso in the agenda of subsequent summonses, except in respect of any item covered by the original proposal which has been amended.

15.2 Provided that if the meeting at which new Clauses should be considered or confirmed coincides with the Grand Festival, such consideration or confirmation may be adjourned to the next meeting.

16. **Date when provisions come into force**

The provisions of this deed shall come into force on the date of this deed and from that date shall replace and supersede any previous rules or regulations relating to the Charity and the Fund of Benevolence.

Provided that nothing in this deed shall render invalid any act done before such date in accordance with the rules or regulations then in force.

17. **Winding up the Charity**

    The Trustees may resolve to wind up the Charity at a meeting called for that purpose and after the discharge of or provision for all debts and liabilities of the Charity the Trustees shall transfer the remainder of the Fund to such other charitable organisation approved by the Grand President having objects similar to the Charity as the Trustees shall decide, at or before dissolution, or in default by a resolution of Grand Lodge.

18. **Governing Law**

    The Charity shall be governed by the law of England and Wales.

    IN WITNESS whereof the parties hereto have executed this declaration of trust as their deed and have delivered it on the day and year first before written.

EXECUTED AS A DEED by	)
GEOFFREY MICHAEL REDMAN-BROWN	)
in the presence of	)
EXECUTED AS A DEED by	)
RAYMOND JOHN SMITH	)
in the presence of	)
EXECUTED AS A DEED by	)
JOHN LAWSON WILIAM WRIGHT	)
in the presence of	)
EXECUTED AS A DEED by	)
MICHAEL HOWARD LAWSON	)
in the presence of	)

Annex B – Rules Mark Benevolent Fund
MARK BENEVOLENT FUND
RULES MADE PURSUANT TO CLAUSE 10
OF TRUST DEED

William Sturges LLP.
Burwood House.
14-16 Caxton Street.
London SW1H 0QY

MARK BENEVOLENT FUND
RULES MADE PURSUANT TO CLAUSE 10 OF TRUST DEED

1. **Relief to Brethren**

1.1. Except as hereinafter provided a Brother shall not receive benefits from this Fund unless he has been registered under Grand Lodge, has paid the full advancement or joining fee, and has been a contributing member of a Lodge or Lodges for at least three years provided that the limitation of three years may be reduced to one year by the Trustees in the case of death or injury in the Naval, Military or Air Services of the Crown, or due to warlike operations, civil commotion, or shipwreck, or of blindness or other illness or misfortune, which in the opinion of the Trustees entitles the applicant to such relief.

1.2. No application shall be entertained on behalf of a Brother after a period of five years from the date when such Brother ceased to be a subscribing member of any Lodge, unless such Brother had been a contributing member of a Lodge or Lodges for at least fifteen years in all, nor unless the Brother has been a subscribing member of a Lodge for five years at least prior to the date of the application. In neither case need the periods of contribution have been consecutive.

1.3. Provided that the Trustees may entertain applications beyond the said periods if in its opinion there are special circumstances warranting such a course.

2. **Relief to dependants**

2.1. The Trustees may grant relief to the wife, widow, civil partner, mother or child of a Brother or the sister or other dependant of a deceased Brother subject to the following conditions:-

(a) If the Brother is living he must himself be qualified at the time of the application to apply for relief under the provisions of Rule 1 hereof or if he is deceased he must have been so qualified at the time of his death.

(b) A widow or civil partner must have been the wife or civil partner of a Brother of at least three years prior to the time that the said Brother ceased to be a subscribing member of the Order. Provided that the Trustees may grant relief in cases where a Brother died within three years of the marriage or partnership, if his death occurred whilst on active service in the Naval, Military or Air Forces or was due to warlike operations, civil commotion, shipwreck or accident. Provided also that the Trustees may, if they think fit, relieve a widow or civil partner not eligible under this Rule, but on one occasion only and to an amount not exceeding such sum as the Trustees shall from time to time in their absolute discretion decide.

(c) For a child of a deceased Brother to be qualified for relief the deceased Brother must have been a subscribing member of a Lodge at some time during the child's life and the child must have been supported at some time by the Brother.

(d) In these Rules "sister" shall not include a sister whose husband is living at the time of the application unless the marriage between them has been dissolved and shall not include anyone under the age of sixty years unless incapable of employment by reason of infirmity.

2.2. A son over 21 years of age or a daughter who at the time of the application for relief is a married woman shall not be eligible for relief. Provided that the Trustees may nevertheless make grants for purposes of his or her own education to sons who are over such age or married daughters.

3. **Grants for curative treatment or convalescence**

3.1. The Trustees may make a grant or grants to a Brother qualified for relief under Rule 1, or to the wife, civil partner, widow, mother, sister or dependant or child of a Brother qualified under Rule 2 to enable the applicant to undergo special curative or remedial treatment, or to pay his or her expenses through a period of convalescence, provided that such treatment or convalescence is recommended by the medical adviser of the applicant or of the person on whose behalf the application is made.

3.2. The application should be recommended as provided in Rule 14 but in a ease of urgency the Trustees may make a grant without a recommendation.

4. **Applicants from other Constitutions**

Brethren from recognised Constitutions may be relieved on production of certificates from their respective Lodges or Chapters, or other satisfactory evidence, but except in a case of illness only one grant which shall not exceed such sum as the Trustees shall from time to time decide shall be made. The provisions of Rule 1 shall not apply to such cases, nor shall a formal petition or recommendation by a Lodge be necessary.

5. **Time of presenting a petition**

Petitions for relief must be deposited with the Secretary at least seven clear days before the meeting of the Trustees at which they are to be considered.

6. **Second application**

    6.1. The Trustees may determine the period within which a Grant is to be disbursed and at the end of that period any undistributed amount of the Grant shall be returned to the Fund.

    6.2. A further petition cannot be received from an Applicant who has been relieved until after the expiration of one year from the date of relief unless there are special circumstances, not considered at the time of the former grant, which in the opinion of the Trustees justify a further grant.

7. **Amount of relief by Trustees**

The Trustees may order the payment of any sum not exceeding five thousand pounds towards the relief of a petitioning Brother or the wife civil partner or child of a Brother, or of a widow, mother, sister or other dependent or child of a deceased Brother.

8. **Amount of Relief by the President**

If in any case the maximum sum which may be paid under the preceding Clause shall appear to the Trustees inadequate to the exigencies of the petitioner's circumstances, the Grand President, on a representation from the Trustees, may sanction an amount not exceeding such sum as the Trustees shall from time to time decide to a Brother, or the wife, mother, civil partner, widow or child of a Brother.

9. **Emergency Grant**

Notwithstanding any provision in this deed, the Trustees may make an emergency grant without the presentation of a formal petition or the recommendation of a petition, and make a further grant on the receipt of a petition or recommendation, but the total amount of such grants shall not exceed the amount of the single grant permitted by this deed.

10. **Grants**

The following provisions shall apply in the case of Annuities granted out of the Fund prior to 13 December, 1977 under the Rules then obtaining:

    10.1. If any Annuitant shall remarry or enter into another civil partnership, that annuity shall thereupon cease and determine unless the Trustees directs its continuance.

    10.2. Where it subsequently appear any material facts have been suppressed or false representations made at or before the date of election or appointment, the Trustees may decrease, suspend or terminate the annuity.

    10.3. The Trustees may increase, decrease, suspend or terminate an annuity should the circumstances change, or should Grand Lodge make any alteration in the conditions for, or limitations on, annuities. In particular the Trustees may decrease, suspend or terminate an annuity if the Annuitant becomes possessed of an increased income independently of the annuity, or becomes entitled to an old-age or other pension.

    10.4. The Trustees may suspend or terminate an annuity if the Annuitant shall anticipate the payment thereof, or charge or encumber the same in any manner, or shall by improper conduct render him or her unworthy to be supported by the Fund.

    10.5. The Annuities shall be paid in advance on the Friday after the first Thursday in January, April, July and October. An Annuitant shall furnish such evidence as to being alive and in the case of a widow, mother, or civil partner, unmarried or not in a civil partnership, on the day when any payment becomes due, or at a date shortly before such day, as the Trustees may direct.

11. **Petitions**

    11.1. Applications for grants must, except as herein specially provided, be by petition on the form by the Trustees from time to time, stating inter alia the name, age, place of abode, and circumstances of the person for whom relief is sought, and the name and number of the Lodge in which, and the time when, he (or in the case of a wife, civil partner, widow, mother or child, the husband, partner or father) was advanced, and any other relevant matter known to the petitioner. The petitioner must, if capable, sign the petition. A petition for relief for a child under sixteen should be presented by a parent or guardian if such there be. When by reason of age, health, or other sufficient cause it is not practical for the person for whom relief is sought or, in the case of a child, the parent or guardian of such child, to present a petition, a petition on behalf of such person may be presented by a Brother having knowledge of the relevant circumstances.

11.2. The petitioner must, so far as possible, furnish any information relevant to the case which the Trustees may reasonably require and, if the Trustees so direct, must verify the statements by statutory declaration.

12. Recommendation

12.1. Petitions should be accompanied by a recommendation by a Brother or Brothers having knowledge of the relevant circumstances.

12.2. Where the recommendation is by a Lodge or by a Brother in a Province or District, it should be forwarded with the Petition to the Provincial or District Grand Secretary or Almoner, who should transmit it to the Secretary with his report thereon.

12.3 In all cases the recommendation should be accompanied by a report from a Brother who has actually visited the Petitioner. Such Petitioner should preferably be a member of the Lodge sending the recommendation.

13. Subscribing Member

13.1. "Subscribing member" shall mean a Brother who (a) has actually paid his subscriptions to a Lodge during the year in question or (b) has been excused from payment of such subscription under the by-laws by reason of his service as Secretary or (c) has acted as Tyler or Serving Brother to the Lodge throughout such year.

13.2 Where reference is made in this deed to a Brother having been member of a Lodge or Lodges for a stated number of years, periods during which a Brother has been a contributing member of different Lodges, whether simultaneously or not, shall be reckoned cumulatively.

13.3 Failure of a Lodge to register a Brother on advancement or joining, or to pay annual dues for a Brother, shall not affect the rights of such Brother, or of those claiming through him, if it be shown that such Brother has paid the requisite fees and subscriptions to the Lodge.

14. Serving Brethren Tylers

Reference in their Rules to a Brother having paid full fees for advancement or joining shall not apply to a Brother obligated as a Serving Brother or advanced as a Tyler and for the purposes of this deed a Serving Brother shall be deemed to have been registered with Grand Lodge on the date when he was obligated.

15. Definitions

15.1. In any Rule from 1 to 17 inclusive, the term "widow"

(a)   shall include a former wife of a deceased Brother but

(b)   shall not include a woman who has remarried after the death of (or divorce from) the Brother through whom she claims.

15.2. When a former wife applies for relief, the term "husband" in any such Rule shall mean the Brother to whom she was previously married.

15.3 Reference to a dependant in such Rule shall mean a person either over the age of 65 years or under that age but not reasonably able to earn his or her living and (in either case) for whose maintenance the deceased Brother on whose record the petition is founded has been accustomed to assume some responsibility.

15.4 The definitions contained in Clause 1 of the Trust Deed shall apply to these Rules and Regulations.

16. Withholding grants

Should it appear that any grant has been obtained by false statements, or suppression of material facts, or that the circumstances of the petitioner have changed so that the need for the grant no longer exists, or is less than at the time the grant was made, the Trustees may withhold or instruct any Province District or Lodge to whom the grant has been paid to return to the Fund the unexpended portion of the grant, or any part thereof.

17. Power to continue relief

Notwithstanding any provision in Rules 1 to 17 the Trustees may continue to relieve a petitioner who has been relieved before the date at which the Clauses contained in this deed come into force.

INDEX

	Rule
ANNUITANTS AND ANNUITIES	165 to167 & Annex B
ANTIENT LANDMARKS	2, 15, 98

APPEALS
Grand Lodge ... 144
Other Authorities ... 144, 145
Procedure ... 57, 66

APPLICATIONS
Annuity ... 165 to167 & Annex B
Benevolent Grant ... 165-167 & Annex B
Centenary Warrant ... 54, 154, 178
Commemorative Jewel ... 155
Clearance Certificate ... 91,135,146
Convalescent Grant ... 165-167 & Annex B
Educational Grant ... 165-167 & Annex B
Grand Lodge Certificate ... 141
Grand Master, to ... 39, 70
Warrant ... 91
Warrant of Confirmation ... 95

APPOINTMENT
Assistant Grand Master ... 31
Assistant Provincial/District Grand Master ... 71
Deputy Grand Master ... 30
Deputy Provincial/District Grand Master ... 71
Officers of Grand Lodge ... 32
Officers of Private Lodges ... 96,97, 100 to 104
Officers of Provincial/District Grand Lodge ... 75, 77
Past Rank ... 32, 77, 87, 164
Pro Grand Master ... 28
Provincial/District Grand Master ... 70

APRONS ... 187 to 193

ARREARS
By-laws – provision as to ... 116
Exclusion for ... 145

ASSISTANT GRAND MASTER
Appointment and Powers ... 31
Fee of Honour ... 164
Jewel ... 172
Precedence ... 4
Visiting private Lodges... 147

ASSISTANT PROVINCIAL/DISTRICT GRAND MASTER ... 71, 172

AUDIT (See ACCOUNTS)

AUDITOR
Elected by Grand Lodge... 23
Must be a Chartered Accountant and a Registered Auditor ... 23(iii)

AUTHORITIES. (See DISCIPLINARY POWERS, GENERAL BOARD, GRAND LODGE, PROVINCIAL/DISTRICT GRAND MASTERS)

INDEX

Rule

BALLOT
- Candidates for membership ... 136, 137
- Casting vote on ... 161
- Exclusion of member ... 144
- Grand Treasurer ... 34
- Master ... 97, 100
- Members of General Board at Mark Masons' Hall ... 49
- Members of Mark Executive Committee ... 54
- Removal of Officer ... 110
- Treasurer and Tyler ... 108

BANKING ACCOUNT.
- Grand Lodge ... 23, 52, 158
- Private Lodge ... 132, 158

BENEVOLENCE – FUND OF
- Administration of ... 165-167 & Annex B
- Rules ... Annex B
- Trustees ... 167

BENEVOLENT GRANTS
- Rules ... Annex B

BOOKS
- Books to be kept by Lodge ... 126, 127, 132
- Books to be kept by Lodge of Instruction ... 150
- Disposal of ... 150, 153
- Inspection of ... 62, 153, 158
- Surrender by Officers ... 150, 156

BUSINESS
- Conduct of ... 161
- Emergency meetings ... 8, 124
- Grand Lodge. (See AGENDA)
- Minimum attendance for transaction of ... 125

BY-LAWS
- Amendment of ... 115, 121
- Approval of ... 115
- Arrears – provisions as to ... 116, 145
- Ballot – provisions as to ... 116, 137
- Contents of ... 116, 117
- Enforcement of ... 99
- General Board – power to require alteration ... 115
- Presentation to new members ... 118
- Provincial/District Grand Lodge ... 84
- Submission to ... 118

CANDIDATES
- Advancement, for – must be Master Masons ... 134
- Ballot for ... 137
- Certificates of ... 135
- Clearance certificates ... 91, 135, 146
- Declarations ... 136
- Election void ... 138
- Fees for ... 164
- Grand Lodge Certificates ... 141

INDEX

	Rule
Joining members	134
Particulars	126, 127, 134
Proposal	134
Returns of	127

CASTING VOTE ... 161

CENTENARY & COMMEMORATIVE JEWELS ... 154, 155, 174, 178 - 180

CENTENARY WARRANT ... 154

CERTIFICATES, CLEARANCE ... 91, 135, 146

CERTIFICATES, GRAND LODGE
- Advancement, on ... 141
- Districts, in ... 141
- Duplicate ... 141
- Fees for ... 164
- Lost or destroyed ... 141
- Posting ... 141
- Presentation in Lodge ... 62,141
- Production of ... 135
- Serving Brothers and Tylers ... 140
- Signature ... 141
- Visitors ... 148

CERTIFICATES FROM OTHER RECOGNISED CONSTITUTIONS ... 91, 135, 148

CHAINS ... 181, 182

CHARITY JEWEL ... 176

CHILD
- Advancement in life ... Annex B
- Educational Grant ... Annex B
- Eligibility for relief ... Annex B
- Petition by or on behalf of ... Annex B

CLERKS
- Control by Board ... 52

CLOTHING – MASONIC (See REGALIA)

COLLARS (See REGALIA)

COMMITTEES
- Business – conduct of ... 161
- Enquiry, of ... 68
- General Board ... 54
- Limitation of powers ... 157
- Private Lodges ... 133
- Provincial/District Grand Lodge ... 68, 86

COMPLAINTS
- Adjudication ... 52, 63, 64
- Affecting members of General Board ... 51
- Honorary Members and Visitors to withdraw ... 144

INDEX

Rule

CONFIRMATION
By-laws ... 115
Constitutions and Regulations – alterations to ... 169
Minutes ... 14, 126

CONSECRATION OF LODGE ... 92

CONSTITUTIONS AND REGULATIONS
Amendment of ... 169
Declaration of obedience to ... 91, 98, 136
Presentation to new members ... 141

"CONTRIBUTING MEMBER" – DEFINITION ... Annex B

CONVALESCENT AND CURATIVE GRANTS ... Annex B

CORRESPONDENCE
General Board ... 55
Grand Lodge ... 39, 52
Grand Master ... 39, 52

DAYS – PROHIBITED ... 122

DEATH OR INCAPACITY
Grand Master ... 29
Master ... 113
Master Elect ... 100, 101, 102
Provincial/District Grand Master ... 73

DECLARATIONS. (See CANDIDATES, MASTER)

DEFINITIONS ... 168

DEPUTIES AND ASSISTANT GRAND OFFICERS ... 32, 164, 172

DEPUTY GRAND MASTER
Appointment and Powers ... 30
Fee of Honour ... 164
Jewel ... 172
Precedence ... 4
Visiting private Lodges ... 147

DEPUTY MASTER ... 106, 107

DEPUTY PROVINCIAL/DISTRICT GRAND MASTER
Appointment and Powers ... 71, 72, 73
Regalia and Jewels ... 172, 182, 188
Fee of Honour ... 164
Not as such a member of Grand Lodge ... 5
Precedence, salutes, etc. ... 4, 6, 71
Visiting private Lodges ... 147

DISCIPLINARY POWERS
General Board ... 57 to 63, 158
Grand Lodge ... 60
Master of Lodge ... 143
Provincial/District Grand Master ... 57 to 63, 158

INDEX

                                                                                                         Rule

DISPENSATIONS
    Fees for 87, 164
    Meeting without a Warrant 94
    Master ineligible without Dispensation... 100
    Master in two Chairs 107
    Re-election for third consecutive year 107
    Not previously served office of Master in a Craft Lodge......................... 97
    Not served office of Warden for one complete year 97
    Change of meeting date or place 104,122

DISPUTES AND DIFFERENCES.. 62, 63

DISSOLUTION OF LODGE 153

DISTRICTS. (See PROVINCES AND DISTRICTS)

DISTRICT GRAND LODGE, GRAND MASTER, GRAND OFFICERS (See PROVINCIAL AND DISTRICT)

DOCUMENTS
    Custody and production of 158
    Lodge of Instruction 150, 158

"DUE FORM" 13, 76

DUES
    Annual 87, 164
    Lodge liable for 87, 164
    Neglect to transmit, penalty... 130, 131
    Neglect to transmit, not to prejudice Brother 131
    None for Honorary Member or Tyler 139, 140
    Suspended Lodge 59
    Transmission of 127, 128

EDUCATIONAL GRANTS .... Annex B

ELECTION
    Candidates 137
    General Board 54
    Grand Master 27
    Grand Treasurer 34
    Master 97, 100, 101, 104
    Treasurer and Tyler 108
    Void... 138

EMERGENCY MEETING 124

ERASURE OF LODGE
    Contumacy, for 59
    Failure to meet 151
    Failure to make returns... 130
    Grand Lodge, sole power of 3, 60
    Numbers less than three 151
    Procedure 60
    Recommendation as to 60
    Surrender of Warrant 151

INDEX

Rule

EXCLUSION
- Arrears – Member in 145
- Grand Lodge, from 20
- Meeting, from 143
- Permanent 144, 145

EXPENSES
- Grand Festival 44
- Suspended Lodge 59

EXPULSION
- Contumacy 58
- Grand Lodge, sole power of 3, 60
- Procedure 60
- Recommendation 60
- Returns, failure to make 130
- United Grand Lodge, by 3

FEES
- By-laws – to state 116
- Failure to pay joining fee 138
- Fees of Honour 87, 164
- Prescribed fees 87, 164, 168
- Tylers 140

FINES
- General Board 57, 58
- Master 143
- Provincial/District Grand Master 57, 58

FORM
- Opening of Grand Lodge 13
- Opening of Provincial/District Grand Lodge 76

FOUNDERS 91

FUND OF BENEVOLENCE. (See BENEVOLENCE – FUND OF)

FUNDS – INVESTMENT OF 23

FURNITURE – NOT TO BE PLEDGED 149

GAUNTLETS 194

GENERAL BOARD 49
- Business of Grand Lodge – Preparation of 9, 10, 11, 14
- Committees 54, 68
- Communications, to and by 55
- Constitution of 49
- Control of buildings, correspondence, employees, finance, property 23
- Deputy President 50
- Disciplinary powers .... 57 to 67, 158
- Exclusion – Powers as to 144, 145
- Masonic clothing, when to be worn 51
- Meetings 50
- Member, complaints affecting 51
- Minutes 56

INDEX

	Rule
Power to reject propositions	10
Powers of	52
President	4, 6, 32, 49, 50, 164, 172
Propositions to be submitted to	9
Quorum	51
Reports to Grand Lodge	53
Suspension by	59

GRAND DEACONS 4, 32, 164, 172

GRAND DIRECTOR OF CEREMONIES 4, 32, 41, 164 189

GRAND FESTIVAL 44, 176

GRAND INNER GUARD 4, 32, 42, 172, 189

GRAND INSPECTOR OF WORKS 4, 32, 40, 172

GRAND LIBRARIAN 4, 32, 172

GRAND LODGE
Absence of Grand Master	12
Absence of Grand Officers	52, 54
Accounts	23, 39, 52, 54
Adjournment of business	16
Agenda	10, 11
Alterations of Constitutions and Regulations by	169
Appeals to	3, 57, 66 to 68,144
Authority of	1, 2, 3
Banking Account	23, 54
Business	9, 10, 11, 14, 15, 16, 17
Business –	
First considered by General Board	14
Order of	14
Calling to Order	18
Certificates	39, 61, 135, 140, 141,163
Communications – Quarterly	7
Constitution of	1, 4, 5
Custody of Property	23, 39, 52
Employees	52
Erasure and Expulsion by	3, 58, 60, 130, 144
Grants by	Annex B
Investments of	23
Laws emanate from	3
Meetings	7, 8
Members not to speak twice	21
Members to address Grand Master	19
Membership	1, 4, 5
Minutes	11, 14
Motions in	9, 14, 15
Opening and closing	13
Order of Service to Mark Masonry	33
Past Rank	1, 4, 5, 32, 48
Porch	42, 44
Precedence of members in	4
Property of	23, 39, 52, 156
Qualification of	5

479

INDEX

	Rule
Reports to	14
Representatives from and to other Recognised Constitutions	52
Returns to	127 to 131
Right of reply	21
Seal of	38, 39
Silence in	18
Sovereign Grand Lodges – Recognition of	24, 25, 26
Special Meetings	8
Style of	1
Summoning	8
Transgression of Rules	20
Visitors to	22
Voting in	17, 161

GRAND MASTER

Absence of	12
Acceptance and rejection of propositions by	15
Applications to	39
Appointment by	
Assistant Grand Master	31
Deputy Grand Master	30
Grand Officers	32
Grand Master's Award	33
Grand Stewards	44 to 47
Holders of Overseas Mark Grand Rank	90
Members of General Board	49
Pro Grand Master	28
Provincial/District Grand Masters	70
Representatives to other Recognised Constitutions	52
Appointment to	
Past Rank	32
Tribunal	64
Correspondence	
Dealt with by Grand Secretary	39
Dealt with by General Board	52
Death or incapacity of	29
Directions by	64, 65, 104, 160
Jewel	172
Lodges meeting in other Provinces or Districts	119
May appoint a Tribunal	64
New Sovereign jurisdictions	24, 25, 26
Nomination, election and installation of	27
Provinces and Districts – formation, etc	69
Removal of Grand Officers	48
Subscriptions – Powers to remit	145
Title and Salute	6
Visiting Lodges	147
Warrant, property of	94

GRAND MASTER'S LODGE

Precedence of	93

GRAND OFFICERS

Absence of	32
Appointment and Investiture	32
Aprons	189
Attendance on Grand Master	37

INDEX

	Rule
Chains and Collars	181, 182, 183
Fees of Honour	164
Installed Master, who must be	32
Jewels	172
One office only	32
Past Rank	1, 4, 6, 32, 48
Precedence, Title and Salutes	4, 6
Recommendation of	45
Forfeiture of	46
Time for submitting	44
Removal of	47
Representatives of and to other Recognised Constitutions	52
Vacancies	32

and (See INDIVIDUAL HEADINGS)

GRAND ORGANIST ... 4, 32, 164, 172

GRAND OVERSEER ... 4, 32, 147, 164, 172

GRAND REGISTRAR ... 4, 32, 38, 164, 172

GRAND SECRETARY
- Applications to Grand Master through ... 39
- Appointment and tenure of office ... 35
- Custodian of Regalia and Grand Lodge Documents ... 39
- Duties ... 39
- Jewel ... 172

GRAND STANDARD BEARER ... 4, 32, 164, 172

GRAND STEWARD
- Appointment ... 44
- Duties ... 44
- Fee of Honour ... 164
- Grand Festival, management of ... 44
- Jewel ... 172
- Lodge ... 47, 93
- Member of Grand Steward's Lodge ... 47
- Nomination ... 44, 45, 46

GRAND SWORD BEARER ... 4, 32, 164, 172

GRAND TREASURER ... 4, 32, 34, 164, 172

GRAND TYLER ... 4, 36, 43, 172

GRAND WARDEN ... 4, 32, 147, 164, 172

GRANTS. (See BENEVOLENT GRANTS)

HOLIDAYS
- Dates of meetings falling on ... 122
HONORARY MEMBERS ... 139

IMMEDIATE PAST MASTER
- Absence of ... 96
- Installing Master, as ... 103

INDEX

	Rule
Position and precedence	96
Ruling Lodge	114
Summoning Lodge	113

INSPECTION OF ACCOUNTS, BOOKS, etc.
    Grand Lodge 23
    Private Lodges 158

INSPECTORATES 89
    Permissive Officers 89

INSTALLATION
    Deputy Master 106
    Grand Master 27, 29
    Master .... 97, 100 to 104
    Meeting, date of 105, 116
    Provincial/District Grand Master 70

INVESTITURE
    Deputy/Assistant/Provincial/District Grand Master 71, 77, 83
    Grand Officers 32
    Lodge Officers 100, 101, 102, 105,109
    Provincial/District Grand Officers 77, 83

IRREGULARITIES, ADJUDICATION ON 57

JEWEL OF THE ORDER 175

JEWELS .... 172 to 180

JOINING MEMBERS. (See CANDIDATES)

JUBILEE JEWEL 155, 179

KEYSTONE JEWEL 177

SESQUI-CENTENARY JEWEL 180

LAWS EMANATE FROM GRAND LODGE 2

LOCAL FUNDS 87

LODGE
    Accounts 132, 158
    Amalgamation 152
    Appeals by 66
    Books of 62, 126, 127, 132
    By-laws 99, 115, 116, 118
    Candidates. (See CANDIDATES)
    Certificates from 146
    Collars 186
    Committees 133, 157
    Consecration 92
    Disorderly conduct in 143
    Dissolution of 151, 153, 156
    Dues payable by 87, 164
    Erasure 3, 130, 151

INDEX

	Rule
Exclusion of members	143, 144, 145
Failure to meet	151
Fees of advancement or joining	117, 138
Fees payable by Lodges	87, 164
Fines	143
Funds of	132, 156
Furniture, not to be pledged	149
Gauntlets	194
Honorary members	139
Inspection of books	62, 158
Jewels	174
Joining member. (See CANDIDATES)	
Master. (See MASTER)	
Meaning of	168
Meetings. (See MEETINGS)	
Minutes	126
Name and number of	93
Officers of	96
Petition form of	91
Precedence of	93
Property	149, 156
Publication of proceedings	163
Register	127
Regular Lodge, meaning of	168
Removal	120, 121
Representatives in Grand Lodge, and Provincial and District Grand Lodges	1, 4, 74
Resignation from	61, 142
Returns by. (See RETURNS)	
Secretary. (See OFFICERS)	
Summons	134
Suspension. (See SUSPENSION)	
Transfer to other Recognised Constitutions	24, 26
Treasurer. (See OFFICERS)	
Tyler. (See OFFICERS)	
Visitors	148
Visits by Grand Master, etc.	147
Warden. (See OFFICERS).	
Warrant. (See WARRANT)	

LODGE OF INSTRUCTION	150

MASONIC CLOTHING

Not to be worn in public	162

MASTER

Absence of	102, 114
Appointment and Investiture of Officers	100 to 105, 109
Apron and Jewel	174, 193
Attending, to produce books and Warrant	62
Casting vote	161
Custodian of Warrant	94
Death or incapacity of	113
Deputy Master	106, 107
Direction in difficulty	104
Dispensation for	97, 100, 101, 105, 107
Duration of office	107
Election and Installation	97 to 105

INDEX

	Rule
Enforcement of Constitutions and Regulations, antient landmarks and By-laws	98, 99
Fines by	143
Installing Master	103
Member of Grand Lodge and Provincial/District Grand Lodge	1, 4, 74
Obligation	98
One chair only	107
Order—maintenance of	99, 143
Outgoing Master	100, 101, 102, 107
Period of office	107
Qualifications	97
Removal of Officers by	110, 111
Vacancies, powers to fill	109 to 112
Visitors, power to refuse admission	148

and (See MASTER ELECT, PAST MASTER)

MASTER ELECT
Absence, death or incapacity of	100 to 102
Dispensations for	97, 100
Installation	97 to 105
Refusal of office	100, 101

MASTER MASON
Candidates, must be	134, 135
Tyler, must be	140

MEETINGS OF PRIVATE LODGES
Absence of Master	114
Adjournment forbidden	123
Alteration of dates	105, 121
Dates and place to be fixed by by-laws	116
Election and Installation	97, 100 to 104, 116
Emergency	124
Lodge of Instruction	150
Minimum attendance	125
Only one on one day	123
Prohibited days	122
Public holidays	122
Regular, cannot be cancelled	123
Temporary removal	120, 122
Warrant—without	94

MEMBERS OF PRIVATE LODGES
"Contributing"—definition	Annex B
Election of. (See CANDIDATES)	
Exclusion for misbehaviour	143
Exclusion, permanent	144, 145
Honorary	139
In arrears	116, 145
Reinstatement	144, 145
Resignation	142
Returns of	127, 129, 139
"Subscribing"—definition	168

MEMORIALS AND PETITIONS TO GRAND LODGE ... 9, 10, 14

MINUTES
Minute Book	126

INDEX

	Rule
Confirmation of	14, 126
General Board	56
Grand Lodge	11, 14
Lodge of Instruction	150
Private Lodge	126
Provincial/District Grand Lodge	85

MISBEHAVIOUR
    Grand Lodge, in ... 20
    Private Lodge, in ... 143

MOTIONS
    Alteration of by-laws ... 115
    Exclusion of member ... 144, 145
    Grand Lodge, in ... 9, 10, 14, 15, 21
    Proposed and seconded, must be ... 161
    Removal of Office ... 48, 82, 110, 111, 112

NAME OF LODGE NOT TO BE CHANGED ... 93

NOMINATION. (See GENERAL BOARD, GRAND MASTER, GRAND STEWARDS, GRAND TREASURER)

NOTICE OF MOTION
    Alteration of by-laws ... 115
    Alteration of Constitutions and Regulations ... 169
    Grand Lodge, in ... 9, 10, 14, 15, 21

NUMBER OF LODGE ... 93

OBLIGATION OF MASTER ... 98

OFFICERS OF LODGE
    Appointment and Investiture ... 96, 97, 100, 101, 102, 104, 109
    Collar and Jewel ... 174, 186
    First Officers ... 91
    Honorary member cannot be Officer ... 139
    Immediate Past Master ... 96, 103, 114
    One regular office only ... 96
    Overseers and Wardens are members of Grand Lodge and Provincial/District Grand Lodge ... 1, 4, 74
    Precedence ... 96
    Regular and additional ... 96
    Removal ... 110, 112
    Secretary ... 96, 116, 126, 146
    Treasurer ... 96, 108, 132
    Tyler ... 96, 108, 110 to 112, 140
    Vacancies ... 109
    Wardens ... 1, 4, 74, 96, 100, 102, 113, 114, 124

OVERSEAS MARK GRAND RANK ... 173, 191

PAST MASTER
    Apron, Collar and Jewel of ... 173, 186, 193
    Definition of ... 168
    Installing Master, acting as ... 103
    Member of Grand Lodge and Provincial/District Grand Lodge ... 5, 74
    Return of ... 129

INDEX

	Rule
Ruling Lodge	114
Summoning Lodge	113
Title and Salute	6
and (See IMMEDIATE PAST MASTER)	

PAST RANK
- Grand Lodge ... 4, 32, 48, 173
- Provincial/District ... 77, 78, 82

PATRONS AND VICE-PATRONS
- Collarettes ... Annex B
- Qualifications ... Annex A

PETITIONS. (See APPLICATIONS)

PRECEDENCE OF OFICERS
- Grand Lodge ... 4
- Private Lodges ... 96
- Provincial/District Grand Lodges ... 77, 80, 81
- Provincial/District Grand Masters and their Deputies and Asisstants ... 70, 71

PREFIXES, TITLES AND ABBREVIATIONS ... 6

PRESIDING OFFICER
- Casting Vote ... 161
- Powers ... 161

PRIVATE LODGE. (See LODGE)

PROCEDURE AT MEETINGS
- General ... 161
- Grand Lodge ... 9 to 22

PRO GRAND MASTER ... 4, 28, 172

PROVINCES/DISTRICTS – CREATION, etc. ... 69

PROVINCIAL/DISTRICT GRAND LODGE
- Accounts ... 88
- By-laws ... 84
- Committees ... 86, 157
- Consent to transfer of Lodge ... 24, 26
- Dues and Fees payable to ... 87
- Local funds ... 87
- Meetings ... 75
- Membership ... 74
- Minutes ... 85
- Opening ... 76
- Past rank in ... 77
- Returns to ... 128, 129

PROVINCIAL/DISTRICT GRAND MASTER
- Absence, death or incapacity of ... 73
- Appeals from ... 66
- Appointment and Installation ... 70
- Appointment of Officers ... 71, 72, 77
- Certificates – issue of in District ... 141

INDEX

	Rule
Clothing and Jewel	172
Communication to Grand Master through	70
Disputes and differences – adjudication	63
Disciplinary powers	57 to 65
Exclusion – powers in case of	144, 145
Fee of Honour	164
Removal of Officers by	82
Summoning Brethren, etc.	62
Suspension by	59

PROVINCIAL/DISTRICT GRAND OFFICERS
Appointment and Investiture	77, 83
Aprons, chains, collars and jewels	172, 182, 184, 190
Fees of Honour	87
One office only	77
Past rank	77
Precedence	4, 77
Precedence, local only	81
Qualification	77, 79
Removal	82
Vacancies	83
and (See INDIVIDUAL HEADINGS)	

PROVINCIAL/DISTRICT GRAND OVERSEER
Qualification	79

PROVINCIAL/DISTRICT GRAND SECRETARY
Certificates – issue by District Grand Secretary	141
Report on petitions for relief	Annex B

PROVINCIAL/DISTRICT GRAND TREASURER ... 88

PROVINCIAL/DISTRICT GRAND WARDEN
Qualification	79

PUBLIC HOLIDAYS ... 7, 50, 122

PUBLIC WEARING OF REGALIA ... 162

PUBLICATION OF PROCEEDINGS ... 163

QUARTERLY COMMUNICATIONS ... 7

RECOGNISED CONSTITUTIONS
Correspondence with	39
Definition of	168
Joining member from	135, 136
Petitioners for Warrant, from	91
Recognition of	24, 25
Relief to members of	Annex B
Representatives from and to	39
Transfer of Lodges to	24, 26
Visitors from	22, 148

RECOMMENDATION OF PETITIONS
New Warrant	91
Relief	Annex B

INDEX

	Rule
RECORDS OF GRAND LODGE	38, 39

REGALIA
- Aprons ... 187 to 193
- Chains ... 181 to 182
- Collars ... 183 to 186
- Gauntlets ... 194
- Jewels ... 172 to 180
- In Private Lodges ... 192, 193

REGISTER – LODGE ... 127

REGISTRAR OF MARKS ... 96

REGISTRATION
- Advancement, on ... 141
- By-laws ... 115
- Fees for ... 87, 164
- Joining members ... 127
- Marks ... 127
- Neglect of Lodge, not to prejudice Brethren ... 131
- Tylers ... 140

"REGULAR LODGE" – DEFINITION ... 168

REJOINING MEMBERS. (See CANDIDATES)

REPLY – RIGHT OF ... 21

REPRESENTATIVES TO AND FROM OTHER
RECOGNISED CONSTITUTIONS ... 39, 168

RESIGNATION ... 61, 142

RESOLUTIONS
- Amalgamation ... 152
- Amendments to ... 161
- By-laws – for alteration of ... 115
- Constitutions and Regulations – for amendments of ... 169
- Disposal of Lodge Property ... 153
- Exclusion, for ... 144, 145
- Irregular ... 15, 161
- Proposing and seconding ... 161
- Removal of Officers ... 48, 82, 110 to 112
- Right of reply ... 21
- Surrender of Warrant ... 151

RETURNS
- Annual ... 127 to 129
- Masters, Past Masters, etc ... 129
- Neglect – penalty for ... 130
- Neglect not to prejudice Brethren ... 131
- New members ... 127
- Provinces/Districts, to ... 128, 129
- Provincial/District Grand Officers ... 77

INDEX

	Rule
RIBBONS	175, 176
RIGHTS OF BRETHREN NOT PREJUDICED BY FAILURE TO MAKE RETURNS	131
SALUTES	6
SAVING CLAUSE	171
SEAL OF GRAND LODGE, CUSTODY	38
SERVICE OF NOTICE, SUMMON, etc.	160
SERVING BROTHERS	140
SOVEREIGN GRAND LODGES	24, 25, 26
Effect of recognition	25
Right of Lodge to transfer	26
STYLE OF GRAND LODGE	1
"SUBSCRIBING MEMBER" – DEFINITION	168
SUBSCRIPTIONS	116, 117, 139, 145
SUSPENSION	
Lodges or Brethren, of	59
TIME, Computation of	159
TIME IMMEMORIAL LODGES – PRECEDENCE OF	93
TITLES AND ABBREVIATIONS	6
TRIBUNAL – SPECIAL	
May be appointed by Grand Master	64
TYLERS	108, 110, 140
UNATTACHED BRETHREN	
Tyler – Status of	140
Visitors	148
UNITED GRAND LODGE	
Expulsion by	3
VACANCIES	
General Board	49
Grand Officers	32
Officers of Private Lodges	109
Provincial/District Grand Officers	83
VISITS BY GRAND MASTER, etc.	147
VISITORS	
Grand Lodge	22
Private Lodges	148

INDEX

	Rule
VOTING IN GRAND LODGE	17

WARDENS
- Appointment and Investiture ... 100 to 102
- Precedence ... 96
- Ruling Lodge ... 114
- Service counts from Investiture ... 97
- Short service of – dispensation for ... 97
- Summoning Lodge ... 113
- When deemed to have served full term ... 97, 100 to 102

WARRANT
- Centenary ... 154
- Dispensation for meeting without ... 94
- Endorsement – forbidden ... 94
- Fees for ... 87, 164
- Lodge cannot meet without ... 94
- Loss of ... 94
- Master, custodian of ... 94
- Petition for ... 91
- Production to higher Authority ... 62
- Property of Grand Master ... 94
- Surrender of ... 151
- Transfer forbidden ... 153

WARRANT OF CONFIRMATION ... 95

WIDOW
- Annuitant ... Annex B
- Relief to ... Annex B
- Remarriage of ... Annex B

WIFE OF BROTHER – RELIEF TO ... Annex B

REGULATION FOR THE DEGREE OF ROYAL ARK MARINER

BY-LAWS ... 21

CANDIDATE
- Certificate for ... 16
- Declaration ... 19
- Fee for ... 23
- Mark Master Masons – must be ... 2
- Particulars of ... 18
- Recognised Constitutions – from ... 2
- Return of ... 18

COMMANDER
- Apron, Collar and Jewel ... 25 to 29
- Election and Installation of ... 14
- Qualifications of ... 14

DATE OF ANNUAL ASSEMBLY ... 1

DEGREE RULED BY ... 3

INDEX

	Rule
FEES AND DUES	23

GRAND LODGE RULES
Application of ... 22

GRAND MASTER
Governs Order ... 3
Nominates additional members of Grand Master's Royal Ark Council... 4
Secrets – to have ... 3

LODGE
Election of Commander ... 14
Mark Lodge – to be attached to ... 15
May be transferred ... 15
Name and number... 15
Officers... 13, 14
Separate books, summonses and Officers ... 16, 17
Warrant ... 11, 12

OVERSEAS GRAND RANK OF THE ANCIENT AND HONOURABLE FRATERNITY OF ROYAL ARK MARINER ... 6, 7, 9, 30

PAST COMMANDER'S COLLAR ... 29

PROVINCIAL/DISTRICT GRAND MASTERS AND THEIR DEPUTIES
Power of ... 5
Secrets – to have ... 5

PROVINCIAL/DISTRICT GRAND RANK OF THE ANCIENT AND HONOURABLE FRATERNITY OF ROYAL ARK MARINER ... 7, 8, 9, 23, 30

REGALIA... 25 to 30

RETURNS ... 18, 20

ROYAL ARK COUNCIL
Appeals to ... 5
Collarette ... 30
Constitution of ... 4
Membership (Honoris Causa) ... 4
Members to be holders of Grand Rank in the Ancient and Honourable Fraternity of Royal Ark Mariner... 4
Powers ... 3, 5
Warrant – Application to Council for ... 12

GRAND RANK IN THE ANCIENT AND HONOURABLE FRATERNITY OF ROYAL ARK MARINER
Appointed by Grand Master ... 6
Fee of Honour... 23, 24
Holders must be Past Commanders... 6
Precedence ... 9
Provincial Grand Rank ... 7
Titles ... 8

SALUTES ... 10

INDEX

Rule

WARRANT
Petition for 11, 12
Recommendation by Mark Lodge 11, 12

PLATES

PLATE NO. 1

PLATE NO. 2

GRAND MASTER AND PRO GRAND MASTER

PAST GRAND MASTER AND PAST PRO GRAND MASTER

PLATE NO. 3

PLATE NO. 4

DEPUTY GRAND MASTER

Assistant Grand Master, as above, but with the word "Assistant" engraved on a bar across the lower part of the jewel.

GRAND SENIOR WARDEN

PLATE NO. 5

GRAND JUNIOR WARDEN

PLATE NO. 6

GRAND OVERSEER

PLATE NO. 7

GRAND CHAPLAIN

(a) Deputy Grand Chaplain, as above, and with the word "Deputy" on a bar on Quarterfoil above the Book.
(b) Assistant Grand Chaplain, as above, and with the word "Assistant" on a bar on the Quarterfoil below the Book.

PLATE NO. 8

GRAND TREASURER

PLATE NO. 9

GRAND REGISTRAR

Deputy Grand Registrar, as above, but in addition the word "Deputy" engraved on upper part of scroll.

PLATE NO. 10

PRESIDENT OF THE GENERAL BOARD
AND DEPUTY PRESIDENT OF THE GENERAL BOARD

PLATE NO. 11

GRAND SECRETARY

(a) Deputy Grand Secretary, as above, and with the word "Deputy" on a bar across the upper part of pens.
(b) Assistant Grand Secretary, as above, but without Laurel and the word "Assistant" on a bar across lower part of pens.

PLATE NO. 12

GRAND DIRECTOR OF CEREMONIES

PLATE NO. 13

GRAND INSPECTOR OF WORKS

PLATE NO. 14

GRAND SWORD BEARER

(a) Deputy Grand Sword Bearer, as above, but with the word "Deputy" on a bar above centre of blades.
(b) Assistant Grand Sword Bearer, as above, but with the word "Assistant" on a bar across hilts.

PLATE NO. 15

DEPUTY AND ASSISTANT
GRAND DIRECTOR OF CEREMONIES

(a) Deputy Grand Director of Ceremonies, as above, but with the word "Deputy" on a bar across the upper part of Wands.
(b) Assistant Grand Director of Ceremonies, as above, but with the word "Assistant" on a bar across lower part of wands.

PLATE NO. 16

GRAND DEACON

PLATE No. 17

GRAND LIBRARIAN

PLATE No. 18

GRAND ORGANIST

PLATE No. 19

GRAND STANDARD BEARER

(a) Assistant Grand Standard Bearer, as above, but with the word "Assistant" on a bar across lower part of staves.
(b) The dexter standard displays the Arms of Grand Lodge. The sinister displays the Arms of the Grand Master for the time being.

PLATE No. 20

GRAND INNER GUARD

Assistant Grand Inner Guard, as above, but with the word "Assistant" on a bar below centre of mallets.

498

PLATE NO. 21

GRAND STEWARD

PLATE NO. 22

GRAND TYLER

DEPUTY GRAND TYLER, AS ABOVE, BUT WITH THE WORD "DEPUTY" ON A BAR ACROSS THE UPPER PART OF SWORD

PLATE NO. 23

PROVINCIAL OR DISTRICT GRAND MASTER

PLATE NO. 24

DEPUTY PROVINCIAL OR DISTRICT GRAND MASTER

Assistant Provincial or Assistant Grand Master, as above, but with the word "Assistant" engraved on a bar across lower part of Keystone.

Plate No. 25

Master

Plate No. 26

Past Master

Plate No. 27

Collar of Grand Officer

Plate No. 28

Centenary Jewel

PLATE NO. 29

JUBILEE OR SESQUI-CENTENARY JEWEL

PLATE NO. 30

KEYSTONE JEWEL

PLATE NO. 31

GRAND MASTER'S ROYAL ARK COUNCIL

PLATE NO. 32

JEWEL OF HOLDERS OF GRAND RANK IN THE
ANCIENT AND HONOURABLE FRATERNITY OF
ROYAL ARK MARINER

PLATE NO. 33

COMMANDER

PLATE NO. 34

PAST COMMANDER

PLATE NO. 35

JEWEL OF THE DEGREE OF THE ANCIENT AND
HONOURABLE FRATERNITY OF ROYAL ARK MARINER

PLATE NO. 36

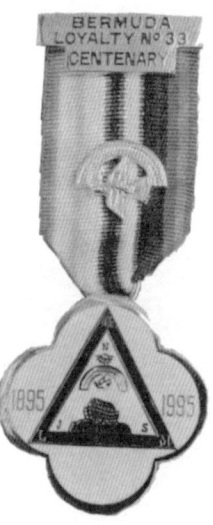

CENTENARY JEWEL

PLATE No. 37

JUBILEE JEWEL

PLATE No. 38

CHAINS – GRAND OFFICERS

PLATE No. 39

CHAINS – DEPUTY PROVINCIAL/DISTRICT
GRAND MASTER

PLATE No. 40

CHAINS – ASSISTANT PROVINCIAL/DISTRICT
GRAND MASTER

Published by Lewis Masonic